1,00

The Developing Nations
A Comparative Perspective
Second Edition

Robert E. Gamer
University of Missouri, Kansas City

Allyn and Bacon, Inc.
Boston London Sydney Toronto

Library of Congress Cataloging in Publication Data

Gamer, Robert E., 1938–
  The developing nations.

  Includes bibliographical references and index.
  1. Underdeveloped areas—Politics and government.
I. Title.
JF60.G35   1981   320.9172′4   81–10839
ISBN 0-205-07647-5   AACR2

Printed in the United States of America.
10 9 8 7 6 5 4 3   91 90 89 88 87

My mother,
Alice Clara Gamer,
says the world would be more sane
if the people who run it,
and try to explain it,
would take the time to appreciate sunshine,
chats with the neighbors,
and birds in their nests.

This book is dedicated to
my mom, sanity,
and nests of all shapes and sizes.

On Using
This Book

A NOTE TO INSTRUCTORS

Political scientists, like anthropologists, economists, and other social scientists, frequently debate among ourselves. For instance, some of us see ourselves as behavioralists, while others prefer to be called traditionalists or post-behavioralists. We have differing ideas about how to apply scientific method. Some claim that developing nations are best understood from the perspective of dependency theory, while others see them best explained through functional analysis, or cost-benefit analysis, or what have you. The fact that we have such debates shows the vitality of our profession, although sometimes these discussions exaggerate the differences among our views. There is far more that unites us than divides us.

Students entering the study of developing nations are not always immediately ready to learn about such nuances in our thinking. Most have never set foot off these shores. They have little opportunity to read about developing nations or see television reports on them except when crises arise. They lead comfortable lives far divorced from the poverty that characterizes much of the developing world. Before we as teachers introduce students to complex scholarly debates we should first help them establish greater empathy for these peoples and some basic comprehension of their problems and political systems.

To begin to comprehend anything as unfamiliar as the politics of developing nations, one needs some methodological moorings. The early chapters of this book use a rigorously systematic approach to introduce the politics of the developing nations. They are filled with discussion about people, places, and processes, but are generally devoid of exotic terminology. Only after the students have acquired this introduction to developing nations are they initiated into debates among political scientists over how to interpret political development. At that point (in Chapter 6), they are strongly encouraged to explore differing approaches to comprehending developing political systems. Similarities among these approaches are emphasized along with differences. To compare these schools of thought before acquiring some empirical knowledge seems out of keeping with scientific method and sound pedagogy. To fail to do so after learning an approach and acquiring some empirical knowledge seems equally out of keeping with scientific method and sound pedagogy.

If you are like me and nearly every reader of this book with whom I have spoken, you will find the last two chapters the most interesting. They analyze land reform, the Green Revolution, industrialization, and political reform policies. They examine population growth, ecology, our diets, food and energy shortages, multinational corporations, and the political and economic interdependence of the developed and developing nations, along with scenarios for the future. You will find me raising the spector that *all* nations could become marginal in resources and power within this century. I also suggest that it is within the power of the inhabitants of this planet to find mutually favorable solutions to the problems we share. However, I look upon the first six chapters as the main courses of the meal and the last two as the dessert. Reading the last two chapters without first methodically examining the political systems of developing nations can lead to superficial conclusions. On the other hand, after examining those systems it seems important to explore the questions raised in the last chapters.

This book is just one of many vehicles by which the politics of developing nations can be understood. It is a means by which teachers, regardless of their point of view, can introduce students to the politics of developing nations in a methodical, comprehensible, comprehensive, and engaging manner.

Most of you will be using the book for survey courses on developing nations or development and change; some will be using it for other types of courses. The following information and suggestions may be of help in adapting the book to your course:

For Courses on Developing Nations.   If you wish to use the book in its most skeletal form, I would suggest having your students read Chapters 1 through 5. As each new argument is introduced, students can get by with using one illustration to give it flesh and blood; they need not absorb all of the illustrations. What is important is that they relate illustrations to arguments so they assure themselves of understanding substance and not just words. Students can use the questions at the beginning and end of each chapter to review the main points covered. Notice that "The Book in Brief" in Chapter 1 goes through the entire model, argument by argument, so that you can quickly get an overview of what the book is all about.

Because of the systematic format, you can also abbreviate your treatment of portions of the book you find less important than others. For instance, if you wish to spend less time on the discussion of historical development in Chapters 2 and 3, have your students pick up the main points of the argument there and then read Chapter 4 in greater detail. All chapters and chapter sections end with a summary. The entire book is summarized in Chapter 1. Chapters 2 through 5 are summarized at the end of Chapter 5 and in the second section of Chapter 6.

If you wish to concentrate on particular countries, notice that a number are covered in some detail. Boxed citations tell the readers where to pick up the discussion next.

The Index is more complete than most. For lectures on bureaucracy, centralization of power, cultural pluralism, elections, ideology, judiciaries, legislatures, military, political leadership, political parties, political recruitment, executives, responsiveness, representation, revolution, colonialism, agrarian reform, foreign aid, taxation, or urbanization, see those topics in the Index for tie-ins. For *communications* see mass media, education, roads, representation, Deutsch; for *institutionalization,* Huntington; *industrialization,* businessmen, multinational corporations; class, artisans, commodities middlemen, laborers, landless peasants, serfs, landowners, middle classes, nobility, headmen, caste, students; *human rights,* freedom of expression; *federalism,* Nigeria, governance of. With a bit of imagination, you can do this for a number of other topics. Often a train of thought introduced about a topic at one point in the book is picked up again at a later point.

For Courses on Comparative Politics. If the developing nations are being treated as part of a course on comparative politics, the suggestions just made still apply. To see whether you can tie in with the theoretical approach used in the European portion of the course, you may want to read "The Patron-Client Relationship" at the beginning of Chapter 4, and look at Chapters 1, 6, and 8. Notice that students are introduced to a variety of approaches to studying comparative politics; that comparisons are frequently made between developing and developed nations; and that policy issues are addressed from the perspective of interdependencies among political systems.

For Area Studies Courses. Each main *generalization* in this book is accompanied by at least one and often several illustrations from each *region* covered: Latin America, Africa, the Middle East, South and Southeast Asia. An extensive introduction to the most populous nations in each region is provided, as well as of some with fewer inhabitants. History and current problems are both discussed. You can use the book to give a methodical introduction to a particular region by having the students concentrate on the illustrations and country studies pertaining to that region. They will have the advantage of seeing how that region compares and interacts with others and of being able to draw upon various theoretical approaches for analyzing it. This frees you to assign supplemental reading that is not comparative (e.g., on a particular country) or is only partially comparative (e.g., on the military in the region, or a textbook with several essays by different authors on different countries). Notice that the Index has regional headings like "Latin America" in addition to headings for individual countries, and breakdowns like Middle classes: in Africa, in Asia, in Latin America.

For Courses on Political Development and Modernization.   To acquaint yourself with the book's potentials in this realm, look at Chapter 1, the "Synthesis" at the end of Chapter 5, and Chapters 6 through 8. The works of several development theorists are introduced, ranging from systems analysis to dependency theory. The historic and contemporary impact of the Industrial Revolution on the political systems of developing nations is analyzed. Modernization and development are treated as separate phenomena, and their interactions are explored at a number of levels. The book contains many statistics and case studies about political constraints on modernization and development. The last two chapters address themselves to the most pressing current issues regarding development and modernization.

For Courses on Political Geography.   Chapters 3, 7, and 8 will be those with the most interest to geographers. Index entries include agrarian reform, agricultural extension, agricultural productivity, bananas, beans, cocoa, coconut, coffee, cooperatives, copper, corn, cotton, cows, day laborers, diet, diseases, exports, fallow fields, famine, fertilizer, fish, foraging, fruit, fuel, grains, headmen, herding, hunting, indigo, intercropping, iron, jute, landowners, plantations, land tenure, livestock, manure, meat, metals, millet, mining, nitrates, oilseeds, opium, palm oil, peanuts, peas, pesticides, petroleum, phosphates, potatoes, potassium, protein, raw materials, seed, shantytowns, soil, soybeans, sugar, tea, technology, tenants, timber, tin, tobacco, tubers, vegetables, and wheat.

For Courses on Political Anthropology.   Chapters 2 and 3 deal with political anthropology. I suspect the rest of the book is of interest to anthropologists as well. Look at the last section of Chapter 8, and Index entries like artisans, caste system, commerce, community councils, cooperative labor, cultural pluralism, day laborers, debt bondage, families, headmen, hunting, kings and monarchs, merchants, dependency syndrome, and warfare.

For Courses on Economic Development.   Read the Model at the beginning of Chapter 1, and leaf through Chapters 1 and 8, the Contents, and the Index. While its primary focus is on politics, the entire book deals with aspects of economic development and draws upon economists. The detailed discussions of land reform, industrialization, international trade, multinationals, and international economics in the last two chapters might be of special interest. Chapters 2 through 4 discuss the stages of economic development in developing nations.

For Policy Studies Courses.   The book has a strong but nontraditional policy orientation. Early chapters deal with historic policies pertaining to land, civil disputes, food, trade, and intergroup relations. Chapters 4 through 6 discuss the constraints that political systems place upon policy. Chapters 6 through 8 deal with contemporary policy issues, as does the end of Chapter 4.

A NOTE TO STUDENTS

This book covers a lot of material, but it is neatly organized. Once you find that organization, it becomes quite simple to read.

The first chapter contains two summaries of the entire book. The summary at the beginning of Chapter 1 is called "The Model" and is one paragraph long; at the beginning of each chapter "The Model" is reprinted and italicized to indicate which portion of it is covered in that chapter. The summary at the end of Chapter 1 appears under the heading "The Book in Brief" and is ten paragraphs long; each additional chapter of the book discusses one or more of these paragraphs.

There are summaries at the end of each chapter and each chapter section. This means you can review the entire book by reading the summaries at the end of the chapter sections and chapters. You can review it by reading "The Book in Brief." Or you can review it by reading "The Model."

This may prompt you to ask why we have bothered to fill the spaces between the summaries with a book. The chances are you will find the summaries highly abstract at first. They must be brought down to human proportions by using illustrations. If you see a lot of these in sequence, they probably apply to the same generalization. When you see an illustration ask yourself what generalization is being discussed. If the first illustration does not bring it down to earth for you, perhaps the second or third one will; then you could move on to the next generalization and its illustrations.

Several special aids are designed to help you study.

These boxes are one such aid. At times the box will translate what you are reading into simpler, more concise, language. Sometimes it will give you hints on how to read. It may call your attention to something by asking a question. Often it will provide a specific example of what is being discussed. It may point to other places in the book where similar material is discussed, or where a discussion about a particular country continues. It may offer a short summary of the chapter.

The world map at the front of the book will help you conveniently check where places are. At the beginning of each chapter are some questions about the locations of countries, and about some of the main points to look for in the chapter. At the end of each chapter are review questions for the chapter, including some page references for locating key definitions you might have missed.

The Index includes many specific places, objects, concepts, and authors, and it is cross-referenced. Each topic is followed by a complete listing of the pages on which that topic appears. With some practice, you will find it useful for pinpointing answers to questions or to get yourself going on a term paper. For term papers, the footnotes also contain useful references to books and articles with different viewpoints on the same topic.

This book will give you a lot of new things to think about, and new ways to look at some things you already think about. If you use these study aids to keep yourself organized, you should be able to benefit from another study aid: the discussion in Chapter 6 of how to develop your own approach to such matters. I look forward to having you join the debate about how best to study and deal with the problems of developing nations.

Contents

The Developing Nations
A Comparative Perspective

CHAPTER

1

GETTING YOUR BEARINGS (see map, front of book)

1. Are any of the developing nations as far north as Europe? As the Tropic of Cancer?
2. Which of them are south of the equator? Of the Tropic of Capricorn?

The Model[1]

A *developed nation* provides most of its citizens with a *stable personal environment*. A *developing nation* does not. Today's developing nations were once developed nations. They changed because their *political systems* separated from their *social systems* when European commerce was introduced. If the structure of international trade changes in the near future, social and political systems may be reintegrated, promoting *political development*. Then the developing nations may once again become developed nations.

---

[1] "A model is an abstraction of reality that is developed for presenting systematically the most important relationships in the situation which is being described. Necessarily the model is less complex than the reality. A theorist hopes to identify all of the basic ingredients of the situation in his model, inducing the representations of all the significant phenomena and all of the significant relationships among them." George J. Graham, Jr., *Methodological Foundations for Political Analysis* (Waltham, Mass.: Xerox College Publishing, 1971), p. 112.

"Models typically include sets of categories, assumptions, and postulates which are used to sort out data, analyze it, determine relationships, and help the model builder to explain or predict. . . A model may be expressed in words, charts and graphs, or mathematical symbols." Jack C. Plano and Milton Greenberg, *Political Science Dictionary* (Hinsdale, Ill.: Dryden Press, 1973), p. 241.

Introduction

QUESTIONS TO KEEP IN MIND

1. What is a model?
2. What are the main definitions in this chapter?
3. Why are history, intuition, and details important for understanding developing nations?
4. How has commerce affected stable personal environments?

If you have not done so, read "On Using this Book—Students," p. ix.

The peoples of southern Asia, Africa, and Latin America remained largely isolated from one another and from North America and western Europe until the twentieth century. A hundred years ago only a few of us "westerners" had any interest in those parts of the world. The kings of Spain, Portugal, and England gained economic advantage over rivals by using their ships and guns to take over and expand gold and silver mines there. The merchants of the Netherlands and Venice did the same with diamonds, and became exclusive agents to Europe for certain exotic trade items. Europe and North America received spices, tea, sugar, tapioca, slaves, hardwoods, and other nonnecessities from these strange outer regions. A few Europeans even went to live there. All this required occasional battles between small armies and navies. It did little to improve or hamper the

---

"The acceptance of the model is justified in the first place by the way in which it helps us to explain, represent and predict the phenomenon under investigation. . . [A] good model . . . suggest[s] further questions, taking us beyond the phenomenon from which we began, and tempts us to formulate hypotheses which turn out to be experimentally fertile." Stephen Toulmin, *The Philosophy of Science: An Introduction* (New York: Harper & Row, 1960), pp. 37–38. Toulmin says (p. 39) that models are more than simple metaphors. Abraham Kaplan, *The Conduct of Inquiry: Methodology for Behavioral Science* (San Francisco: Chandler, 1964), p. 265, calls them "scientific metaphors . . . those theories which explicitly direct attention to certain resemblances between the theoretical entities and the real subject matter." See note 11.

standard of living of any but a select (or unfortunate) few. There was but minimal contact among continents and regions.

The Industrial Revolution changed all that; it made interdependence a necessity for the many rather than a luxury (or burden) for the few. To run their factories, the European nations demanded raw materials—cotton, indigo, rubber, metals, chemicals, vegetable oils, woods, crude oil, and large ships to carry them. The movement to the cities in Europe required grain imports, and mechanization of agriculture produced a need for large quantities of phosphates and nitrates. The new urbanites came to look upon coffee, tea, and sugar as vital necessities. North America could provide many of these commodities, and Europe a few. Latin America, Asia, and Africa were mobilized to supply the rest. In addition, they provided valuable markets for manufactured goods. World War I accelerated this; no nation could compete in warfare requiring high technology if its supply lines to the developing areas[2] were interrupted. Since World War II the percentage of vital commodities produced by developing nations[3] has steadily risen; so has their role in providing factory labor and markets. Developing nations contain an increasing percentage of the world's population, and consume increasing quantities of food, fuel, metals, and other materials that were previously a virtual monopoly of the North Atlantic nations. Many of these commodities are in short supply. The cost of human life and materiel in conflicts like Vietnam to both developed and developing nations is vastly greater than the losses in the Boer War or even the Malayan Emergency. An increasingly sophisticated leadership in developing nations may gradually improve their ability to compete for the use of and profits from these resources.

A WAY TO MEASURE THE GROWING INTERDEPENDENCE

The galleons and carracks of the fifteenth and sixteenth centuries seldom exceeded 100 feet in length and 35 feet in width. The largest wooden ship ever built, the Yankee Clipper *Great Republic,* launched in 1853, was 325 feet long and 53 feet wide—about the length of a football field. It never sailed. Most clippers were 200 feet long, with about 900 tons cargo capacity. In 1858 the steamship *Great Eastern* was launched; its metal hull was 692 feet long and 83 feet wide, with 274,000 tons displacement. *The Normandie,* launched in 1932, was 1,029 feet long and 118 feet wide (wider than the length of a galleon). Today's supertankers exceed 1,350 feet in length and 350 feet in width (wider than the length of the *Great Republic*). They can carry 550,000 tons. The nineteenth century brought a revolution in the capacity of ships to carry cargo,[4] and thus to link the developed and developing nations.

In short, Europe and North America are heavily affected by the course of events in developing nations, yet this interdependence has crept up so quickly

---

[2] See note 14.
[3] See p. 9 for an explanation of this term.
[4] See Björn Landstrom, *The Ship: An Illustrated History* (Garden City, New York: Doubleday, 1961).

that few people have noticed the extent of its ramifications. In fact, few people know much of anything about the developing nations, even in the developing nations themselves![5] Most of what is written on the subject in any systematic fashion is to be found in journals, low-circulation books, and pamphlets read only by a select scholarly community. To be sure, newspapers and television carry stories on developing nations, but they do not probe very deeply. It seems imperative that the considerable body of knowledge that has been accumulated by scholars be assimilated in a form that can be comprehended by a wider audience. It is the intention of this book to contribute in this direction.

Poor information often leads to unfounded fear. Some fear that the developing nations might combine forces against Europe, Japan, and North America to deprive us of resources. In my opinion, there is not much chance of that happening. Some are speculating that there is little hope for the developing nations, or for the planet as a whole; the human race is fighting a losing battle against rising population and diminishing resources. This book challenges that conclusion, yet it also suggests that there is no room for complacency. It argues, in fact, that greed (yours, mine, and theirs) is responsible for a great many problems that we often blame on the scapegoats of overpopulation and scarce resources. The energy crisis, for example, results more from greed than from an actual shortage of resources.

Greed is growing in magnitude (perhaps even faster than population, if one could produce such a scale). It leaves a few fat, and many lean. That greed, however, can be rechanneled in directions that would make effective use of resources and cater to the needs of all human beings who might populate the planet in the foreseeable future. Let me explain:

We have developed a tendency to judge Africa, Asia, and Latin America by some of the standards that appeared to apply in Europe and North America during the past century. The best way to spread benefits, according to that perspective, is to become more "modern." Modernization brings humankind a greater capacity than ever before to specialize in tasks, to accumulate knowledge, to organize labor and materials, to assess options, and hence to achieve some desired results. It also increases the capability of individual men and women to control their own destinies. To do so, they must build interest groups, parties, and communication networks to express their interests, institutions to make laws in the public interest, and other bodies to administer and enforce these laws. Technology has already produced a great institutional capacity to mine, manufacture, and distribute things; when the public's institutional capacity to control and channel technology reaches comparable complexity, we are on our way toward using resources more effectively and equitably. The spread of literacy and higher education, the research projects of scholars and foundations, the gradual growth of the middle classes, greater global interdependence and communication, and increasing sophistication in leadership and organizational capacity will help this process along.

---

[5] The reasons for this lack of knowledge within the developing nations will become apparent in Chapters 4 and 5.

SUMMARY

Some people think that modernization will solve the problems of developing nations.

The knowledge we are accumulating about developing nations, however, may warrant different conclusions. Modernization does not necessarily create greater capacity to assess options and achieve desired results in the political realm. Viewed as a complex whole, it increasingly *reduces* the capability of individual men and women to control their own destinies or to experiment with new approaches to solving problems. The efforts of developing nations to bring technology under control mask a colossal paradox. The more education permeates, research projects proliferate, consumer goods spread, and computerized office networks replace homely officials in the affairs of government, the more those few who own or run the technology will control the public interest. The greater the modernity of a developing nation, the greater the capacity for a few individuals to keep the bulk of its benefits for themselves. And modern institutions (governmental and otherwise, whatever their avowed purpose) *increase* the chances that these few individuals will continue to hoard resources. Corruption—viewed in the broader sense of an inequitable distribution of resources—actually *grows* when one applies education, communications, political parties, legislative processes, concerned capable national leadership, and modernized bureaucracy to fight it. It will inherently continue to do so, no matter how these instruments are applied, so long as modernization proliferates. Modernization does give lipstick, soft drinks, travel, knowledge about faraway places, and many other such options to the poor, but, basically, choices shrink and inequities magnify as technology spreads.

EXAMPLE OF HOW TO LIE WITH STATISTICS

At several places in the book we will be demonstrating that statistics can be misleading. I will be providing considerable support for the contentions in the previous paragraph as we proceed, but here are some statistics that seem to support them which must instead be approached cautiously. A study of thirty-seven developing nations around 1965 showed that those with higher per capita incomes had greater disparities between the rich and the poor than those with less modernization and lower per capita incomes. In the nine countries with average per capita incomes below US$100, the poorest 60 percent of the populace received 30 percent of the total incomes, while the richest 5 percent received 29.1 percent. In the nine countries with average per capita incomes of US$301–500, the poorest 60 percent received 24.7 percent, while the richest 5 percent received 30 percent.[6] The higher

---

[6] Felix Paukert, "Income Distribution at Different Levels of Development: A Survey of Evidence," *International Labour Review* 108 (August–September 1973): Table 6. Per capita income is based on Gross Domestic Product, and the survey includes all countries with per capita incomes below US$500.

the per capita income, it would seem, the worse the relative income position of the poor. Yet West Germany, which has higher per capita income than the United States, exhibits less disparity between rich and poor. In 1970, the poorest 60 percent of the West German populace had 29.1 percent of the national income, but the top 5 percent had 33.7 percent; in the United States the poorest 60 percent received only about 15 percent of income, while the top 5 percent received 19 percent.[7] So the generalization does not apply to these two countries. There is no "quick-fix" way to support hypotheses like those in the preceding paragraph. They must be approached through careful, systematic argumentation and documentation. These statistics by themselves do not tell us much.

These are probably not familiar conclusions, and they become even more unfamiliar when we look for ways to end this corruption. I do not think the continuing expansion of modernization in developing nations is inevitable for, as we shall see, the very interdependence it has created may be its own Achilles' heel. Should modernization cease to proliferate, the prognostications are not entirely gloomy. While these nations' *technical* capacities to solve problems might be decreased somewhat, *political* capacities to solve basic human problems might be augmented. Ironically, this augmentation would take place because political power might partially slip from the hands of those with great technological capacities back into the hands of those with fewer technological capacities (not to mention inferior educations), namely, the peasantry and indigenous rural aristocracy. Though the latter have simpler and more rigid attitudes toward problem solving, they might prove better at accommodating human need than present national leaders. To many this will seem a preposterous argument; at one time it seemed so to me. It was only after I began to explore a number of areas not usually given much attention by political scientists that it began to seem increasingly viable. I am going to share these same matters with you so that you may judge for yourself whether the argument holds water.

If you are to understand my argument, then, you will need to draw your attention to three areas that tend to be covered with dust, rust, and barnacles nowadays—intuition, history, and detail. Our society does not like to explore these areas. We try to avoid questioning the assumptions on which our behavior is based. For example, our personal experience and intuition often suggest to us that technology has not brought us much progress, or that the groups to which we belong are not behaving morally. Rather than explore such fundamental questions, it is easy to spend our thought time on "data" and charts and graphs. We tell ourselves that this is somehow more "objective." Perhaps we fear that if our assumptions are wrong the future will seem more frightening. On the contrary, by exploring assumptions we can plan for the future and make it less frightening. In the words of Sheldon Wolin:

---

[7] William Loehr, "Economic Underdevelopment and Income Distribution: A Survey of the Literature," in *Economic Development, Poverty, and Income Distribution,* ed. William Loehr and John P. Powelson (Boulder: Westwood Press, 1977), p. 10. This article contains references to many other articles dealing with this sort of statistic. We shall be using more of them presently.

Modern social science, in its way, displays the same syndrome of attitudes and activities as that found among revolutionaries and technocrats: it objectifies the world, then converts it into data, processes the data, and describes the results as "findings." It, too, depletes the world by depriving it of history, value, and common experience.[8]

Far from ignoring their experience, intuition, and values, good scientists make full use of these attributes.[9] Successful discoveries are usually preceded by an intense desire to solve some particular problem. The discoveries usually evolve from a lively mind that notices a great deal around it and is interested in a great many subjects. Early in the process, scientists formulate some hypotheses to tentatively explain the phenomenon into which they are inquiring. They begin experiments to gather information that might confirm or deny the validity of these hypotheses. They must ask themselves why and how this information might be pertinent. They go out to observe people or animals or things involved in the phenomenon they are studying. They talk to these people, they talk to other scientists who have observed the phenomenon, and they read varied related materials. They constantly ask themselves whether their experiments and information square with their own personal observations and those of others. Only then do they begin to invent big words and draw together information to describe what they have done.

A student wishing to understand the work of these scientists cannot do so simply by memorizing the technical terms or charts and graphs that are the end products of this research. The student must go back to share the more intuitive portions of the exercise by learning what questions the scientist asked, why the questions were asked, what other observers said about the phenomenon, in what setting the scientist observed the phenomenon, and so forth. Only then can the student begin to share in the science itself.

Suppose a man shoots another man in the neck. One expert calls this a protective reaction, and hence third-degree murder. Another testifies that it was deadly assault with intent to kill, and hence first-degree murder. A jury would be remiss in its duty to take either of these explanations at face value. It would want to know a great many details and to compare some testimonies. It would be acutely aware that the information filters through each juror's values and experience. If it does not do this, the jury will be easy prey for some lawyer with a slick courtroom manner. Of course, the biggest loser could be the defendent unjustly jailed, or the society unjustly saddled with a freed killer.

Returning, then, to intuition, history, and detail, we are trying in this book to understand the nature of the developing nations and their potentials in the future. We begin by introducing some hypotheses about them, and sharing with you some of the values that led to their formulation and some of the information that we have used to test them. Later we will discuss how you can square your

---

[8] Sheldon S. Wolin, "The Politics of the Study of Revolution," *Comparative Politics* 5, no. 3 (April 1973): 356.

[9] See W. I. B. Beveridge, *The Art of Scientific Investigation* (New York: Vintage Press, 1957) for a good discussion of the role of intuition and creativity in scientific discovery.

own values against the hypotheses and information, and develop hypotheses and information of your own.

At the heart of our inquiry is the history and development of the special relationships that exist among politicians, businesspersons, and bureaucrats. It is no secret that such special arrangements do exist. Treatises and exposés have been written about them. These arrangements are sometimes viewed as applying especially to contracts, public construction, and political donations from special interests. In this book we view them more broadly as the most fundamental aspects of present-day politics in developing nations, far more important, for instance, than political parties, interest groups, legislatures, or even military organizations.

In order to understand why these special relationships are so important today, we will have to go back in time to their beginnings (in the sixteenth century or so), and trace the buildup of their economic and political power. Then we will examine how the role of businesspersons and bureaucrats has increased in importance since World War II. To understand how these groups might lose their prominent political role in the future we must (ironically) look even further back in time than the sixteenth century to comprehend the nature of the political arrangements that preceded their ascendancy.

This argument, then, requires focusing attention on some processes that are seldom explored and even less often analyzed systematically by political scientists, economists, or others who think about these matters:

1. the conditions and political arrangements that prevailed before the businessperson-politician-bureaucrat relationships became important;
2. the forces that moved the central decisions of politics into the hands of the latter (which we term patron-client networks);
3. the nature of these patron-client networks;
4. the evidence that these networks are increasing their power as technology and modern government spread;
5. the reasons to believe that this situation might change, and the role played by the remnants of (1) in that change.

An indigenous rural aristocracy reinfused with power would have different options than it had when it held power in the past, if only because of the existence of the modern sector. But the evidence that these groups husbanded and distributed resources sensibly in the past has important ramifications for the argument that they could do so again in the future. This, too, requires turning attention to the period before the sixteenth century. From all this you can see the important role that intuition and history will play in our inquiry.

If we devote several pages of one of the following chapters to a discussion of the details of life in an obscure village, it is not to present a human interest story, but rather to allow you to make some judgments about one of the hypotheses in the paragraph that follows this one. If the hypothesis stays in the forefront of your mind, the details will help link the village with that hypothesis. Later in the book, when alternative hypotheses are presented, the details will again help you decide which one seems most *apropos*. Then you can turn to objectified words like *insti-*

tutionalized capacity, authoritative response, productive capability, or *instability* with some comprehension of what they mean in human terms, and apply them to the model as you see fit. After that you can devise theorems, experiments, and data to confirm or deny the validity of *your* model.[10]

Here, then, is the model (see footnote 1)[11] that summarizes this book:

> A developed nation provides most of its citizens with a stable personal environment. A developing nation does not. Today's developing nations were once developed nations. They changed because their political systems separated from their social systems when European commerce was introduced. If the structure of international trade changes in the near future, social and political systems may be reintegrated, promoting political development. Then the developing nations may once again become developed nations.

COMMENT

Notice that this model covers the five processes we mentioned three paragraphs earlier. The condition that prevailed before the businessperson-politician-bureaucrat relationships became important was that of development. When the businessperson-politician-bureaucrat network took power away from social systems the development ended. Changes in international trade would allow some power to return to social systems and thus open the way for development once again.

Obviously, some of the words just used need defining. First of all, what could be meant by a developed nation? According to this model, a developing nation is not developing, but decaying. There is also an implication that this decay is not necessarily permanent; it may be a stage through which a nation is passing, a temporary setback. A temporary setback in what? In personal environments. We are defining a developing nation here in terms of its effects on individuals or, more exactly, families. Those effects have to do with a *stable personal environment;* to experience this, an individual's housing, cultural setting, job, and education must all be in balance. Good education and poor job, low income and expensive house, affordable house but hostile neighborhood, good job with insecure future—all result in imbalances. A stable personal environment requires enough food to eat;[12] health care; housing that is affordable and satisfying

---

[10] See Mark E. Kann, *Thinking About Politics: Two Political Sciences* (St. Paul: West Publishing, 1980) for more discussion on how to proceed with scientific inquiry in political science.

[11] Abraham Kaplan, *The Conduct of Inquiry,* p. 263, says that models should be in postulational or formal style. Ours is postulational: The foundation is a set of propositions whose "truth is dependent on matters of fact" (pp. 260–261). The language used is that of logic rather than mathematics. The "emphasis is on the system as a whole, bound together by the chains of logical derivation," and on the "validity of the proof" rather than "the content of the propositions." The rules for the logical derivation are explicitly formulated and applied. From these propositions theorems will be derived. "What is wanted is the simplest set [of propositions] which will suffice for the derivation of the theorems in which we are interested, one which will allow for elegant proofs of the important propositions about the subject-matter." The propositions are not likely to be demanding of extensive measurements or quantitative scales; the theorems derived from the propositions may be.

[12] This need can be fairly accurately determined by nutritionists; the other parameters of this definition, however, will vary according to the values held by the individual.

to live in; neighbors and cultural facilities with which individuals feel comfortable; a job offering a modicum of satisfaction, continuity, and above-subsistence income; and an educational system that can promise children the same advantages. A person with *no* monetary income can have this as well as one with high income; *the key lies in the balance of the parts.* Modernization creates imbalances in these parts and also provides means to correct those imbalances.

COMMENT

One could call a stable personal environment a balanced personal environment—a state of equilibrium among one's values and environment. We all have our own notions of what suits us. What seems a castle to one individual is a hovel to another. These two individuals would probably disagree on what constitutes a good job, education, and cultural setting as well. Our own values may *change* in the course of our life. If so, our education, job, housing, and cultural setting may need to be adjusted accordingly. The absence of such adjustment brings instability, or imbalance, to our personal environment.

Some nations, which we term *developed nations,* have already achieved stable personal environments for a majority, or at least increasing percentages of,[13] their citizens. Other nations once (usually before the advent of nationhood) had such balances for a majority of their people; today, a *decreasing minority* of their total populations experience such stable personal environments, though this trend may be reversed in the future. These are the *developing nations;*[14] specifically, those in Latin America, the South Pacific Islands, Southeast Asia (excluding Australia and New Zealand), South Asia, the Middle East (excluding Israel), and Africa. We are classifying all the other nations on the globe as developed (i.e., offering stable personal environments to a majority, or an increasing number, of their citizens).[15] Whether they will stay in this category remains to be seen.

This definition groups together nations that seem to have little in common. Some classed here as developed have high living standards, and others, lower living standards. Some have much technology; some little technology. Some have capitalist economies, while others are socialist or communist. Degrees of per-

---

[13] All nations experience periods of economic recession that temporarily reverse such a trend; developing nations seldom have such a trend even during periods of economic prosperity.

[14] When discussing these places in periods before they acquired nationhood, we call them developing areas.

[15] There are a few borderline nations that should perhaps not be included as developed nations. Taiwan and South Korea may be poor, but are extending stable environments to increasing percentages of their populations. Many developed nations also have economically depressed regions, or regions that are dominated by other regions; in this sense Great Britain, the United States, the U.S.S.R., Spain, Portugal, and Italy are less developed than China and Romania. I have thought in terms of the nation as a whole.

Turkey, Kuwait, and Singapore are at the upper edges of those classified as developing nations in terms of extending stable personal environments; their social systems do remain separated from the political system, and there appear to be narrow limits on how far the stable personal environments can extend.

sonal freedom vary widely. They speak many languages and have divergent cultural traditions. Yet, in different ways, they are all creating stable personal environments. They have something else in common as well. All have in some degree meshed their social and political systems. Those I have classed as developing nations also exhibit many varieties of culture, resources, absorption of modernity, and the like. But they have been far less successful in creating stable personal environments, or in meshing their social and political systems. They share the experience of being dominated by commercial interests emanating from the nations we have defined as developed.

What do we mean by political and social systems? Social science literature contains a number of definitions that we could use for each concept. It is useful to think of a political system in two ways: as a group and as a process. Politics has something to do with the manner in which limited resources get distributed to people (who gets what, when, where, and how) and in which they are prevented from doing things (an organized system of coercion or restraint of conflicts). Hence we shall define a *political system* in two ways: (1) as those individuals in charge of the authoritative allocation of values (i.e., who have highest say in distributing advantages and disadvantages) with a monopoly on the use of force; and (2) as the processes involved in that authoritative allocation of values and monopoly on the use of force. We shall define a *social system* as people united by some form of regular interaction and interdependence. Most nations contain a variety of social systems, partially overlapping, based on class, ethnic background, regional identities, religion, and other factors.

Our contention is that those who control the political system in develop*ed* nations come from a variety of social systems in their nation and interact with a large number of people in the processes of politics. In develop*ing* nations, those who constitute the political system come from *one* small social system revolving around the capital city and interact with few other people in connection with the processes of politics. The political leadership is not far removed culturally from other social groups in the nation; it simply does not interact with them.[16] Most people are thereby excluded from membership in and the rewards of political processes. It is the lack of basic contact between the political system and various social systems—cultural groups, villages, neighborhoods, trades, religious congregations—of the nation that causes the destabilization of personal environments. While the political system can do little to aid these social systems, commercial interests steadily destabilize them by gaining ever-increasing control over their resources, their labor, and their behavior. Hence, most social systems within a developing nation have little control over their own environments, or over those who control their environments. They first began to lose this control when commerce was introduced to their nations and have continued to lose it as the extent of commercialization increases. Most of the income from commerce is

---

[16] In the words of Gerald A. Heeger, *The Politics of Underdevelopment* (New York: St. Martins, 1974, p. 6): ". . . social change often produces groups that may be as localized as their traditional counterparts. The emergence of small, urbanized middle-class groups. . . is an example of this. Such groups may be very limited in membership and interests and only intermittently linked to other groups elsewhere in the territory. Social change, in other words, may not only cause the demise of traditional forms of particularism, it may also create new particularisms."

circulated within the closed social group that surrounds the political system and to the organizations in the North Atlantic nations and Japan which supply this group with markets, technical assistance, and military prowess. Once these two sectors have absorbed their share, there is little left to filter down to other social systems within these nations. This results in political systems that are more responsive to the demands of other nations than to the needs of their own societies, and produces unstable personal environments. The political leadership in these nations is poorly integrated into any of the existing social systems; by contrast, *political development* means broadening the social base of the political system and increasing the percentage of the populace experiencing stable personal environments. That reintegration may some day take place.

SUMMARY

"Developing nations" are not currently experiencing political development because their leaders are more closely affiliated with *our* political system than with the social systems of the majority of people in their own countries.

This may sound like a very different approach to the problems of development from that of someone who defines development as, say, modernizing the economy and political institutions. It is not. In Chapter 6 we shall show how this model can be rewritten to accommodate the values, observations, and experiments of other scholars. It will become apparent at that point that their views about these matters are quite similar to those presented here, although their thinking about the *future* may differ. The real difference lies less in the hypotheses than in the material they examine to support the hypotheses and additional related concepts that they explore. Absorbing the material in the next four chapters will allow you to view these hypotheses from perspectives not otherwise possible and to reject some ways of stating these hypotheses while favoring others. For instance, nearly all of these authors see an increasing separation of the political from the social realm, physical displacement of people in a manner which reduces both the stability of their personal environments and their political efficacy, proliferating conflicts among competing social systems, and increasing subordination of political decision making to the exigencies of the world market. *If, before dealing with these complex intellectual constructs, one first has a clear conception of what they mean—rooted in examples—it is easier to be precise in describing them and to avoid drawing mistaken conclusions from them.*

This leads me to reiterate the role of discovery in learning: For virtually every argument you encounter in this book you will be introduced to a counterargument and empirical data to help you choose between the arguments. I hope you will deal with the arguments more by thinking through the ramifications of the empirical examples than by resorting to ideological orthodoxy. I argue that revolution is not in the cards for the developing nations. This is not left-wing orthodoxy, nor is the argument presented here that left-wing ideologists are not ideological, or that the developed nations could continue to increase their standard of living without exploiting the developing nations. While ideologues on the right should take kindly to the argument that colonialism *per se* was not a disintegrative force and that centralization of government power is a disruptive force, they will probably not favor the discussion about social disintegration resulting from economic development. But it is not the purpose of scholarship to cater to orthodoxies. To be scientific, theory must develop some flexibility in relating data to hypotheses and arriving at conclusions. Hopefully, that is what is happening here, and hopefully, it will develop your ability to apply further data to your own further hypotheses.

There is also considerable information here for hypotheses about the future of North Atlantic nations. Their role in providing raw materials—oil, iron ore, aluminum, copper, cobalt, nickel, agricultural products—labor, and markets for the Industrial Revolution has expanded markedly. The cost of humans and materiel in warfare and aid programs to keep these supply lines open has risen steadily. Future trends in the politics of developing nations can affect the flow and cost of goods basic to advanced technological society in North America, Europe, and Japan. The last chapter of the book expands on this situation in some detail.

The basic material here concerns the developing nations themselves. The next two chapters discuss what life was like when social and political systems were combined and what the forces were that drove these systems apart. Chapter 4 describes the new political systems that have emerged to replace the former ones and the strengths and weaknesses of these new systems vis-à-vis the older ones. Chapter 5 analyzes why these new systems are likely to remain in ascendancy as long as the world economy permits. Chapter 6 introduces alternative perspectives from which to view these political systems. Chapter 7 describes why the continuing separation of the political and social systems hinders the efficacy of the most popular means of reform: land reform, economic growth, and political reorganization. Chapter 8 discusses the interactions of the developing nations with developed nations, and the future.

THE BOOK IN BRIEF

To close this chapter, we shall summarize the entire book. Keep in mind that the relationship among *stable personal environments, social and political systems,* and *political development* remains at the heart of this discussion.

STUDY AID

The ten paragraphs that follow this study aid are a summary of the entire book. Every sentence constitutes an argument—an hypothesis or theorem. Together, they form a description of a political system of a developing nation. The Model that appears at the beginning of the chapter is a set of propositions concisely describing the system as a whole (see footnote 11). These ten paragraphs contain the theorems derived from those propositions.

Since each sentence or theorem needs to be verified by facts, we shall proceed to illustrate them in order. The next chapter deals with the first paragraph, and so forth through the book; the end of Chapter 8 deals with the tenth paragraph.

Some of these theorems will seem clear to you when you first read them. Others will be confusing; you might underline these. Use the illustrations to clarify the meaning of the theorems you find confusing. When you are able to read through all ten paragraphs understanding each sentence clearly you should be able to see how they are related (as Kaplan puts it, "bound together by the chains of logical derivation"). Then you will be ready to be critical of the description as a whole, the Model.

Prior to the arrival of European and Sino-European traders, people in developing areas tended to live in herding, hunting, and village settings. Extended families lived together, usually in clusters with other extended families. Their interactions constituted a primary social system. They also formed the basis for a primary political system. Members of these families were the rulers of these systems; some with ceremonial titles had ultimate power to allocate goods and privileges authoritatively and use force, while other members of the families discussed political decisions with these leaders. Each individual within the social/political system was guaranteed land, food, affection, continuity of relationships, and a sense of individual worth. Leaders were limited in their powers and answerable to those over whom they had influence; in most instances, authority was spread among several leaders, each of whom had different responsibilities. No one had ultimate control over the use of force without community consent.

The political autonomy of social groups began to break down, however, when some lineage leaders learned to collect grains and mine metals. They could then feed and outfit militia, accumulate goods through trade, and become kings. The king and coterie generally lived together in a separate town, where they all watched one another. Hence, the political system—the authoritative allocation of values by those with a monopoly on the use of force—was beginning to move away from the social system of the village. The move was by no means complete. The king shared the same customs and traditions as his subjects; his lifestyle (in terms of type of food eaten, the material from which his home was constructed, etc.) was not radically different from his subjects (though he had considerably *more* of everything); his courtiers kept frequent physical contact with the villages. The courts of these rulers were the first proving grounds of patron-clientism; the courtiers themselves were subject to the personal whims of the ruler and the leading families, unrestrained by any of the rules that governed village life. However, basic political decisions such as the distribution of land, punishment of wrongdoers, organization of public functions, and regulation of family affairs still took place within the village. The villagers continued to feed themselves, settle their own internal disputes, distribute their own land, and select their own leadership. The king had an interest in their doing so since the food produced in these villages was the basis of his power. The mass of people continued to live in villages, generally unaffected by the king except when the tax collector arrived, a battle or war was fought in their midst, or the king took an interest in a family feud or other civil altercation among them. The king was heavily dependent on the prosperity of the villages for his own prosperity.

Then, usually after the fifteenth century, came a broad expansion of trade. This often occurred after the opening of a new overland or sea route connecting the region with Europe or China. For the first time, ordinary people who had never thought of being anything but peasants or hunters were offered opportunities to make money by producing something like spice, sugar, hardwood, or ivory. For the first time, individuals could make profits and even acquire metals without the intervention of the king. Outsiders organized transportation and storage facilities far from the royal court. In short, the number of people engaged in commerce and bureaucracy greatly expanded in a manner that diminished both the king's power to supervise them and his ability to directly control the most lucrative resources. The new elites could set up trade relations with villages that made the villages dependent upon *them* for food. Even the king had to obtain his food by import rather than from the villages. The commercial elites might abduct an individual from his village and force him to work; land was sold to outsiders. Royal prosperity came to rest more on healthy commerce, the taxation of this commercial activity, than healthy villages. When the villages were being plundered by entrepreneurs, the king no longer had the power nor will to intervene if his interference might weaken the commerce which constituted his new tax base. The village was no longer the basic unit of economic production.

As a result, by the mid-twentieth century there were few villages that could guarantee their members a piece of land, a subsistence diet, a tightly-knit nuclear family, or an unquestioning sense of worth. Worse yet, kings and emerging national governments are not in a position to do this either for villages or individuals. Many people, in fact, have moved out of villages and lost all contact with the rules under which they operated. Far more of them have been displaced than can be absorbed into the new commercial pursuits. This situation provides the commercial leaders with a subservient labor pool and with the power to become politically influential themselves. In settings of social fluidity and uncertainty, many have sought out a means of security that had once existed only in royal courts: the patron. The individual works long hours for the patron, in return for subsistence and some entrée to the political authorities when it is needed. This patron in turn carries on commercial or political dealings with a patron higher up. In this manner a link is created with those at the center of political authority and commercial enterprise. Political activities and commercial pursuits increasingly center around the capital city. Here there are developed universities, fine restaurants, a prevalence of foreign languages, airports, imported goods, many automobiles, and other accoutrements generally unfamiliar to those living in the outer reaches (even of the capital city). These trappings do not radically change the cultural behavior of those caught in them (e.g., make them more modern), but they do serve to cut the participants off socially from others in the nation. Here it is possible for those in positions of political, economic, and bureaucratic power to operate with great independence, even from the kings in the countryside. Their links with the countryside come through their patrons and clients there who pass more goods up the ladder than they pass back down. Their power ultimately derives from the fact that they can sell the goods obtained in this manner abroad. Now it is the traders who control the mines, the grain, the taxes, and the armies.

Those with a patron who resist this system will lose that patron, and hence their only means of security. Those without one can easily be arrested, if they are to resist. More important, the principal means of conflict has come to involve struggles between competing social systems: Most developing nations contain a number of different racial, cultural, and religious groupings. As urbanization advances, they come into increasing contact with one another. Members of some groups have better contacts with the political center than others (though, significantly, none of them control it), causing resentments among competing groups. Yet, because of the disintegration caused by urbanization, no social group forms a well-integrated or autonomous system, as had been the case during village life. The result is continuous unresolved conflict among the various social groupings, which serves to divert hostility from coming to bear on the political system itself; divide and rule.

Meanwhile, economic development continues, including a portion of the national budget spent for public welfare. Economic development means diverting increasing portions of land to export crops; building roads to mines and timber claims; and building offices, factories, and government buildings. Those in the best position to benefit from these activities are economic elites most closely affiliated with the political system. Even the recipients of welfare are likely to be those affiliated with a well-connected patron. This system offers benefits to commerce, but it often has few direct effects for the bulk of the populace. Population continues to grow. Unemployment continues to rise. Income and land distribution become more markedly lopsided; there are few harbingers of a vigorous middle class. Wars, periodic famines, epidemics, and other hardships show—to put it generously—little sign of diminishing.

If this situation is to improve, methods must be devised to distribute resources more evenly among the populace, to reestablish community life, and to help people regain economic security. Kings and kinship groups showed concern for these priorities, but control of government leadership no longer rests with them. Commercial interests, large investors, landowners, and bureaucratic leaders who form the backbone of today's ruling parties and governments have encouraged quite opposite trends for the past several centuries.

Most scholars recognize that these problems exist. They differ, however, in their assessments of how to deal with them. Some suggest increasing popular participation in politics. Others suggest simple continuing expansion of economic development; land reform; decentralization of politics; strengthening the political elites so they can resist the economic elites; an expansion in the number of political parties and in the power of legislatures, which tend to be weak; and expansion of governmental institutions. The problem with all these proposals is that they are easy to exploit for personal gain if one is wealthy or has political connections, and not easy to exploit if one has not. In short, all these proposals can further strengthen those socially isolated people who control the political and economic systems without materially benefitting those for whom the reforms were originally intended.

North Atlantic proponents of such reforms are often interested in stability: continuing inexpensive raw materials and markets, prosperity at home, and freedom from military threats. So long as these goals materialize, these "reformers" can and often do overlook the fact that the reforms do not widely benefit the citizens of developing nations. Viewed in terms of the national interest of the developed nations, a developing nation is one that supports the political and economic viability of the developed nations. The day may come (even soon) when the developing nations no longer support the viability of the developed nations, when the former cost the latter more than they contribute. At that point, the developed nations may seek resources elsewhere. Siberia, Canada, Antarctica, and the oceans contain vast deposits of raw materials. Some non-necessities like coffee, tea, sugar, and palm oil can be grown further north or replaced with other foods.

This development of new sources would leave leaders of developing nations with greatly diminished foreign markets, and hence without support for their patron-client networks. Their nations would have to turn inward for sustenance. Most have considerable potential for improving agricultural productivity, but only if they make full use of marginal lands and human labor. The old communally organized village can perhaps exploit these resources more fully than can experiments of recent years. Even with today's expanded populations, there is sufficient arable land to effect a return to communal tenure for much of the populace of developing nations. If both communal towns and some individual farmers kept intact on better lands concentrated on growing food, and received technical support from the cities, their nations could become self-sufficient in food. The cities, besides their technical support, could produce additional consumer products to raise standards of living somewhat. Since the cities would largely be dependent on the countryside both for food and markets, the balance of political power would also tend to shift from the city to the countryside. As a result, political leadership would emerge from wider strata of regions and social systems. The political leadership would no longer be able to ignore the health of the communities that support it. In some ways that would be quite new; in others, it would be quite traditional.

Is this argument realistic? A careful perusal of the book should provide raw material to judge where it is strong and where it is weak. That raw material may hold some surprises.

SHORT SUMMARY

To understand developing nations it is necessary to make some generalizations and test them against some details. The main generalizations are in the Model at the beginning of this chapter. To understand them, you need to take note of the key definitions that appear in this chapter, and of some (a sampling if you like) of the illustrative stories that appear in the following chapters. If you do not try to perceive how the stories illustrate generalizations, you will not understand developing nations.

Have you caught these definitions?

Can you answer each with one sentence?

1. From where do we get spices?
2. Why was it impossible to import much phosphates and nitrates prior to the Industrial Revolution?
3. How can living in an attractive house decrease the stability of a family's personal environment?
4. How can a family with no monetary income have a stable personal environment?
5. If the percentage of income in a nation going to the poor declines, does this show that the stability of their personal environments is declining? Why?

From what you have read this far, can you make and support judgments about these questions?

1. How did sugar and spice affect the power of kings and the stability of village life?
2. If you are a member of a jury, how can you tell first-degree murder from second-degree murder?
3. According to the definitions used in this chapter, does a nation need to have high living standards to be a developed nation? Does a developing nation have to have low living standards?
4. When does a social system have maximum control over its own environment? Will it then try to create stable personal environments for all its members?

CHAPTER

2

GETTING YOUR BEARINGS (see map, front of book)

1. Locate the nations where the groups in this chapter live.
2. Do any of these groups live in more than one nation?

The Model

A developed nation provides most of its citizens with a stable personal environment. A developing nation does not. *Today's developing nations were once developed nations.* They changed because their political systems separated from their social systems when European commerce was introduced. If the structure of international trade changes in the near future, social and political systems may be reintegrated, promoting political development. Then the developing nations may once again become developed nations.

Yesterday's Political Systems: Friends and Relatives

QUESTIONS TO KEEP IN MIND

1. Why did people in traditional societies have stable personal environments?
2. Why were kings and empires unable to disrupt the stability of those personal environments?

A book on developing nations[1] states that "the traditional milieu is characterized by high birth rates, high disease rates, near total illiteracy, minimal or subminimal calorie consumption, short life spans, early aging, and early deaths . . . suspicion and distrust between tribes, clans, families, and religious groups are intense. People mix primarily with their own kind." Hence, "the traditional individual is forced to rely on his own experience and on the beliefs, customs, and traditions of his societal unit for information and guidance." Palmer continues:

> The traditional environment is also marked by insecurity. The traditional individual is insecure because his rudimentary existence leaves him totally vulnerable to the capriciousness of nature: to flood, drought, famine, plague, and all manner of pestilence. His social isolation maximizes distrust and suspicion between units and between individuals within units; his limited sources of information make him prone to superstition and awe of the supernatural; and his physical isolation has increased his vulnerability to theft and pilferage.

This is not a pleasant picture. Social structures centered around kinship groups do try to minimize these insecurities, but they are too fragmented to be effective. Palmer says that they "tend to be affective, self-oriented, par-

---

[1] Monte Palmer, *The Dilemmas of Political Development: An Introduction to the Politics of the Developing Areas* (Itasca, Ill.: Peacock, 1973). All references to this work are taken from pp. 11–30 unless otherwise specified.

ticularistic, ascriptive, and diffuse.'' There is a basic assumption that other individuals are going to put themselves and their groups first, and everyone else
must do the same; people are not willing to play by the rules in a fair-minded and
disinterested manner. They obey more from the fear of being humiliated than
from any abstract concern for the community good; they desire preferential
treatment for their own family. Status is accorded to individuals without any
particular need for them to demonstrate their proficiency. Economic systems are
particularistic (social considerations take precedence over economic ones) and
diffuse (economic decisions are made by the same individuals who make other
decisions and who have no economic competence). Surpluses and technology are
minimal (though there is congruity between social and economic relationships).
Those who dissent or show innovative tendencies are reprimanded and cajoled to
continue family solidarity. Family heads demand absolute loyalty from family
members. Demands and expectations made on the system are minimal (''people
are too *weary* to demand better''), while identification with the system is high.

> In their simplicity, traditional political systems are equipped to perform few
> functions beyond those directly related to the perpetuation of the system.
> Specifically, they organize the tribe or village for defensive or offensive pur-
> poses, adjudicate disputes that exceed the scope of the smaller kinship units, ex-
> act tribute to be paid to external authorities, assign tasks when cooperation is re-
> quired, allocate wealth and other values in such a way as to avoid excessive con-
> flict, reinforce established norms by focusing shame on the individuals and
> families concerned, and generally uphold the values and myths of the society.[2]

Colonialism, Professor Palmer continues, brought with it fixed rules; native
technicians, administrators, and police; modern health practices; transportation
networks; a money economy; education; rising expectations; new chances for
personal income; and a takeoff into modernization. Unfortunately, traditional
political/social structures resist such influences that threaten their solidarity. A
principal problem of modernizing regimes is to overcome this resistance while at
the same time re-creating some of the better features of traditionalism (such as
group identity) in a modern setting. Frustrated in this attempt, such regimes have
frequently turned to coercion.

Palmer's analysis echoes that of many observers of developing nations. This
book *agrees* with a number of the features of his argument: Death rates are high
and consumption low in traditional settings. People are subject to the
capriciousness of nature. There is suspicion between tribes, parochialism within
them, and no dissent from basic mores. Yet we find ourselves *disagreeing* with
the overall argument. Palmer's analysis implies that traditional societies do an
inherently inadequate job of providing for their populace, and that their
resistance to change is a principal cause of the poverty, social unrest, and
disparities in wealth to be found in developing nations today. In contrast, we
would argue that these societies were more adept at serving the citizenry than this
analysis suggests, while the forces that prevent the equitable distribution of the
rewards of modernization are a by-product of modernization itself. The distinc-

---

[2] Ibid.

tion is more than academic. If one thinks that modern forms have more potential for aiding people than traditional ones, one might feel prone to replace traditional forms with modern ones even though no immediate advantage to the citizenry might be apparent. If, on the other hand, traditional forms commend themselves as having intrinsic value, one might be more hesitant about uprooting them until clear and present rationale appeared for doing so. The presumption is often too readily made that if modernization is occurring, progress is in the works. This book intends to make a frontal attack on that presumption. As a first order of business, I intend to demonstrate (in this chapter and the next) that the initial phases of modernization—which are still in process in developing nations—bring decline along with progress.

Palmer argues that suspicion and distrust between clans and families in traditional societies are intense; I will note that the means for resolving such suspicion are complex and effective. Palmer sees traditional man as isolated; I will see him as integrated into a social unit. Palmer sees him vulnerable to theft; I will note his recourses against theft. He sees individuals and groups placing themselves first; I will point to evidence of concern for the community good. He sees an unwillingness to play by the rules; I will disagree. He sees status as unrelated to a demonstration of proficiency; I will prove a close relationship between the two. He sees social elites making incompetent economic decisions; I see them making sensible economic decisions. He notes that colonialism brought health, education, and new chances for personal income; I argue that it also brought a loss of free land tenure and considerably greater personal insecurity. I will proceed now to support these emphases with data and argumentation. You will need to decide whether these theories hold water in the face of Professor Palmer's counter-emphases.

To begin, we shall examine two hypotheses about developing areas that describe more positive aspects of the interaction between their social and political systems before the arrival of the Europeans:

1. People lived in *integrated communities* (i.e., communities guaranteeing nearly everyone help in maintaining stable personal environments). This guarantee resulted from *self-governance* (i.e., political decisions most affecting stable personal environments were made by individuals within the community limited by custom and close interaction with fellow villagers).
2. Political decisions were sensible (i.e., characterized by good or common sense; intelligent; reasonable) in terms of creating stable personal environments, but not necessarily in terms of other goals like modernizing.

STUDY NOTE

You may prefer to substitute the word *rational* for *sensible*. Be sure to define your term.

After examining these two propositions in this chapter, I shall proceed in the next chapter to illustrate that modernization subsequently reduced the amount of integration, self-government, and attention to the needs of the populace. Since these propositions at least partially contradict those of Professor Palmer, and much conventional wisdom about developing nations, it seems safest to illustrate them by referring to specific field studies. I shall use the following studies and tribal groups which, because they are diverse and geographically scattered, allow us to test the propositions in a variety of settings. I will be generalizing about these groups *before* they were introduced to extensive commerce:

- *The Nuer*[3] inhabit areas adjoining tributaries of the lower Nile, in the Sudan. They were studied during the early 1930s by a British anthropologist, E. E. Evans-Pritchard. His work on them is widely known.
- *The Yakö*[4] live to the east of the Niger River in Nigeria. They were studied by the British anthropologist Daryll Forde during the 1930s.
- *The Nambikuara*[5] live deep within Brazil. Studies on them by the anthropologist Claude Levi-Strauss made in the 1930s are also well-known.
- *The Eskimo*[6] live in northern stretches of North America, basically from the Hudson Bay area west.
- *The !Kung*[7] live in the Kalihari Desert of Namibia and Botswana. Lorna Marshall carried out her studies of them in the 1950s, and many anthropologists have been studying them since.
- *The Navajo*[8] occupy the southeastern portion of the United States.
- *The Konds*[9] occupy the hills of western Orissa, in India.
- *The Kachins*[10] live along the upper valleys of the Irrawaddy River in Burma. British anthropologist E. R. Leach studied them from 1939 to 1940.
- *The Nupe*[11] live to the north of the Niger River in Nigeria. They were studied by anthropologist S. F. Nadel during the late 1920s.

---

[3] E. E. Evans-Pritchard, *The Nuer* (Oxford: Clarendon, 1940).

[4] Daryll Forde, "The Governmental Roles of Associations among the Yakö," in *Comparative Political Systems,* ed. Ronald Cohen and John Middleton (Garden City, N.Y.: Natural History Press, 1967), pp. 121–141.

[5] Claude Levi-Strauss, "The Social and Psychological Aspects of Chieftainship in a Primitive Tribe: The Nambikuara of Northwestern Mato Grosso," in *Comparative Political Systems,* ed. Cohen and Middleton, pp. 45–62.

[6] E. M. Weyer, "The Structure of Social Organization Among the Eskimo," *Comparative Political Systems,* ed. Cohen and Middleton, pp. 1–13; Charles C. Hughes, "From Contest to Council: Social Control Among the St. Lawrence Island Eskimos," in *Political Anthropology,* ed. Marc J. Swartz, Victor W. Turner, and Arthur Tuden (Chicago: Aldine, 1966) pp. 255–264.

[7] Lorna Marshall, "'!Kung Bushman Bands," in *Comparative Political Systems,* ed. Cohen and Middleton, pp. 15–43; Richard B. Lee and Irven DeVore (eds.), *Kalihari Hunter-Gatherers: Studies of the !Kung San and Their Neighbors* (Cambridge: Harvard University Press, 1976); Richard B. Lee, "The !Kung Bushmen of Botswana," in *Hunters and Gatherers Today,* ed. M. G. Bichieri (New York: Holt, Rinehart and Winston, 1972), pp. 326–368; Richard B. Lee, "'!Kung Bushmen Subsistence: An Input-Output Analysis," in *Environment and Cultural Behavior,* ed. Andrew P. Vayda, (Garden City, N.Y.: Natural History Press, 1969), pp. 47–69.

[8] Mary Shepardson, "The Traditional Authority System of the Navajos," in *Comparative Political Systems,* ed. Cohen and Middleton, pp. 143–154; Ruth Underhill, *Here Come the Navaho!* (Lawrence, Kans.: Bureau of Indian Affairs, 1957).

[9] F.G. Bailey, *Caste and the Economic Frontier: A Village in Highland Orissa* (Manchester, Great Britain: Manchester University Press, 1957); idem, "Political Change in the Kondmals," in *Comparative Political Systems,* ed. Cohen and Middleton, pp. 415–437.

[10] E. R. Leach, *The Political Systems of Highland Burma* (Boston: Beacon Press, 1965).

[11] Siegfried F. Nadel, *A Black Byzantium* (London: Oxford University Press, 1951); idem, "Nupe State and Community," in *Comparative Political Systems,* ed. Cohen and Middleton, pp. 293–337; H. A. S. Johnston, *The Fulani Empire of Sokoto* (London: Oxford University Press, 1967).

- *The Bantu*[12] occupy southern Africa.
- The inhabitants of North Kiriwina Island in the Trobriand Islands to the northeast of New Guinea in Southeast Asia were studied by the Polish anthropologist, Bronislaw Malinowski, from 1915 to 1918. His voluminous writings about the *Trobrianders*[13] are among the most famous in anthropological literature.
- *The Inca Empire,*[14] which extended along the coast of South America between the Andes Mountains and the Pacific Ocean from 1476 to 1534, was preceded by a number of other political systems within that region. The major archeological investigations there have taken place in the vicinity of the modern town of Trujillo, Peru, especially in the late 1940s. Scattered digs have been carried out up and down the coastline. Vast regions remain unexplored by archaeologists.

It is my intention in this chapter to demonstrate that traditional communities were integrated, self-governing, and made sensible decisions. First I shall briefly introduce the elements that made these groups integrated and self-governing. Then I shall examine more closely the Inca, the Nupes, the Hindus, the Kachins, and the Persians; although involved with empires, their villages were also integrated and self-governing. In the third section of the chapter, we shall peruse some decisions affecting personal environments relating to getting enough to eat, health, sharing, using talents, fighting, limiting power, and belonging. Were they sensible? And does the sum total of all this add up to stable personal environments?

The minor guarantees of land, food, companionship, a sense of worth and belonging, contact with leaders, and full use of scarce resources discussed here may seem somewhat trivial in an age of computers and space technology. Our talk of returning to them may well have a pathetic ring. It will, I hope, seem less pathetic once it becomes apparent that these attributes—taken for granted among middle classes in advanced industrial societies—are largely absent in contemporary developing nations.[15] For the moment, our problem is to ascertain whether they ever existed.

Before we proceed I should alert you that there are those who will argue that everything in this chapter should be examined warily because the anthropologists whose work we cite are prejudiced. It is true that most of them liked the societies

---

[12] I. Schapera, *Government and Politics in Tribal Societies* (New York: Schocken Books, 1967).

[13] Bronislaw Malinowski, *Coral Gardens and Their Magic: A Study of the Methods of Tilling the Soil and of Agricultural Rites in the Trobriand Islands,* vol. 1 (American Book Company, 1935); idem, *Argonauts of the Western Pacific* (London: Routledge & Kegan Paul, 1922); idem, *Crime and Custom in Savage Society* (London: Routledge & Kegan Paul, 1926); idem, *A Diary in the Strictest Sense of the Term* (New York: Harcourt, 1967); H. A. Powell, "Competitive Leadership in Trobriand Political Organization," in *Comparative Political Systems,* ed. Cohen and Middleton, pp. 155–192.

[14] Edward P. Lanning, *Peru Before the Incas* (Englewood Cliffs, N.J.: Prentice-Hall, 1967); Sally Falk Moore, *Power and Property in Inca Peru* (New York: Columbia University Press, 1958); Paul Kosok, *Life, Land, and Water in Ancient Peru* (New York: Long Island University, 1965); John V. Murra, "On Inca Political Structure," in *Comparative Political Systems,* ed. Cohen and Middleton, pp. 339–353.

[15] I should add that some of you may discover a further perplexity: perhaps only traditional society offers anyone these minor guarantees. The guarantees perceived among the middle classes (save for food) may be pseudo-guarantees.

they studied and were anxious to present them in a favorable light to their readers. Chapter 6, however, will make it clear that comparative politics theorists are also prejudiced. They feel that "modernity" is superior to "tradition," and are anxious to prove to their readers that the rigors of progress can be made to work.

A juror would be most remiss to decide a case only on the basis of the summaries by two contending lawyers. Summaries are designed to put the best foot forward—to make prejudices sound tenable. It is in listening to cross-examination that the observer learns the most at a trial. The kinds of questions asked have a strong bearing on the information one receives. By having lawyers with differing prejudices (or, as we shall call it in Chapter 6, differing perspectives) ask questions of the same witness, the judge and jury receive more information than if only one lawyer were asking the questions.

Today's comparative politics theorists are easy on their client ("modernity") in many regards. Many of them do not ask how increased Gross National Products can be expected to translate into higher standards of living. They do not explore why higher flows of information (e.g., from introducing democratic institutions) should cause governments to be more sensitive to the needs of their citizens, nor do they explore why improved capacity to distribute goods should be accompanied by improved motivation to do so. They simply imply that these attributes go together. Likewise, anthropologists often "see" a fair distribution of food and physical vitality in the villages they study, yet make no attempt to measure nutrition levels and life expectancies. They mention the existence of channels of communication between subject and ruler without exploring how they were used. They suggest that incompetent leaders can be removed without closely examining any specific attempts to do so. They do not look for personal biases in decisions by leaders.

If comparative politics theorists could have been in the field to question the anthropologists' clients, and anthropologists were to ask questions about today's ruling governments, we might find out more about each. This is precisely what is not happening. As a result, important searching questions are not being asked about either end of the spectrum. If the answers you find in this chapter still leave you with further questions, rest assured that you will face the same problem when we focus on modernization. If we determined to give up listening to prejudiced people, we would have to give up listening. Instead, we are using the same approach to both anthropologists and comparative politics theorists. We are focusing on the questions they ask and the manner in which they apply these questions to the data—not on their summary statements. Perhaps by doing so we can induce, from the next generation, some cross-examination in both realms. If those who are critical of the questions asked by the anthropologists apply the same standards to the questions asked by comparative politics theorists, they are liable to develop doubts about some matters that have become virtual articles of faith in today's generation. That alone is sufficient reason to read this chapter with care.

I also have a personal word of warning. The societies we will explore did not allow the pursuit of individual thought or the growth of science. There was no such thing as anonymity or privacy. The village peasants had little freedom to innovate or acquire goods for themselves. They were parochial and narrow in outlook. Their amusements were far less sophisticated than daytime television. A person who strayed out of the village into a royal capital might find himself or herself incarcerated or headless at the whim of some elite personage. To be frank, I think that most readers of this book would be quite miserable living in such a place. To assure you of your safety, I should also add that few such places exist anymore, for reasons that will soon become apparent. However, former inhabitants of such places, and their descendents, do exist—and in large numbers. Most of them, too, have little chance to pursue individual thought or science, little anonymity or freedom to innovate or acquire goods. They are parochial and enjoy unsophisticated amusements. Those in the cities still face dangers of bodily injury and even murder in the unstable atmosphere of the shantytown. To understand them, one needs to know something about the village life from which they emanated. For them, village life might be a more feasible option than it is for you.

INTEGRATED SELF-GOVERNING COMMUNITIES

STUDY NOTE

In this section and the next we are discussing the first hypothesis on p. 21. What is a social system? A political system? How would the two need to interact to create integrated self-governance? (See p. 10.)

Kinship groups, ritual leaders, and ritual organizations formed the heart of both the political and social systems in all these pre-modern communities listed on pp. 22–23. Kinship revolved around father and mother, grandparents, brothers and sisters, nieces and nephews. Usually one would spend an entire lifetime with these relatives subject only to the limits of patrilocalism and matrilocalism; in the former system the bride moved in with the groom's family, and in the latter the groom moved in with the bride's family. Uncles, aunts, and cousins also tended to live in proximity, creating a clan. The several clans living in the immediate vicinity had probably done so for several generations, providing a strong sense of continuity. Should an individual lose his or her family by deaths, war, or moves forced by extended drought, family and clan would adopt this person; so no one needed to be without a clan. If differences in a community or a clan became irreconcilable, there was usally a system that permitted a group of brothers or other sets of relatives to take their families and create a new homestead elsewhere. Such moves were made on a group, and not an individual, basis.

Ritual leaders, chosen from within the kinships groups and responsive to them, authoritatively allocated values and (even in empires) monopolized most of the legitimate use of force. Rather than being self-oriented and particularistic, their position demanded that they show concern for the community as a whole. They were selected as much for their talents as for their family of birth. Their duties were usually quite specifically defined by custom, and they had to share power with other ritual leaders in the community. People obeyed ritual leaders because the positions they held were ordained by custom with sacred ceremonial importance; obeying them bound the inhabitants to the community, their surroundings, and the natural order. The individual found meaning by identifying with the community and its leadership. Some of the most important decisions of these leaders were economic in nature. Every extended family in the community was entitled to a piece of land, and the leaders helped to assure that it was divided equitably. After a hunt, they saw that all participated in eating the meat. In case of theft or murder, they interceded to assure repayment. They organized community functions, and members of the community frequently turned to them for assistance.

The heads of families and clans constituted primary ritual leaders in any community. In addition, there were always other groups with ritual leaders, and ritual leaders without groups. The latter were sometimes priests who presided over ceremonies relating to planting crops, the founding of the village, initiations, blessing pregnant mothers or infants, changes of weather, divining, or any number of other functions. Sometimes they were in charge of leading warfare or hunts or settling feuds and disputes. Such individuals seldom presided over more than one type of ritual activity; during that ritual others obeyed them, and during other rituals they obeyed others.

Examples of groups requiring ritual leaders included age-sets, community councils, hunting and healing societies, priestly councils, and organizations to decide about thefts or land disputes. Boys were often initiated into age-sets at puberty. In addition to providing camaraderie, these groups of same-aged boys performed functions together like organizing weddings, building a roof for a large building, or helping to enforce a decision of a council regarding restitution for a theft. They became training grounds for leadership. Other groups often chose and replaced their own members, picking new ones partly on the grounds of the clan to which they belonged, and partly because of their capabilities for the job. On occasion, when tradition called for a son to replace his father in a particular ritual leadership role, he could be by-passed in favor of someone else if he was not deemed suitable. Such groups and leaders also had strictly defined duties, and were obeyed only in the realms over which they traditionally presided. No community had only one leader, nor did one group make all decisions. Most members of the community had more than one group identity. If someone felt he or she had received insufficient land or share of food, or had been harmed in some way, there was usually a group constituted to handle such appeals. People had frequent face-to-face contact with their leaders. Litigants could plead their own cases, often with other interested parties looking on. The lifestyle and living standards of ritual leaders tended to differ little from the other members of the community; they participated in its daily routine and regimen.

Villages often had one ritual leader designated as headman. This role was sometimes hereditary, with provisions for by-passing one unpopular heir in favor of another. One of the principal duties of this leader was to be "owner" of all the land of the village. This was the supreme symbol of continuity and solidarity in the village. Sometimes he would retain portions of this land for his own or general community use, but it was never his to keep. He was the custodian who presided over its distribution to the community, using other ritual leaders to help him in this task. On matters that were the prerequisites of other ritual leaders alone, the headman obeyed just like other members of the community.

Hence, there is evidence that these communities were integrated and self-governing and offered all their members land, food (except during periods of general drought), affection, continuity of relationships, and a sense of worth. Leaders were limited by custom and face-to-face contact with members of the community. The political systems grew out of the social systems.

SELF-GOVERNING COMMUNITIES UNDER EMPIRE

STUDY NOTE

This section continues discussion of the first hypothesis on p. 21.

The integrated self-governing community may be believable among herders and isolated villages, but what about those large territories in the pre-industrial world under the thumb of empire? Does this characterization apply to Egypt under the Pharaohs, India under Aqbar, Cambodia under the Khmer Kings, ancient Mesopotamia, Mexico under the Aztecs, or Peru under the Incas? Very little information is available to tell us about villages within these empires, but we are at least in a position to pursue the question with regard to villages under the Inca Empire. And we know a good deal about the question as it pertains to the Nupes, the Kachins, the Hindus, and the Persians, all of whom were involved with large dynastic systems. So we shall explore these five systems in some detail to see how the integrated self-governing community fared within them.

The Incas

These opening words of a chapter entitled "The Inca and His City" echo many other discussions on the subject:

> Louis XIV, the Sun King of France, actually had to insist that *he* was the state; "L'etat c'est moi." The Sun King of Peru, the Sapa Inca, never had to emphasize this—all which lay under the sun was his; it was known to everyone and accepted.[16]

The Sapa Inca may have been the state; but he did not govern villages. His power was not as great as this quotation implies.

The earliest known settlements on the north-central coast of Peru date back

---

[16] Victor Wolfgang von Hagen, *The Ancient Sun Kingdoms of the Americas* (Cleveland: World Publishing Company, 1957), p. 493.

to 2500 B.C. They were fishing and farming villages on the mouth and shores of rivers, probably organized along the lines we have just described in the previous section. By 1500 B.C. the men were already building large temples outside their villages, and later they experimented with irrigation. Then, around 200 B.C., the extent of irrigated land vastly expanded. The population shot up from a prior figure of around 25,000 for the entire coast to some 4½ million. The ceremonial centers grew in size, with walls hundreds of feet in length and towering into the air as pyramids. Military conflicts ensued. Cities developed, populated by administrators, architects, soldiers, merchants, artisans, and politicians. Class differentiations increased. Though the Inca Empire was still a thousand years in the future, this was the high point of the culture. The ceramics of this period are the finest, the pyramids the greatest, and more land was under cultivation than even during the Inca Empire or the twentieth century.

Obviously, individual valleys were well-organized by this time to make such great achievements. The flow of water in the irrigation canals had to be regulated. A villager would probably have to pay a percentage of his crop in order to support various pursuits of the city, and might have been drafted to fight in battle against a neighboring valley. (Political territories seldom seem to have extended beyond two or three valleys.) Many work hours must have been donated during these centuries for construction of the temples. Neighbors might have moved a few miles away to town to take up a craft or perhaps go to work for the government. For the great majority who stayed behind in the village to tend the extensive fields, there would be a new need for deference to some elders from higher status clans who had positions of power in the city, in addition to the inhabitants' own village elders and priests. But most decisions about community life probably were made within the communities themselves.

Starting about 600 A.D. a new phase came, which lasted some 600 years, during which warriors sought to consolidate groups of these political entities into empires. Each of these attempts was short-lived, and brought in its wake the disintegration of many of the old cities and shifts and instability in population. Cemeteries of this era are filled with the wounded and decapitated bodies of youths. Building temples gave way to building defensive fortresses. Finally, around 1250 A.D., some leaders in the north-central plain were successful in conquering much of the coastline from north to south and establishing Chan Chan, a city of some 50,000 inhabitants (who were called Chimu).

Each region still retained its own culture. The Chimu must have used indirect rule and experienced dissension among their own ranks. On the periphery to the south, the small farming village of Cuzco rose as challenger to the throne. Between 1471 and 1493—only thirty-nine years before the Spaniards in turn conquered the Incas[17]—the Inca leaders of Cuzco finally conquered the Chimus, to set up their own last great empire.

Cuzco was a cultural backwash; Chan Chan, its new subject, was the center of a region which for centuries had been the cultural mecca of South America. Furthermore,[18] the Incas felt they needed to demand more uniformity than the

---

[17] Kosok, *Life, Land, and Water*, p. 73.

[18] From this point, the discussion largely depends on Moore, *Power and Property in Inca Peru.*

Chimus had if they were to succeed. They recognized that they had two great tasks: to maintain an adequate flow of taxes, and to keep the peace.

To deal with taxation, the rulers determined that some land should be set aside everywhere in the kingdom for the Inca. Every able-bodied family head would be expected each year to work this land or (if not near such land) to contribute a percentage of produce from his own land, or to serve in the militia or as a temporary servant for one of the ruling families. Artisans would be expected to contribute a percentage of their output, and officials to contribute gold ornaments or other quality goods. This fed the militia and the officials and provided wealth for Cuzco. One problem was that much of the tax was to be received in the form of food. The Incas were unfamiliar with the wheel and the horse; llamas, the regional beast of burden about the size of a large sheep, would have been an inconvenient means for transporting the entire food supply back to Cuzco. Hence, it is not surprising that Spanish chroniclers record that Governors used much of the food at the local provincial capitals to feed the militia, government workers, state guests, road-building crews, and the like. Another problem was to keep the tax collector honest. To deal with this the Inca devised the famous decimal system by which a hierarchy of officials ruled over 10,000, 5,000, 1,000, 100, 50, and 10 persons respectively. Each rank carried identical—and rather generous—emoluments in the form of servants and payments; each official of the same rank was expected to bring in approximately identical tax revenues. If you knew the man's rank, you knew how much he should be worth. From a theoretical angle the idea is well adapted for taxation; it would obviously be difficult to implement for other ruling functions, since groups of people seldom come in such conveniently uniform sizes.

The Incas' second problem, keeping the peace, was a more serious one. To replace the old nobility with a new one at a time when the Incas were just beginning to consolidate power carried the risk of alienating local populations and substituting trial and error for experience. Yet it was the old nobility that had fomented much of the warfare to begin with by constantly raising armies to conquer more land. If the Inca would both pay for the army and give the nobility land, he might have hopes of retaining a local leadership with both popular following and loyalty to himself. The Spanish chroniclers record that the Inca did just that. To the north were areas where the nobles owned all the land and received produce back from the peasants, a carryover from Chimu times. In other regions, whole villages were producing surplus only for a particular temple. Frequent mention is made of lands associated with official positions, and of lands given by the Inca to individuals for outstanding service in war and the like. It is mentioned that nobles owned mines and plantations. There is reference to one of the duties of the provincial governor being that of assigning land to nobles. In each village lands were set aside to support the local temples in addition to those plots reserved for members of the village. The Inca did not have a real monopoly on the use of force; he had to share power with the nobility.

QUESTION

How did the Incas tax villagers?

The Inca did not allocate all values. An interesting omission from the chroniclers' discussions is any mention of how to deal with disputes regarding local land. If a peasant fooled around with the wife of a nobleman, say the chroniclers, he might be put to death. Should he move the landmark that separates two communities, he might be beaten with a stone, or put to death. But what if he proceeds to till another man's land for his own use? Or a younger son claims an elder son's inheritance? The chroniclers are silent on these issues. The boundary line between two communities might disrupt jurisdiction for taxation purposes and hence was a matter of great interest to the Inca; in contrast, the Inca had no interest in how untaxed land assigned to the villagers should be subdivided, or in inheritances that he did not tax. Those situations, along with local quarrels that did not involve officials, outside nobility, or potential hazards to the state, *could be handled at the local level.* There were not even provisions to appeal to a higher authority on such matters. Roads continued to be maintained by local citizenry, with tolls sometimes collected for local use. Though the principal statues in all local shrines were transported to Cuzco, the local priesthood stayed behind. Some receipts from temple lands also went to Cuzco; others stayed to be used at home. In times of peace, if a villager served his state service time and committed no crimes, he might expect to be left alone by the Inca. Even his period of state service need not have been entirely disruptive, for, since only able-bodied married men were subject to this obligation, his wife and children could tend the family fields while he was tending to the Inca's fields, roads, or battles.

With all this in mind, it is hardly surprising to find the chroniclers describing local political organization. When clearing land, planting, and harvesting, the whole community helped one another.[19] When a couple married, their lineage got together to build them a house. Before such tasks were begun, they sat down to figure out exactly what share each household was to contribute, according to customary formulas. The community also assumed responsibility for the aged, widows, orphans, the sick, and the lame; sometimes such individuals were placed in charge of distributing the villager's share of irrigation waters, supported by temple receipts. The community as a whole also cultivated some patches of ground to produce the maize beer needed for ritual libations. Villages had their own headman; clans took turns tending the fields of these individuals and providing them with water and wood, although headmen worked in the fields themselves as well. The lifestyle of a headman does not appear to have differed markedly from that of other villagers, and there is every indication that he shared his powers with other clan and ritual leaders and consulted with fellow villagers about decisions.

The Inca may have held supreme power for the thirty-two years that separated the conquest of the Chimus and the beginning of the civil war. He may have been considered the owner of all the lands in the kingdom in a geographic broadening of the type of power claimed by Trobriand, Kachin, Nupe, Yakö, and !Kung chiefs and cluster leaders. He may well have been absolutely ruthless and brutal in dealing with sexual rivals and political enemies. But this did not

---

[19] On this, cf. Murra, "On Inca Political Structure."

prevent men from looking after their own affairs through local leadership, in accordance with established customs. The Inca himself does not seem to have extended his power to all levels of decision making. Those at the lower levels of decision making were limited in their powers by custom and by their interaction, at least, with other local ritual and clan leaders.

Further discussion of Incas may be found on p. 69.

The Nupes

Nupe villages in north-central Nigeria were part of a broader political world. Some 200 miles to the south along the Niger River was a kingdom called Benin, whose rulers sent out military expeditions to make vassals of neighboring groups. From about the tenth to fifteenth centuries Nupeland paid tribute to one of Benin's vassals. Then in the fifteenth century a figure whom legend calls Tsoede set up a Nupe dynasty to rule Nupe territory. Tsoede and his successors established a capital that remained, save for some occasional lapses during dynastic feuding, at a town called Bida. The throne was hereditary and a royal clan grew up around it, along with some clans into which it had married. To provide these nobility with livelihood, a system of fiefs was established by which the king, *Etsu Nupe,* assigned villages to various royal extended families. These families, or parts of them, would go to the villages to reside for at least part of the year; the villages were expected to support them during their stay. While there, they could supervise tax collection, and perhaps interfere with decisions of the village elders. Every few years villages would be reassigned, so that no fief holders could entrench themselves. Not all villages became fiefs. The *Etsu Nupe* created a permanent army, which continually conducted missions both within Nupe territory and beyond it to the south, and they brought back slaves. Some of these military leaders with higher rank were permitted to use the slaves to open new land to farming. These slave villages may have been run in a brutal manner; we know nothing about them. Other slaves became attached to the royal court as trusted assistants. They inherited the duty of making annual or biannual trips to villages that were not fiefs to collect taxes. Both the fief holders and the slave assistants were empowered to collect taxes; *village elders governed other village affairs.*

Meanwhile, even broader forces were brewing that would come to bear on the Nupe. In the seventh century Arab raiders,[20] newly converted to Islam, moved westward from Egypt and conquered most of North Africa. They settled in the towns and imposed themselves as a ruling aristocracy, leaving the Berber farmers in the countryside to continue their livelihood. The Berbers remained uneasy under this foreign yoke, and continually attempted to revolt. Some of them probably began drifting into the broad territory north of the Nupes about that time. Then in the eleventh century came a new round of Arab invasions in the north, this time by Bedouin groups who were determined to push the Berbers from their farmland in order to use it for pasturing their herds. In these fierce

---

[20] Cf. Johnston, *The Fulani Empire.*

battles, towns were laid flat, and many were killed and enslaved. Those who remained retreated into the less fertile land of the surrounding hillsides. Many of the hardier males, however, seem to have made the long caravan journey across the Sahara to the south, filtered into the territory north of the Nupes, took wives among the groups already inhabiting the region, and settled down to farm. In this manner a major new African ethnic group, the Hausas, came into being.

The people with whom the Berbers intermarried appear to have themselves migrated into the region at an earlier date, probably from Chad or the Sudan, and were already settled into farming communities, with some clusters ruled matriarchally by queens.[21] As the new Hausa group emerged, its political system divided into seven states, each ruled by an hereditary chief. Capital cities evolved for each state (some outstripping others) and armies were created to allow these cities to make war against one another. Under this system, too, villages that paid their taxes continued to rule themselves.

The fourteenth century saw the reopening of two caravan routes, one linking the Hausas with North Africa, and the other joining them with the lower Nile. Within a short time the Hausa city of Kano was transformed into a major trading center linking the north, east, and west coasts of Africa. With the new prosperity came war, as neighboring kingdoms and internecine challengers sought to claim Hausaland for themselves, taking slaves and booty on the side. The former states disintegrated into warring factions. Meanwhile the route to the east brought from the Sudan a new social force: the Fulani. Like their former neighbors, the Nuer, they were herders of cattle. Among them were men of learning, converted to Islam. They traded their dairy products for the grain grown by their new Hausa neighbors, and their numbers grew. By the seventeenth century, Hausa village heads expected to receive tribute from the Fulani, and the state placed a tax on cattle. Both moves greatly disturbed the Fulani. The year 1755 marked the birth of a Fulani named Shehu, who devoted his life to rousing his fellow Fulani into a holy war against the Hausa. By 1817, after a long battle, the Hausa territory had been partitioned into two Islamic Fulani states.

Meanwhile the Nupes were divided into two camps by a dispute over succession. With the aid of the new powerful allies to the north, some of the few Fulani in Nupe territory took advantage of the feud to move for power themselves. They succeeded behind the scenes in 1810 and formally assumed the title of *Etsu Nupe* in 1836. They attempted to expand the boundaries of their rule, inducing civil war in the 1850s, and then settled down for a period of relatively stable rule.

Once again, one wonders how all this affected governance at the village level. Clearly a great many villagers were killed, enslaved, uprooted, burned out of their homes, conscripted, and heavily taxed. According to one European traveler, nearly half the population of the Hausa Emirate of Kano consisted of slaves.[22] Yet this narrative has covered a vast territory and span of time. If one

---

[21] This is the first point at which matriarchy (females holding ritual offices) has come up in our discussion. A society can be *matrilineal* (inheriting through the female line) and *matrilocal* (couples residing near the wife's parents) and still *patriarchal* (males holding offices).

[22] Heinrich Barth, *Travels and Discoveries in North and Central Africa,* vol. II (London, 1957) pp. 124–25; 143–44. Generally such slaves were adopted into the households of their owners, living in a synonymous lifestyle with them but keeping their subordinate roles.

were to examine the period village by village and add up the years that individual villages were unaffected by war, the total would be considerable. Save for the concerted Bedouin attack on the Berbers, much of the fighting was dynastic, with fixed armies fighting one another around towns and probably avoiding villages as much as possible. All towns (and the Nupe villages) were walled. The major Hausa city of Kano had walls with a perimeter of eleven miles. Peasants were invited inside the walls during periods of siege.

Among the Nupe, taxation seems to have had undesirable effects. The only recourse a village could have against unscrupulous taxation was appeal to the *Etsu Nupe*. In the period before the Fulani conquest there are records of villages succeeding in having the *Etsu Nupe* recall both holders of fiefs and slave tax collectors because they were imposing taxes greater than those prescribed. During the long period of civil wars, however, this recourse was weakened and remained so afterward.

Despite such actions, anthropologists who visited Nupe villages still under Fulani rule in the 1920s, both as fiefs and directly under royal domain, found them headed by a village council of elders, with a chief who distributed land, a priest, age-sets presided over by boys from the next highest age grade, and the general form of governance described earlier in the chapter. Local governmental systems like this existed throughout what is now northern Nigeria. The Fulani *Etsu Nupe* interfered with these systems by taxation, by trying certain criminal cases that were felt to be crimes against the state, and by approving all choices of village chiefs. At times, the *Etsu Nupe* did not approve the village's choice, and demanded another candidate. In these circumstances it was not uncommon for the village to simply ignore the royal choice and continue to treat its own man as *de facto* chief. The king's rule was administered by the nobility or slave officials who came out to stay at irregular intervals for unpredictable periods of time, with an eye fixed principally on collecting taxes. Since the king would not support these individuals in their efforts to overtax, the amount they took partly depended on the guile of the villagers. A few villages even succeeded in buying away fiefs in exchange for an annual payment. Meanwhile villagers were left with the task of dealing with community problems as they arose each day; the only machinery adequate for this task was their own. The rule of the *Etsu Nupe* was less beneficial to villagers than that of the Inca, although it in no way destroyed the integrated, self-governing community. In fact, it helped keep that community intact.

Further discussion of the Nupe may be found on p. 68.

The Kachins

The Kachin hill tribes of highland Burma have apparently had a rather constant pattern of internal politics for about 1,600 years. A council of lineage heads, containing a headman, presided over each village. They farmed by slash-and-burn techniques (see the index) with the council deciding where to clear the next fields and each lineage entitled to a piece of land. Each cluster was presided over by a chief, and clusters sometimes engaged in feuds.

In the valley below the Kachins lived the Shans, whose economy centered around rice paddies and trade with China to the north. Sometimes the Chinese sent in fighters instead of traders; during the nineteenth century the challenge came from Burmans and British to the south. On these occasions the Shans allied with the Kachins, who furnished them with mercenary soldiers and with intelligence on troop movements. During times of peace, trade over the mountain passes was active. The Kachins capitalized on this by charging tolls; mining salt and iron, and later, jade; making ceremonial swords for sale; and selling protection to the Shans in the valleys below.

The Shans had their basic origins in China, and Shan princes were influenced by Han Chinese principles. They lived apart from their people in palaces and did not marry commoners. While Shan villagers actually owned their own land and ran the affairs of their own villages, the princes looked upon them as vassals. Being polygamous, the princes sometimes married the daughters of commoners; their parents were then viewed as tenants of the princes. The princes helped one another in times of internal insurrection or external attack. They cemented these alliances by marrying one another's daughters. When a prince died, his oldest son would take over and continue the rule unless there was a challenge to the throne by some other relative.

QUESTION

What power did Shan princes have over villagers?

Kachin chiefs were often envious of the glitter and pomp of the Shan nobility. A Kachin chief frequently held his position because he was from the most prominent lineage of a cluster of villages. His status was largely ritual. The judicial powers of Kachin villages were in the hands of a judicial council, composed of respected elderly men in the village. Since the Kachin had a custom whereby the *youngest* son normally succeeded to chieftaincy on the demise of the father, he was often younger than other council members. Because of his central position in the lineage network, he was frequently a litigant rather than an arbitrator. The chief, in fact, did not always preside over the council of elders; that was often left to the headman of another village in the cluster. Says Leach:

> The executive decisions had to be made by the Kachins themselves without waiting for orders from above concerning such matters as where to make a field clearing, when to burn the felled brushwood, when to make the first sowing, where to place a house site . . . in my actual fieldwork I seldom identified any instruction which had issued from a chief acting on his own initiative.[23]

The chief was entitled to tribute, but he was also expected to give the best feasts. There were minor variations of wealth within an individual village, but it was not always the chief who was wealthiest. To increase his prestige within the cluster, he would tend to marry his daughters (Kachin chiefs could also be polygamous)

---

[23] Leach, *Political Systems of Highland Burma,* p 189.

to people in his villages, making them his (subordinate) sons-in-law; at the same time he acceded to a number of ritual kinship obligations to them.

Hence, if a Kachin chief had ambitions to raise his status to one of importance, he was tempted to emulate and imitate the Shan princes. Ordinarily he did not even attempt this. When he did, it was usually because of the power to surreptitiously hoard tolls collected from trade caravans. He would then—in Shan style—give wedding dowries to sons-in-law in exchange for their loyalty to him. To move closer to the Shan alliances, he would try to marry the daughter of a Shan prince, but this usually backfired. In the eyes of his villagers, and especially his own sons-in-law, this put him in the same inferior position to the Shan prince as his sons-in-law held to him. Furthermore, once he had reached the state of some economic independence and a Shan alliance, he often began breaking Kachin kinship rules in his efforts to imitate the Shans (e.g., pressing his *oldest* son as his successor, and treating his sons-in-law as vassals by ignoring his kinship obligations to them).

Once a Kachin chief had reached this state, some of his own villagers usually began a revolt against his rule. This extended feuding would weaken his own real power—to recruit his villagers as troops for the Shans or to enforce the tolls—and he would be forced to leave the village. Often villages that had gone through such a revolt reverted to a system in which they thereafter recognized no nobility at all.

If a chief was to gain real independent power, he needed to take control of some Shan-inhabited valley lands, as sometimes happened. This occurrence would only strengthen and speed up the tendency for his own villages to revolt, and thus deprive him of the very militia with which he had suppressed the valley.

The Shans, meanwhile, were entirely dependent upon their system of alliances, their paid courtiers who collected taxes and arranged the wars, some court favorites to whom they had given land, and the questionable loyalty of the fathers of their commoner wives. Shan commoners did not feel strong kinship ties beyond the nuclear household. The Prince had little in the way of kinship ties to his people, and no standing army, and was dependent on Shan villages for his tax base.[24] Perhaps because they had permanent investments in their rice fields, Shan subjects did feel loyalty to their villages and involved themselves in directing village affairs. There would appear to be little to prevent them from doing so. Thus, both the Shan and the Kachin villages ruled themselves with little interference from nobility or would-be nobility.

Further discussions of Shans and Kachins may be found on p. 68.

The Hindus

Alexander the Great entered India in 327 B.C. He discovered ruling dynasties there, and one of his camp followers founded a new dynasty after his departure. Megasthenes, his ambassador to this court, reported on the existence of seven

---

[24] During the 1960s, the Shan's key role in the opium trade and CIA counterinsurgency gave them new independence. For a fascinating discussion of this see Alfred W. McCoy, *The Politics of Heroin in Southeast Asia,* (New York: Harper & Row, 1972), pp. 242–354.

castes: philosophers, husbandmen, shepherds, artisans, soldiers, inspectors, and counselors of the king. Obviously dynasties and the caste system have early roots in India. In later centuries, some rulers were converted to Buddhism. During the fifth and sixth centuries Huns gained temporary control of northern India. In the eleventh century Turkish Muslims entered India, and proceeded to extend their rule. Some conquered most of India. Then members of the old Hindu nobility would drive them back, only to have them return in a later generation. Much of this fighting, and the demeanor of court life, was savage and brutal. Entire villages would be flattened during battles, and the surviving inhabitants would have to rebuild. Throughout all this turmoil, however, the caste system remained. Successive rulers of all strains superimposed their court systems upon it. Sometimes a community's land would be divided among several high-caste lineages (perhaps Brahmin, perhaps another high caste). Each lineage would have relatives in several villages of the region, and hence had land in several villages. Sometimes a single patrilineal extended family controlled a village's land. At times, a Brahmanical temple, or a kinsman (or kinswoman, or concubine) of the royal family would control a village's land. Some village land (e.g., among the Konds) simply belonged to village headmen, who distributed it in the same manner as most of the societies surveyed earlier in this chapter. Succeeding rulers might vary the revenue-gatherers who had jurisdiction over a group of villages (e.g., rewarding the role to their best warriors). As we shall see in the next chapter, the Muslims effected some changes in the method of revenue gathering in parts of the north. But there seems to be long continuity to the form of rule in individual villages themselves.

Kathleen Gough[25] reconstructed the social pattern of one village in southern India as it existed before the arrival of the British. In 1952, the village comprised 483 acres of wet paddy land and 114 acres of dry garden and waste (all of which grew two crops a year), and had a population of 962 (which probably means it had half this population two centuries earlier). Prior to 1780 it was located a mile away, but was laid flat by a Muslim invasion that year and had to be rebuilt. Three to five Brahmin patrilineages controlled the crop land. Each lineage controlled a fixed number of shares, but lands corresponding to the shares were rotated between the lineages every three years. At that time the eldest competent man of each lineage allotted a portion of his lineage's share to each extended family within his lineage. Twice annually, after each harvest, these families collectively paid 40 to 60 percent of the harvest as tax to the king and his intermediaries. They also sold some of the additional surplus crop individually to merchants in a nearby town. In addition, some land was set aside for the upkeep of the two Brahmin temples. A hereditary trustee managed these lands and paid a biennial stipend in grain to the temple priests.

The Brahmins' land was worked by members of lower castes. Some of these (who grew the grain crops) were serfs, permanently indentured to the Brahmins; others (who herded goats and cows, and raised chickens and vegetable gardens)

[25] E. Kathleen Gough, "Caste in a Tanjore Village," in *Aspects of Caste in South India, Ceylon and North-West Pakistan,* ed. E. R. Leach (Cambridge: Cambridge University Press, 1969), pp. 11–60.

came from independent pastoral communities to the south, and were free to return if they wished. A serf might be transferred from one lineage and village to another if rearrangement of numbers became desirable. All received daily payments of grain, materials for house building, the use of a garden to grow family crops, the right to fish in the bathing-pools, and gifts like clothing at marriages, deaths, and festivals. The serfs, however, were not as well remunerated as the pastoralists, and worked harder.

In addition, the village was served by a family of barbers, carpenters, and potters. These received biennial payments of grain from the Brahmins, and also some payments in kind when they performed their services for individuals. Sometimes a family would serve more than one town; washermen, blacksmiths, and goldsmiths from a village to the south served this village as well. If such a family grew too large to be useful in a community, some of their members could move to another village that was short of a barber, carpenter, or potter. The entire caste could switch to a new occupation, or unemployed members of such castes might be supplied with wet lands, from which they could keep a fourth to a fifth of the crop. A few serfs were periodically appointed by the Brahmins to guard the fields, and during this period of service the guards were paid in the same way as the potters.

Though there was considerable disparity between the wealth of the Brahmins and of the field workers, each caste was quite homogeneous in wealth within itself. Strict religious scruples governed the performance of all these obligations. Since all major exchanges within the community were in grain, and taxes were paid by the Brahmins as a percentage of total crop, no one was in monetary debt to anyone else. The Brahmins were not free to sell the land, which had been given them as a trust by the royalty, or to remove the serfs from it; they were morally obligated to create distributions which provided a livelihood for other members of the community. They furnished the seed and farm implements. The community was self-sufficient in providing for its members, while at the same time providing a surplus for the king. Each caste group chose its own leaders, worshiped in its own temples, and engaged in its own festivals, in addition to those which were community-wide. Disputes were settled by caste leadership, or by the Brahmins. Castes dealt with one another through these leaders. These villages were integrated and self-governing.

Further discussion of India may be found on p. 82.

The Persians

The people of Iran[26] perhaps experienced more empires, and more years of suffering from them, than any other inhabitants of the developing areas. Already in the second milennium B.C., they were ruled by their own powerful kings. In the sixth century Cyrus the Great extended their empire to include most of the lands

[26] Ann K. S. Lambton, *Landlord and Peasant in Persia: A Study of Land Tenure and Land Revenue Administration* (London: Oxford University Press, 1953).

of the eastern Mediterranean and the Middle East. Then they were conquered by Alexander the Great. His rulers were in turn thrown out by Scythian nomads, who were in turn replaced by new Persian rulers. In the seventh century A.D. Islamic Arabs injected themselves into Persia. They were overthrown in the eleventh century by Seljuk Turks, who in the thirteenth century were unseated by Mongol invaders. These invaders were thrown out in the sixteenth century by the Safavids, Persians who established a capital at Isfahan, which was sacked by Afghans at the end of the seventeenth century, but was recovered. In the eighteenth century the Qajars, of Turkish origin, overthrew them and established a capital in Teheran. They were overthrown in 1925 by an officer in a Cossack regiment who declared a new dynasty, which was overthrown in 1979.

All of these invasions and reigns were accompanied by bloodshed. Probably the most radical devastation came with the Mongol invasion, when whole regions were depopulated by flight and massacre. After the Afghans were turned out, large numbers of tribal families were moved forcibly into the region bordering Afghanistan. Especially from the Seljuk Turks onward, new invaders usually wanted booty. They seized property, land, and people to give as rewards to their warriers and administrators. While most recognized, as did the Code of Hammurabi and the writings of Islam, that their prosperity depended upon the well-being of the peasantry, overtaxation was frequent, especially after the twelfth century. The court retainers often took too much for themselves, and expensive military campaigns strained treasuries. This, combined with drought, brought famine and poverty to many peasants.

Beneath all the pillage, however, self-governing villages were able to survive. While the system of administration changed repeatedly with succeeding regimes, most of it was preoccupied with collecting taxes. As with the Incas, there was little concern to interfere with the internal affairs of villages once the urge to tax was satisfied. From the very earliest times district tax collectors and bailiffs oversaw taxation and military conscription at the village level. In 550 B.C., Achaeminids replaced tribal leaders with appointed provincial governors. Every family was permitted to retain at least one able-bodied man to work the fields; all others had to serve in the military campaigns led by great landowners on horseback. The villagers also helped build and maintain roads, and contributed other labor services. This system continued under Alexander and the Scythians. Power seemed to be concentrated in the landowners and provincial governors, while the king retained tax collectors at the village level. Villagers and landowners often cooperated to resist taxation. Landowners came to acquire their own armies composed of peasants from their lands. All villagers seem to have had a piece or pieces of land to grow crops, plus access to pasture land. The landowners paid for construction of irrigation systems, which the peasants helped maintain. After the Arabs conquered, some land was set aside around villages for the caliph's private flocks, but local officials did not change. Some landowners were converted to Islam, while Arabs took ownership in some provinces.

Most villages specialized in herding and tilling. Some families specialized as blacksmiths, barbers, potters, carpenters, and in other crafts. Villagers paid for these services with a portion of crops, and sometimes with a community levy. At times they hired an individual to watch irrigation canals. Village elders were involved in settling disputes. Until the arrival of the Arabs, villagers were probably involved with the priests in tilling and deciding how to distribute the proceeds of lands set aside for charity.

Further discussion of Iran may be found on p. 88.

Summary

Taxes, the threat of military reprisals, the chance for limited mobility outside the village, the percentage of time devoted to labor for the emperor, and the exposure to new cultural artifacts obviously changed village life after the introduction of empire. But empires did not produce the same fundamental changes in integrated self-governing communities that expanded commerce would cause later in history. For the most part, communities continued to tend to their own basic life needs, to settle their own disputes, to see that land and food was distributed among their members, to choose their own leaders, and to join together for ritual functions.

POLITICS AND PERSONAL ENVIRONMENTS

STUDY NOTE

This section discusses the second hypothesis on p. 21. Would it matter if we substituted *rational* for *sensible*?

These communities may have been self-governing entities, but questions still remain as to whether they used this condition to promote stable personal environments. Professor Palmer suggested that individuals in these communities put their own families first and did not think in terms of the good of the community, did not play by the rules, cared more about status than proficiency in choosing leaders, let social customs and superstitions override sensible economics, and let themselves be bossed around by their leaders. A self-governing community that is selfish, shortsighted, wasteful, and does not demand competency from its leaders may sound theoretically good while in reality creating unstable personal environments for many of its members. It may be obvious that these communities had means to govern themselves and rules that suggested humanitarian goals, but did they really obey their rules? Did they show common sense and concern for the weal of the community when they made actual decisions?

Traditional villages do not always immediately commend themselves as being highly embued with common sense. For instance, to the outsider, the Trobriand sociopolitical system seems to be almost comically confused and nonsensical. Parents raised sons to maturity, yet these sons owed their ultimate allegiance to the mother's oldest brother who lived in another village and whom they (and their mothers) hardly knew. Instead of just raising crops and storing them away, everyone went through an elaborate charade of giving away food (at times transporting it for miles) only to find they had an almost equal amount of the same commodities as they had started with once others had bestowed their gifts on them. No matter how emotionally close a village leader felt to his sons, he must ordinarily pass his title along to a nephew who grew up in another village. When you asked a Trobriand villager who owned the land, he would change his story according to who was listening to the conversation. Villages sometimes fought about who had the larger crop, the argument culminating in one village carrying its entire crop of yams over to the other simply to ascertain via an elaborate display and measuring system which crop was indeed the larger. When this was over, they picked up their crop and returned home, perhaps after exchanging some of their yams for those of the other village (of comparable quality, of course!). There was a pecking order on gardens as elaborate as any office arrangement among executives of an American corporation; no one was allowed to have a garden as well laid out or tended as those of the chief. People spent hours decorating their gardens above and beyond what they knew to be necessary for optimal growth of the crops. They also spent a lot of hours just dancing and prancing around in bizarre costumes, all the while insisting there was some serious purpose behind it. Let us see, then, if we can make any sense out of this strange tangle and some similar exotic behavior to be encountered among other groups. Did it aid in creating stable personal environments?

Food

> **QUESTION**
>
> How does food relate to a stable personal environment? To building a modern nation? How can we determine whether a political decision regarding food is sensible (or rational)?

The most immediate problem of all these societies was getting enough to eat. The question we ask here is whether the political systems organized by these groups helped provide inhabitants with enough food. We shall begin by taking a look at those enigmatic Trobrianders.

North Kiriwina Island, although filled with lush green foliage, furnishes very little that is edible beyond a few wild mangoes and breadfruits. The land must be cleared to plant crops. One can plant bananas and coconut palms and leave them virtually unattended for a number of years. Although the coconuts provide valuable protein, these fruits would not provide sufficient nourishment to maintain human habitation. Coastal villages catch occasional sharks and a smaller fish called mullet. These fish also add protein to the diet, but appear only sporadically and unpredictably. There are also pigs, but it is yams and taro roots that provide most calories for the diet. To grow these the farmer must cut away heavy undergrowth, burn off the remainder, dig through thick soil, sort out and plant tubers, and then weed incessantly. Following the harvest it is necessary to start the process all over again. If the rains do not come, the crop may fail. Hence, a good deal of work is entailed in producing a subsistence diet; to be safe against famine, more than subsistence is needed.

The Trobriand political system created strong incentives for producing such surpluses. A Trobriand man was responsible for much more than merely feeding his family. It would be considered a disgrace if his harvest gifts to his sister's family, the chief of his wife's village, and whomever else he might owe tribute, were not up to the quality and quantity of those his family received. Major ceremonies were performed over the fields, and food had much more significance than mere sustenance; it was conspicuously displayed and a great deal of pride was taken in yam and taro tributes. This custom encouraged a substantial crop; it also provided an emotional outlet for creative urges and a sense of being part of a community effort. The rivalry among villages undoubtedly gave incentive to tend plots with care, and assured that an industrious village would not be called upon to tide lazier neighbors through a dry season. Furthermore, when a young man moved to his uncle's village, he was expected to assist with the family's plots; a young man who was not diligent in these regards would not be considered worthy of receiving a plot of land. So a lazy son could not anticipate an inheritance from indulgent parents. Ambitious young men might tend part of the chief's land as well and be rewarded for doing so. If someone did not tend his own fields, he was required to allow someone with insufficient fields to do so and retain all but one-twentieth of the harvest. Those who kept too much to eat for themselves were criticized. And chiefs could see that gardens were grown and rotated in a manner that was in harmony with the ecology of the island.[27] So effective were these incentives that villages generally produced twice what they needed to eat,[28] and plenty to tide them through the occasional dry year. There was some reason behind the madness.

Further discussion of Trobrianders may be found on p. 50.

The Nuer, like the Trobrianders, had some strange habits. Says Evans-Pritchard: "They were always talking about their beasts. I used sometimes to despair that I never discussed anything with the young men but livestock and girls, and even the subject of girls led inevitably to that of cattle."[29] They decorated their cows with tassels, gave them elaborate ritual names, composed songs about them, even washed their hands and faces in the animals' urine. The men were at their happiest when they could spend their days with the cows. Every family's chief ambition was to collect for itself as many cows as possible. The cows provided the Nuer with milk, meat, blood to drink, bones for tools,

---

[27] Garden magician at the village council: "Yes, O Chief, I want to strike Tubuloma, Kavakaylige and Ovabodu. The *odila* (bush) has grown well there, it is a wet year, and it will be good for these lands, which are all galaluwa (black, heavy, but dry soil) and butuma (light, red soil). Let us make our gardens there." Malinowski, *Coral Gardens*, p. 89.

[28] Malinowski, *Coral Gardens*, p. 8.

[29] Evans-Pritchard, *The Nuer*, p. 19.

and dung for fuel. They would have been quite happy as a purely herding people simply following the cows about the countryside as they grazed.

That would, however, have been risky. If epidemics spread among the cows, or they all ceased to lactate at the same time, the Nuer would have faced starvation. So they reverted to a backup activity which none of them enjoyed, raising millet, and to fishing during the dry season. There were probably seasons in the past, before the introduction by Arab raiders of the cattle-killing rinderpest disease, when they could have gotten by on the cows alone, but even then they raised millet. To sustain the three occupations—herding, gardening, and fishing—required considerable coordination. Each activity took place at a different spot. The men had to leave the women behind to harvest the grain while they opened the fishing camps. To guard against rinderpest the herds were separated into a number of encampments at the same time. When the rains began once again, part of each family had to return to plant the millet. The village elders coordinated all these moves, provided rituals for each requisite function, and organized community life during the periods when families were separated.

It is possible that the cultural bias toward cows created overgrazing. Perhaps if the Nuer had focused on better fishing technology (such as permanent ponds, for instance), a steadier supply of food could have been assured (although this could have led to population increases and subsequent disaster in the event that the ponds dried out). As it was, the food supply sometimes proved inadequate. At other times it would appear that herds were allowed to become larger than needed, simply to inflate the egos of the owners.

Especially during the 1960s, governments took steps to aid herding groups like the Nuer by building tube wells and aiding them in planting commercial crops, along with providing vaccinations for men and cattle. As a result, both human and cattle populations increased. Cattle began to overgraze the land. Cultivation for commercial crops reduced savannah forests and grasses which had once held the topsoil and compensatory practices like contour plowing were often not employed. Individual land ownership began to break up village life. Then in the 1970s an intense drought—probably the worst in the history of the regions bordering the Sahara to the south—fell upon the area, drying the wells and many of the rivers. Cut off from relief supplies, at least 250,000 people died. Others set up shantytowns in the cities. Food had to be imported, but funds were not available for adequate supplies and there was much bureaucratic bungling on shipments. In the midst of this food *exports* from the region continued to increase.[30] A report of the European Development Fund (in Niger) concluded that even with good rains for the next ten years, the food-population ratio in sub-Sahara Africa will be worse in 1982 than in disastrous 1973.[31]

During times of drought the Nuer had learned to burn off the savannah so that the grasses with the deepest roots could send up fresh shoots, providing high-protein feed for the cows. They would also migrate to the banks of larger

---

[30] See Food and Agriculture Organization, *Yearbooks of International Trade Statistics* and *Trade Yearbooks* (Rome: United Nations); Frances Moore Lappé and Joseph Collins, *Food First: Beyond the Myth of Scarcity* (Boston: Houghton Mifflin, 1977), pp. 259–261.

[31] Martin Walker, "Drought," *New York Times Magazine* (June 9, 1974), p. 42.

rivers. When rivers were dry, two days of hard work by all able-bodied men of a community would produce a thirty-foot well in a dry river bed to tap the most likely source of water in the region. Fixed national and regional boundaries, individual land ownership, disintegration of community life, and dependence on permanent wells have probably reduced this kind of maneuverability. The drought of the 1970s is so severe that even these techniques would still bring disaster to many, although probably not as many. Since we have no records of earlier periods, it is possible that others have suffered similar disasters in times past, with which even their more flexible techniques could not cope. Certainly the Nuer made three ecological errors even in times of more adequate rainfall. Burning the grasses, while providing the tender shoots and killing insects harmful to cattle, also destroys humus and microorganisms needed for soil fertility and erosion control and increases evaporation. They failed to use the prevalent manure to fertilize their gardens. And they did not fallow fields, but instead planted on the same plots year after year until yields were noticeably depleted. But it is hard to make a case that modern techniques for feeding people in the region are more effective than former ones.

The Nuer have survived a long time. If we go back two or three million years in time to nearby Lake Turkana in northern Kenya, we find mingling there late *Ramepithecus, Australopithecus africanus, Australopithecus boisei,* and *Homo habilis*. Were we to return to those same shores a couple of million years later—or about three-quarters of a million years ago—we would find only one hominid creature there, a descendent of *Homo habilis* called *Homo erectus*. What happened to the rest? If you covered their heads they would have looked remarkably like today's humans. *Ramepithecus* walked with a rather stooped gait, and had poorly developed thumbs and toes and a good deal of body hair. The others had hands almost identical to us, and little body hair. Of them all, *Homo habilis* had the greatest need for water, since he had highly developed sweat glands and therefore lost more water through perspiration than the others. This helped him keep his body cool while running, but tied him to steady water supplies.

Why, then, did only *Homo habilis* survive while the other hominids became extinct? According to Richard Leakey, the answer lies in the brain. The brain of *Homo habilis* was far larger than those of his hominid contemporaries, and contained more folds—especially in the frontal and temporal lobes which house powers of intuition, persistence, restraint, motivation, word association, speech, and memory.[32] These frontal and temporal lobes continued to grow and develop additional folds in *Homo erectus, Homo sapiens,* and *Homo sapiens sapiens*. Our nasal cavities, palates, tongues, pharynx, and larynx also developed in a manner that made it easier to speak. The rest of our anatomy did not change much in all that period of time. Two or three million years ago the water in Lake Turkana and the plant and animal life there was far more abundant than it is today. Hominids could eat plants, scavenge, and do some sporatic hunting, much as other animals in the region. Since then, however, the level of the lake has risen and fallen a number of times, indicating severe climatic changes. Unlike the

---

[32] Richard E. Leakey and Roger Lewin, *Origins* (New York: E. P. Dutton, 1977), p. 192.

other hominids in the region, *Homo habilis* and his successors were able to organize so as to face these challenges. There are remains of his camps which, unlike those of his contemporaries, were occupied for days at a time. He had learned to transport and store food and plants. He learned to divide his labors in collecting food (such as the men hunting while the women gathered plants) and to share food—something no other primate does to any substantial degree apart from parents feeding their young. He learned to carry water in egg shells. Food-sharing within an organized social group requires restraint, initiative, and persistence. When climatic changes occurred, these powers probably served the Nuer's ancestors well. There are early signs that they might have set up camps along the lake during dry season and on the higher ground during wet season, just as the twentieth century Nuer do.

So the Nuer have behind them some three million years of successful adaptation to a very changing environment through constant food-sharing. Those who are quick to suggest that primitive people are not good at adapting to change, or that modern scientists and social planners are better at this than primitive people, should keep this in mind. They should also take note of what happened to many of the Nuer who departed from the ways of their ancestors during the Sahel drought.

Further discussion of the Nuer may be found on p. 54.

The !Kung social system also encouraged sharing. The Kalihari Desert, in which they live, is dry and has only periodic rainfall; sharing in gathering and preparing food is essential for survival. Lorna Marshall reports that "altruism, kindness, sympathy, or genuine curiosity are not qualities that I observed often in their nature."[33] She tells of how they would laugh when a certain lame man fell down, and of their failure to help him up. Yet !Kung also crave social acceptance. They cannot bear even mild disapproval. And group norms made it socially unacceptable to fail to share food or to accept or reciprocate gifts. This was the key to feeding everyone.

About 65 to 80 percent of the !Kung diet came from roots, fruits, nuts, and beans gathered by the women. In the evening each woman provided these to her extended family around her campfire. If there were visitors from neighboring huts they were invited to join in. It was bad manners for visitors to take large portions. If a male member of the family caught a spring hare or other small animal that, too, was shared by the family. It was common during dry seasons to visit relatives and friends in other bands which might be located in areas with more food and water. These visitors were welcomed around the fires for meals, with knowledge that the favor would be reciprocated someday.

When men hunted large game the prey belonged to the person whose poisoned arrow first pierced the animal. It was not unusual for someone who could not hunt to give an arrow to someone who could; in effect, the hunter killed the prey

---

[33] Lorna Marshall, "Sharing, Talking, and Giving: Relief of Social Tensions among the !Kung," in *Kalihari Hunter-Gatherers,* ed. Lee and DeVore, p. 350.

for someone else. The meat was then divided among relatives and friends by elaborate formulas, with everyone in camp taking careful note of what they had and had not received. It would have been especially ungracious to fail to share some future prey with a person who shared their prey with you. Newlywed grooms were expected to show their skills by providing their bride's parents with meat for some months after the marriage.

!Kung women learned to space their children three to four years apart; !Kung children were nursed for about that long. This provided food for the young and a limit on population.

Careful studies by anthropologists show cooperation of the most practical kind. During the course of the year the !Kung migrated to campsites which always placed them as closely as possible to their favorite foods, so they need not walk far each day to collect their dinners. During the last three weeks of July in 1964—the middle of the dry season—Richard Lee conducted a nutritional study among !Kung living just to the east of those studied by Lorna Marshall (who had by that time been resettled in camps by the South African government and hence could no longer be studied as hunters and gatherers).[34] This area generally has more moisture than the region studied by Marshall, but had just suffered from two years of severe drought which was causing food shortages among surrounding pastoralists and farmers. Despite the season and the drought, Lee found about a third of the populace (children and older people) doing no work at all. The rest worked twelve to nineteen hours a week at food gathering.[35] Women usually went out to gather plants two or three days a week. A man might hunt three days in a row and then not go hunting for two weeks. Yet members of the communities were bringing back and consuming an average of 2,140 calories and $3\frac{1}{3}$ ounces of protein per person, a third in the form of meat—well above adequate for people even with high activity levels like these. The vegetables consumed were also rich in minerals and vitamins. Everyone ate every night, often switching from fire to fire to partake of food and conversation. About a third of the total populace was visiting friends or relatives at another waterhole that month, which helped to even out the population around each waterhole. With the ability to provide for themselves this well, even at a time when modern settlers in the region were finding their fields parched and their cattle dead, it is small wonder that working women could walk 900 miles a year, that young !Kung could run for hours on end, and that about 10 percent of the populace was over sixty. Of the 11 percent of Americans over 65, few have as many teeth, nor can look back on a life involving so few work hours, nor can still walk 200 miles a year for seasonal changes of camp and scenery.

Levi-Strauss[36] tells of an incident with the Nambikuara, who, it must be noted, have as little fondness for grasshoppers as the average New Yorker. He had persuaded a band leader to take him inland to see that band's seasonal

---

[34] Lee, "!Kung Bushman Subsistence."

[35] Jiro Tanaka, "Subsistence Ecology of Central Kalihari San," in *Kalihari Hunter-Gatherers,* ed. Lee and DeVore, p. 115, studying a group of !Kung living in an even drier part of the desert, found them working $32\frac{1}{2}$ hours a week.

[36] Levi-Strauss, "The Social and Psychological Aspects of Chieftainship," p. 56.

gardening site. Because Levi-Strauss had brought some animals on the journey (an encumbrance without which no shortage would have been experienced in the first place) it was necessary to pass through some country unfamiliar to the chief and they did not reach their destination on the scheduled day. They ran out of food. Ordinarily the chief would have involved everyone in gathering some, but this expedition had been his own piece of folly.

> He did not wait or discuss; but, taking the incident as a matter of course, he simply left the camp accompanied by one of his wives. At the camp the day was spent sleeping, gossiping and complaining. There was no lunch or dinner. But, late at dusk, the chief and his wife reappeared, both heavily laden with baskets filled to the brim. They had hunted grasshoppers all day . . . the food was enthusiastically received, shared and consumed, amidst restored good humor. The following morning everyone armed himself or herself with a leafless twig and went grasshopper hunting.

The Eskimo faced a situation where they could not—especially in the cold season—travel long distances to find food, or to haul back a carcass. Their social system was a flexible one which allowed them to change the size of their group with the seasons to adapt to whatever form of food-gathering was best for that time. The Navajo, who appear to be Eskimos who gradually migrated southward through the mountain ranges of the west over the centuries,[37] have also shown flexibility in adapting to food-gathering situations. When they relied on hunting alone, the Navajo adopted smaller bands. When they later raided other Indians for food, the size of their bands increased. When they were finally introduced to maize, they settled down to farming. After Europeans brought in sheep, they developed vast herds and scattered themselves into separate family homesteads. Their social culture remains intact despite the isolation of the homesteads; time is set aside for coming together into larger groups to peform ritual functions and discuss mutual problems with their ritual leaders. They have combined great flexibility in food gathering with tight social solidarity.

People in many of these societies suffered from periods of hunger; they had to learn to abide with shrunken stomachs until the harvest or the return of the hunters. But they did demonstrate ingenuity in extracting available food resources, and equitability in distributing them.

Health

QUESTION

How does health relate to a stable personal environment? To artistic expression? To running a marathon race? How can we determine whether a political decision regarding health is sensible (or rational)?

---

[37] That is, both the Navajo and the Apaches speak Athabaskan languages, which are otherwise principally confined to Eskimo groups.

We know little about health among groups not yet subjected to European contact. Some studies among the !Kung offer a unique glimpse into health patterns among people with only minimal contact with outside influences.[38]

Between 1963 and 1969, Nancy Howell studied some 165 !Kung mothers and their offspring. Infant mortality was high. Of 500 children born, 96 died in their first year, mostly during their first few days of life,[39] and 59 more before reaching the age of five. Mortality among those over five years of age was not especially high. The Crude Death Rate ranged from 6 per 1,000 in 1968 to 26 per 1,000 in 1965, for an average of 16 per 1,000. (The 1971 Crude Death Rate in the United States was 9 per 1,000, and in nearby Angola 30 per 1,000). While there were no regular medical facilities, members of the expedition did administer some antibiotics, which may have reduced the rate. Smallpox, measles, pneumonia, and malaria are potentially fatal among the young; some of these may have been introduced by European contact.

In 1967 (in the height of the dry season), 1968 (in the wet season), and 1969, Stewart Truswell and John Hansen visited a small group of people in the same region to see how their health varied over time. They found that many of the people had pot bellies, probably due to the excessive amount of indigestible fiber in their diet. Some women over fifty had excessively wrinkled skin caused by too much exposure to the sun and campfires. Positive tuberculin tests were common. There were a few cases of tonsillitis, rheumatic fever, and asymptomatic mitrol valve disease; it is not known whether any of these are European imports. There was also some syphillis and gonorrhea. Around the permanent waterholes malaria was common; this (and viral diseases) were less of a problem among those living in drier regions with only temporary waterholes during the rainy season. The latter did suffer more from scalp-fungus. "Pinkeye" was common among children, and some older people developed cataracts. As people aged, their teeth were worn down to the gums by the rough food. Teeth did not develop cavities, but did exhibit peridontal disease in their roots and gums. Some of the elderly had arthritis, especially in the fingers but never in the legs. One old man who had killed a leopard with his bare hands had facial paralysis and a chronic ache in his shoulder. A man who had stepped on a poisoned arrow had amputated his foot at the ankle and walked long distances on a crutch he had made for himself.

Obesity was not encountered, nor was there high blood pressure (even among the elderly) or evidence of heart disease. No one had ever heard of or seen a heart attack. Among !Kung seventy to eighty-three years of age mean blood pressure was 120/67, as opposed to 168/90 in the London sample. There were no signs of sleeping sickness, varicose veins, hemorrhoids, hernias, gastroenteritis, or cirrhosis of the liver. The !Kung defecate into sand some

---

[38] Nancy Howell, "The Population of the Dobe Area !Kung," in *Kalihari Hunter-Gatherers,* ed. Lee and DeVore, pp. 137-151.

[39] Only six of these deaths occurred through infanticide, which was previously believed to be heavily practiced among !Kung. Infanticide was practiced on babies with birth defects, one of two twins, or when a baby followed too soon upon another and would force the mother to nurse two children at once. Mothers with gonorrhea had lower fertility rates than others. This disease seems to predate European contact.

distance from camp about a mile from their water supply so problems do not emanate from these sources. Hearing was good, even among the elderly. Injury from interpersonal violence was rare, and there was no indication of suicide or neurological disease.

Among the children—all breast fed—there was only one case of protein-calorie malnutrition (a child with malaria). Once taken off breast feeding, however, their growth seems to be retarded; they are thinner and shorter than they might be. The poor diet during the three driest months contributes to this. Light weight does have an advantage for walking long distances and reducing tension on the heart. Blood tests showed no signs of protein, thiamin, or riboflavin deficiencies. Vitamin A, folic acid, and vitamin B_{12} concentrations were high, while niacin was somewhat low. Vitamins C and D, iron,[40] calcium, iodine, zinc, and copper all were adequate. Sodium and chloride were deficient—which reduces tension—as was phosphorus. Their serum cholesterol ranked among the lowest in the world; mangodango nuts and wild animals are high in polyunsaturates, and prolonged exercise lowers cholesterol as well.

It is unfortunate that similar teams have not surveyed other groups. The !Kung suffered from serious diseases, some of which could be eradicated by simple traveling teams of health technicians. They were remarkably free of other diseases that are heavily debilitating in industrialized societies. The !Kung habits of child bearing and nursing, diet, and exercise—matters in which they make some choices—seem to have been largely sensible.

Sharing

QUESTION

How does sharing relate to a stable personal environment? To developing modern industries? How can we determine whether a political decision regarding sharing is sensible (or rational)?

While these groups may be somewhat effective at extracting food from their environment and sharing it with one another, they may not be willing to share work or other goods. Leaders are especially often prone to avoid sharing the emoluments that come their way.

Sharing is an engrained part of the cultures we have met. Besides food, one of the most important resources shared among !Kung was information about where food could be obtained. !Kung liked to eat only the tastiest plants and animals available at a given time, and they constantly shared with one another information about where these were located. The position of band leader was seldom coveted among the Nambikuara because he was expected to share everything he obtained with everyone in the band; he was permanently without possessions. The !Kung band leader, too, was expected to be more generous than others and so had to be sensitive to have fewer small personal possessions than

---

[40] Hookworm was found in three out of eighteen fecal samples, but was not serious enough to cause anemia. From A. Stewart Truswell and John D. F. Hansen, "Medical Research Among the !Kung," in *Kalihari Hunter-Gatherers,* ed. Lee and DeVore, pp. 166–194.

his fellows. One of the difficulties with being "bull of the camp" among the Nuer was that he was expected, like the Nambikuara band leader, to give away all his personal possessions aside from his cows and household utensils. Sharing of tasks was also taken for granted. We have pointed to a number of shared tasks in Inca villages. The Trobrianders, Konds, and Kachin—with their slash-and-burn agriculture—shared the heavy duties of clearing, planting, weeding, and harvesting.

This sense of sharing did not always come naturally. It often had to be prodded by the social system. An incident related by Evans-Pritchard indicates how the age-set system worked in this regard:

> When I was sick and being removed by steamer, I asked the people to carry my tent and belongings to the river's edge. They refused, and my servant, a Nuer youth, and I had to do it ourselves. When I asked him why the people were churlish, he replied, "You told them to carry your belongings to the river [an affront to their dogged independence]. That is why they refused. If you had asked them, saying, 'My mother's sons [invoking the age-set etiquette], assist me,' they would not have refused."[41]

The Yakö kinship system encouraged people to view their responsibilities on a community-wide basis. Within each compound lived wives who had grown up in different parts of the town (the largest town had 11,000 inhabitants). Each of their matriclans was represented by a shrine and priest. These priests, who were from scattered parts of town, constituted the town's highest council. It was they who supervised the various ceremonies in which community members took part throughout the year. Because the Head of the Village held his office by virtue of his mother's family—which probably had members in every corner of the town—he could be looked upon as a community-wide leader rather than a representative of his father's household, which was located in one section of one ward.

The question of distributing land could be a source of explosive tension in towns as large as the Yakö. The town association (another community-wide organization separate from the priests' council) assigned parcels of land to each ward (each town had several wards), leaving the ward associations responsible for seeing that it was properly parcelled among its component patriclans. Ward associations contained members from each of the five to eleven component patriclans, plus matriclan priests. This meant that no two individuals residing in separate wards would ever be engaged in disputes over their fair share of land. As couples married and people died, the ensuing redistribution could be made by the ward, rather than through inheritance. Should any family or any ward feel that it was being cheated out of adequate land, it could appeal to a special community-wide organization devised for this purpose, which allowed the priests' council to make the ultimate decision on each case. There were no surveyors' boundaries to tie the town fathers to any fixed and unchanging intra or interward distribution. Most important of all, there were no few elite families who could hoard all the land for themselves. If one were to devise an ideal

---

[41] Evans-Pritchard, *The Nuer*, p. 182.

system for sharing land equitably, the techniques described in this paragraph might well commend themselves for consideration.

Discussion of Trobrianders is continued from p. 41.

On North Kiriwina Island it would have been easy for eighty small villages scattered among heavy tropical foliage to isolate themselves from one another's problems. The Trobriand system provided ample reasons to feel attachments beyond those to one's own immediate family, even beyond gift-giving. Every male belonged to two kinship groups: his father's and his maternal uncle's. A boy grew up with his father and then went to another village to live with his uncle after reaching puberty. He would bring his bride to live with him there. He felt responsible to his uncles and aunts, who might be scattered among various villages, and later to his nieces and nephews. No commoner man could live his life in only one village; he always lived in two. Everyone had sisters living in another village. This helped to create a sense of interdependence among the villages.

Should a member of a sub-clan marry the chief of another village, that whole sub-clan would pay the annual tribute to express the allegiance they now felt toward that chief. Chiefs of more important villages were polygamous. By marrying daughters from several towns, they could create a powerful political alliance and considerable tribute. Such a chief was entitled to a percentage of the yield on all coconut palms and slaughtered pigs (allowing him to store part of their precious protein). In return, he had obligations. He was also expected to grow on his land much of the surplus that would be needed by the island in case of a drought. Much of his gardening was carried out for him by young men who received a major portion of the crop from the fields they tilled. Ceremonies—even involving several communities—were frequent, and it was the chief who was expected to furnish everyone with food. When new canoes or storage bins were needed, he was expected to pay for them. And it was incumbent upon him to see that every family resident in his village was apportioned as much land as they would need to raise their crops and carry out their obligations.

Those latter obligations also helped elevate the position of wife and family in Trobriand society. The annual yam tribute was given to the wife's married sisters. Separation from his wife would leave an adult male unentitled to receive annual tribute. Single adult males, separations, and divorce were rare.

Further discussion of Trobrianders may be found on p. 56.

The Bantu tribal chiefs were blessed with large entourages of clients and nobles and marked personal wealth, in the manner of the *Etsu Nupe*. The tribal chief had first choice of land, fields, and hunting spoils, and the largest cattle herds. Commoners were expected to till his fields and give him a portion of their own yield. He could lead raids on other tribes and collect booty and slaves. He was the richest man in his tribe; should any of his relatives begin to vie with him for wealth, they might be murdered or otherwise put out of the way. The Bantu chief maintained the affections of his clients—who ranged from court advisers to soldiers to beggars—by giving them money, land, cattle, and doles. His relatives also received personal privileges. Despite this, the Bantu chief was heavily obligated to all his subjects. He was responsible for distributing free land to all married men, and this often entailed giving portions of his own land to immigrants. When thatching grass or certain trees fell into short supply, he set up regulations to ensure there would be enough to go around. He regulated the agricultural calendar to be certain that each function was performed at the optimal time. He organized collective hunts or parties to destroy beasts of prey or round up lost cattle. He collected medical knowledge and saw to the training of medical practitioners. He sponsored great public festivals, for which he furnished the food and drink. He lent cattle to subjects whose herds had diminished, supported destitute widows and children, and made general distribution of grain during famine.[42] The local chief shared these obligations too; in addition, he knew all the villagers personally and was expected to help them with personal problems such as cattle transactions or mediation with authorities.[43]

> "The chief is the wife of the tribe," says the Tswana, i.e., he looks after the needs of his subjects, and Zulu refer to him as "the breast of the nation," i.e., the source from which all draw sustenance; in the same context, he is often greeted as "mother of the people" or "mother of orphans." One quality always expected of him is generosity, and should he fail in this respect he soon becomes unpopular.

These are only scattered examples. They do, however, cast some doubt on the assertion that traditional villagers thought of their own families as taking precedence over others, and that selfish motivations superceded community needs. There is considerable evidence of sharing in these societies, and in a manner that makes sensible use of scarce resources.

That sharing, it should be noted, was within one's own village. It did not extend to other villages. Weaker groups were often driven from the best lands by stronger groups.

Using Talents

QUESTION

How does use of talents relate to a stable personal environment? To building a pyramid? How can we determine whether a political decision regarding the use of people's talents is sensible (or rational)?

Societies like the ones we have been looking at are frequently accused of allowing nepotism to stand in the way of talent. The point is worthy of attention. Though the "bull" or leader generally came from the same clan as his predecessor, there was considerable flexibility as to who among the Nuer would be eligible for titles of "bull of the camp" and leopard-skin chief. Evans-Pritchard found both these

[42] Schapera, *Government and Politics*, p. 73.

[43] Ibid., pp. 75–76.

title holders in the village he studied to be effective in dealing with their fellow villagers. This probably was more than accidental, since pertinent qualifications were taken into consideration when the villagers chose these men for the roles. In the Yakö villages there was flexibility about who could become a member of various associations, and all the major association leaders were elected by the members. As we have noted, there was considerable specialization of roles. All this would seem conducive to allowing talent to rise to the top. The Eskimos rewarded those who made the greatest contribution to the group, while giving lesser positions by the fire to those who contributed less. The Navajo divided their leadership functions (e.g., hunting, curing) giving them to those who performed them best, and only following each leader when his particular function was being performed. If a Nambikuara band leader did not perform well, he was likely to find his followers joining a new band leader the next time they went foraging.

Likewise, there were frequent changes in !Kung band leadership as people simply regrouped themselves around leaders they liked better. The Nupe age-sets, led by a youth from the next-highest age-set, offered an excellent training ground for potential new leaders; there would appear to have been flexibility as well in choosing new chiefs. The Trobriand system allowed ambitious, hard-working young men to acquire land and prominence; it also allowed nephews to be bypassed in acquiring hereditary titles if they did not perform the duties expected of them by the community. Inca villages were remarkably well adapted for allowing the individual to adapt his chores to his age. Wealth and family name played a role in many selections of leaders, but a man with those attributes but no talent was a far more likely candidate for being by-passed in the selection process here than in settings we shall encounter in subsequent chapters.

Fighting

QUESTION

How does fighting relate to a stable personal environment? To maintaining cultural integrity? How can we determine whether a political decision regarding fighting is sensible (or rational)?

The !Kung, widely scattered in an inhospitable territory, have no history of martial arts. Fighting was virtually nonexistent. As one headman put it, "someone might get killed."[44] They did develop more subtle means to settle disputes, however. The most common conflict was over distribution of large game. One night N!eisi pointedly failed to share part of his wart hog with his sister's husband. Three days later the latter took his family for an extended visit to another band. The behavior was not unusual; it had happened every other year or so. They would return and be friends again. Another part of the ritual is violent verbal battles over the evening campfire. Suddenly one person accuses the other of

---

[44] Marshall, "!Kung Bushman Bands," p. 17

being arrogant and lazy. The other responds by accusing his antagonist of not being generous. The rhetoric usually becomes quite exaggerated, until some third party finally tells a joke. This reduces the entire camp, including the disputants, to helpless laughter. Then they would normally return to immediate amiability. If not, they would take the route of N!eisi's sister's husband.

The ability to change camps thus served as a valuable outlet for tensions among the !Kung. Early marriage, and something called bilateralism, enhanced this outlet. A boy usually married in his early twenties, a girl in her early teens. The boy was expected to hunt for his bride's family, but also to refrain from having sex with her for three or four years. If the parties did not get along, divorce was simple. The boy could just return to his own family. By the time the young couple started having children they were usually settled in for life. At this time they were free to go and live near *his* parents (bilateralism), or perhaps join an entirely different band. There was great flexibility in choosing where you would live.

!Kung took great delight in being together. Families often sat around the fire, ankle across ankle, shoulder across shoulder, a hand casually touching another's body. The rhetoric around campfires was sometimes indirect. Someone late at night might sing a song which pointed to some disapproved behavior without mentioning anyone by name. Or after a hut burned down due to someone's indiscretion there might be general shouting aimed at no one in particular but mentioning specific acts. The intended party has a tendency to correct the behavior. With every man possessing a supply of poisoned arrows, homicide could have been common; however, it was rare.

Further discussion of !Kung may be found on p. 92.

Most cultures do fight. Not only were there fights within the villages and bands we have surveyed; they fought larger-scale battles. The Trobriand leaders at times rallied their clusters to make war against other clusters. The same was sometimes true of Nambikuara band leaders and Eskimo chiefs. At times these battles involved what would appear (from an outsider's perspective at least) to be petty animosities among the leaders. The Nuer and Konds attacked neighboring villages to steal cattle and lands. Later Chimu, and Inca, battles were largely organized in cities; but there also seem to have been battles between villages at an earlier stage. The Navajo organized raids on other Indian tribes. Traditional villagers, in short, were prone to fight. A case might be made, though, that most of them placed greater limits on their fighting than did societies after the introduction of extensive commerce.

Open warfare involved traditions not unlike the chivalric traditions of Europe. The Konds conducted raids on neighboring Kond villages to obtain land. The fighting apparently was often fierce and many were killed. After the fight, however, the victorious side adopted the survivors of the other side into their clan. The Nuer had an advantage in their attacks on Dinka villages: the Dinka usually ran away. The Nuer rounded up whatever Dinka they caught and adopted them directly into their clans. When Kachins engaged in family feuds they would burn houses and steal animals from their enemies; at the same time they tried to avoid killing. Village councils provided arbitration machinery. Unless the feud involved an attempt to overthrow an ambitious Shan-oriented chief, feuds could usually be settled eventually by arbitration; one side would agree to redress the grievance it had caused the other. Trobriand wars were never very bloody or long. The villages of the losers were destroyed, and the inhabitants went into exile for two years. After that period, a ceremony of reconciliation took place, and friend and foe helped to rebuild the villages.

Discussion of the Nuer is continued from p. 44.

Among the Nuer, a mere verbal insult (even to a man's cow) could lead to a fatal (though usually accidental) stabbing, followed by an intractable family feud involving attempts to murder the offender. Evans-Pritchard[45] partially attributes this to their egalitarian upbringing:

> . . . they strut about like lords of the earth which indeed they consider themselves to be. There is no master and no servant in their society but only equals who regard themselves as God's noblest creation. A child soon learns that to maintain his equality with his peers he must stand up for himself against any encroachment on his person and property. This means that he must always be prepared to fight, and his willingness and ability to do so are the only protection of his integrity as a free and independent person against the avarice and bullying of his kinsmen.

There are some aspects of this system that moderns might envy. The Nuer did not respect wealth or rank. They held their heads high and did not suffer from pangs of insecurity. They always knew their families would stand behind them—and they were so sensitive to verbal insults that stabbing seemed a natural retort. After stabbing someone, the offender would usually seek refuge with the leopard-skin chief who was by custom permitted to offer him sanctuary from the clan of the stabbed man, which would be seeking to kill him in turn. The leopard-skin chief's only major public duty, in fact, was settling such disputes. He would not push the issue immediately but allowed time for feelings to cool. Then he approached other families in the village and suggested that the feud should not be allowed to split the community. With the community behind him, he would ask the aggrieved family to accept restitution from the family of the offender in the form of a prescribed number of cows. They usually refused, but they knew that their continued refusal would force the leopard-skin chief to sacrifice a bull, an act for which they would be blamed by the community. So in the end they usually accepted the offer. Payment was often slow, and enmity continued between the families far into succeeding generations. Yet by these methods the system did succeed in preventing family feuds from ripping the community apart.

The Yakö faced the problem of feuds that began when someone stole crops from an unattended field. A prestigious body of men composed of prominent members of both matriclans and patricians specialized in cases of trespassing and

---

[45] Evans-Pritchard, *The Nuer*, p. 182.

crop stealing. Once it had amassed facts on a case, the body took the case before the ward leaders or town heads or priests (depending on where the litigants resided) and served as prosecutor in trying it. After judgment, if the party did not pay the prescribed damages, age-set societies were brought into play to enforce payment through informal means. In more recent times, disputes over theft of cows and land boundaries grew in importance. A similar body was formed to deal with these problems. When other kinds of disputes arose, there was encouragement to settle them within the family or ward. Only when they became intractable, or involved people in different parts of town, were disagreements taken to the town heads or priests. The decisions of the latter groups, however, carried great moral weight with everyone and were generally accepted as the last word.

Eskimos had a habit of settling lesser disputes through wrestling matches. Greater ones came to involve clan leaders and shamans. There seems to have been incentive to see that clans as a whole did not get involved in disputes among individuals.

A principal function of local Bantu chiefs was the mediation of personal disputes. A hierarchical system of local courts allowed appeal of cases to the revered tribal chief. The Bantu also engaged in frequent conquest of neighboring tribes—Bantu and others. Those conquered were generally assimilated into their own tribe, though sometimes with diminished status. Only captives considered culturally inferior, such as !Kung, were treated oppressively. The latter, it should be noted, often *were* treated cruelly.[46] The !Kung fought back fiercely, especially when their land was at stake, inflicting death and being killed in turn.

In his battle to survive in competition with other species, man is better served by cooperation than by killing off his own species. Even cannibals demonstrate more proclivity toward cooperation than murder. Japanese funeral rites have long involved the funeral guests taking home portions of the cremated remains of the deceased. Many South American Indians eat a portion of their deceased relatives, hoping thereby to retain a part of the strength and spirit of the departed. This is not cannibalism, but rather a symbolic means to cement kinship and cooperative bonds. Some groups take this practice further, however, to the point of attacking and killing members of other tribes in order to devour portions of their bodies. A survey of fifty-four tribes in the Amazon area found thirty-eight of them engaging in this latter practice.[47] Of the thirty-eight, thirty-two were settled agriculturalists. All but two of the groups that did *not* engage in the practice were hunters. Agriculture is virtually a prerequisite for such cannibalism, which involves months of ritual preparation before the raid in which the victims are taken, and additional weeks of ritual before the specific portions of the victims are consumed. Contrary to popular myth, these people do not simply nab people and cook them in a kettle; the exercise is highly ritualized and the number of victims few.

Fighting thus seems to have been provided with limits which prevented it from escalating beyond certain levels and with mechanisms to aid in settling

---

[46] Schapera, *Government and Politics,* pp. 128, 132.

[47] Leakey and Lewin, *Origins,* p. 221.

disputes. The fierce fighting in North Africa described earlier in this chapter, which resulted in serious dislocations, was subject to some outside influence which we shall explore in the next chapter. In Iran, which was subject to so many invasions, the Mongols were the only group to leave behind widespread desolation. In comparison to these extreme cases, and to modern warfare, the ferocity of fighting within and among most of these groups borders on benign.

Limited Power

QUESTION

How does limiting the power of leaders relate to a stable personal environment? To building a modern nation? How can we determine whether political processes to limit power are sensible (or rational)?

Limiting the power of leaders is one of the highest and most elusive goals of modern nations. We have already given a good deal of attention to noting limitations on power in traditional societies. It will be of interest, however, if we take a last look at the most powerful villager discussed in this chapter: the chief of the Trobriand village of Omarkana. There is a refreshing directness about this episode in comparison with the ineffectiveness of more recent attempts to control the actions of government leaders.

Discussion of Trobrianders is continued from p. 50.

Malinowski tells the story[48] about Chief To'uluwa of Omarkana—the towering figure of the island whose henchmen could put enemies to death through witchcraft, who alone could summon the rain, who received tribute from virtually all the island, and who led wars against villages in disfavor. By custom, he was to be succeeded by his eldest nephew, but he had exercised his prerogative (allowed only to chiefs) to keep his sons in the village, and it was known that he favored his eldest son for the succession. The villagers were split on the issue. Then one afternoon the controversy was brought to a head. The eldest son and one of the younger nephews—who disliked one another intensely—had a fist fight near the British Governor's residence. The Governor arrested the nephew but, perhaps in deference to the chief, did not arrest the son. When the news reached the village, the nephew's kinsmen seethed with anger. The chief retreated to his hut, and villagers stayed close to theirs.

> Suddenly a loud voice rang out across the silent village. Bagido'u, the heir apparent, and eldest brother of the imprisoned man, standing before his hut, spoke out, addressing the offender of his family:
>
> "Namwana Guya'u [the offender] you are a cause of trouble. We, the Tabalu of Omarkana, allowed you to stay here, to live among us. You had plenty of food in

---

[48] From *Crime and Custom in Savage Society* by Bronislaw Malinowski, © 1926, Humanities Press, Inc. Reprinted by permission of Humanities Press and Routledge & Kegan Paul Ltd.

Omarkana, you ate of our food, you partook of the pigs brought to us as a tribute and of the fish. You sailed in our canoe. You built a hut on our soil. Now you have done us harm. You have told lies. Mitakata is in prison. We do not want you to stay here. This is our village! You are a stranger here. Go away! We chase you away! We chase you out of Omarkana."

These words were uttered in a loud piercing voice, trembling with strong emotion, each short sentence spoken after a pause, each like an individual missile, hurled across the empty space to the hut where Namwana Guya'u sat brooding. After that the younger sister of Mitakata also arose and spoke, and then a young man, one of the maternal nephews. Their words were almost the same as the first speech . . . the speeches were received in deep silence. Nothing stirred in the village. But, before the night was over, Namwana Guya'u had left Omarkana forever. He had gone over and settled in his own village . . . whence his mother came. For weeks his mother and sister wailed for him the loud lamentations of mourning for the dead. The chief remained for three days in his hut, and when he came out looked older and broken for the grief. All his personal interest and affection were on the side of his favorite son, of course. Yet he could do nothing to help him. His kinsmen had acted in complete accordance with their rights and, according to tribal law, he could not possibly dissociate himself from them. No power could change the decree of exile. Once the "Go away"—"we chase thee away"—were pronounced, the man had to go. These words, very rarely uttered in dead earnest, have a binding force and almost ritual power when pronounced by the citizens of a place against a resident outsider. A man who would try to brave the dreadful insult involved in them and remain in spite of them, would be dishonoured for ever. In fact, anything but immediate compliance with a ritual request is unthinkable for a Trobriand Islander.

This passage is remarkable when we compare it with the wars fought over succession in Europe. It also outlines with breathtaking clarity the established force of law in this society, indelibly binding on governed and governor alike.

Malinowski's writing excels in presenting such detailed observation about the operation of the political system. We can well imagine that other traditional systems about which we have somewhat more detached observations witness similar dramas.

Such limits of custom were probably less binding on leaders who lived outside the confines of villages, however, surrounded by their own entourages. For instance, heads of marauding desert bands were undoubtedly very cruel. Sir Hugh Clifford tells stories of how Malay sultans mutilated or murdered young men who slept with one of their wives, and allowed petty thieves to literally rot to insanity and death in small wooden cages under sadistic guards without any sort of trial.[49] We have already referred to the Inca death penalties for sexual of-

---

[49] *The Further Side of Silence,* (Garden City, N.Y.: Doubleday, 1927). Clifford, too, had his biases. He concludes his chapter on the cruelties to occupants of the twelve individually-occupied cages belonging to a certain Raja (which were, incidentally, six feet long, two feet wide, and five feet high, larger than the tiger cages used for similar tortures to thousands of political prisoners during the Vietnam War): "Readers of this true tale will perhaps realize how it comes to pass that some of us men of the outskirts—who have *seen* things, not merely *heard of them*—are apt to become rather strong 'imperialists' and to find it at times difficult to endure with patience these ardent

fenses. Palace intrigues probably abounded, and there were frequent wars over succession. Nobles and warriors in the retinues of princes probably dealt with one another more cruelly than did villagers when they fought. Since (as in the example in Chapter 4 of the *Shaba,* number two man of the Nupe capital) nobles also had their own personal retinues of clients, this served to limit their power somewhat vis-à-vis one another. The Aztecs were not alone in their seizure of villagers to use as personal sacrifice; for instance, Schapera[50] indicates that tribal chiefs in South Africa nearly all used an occasional "human being specially killed for the purpose" when brewing medicines.

Schapera also offers insights into the limitation of powers, this time among chiefs far more powerful than the Chief of Omarkana. There were bloodthirsty chiefs such as the Zulu leader Shaha who had thousands of his subjects put to death as a personal whim and had others who failed to perform the duties expected of them murdered.[51] Shaha's career ended when he himself was murdered by a rival who took over his position. Noblemen were constantly vying for the power of tribal chiefs. If they could organize a personal following, they could secede from the tribe with their personal followers or replace the tribal chief in office. Successions were frequent and often accompanied by civil warfare.[52] It was common for local chiefs to be abandoned by their villagers in favor of a new leader who established himself as chief.[53]

---

defenders of the Rights of Man, who bleet their comfortable aphorisms in the British House of Commons and cry shame upon our 'hungry acquisitiveness' " (p. 147). Talib, whose lingering agonizing death in one of the cages is described, was a slave-debtor to the Raja; he was paying off a money debt by becoming the Raja's slave. He was suspected of stealing a ceremonial sword from the Raja. Though the charge was not proved, the Raja personally ordered him committed to the cage. The cages were located outdoors in the most crowded part of a trading town which was (1895) trading with the British but not yet governed by them. It is hard to tell from the account how the Raja ruled the villages, or whether the debt-slavery had existed before the introduction of foreign trade (see the discussion of India in the next chapter). Clifford notes that this particular Raja's "reputation for kindness of heart stood high among the people."

In pages 208–209 Clifford discusses how the white man placed Pahang under his protection "with the amiable object of quieting that troubled and lawless land." Malay village elders were shocked that the white men should think "to sentence lepers to imprisonment for life, precisely as though it were a crime for a man to fall a victim to disease." Mînah (whose lover was a leper) listened. "The wanton cruelty of the notion was what chiefly struck her. The old native rulers had been oppressive, with hearts like flint and hands of crushing weight, but they had always been actuated by a personal motive, a motive which their people could recognize and understand, the sort of motive whereby the peasants felt that they themselves would have been impelled if their relative positions had been reversed." Leper asylums in the tropics are, at best, deplorable institutions," he adds (p. 212). They, and mental institutions there, still often are (speaking as one who has *seen* things, not merely *heard of them*).

Are the Raja's cages more deplorable than the leper asylums? Stephen Chapman, "Ayatollah's Barbaric Tortures Less Cruel than Prison?" *Kansas City Star,* March 23, 1980, points out that one Louisiana prison confined four or five prisoners in a single six-by-six cell. There were 211 stabbings in three years. Robbery, rape, extortion, theft, and assault are everyday occurrences in American prisons. In contrast to such imprisonment, the Ayatollah Khomeini advocates using the Koranic law to cut off the hands of the thief, kill the murderers, or flog the adulterous man or woman. Would it be preferable to be humiliated and pained for a few minutes, or even mutilated, to spending ten years in a typical state prison? And is it better to develop a sense of public tolerance for cruelty by performing it in the open, or indifference to cruelty by concealing it? There are no easy answers to such questions.

[50] Schapera, *Government and Politics,* p. 72.

[51] Ibid., p. 149.

[52] Ibid., pp. 155, 179, 196.

[53] Ibid., pp. 185–186.

Perhaps more important than this limitation on power were the regular meetings of tribal leaders with councils consisting of local chiefs. In addition, all Bantu chiefs held hearings to which commoners could bring grievances, and abuses of power by local authorities could be appealed through judicial processes. Court hearings at all levels were held in public. If a tribal chief personally wronged someone (e.g., his cattle injured their crops) he might be asked to pay reparations.[54] In practice, individuals of low rank were fearful of criticizing a tribal chief; but councilors were known to secretly fine him for misconduct. Among the Tswana, the regular popular assemblies with their tribal chief provided the ultimate in limits on rule. Subjects there were rather free to deliver reprimands personally to the tribal chief. One chief actually fled his kingdom after an especially vituperative popular assembly and another was publicly assassinated in full view of such an assembly.[55]

The chiefs Schapera describes are not the spartan individuals who governed the more primitive villages:

> As a widespread proverb says, "Hunger does not enter the chief's home;" one praise-name for chiefs among Venda is *tsetsema*, "shuffler," because he is "supposed to be so fat he can only shuffle along."[56]

But he also concludes:

> As the proverb says, "A chief is a chief by grace of his people," and rarely has any chief been able to rule oppressively for long. If not democratic in the sense of being able to elect their rulers, South African communities can at least often restrain them and if sufficiently provoked get rid of them.[57]

The generalization might be extended to other traditional political systems as well.

Praxis

QUESTION

Can there be praxis or a stable personal environment without technology? When can technology harm praxis and stable personal environments?

Some say technology relieves people from helplessness; it makes them masters of Nature, rather than its servant. Others fear that technology has alienated us from Nature, and from one another, and hence we are more helpless than before. To many modern people of all ideological callings, this description of how we should blend with nature has taken on new meaning as a definition of rational society:

> Labour is, in the first place, a process in which both man and Nature participate, and in which man of his own accord starts, regulates, and controls the

---

[54] Ibid., p. 150.
[55] Ibid., p. 151.
[56] Ibid., p. 114.
[57] Ibid., p. 211.

material reactions between himself and Nature. He opposes himself to Nature as one of her own forces, setting in motion arms and legs, head and hands, the natural forces of his body, in order to appropriate Nature's productions in a form adapted to his own wants. By thus acting on the external world and changing it, he at the same time changes his own nature.[58]

This is a definition of *praxis,* or practicing an art or discipline as opposed to simply theorizing. To practice any creative art, be it farming or music, one must use tools, land, food, and the aid of others. Those directly engaged in creating food, crafts, and entertainment using their own tools must develop a number of talents, must learn to cooperate with nature and their social group, and must respect their tools. Modern individuals have often been freed from having to create their own food, clothing, and shelter. They have become dependent on other people's land and highly automated tools to provide these. They have lost the need to cooperate with others for anything other than to earn money. As a result, we are often less creative and less at one with our social and natural environment than we might otherwise be. Wasted natural resources, pollution, crime, poor eating habits, economic inequities, neglect of the poor and of property, declining quality of workmanship, drug addiction, divorce and child abuse, boredom, and arrogant behavior occur more easily when praxis is absent. Praxis can occur in modern society. Though we will see little sign of it in contemporary developing nations, it was a natural part of their traditional societies.

Malinowski's study of the Trobrianders provides a closing thought about traditional systems and stable personal environments. In every Trobriand village there were two sacred spots: a hole of emergence, and a mass burial grave. Trobrianders believed that the soul of every individual in their sub-clan emerged from this hole, from the soil; after death the body went to the mass burial grave and its spirit to another nearby island where it tended fields with the other spirits.

To the Trobriander land, the territory, the soil he treads and the soil he works, the rocks, groves, and fields where he plays and lives, are actually and not merely legally bound up with him. Land for him is the real mother earth who brought forth his lineage in the person of the first ancestress, who nourishes him and will receive him again into her womb.[59]

The garden magician's incantation for all the community's fields before the garden teams strike the first soil gives additional feeling for this oneness:

The belly of my garden leavens,
The belly of my garden rises,
The belly of my garden reclines,
The belly of my garden grows to the size of a bush-hen's nest,
The belly of my garden grows like an ant-hill;
The belly of my garden rises and is bowed down,
The belly of my garden rises like the iron-wood palm,

---

[58] Karl Marx, *Capital,* vol. I (New York: International Publishers, 1967), p. 177.
[59] Malinowski, *Coral Gardens,* p. 350.

The belly of my garden lies down,
The belly of my garden swells,
The belly of my garden swells as with a child.
I sweep away . . . the grubs . . . the blight . . . the beetle[60]

Modern writing is filled with talk of humanity's alienation from nature and from fellow humans.[61] This incantation—this poem—would seem to expresss the sentiments of people without the ability to decipher the meaning of alienation, whose sense of belonging and purpose and wholeness is very complete. Land is no mere possession; food, no mere commodity of exchange; neighbor, no mere common property-owner; labor, no mere means of survival.

SUMMARY

We have looked at a series of political systems. They differ in many regards, yet all provide a means to divide land among their members, to mediate disputes, to assure that everyone is fed even in times of hardship, to bring together willing hands when there is work to be done, and to keep leaders in check. These systems also have their weaknesses, such as the threat of famine, war, and pillage. Whether the solutions they found were the *best* under the circumstances remains a moot point. Yet it seems obvious that the solutions they devised to many of the most serious problems that confronted them were sensible, reasonable, and devised within the communities themselves.

During war, famine, and pestilence the environments of individuals living in traditional communities were anything but stable. But times of wars, famine, and pestilence in traditional societies were interspersed with longer periods which were free from these maladies. Food to eat, housing that was satisfying to live in and affordable, neighbors and cultural facilities with which people felt comfortable; a job offering satisfaction, continuity, and above-subsistence income; and an educational system which could promise children the same advantages were probably more the norm than the exception in traditional societies. These systems provided most of their members with stable personal environments.

SHORT SUMMARY

Prior to the introduction of extensive international commerce, people in developing areas tended to control most aspects of their own lives in a manner that was satisfying to them.

Have you caught these definitions?

	page
integrated	21
self-governing	21
matrilineal	32

---

[60] Ibid., pp. 96–97.
[61] For a discussion of alienation, see p. 179ff.

	page
patrilocal	25
bilateralism	53
ritual leader	25
age set	26
praxis	60

Can you answer each with one sentence?

1. What are some important questions that anthropologists often fail to explore?
2. In what sense did a village headman own the land in the village?
3. How did empires interfere with village integration and self-governance?
4. Why could villages continue to govern themselves even under empires?
5. Can a community be integrated without being self-governed?

From what you have read this far, can you make and support judgments about these questions?

1. On what points would Professor Palmer disagree with this chapter?
2. What does it mean to say that political systems once emerged from the societies in which indigenous people lived?
3. What are some examples in this chapter of social systems causing people to behave more sensibly than they otherwise would?
4. What sorts of factors reported on in the chapter interfered with stable personal environments?

It is important that you understand how the parts of this book fit together. Reread the entire "Book in Brief" section of Chapter 1, with particular attention to what you now know about traditional political systems.

CHAPTER

3

GETTING YOUR BEARINGS (see map, front of book)

1. Which of today's developing nations could ancient Athens reach by sea?
2. In the seventeenth century, how would a Portuguese sailor get to Java? Peru? Mozambique?

The Model

A developed nation provides most of its citizens with a stable personal environment. A developing nation does not. Today's developing nations were once developed nations. *They changed because their political systems separated from their social systems when European commerce was introduced.* If the structure of international trade changes in the near future, social and political systems may be reintegrated, promoting political development. Then the developing nations may once again become developed nations.

The Disruptive Forces

QUESTIONS TO KEEP IN MIND

1. How did international commerce permit rulers to ignore the prosperity of villagers?
2. How did international commerce take land away from peasants?
3. How did international commerce separate political systems from social systems?

The political systems discussed in Chapter 2 are for the most part in retreat. Stable personal environments have largely joined them in this withdrawal. In this chapter and part of Chapter 4 we shall try to discover why. We shall explore several processes, grouping them into three subtopics: (1) the introduction of grains and metals and the rise of kings and empires; (2) the eclipse of kings and empires by independent traders and bureaucrats; and (3) the activities of those traders and bureaucrats: the alienation of land ownership, the introduction of plantations and commercial mining, and (reserved for the next chapter) the co-optation of local leadership and the beginning of industrial pursuits.

Normally, texts hurriedly introduce these processes as a sort of background briefing on how nations began their takeoff into modernization; that is how Professor Palmer handled them in the discussion we quoted in the last chapter. Discussion then focuses on how to deal with modernization (and the traditional forces that hamper it) in ways that will spread its blessings. In contrast, we are pausing to examine these modernization processes in greater detail because they are the forces that brought instability to personal environments. If we are to discover how to regain that stability, we must understand how it was lost. The introduction of modernization to developing nations, in short, brought social disruption—not social progress. Later events, we shall see subsequently, have eased the effects of this disruption in some places. However, in most places the disruption has continued to grow in magnitude, with no change in sight. The processes of disruption discussed in this chapter are still with us today; they are simply more severe.

It may seem strange, in the light of this assertion, that we should begin by discussing something that appears on the surface to be anything but disruptive: a reliable source of food. Ironically, the need for that reliable source of food started all this turmoil. There are many more ironies to come in the story that is about to unfold.

STAGE ONE: GRAINS AND METALS

To survive, the human body needs carbohydrates, protein, and a number of vitamins and minerals.[1] There are many plants and animals that can supply these essentials. Still, if people are to have more than hand-to-mouth existences—and especially if people are to move away from farming areas into the city—it is important for them to gain access to types of food that have three characteristics. First of all, they must yield large quantities from a compact area; if it takes several acres to grow enough food for one family, farming remains at subsistence level. There must be enough left over to support people who are not engaged in agriculture. Second, this food must be easy to store for long periods of time; otherwise it will be available only at harvest season, and there will be insufficient time to move it from the farm to the consumer. And third, this stored food must supply sufficient proteins, carbohydrates, and trace elements to sustain life. The need is for high-yielding, storable, nutritious food. Before the age of refrigeration, it was impossible to store fish or meat for long; those items remained at best a peripheral part of the diet. Dairy products were useful only to those actually herding the animals. Most fruits and leafy vegetables spoiled quickly. This left only three groups of plants that satisfied these three requirements: cereal grains, tubers, and legumes. Of these, cereal grains were the most satisfactory overall.

Whole cereals contain 8 to 16 percent protein, can give high yields, and are relatively easy to store and transport. Wheat, rice, barley, rye, millet, maize (corn), sorghum, and oats are the principal cereal grains consumed by humans. Wheat, barley, millet, and oats were first cultivated in the region to the east of the Mediterranean, and, until after the time of Christ, were largely confined to China, India, the Middle East, North Africa, and Europe. Maize was indigenous to the Americas, and was cultivated from southern Peru to the Mississippi Valley when Columbus arrived. Rice was found mainly in mainland Asia and Java. If kept dry and rodent-free, rice and maize can be stored for several years, but they are a bit lower in protein than other grains. Maize has become a popular secondary crop around the world today. A number of tubers, including the sweet potato and potato, were raised in Central and South America before European contact; they were later exported to Asia and Europe. Another tuber, the yam, was a staple crop in the Pacific Islands. Tubers are bulkier to transport, more limited in their uses in cooking, cannot normally be stored over a year, and are basically carbohydrates. Beans, which are legumes, have been raised by cultures around the globe for many centuries, though it was the New World farmers who devel-

---

[1] We shall examine more precise figures in Chapter 7, especially p. 323ff.

oped the most advanced species. They are high in protein (20 to 32 percent) but also susceptible to disease and drought and more limited in their potential growing area than grains; they have usually been relegated to a secondary position in diets. Hence, all the major continents and island groups have had access to these food sources for a great while, though, as we have seen, such food sources did not grow everywhere on these continents and varied in yield, quality, and usefulness. Of the groups discussed in the previous chapter, only the Nupes, Shans, Navajo, and Trobrianders produced significant surpluses of any of them.

The grains were ultimately to play the biggest role in allowing leaders to free themselves of cultural norms and interactions with fellow villagers. A ruler who wished to exercise independent power needed grain at his disposal: local ritual leaders (in the systems discussed in the previous chapter) kept power only as long as they lived up to the obligations expected of them by their family and their community. If a leader was to develop genuine power in his own right, he had to set up his own base of operations, complete with henchmen to do his bidding, whom he could feed, clothe, and shelter without constant reliance on either relatives or outsiders. The henchmen would need to be able to force the peasantry or slaves captured in war to provide the base of operations with this food and labor. Peasants can fight and produce weapons from wood and stone. To counteract this, the king's men needed stronger weapons—made of metal. *In short, the king needed both storable food and metals to assure his independence from the peasantry.*

Grains were available to rulers, either on fields opened for them by slave labor or by taxing a percentage of the yield of villages within the kingdom. Because they were compact and storable, grains could be transported to storehouses built for the convenience of the ruler. The great empires of Egypt, Mesopotamia, northern China, India, Cambodia, Indonesia, MesoAmerica, and the Central Andes all grew from grain-producing valleys. The transformation of the Mesopotamian political system circa 3500 B.C. to circa 2500 B.C. from one centering around an assembly of adult male members of the community to one concentrating power in a secular personage or class wielding independent power was accompanied by a change in temple architecture, which went from central cells flanked by rows of small rooms to a massive complex surrounded by dwellings, workshops, granaries, and storehouses.[2]

Once a king was in a position to collect and store his own grain to feed a retinue of men subject to his control, a process which may initially have begun through village leaders paying him tribute in return for his performance of mutual obligations, he could establish his independence by mining. To cast weapons and shields sufficient for a militia or to coin any quantity of money, it was necessary to dig some depth into the earth for iron, copper, or tin. This was heavy work, requiring sustained effort by a number of men. No farming village

---

[2] Paul Wheatly, *The Pivot of the Four Quarters* (Chicago: Aldine, 1971), pp. 227, 228. It is difficult to make comparisons of this nature elsewhere because of the absence of a written language to accompany the archeological finds. In this case the language itself seems to have been an outgrowth of the need to keep records in connection with storing grain. Wheatley records a similar phenomenon in connection with the early growth of Shang cities, in China, which became increasingly laced with storage pits for millet, barley, and rice. Ibid., pp. 34, 35.

could organize this effort and feed itself at the same time, but a ruler backed up with storehouses could. Once he had taken this step, he controlled the metals produced in the mines, and hence both weaponry and coinage could come under his survelliance. Then he no longer had to worry about cooperating with villagers to support his army and bureaucracy.

Discussion of Shans and Kachins is continued from p. 35.

The Trobriand chiefs had half of the prerequisites for independent power, yams and coconuts, but they had no metals. Those Kachin chiefs who controlled iron mines and tolls from overland trade came closer. Yet they were hampered by Shan control of the rice-producing valleys. Each ruler had only part of the equation (the Shans with the grains; the Kachins with the metals), and their position remained tenuous. Only when they combined control of the valley with their control of trade routes, mines, and weaponry, did they achieve independent power, as this quote from a modern Burmese historian attests:

> Four hundred years ago the six (Shan) chiefs (of the Hukawny Valley) had 7,000 households in their tracts. The Kachins followed the Shans by a slow infiltration which subsequently led to . . . fighting. . . . The people on the losing side of this fight ran away from the Hukawny and had their land taken over by the Kachins. As more and more Shans ran away, more and more Kachins entered into their land. . . . The Ningbyen Shans . . . still in the valley . . . accepted the overlordship of the Ningbyen Kachin chief. They remain subordinate to him even now.[3]

Leach points out that this situation was highly unusual; elsewhere "Kachins seem to have been satisfied with the status of political parasite rather than acknowledged overlord."[4]

Further discussion of Burma may be found on p. 80. Discussion of the Nupe is continued from p. 33.

An aerial photograph of Bida, the Nupe capital, or indeed of nearly any of the capitals of the Hausa states to the north, reveals a palace section, a mosque, and a residential section; there is no visible means of support in the form of surrounding farms. The invisible means of support for such capitals were cowrie shells (tiny shells for which swimmers must dive in tropical seas) and, later, English currency paid by the villagers as taxes. The villages could never have obtained cowries or English currency to pay their taxes without a product to sell to small traders. Their millet, guinea corns, maize, and yams (or kola nuts and fish, in the case of some of them) furnished that product. The *Etsu Nupe* could use the cowries to buy part of the food from traders and hence support his retinues.

---

[3] Kawlu Ma Nawng, *The History of the Kachins of the Hukawny Valley* (Bombay, 1942) quoted in E. R. Leach, *The Political Systems of Highland Burma* (Boston: Beacon Press, 1954), p. 254.
[4] Ibid.

About 3,000 shells could be exchanged for one-eighth ounce of gold, which would in turn buy the chief weapons, regalia, or whatever else he might like.[5] Grains and tubers grown in the village were thus inherently translated into food and metal for the king and his retinues. Significantly, *only the king could amass enough cowrie shells to purchase important quantities of metals to make weapons.*

Further discussion of the Nupe may be found on p. 70. Discussion of Incas is continued from p. 31.

Gold and silver ornaments began to appear in the northern part of the coastal Andes between 900 and 200 B.C. In the period from 200 B.C. to 600 A.D. came spearthrower hooks, fishhooks, copper chisels, spear points, and digging points, all small items.[6] By the time of the Inca conquest there was general familiarity with alloys (especially bronze) and more advanced metalworking techniques. The Incas gave great emphasis to metallurgy. Their artisans made extensive use of bronze, setting aside stone tools in favor of bronze crowbars, chisels, axes, club heads, points, and knives for farmers throughout the empire. This helped produce surpluses of potatoes, maize, beans, squash, and several other tubers, legumes, and grains, which supported the Inca under the labor system of taxation. To assure that the soldiers remained even better armed than these farmers, they were equipped with heavy metal war clubs and headbreakers as well as spearthrowers and companies of bowmen using metal-tipped weapons.

The more powerful rulers among those we surveyed, in short, were in a position to control grains and metals.

It is not possible to make a pure cause-and-effect diagnosis, but these changes were also accompanied by an increase in the ferocity of warfare.

By the time metals were introduced, the coastal people of the Andes had already built pyramidal temples measuring 600 ft. × 2100 ft. at the base. They had also been growing maize for 1,000 years and were trading extensively. There is no evidence of burials or fortified architecture that would indicate that fighting among villages was a common activity. It was after the spread of agriculture and irrigation, the growth of cities, the introduction of metal weapons, and the increase of population that warfare became endemic.[7] Whereas battle scenes had been rare in prior art, they now came to dominate it. Headless bodies of youths are found throughout cemeteries. Cities were surrounded by high walls. Later there is evidence of entire towns—and even sectors of coastal plains—being abandoned or drastically thinned in population. Art shows a highly stratified society: from kings on thrones to naked prisoners with ropes around their necks. Finally, at the end of the Huari Empire, cities were abandoned altogether, and land under cultivation was greatly reduced. Even then, fighting continued, leading to the rise of the Chimus, then the Incas, the dynastic fighting of the Incas,

---

[5] At the end of the sixteenth century the exchange rate in Timbuctoo was 3,000 cowries for one-eighth of an ounce of gold; in Ashanti in 1820, 3,500. See H. A. S. Johnston, *The Fulani Empire of Sokoto* (Ibadan: Oxford University Press, 1967), p. 265.

[6] Edward P. Lanning, *Peru Before the Incas* (Englewood Cliffs, N.J.: Prentice-Hall, 1967), p. 126.

[7] Ibid., pp. 120–122.

and finally the Spanish conquest. Few people who lived during these centuries could have escaped some of the effects of war.

| Further discussion of Incas may be found on p. 95. |

Once a ruler had control of grain and metal, he had at least the potential to carry on protracted wars without consulting his populace and without any traditional restraints, to tax excessively, and to demand considerable labor time for the peasant for state purposes. He did not, however, have the capability of eliminating government at the local level. Villages were still in a position to support themselves, and the king was dependent on at least some of them for his own support, and he remained unable to interfere in their affairs except on an intermittent basis. Any king who had to feed his capital city by caravans alone would be in a fragile and subordinate position; the health of village agriculture and peaceful village life was still important to him. Those taken as slaves in warfare were likely to be reintegrated into the social structure of the empire. The grain-producing village under a king with independent power had less control over the personal environments of its members than it had possessed before it produced surplus grains. But the village still had considerably more control under the king than it would have after it ceased to grow staple foods. The peasant, whether under empire or away from it, still had something his descendents could lose: control over his own food supply. *The king wishing to tax that food supply had an interest in good yields of edible foods from the villages.* There was a symbiotic relationship between a healthy self-sufficient village and a powerful court.

STAGE TWO: INDEPENDENT TRADERS AND BUREAUCRATS

Kings were dependent upon controlling grains and metals to establish their power. To keep that control, they needed the assistance of traders and bureaucrats. In time, however, these traders and bureaucrats gained control over the grains and metals, and thus over kings and their subjects as well. It is this process we will discuss next.

Several of the cultures we have surveyed to this point had developed trade, but none that we have looked at so far, save the Incas, had government bureaus with paid civil servants.

| Discussion of the Nupe is continued from p. 69. |

Bida, the capital of Nupe territory, contained several distinct layers of what could be called bureaucratic types: the military, tax collectors, and "white-collar" clients. Yet these people differed in some important ways from their modern counterparts. As members of ranking or inferior sub-clans, they inherited the right to perform their roles, or were actual slaves of the *Etsu,* rather than being hired workers. The *Etsu* saw his leading court slaves on a daily basis; they were lower-status members of his extended family. He met every Friday with leading members of the nobility to discuss all matters of administration. The social structure of the king's court, with its various clans, was in many ways similar to that of the village. The major difference, perhaps, was that the king held more power over his courtiers than the headman exercised over his villagers; power was hierarchical and capricious, rather than shared and limited.

Near the bottom of this hierarchy were some sub-clans that engaged in trading. Their social status was even lower than that of the court slave officials. The *Etsu* also had a means to watch over the sub-clans: a personal private police force whose duty it was to guard the town markets. Some of these traders became quite wealthy. Yet, as we have indicated, the *Etsu* controlled much of the town's investment capital; he was their major customer. This sort of involvement in trading by low- or middle-echelon members of the nobility—trading in which even prices are controlled by the king—may be reliably inferred to have prevailed in the ancient Sumerian, Mesopotamian, Egyptian, and Aztec Empires as well.[8]

| Further discussion of the Nupe may be found on the next page and on p. 110. |

It is possible, however, for trading and bureaucracy to go some steps beyond this. Ancient Athens illustrates these steps so clearly that I hope you will excuse a brief excursion farther back into history and the borders of Europe. Using Athens as an example also helps illustrate a point made in connection with defining developed nations in Chapter 1: Europe, China, and Japan developed trade far earlier than the rest of the world. In Chapters 4 and 7 you will witness virtually these same processes taking place in developing nations during the twentieth century—more than *two millennia later*.[9]

The Greeks originally moved into their territory from the Black Sea. The higher ranking clans among them took the land in the valleys, while lower ranking clans subdivided the surrounding hills. The heads of leading clans eventually set themselves up as kings. That took them to the point reached by the Nupes in the narrative just mentioned. Then the arts of shipbuilding, metallurgy, and pottery grew, and with them Greek trading towns. As the trade and warships plied the seas, the nobility who operated them increased in stature, not only in the inner councils of the city government but within their clans as well. They began to accumulate capital that they controlled independently of the king, whose courtiers could not watch all the transactions in all the ports. Ships in port towns are harder to oversee than caravans moving from kingly capital to kingly capital. These noble families came to own their own estates, scattered apart from the king's residence. Their surplus wealth gave them a chance to loan money to their poorer neighbors, and thus place them in various degrees of debt bondage, including outright slavery. They could choose what crops could be raised. Only a man who could furnish his own suit of armor could fight in the military; hence, the king's officers were these same men of independent means. These country gentlemen hunted on their estates with horses and dogs. Their homes contained

[8] Wheatley, *Pivot of the Four Quarters,* pp. 283-284.

[9] See especially Richard Mansfield Haywood, *Ancient Greece and the Near East* (New York: David McKay, 1964); Alfred Zimmern, *The Greek Commonwealth,* 5th ed. (London: Oxford University Press, 1931).

fine artifacts from all over the Mediterranean. They were leaders in their own districts and town government.

This is a far cry from the Nupe gentry who were moved from one village to another, or who owned a district of slaves and lived in the capital of Bida, or the merchants who acted as middlemen for the king's trade and lived in the commercial section of Bida, where they could all be closely watched by the *Etsu Nupe*. The *Etsu* could transfer a military leader or feudal lord from his village; these men were permanent heirs of their estates. The Nupe courtier was directly dependent on the *Etsu* for his moderate wealth; these men achieved their great wealth in transactions that did not involve the king. The Nupe traders' customers were kings; these men were trading with others much like themselves, outside of Attica. The Nupe's military leaders, civil servants, and traders were different classes of people. These landed, independently wealthy individuals served all three roles for their king. *They—not the king—had the chief access to food, military prowess, civil service functions, and investment capital.* At the same time, they were freed from the restraints of clan control. On their estates they held sway over the members of their own clans. They were the employers of individuals from poorer clans—not their peers. There was no presumption of equality in the distribution of food, land, or wealth. The poor did at least have their own key to freedom from both king and nobility; new colonies continued to proliferate—sponsored by existing city-states. A talented man from a poorer sub-clan might hope to marry into a wealthier sub-clan and prosper in a new colony. This served to create new aristocrats and broadened the scope of aristocratic power; it left most members of the poor clan poor. It also extended the power of Athens and its trading aristocracy, who had these new cities as satellites.

It is therefore not surprising that in the seventh and early sixth centuries B.C. aristocrats who already controlled both grain and metals took power from the kings. In the process of weakening king and clans, however, they had created a new problem not unfamiliar today: a surplus of poor people and a shortage of food. The landed nobility accrued their wealth by selling the cereal grains and olives they grew on their estates to townsmen and surrounding islands, leaving little food behind for the members of the poor rural clans. Their return payment from the townsmen came in pottery, which could be sold abroad for other goods. They profited from these transactions because the use of debt-bondsmen on their estates kept the cost of production low. The land of Attica is not well suited for growing cereal grains, and farms of poorer clansmen on the hillsides did not produce sufficient grain to feed the countryside. This aristocracy had replaced the king. They had taken the best land away from their fellow countrymen. They could produce enough exports to purchase attractive artifacts for their homes, but in doing so they were leaving the country short of food. They needed to find a way to hold onto their prerogatives and yet produce enough food.

In 594 B.C. the nobility on the ruling council elected a man named Solon as their head. He initiated a series of reforms[10] that would have the effect of transforming the landed nobility into still a different kind of ruler—the town-based

---

[10] Solon may not have been personally responsible for all the things mentioned here as attributed to him. What is important is that they happened during this period.

businessman-tyrant. He decreed that henceforth a substantial portion of land would be used to raise only olive trees, in an intensive manner. Olive trees require little tending and are ideally adapted to Attican soil; they would provide a lucrative export crop, involving low labor costs and contributing high yields. The aristocracy would thus be free to move to the city and sell olives and pottery abroad in exchange for grain. Solon outlawed debt-bondage and returned all bondsmen to free status, absolved of debt, so they could also move to the city, where new crafts and industries and needs for troops would provide them with incomes independent of the land and they could buy the imported grain from the aristocracy. To aid trade further, Solon introduced coinage which would be accepted throughout the Mediterranean. In Sparta, the rural nobility grew grain, but had no Spartan coins that would be accepted in other states. So when foreign ships arrived they might, say, trade some foreign coins and some manufactured goods for some Spartan grain. The aristocracy would tend to buy from the ship some household goods or armaments for themselves but none for trade, since they could make more by selling needed grain than fancy imported household goods to their fellow Spartans. Also, foreign coins could not be used much in the markets at home without giving the merchants too much freedom to deal with foreigners on their own. An urban citizen would be left out of these foreign trade transactions because he could not pay the ship's captain with Spartan currency. The captain could only deal with people who had a commodity he cared to haul away in his ship, or foreign coins. Up until Solon's reform this is what happened in Athens, too. The situation was beneficial to an aristocracy living on their rural estates. They sold grain to townsmen in exchange for pottery to sell abroad. This had given the rural aristocracy a monopoly on foreign trade. Now, with an international currency, anyone could save the coins they would normally spend domestically on bread or at the local bazaar, and go down to Athens' port of Piraeus and trade directly with the ships.

Solon's reform—the relief of debt-bondage, the switch to export crops, the introduction of international coinage, and the democratization of politics—would later be introduced by nineteenth century colonialists and "progressive" twentieth century leaders in the developing nations. Solon made it possible for more people to move to Athens—including many from other parts of Greece—and gain a livelihood there. At the same time he made all Attica, including the peasantry, *dependent upon the transactions of traders, and the success of warriers abroad in securing trade outlets;* without their successes in trade and war Attica would not eat. A man's (and the city-state's) livelihood no longer depended upon obeying the norms of his village or cooperating with the leaders of his clan; it simply meant sharing at some level in the monetary returns of trade. One need not come from the nobility to achieve a key position in trade, though most people in such positions probably did come from there.

Recognizing that new social forces had been set loose, Solon or one of his successors introduced a system whereby the ruling council was no longer chosen from among the leading clans but rather by lot from all strata of the society. Concomitantly, the regulation of taxation, commerce, justice, and the like shifted from the hands of clan leaders into the impersonal system of lots or elections, or hiring of those who seemed most competent. It was not necessary for individuals to consult with their clan groups before voting or accepting office;

quite the contrary. Factions grew up centering not around clans, but economic interests. There was a party of the smallholders in the hills; another of the large estates in the plains; another with trading and commercial interests; another of dockyard workers, sailors, and fishermen on the coast. When one of the elected leaders (the military commander Peisistratus) seized the Acropolis in 561 B.C. and made himself a tyrant, there was no one to say, "Go away! We chase you away!" He had paved the way to power earlier by taking over a mine and using it to support his own personal retinue of soldiers. While once it was understood that all clans were entitled to estates (however disparate in size), he now confiscated estates and distributed their lands to poorer farmers, leaving members of formerly wealthy clans landless. Their members who had already moved to Athens and absorbed themselves in its commerce were not harmed by the move—only those who had kept their roots in the countryside.

Where once court cases had been heard by family and clan leaders, or leaders of higher status clans, Peisistratus now sent hired justices of the peace around to the villages to hear cases. He owned mines in Thrace; he used part of this income to make loans to small farmers so they could plant olive trees and vineyards. He listened to complaints personally. With this residue of support, he was assured of followers who were beholden to him not under the rules of kinship, but out of personal loyalty. He disarmed the military and civilians and created his own mercenary force. He removed the holders of all governmental posts and replaced them with his men.

Such personal regimes have their own limits. Within a few years some of the very military leaders, commercial interests, and bureaucrats whom Peisistratus had helped to foster overthrew him. Athens returned to elected leadership. Neither clans nor elected leaders were destined to rule however. The traders and military leaders involved in foreign wars had begun to bring back slaves, for which they soon found a use. In 483 B.C., a rich vein of silver was discovered in Attica.[11] The state promptly sold the mining rights to various traders and manufacturers for enough annual fee to build a large navy. Some 20,000 slaves appear to have worked the mine. There were some 2,000 shafts (up to 250 feet deep) and over one hundred miles of tunnels. The slaves worked twelve-hour shifts around the clock in the two- to three-foot high tunnels, wearing chains and branded with their master's stamp. So now such wealthy individuals could grow even wealthier without any assistance from their fellow Atticans. No one was in a position to interfere. They already had access to most of the olives and ran the factories. Now they could literally mint for themselves all the coins they wanted, too. Unlike the Spartan nobility, they did not even need to operate rural estates and hire workers there. Yet while they were freed from others, others depended on them. The people needed them for their food and jobs. The government was run by amateurs who could not produce a navy without the money and expertise controlled by these new aristocrats. And no new Peisistratus could compete by turning out money faster.

The government turned the navy into the best in the Mediterranean. It proceeded to defeat the powerful Persian fleet and assure free access to the most im-

---

[11] Zimmern, *The Greek Commonwealth*, pp. 398–400.

portant grain belt along that sea—the Nile. Egypt would now both trade wheat and send free shipments of it as tribute. The navy assured for the time being that no one else could accumulate greater mining capabilities. It was also able to round up even more slaves to help with mining and manufacturing. Very soon, under the leadership of Pericles, the slaves would also be used to build the Parthenon and other spectacular monuments of the great era of temple and wall building. Athens' great age of literature, art, and prosperity was paid for largely from the tribute and trade it received from the other Mediterranean states.

Then the defeat of Athens' navy in the Peloponnesian War would bring the great prosperity to an end. Unable to control the trade in grain and output of mines in the Mediterranean, Athens would soon find itself doing the bidding of other cities and empires, but it would not again return to self-sufficiency. It continued with the olives and grain imports and international currency. And Athens' trading and mining community found new capitals from which they could continue their operations. Clans continued to try to assert their influence in the centuries ahead. Yet functions that had formerly been the exclusive prerogatives of clans had slipped out of Pandora's box. A populace that formerly did not need metals and grew its own food now had come to rely on total strangers, aristocrats, and bureaucrats to obtain both. Political leaders who formerly controlled both grains and metals had found that they must bargain with mine leasers, traders, and bureaucrats in order to obtain them.

First the leading clans had achieved independence from the king. Then the urban traders and officials achieved independence from the leading clans. No future regimes were in a position to function without the aid of those traders and officials, whose assistance was needed in obtaining food, basic raw materials, armaments, and especially working capital. It was people like those traders and officials who started to show up in the sixteenth century in the developing areas. They could buy more cannons than any king. They could pay peasants more for crops than could kings. They would soon place the *Etsu Nupe* on what seemed to him a handsome salary and help him build a new palace just outside Bida, thus relieving him of the need to collect taxes and of the opportunity to spy on commerce so closely. They could ask the peasant to shift into growing crops for export. They could even ask peasants to vacate areas, which they would begin to cultivate using their own laborers. This was the shift in control over food and metals, and thus power, from clan and nobility to trader and bureaucrat, which began when European commerce was introduced to the developing areas.

STAGE THREE: LAND, PLANTATIONS, AND COMMERCIAL MINING

For developing areas the structure of international trade changed when trade ceased to revolve around kings and began to revolve around people like Athens' mine leasers and traders. Unlike the kings, who had depended upon integrated villages for their livelihood, these outsiders had no use for clans. What they wanted was land and laborers who would work for them, rather than to fulfill reciprocal obligations within the village. Kings were mere nuisances who could be bought off easily, but clans were a threat. Left intact, they used up land and labor on unprofitable activities that fed, clothed, and sheltered the populace but left little room for commercial advantage.

So when these international traders arrived, their first order of priority was to destroy the integrated, self-governing village so that the land and labor would be freed up to produce profitable exports, including metals to provide the traders with more immediate working capital. In the remainder of this chapter we will literally circle the globe to show how successful they were in this endeavor. The second order of priority was to establish governments in all these countries similar to that established by Solon, so that they could assure their own perpetual ascendency to political power. The next chapter will show how successful they were in that endeavor. Chapter 5 demonstrates that there is little danger of kings or clans, or Peisistratus and his mobs, returning to power. In Chapter 7 you will meet many more Solons, battling to drive the aristocracy from their country estates, and the clans from their villages. At that point you will begin to appreciate the staggering dimensions of those reforms, and the frightening potentials of the world order we have created for ourselves today. In the last chapter we shall explore our own age of Pericles, to see where it might be leading us.

Southeast Asia

QUESTION

What hypothesis are we examining here?

During the seventeenth century, Chinese merchants began renting land in the East Indies and hiring labor to grow spices and other export crops for sale to Portuguese traders. Villagers themselves began to grow export crops for sale to these traders. These two approaches—renting, and converting village farming to export crops—gradually grew from the exception into the rule. By the nineteenth century the Dutch (who meanwhile had intervened in the area) had introduced a cultural system in which every villager was expected to contribute a percentage of his crop to them. Unlike earlier exactations by kings, the crop taxed was not staple food, but sugar cane strictly for export.

A brief look at a town in a rice-producing region of Java in the 1920s illustrates the effects of these processes on the populace.[12] The town contained a large mill for processing sugar cane. In a neat row alongside were houses for the twenty Dutch employees who operated the mill. The company had an agreement with the community leaders by which it rented one-third of the rice paddy fields at a time, rotating fields every eighteen months. The company used the fields for sugar cane rather than rice, hiring villagers at low wages to plant and later harvest it. The remaining fields were divided among the villagers by the village leadership in a traditional manner to grow rice. The company shared a small percentage of the profits from the export of the sugar with the regional indigenous rulers

---

[12] Clifford Geertz, *Agricultural Involution* (Berkeley: University of California Press, 1963); idem, *The Social History of an Indonesian Town* (Cambridge: MIT Press, 1965).

and the Dutch government in Bandoeng. The new forms seemed to be coexisting with the old.

The growth in sugar cane production brought with it a growth in population, if for no other reason than that food could now be imported during occasional years of famine. The fact that one-third of the land was now perpetually in use by the outsiders created a paradox. Total production for the region in *both* sugar cane and rice grew to record highs, thanks to the greater labor-intensiveness in cultivation. Yet *per capita* production of rice was below what it had been a hundred years before, and each family was tilling less land. In addition to working his own inadequate-sized plot, a man would devote some time to wage-labor in order to bring his family to the subsistence level. He might even sell off his rice crop and purchase family food at the store. At the end of World War II most of the sugar mills did not reopen, and his plight became even more severe. Many nuclear families claimed the plot of land they occupied was theirs, though it was understood within the village that they would not sell it to outsiders. By the 1950s, 76 percent of the land was in small individual holdings of this type, and only 23 percent was distributed through the traditional community structure.[13] Average daily caloric intake on Java was 1,946 calories in 1960, down to 1,730 in 1967, and continuously dropping to the present time.[14]

The traditional system of local land control, communal land tenure, which had initially coexisted with the new economic forms, was subtly being destroyed. The villagers, originally self-supporting, had become increasingly dependent on the outsiders for their subsistence. Local leadership—with little flexibility in land distribution or adjustment to population growth—could no longer aid them in times of emergency. When productivity of export crops was down, the outside merchants were not in a position to help the people either. The nobility, who had come to rely on those merchants to collect their taxes, had lost contact with the village leadership that had formerly been its local ally; they had declined in tandem. Land was still in the hands of local people, but it was too little land in too few hands, removed from a social context that would maintain top productivity by means of cooperation in labor, irrigation, or marketing. The privatization of land was not accompanied by the introduction of new means of livelihood for the landless or those with insufficient land.

Further discussion of Java may be found on p. 307.

Meanwhile, Deli, on the east coast of Sumatra, had become a center for plantations. The villages there practiced slash-and-burn agriculture: burning off a patch of jungle, farming it a few years, and then moving on to a new site. These villagers were left free to rotate their plots in the hills; however, the plantations burned the patches for them and raised tobacco there the first season. The villagers were then given use of the patch for the second season (when the land's productivity had been lowered) while the plantation opened a new field. Once again, the old and the new seemed to coexist. This system ended when rubber

[13] Geertz, *Social History,* pp. 24ff.

[14] Richard W. Franke, "Miracle Seeds and Shattered Dreams in Java," *Natural History* 83, no. 1 (January 1974): 11.

replaced tobacco as the principal crop. Rubber trees require several years of gestation; they simply took over much of the land formerly used by the slash-and-burn farmers. Imported Chinese and Javanese laborers worked for the plantations, living in company-built towns. By 1930, there were 645,000 Javanese and 195,000 Chinese in the region, either working on plantations or in commercial pursuits connected with them.[15] The plantations averaged 8,000 acres and were complete societies with their own housing, processing plants, law, and government closely monitored by the plantation owners who had created the new social system. Meanwhile, original inhabitants were finding land so scarce that some of them were squatting on plantation land. Smallholdings elsewhere in the Outer Islands of the Indies grew coffee, pepper, tea, and coconuts for export to supplement their regular food crop. Some farmers became wealthy on these crops, inducing many of their neighbors to abandon rice production in favor of the more lucrative (until the Great Depression) export crops. By World War II some of these small former rice farmers in the Outer Islands were export farmers in debt and importing rice. Some found jobs in town; many were separated from their villages and without jobs.

In 1781, Spanish traders in Manila established a system through which they controlled crop volume, price, and marketing of tobacco, with forced delivery from the regions of northern Luzon. It proved to be so profitable that the Spanish monarchy authorized the establishment of the Royal Philippine Company. By 1790, this company was investing in indigo, pepper, sugar, and cotton crops—also obtained by indirect taxation of farmers arranged through local leaders. Spanish friars, too, were given large tracts of land—gifts sometimes involving the eviction of whole villages—which they used native-hired labor to cultivate. Then during the nineteenth century came American, European, and Chinese investment firms that broadened the scope of these enterprises. In 1857, a British firm began building sugar mills on the island of Negros; soon the island was filled with sugar fields tended by seasonal workers who had heard about the wages to be made at such work. Formerly the islands had produced sufficient rice for both home consumption and export; by 1870 so many small farmers had shifted to raising sugar, hemp, and hillside coffee that it became necessary to import rice. After the American takeover, an extensive sugar industry also grew in the Huk territories of the central plain of Luzon. Throughout the Philippines, control of land was clearly shifting from village to landlord and use of land was increasingly for export crops. Villagers were becoming directly dependent on commercial enterprises for their livelihood.

Further discussion of the Philippines may be found on p. 115.

Polynesia has a long history of intra- and inter-island warfare.[16] These bloody wars forced inhabitants of entire villages into the mangrove swamps.

[15] David J. Steinberg et al., *In Search of Southeast Asia* (New York: Praeger, 1971), pp. 219, 220.

[16] Polynesia is bounded by the Hawaiian Islands to the north and Easter Island on the east. The Trobriand Islands lie on the cultural fringes of this area, to the west. See Irving Goldman, "Status Rivalry and Cultural Evolution in Polynesia," in *Comparative Political Systems*, ed. Ronald Cohen and John Middleton (Garden City, N.Y.: Natural History Press, 1967), pp. 375-395.

Many clans broke the custom and moved in with the wife's family. This meant the scattering of some villages, and weakened kinship solidarity in others. Chiefs took advantage of this situation, claiming tracts of land in their own or defeated villages as personal property. Many families, made poor and weak by battles, were available to work this land. When families from leading clans were not cooperative with a chief, he was able to hand out land to supporters from lesser lineages and thus create new allies. With danger from outside attack always imminent, it was difficult to argue with a chief and his warriors. So large plantations, privately owned land, and landless families existed even before the arrival of European influence. Clan control of land had collapsed from within. The means of livelihood had become uncertain for many people.

In Thailand, Chinese planters introduced commercial sugar production around 1816. Thai rulers sold the right to collect internal taxes to Chinese immigrants. Various members of the nobility extended their right to labor services from subjects to the point that by the 1850s foreign observers estimated that half the population of the kingdom lived in a state of voluntary servitude.[17] The system was later outlawed and, unlike developments in neighboring countries, much of the succeeding expansion of rice production took place on peasant-owned plots. By this time, however, Thai peasants in rice regions had been largely removed from former kin leadersip and associated with Chinese middlemen. Sugar exports were high. In 1855, the king signed a treaty with the British opening up free trade, and Thailand became one of the world's largest exporters of rice and teak. Later, Thailand also developed extensive rubber plantings, largely on smallholdings operated by tenant laborers. Villagers were concentrating on crops for export; they were under pressure to cooperate with those who marketed these crops. The king became more dependent upon his alliance with the merchants than upon his contact with the local kinship structure. But here we may find an exception to the rule. This introduction of private land ownership may not have been accompanied by a loss of livelihood for significant numbers of people—in the rice growing regions. In the northeast and northwest where productivity was low, job displacement became a far more serious problem.

In Vietnam, most villagers originally lived in the north; the first census of 1847 revealed that only 165,598 of 1,024,338 male taxpayers lived in the six southern provinces.[18] During the late eighteenth century imperial exactions of land, taxes, and labor dues had weakened the position of the peasant in the north. When the virgin lands to the south were opened, individual ownership became the norm there; an 1836 court survey in the south found landlords, many poor landless people, and many illegal squatters. This paved the way for French efforts in the 1860s to reassign old lands and colonize new ones. The French drained and irrigated large tracts of new land and sold lots at low prices. By 1938, half the arable land was planted in rice, with half of this in the hands of 2.5 percent of landowners. Some 70 percent of all landowners owned 15 percent of the arable land, while 350,000 (or 57 percent of the rural population) were land-

---

[17] Steinberg, *Southeast Asia*, p. 112.
[18] Ibid., p. 125.

less tenants. Of the 7,000 large landowners in Vietnam just before World War II, 90 percent were located in the south. They lived on rent paid by tenants, interest from loans advanced to the peasantry, and rice exports (which were handled by Chinese). There were 1,005 rubber plantations using laborers from the north;[19] extensive rubber plantations also developed in southern Cambodia. Meanwhile, the land ownership pattern had changed in the north as well. In Tonkin Province 500 large landowners—both French and Vietnamese—came to own 20 percent of the land; another 17,000 held a further 20 percent. The rest of the land did not remain in village control but was divided among a million smallholders, at an average of one- and one-quarter acres per family.[20] On top of the cost of loans, these cultivators and tenants had to pay heavy head and land taxes to the French colonial government. Hence, in Vietnam the transformation from village to individual control of land and the move from subsistence to export agriculture came quickly. Clearly, a significant percentage of the populace was forced to eke out an existence on minimal land, or as a complete subordinate to a landowner.

Still, as of 1930, some 20 percent of the land in Tonkin to the north, 25 percent in Annam in the center, and 3 percent in Cochin to the south was under the control of village leaders. Yet, similar to what we saw tried by the *Etsu Nupe,* the French instituted a system by which the province chief had to approve the election of a village chief, interfering with the choice of the elders. Unlike the case with the Nupe villages, these villages were not in a position to ignore the outside choice. Hence, the village chiefs ceased to be representative of the community, and corruption became common.[21] Many village chiefs, epsecially in the south, rented out major portions of the communal lands, or simply gave several hectares of land to village notables, who in turn rented them out to landless peasants. Those who ran the village, then, were those with ready cash; they were dependent on the French for that cash, and so they were attractive to the French as cooperative candidates for village leadership. Local clan leadership had given way to control by outside commercial interests.

Further discussion of Vietnam may be found on p. 117. Discussion of Burma is continued from p. 68 and continues on p. 194.

When the Burman king in Mandalay surveyed the population of his territories in 1803, he found only two million people, mostly engaged in the production of rice and other staple food.[22] After the British occupied lower Burma in 1852, the Burman ruler realized he must modernize his people if the British were not to capture his kingdom in upper Burma as well. He ended the tax-collecting power of princes by establishing a state income tax and placing the princes on salaries and stipends. He purchased several river steamers and with the assistance of European managers set up processing plants for tanning and dying resins, shellac, sugar, cotton, and silk. He also began to stimulate rice pro-

---

[19] Eric R. Wolf, *Peasant Wars of the Twentieth Century* (New York: Harper & Row, 1969), p. 168.

[20] Ibid., p. 166.

[21] Ibid., pp. 174–175.

[22] Steinberg, *Southeast Asia,* p. 99.

duction. He had opened the door to dependence on export agriculture, while weakening the power of princes and—probably—clan leaders as well. Unknowingly, he was also contributing to the decline of his own throne. In 1855, when the British began to work on rice production in the lower valley, the Irrawaddy delta had 1 million acres under cultivation, mostly in smallholding plots of two and three acres; by 1930, that figure had grown to 10 million.[23] Meanwhile, population there rose from 1.5 million to 8 million. Much of this expansion was in the form of land sold in plots of fifty acres and more and worked by seasonal laborers. By 1928, 42 percent of rice-planting land was farmed by tenants; the Great Depression then caused considerably more of the smallholders to sell their land, raising that figure to 58 percent by 1935.[24] With so many landless, and new land now scarce, rents for tenants rose and tenants were frequently forced to move. Only one who already owned a plow animal could find a tenancy; he could soon be moved if a poor yield caused him to default on rent.[25] A great many farmers who remained on their own land were heavily in debt to moneylenders. Individual land ownership, export crops, and dependence on commercial interests had become the norm here as well. Access to means of livelihood had become more uncertain. The area around Mandalay, formerly the heart of the kingdom, had receded to the economic periphery of the delta region.

In 1876, Sir Robert Wickham smuggled seeds of the Amazon rubber tree to England, from whence seedlings were subsequently taken to Ceylon and Malaya. In Malaya vast tracts of sparsely inhabited jungle awaited the new crop. Some trees were planted by Malays already there, and others by small planters who migrated from various parts of the Indonesian archipelago. These small planters began to supply the new motor car industry from their smallholdings of one hundred acres and less. In 1903, Harrison and Crossfields of London invested in a large estate. In 1910, the first year its trees produced, it netted its investers 200 percent of their entire original investment.[26] From that point on, encouragement of these large plantations became a major objective of British colonial rule in Malaya. Policy was deliberately slanted to favor the plantations and discourage smallholdings. Malays preferred to work their smallholdings, rather than live on the large estates, so workers were imported from southern India (dispossessed people discussed shortly in the next section) and China. As of 1932, the Malayan smallholder could produce rubber for 0.5 cent per pound, versus 12 cents on the large estates, while the market price had dropped to 5 cents. This threatened the large estates. In 1934, smallholders produced 217,000 tons compared with 260,000 on the estates. During that same year, 83 percent of the world's rubber output came from Malaya and the Dutch East Indies.[27] So by squeezing out small producers there, it was possible to make world markets dependent on

---

[23] Ibid., p. 223.

[24] Ibid., pp. 225, 226.

[25] In one study of 325 tenants in three areas in the early 1920s, only 19 had been on the same plot for twelve years or more. James C. Scott, *The Moral Economy of the Peasant: Rebellion and Subsistence in Southeast Asia* (New Haven: Yale University Press, 1976), p. 72.

[26] Ozay Mehmet, *Economic Planning and Social Justice in Developing Countries* (New York: St. Martins, 1978), pp. 102–106.

[27] League of Nations, *Statistical Yearbook 1934/35*, Table 47.

estate rubber.[28] The Malayan Controller of Rubber instituted a policy of merging smallholdings into large estates and restricting exports of smallholding rubber. Only the larger smallholders tended to survive. So Malays had been moved from communal agriculture into private ownership and thence into unemployment, while large private holdings took over much of the land. In the meantime, the Sultans were receiving generous payments for land to which they had laid claim.[29] With competition from smallholders eliminated, world rubber prices would rise.

Further discussion of Malaysia may be found on p. 119.

South Asia

Discussion of India is continued from p. 37.

Britain's East India Company came to India in 1601, and established itself in the Bay of Bengal in 1611. By the end of that century it had settlements in Madras and Bombay. It was not until 1859, after many military campaigns, that Britain gained hegemony over all of India. Nevertheless, British reforms (largely begun toward the end of the eighteenth century) were to have a more profound effect on India's land tenure system than those of any of their predecessors. On the surface the changes seem rather innocent: *The intermediaries for collecting land taxes were given hereditary, rather than moveable, posts, with contractual rights over the lands from which they collected revenue. Taxes could be in money as well as kind, and were paid directly by the peasant.*

The idea of collecting land tax in money through intermediaries did not originate with the British; the Delhi Empire began this practice early in the fourteenth century.[30] The Muslim emperor who ruled from 1296 to 1316 decided to deviate from the longstanding practice of collecting all land revenue from the highest caste members of a village, and claimed the right to deal directly with the peasant. The reform was intended to be a progressive one, and first began around Delhi. Between 1325 and 1351, administrative officers were placed in

---

[28] Soon synthetics, based on coal and petroleum mined by large companies, would replace estate rubber. Then small producers, on which tire manufacturers relied at the beginning of this century, would have virtually no part in the production of tires. The industry that encouraged these smallholders to break away from village life would leave them with no village to which to return.

[29] With regard to nonrubber land, Robert Ho, "Land Ownership and Economic Prospects of Malayan Peasants," *Modern Asian Studies* 4, no. 1 (January 1970): 84–92, gives statistics on the state of Perak in Malaya. There the area of land devoted to rice and village crops has grown more slowly than the population. Holdings of land are both small and physically fragmented. Until the 1960s two-thirds of all paddy land and three-fourths of kampong (village) land changed hands each decade. The more recent phenomenon is a growth in joint ownership of land, especially where several people inherit the same patch of land. It is not unknown in Malaya for an individual to own 1/2000 of a two-acre plot of rice. In Perak, Kedah, Perlis, Kelantan, and Malacca about half of the rubber and rice workers are tenants. Chapter 4 contains a further discussion of Malayan land tenure.

[30] Irfan Habib, "Usury in Medieval India," *Comparative Studies in Society and History* 6, no. 4 (July 1964): pp. 393–419.

charge of particular regions. During a famine, the officers *(talukdars)* would order the digging of wells, and give money and seed to the peasants; the peasant was in turn expected to contribute a third to a half of his harvest (or its cash equivalent) to the state granaries (allowing the peasant to retain more for himself than under the former system). A whole body of officials *(zamindars)* was set up to advance these loans, each given charge of advancing loans to and collecting taxes from several villages. By the seventeenth century this had become standard administrative practice. The money was generally advanced through the village headman or highest caste members, who stood surety for the repayment, which was always due at the next harvest and could be deferred if the harvest failed. No interest was charged; the officials probably took commissions. These officials, later joined by warriors and merchants, did advance personal loans on the side, charging high rates of interest (on the order of one-eighth of the principal each month) to peasants who needed money to pay their land or poll tax, buy a draught animal, or pay for a wedding or funeral. If a *zamindar* could not collect on personal loans, or overextended himself so that he did not have sufficient state revenue to turn over to the *talukdar,* he could borrow money from merchants in the town. Sometimes the latter hoped he would not be able to repay, so they could become *zamindars* themselves. Should a village fall too far behind in paying taxes, the *zamindar* might persuade the leaders to take out a private loan to pay them. Nobility also borrowed heavily to support their huge retinues; they repaid handsomely after receiving their shares of the harvest, enriching the moneylending merchants and depleting the size of the state granaries.

Personal loans began to take their toll on the peasantry. If crops failed, they could defer payment on the interest-free government loans until the next crop. But the interest on the personal loans added up at the rate of 15 percent of the principal or more each month. A 1684 imperial order provided for exemption from the poll tax of "the poor peasants who engage in cultivation, but are wholly in debt for their seeds and cattle." The arrival of the East India Company had added new temptations. In seventeenth century Agra, indigo merchants advanced money to peasants on the condition that they grow indigo on their land, and took repayment in indigo at high interest; they sold the indigo to the East India Company. Gujarat merchants were giving out worm-decayed grain for cotton yarn, inflating the value of the grain and deflating the values of the yarn in calculating the transactions. Since their own officials had become so dependent on the system of private loans, the Moghul emperors supported the collection of debts. The government sent out memoranda ordering *zamindars* to make debtors pay. Since they were themselves in debt to the moneylenders, they had a double incentive to do so. The emperors permitted taking children as security on loans, creating a class of debt-servants. By 1750, just before the British conquest of Bengal, one writer reports that most peasants were in debt. Rich and powerful debtors could often escape paying debts, while poor debtors continued to owe and to pay out high percentages of the crops to cover them. Still, because the caste system remained intact, they could not be removed from their community or their land.

Prior to the British presence, the position of the *zamindar* was rather tenuous. He could be removed from his position by the *talukdar* or the emperor. He was expected to bring in adequate revenues, and to repay his own debts to the moneylenders; this meant he needed a good working relationship with the local leaders. The British strengthened the power of the *zamindars* by making their posts (or, in some regions less under Muslim control, other similar functionaries) hereditary. The *zamindars* hired retainers, responsible only to them. The *talukdars* were also made hereditary. They were sometimes given waste lands to cultivate, or a specific percentage of revenue. Warriors, bankers, or government officials were sometimes made *talukdars* to give them extra status in exchange for their services to the government. They, too, hired large staffs of retainers.[31] By these moves, the British were seeking to establish a set of powerful local supporters.

The relations between the villages and the *zamindars* became something of a show of strength. The *zamindar* generally took around half of the crop, plus a percentage for his servants. Those of higher status in a village might develop an understanding with *zamindars* to help extract more revenue from those of lower status in the village, and there was little to stop this, especially during the final wars between the British and Indian nobility that culminated in the ascendency of the British Crown in 1858.[32] The peasant's one resort was to move to uninhabited lands, which were still available in many regions.

Conflicts between *zamindars* and *talukdars* also increased. A *zamindar* might pass on a fourth of each of his villages to each of his four sons. The sons lost contact with peasants; residing elsewhere, they knew only about revenue collection.[33] They might argue among themselves about who should get what revenue from what village. They ran up large debts to moneylenders to support their expensive retainers and lifestyles. Sometimes a moneylender would try to foreclose and the peasant would find two people demanding his harvest, both claiming to be the *zamindar*.[34] Sometimes a *zamindar* would not give the *talukdar* what he considered his fair share; then the latter would try to replace him with another who was paying.

When the British Crown took full control in 1858, it attempted some reforms. Serfdom was outlawed. Government civil servants would henceforth assess all land themselves, establishing fixed biannual payments based on the type of land and the crops normally grown there. The civil servants would deal with a villager, the *lambardar,* chosen by all the villagers at an open meeting. Taxes would be paid directly to the revenue department. At the same time, British civil servants would be given furloughs to England every four years to revitalize them and reestablish their contacts with the homeland. This reduced their command of information about their districts. Their underlings—too few and too poorly paid—became dependent upon the employees of the *zamindars* to make the assessments. These employees generally kept two sets of books.[35] The *zamindar* or his retainers had the power to be present at the harvest. He had

---

[31] Elizabeth Whitcombe, *Agrarian Conditions in Northern India, Vol. 1 The United Provinces Under British Rule, 1860-1900* (Berkeley: University of California Press, 1972), pp. 41–42.

[32] Ibid., p. 44.

[33] Ibid., pp. 53, 55.

[34] Ibid., p. 58.

[35] Ibid., pp. 241–242, 258

good working relations with the largest urban traders who were handling exports to Britain. Unlike the civil servant, he could also help keep civil order. Hence, the *lambardar* and the civil servants were effectively by-passed. Because the land rents were now fixed, peasants were liable for payment even when the crop failed. This made resort to moneylenders necessary, and created permanent debts.

The *zamindars* were empowered to evict tenants who did not pay rent, or to forcibly take crops at harvest time to cover back rent.[36] As irrigation (discussed in Chapter 7) progressed, they took land along the canals, or were able to charge a higher rate of rent. The local high-caste leaders were only responsible for paying tax on the land they had worked themselves. They could hire landless laborers for this, or pay wages to landed laborers wanting more income. They owed obligations only to those who worked directly for them, or who performed services for them; many were not even Hindu. *Zamindars* sometimes even demanded taxes from local craftsmen in the form of blankets or shoes and the like.[37] Many of them rarely visited the villages; if improvements were to be made, the tenants were often expected to make them.

A sharp line grew between those who owed money and those who did not, and between those with roads and irrigation and those without. One had to pay for irrigation water, but the crops of wheat, indigo, cotton, opium, sugar cane, tobacco, and vegetables that could be grown would bring a good price. The profits could be lent to others at high interest rates, increasing assets. The native grains grown on the unirrigated land brought a low price and were subject to failure during drought, requiring the peasant to take out a loan to pay taxes. *Zamindars* whose estates constituted unirrigated land, or which were shrinking in size due to divisions at time of inheritance, might also find themselves in this position. The peasant could be evicted if he did not repay; the *zamindar* would often sell out to a wealthier *zamindar* or sometimes to an urban investor. Furthermore, when drought approached, solvent owners of irrigated fields could draw on their grain reserves and fields to command a large price for their crops; insolvent peasants with unirrigated fields could not get further loans and had to pay high prices at the market for food after their crops failed. The only recourse was to sell the land to some buyer. Once land was lost, the peasant was left to the uncertainties of the labor market. The cotton, sent to Britain and then returned to India as manufactured cloth, destroyed the cottage industries that had previously produced most of India's cloth, and many of her nonagricultural jobs. Serfdom to the land had been outlawed and replaced with economic serfdom.

In the 1860s the village studied by Kathleen Gough (introduced in the previous chapter) was parcelled out and purchased by the former Brahmin "owning" families, some other local Brahmin families, and some Muslim and Hindu traders from the town three miles away. The former serfs stayed and continued to work the Brahmins' land; they borrowed money from these Brahmins and became indebted to them. Land tends to change hands frequently, and as of 1951

---

[36] Ibid., p. 159.
[37] Ibid., p. 44.

these individuals were employed on a year-to-year basis, often working for new owners. Only 22 percent of them were still tied laborers, 38 percent leased land, while 39 percent were day-laborers.[38] Many have become detached from their families, and wander from village to village looking for work as day-laborers. This particular village is more sparsely populated than many around it, and has absorbed some such individuals and families. The nonfarming service families have lost their hereditary rights, and have sometimes found competitors moving into the village. Some have had to seek other occupations. Some of the service castes have raised their status (e.g., some former cattle raiders have become successful rice traders); the status of others has diminished (e.g., Brahmins are working as waiters in a restaurant). Some new castes have moved into the village. The Brahmins own about 65 percent of the land, and most of the rest belongs to town traders and Brahmins from other villages. One former serf family owns a very small plot. The bathing pools are now for the exclusive use of the Brahmins, and their fish are annually auctioned to professional fishermen outside the village. The Brahmins do offer food to their tenants and servants at weddings and festivals.

By 1950, some 17 percent of all farm-related families in India owned half of all the land under cultivation and had it worked by tenants, sharecroppers, or hired labor. Half of the income derived from these farms was from export or industrial-related crops. An additional 45 percent of farm families worked as tenants on the above farms or owned (directly or indirectly) farms of their own, ranging from two to sixteen acres. The remainder of farm families had no access to the land and made a living by working for others.[39] In those cases where the landlord still lived on the farm, he developed a parent-child relationship with his tenants; otherwise the relationship was purely economic. Private ownership had moved from the exception to the norm. As we shall see from a futher discussion of India in Chapters 4 and 7, the means of livelihood were becoming increasingly uncertain.

Further discussion of India may be found on p. 110.

During the 1840s and '50s, the British began raising tea on a large scale in northern and southern India and central Ceylon.[40] These schemes varied from large estates and small proprietorships relying on outside labor—from Nepal and Sikkim in Darjeeling, Bihar and Orissa in Assam, and Tamils in southern India and Ceylon—to small individual landholdings. Later on, rubber growing organized in a similar mixed manner was added in southern India and especially central Ceylon. Land tenure in all these regions came to center around individually owned plots of land large and small, raising export crops.

---

[38] A study of six districts in South India compared the wages of laborers in 1873–75 to 1898–1900. In one district they rose 29 percent. In the others they fell 13 to 48 percent. Dharma Kumar, *Land and Caste in South India* (Cambridge: Cambridge University Press, 1965), p. 164.

[39] Charles Bettelheim, *India Independent* (New York: Monthly Review Press, 1971), pp. 26–27. K. Ishwaran, *Shivapur: A South Indian Village* (London: Routledge, 1968), pp. 2, 11, like Kathleen Gough, brings these figures to an individual village level. There, 5,621 acres (a mean average of 1.5 per individual) is owned by 47 percent of the families; 20 percent of the families are tenant farmers, while the rest have no direct connection with the land. The largest farm contains 200 acres.

The Middle East

Scattered through the hill regions of eastern Turkey, Soviet Armenia, northeast Iraq, and northwest Iran live a people called the Kurds. Once entirely a herding people, part of them later settled in farming communities. These villages were governed and distributed land in a traditional manner. Certain lineages claiming descent from Muhammad were known as *shaikhs* and were considered of higher status, both within villages and herding groups, and in tribal organization above the village level. Within each village or herding group were about fifteen mounted riflemen who were ready to form a militia for the *shaikh* of their region should they be needed for a raid against a caravan or village. It was these militias that became the nuclei for the introduction of individual land ownership. They expanded Kurdish power by conducting raids on non-Kurd farming villages and demanding that these villages submit to leadership by a group of Kurds who would then move into the village and support themselves by collecting a portion of the year's crop as taxes. In addition, some of their number would take individual plots of land to farm themselves, as individual inheritable property. When the corrupt and declining Ottoman Empire took control of the region in the mid-nineteenth century, they brought with them a rule—a bastardization of an approach we shall examine in a moment—that all land belongs to the emperor. Immediately, *shaikhs,* wealthy merchants, and others purchased large tracts of land that had formerly belonged to peasant villages from "representatives" of the emperor.[41] Once they owned part of a village, they would forcibly take over the rest of it. In this manner the region became divided among villages composed entirely of tenants or wage earners, and villages composed of freemen. Usually the landowner assigns a village to an intermediary capitalist who looks after the tenancies and tax collections for a fee; he has considerable flexibility in the rent he actually charges. The landowner appoints the village chief—and often the chiefs of surrounding freeholding villages as well—and has final say in all its affairs. *Shaikhs* who own villages came to rely on displaced individuals to form their personal militias. A *mullah* (religious leader) from a village that was purchased by a prominent *shaikh* summarizes the changing status of kinship and tribal loyalty:

> When Shaikh Mahmud was a religious leader, I was a mullah. He became King,
> I became a rifleman. Now he is a landowner, I am a farmer.[42]

In Iraq in 1953—with a population of 900,000 Kurds and 6,200,000 other people—2 percent of the landowners owned 68 percent of the total agricultural holdings, and 89.4 percent of peasants owned no land at all.[43] This process of replacing village land tenure by individual ownership was, in short, by no means limited to the Kurds, but was happening throughout the former regions of Meso-

---

[40] See P. P. Courtenay, *Plantation Agriculture* (New York: Praeger, 1965).

[41] Fredrik Barth, *Principles of Social Organization in Southern Kurdistan, Universitetets Etnografiske Museum Bulletin* No. 7 (Oslo, 1953): 53.

[42] Ibid., p. 127.

[43] Fuad Baali, "Social Factors in Iraqi Rural-Urban Migration," *American Journal of Economics and Sociology* 28, no. 1 (January 1969): 62.

potamia. It clearly brought with it great uncertainties regarding means of livelihood.

Discussion of Iran is continued from p. 39.

Iran's land tenure began to change its character after the conquest by the Seljuk Turks in the eleventh century. Former armies had been recruited directly off the land. The Seljuks instead used mercenaries from Turkey, and rewarded these troops by giving them large portions of the best land in northern Iran. Military leaders replaced the former provincial governors and tax collectors. With local landowners deprived of their armies, and the Seljuk rulers weak, these tax collectors began to behave like landowners. After the Mongols swept in, the large tracts of land that became vacant or underpopulated were taken over by minor government officials. They farmed some areas with the aid of slaves, and others with the help of peasants whom they taxed mercilessly. They also supported banditry on the roads, though few of those revenues ever reached the Mongol rulers. Before the eleventh century, the peasant could play landlord and tax collector against one another, while the king had an interest in keeping agriculture viable and productive. Now the peasant had no one to turn to, and the landlord's prosperity depended more on plunder than viable agriculture.

The Safavids, who replaced the Mongols in the sixteenth century, continued a similar system, using Armenian and Georgian mercenaries, but they were less harsh. They set up Shiite Islam as the official religion, and gave much land to religious leaders, in addition to that given to the military. Many large private landholdings from the previous regime were also left intact. The right to private landowning was asserted. The Shahs themselves took over large tracts of land as their own, and toward the end of the dynasty some religious land was sold to private owners. Still, peasants had rights guaranteed as sharecroppers. Usually the landowner furnished water, seed, manure, and sometimes oxen, and the peasant retained a portion of the crop for his labor. Meanwhile, the more nomadic tribes roamed relatively free in the countryside.

After the takeover by the Qajars in 1785, much land went out of production and reverted to the state, thanks to high costs for paying the army and courtiers, tribal warfare, banditry by Russians and Turks, confiscations of land and excess taxation by the tuyuldars sent to the countryside as tax collectors, and a famine from 1869 to 1872. Much land was given to religious leaders. The Shah took some as his own, some was sold to private investers, and the state hired bailiffs to cultivate that which it retained for itself. The policy was continued under Riza Shah Pahlevi after he overthrew the Qajars. Much land was owned by absentee landowners; some by tuyuldars, some by the state, some by religious leaders, and some by tribal leaders. Furthermore, these individuals had often become the highest court of appeal in civil suits, and the tax collectors for their regions. They negotiated their own sharecropping agreements with the peasants, and controlled the waterways. Most seriously, these government officials, merchants, bailiffs, and tribal and religious leaders often acquired as much land as they could simply for prestige. They needed only as much income as would give them a good standard of living, and did not have the time or interest to improve their holdings.

Much land had been rendered unproductive. So the peasant was more than ever before subject to the whims of the landowner. Those peasants who had lost their sharecropping status in the course of the many upheavals were by no means assured of employment as casual labor. Sharecroppers could be removed from the land at any time.

Further discussion of Iran may be found on p. 145.

Africa

Discussion of North Africa is continued from p. 32.

Approaching Africa, we find a new phenomenon: the displacement of indigenous people to make room for Europeans. The previous chapter discussed the attempts of Bedouins to displace Berbers in North Africa during the eleventh century. Even after the bloody warfare of that period, a pattern emerged in which Berber villages adjoined Bedouin grazing grounds, with the sheep even grazing in the fields during fallow season. Ottomans conquered the coast, where they raised crops on the fertile coastal plain and controlled the ports. So although the Berbers had been pushed into the poorest land, they still retained land and coexisted with the Bedouins, and Ottomans. The ruling *bey* claimed some lands as his own and in turn he gave them out to villages to distribute in a traditional manner. Other lands were thought of as belonging to various tribes; any tribesman who worked the land with his plow was entitled to a share. Of the total yield, 2 percent was given over in taxes. In addition, some of the best irrigatable land was retained by the *bey* himself, to be worked by sharecroppers or by peasants contributing labor in lieu of taxes. Some grazing and agricultural lands taken from rebellious tribes were given by the *bey* to his officials, who had hereditary right over them and worked them through sharecroppers. Hence, contrary to the situation with the Kurds, the Ottomans in North Africa distributed land in a traditional manner through village leaders and the king.

Then, early in the 1840s, the French conquered Algeria. One of their first acts was to remove the sharecroppers—some of whom had been there for generations—from the *bey's* land and replace them with French settlers. They also seized the lands belonging to Muslim religious foundations and increased taxes on remaining land. Finally in 1863 they threw all land onto the open market. Soon Frenchmen owned large tracts of land on the coast and in Berber regions, pushing Bedouin pastoralists into the hinterlands where they were shut off from sharing fields during fallow season; herd sizes decreased by four-fifths.[44] The French also instituted a very deliberate policy of creating new villages in which each member would be entitled to a share of land, and then populated these villages with regionally and culturally heterogeneous people. In this manner they effectively neutralized the influence of tribal chiefs who opposed them and

---

[44] Wolf, *Peasant Wars,* p. 214.

destroyed the former kinship structure. After 1900, much of the coastal land was devoted to vineyards owned by Europeans. Grapes require much seasonal labor, which was provided by landless Muslims. At the other end of the scale, about a third of all Muslims had acquired individual holdings of 125 to 500 acres of wheat or $2\frac{1}{2}$ to 50 acres of vines.

Similar kinds of European takeovers occurred in Tunisia, Kenya, Zambia, Zimbabwe, and the Union of South Africa (though with different European actors and generally without the associated large holdings for indigenous people). The 1950s marked the beginning of a comparable policy in Angola. In the cases of Zimbabwe and Kenya, original tribal units were not as deliberately scattered. In all these countries, original tribal organization of landholding was probably affected more than elsewhere in Africa. Increasing numbers of people had become dependent for their livelihood upon the minority who owned land.

Tropical Africa became the site of a few plantations. In Katanga province of the Congo large plantations were established, concentrating especially on oil palm, as well as bananas, coffee, rubber, cinchona, and tea. Nyasaland, Mozambique, and Kenya hosted tea estates of moderate scale. Vast American-owned rubber plantations were opened in Liberia in the twentieth century. Uganda, Kenya, and Tanzania developed smallholding coffee estates, worked by tenants. These estates, and a few additional ones not mentioned, were generally not near populous areas.

To a much greater degree than was true in Asia and Latin America, land occupancy in tropical Africa has been left undisturbed by the land consolidators. This does not mean, however, that land tenure there has not gone through the same transformation from lineage control to individual property. The processes have simply been more subtle. Colonialists introduced European legal concepts of land ownership. Throughout Africa villagers began to switch their production from foodstuffs for local consumption to coffee, oil palms, cacao, peanuts, tobacco, bananas, cotton, and a variety of other crops for sale on the world market. Some examples will give an idea of how land tenure was affected: In Tanganyika (now Tanzania) in the 1950s, an anthropologist found several tribes in which chiefs were allowing the villagers to sell their plots of land to outsiders, so they would no longer revert back to the village.[45] One village in Uganda[46] began raising chrysanthemums, tea, hybrid cattle, and corn during the same period. While villagers had once allowed the cattle to graze through the fields, they now found it necessary to fence off their high-profit fields for protection. By the mid-1960s, security had gone so far that "brothers who cultivate adjacent holdings would have individual paths leading into their respective holdings and homesteads." This type of situation is hardly conducive to kin group solidarity. Nor was it entirely accidental. It was encouraged by both conservative and liberal colonials. A liberal London weekly editorialized during the Mau Mau uprising in 1953:

---

[45] E. B. Dobson, "Comparative Land Tenure of Ten Tanganyika Tribes," *Journal of African Administration* VI, no. 1 (January 1954).

[46] Victor C. Uchendu, "The Impact of Changing Agricultural Technology in African Land Tenure," *Journal of Developing Areas* 4, no. 4 (July 1970): 484.

... a limitation of the franchise to those able to establish an *individual* title in land would exclude tribal societies, and expedite that individualization which alone can support a system of representative government.[47]

In the Sudan surveyors went to villages in several provinces, plotted boundaries of fields as they happened to exist at that time, and (in keeping with the precept of individualization) registered them, not in the name of the village chief who had probably been their customary owner, but in the name of the man farming the plot. Soon judges found themselves litigating cases in which forty or fifty names appeared on the register as heirs to a plot of land; at times none of these people even lived in the village where the plot lay.[48]

The British introduced cotton to many Busoga villages and gave the regional nobility power to collect taxes from the resultant revenues; later they simply placed this nobility on fixed salaries and freed them from all economic dependence on their own territories.[49] Meanwhile, local headmen were deprived of their traditional annual tribute payments. An epidemic of sleeping sickness took a heavy toll of lives in southern Soga villages. Strangers moved to these villages—people who passed their land along to their sons instead of to brothers or back for redistribution by the village headmen as in earlier days. The divorce rate peaked, and many sons were raised by their mothers alone. People had more dealings with their neighbors than with their kin. In such villages land was quickly individualized. Even in villages where land remained largely under the control of the headman, change was evident:

> The concern which most often draws visitors to the headman's homestead and forms the topic of the endless discussions which take place there is land. More than anything else, it is the headman's rights in all the land of his village or sub-village which form the basis of his prestige and authority.[50]

With tribute abolished, the headman's only income derives from fixed payments (allocation fees) made by villagers at the time they are allotted land. "The headmen were aware, however, that the government is not sympathetic to their position in the land-holding system.[51] When the government takes over peasant land for development purposes, for instance, it tends to compensate the peasant but not the headman. Headmen are tempted to redistribute land lawfully occupied by tenants in order to collect allocation fees, to rent land to outsiders, or seek civil service posts while leaving their village duties to stewards. This increases land litigation in the courts and decreases land security and careful husbandry.

---

[47] Sir Olaf Caroe, "Land Tenure and the Franchise," *Journal of African Administration* VI, no 1 (January 1954).

[48] A. B. Miskin, "Land Registration," *Journal of African Administration* V, no. 1 (January 1953): 77-78. A. J. B. Hughes, "Some Swazi Views on Land Tenure," *Africa* 32, no. 2 (1962): 253-277, provides additional insight into the social consequences of this type of process.

[49] Lloyd A. Fallers, *Bantu Bureaucracy* (Chicago: University of Chicago Press, 1965).

[50] Ibid., p. 163.

[51] Ibid., p. 177.

Discussion of !Kung is continued from p. 53.

In 1650, the number of !Kung in southern Africa can be estimated between 150,000 and 300,000. The Dutch brought with them a systematic campaign to wipe out or carry into slavery all !Kung south of the Orange River. Many !Kung lost their language and culture and became part of the "colored" population of the Republic of South Africa.[52] Most of today's 50,000 !Kung live in Botswana and Namibia; only 5 percent of them live in the traditional way. In 1899, poor European settlers set up ranches on land formerly inhabited by !Kung.[53] They hired the !Kung to tend their scrawny cattle, paid them a small monetary wage plus small rations of corn meal, tea, sugar, and tobacco, and let them live in nearby settlements. They also protected the !Kung against raids by the Bantu. These early white Boer settlers were often so poor that they depended on marama beans collected by !Kung women, for which they exchanged meat, blankets, and tobacco. Then, in 1950, British investors from South Africa began setting up modern cattle ranches in the area. They preferred hiring Bantu, who had long been skilled cattle raisers. Most !Kung had lost the skills to live a completely nomadic life again. Some went to work for the Bantu who acquired their own small cattle ranches. Some squat near water pumps on outlying regions of farms, where they keep donkeys and goats (either stolen or received as part of wages), hunt, and gather. Many have developed tuberculosis, upper respiratory infections, and smallpox—diseases they had not suffered in the past. Many express envy of their neighbors' possessions, and disaffection at the fact that they are regarded as the lowest social group. !Kung displaced from farm jobs would like to have some land of their own. Bantu would like the !Kung to stop squatting on their land and stealing cattle. Whites favor separating people under Apartheid. Government proposals for dealing with these !Kung generally involve moving them to reservations in remote hinterlands where they could hunt, gather, and raise cattle. They might also be taught leather work, carpentry, tool-making, pump maintenance, hygiene, domestic sciences, and handicraft marketing.

Further discussion of !Kung may be found on p. 327.

The Akwapin of southern Ghana developed a more delicate adaptation between their old village life and modern capitalist pursuits.[54] Late in the nineteenth century they began buying surplus land for cocoa raising from chiefs of neighboring tribal groups. This land was purchased individually; the sale was negotiated by an Akwapin spokesman for a group of potential investors. At first the fields were close to home and other members of the family helped with weeding and upkeep chores; part of the land could grow food for home consumption. When the cocoa bushes began to yield, more land would be purchased

---

[52] Richard B. Lee and Irven DeVore (eds.), *Kalihari Hunter-Gatherers: Studies of the !Kung San and Their Neighbors* (Cambridge: Harvard University Press, 1976), p. 5.

[53] Mathias G. Guenther, "From Hunters to Squatters: Social and Cultural Change among the Farm San of Ghanzi, Botswana," in *Kalihari Hunter-Gatherers,* ed. Lee and DeVore, pp. 121-134.

[54] Polly Hill, *The Migrant Cocoa-Farmers of Southern Ghana* (Cambridge: Cambridge University Press, 1963).

farther away. Here tenants were hired from other tribal groups; they would bring in their families and get paid on the day the cocoa was sold. Some seasonal labor was also hired around weeding time. Although land was owned and inherited on an individual basis and profits accrued to individual families, the owners never left their home villages. They continued a traditional family structure, submitting to the authority of their village chiefs. They did not sell land to outsiders. More prosperous members lent money on a long-term basis so that other villagers might invest in the cocoa land. Everyone in the village lived in the same style of housing and at the same standard of living. When swollen shoot disease devastated their trees in the 1950s, these villages remained intact, turning more toward subsistence agriculture and rental of some houses they had built in Accra and other places to replace the lost income.

Further discussion of Ghana may be found on p. 111.

A similar trend is observable in the Yakö villages. There it became customary during the 1930s for young men who were especially prosperous from participation in oil palm trade to be accepted into membership in the ward associations along with family heads and other more traditional members of those bodies.[55] Individual personal wealth was becoming a factor in the community power structure.

All of these examples serve to emphasize that changes were taking place both in village structure and in land tenure throughout tropical Africa. These changes were related to the bureaucratic introduction of European legal concepts of land ownership, the growth of trade, the replacement of edible crops with those for export, and the spread of the money economy. Yet both village structure and village independence—and security of access to a means of livelihood—eroded far more slowly than in most parts of the rest of Africa, Asia, and Latin America.

Latin America

The portion of the globe that experienced the most cataclysmic changes in land tenure lay in Latin America.

In 1576, the Portuguese introduced sugar cane into frontier portions of northeast Brazil.[56] A smallholder with fifteen acres would buy twenty Negro slaves from Africa to run a typical operation. In the Caribbean the few original American Indian inhabitants—the only vestiges of traditional village structure—were eventually massacred or moved, being replaced by self-contained sugar estates of about a thousand acres, with 200 to 250 African Negro slaves. When the mid-nineteenth century brought the general demise of slavery, sugar production centered largely upon Cuba. There American investors opened estates of 500 acres or more that were greatly dependent on seasonal labor from the other islands, leaving the remainder of the Caribbean to subsistence small-

---

[55] Daryll Forde, "The Governmental Roles of Associations Among the Yakö," in *Comparative Political Systems,* ed. Cohen and Middleton, pp. 125–126.

[56] See Courtenay, *Plantation Agriculture.*

holdings and some plantations worked by the assortment of people who had been thrown together by the plantation movement. By 1955, 1.5 percent of Cuban landowners controlled 46 percent of the cultivated acreage.[57] In the 1870s, the Boston Fruit Company began buying bananas from smallholders in Jamaica; this company, later reorganized as the United Fruit Company, purchased large tracts of land in Costa Rica, Colombia, and Guatemala which later became self-contained plantation operations. Private ownership of land was clearly established. Sugar and bananas create great uncertainties for stable livelihood, since they require seasonal labor with little work in between crop harvests.

Many estates of fewer than 500 acres were also chartered or sold to smaller investors. In the 1840s, owners of such plots of land began offering alternatives to Europeans who had come to the vicinity of the Paraiba Valley of Brazil in an unrequited search for gold. They could set up a homestead, cultivate their own garden plots, and receive small incomes in exchange for planting and tending coffee bushes for the landowner. This practice later spread to the São Paolo hills. Between 1887 and 1906, some 1,200,000 immigrants—mostly Italian—moved into that area to work as homestead tenants.[58] Beginning in the 1860s, many Italians and Spaniards immigrated to Argentina and northeast Brazil, hoping to raise cattle. In periods of depressions these immigrants were to find themselves with little food or income.

The plantations we have discussed in this chapter are commercial ventures. A European or American company buys or rents land and sends out employees to operate the venture, which it will discontinue if it becomes unprofitable (freeing the capital for other commercial pursuits elsewhere), or the investors set up marketing and processing operations and depend on smaller operators to produce the raw materials. Latin America (especially Brazil, Argentina, Chile, Peru, Bolivia, Ecuador, Colombia, and Mexico) also has two other institutions which, though reminiscent of pre-Solon Attica, are virtually without parallel elsewhere in the modern world except for central Luzon in the Philippines. These are the *latifundio* (or *fazenda*) and the *hacienda*, great landed estates. Most had their origins during the sixteenth and seventeenth centuries when Portuguese and Spanish royalty gave large tracts of land in the New World to members of their nobility or other favored Europeans.

Some *latifundios* and *haciendas* cover more than a million acres.[59] This means that five tracts of this size cover as much territory as all the land formerly occupied by white settlers in Kenya. Other *latifundios* are in the range of 500 acres. All these estates center around a great manor house occupied by the lord of the manor, whose eldest son would usually inherit the estate while younger sons joined the military or commercial pursuits. The manor house often had fifty or more servants. A large hacienda generally made everything it consumed: food, clothing, building material, even salt. With no outside owners, the manorial lord could maintain his lifestyle without much contact with the outside economy. His desire for consumer goods, however, often induced him to wish to produce some export crops, usually only on a small portion of his territory, leaving vast

---

[57] Frank Tannenbaum, *Ten Keys to Latin America* (New York: Vintage, 1962), p. 78.

[58] Courtenay, *Plantation Agriculture,* p. 37.

[59] Ibid., pp. 31, 78.

acreages unused. If his estate was in sparsely inhabited territory, he might import a few workers to work his land; he had complete control over these individuals. The estates in older settled regions of the Aztecs, Mayas, and Incas already contained whole villages that were in theory free to manage themselves and their traditional lands as long as they raised a specified commercial crop for delivery to the owner or contributed labor to the owner's fields. In practice, owners forced resettlements and expropriated community lands. Increasingly, investors made efforts to purchase large tracts of land. For instance, between 1867 and 1910, it is estimated that a fifth of the national territory in Mexico changed hands, much of it ending up under control of foreign investors.[60] Only around 15 percent of Mexican villages, mostly in regions useless for any commercial crops, seem to have been able to retain their communal lands.

Discussions of Incas is continued from p. 70.

When the *conquistadores* conquered the Inca Empire at least 6 million people[61] worked fields of more than sufficient size to support themselves and their families. Interspersed with these were plots they tended for the state. By 1965, 88 percent of Peruvian farms occupying 7.4 percent of the arable land were too small to adequately support a single-farm family (i.e., were *minifundios)*. Meanwhile, 1.1 percent of farms, the *latifundios,* occupied 82.4 percent of arable land,[62] primarily in the irrigated portions of the plain that had constituted most of the Inca Empire's growing area. These farms grew mainly sugar and export crops. The original Indian village inhabitants once again number around 6 million (after millions of them lost their lives working mines and fields of the *conquistadores*). They are now mostly relegated to the mountain territories and received only around 13 percent of Peru's national income in 1963 (although they represented 56.7 percent of the population.)[63] Two-thirds of their villages contain private landholdings.[64]

Further discussion of Peru may be found on p. 111.

The result of these movements is a land-holding pattern in which the vast majority of the peasant communities have lost control over their own affairs and benefit little from what they produce past the subsistence level, while many other peasants are uprooted from any kind of community life or contact with the land whatever. In 1960, 65 percent of the arable land in Latin America as a whole was

---

[60] Moises Gonzalez Navarro, "Mexico: The Lop-Sided Revolution," in *Obstacles to Change in Latin America,* ed. Claudio Veliz (London: Oxford University Press, 1965), p. 207.

[61] Lanning, *Peru Before the Incas,* p. 115.

[62] Celso Furtado, *Economic Development of Latin America* (Cambridge: Cambridge University Press, 1970), p. 54.

[63] Jacques Chonchol, "Land Tenure and Development in Latin America," in *Obstacles to Change in Latin America,* ed. Veliz, p. 86.

[64] Susan C. Baurque and David Scott Palmer, "Transforming the Rural Sector: Government Policy and Peasant Response," in *The Peruvian Experiment: Continuity and Change under Military Rule,* ed. Abraham I. Lowenthal (Princeton: Princeton University Press, 1975), pp. 210–211.

in estates of 2,500 acres or more and 23 percent in holdings of 250 to 2,500 acres, the kind of holdings normally worked by tenants and laborers and devoted to export crops. Meanwhile, only 3.7 percent of arable land was divided into $5\frac{1}{2}$ million holdings of fifty acres or less, most of these probably also worked by tenants.[65] Many others remained landless. Clearly there have been vast changes. The crops that once sustained the greatest empires and the most isolated village alike are relegated to a secondary position along with the peasants who tilled them.

In Asia, Africa and Latin America the trend was the same. Land shifted to the private control of commercial interests. Its use changed from crops for sustenance to crops for export. Communities disintegrated. Many were forced to leave the land and, on an individual basis, find new means of livelihood elsewhere.

Commercial Mining

When the Spaniards first took over the Inca and Aztec Empires, they were not yet interested in sugar plantations. Their eyes were on the gold. Initially they pillaged what had already been mined. Then they turned their attention to the source of the gold and led large forced expeditions into the mountains to extract gold from placer deposits and silver from the mine at San Lúis de Potosi in Mexico. Between 1503 and 1660, 85,000 pounds of gold and 7.3 million pounds of silver were shipped to Spain. This was more than three times Europe's monetary reserves at the time. The silver was extracted with mercury, which killed several million of the indigenous Indian workers, who were recruited by force from the prosperous lands that once constituted the Aztec Empire.[66] Later, vast silver mines were opened deep in the earth below Guanajato, Mexico, worked by thousands of Indian miners. Galleons carried this silver to Spain and Manila. Each year, for 250 years, Manila merchants organized a galleon that headed for Mexico with Chinese silks and other luxuries and returned laden with silver pesos. So completely dependent were the Manila merchants on this process that the colony was bankrupted when the British seized one shipload at sea.[67] Discovery of gold in Brazil attracted a great gold rush and, thanks to an Anglo-Portuguese trade agreement, furnished Britain with the international reserves she used to fight her war against Napoleon.[68] Discoveries of diamonds in southern Africa and in Sierra Leone began similar trends.

During the nineteenth century, copper, tin, and iron came into great demand to feed the Industrial Revolution in Europe and North America. From high in the mountains of Bolivia, the plains of Peru and Chile, various parts of Mexico, the northwest plain of Malaya, Pretoria in the Union of South Africa, and the north-central stretches of Zambia came great quantities of these minerals. The extraction of nitrates began in northern Chile. Coal fields were opened in Bihar and Bengal. The twentieth century brought large-scale

---

[65] Tannenbaum, *Ten Keys to Latin America,* pp. 81–82.

[66] Bernard Lietaer, *Europe + Latin America + the Multinationals* (Westmead, Eng.: Saxon House, 1979), p. 144n.

[67] Steinberg, *Southeast Asia,* pp. 53–54.

[68] Furtado, *Economic Development of Latin America,* p. 20.

petroleum production to the Middle East, Venezuela, Indonesia, and Mexico. All of these developments except the petroleum production attracted large numbers of laborers who worked for low pay and transformed the economic base of the regions in which they settled.

Between 1801 and 1810, Chile produced an average of 6,850 pounds of gold per annum; from 1781 to 1800, 11,000 pounds per annum of silver; and from 1761 to 1810, 24 million pounds of copper per annum. By 1800, Mexico produced 66 percent of world silver output, mostly at Guanajuato; Spain's American colonies combined produced 90 percent of world silver output.[69] Yet, despite the fact that mining had often been carried on for hundreds of years in these nations, colonial powers often prohibited ownership of mines by inhabitants of the colonies. They set up their own marketing boards, and denied licenses to locals. They gave tax exemptions to these foreign owned and managed enterprises, so they did not even contribute to local economies.

Mining is at the heart of European domination. European mines and technology produced the arms and ships that permitted Europeans to establish the world-wide trade links and control of foreign mines. The income from the mines and land abroad allowed the Europeans to produce bigger ships and arms, which gave them the power to control still more land and mines abroad. The more the output of the mines, the bigger the ships to carry that output, and the greater the potential for increasing the commercialization of agriculture.

Before the Europeans arrived the Javanese and Burmese royalty had extensive trade with China and India over land and sea. Their countries had navigation instruments and cottage industries that compared favorably with those in Europe. By world standards, both countries had high literacy rates and a refined artistic tradition. The Incas had roads, astronomy, farming technology, theater, poetry, and mines that rivaled Europe as well. What they lacked was the technology to produce big enough guns and ships. Using those guns and ships, the Dutch and British, and the Spanish and Portuguese, were able to close down their ship-building industries, their iron working, their weaving, and their merchant guilds, and to transform their systems of agriculture. This was the white man's burden of which Rudyard Kipling did *not* write.

A king controlling grains and metals has power over villagers. Merchants who can collect agricultural surpluses and metals independent of the court nobility have power over kings, and even more power over villagers than kings had. An industrialized and bureaucratized society with access to vast growing areas and to mines has power over kings and smaller merchants. Its power to disrupt villages and the individual environments of their members is vast, and it uses the power to do exactly this by commercializing labor, taxation, land ownership, governmental authority, consumption, and reciprocal obligations.

SUMMARY

To sum it up in a word, then, it is *commerce* that transformed a world composed almost entirely of villages capable of handling their members' daily needs into

[69] Stanley J. Stein and Barbara Stein, *The Colonial Heritage of Latin America* (New York: Oxford University Press, 1970), pp. 100–101.

one where few men or women could look to a village or anywhere else for help with the most pressing problems of daily life. Whereas the old village systems were most concerned with helping their constituents support themselves from the land, and the kingly states that grew up above them were motivated to preserve those village systems which supplied their retinues with food, the interest of today's political systems in maximizing the monetary yield per acre of ground has little relationship to village welfare. British, French, Spanish, Portuguese, and German colonialism transformed land from homesteads supporting entire villages into investments supporting select private individuals, who often lived outside the villages. This increased the economic productivity of the land. (In Attica, olives grown on a plot of land were worth more money than cereal grains grown on that same plot.) It also gave new power to the traders (who sold the olives in exchange for the city-state's food) and the officials (who regulated those exchanges); it turned land into a commodity that could be bought and sold (with no limit on the size of the largest holdings, as in Attica's case) by city-based investors; it weakened the power of the local clan leadership by taking away their right to distribute land. In Attica, this had involved a political battle among Attican clan leaders, Attican debt bondsmen, and Attican traders and officials. In the case of the British in India or the Dutch in the East Indies the traders and officials in the fight happened to be aliens from another continent, who in time developed local counterparts. The consequences—land alienation, diminution of clan power, and removal from the local level of control over individual personal environments—were much the same as if these initial traders and bureaucrats had been indigenous.

Though the specifics of this transformation differed from region to region, there is a theme running through the process: Whereas in the sixteenth century nearly all the cultivated or hunting lands in the developing areas were distributed and regulated by clan-related community leaders, by the middle of the twentieth century most land was in the hands of people who controlled it independently of clan-related community leaders, or of people who could choose their own community leaders. Land had been transferred from clan to private control. Furthermore, whereas in the sixteenth century most cultivated land in these regions was growing crops central to the diet, by the mid-twentieth century much of this land grew crops peripheral or unrelated to the diet, and they were usually destined for export.

No modern Prime Minister can meet each week with his top bureaucratic and commercial leaders to coordinate commercial, governmental, and political decisions as could the *Etsu Nupe,* because he or she is no longer their chief customer, tax collector, or decision maker. Nor are there powerful groups at the local level. The political, governmental, and commercial leaders all have their own networks of supporters, who can trade, collect taxes, and make decisions independent of both clan and king. All this is not necessarily beneficial to those whose birthright to own land has been taken away. The forces that deprived people of land have moved with much greater swiftness than those that produce alternative means of livelihood. Once villagers are dependent upon income from uncertain markets, their food, jobs, housing, cultural surroundings, and education become manipulable by the same people who manipulate the marketplace and make the decisions in place of the kings. Those are not clan leaders, but landowners, bureaucrats, traders, mine owners, and manufacturers. How do they operate politically? That is what we shall explore next.

SHORT SUMMARY

International commerce paid kings money so they would no longer need their taxes from villagers. With the kings' backs conveniently turned away, it proceeded to take land away from the peasants and changed them into sharecroppers, day laborers, or unemployed wanderers. In so doing it made their personal environments very unstable. It also transformed the nature of political life.

Have you caught these definitions?

	page
tubers	66
communal land tenure	77
debt bondage	71
plantation	77
slash-and-burn agriculture	77
latifundio	94
minifundio	95
zamindar	83
talukdar	83

Can you answer each with one sentence?

1. What are three characteristics food must have if people are to be freed to move into cities?
2. Why does the rise of traders and bureaucrats often leave a surplus of poor people and a shortage of food?
3. Why do changes in land tenure, and money lending, go together?
4. How did the French neutralize the influence of tribal chiefs in North Africa?

From what you have read thus far, can you make and support judgments about these questions?

1. Why did kings need grains to get metals, and both to attain independence?
2. In social and political terms, what difference does it make whether Attica grew grain or olives?
3. Do plantations seem more disruptive of traditional village life than privately-owned smallholdings?
4. Why were kings weakened by the changes in land tenure policies?

I hope you are getting a better sense of how the parts of this book fit together. To see whether this is so, reread the entire "Book in Brief" section of Chapter 1, with particular attention to what you now know about the breakdown of traditional political structures.

CHAPTER

4

GETTING YOUR BEARINGS (see map, front of book)

1. In terms of territory, what is the biggest developing nation?
2. Which of the following nations border on one another?: Ghana, Liberia, Ivory Coast, Senegal, Peru, Brazil, Chile, Costa Rica, Malaysia, India, Pakistan, Iran.
3. Consult an atlas to find how many capitals of developing nations are not located on the sea.

The Model

A developed nation provides most of its citizens with a stable personal environment. *A developing nation does not.* Today's developing nations were once developed nations. They changed because *their political systems separated from their social systems* when European commerce was introduced. If the structure of international trade changes in the near future, social and political systems may be reintegrated, promoting political development. Then the developing nations may once again become developed nations.

Today's Political Systems: Patrons and Clients

QUESTIONS TO KEEP IN MIND

1. What is the difference between the way today's developing nations are governed and the way traditional societies were governed?
2. What is the difference between the way today's developing nations are governed and the way advanced industrialized nations are governed?
3. Why do developing nations fail to distribute resources to the poor?
4. Why don't the developing nations turn into developed nations?

If the former political systems composed of kings and ritual leaders were disrupted by the introduction of commerce, what replaced them? This chapter addresses itself to that question. We often have the impression that the political systems in developing nations are chaotic, but they are far from it. The political systems that replaced the old coalitions of kings and ritual leaders are just as tightly woven as those former systems. Who, then, composes the new coalitions? The first thought that might come to mind is that European colonialists took over where the ritual leaders left off. This is only partly true. During the 1930s, England's largest colony, India, had a population of 300 million people. Yet Britain had only 154,000 Britishers in that country—4,000 civil servants, 60,000 soldiers, and 90,000 businessmen and clergy. Clearly, the British needed a number of local collaborators to run the country. To understand the political systems of developing nations we must understand who those collaborators were and are.

The political systems of developing nations center around patron-client relationships in which entrepreneurs and client-bureaucrats play a major role. Many individuals who need work because the job security of their traditional village has been eroded develop complex special relationships with men who can offer them income in exchange for their services and loyalty. These men in turn develop special relationships with economic and political elites, and they form chains of individuals who exchange both economic assets and political supports. These patron-client networks have displaced clans and kingly courts as the authoritative allocators of values with a monopoly on the use of force; they also control commerce. Kings and clans are often peripheral to them, or have transformed themselves into the hub of such networks. Any analysts who might ignore these networks fail to understand why developing nations behave the way they do. Some think of developing nations as being run by presidents or military leaders; to understand how those individuals "run" things we must first understand patron-clientism. Some think that multinational corporations run developing nations; they have helped start, support, and perpetuate patron-clientism, but their removal from the scene would not eliminate it. Especially in times of crisis, we sometimes think that no one is running a developing nation; comprehension of patron-clientism can help policy makers avoid costly errors based on such a misperception. Premiers and policy makers may become temporarily isolated from the political structure, but that structure does not disappear. Their task is to locate the structure, and comprehend how to work within it. This chapter will help you do that.

We begin by defining and illustrating some patron-client relationships. Then we will proceed to differentiate those at the bottom of the networks (the minor network) from those at the top (the major network). In the third section, we will suggest that the members of the major network tend to live together in the capital city, where they control both the commerce and politics of the nation and develop a social system of their own that is cut off from the rest of the nation. Because of their dependence on special relationships they are not free to distribute political rewards beyond the boundaries of the minor network of patrons and clients. Most rewards are circulated and recirculated within the major network, with little residue even for the minor network.

At the hub of the major network are the presidency, the client-bureaucracy, the military, business leaders (including big landlords) and their immediate associates (including middle-class groups and labor unions). Hence, it is meaningless to speak of regulating the client-bureaucracy, the military, or business; these groups are themselves part of the regulatory mechanisms. The most vulnerable of these groups is the presidency; if the president leans too heavily toward one group, he may be replaced by a representative of another. A continuing game of musical chairs keeps all partners of the major network satisfied. Unfortunately, this does not stabilize the personal environments of citizens. Little filters down from the top. The major network has little control over what does filter down.

A basic characteristic of the minor network is that its members, as intermediaries in the chain that passes supports and resources upward to the major network, tend to retain for themselves only enough resources to support their own immediate families and to spread little residue of resources beyond those who are not direct clients. In an atmosphere of scarce resources, an individual who is not a client must devise some service he can perform that will be needed by the major network if he expects the total network to extend out to benefit him. It is a basic principle of patron-clientism that more resources flow up the network than flow down, and that those at the very bottom of the network who contribute the most labor receive the sparsest rewards.

Those in the major networks have surpluses to use for investment capital and conspicuous consumption. It is because they control these surplus resources that they wield political influence.

> The essence of this system consisted in a bargain whereby patronage was accorded in return for the promise of support. The state served to foster and protect the existing regime, and at the same time provided the necessary number of sinecures to ensure the political support which the ruling class would otherwise have lacked, and which it needed in order to preserve its economic and political control of the country.[1]

The major networks have at their disposal techniques not often available to western European or North American leaders that allow them to coerce any inside or outside the networks who resist their hegemony. Regardless of the form or ideology of government, top priority goes to raising the gross national product through expansion of industry and export agriculture and to ironing out internal conflicts in (or adding to and subtracting from) the patron-client networks. The political systems of developing nations consist of the authoritative allocation of values primarily among a limited network of patrons and clients, and a monopoly on the legitimate use of force by those at the top of this network.

THE PATRON-CLIENT RELATIONSHIP DEFINED

Extended families and kinship loyalties remain far more intact in today's developing nations than in North America or northern Europe. *Yet the power of kinship leaders—except from the wealthiest families—is largely gone.* National leaders seldom consult local kinship leaders when making policy decisions. Instead, they often work through individuals who may not even be of the same racial background as the local constituents for whom they speak. Social science literature is increasingly referring to these new power brokers as *patrons.*

As is usually the case when one word or phrase is used to describe a wide variety of individuals or relationships, the patron-client relationship has been defined in many ways.[2] The following definition seems especially lucid:

> First, the patron-client tie develops between two parties *unequal* in status, wealth, and influence. . . . Second, the formation and maintenance of the relationship depends on *reciprocity* in the exchange of goods and services. . . . Third, the development and maintenance of a patron-client relationship rests heavily on *face-to-face* contact between the two parties.[3]

---

[1] Helio Jaguaribe, "The Dynamics of Brazilian Nationalism," in *Obstacles to Change in Latin America,* ed. Claudio Veliz (London: Oxford University Press, 1965), p. 168. Jaguaribe calls this the cartorial system, operating in its classic form earlier this century but extending into the present.

[2] E.g., see Peter M. Blau, *Exchange and Power in Social Life* (New York: John Wiley, 1967).

[3] John Duncan Powell, "Peasant Society and Clientist Politics," *American Political Science Review* 64 (June 1970): 412–413. Emphasis added.

FIGURE 4.1
The Patron-Client Chain

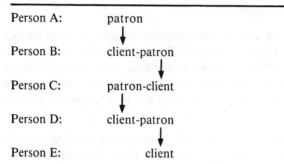

Patron-clientism involves sets of patrons and clients cooperating with one another to retain maximum benefit for themselves from all assets which any of them handle *by personally exchanging these assets among themselves.* (See Figure 4.1.)

A client-bureaucrat within a patron-client system is expected to place the interest of his patron (who is often not a part of the formal bureaucracy) above that of the bureaucratic organization; the orders coming from his patron supercede those from his superiors within the bureaucracy. He distributes and withholds favors in keeping with the needs of his patron, breaking the rules if he needs to. A person wishing to receive from government a service due him under the law must develop a personal reciprocal relationship with a client-bureaucrat (e.g., through a bribe) in order to receive it; otherwise he cannot expect the law to be obeyed. A businessman-patron cannot hire and fire employees strictly on the basis of their job performances; he must hire those his patron (who may not be a part of his business) approves, and who will obey him in performing services unrelated to the business. A business is likely to develop working relationships with other businesses which continue even when their profitability is not optimal. Those at the bottom of the hierarchy are heavily dependent on those at the top. James L. Payne, discussing the Peruvian bureaucracy, describes the matter succinctly:

> Patronage is entrenched from top to bottom. It works something like this: public figure (A) recommends close personal friend (B) to head a department. (B) makes his cousin (C) section head. Nephews (D) and (E) obtain jobs through (C). (F) owns a small factory which owes back taxes. (F) is a close friend of (A), and (G) who is second manager of the factory is brother-in-law of (B). *Will (E) collect the back taxes? Not if he is a normal human being.*[4]

Contrast the client-bureaucrat with a real bureaucrat. The latter may actually happen to be wealthier than his immediate superior; the client-bureaucrat never is wealthier than his patron. The relations of the real bureaucrat with her

---

[4] James L. Payne, *Labor and Politics in Peru: The System of Political Bargaining* (New Haven, Conn.: Yale University Press, 1965), p. 233. Emphasis added.

superior may or may not be face to face; those of the client-bureaucrat with his patron always are. Continuance of the real bureaucrat in his job or his promotion depends strictly on what he does for the organization—not even for his immediate superior. Regardless of what he does within the bureaucratic organization, the client-bureaucrat will lose his job if he offends his patron (who may not even be a part of the bureaucratic organization). The real bureaucrat may switch from one post and superior to another, while the client-bureaucrat may not unless his patron arranges it. The real bureaucrat's distribution of favors and punishments to the public is likewise based on rules applying equally to all members of the same genre—not on his personal relationships or favors exchanged with those with whom he deals. For instance, when the real bureaucrat is dealing with the elderly she must treat all elderly in the same manner; the client-bureaucrat might favor only those who bribed him or were recommended by the patron. The personal life of the real bureaucrat is normally not considered to be of concern to the organization, so long as it stays out of his job. Personal exchanges of goods and services between a superior and his subordinate, or an official and a member of the public, might in fact be looked upon with more than raised eyebrows by the organization. The client-bureaucrat, in contrast, is expected to exchange personal favors with his patron. The private affairs of those with whom the real bureaucrat deals are none of his business, unless specified by statute; the client-bureaucrat is the part of their personal lives. In genuine bureaucratic organizations, in short, authority relations hold between offices and positions, not between persons who fill them. *In client-bureaucracies, authority relations hold between persons who fill offices and positions, not between offices and positions themselves.*

Compare the patron-employer with the modern private employer. The latter creates work slots to be filled (clearly defining what is expected of the occupants of those slots) and marketing systems to distribute his or her products. When employees do what is expected of them, they are paid; when they do not, they are terminated. Individuals could appeal such termination, and would be reviewed on the basis of job performance and not merely on how well they got along with their superior; one set of bureaucrats or employers can overturn the decisions of another set of bureaucrats and employers. Whoever pays the company for the product is welcome to buy it. The patron-employer, in contrast, can fire employees at whim, unless a patron disapproves. The patron-employer may also choose to sell products only to those with whom personal favors have been exchanged.

The village ritual leader was largely in the same position as the modern bureaucrat or employer. He was obeyed because of the office he held. He was expected to follow strict procedures and to be even-handed in distribution of favors, sharing with all members of the community. As offices changed hands, existing ritual leaders were expected to deal with the new occupants as they had with the old, and those stepping down ceased to receive the benefits of office. The leader was expected to share his own goods with everyone in the community and often had no more personal wealth than others in the community.

Hence patron-clientism is a phenomenon that lies somewhere between the introduction and the ascendancy of commerce. The following list of some of the

FIGURE 4.2
Five People—Three Systems

Traditional

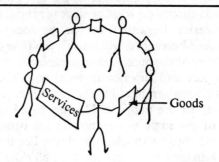

Patron-Client

Bureaucratic

sorts of individuals in a position to become patrons, and clients of larger patrons, translates this statement into social terms:

- small traders
- commodities middlemen
- retail merchants
- plantation owners
- traditional headmen and chiefs
- nobility
- kings and courtiers
- slave officials
- military men
- owners of moderately-sized private plots
- *hacendados* and *latifundistas*
- moneylenders
- managers of estates
- owners of villages

- mine owners and managers
- organizers of village crafts
- religious leaders
- *caudillo* leaders
- managers of admission-charging cultural and sports events
- bureaucrats
- elected political leaders
- political party functionaries
- factory owners
- investors
- large entrepreneurs

Patron-client relationships stand on a middle ground between traditional social systems and the bureaucratic hierarchies and market relationships of the developed nation-state. None of the roles listed above (save that of village head-man and some religious leaders) are common to traditional village life. Several of them existed in the courts and towns surrounding kings: the historic breeding

TABLE 4.1
Three Systems

INTEGRATED SELF-GOVERNING COMMUNITY (traditional societies)	PATRON-CLIENTISM (developing nations)	GENUINE BUREAUCRACY (developed nations)
1. exist before introduction of foreign commerce	exist after introduction of foreign commerce	exist after foreign commerce creates a strong domestic market
2. face-to-face relationships	face-to-face relationships	impersonal relationships
3. behavior based on custom	behavior based on the wishes of the patron	behavior based on law
4. each organization has its own command structure	command by patron supersedes all other commands	each organization has its own command structure
5. principals may be removed for breaking custom	principals cannot be removed	principals may be removed for breaking law or procedure
6. subordinates may be dismissed for breaking custom	subordinates may be dismissed without reason	subordinates may be dismissed for breaking law or procedure
7. principals and subordinates have similar wealth	principals always wealthier than subordinates	principals not always wealthier than subordinates
8. people receive about as much as they give in exchange of favors	patrons receive more from exchange of favors than clients	no exchanges; bureaucrats receive salaries and the public receives services
9. everyone included in reciprocities	only patrons and their clients included in reciprocities	salaries and services stipulated by laws and procedures
10. exchange is between offices and positions	exchange is between persons	transactions are between offices and positions

places of patron-clientism. Many of them began with the sixteenth century introduction of commerce. *These roles usually emerge when the individual gains access to resources or followers outside his village.* Some of the roles might be inherited; yet in order to keep the role, it is seldom necessary to cooperate with one's extended family or traditional village hierarchy (unless they happen to in turn control some resources to which one needs access). These positions are more dependent upon control of resources and personal relationships with individuals who are not relatives or with relatives who owe more loyalty to one person than to the rest of the family, than on one's corporate relations to a broader kinship/social structure.

An individual might theoretically hold one of these positions without being a patron. To become a patron, one must *use* the resources one controls, or one's relationships, to enrich oneself, and a set of specific individuals of lower status, wealth, and influence with whom one regularly exchanges goods and services. The patron must place this enrichment first in his or her order of priorities. If this is done, the patron will still not necessarily become political, even though many patrons are involved in politics. *The political structures of today's developing nations are composed only of those patrons and clients involved in politics,* not of all patrons and clients, or all factory owners and religious leaders.

The political structures of North America and northern Europe contain considerable patron-clientism. Political patronage, city boss politics, the nexus of campaign contributions, party and interest group organization, electoral politics, hierarchies within legislatures and the bureaucracy, and even the court system involve patron-client relationships. Yet, except for some individual states within these nations, patron-client relationships probably occupy a less central place in the politics of developed nations than of developing nations. Some institutions control other institutions. It is rare for any individual, or small circle of individuals, to control institutions for long. One can rise high in institutions without personally exchanging goods and services with anyone. Many North Americans are involved in politics who are not part of patron-client networks; *few who are involved in politics in developing nations are not a part of patron-client networks.* It is possible to receive substantial material rewards in northern Europe without involvement in such networks. It is less possible to do so in developing nations. In short, *patron-clientism thrives in a situation of scarce resources.* For reasons we shall examine later resources are not so scarce in developed nations. To stay in power, leaders of developing nations merely have to divide up proceeds from the sale of commodities on world markets and hold their people in check. To develop a strong domestic market, keep control over world markets,[5] and respond to a great variety of competitive issues,[6] developed nations must turn to genuine bureaucracy and modern business practices. A nation cannot prosper with its resources locked into a few hands. The developed nations still contain some patron-clientism but have moved beyond it; *the developing nations are ruled by patron-clientism and cannot move beyond it.*

---

[5] Chapter 8 discusses this point at length.
[6] Chapter 6 discusses this point at length.

Forms of Patron-Clientism

Since patron-client relationships take on so many forms, there is no better way to introduce them than to describe several different patron-client relationships. Here are nine variations on the theme:

---

1. In the nine illustrations that follow can you find all of the roles on the list of occupations (small traders, commodities middlemen, etc) in the previous section?

2 . What makes these patron-client, instead of bureaucratic or traditional, relationships?

---

1. In Kuching, Sarawak, rows of small shops all sell a virtually identical combination of goods and hence seem to be in competition with one another—but they are not. The secret lies in patron-client relationships.[7] Each merchant selects a few small rubber planters whom he trusts. He permits them to purchase groceries, kerosene, and hardware on credit. In turn they send in sheets of rubber every afternoon in payment, with the merchant keeping account of the outstanding balance. The rubber planter's debt is usually perpetual. The merchant himself is likely to have a similar credit arrangement with someone higher up: he exchanges the sheets of rubber and some cash for his inventory. Since the planter owes the shopkeeper he cannot switch to selling his rubber to a neighboring shopkeeper. Since the shopkeeper owes the middleman he cannot switch to another middleman. Since the middleman probably owes the rubber company he probably cannot switch to selling to another rubber company. So there is no competition. The rubber company simply has several clients, in the form of shopkeepers who have their shops along the same street.

2. In East Nepal the Limbus have developed the habit of giving their traditional lands as pledges in exchange for credit extended by Brahmins.[8] About 70 percent of Limbu lands are thus pledged in transactions that can extend for several generations. Most Limbus would have to pay about US$750 to repossess their lands, although average annual income is only around US$125. The only catch from the point of view of the Brahmin is that another Brahmin can always offer the Limbu owner the price of the land plus an additional increment for good measure and thus take over use of the land for himself. Hence, the average Brahmin patron periodically offers his Limbu client additional loans to prevent this from happening. The inflation of land prices, caused by an increasing scarcity of freehold land, keeps the process going. The Limbus owe the Brahmins so much money they cannot get their land back. As the value of the land increases, the Brahmin simply loans the Limbu a bit more money—putting

---

[7] Barbara E. Ward, "Cash or Credit Crops? An Examination of Some Implications of Peasant Commercial Production with Special Reference to the Multiplicity of Traders and Middlemen," *Economic Development and Cultural Change* 8, no. 2 (January 1960): 151.

[8] Lionel Caplan, "The Multiplication of Social Ties: The Strategy of Credit Transactions in East Nepal," *Economic Development and Cultural Change* 20, no. 4 (July 1972): 691–702.

him further into debt. The Limbu soon spends the money, and is still without use of his land.

Discussion of India is continued from p. 86.

3. In previous chapters we saw the ancient origins of the Hindu caste system, and its persistence into modern times. We also noted how changes in the landholding system have removed many individuals from caste protection, forcing them to seek jobs as day laborers and wage earners. Those of high caste no longer have an obligation to find a position for everyone born within their communities; they can choose those with whom they will deal. Since everyone will not be included, there is competition among members of a caste to be chosen. When services are no longer needed, they will be terminated. Carpenters, potters, blacksmiths, water carriers, sweepers, and laundrymen still perform these services and assist in the rituals of birth, marriage, and death for those of higher caste. In return they are rewarded with grain, clothing, sugar, fodder, and animal products like butter and milk. But they understand that this is no longer simply the natural order of things; they are individuals exchanging reciprocities with individuals (to whom they may in addition be in monetary debt) who could dismiss them at any time.

Further discussion of India may be found on p. 118.
Discussion of the Nupe is continued from p. 71.

4. In the Nupe capital of Bida[9] it was common for craftsmen seeking prosperous customers, *mallams* (Muslim scribes) seeking sons of nobility as students or looking for bureaucratic posts, various social climbers, or individuals seeking jobs as servants, messengers, or soldiers to become clients of wealthy men. In the mid-1930s the *Shaba*, the second highest Bida nobleman, had nineteen clients. The clients of his sons and younger brothers numbered forty, while eight or ten of his other relatives with whom he was on good terms had a hundred clients among them. In addition, he was of course the most important man on the street where he lived, which meant he could generally count on the support of twenty or thirty immediately adjacent households. This gave him a following of 400 men or 1,000 persons in a town of 30,000—a major political power bloc. If any of these 400 men crossed the *Shaba* they could lose their means of livelihood.

5. In 1950 and 1951, a researcher in northern Nigeria sent two sets of agents with cotton from the same fields to be graded in markets by government officials (the grading process determining the ultimate price the cotton will receive in the marketplace).[10] Only those agents who bribed the officials received the highest grade. This, too, is raw material from which a patron-client relationship could

---

[9] Siegfried F. Nadel, *A Black Byzantium: The Kingdom of Nupe in Nigeria* (London: Oxford University Press, 1942), pp. 123–165.

[10] M. G. Smith, "Historical and Cultural Conditions of Political Corruption among the Hausa," *Comparative Studies in Society and History* 6, no. 2 (January 1964): 187–188.

grow. The sellers are at the mercy of the officials. No bribe—no profit. If the officials have this much power, they have more. A political dissident, for instance, might find it impossible to receive anything but the lowest grade for his cotton.

6. The Ibo Chief Onyeama was born into a poor chiefly family.[11] He later managed to weaken his traditional position in the village while enhancing his material well-being by becoming a client to the coal mines of Engu in East Nigeria. He allowed mine agents to round up people in his village to serve as laborers in the mines (or attend mission schools) and beat those who resisted. In return, he received a financial subsidy.

Further discussion of Nigeria may be found on p. 215.
Discussion of Peru is continued from p. 95.

7. A classic patron-client relationship is that between the *hacendado* (owner of a *hacienda*) and *campesino* introduced by the Spanish and Portuguese. Hector Martinez clearly describes the relationship as it exists on a contemporary *hacienda* in highland Peru.[12] The service tenants (*campesinos*) are obliged to work on the estate 160 days a year. In addition, they must (when required) watch over the estate's crops, look after harness and the harness room, supervise field labor, and do domestic service in the owner's home and yard. They are expected to loan their cattle to the owner for use as beasts of burden and to manure the estate's fields, to turn over a percentage of milk yield, and pay fines when something happens prejudicial to the owner's interests during the tenant's work period. In exchange they are entitled to a plot of land to use as they please, pasturage for their cattle on the owner's land, the right to rent additional land for raising corn and potatoes, one lamb per year from the owner's flock, meals when special services take place at mealtime, a ration of coca or corn beer, and fifty centavos per week. The patron may also be expected to serve as godfather to some of the more faithful tenants and to know everyone by his or her first name, tend to people when they are ill, and contribute to their fiestas.[13]

Further discussion of Peru may be found on p. 129.
Discussion of Ghana is continued from p. 93.

8. Along the coast of Togo and Ghana it takes common fishermen years of capital accumulation to produce a net (200 to 350 yards long).[14] Once an individual has done so, either alone or collectively, he is in a position to form a

---

[11] Robert L. Tignor, "Colonial Chiefs in Chiefless Societies," *Journal of Modern African Studies* 9, no. 3 (1971): 347.

[12] Hector Martinez, "La Hacienda Capana," *Peru Indigena* 10, nos. 24–25, 40–42.

[13] For extensive additional bibliography on and analysis of such arrangements as they exist throughout Latin America, see Peter M. Singelmann, *Structures of Domination and Peasant Movements in Latin America* (Columbia, Mo.: University of Missouri Press, 1981).

[14] Robert W. Wyllie, "Migrant Anlo Fishing Companies and Sociopolitical Change: A Comparative Study," *Africa* 39, no. 4 (October 1969): 396–410.

company with himself in charge of net casting, a second acting as coxswain and disciplinarian, and a clerk to keep records. The company rents part of a town and hires men from other towns to live there. This community generally has a headman who is a net owner and a council composed largely of net owners. In the town of Muniana the council passed curfews, declared certain areas off-limits to workers, and issued other decrees to which workers objected strenuously. The workers were not part of the decision-making process, but were generally far enough removed from their traditional villages that they did not allow such grievances to divert them from continuing their clientage to their employer-patrons. Where else would they find work?

Further discussion of Ghana may be found on p. 158.

9. In Mandande chiefdom among the Korekore of Zimbabwe the land is ill-suited for the millet and sorghum that constitute the principal crops. Preparation of the soil, two weedings, and harvest require much young labor.[15] The traditional solution to this problem had been a twenty-year bride service performed by grooms for their in-laws. By 1961, however, over 72 percent of the men between fifteen and forty-nine were away working as day laborers. The more traditional substituted for their work obligation by sending home money payments to their brides. A few made brief trips home to help at critical stages of the growing cycle. Others simply eloped. With lowered yields, most villagers were forced to buy more grain from stores. In most instances, unemployment, sickness, or old age forced the young emigrés to return to the village at some stage in life, usually to find that their inherited land and titles[16] had been passed on to those who had stayed behind. This produced a serious rift between the latter and the emigrés who had to develop a means of livelihood apart from the village system.

Into this setting came a fundamentalist Protestant church that was largely attended by returned emigrés, by people who had started cash crops, and by those who had begun raising cattle for sale. The church forbade its members to take part in ancestral rituals. Members showed an interest in building roads to improve commerce, a school, a clinic, and a general store. Some of them owned a plow (a very substantial investment) and wanted this inherited by their eldest son, rather than by other of their father's relatives in the traditional manner. Instead of *giving* gifts of grain to kinsmen as was customary in times of shortage, they demanded cash payment. And leading their congregation (89 percent of whom were of commoner lineage) was one of the sons of the Madande chief. When the District Commissioner arrived in 1964, offering economic assistance to the valley under a new program, he met resistance from the chief and chose to work instead through the chief's son, the church leader. The latter soon suc-

---

[15] See G. Kingsley Garbett, "Prestige, Status, and Power in a Modern Valley Korekore Chiefdom, Rhodesia," *Africa* 37, no. 3 (July 1967): 307–326. William O. Jones, "Turnips, the Seventh Day Adventist Principle, and Management Bias," *Food Research Institute Studies* 16, no. 3 (1977–78): 149–151, contains similar reports from Kenya and Zambia.

[16] The title of chief developed a special attraction after the government began paying chiefs eighty to one hundred pounds per annum, more than the yield from day labor.

ceeded in obtaining government funds for a school, which his congregation built without permission on traditional village land, and in beginning an irrigation scheme in the sector to which his followers had moved. The government was rewarding only those who broke away from the traditions of the village *and* submitted to the leadership of the chief's son. With 72 percent of the able-bodied men gone, the traditional village found it hard to produce crops. What sort of power did this leave villagers other than the chief's son?

Each of these examples involves interaction between parties unequal in status, wealth, and influence. It involves reciprocity in the exchange of goods and services between parties who have face-to-face relationships. The individuals involved in these interactions are not related. They often come from different communities and sometimes from different racial and tribal groups. They are not always bound by the same customs. In fact, the only customs they necessarily have in common are those that surround the particular interactions they have with one another. But their relationship is cemented by interactions beyond the simple exchange of goods and services such as the patron becoming the godfather of one of the client's children, the leader of a church, the provider of meals, or the arbiter of the hours during which people can be on the streets. The only people who benefit from the relationships are the participants themselves, and those at the bottom can be severed from the ties at any time.

Links between City and Countryside

The patron-client relationship is inherently less stable than the kinship obligations that held together the traditional community, and it grows even more unstable as ties with the city increase. Robert Murphy reports on the construction of an emergency airstrip near Belem, Brazil, in the Amazon.[17] The chief of the project offered laborers thirty-five cruzeiros a day plus room, board, medical services, and the privilege of buying goods at a discount at the airfield store. Those he hired had been tapping rubber and selling it to traders. Satisfied with their new employment, his workers did not return to tapping when that season began. At the same time, they failed to pay the traders the back accounts they owed; that is, they accepted as a gift the groceries they had received as an advance on future tapped rubber. The traders were irate. The chief of the airport project had no sympathy for their case and would give them no aid.

Here is a case of a clear clash between two economic and social systems: the patron-client system of the countryside, and the open market arrangements of the city. The trader—the patron—makes his money at two ends. He gives the tappers credit for their crude rubber at so much per pound (e.g., ten cruzeiros) while selling it in turn to another middleman for a higher figure (e.g., twenty cruzeiros). Then he buys foodstuffs and supplies at wholesale (e.g., five cruzeiros) and advances these to his clients at retail value (e.g., ten cruzeiros). The middleman makes fifteen cruzeiros on this transaction—minus some possi-

[17] Robert Murphy, "Credit Versus Cash: A Case Study," *Human Organization* 14, no. 3 (Fall 1955): 26-28.

ble interest—while his tappers never see any cash. His economic liability is that he must usually advance groceries faster than the rubber comes in. His "collateral" is the fact that his tappers all live in the same little community in which he is perhaps religious leader and arbiter of disputes. This works in turn to the advantage of the client who can seek his help in times of trouble or economic scarcity. The urbane chief of the airport project pays considerably better wages and charges lower prices. Yet when the airstrip is completed he will return to São Paulo, leaving his workers high and dry. As he told the traders, he is not responsible for his workers' debts; he is responsible for paying them but not for what they do with the money. The instability of the patron-client system is demonstrated by the speed with which the clients deserted it when presented with what seemed to them a lucrative opportunity. Patron-client ties are perhaps cemented most firmly by the fact that such opportunities to escape them do not arise often, and when they do, they are often even less stable than the patron-client relationship!

Further discussion of Brazil may be found on p. 133.

Left to itself, patron-clientism at the village level can provide fairly stable reciprocal obligations, benefitting both patron and clients. If a rubber planter around Kuching, which we introduced a few pages back, were to decide to default on his debts he would have only one choice: to sell his rubber to another shopkeeper down the street. This would not work, however. These shopkeepers must live with one another, and they could not take the same hands-off attitude as the man from São Paulo. They would not buy the rubber, but would instead send the planter back to work out his debt with the original shopkeeper. As the cash economy expands in the countryside, however, it permits local patrons to buy land,[18] increase the indebtedness of their clients, and hence gain more power over them. The patrons can then ignore their obligations to the peasants and demand more from them. The peasants in turn can look for new jobs and new patrons farther away. This weakens kinship ties and makes it even harder for villagers to demand that the patron perform his obligations to them. Most must stay behind and accept the hegemony of the local patrons.

The greater the dependence of the peasant upon the local patron, the easier it is for these patrons to establish links with outside bureaucrats and politicians. Others who are not patrons (such as village councils or religious leaders) can also *become* bureaucrats and politicians in this manner. The arrangement works well from the perspective of the outside patrons. The bank manager approves loans

---

[18] James C. Scott, "The Erosion of Patron-Client Bonds and Social Change in Rural Southeast Asia," *Journal of Asian Studies* 32, no. 1 (November 1972): II, and Benedict J. Kerkvliet, *The Huk Rebellion* (Berkeley: University of California Press, 1977), pp. 5–25, suggest that any land shortage weakens reciprocal obligations in patron clientism. While there is enough land to which they can threaten to migrate, peasants can demand assistance in caring for elderly parents and in celebrating rituals, help during sickness, protection against outsiders, food and money loans, and other services from their patrons. When land becomes short, the balance of power shifts into the hands of the patrons.

for landowners who will support his party in the next election; the bureaucrat offers government programs to village councils that will do the same. With this new access to outside money and influence (beyond their former purely economic contacts) the patrons are freer still to ignore reciprocal obligations to clients. Once central government has tied into these networks, furnishing additional outside support yet with weak supervisory power at the local level, these middle-echelon patrons become even more powerful. *The more local patrons tie in with national and international patrons, the less the client at the bottom receives.* A few more examples illustrate:

Discussion of the Philippines is continued from p. 78.

1. Manuel Tinio[19] helped his peasants on central Luzon in the Philippines by providing rice until harvest time, interest-free loans, wood from his uncleared land, gifts of money for illness and weddings, and much else. In return, the peasants served him loyally. They developed his undeveloped lands, and supported him as a local political leader. During the 1910s, to help the natives, the American colonial government, ordered cadastral surveys of all land and the opening of government land to homesteading. The move helped only the wealthy natives. The big landowners used their influence with the courts and bureaucracy to proceed to take or buy most of the unoccupied land on Luzon for themselves. They even used the courts to claim title to land that had been occupied by peasants prior to the cadastral surveys. This left peasants with no new plots to occupy on their own.

The colonial government also offered the landlords an opportunity to invest in export businesses, and increased opportunities to market crops. Manuel's son, Monolo, attended Cornell University in the United States, where he studied engineering. When he took over for his father he began to deal with the peasants on what he thought was a strictly businesslike basis. He stopped giving interest-free loans, advances of rice, access to the forest, and gifts at weddings. He demanded a greater percentage of the crop from them, and he wanted to mechanize production. His father had expanded wealth by buying more land and using the good will of the peasants to develop it. Monolo was expanding wealth by increasing the crop and his profit from it, while the peasant was receiving less than ever before. Since other landlords were doing the same, the peasants had no place to turn.

2. Recall from Chapter 3 that sugar plantations were begun on the island of Negros and in central Luzon in the Philippines. Negros was a locally owned, relatively low-capital operation. The plantations in central Luzon were heavily financed by American investors. In Negros, investors opened mills and took title to frontier lands. They invited laborers from other parts of the Philippines to work small plots of this land in exchange for a payment of a percentage of the crop when it was brought to the mill. The tenant dealt directly with the mill owner. When the tenant faced personal problems, he could turn to the owner for

---

[19] Kerkvliet, *Huk Rebellion,* pp. 5-25, 35ff.

assistance[20] in much the same manner as the Brazilian rubber tapper. In contrast, the Luzon mills were much larger. Their owners lived far away and hired *hacenderos* to control the *hacienda* and its output. These hired managers had no personal relationship with the laborers. The mill owners did not buy the cane from the laborer but from the *hacendero*. He in turn was supposed to divide the proceeds among the tenants. He often cheated on this obligation. Nor did he carry through with other traditional obligations of patrons. Ben Kerkvliet and James Scott describe the results:

> Gone was the crucial subsistence insurance for the subordinate peasantry; gone was the personal assistance brokerage of the landowner; gone was any palpable contribution of the landowning class to village welfare; gone was any recognizable contribution to cultivation itself. Left was a peasant who shouldered almost all the tasks and risks of farming and a landowner who did nothing at all except to collect rents.[21]

Further discussion of the Philippines may be found on p. 198.

3. Barraclough and Domike summarize the problem as it exists in rural Latin America when peasants become entirely dependent upon large *haciendas* that have gone heavily into cash-cropping:

> Wage and rental agreements can be adjusted to suit the landowner's convenience so that all productivity increases and windfalls accrue to him. Permanent improvements such as buildings or fruit trees belong to the estate even when all the costs are borne by the tenant. On many large plantations residents are strictly forbidden to make improvements without permission for fear they would acquire vested interests in the land or take resources away from the production of the cash plantation crop. Residents of the large estates can be expelled at will in traditional areas where there is neither a strong central government nor a labor union to defend them . . . Even though it was prohibited as long ago as the seventeenth century, the practice of "renting out" workers still persists.[22]

4. Countering these barons were some "Robin Hoods." Various charismatic strongmen, often of humble origins, once took power in various

---

[20] In the 1970s, this situation changed. Some 60 percent of Agriculture Bank loans went to Negros. President Marcos himself was an owner of a Negros sugar estate. The *hacendero* had arrived in Negros, too. Charles Elliott, *Patterns of Poverty in the Third World* (New York: Praeger, 1975), pp. 75, 140.

[21] James C. Scott and Ben Kerkvliet, "The Politics of Survival: Peasant Response to 'Progress' in Southeast Asia," *Journal of Asian Studies* 4, no. 2 (September 1973): 249. The generalization is intended to apply to central Luzon, lower Burma, and southern Vietnam.

[22] Solon L. Barraclough and A. L. Domike, "Agrarian Structure in Seven Latin American Countries," in *Agrarian Problems and Peasant Movements in Latin America,* ed. R. Stavenhagen (Garden City, N.Y.: Doubleday, 1970), pp. 53–54. See Ernest Feder, *The Rape of the Peasantry: Latin America's Landholding System* (Garden City, N.Y.: Doubleday Anchor, 1971), pp. 121–167, for a brilliant discussion of the increasing power of the *latifundista* over the peasantry.

regions in what is known as the *caudillo* or *cacique* system. The *caudillo* leader would simply seize loot by force with the aid of his band of brigands and redistribute part of it to the peasants.

> In an important sense *caudillo* rule was not strong-man rule, but weak-man rule. Pillage had its limits, and if one man did not deliver booty, another could rise up to challenge his right to leadership.[23]

(As we shall see, the *cacique* has a present-day counterpart in rural administration and big city neighborhoods.) This kind of patron could hardly be expected to insure his clients the same thorough reciprocity as the patron who spent his life in the village. The conflict between landlords and *caudillo* leaders for control of the countryside further weakened the position of the peasant who had to keep on good terms with both sides without assurance of continuing reciprocities from either. That conflict was not an important feature of the old self-contained *latifundio*; it is an outgrowth of the advent of cash-cropping.

Discussion of Vietnam is continued from p. 80.

5. Frances Fitzgerald describes the consequences of Ngo Dinh Diem's administrative system in South Vietman:

> The story as told by villagers throughout the country had its stock characters: the government-appointed village chief; the "haughty," "arrogant" official who took bribes from the local landlords and forced the villagers to work for him; the village security officer—a relative, perhaps, of the village chief—who used his position to take revenge on old enemies or to extort money from the villagers; the government soldiers who, like juvenile delinquents, drank too much, stole food, and raped the village girls . . . the district and provincial officials who, like Kafka's bureaucrats, seemed to inhabit a world impossibly remote from the village . . . when the Front cadre moved into the village and assassinated one or two of the government officials, the villagers reacted with enthusiasm or indifference.[24]

Those who dealt directly with the peasant were so necessary to the central government that it could not intervene in their activities. Vast efforts by the United States to wipe out these behavior patterns during the 1960s proved to be largely ineffective, according to reporters from all frames of reference. Later in the Vietnam War, the government agents found they could make more money trading narcotics or selling American army goods on the black market. Then Saigon lost touch with the villages entirely. The peasant, cut off from seeds and

---

[23] Eric R. Wolf and Edward C. Hansen, *The Human Condition in Latin America* (London: Oxford University Press, 1972), pp. 223-224. See also Robert Kern, ed., *The Caciques: Oligarchical Politics and the System of Caciquismo in the Luso-Hispanic World* (Albuquerque: University of New Mexico Press, 1973).

[24] Frances Fitzgerald, *Fire in the Lake: the Vietnamese and the Americans in Vietnam* (Boston: Little, Brown, 1972), p. 106.

other supplies, had to rely on contacts with North Vietnamese forces when he needed help, or simply on his own wit.

Further discussion of Vietnam may be found on p. 221.
Discussion of India is continued from p. 110.

6. When the Congress Party in India "outlawed" the caste system and set up elected village *panchayats,* it, too, found itself strengthening the power of local patrons and ignoring the needs of its poorer clients. For instance, in Gaon, in Maharastra,[25] the leaders of the three major castes in the community had met together to rule the village informally.[26] The only government agency in town was the Revenue Department. The caste system, involving clearly defined reciprocities, was intact. The introduction of irrigation brought cash crops, and the opportunity to move out to individual farms. It also brought land surveyors, canal inspectors, and increased interaction with the merchants of nearby Mot. In 1947, the government began to sponsor cooperative societies. Together with the increased number of government agents, these societies provided competition to the three caste leaders in their efforts to rule the community. Anyone with more than half an acre of irrigated land could join the sugar cooperatives, which had access to bank loans; those with more than half an acre were usually people of higher caste. No cooperative was created for untouchables like scavengers.

> It was said that powerful people could get loans more easily and that they were more likely to use the money for non-agricultural purposes. Fellow villagers were "supervisors" who, of course, would take no action against the powerful. Such men were also the slowest to repay. Nonpayments of loans resulted in the closure of the original society by the Central Bank.[27]

In addition, when disputes arose between poorer co-op members who wished to purchase cheaper used equipment and the wealthier who preferred to wait for expensive new items, it was usually the latter who won out.

COMMENT

Notice that only higher caste people were able to join the cooperatives, which united these castes, the bureaucracy, and lending institutions into a powerful counterforce against the more democratically-chosen *panchayats.*

---

[25] Henry Orenstein, "Village, Caste, and the Welfare State," *Human Organization* 22, no. 1 (Spring 1963): 83–89.

[26] The original *panchayats,* established by the Muslim emperors about the seventeenth century to aid revenue collection consisted precisely of this group. E. Kathleen Gough, "Caste in a Tanjore Village," in *Aspects of Caste in South India, Ceylon and North-West Pakistan,* ed. E. R. Leach (Cambridge: Cambridge University Press, 1969), p. 36.

[27] An historic parallel: In 1871 the British Crown Government passed the Land Improvement Act. By 1875, Rs. 26,322 in land improvement loans had been advanced under this act. Rs. 24,293 of this had gone to landlords, while the rest was divided among fifty-two tenants, scattered throughout the provinces (some tokenism). Elizabeth Whitcombe, *Agrarian Conditions in Northern India* (Berkeley: University of California Press, 1972), p. 116.

This was the setting into which elected *panchayats* were introduced. The groups often contained individuals—including untouchables—who were entirely unrepresented in the upper castes, the cooperatives, or the bureaucracy (which were all generally of higher caste). When six members of the Gaon *panchayat* attempted to take effective action with regard to equalizing benefits and cutting back on favoritism, the community influentials saw to it that new elections were called. The Congress Party's effort to use popular intervention to limit upper caste rule and favoritism failed. The effort may, in fact, have increased the power of that upper caste. The situation in Gaon is probably not exceptional. Referring to the *panchayati* system, Iqbal Narain says:

> . . . benefits are not being equitably distributed and there is a lot of misuse of funds. It is common knowledge that sections who belong to the higher strata of rural society have captured power and they are trying to monopolize the benefits . . . *panchayat samitis* [heads of *panchayats* formed into a regional council] get divided between dominating and minority groups and there comes about the phenomenon of *political haves* becoming also the *economic haves* and *political have nots* becoming the *economic have nots*.[28]

Thus a *panchayat* dominated by those who do not have some other base of power is likely to be ignored[29] by those with power, both in its own community and in more powerful surrounding communities. Using their own network of patron-client relationships, those in power are in a position to by-pass or replace any *panchayat* not blessed with its own powerful patron. They are also increasingly free to ignore their obligations under the caste system.

Further discussion of India may be found on p. 123.
Discussion of Malaysia is continued from p. 82.

7. In the 1961 elections, the ruling Alliance Party in Malaysia finally won the assembly seats formerly occupied by the regional PMIP party in the state of

---

[28] Iqbal Narain, "Developmental Administration under Panchayati Raj: The Rajasthan Experience," *Indian Journal of Public Administration* 14, no. 1 (January-March 1968): 71-72. Other sources supporting this contention: George Rosen, *Democracy and Economic Change in India* (Berkeley: University of California Press, 1967), pp. 92-101, 145-146; Gunnar Myrdal, *Asian Drama: An Inquiry Into the Poverty of Nations* (New York: Pantheon, 1968), pp. 887-891, 1339-1346; and Reinhard Bendix, *Nation Building and Citizenship: Studies of Our Changing Social Order* (Garden City, N.Y.: Doubleday, 1969), pp. 338-356. André Béteille, *Caste, Class, and Power* (Berkeley and Los Angeles: University of California Press, 1965), reports on a Madras situation where Brahmin political control has been challenged at both the local and state level. Thus local Brahmin landholders do not directly control the *panchayats*, yet the *panchayats* have not challenged their economic control. M. V. M. Mathur, Iqbal Narain, V. M. Sinha, et al., *Panchayati Raj in Rajasthan* (New Delhi, 1966), pp. 234-235: ". . . village Mahajans [money-lenders] capture seats of power in *panchayats* and *panchayat samitis* help the peasants in getting loans and taccavis and ultimately see to it that the money the villager gets is used for repayment of loans he has taken from them."

[29] This will probably happen in the same manner as *lambardars* were ignored during the nineteenth century. See pp. 84-85.

Trengannu.[30] It then decided to extend schemes of the Federal Land Development Authority into that state. The programs quickly became entangled in patron-client relationships that prevented implementation from the top in a rational manner. Committees were selected, consisting of the district officer, an agricultural officer, and citizens who owed allegiance to the Alliance Party. The assemblymen suggested sites for the schemes. Paid field assistants spent more of their time organizing political party branches than in surveying land. The individuals resettled into the schemes (each receiving a few acres from which to tap rubber) seem to have been chosen more on the basis of their political affiliation than on their ability as agricultural workers. Those placed on the scheme received this benefit in exchange for at least a tacit understanding that they would support the party. The civil servants found it difficult to enforce standards. They were in a position both to be outvoted by the other committee members and to be removed from office by a government controlled by the Alliance Party. The rubber trees did not grow properly (ironically, a fact that did not contribute to the Alliance's hold over its new clients). Neither the patrons nor the clients received a long-range benefit from this particular relationship; the opposing PMIP experienced a resurgence in the 1969 elections. Cultivation of patron-client ties seemed to take precedence over the cultivation of rubber, however. Functional control from the top to insure success of the schemes did not materialize, nor did substantial benefits for those at the bottom.

Further discussion of Malaysia may be found on p. 212.

Patron-client relationships, then, exist in a variety of modern cultural settings. Whether they like it or not, politicians must rely on middle-echelon patrons to implement policy at the local level. By supplying these middle-echelon patrons with resources, the government strengthens their ability to ignore their reciprocal obligations to those below them. Hence, ironically, the introduction of governmental programs to aid the people often allows middle-echelon patrons to diminish aid to the people; contacts with central government strengthen patrons at the expense of the lowest clients.

THE MAJOR AND MINOR NETWORKS DEFINED

We come now to the question of how all this ties together. We have seen how patron-client relationships form. We have seen benefits become more unequally apportioned as links with capital cities and international commerce, and competition for scarce resources, intensify. Now we will focus more closely on how those links between local and national patron-clientism came into being, function, and affect people.

---

[30] Dorothy Guyot, "The Politics of Land: Comparative Development in Two States of Malaysia," *Pacific Affairs* 44, no. 3 (Fall 1971): 368–389.

A government is in a strange position. Most patrons were around before it took office, and will be around long after it leaves. Any government which displeases most patrons will fall. But in order to function the patrons depend on the government—and it depends on them. *If government is to have either rewards to distribute to the people or armies with which to coerce, it needs access to both money and expertise.* Yet those who come to power in developing nations are often not wealthy. Their governmental systems and methods of succession are not legitimized by long tradition. Governments seldom have large monetary resources or efficient, well-trained bureaucracies. This money and expertise lies in the hands of the investment banker, the large corporation, the plantation and mine operator, religious institutions, various entrepreneurs, and perhaps some nobility allied with these groups. Should the government offend these institutions, they are usually in a position to take both money and expertise abroad. On the other hand, by becoming a patron to these individuals and institutions—helping them to maintain a safe investment climate and a minimum of popular unrest—the government can gain access to the resources it needs to stay in power. This implies that government in turn must become patron to the smaller patrons who control men and resources at the local level.

By involving itself in this complex set of patron-client relationships, a government finds itself caught in some crossfire. The patrons valued for their control over the populace (e.g., small traders, union organizers, traditional headmen, small landlords and moneylenders, political party functionaries, craft guilds, caste leaders, lower-level bureaucrats) sometimes fall into conflict with those who control large quantities of money: Large institutional investors sometimes try to drive small entrepreneurs out of business. Union organizers pressure management for wage increases. Regional politicians sometimes prefer to carry out projects without interference by corporations.[31] Commodities middlemen often buy for prices considered too low by local elites.[32] Under such circumstances there *is* a means by which government can successfully maintain both its sets of alliances—it can act as a friendly broker. For instance, the manufacturing firm is required to make concessions to urban labor leaders; in return, labor leaders are asked to help keep down unrest in the countryside (e.g., by inhibiting the organization of farm workers). Or local elites can receive bureaucratic posts to compensate for low commodities prices. Taxes derived from larger institutions can be used to benefit smaller entrepreneurs in exchange for their support of larger institutions on other matters.

[31] E.g., the Mentri Besar of Trengannu, wishing to start an oil palm estate and disobeying orders from the capital that he must first run a feasibility study, illegally diverted Public Works Department equipment to begin the project. He placed his brother in charge, hoping to sell the project in small plots to small investors and make funds for the family. It was only after mismanagement had left the project a tangle of weeds that the federal government intervened and placed the project into the hands of a Dutch firm. Guyot, "The Politics of Land," p. 379.

[32] In Kita, Mali (discussed later in this chapter), the local party functionary defended a 2 percent cut in the price paid peasants for their peanuts. Later, a rival for his post criticized him for this defense and received much public support for doing so; the functionary backed down from his position. It would appear that the former price was restored. The government showed an ability to make minor modifications in policy, trading—when it had to—price increases for the middle-manning operation in exchange for local supports. Nicholas S. Hopkins, *Popular Government in an African Town: Kita, Mali* (Chicago: University of Chicago Press, 1972), pp. 148–150.

The government helps the major network settle its own internal feuds, and their feuds with the minor network. *Hence, the government does not deal with the middle-echelon patrons by itself; it deals with them in concert with those who control wealth, expertise, and resources.* Without rewarding the latter, it would not have the means to reward or coerce these middle-echelon patrons, or the populace at large. And once government has rewarded all of its patrons, it may have little left for the populace. One can think of this process as having three groups of participants: the major network, the minor network, and everybody else.

The *major network* of this system, then, consists of investors, bureaucrats, and politicians interacting with one another. They principally derive investment capital and political power from the system; they are the ones who handle surplus capital. From the general populace, the major network needs political quietism and support (e.g., votes), labor, and agricultural commodities. To extract these, they employ the services of a *minor network* of the middle-echelon patrons. These patrons receive personal rewards for these services that allow them to maintain a·modest to high standard of living, with some savings laid away but not enough to control investments. Below these two networks lie the *great bulk of the populace* who ultimately supply economic growth and political quietism. The minor network is moderately well designed to pass labor, raw materials, and political support upward to the major network and to extract its own payment for these transactions; it is poorly designed for passing economic benefits back downward to the populace.

You can almost recognize members of these networks by visiting with them. If they are prosperous, and they have someone's money to invest, they are probably members of the major network. If they are at least fairly prosperous, but have no money to invest, they are probably members of the minor network. If they don't have much, they are everybody else. You might chuckle and think that hits pretty close to home: Join the club, aren't we all "everybody else"? Look at the following examples and see if you still think so.

Some Examples of Network Systems

The major network has the surplus capital. The minor network helps them extract the resources that will create more capital. In *Liberia,*[33] a nation of a million and a half people, the two groups are easy to identify. Liberia was founded by ex-slaves from the United States who landed in west Africa and set up a colonial-style government. Their descendents, known as the Americo-Liberians, combined with some Europeans and Lebanese, constitute the major and minor networks. Together, they comprise only about 5 percent of the total population. In conjunction with foreign firms, they control the iron ore, rubber, and timber firms from which most of the country's revenue is derived. These families are on the boards of directors of virtually every firm in the nation. These

---

[33] Ozay Mehmet, *Economic Planning and Social Justice in Developing Countries* (New York: St. Martins, 1978), pp. 123–140.

firms, and top government posts, are nearly all operated by Europeans and Lebanese. Together, they comprise the major network.

Members of the tribes that constitute the original, and most numerous, inhabitants of the nation play no part in the major or minor network. Between 1950 and 1972, especially because of the growth in iron mining, the gross national product increased 1,300 percent, government revenues by 4,000 percent, and road mileage by 1,100 percent. Yet over one-fourth of the tribal lands were given to business firms. Some of the tribesmen were hired to work in the new mines at 12¢ an hour. Virtually the entire government budget was spent to provide buildings, education,[34] and salaries for Americo-Liberians and the few Europeans and Lebanese. Those of them who do not belong to the major network constitute the minor network. Original inhabitants received no benefits. They must support themselves with subsistence agriculture, though Americo-Liberians are taking control of increasing amounts of their land for cash-cropping.

In 1980 the government was overthrown by a military coup. The new government will be unable to function without the revenue from the iron mines, rubber estates, and timber concessions. They will be unable to operate without the assistance of the foreigners and the Americo-Liberians. Everyone else will probably still remain impoverished.

Discussion of India is continued from p. 119.

India is a much more populous and complex nation. Yet its major and minor network are also easy to spot. One can do so by focusing on who has the most capital and income.

Working backward, who does not have much income? In 1950, 38 percent of peasant families worked intermittently as hired help or owned no land.[35] Some 45 percent of peasant families owned sixteen acres or less. Some of these individuals worked for the minor network as laborers and thus might be considered lower clients within that network. The rest remained outside of it.

The heart of the minor network is likely to have derived more from among the 17 percent of families who owned more than sixteen acres of land (or 57 percent of total farmland). These larger farmers averaged US$650 annual family income (versus US$90 for the hired help). This meant that even most of the larger landowners could live only modestly, with few savings. About a tenth of the larger landowners owned more than seventy-five acres[36] and an additional 300,000 Indian families derived capitalist income from mines and manufacturing; 96 percent of these people earned declared incomes below US$14,000 per

---

[34] Of the total education budget, 30 percent went to foreign scholarships for Americo-Liberians, and to a university that graduates about one hundred people a year. In 1973, the university was moved at a cost of about US$90 million—more than the entire 1973 government budget—so it could be near President Tolbert's country estate.

[35] Charles Bettelheim, *India Independent* (New York: Monthly Review Press, 1968), pp. 25–27.

[36] Ibid., pp. 54–59.

year.[37] It is from these latter sectors that most minor patrons were likely to derive.

Meanwhile, .0006 percent of the Indian population—mostly from among the larger landowners and from mining and manufacturing—had a declared income of over US$14,000. This group contributed half the capital in banks and industries; the other half came from foreign investors.[38] These people provided the core for the major network. As indicated in the discussion of cooperatives earlier in this chapter, most bank loans were handled through members of the minor networks. Loans often carried the stipulation that the recipient must sell his produce through the bank agent. So only a tiny fraction of the populace owned all the investment capital and productive assets, and another small fraction with modest incomes served as their minor network. Meanwhile, 45 percent of the populace with incomes below US$50 a year has experienced a continuing decline in their per capita income.[39]

Further discussion of India may be found on p. 199.

COMMENT

Simple statistics unaccompanied by further information are not sufficient to demonstrate either the existence of major and minor networks, or the extent of inequalities. For example, if you compare the income of the top 5 percent of a country with that of the bottom 40 percent, the actual inequalities still remain well disguised. For instance, 5 percent of Libyans receive 46 percent of the national income, while the bottom 40 percent receive an astonishing .05 percent. In India, the top 5 percent receive 20 percent of declared income, while the poorest 40 percent receive 20 percent.[40] But India's top 5 percent includes 4.9994 percent with incomes below US$14,000. So actually, .0006 percent control close to one-fifth of the nation's income. And India's wealthy may have far more undisclosed income (so as to hide from the tax collector) than Libya's, since much of Libya's income derives from oil and thus may be harder to disguise. India and Libya may be more similar in their income structures than the figures would initially seem to indicate.

---

[37] Today, the "Green Revolution" (discussed in Chapter 7) is probably allowing additional percentages of this group to earn more than US$14,000.

[38] The proportion of foreign investment has since been substantially reduced, probably adding even more to the control of this tiny fraction of the population.

[39] H. B. Chenery, M. Ahluwalia, C. L. G. Bell, J. Duloy, and R. Jolly, (eds.), *Redistribution with Growth* (London: Oxford University Press, 1974).

[40] I. Adelman and C. T. Morris, *Economic Growth and Social Equity in Developing Countries* (Stanford, Calif.: Stanford University Press, 1973), pp. 245–246. See Keith Griffin, *International Inequality and National Poverty* (London: Macmillan, 1978), pp. 121–136 for another such study.

In Pakistan in 1968, 66 percent of industrial capital was controlled by twenty families,[41] who also controlled 80 percent of the banking and 97 percent of the insurance businesses.[42] Nearly all of these families descended from West Indian minority groups who had fled to Pakistan when it separated from India.[43] They lived for the most part in and about Karachi, the principal city of West Pakistan. The government artificially held the price of the rupee at about 50 percent above market value. Hence, when an East Pakistani farmer sold his jute on the foreign market, the foreign buyer paid about 50 percent more than the farmer received; the government kept the difference. Under an import licensing system, this money was allocated to the industrial sector to import goods; import controls also enabled the industrialists to sell their products on a protected domestic market.[44] In this way the government established a major patron-client network with the twenty families using the proceeds of the exports of the rural sector to support themselves. The families, in turn, invested the money in growth: industrial production rose 160 percent between 1960 and 1968.[45] The government's no-strike law and the tendencies of its protectionist policies to raise the cost of manufactured goods for Pakistani consumers further increased the amount of money available to these patrons for investment. To make low wages possible, the government compulsorily procured foodstuffs cheaply from small farmers, so that food could be rationed at low prices in the cities.[46] Here, clearly, was a system in which a major network reaped strong benefits from rural productivity.

In addition, the government spent US$2 billion on the Indus River project, creating vast stretches of irrigated land in the Punjab. Here agricultural production was increasing by 10 percent a year between 1965 and 1968 (versus 3 percent in East Pakistan, now Bangladesh).[47] The Punjab, where most of Pakistan's larger farms are located, enjoys a per capita wealth 2½ times that of the rest of West Pakistan (and West Pakistan's per capita income in 1969/1970 was 37.9 percent higher than East Pakistan's).

In the Punjab, 0.6 percent of landowners owned 21.6 percent of the cultivated land, in farms over one-hundred acres.[48] Some of these belonged to

---

[41] Henry Heitowit, "Regionalism and Public Policy Making in Pakistan: The Failure of Development from Above," Paper delivered to the American Political Science Association, Washington Hilton Hotel, Washington, D.C., 1972.

[42] Wayne Wilcox, "Pakistan: A Decade of Ayub," *Asian Survey* 9, no. 2 (February 1969): 91.

[43] Gustav F. Papanek, *Pakistan's Development: Social Goals and Private Incentives* (Cambridge: Harvard University Press, 1967), pp. 40–42. See also Walter P. Falcon and Gustav F. Papanek (eds.), *Development Policy II—The Pakistan Experience* (Cambridge: Harvard University Press, 1971), p. 238.

[44] Richard Nations, "The Economic Structure of Pakistan: Class and Colony," *New Left Review* (July–August 1971): 6–8; Stephen Lewis, *Pakistan: Industrialization and Trade Policies* (New York: Oxford University Press, 1970), pp. 20–37.

[45] Richard Wheeler, *The Politics of Pakistan: A Constitutional Quest* (Ithaca, N.Y.: Cornell University Press, 1970), pp. 82–83.

[46] Heitowit, "Regionalism and Public Policy Making," p. 18.

[47] Ibid., pp. 18–20.

[48] Keith Griffin, *The Political Economy of Agrarian Change: An Essay on the Green Revolution*, 2nd ed. (London: Macmillan, 1979), pp. 19–20, 215–216.

the major network, and the rest to the minor. The minor network also included some of the 20.7 percent who owned an additional 46.7 percent of the cultivated land, in farms over ten acres. These individuals received from government free applications of pesticides, government-subsidized fertilizer and tractors at half price, and exemption from virtually all taxation. The poorer farmers received nothing.

In 1960 President Ayub Khan instituted a system of Basic Democracies as a means of developing political support for the government in the countryside. Some 40,000 Basic Democrats were to be elected in East Pakistan (one from each 1,000 citizens), with a like number from West Pakistan. These people would form councils (not unlike *panchayats*) to promote agricultural, industrial, and community development. A study of these councils in East Pakistan showed that whereas only 10 percent of East Pakistani farmers had holdings above 7.5 acres, 63 percent of council members did.[49] And while 15 percent of East Pakistani farmers earned over 3,000 rupees a year, 48 percent of council members did. When interviewed, 63.6 percent of the respondents felt that the council members were corrupt; respondents who did not think so were usually those who had larger holdings of land.[50] It would not be surprising if these "Basic Democrats"—like the *panchayat* members—were often elected because they were patrons to members of their community. The government was using rural works funds as a means of gaining favor among the council members; many of these funds were used by council members to buy land from poorer villagers. A minor network of patrons appeared to be looking after their own needs, thanks to the intervention of the political structure. Obviously the cream of the system was going into the hands of the major network in Karachi.

Further discussion of Pakistan may be found on p. 316.

Senegal derives most of its income from exporting peanuts. Here one can spot the major and minor network by giving attention to how the peanuts are marketed. In 1910, the French established Providence Societies.[51] Seed, fertilizer, and agricultural implements were distributed on easy terms to members, each of whom contributed small dues. Any peasant could belong. Between 1915 and 1947, membership in these societies was made compulsory for all heads of households. Through the societies, those with adequate credit could obtain loans at interest rates much lower than those available from private sources. These loans were administered by government bureaucrats; they tended to go to local notables. The money was used to clear tracts of undeveloped land and create huge private estates. "Fungicide, fertilizer, food, and seed loans were allocated preferentially to those who were already wealthy and powerful," using the funds

---

[49] Rehman Sobhan, *Basic Democracies, Works Programme, and Rural Development in East Pakistan* (Dacca: Oxford University Press, 1968).

[50] Ibid., pp. 121–126.

[51] See Donald B. Cruise O'Brien, "Co-operators and Bureaucrats: Class Formation in a Senegalese Peasant Society," *Africa* 41, no. 4 (October 1971): 263–278. See also idem, *The Mourides of Senegal* (Oxford University Press, 1971).

contributed by poorer members.[52] By the time of independence in 1960, a minority of households controlled most of the land.[53] The wealthier made loans to the poor, let land to tenants, and sometimes handled outside trade; hence, patron-client relationships were well in progress. In some instances these owners created their own private cooperatives, which in turn became affiliated with political parties. Patrons would pay subscription fees for their clients (in addition to casting the client's votes) and force the latter to market their crops through the cooperative.

With the advent of independence in 1960, the government sought to increase the control of the national leadership over the countryside. They set up new cooperatives. Once again, local notables filled the offices channeling credit, relief food supplies, medical supplies, and refunds for crop sales into the hands of friends.[54] Peasants who did not join tended to lose their marketing license, so 80 percent were members by 1966. Members were required to market all their produce (which consisted principally of peanuts) through the cooperative. Under this system, the net *profit* per kilo received by the government after the final sale of the peanuts tended to exceed the *price* paid the farmer for his kilo in the first place;[55] while world market prices, and the national marketing board's profits, were increasing, the price paid to peasants was declining. Between 1967 and 1970, peasants became increasingly aware that they would make more money by smuggling their peanuts across the border to Gambia where they received 3½ francs more per kilo, in cash, without paying back their fertilizer advances. Or else they returned to growing millet. Since rainfall was also down, the 1960–61 official production figure of 786,000 kilos had declined to 423,000 kilos by 1970–71. Since the half of Senegal's population that grew peanuts had produced 80 percent of her export revenue, this created a national crisis. The government announced in 1970 that it would pay 22 francs per kilo, in cash. The official 1971–72 harvest was up to around 800,000 kilos.

As in Kita (see note 32), the Senegalese peasant had learned that he could exert some pressure (in this case, by smuggling) on the government and win some concessions. The major network continues to retain a considerable portion of the income from these rural resources within its bureaucratic and business apparatus in the capital. The minor patrons in control of the cooperatives at the local level were restored to full command of the situation. The speculators who had been

---

[52] O'Brien, "Co-operators and Bureaucrats," pp. 268–269. In the region studied by O'Brien estates ranged from ten acres to thousands of acres.

[53] E.g., 10 of 33 in one village, and 12 out of 102 in another six villages surveyed.

[54] O'Brien, "Co-operators and Bureaucrats," p. 271. One effect, however, was to drive out French and Lebanese traders and concentrate the process in the hands of African traders. Interest rates charged peasants were also somewhat lowered. Cf. Jonathan S. Barber, "The Paradox of Development: Reflections on a Study of Local-Central Political Relations in Senegal," in Michael F. Lofchie, *The State of the Nations: Constraints on Development in Independent Africa* (Berkeley: University of California Press, 1971), p. 53.

[55] The actual price paid the farmer was even lower. Upon receipt of his peanuts, the government paid him with a chit redeemable only four months later after the final transaction abroad had been completed. If he received 19.5 francs per kilo, the government would subtract the cost of the fertilizer and other supplies advanced, leaving him with 10 or 11 francs. During the four-month wait, he might have to redeem his chit to a speculator for 6 or 7 francs in cash.

buying chits from the farmer without obligation to either the cooperatives or the government were frozen out. The government had intervened to keep the network in balance.

In 1974, 47 percent of Senegal's budget went into salaries of bureaucrats, and 23 percent of her foreign exchange was spent for refrigerators, air conditioners, television sets, and other such imports.[56] Her total agricultural imports continue to exceed the value of her agricultural exports; much of this also goes to feed the urban middle classes. As Sheldon Gellar concludes:

> In terms of income distribution . . . the gap between rural and urban incomes has increased and . . . most of the gains in the urban areas have been made by the educated inheritance elite.[57]

There is considerable continuity in that educated inheritance elite. Claudio Veliz could be talking about nearly all developing nations in this comment about Latin America:

> If a list were compiled of one thousand families that two or three centuries ago were near the centers of political and economic power and monopolized social prestige, and the same list were examined today, it would probably be discovered that a large proportion of those names are still prominent in the ruling circles of their respective countries . . . many new names would [also] have been added . . . . [But] these families have . . . a capacity to adapt to changing circumstances that compares favorably with that of the more resilient European aristocracies.[58]

That is the major networks. The minor networks probably turn over more rapidly.

Special Members: Neighborhood Groups and Trade Unions

Urbanites have at least one political advantage over villagers: They are close to the president's palace, so can cause embarrassment by forming a mob outside it, or they can interrupt commerce at its hub by terrorizing businesspeople or sabotaging business institutions. This gives a unique reason for governments to create some patron-client links with urban groups who might otherwise have little of material value to contribute. When, occasionally, rural movements create disturbances in the countryside, as we shall see later, patron-client networks are shifted around to co-opt and incorporate their leadership. But the constant danger of interruption calls for special, more permanent, means of doing this in

---

[56] "Social Institutions," a study commissioned by the Special Sahelian Office, March 28, 1974, p. 80, quoted in Frances Moore Lappé, *Food First: Beyond the Myth of Scarcity* (Boston: Houghton Mifflin, 1977), pp. 103–104.

[57] Charles K. Wilber and James H. Weaver, "Patterns of Dependency: Income Distribution and the History of Underdevelopment," in *The Political Economy of Development and Underdevelopment,* 2nd ed., ed. Charles K. Wilber (New York: Random House, 1979), p. 116.

[58] Claudio Veliz, *The Centralist Tradition of Latin America* (Princeton, N.J.: Princeton University Press, 1980), p. 275.

marketing towns and cities. In addition, it is necessary to deal with those who are working in factories, public utilities, and other urban jobs. For these continuing contacts, major networks make use of neighborhood groups and labor unions.

These institutions have no surplus capital, and they do more than simply extract resources. They are unique in at least three ways. For one thing, they provide an avenue through which individuals can occasionally hope to rise from minor network status to at least the lower echelons of the major network. For another, while they involve reciprocities, they are also designed to prevent civil disturbances, so the main rewards go to those who can aid in this. This means that their members are often more interested in how they can rise within the ranks than in simply how they can keep established reciprocities alive. So these institutions, like government, hold a special place in the major and minor networks. Government is a part of the major network but must act as an intermediary betweeen the major and minor networks. Unions and neighborhood groups are part of the minor network but deal directly with the major network. Because they are unique, it is well to focus on them a bit to round out your understanding of how patron-clientism works. In the next section you will see there is another reason for giving special attention to these particular urban coalitions; they perform unusually important functions in the governance of developing nations, considering their size, lack of capital, and the relatively meager rewards they provide their members. They also provide a convenient point of contact for intelligence agencies of developed nations who wish to infiltrate the politics of the developing nations.

Discussion of Peru is continued from p. 111.

Blas, son of a plantation worker, moved to Lima when he turned eighteen.[59] He married and found a small job. When his family was about to be evicted from the room they rented, Blas affiliated himself with a group of about forty families who took over a stretch of state land during Independence Day holidays. They carried Peruvian flags and gave interviews to reporters about their plight. The government could not move them without embarrassment, and they stayed, built homes, and set up their own governing council to approve changes in home ownership and the like. They tended to shy away from involvement in national politics, lest a change in government put them on the wrong side of the political spectrum or rouse public fears that they might be radical.

Further discussion of Peru may be found on p. 256.

Many urban neighborhoods have similar beginnings. They are known as squatter settlements. In Caracas, Venezuela, squatter neighborhoods do not like to ally themselves with any one political party either. Instead, they have their

---

[59] William Mangin, "Urbanization: Case Study in Peru," *Architectural Design* (August 1963): 367–70.

own competing political groups called *juntas.*[60] These groups seek to obtain materials, money, and other services for their neighbors through government contacts. A *junta* is led by a *cacique,* a tough man with little formal education and few scruples. He lives on a share of what he gets for the neighborhood and on payments from the dwellers for providing political contacts. Each *junta* has only about four active members. One of these is usually a woman who maintains contact with public and private groups, including political parties, outside the neighborhood. Youths in the neighborhood often organize themselves and bargain with the *juntas* rather than join them. A neighborhood may have as many as three competing *juntas* or it may have none at all.

Politicians prefer to deal informally with the *juntas* rather than with large groups. Municipal council members, for instance, might talk to *caciques* while walking to church (a secretary will jot down any promises made), or private conversations are held indoors. One reason for the informality is that promises are seldom kept in full or on time. When one notes that Caracas alone contains some 300 squatter settlements, this is understandable. Another reason is that by announcing favors through the *junta* the politician creates a reciprocal obligation. Recipients of the favors are expected to enroll in his political party. Local politicians are generally content with forty or fifty party members out of an area of 1,500 people. Given the high degree of political apathy, this usually gives them sufficient support to win an election. Hence, few favors need to be distributed to maintain an adequate following. In fact, *juntas* have a vested interest in delaying substantive action; so long, for instance, as desired land titles are held back, the community has a continuing dependence on the *junta* to negotiate for them.[61] This particular patron-client relationship is important to those in power, lest it be usurped by a political enemy. It also absorbs those in the neighborhood with any political proclivity into the political system. It costs the party very little.

A study in the 1960s of Kita, Mali, provides some insight into another variation on urban patron-clientism.[62] Kita congealed around several villages and a French fort late in the nineteenth century and became a marketing center for peanuts, eventually reaching a size of about 10,000 inhabitants. Town merchants set up patron-client relations with the peasants from whom they purchased peanuts. The merchant offered the peasant credit (and high interest rates), consumer goods, lodging during town visits or for children attending school in town, intercession in dealings with administration, sometimes even a son in marriage. The peasant would in turn keep some cattle for the merchant, bring him occasional honey or other specialty foods, and provide him with millet for his family in times of shortage.

[60] Michael Bamberger, "A Problem of Political Integration in Latin America: The Barrios of Venezuela," *International Affairs* 44, no. 4 (October 1968): 709–719. See also Talton F. Ray, *The Politics of the Barrios in Venezuela* (Berkeley and Los Angeles: University of California Press, 1969).

[61] Wayne A. Cornelius, "Local-Level Political Leadership in Latin American Urban Environments: A Structural Analysis of Urban *Caciquismo* in Mexico," Paper presented at American Political Science Association Annual Meeting, Chicago, September 7-11, 1971, argues that this is sometimes a deliberate *cacique* tactic.

[62] Hopkins, *Popular Government in an African Town.*

During the 1960s, a socialist political party that had come to power in Mali switched to government marketing of peanuts (as in neighboring Senegal) as well as introducing consumer's cooperatives which offer no credit to buyers.[63] These policies diminished the status of the merchants and brought an influx of salaried civil servants to Kita. Political party functionaries became influential in the power structure of the community and various factions vied for these party posts, including traditional kinship leaders, merchants, and civil servants. The ideology of the party called for frequent open meetings, and those not holding party office would raise sensitive issues on these occasions to win public favor. Hence, the nature of patronage changed. People turned to party leaders to get children accepted into school, find them jobs or house lots, deal with unjust treatment by a government official, or when they were destitute. Since this was an important aspect of maintaining popularity, the party leaders responded to such requests for help. Their response usually involved pressuring a civil servant to comply with the request. The civil servant, wishing to have good relations with the party, tended to comply if the request did not interfere with some other priority. Petitioners did not seek to establish a permanent relationship involving more complex ties. They reserved their freedom of movement to turn to the opposing factions, should their position shift.

The new system was effective for dispensing favors, but not necessarily stable resources. Civil servants were not free to perform their duties in a purely professional manner. Patrons had no real responsibilities toward their clients, and the system of favors meant that the party and civil service leaders were in a position to get the best favors for themselves. Government could not interfere too deeply in the personal life of the villagers (e.g., an attempt to ban grass burning could not be enforced).[64] Yet the ability of the factions to pressure the government to change its policies on marketing (except minor matters like the 2 percent lowering of peanut payments discussed in footnote 32), commerce, taxation, electrification (the town was still waiting for it), food shortages in the cooperatives, and cattle registration was extremely limited. The government could move civil servants and remove party leaders. The national leadership had placed itself into a position to control major resources and political loyalties of the community. It had produced its own minor network which passed on to clients less than the merchant-patrons who had preceded them. It asked of the townfolk not raw materials, but loyalty. In return, it gave them very little.

Trade unions in developing nations are in many ways more similar to these meetings in Kita than to, say, an American trade union. They do bargain over wages, receive periodic modest wage increases, and become involved in political campaigns, but they have some other stranger features. Their leaders are often government officials. Because of this, factions grow within their ranks which government tries hard to control. Members attempt to use the unions to bargain

---

[63] After the [merchant-centered patron-client] system had disappeared, peasants tended to recall the advantages of the system—the availability of goods even when they did not have ready cash and the establishment of a personal link with someone who would intervene on their behalf if need be—rather than any disadvantages arising from indebtedness." Nicholas S. Hopkins, "Socialism and Social Change in Rural Mali," *The Journal of Modern African Studies* 7, no. 3 (1969): 459.

[64] Inspectors might be told that the fire was started by a fire-breathing antelope.

over issues which in America would be dealt with by parties and interest groups other than unions. They are usually unsuccessful in this. But government does reward them by occasionally pressuring their employers to raise wages. It also allows their leaders to rise even higher politically and economically than would be the case in the United States. If you look at a couple of the following illustrations you will get a feel for this.

In 1953, Tom Mboya was elected Acting General Secretary of the Kenya Federation of Registered Trade Unions.[65] When this became the Kenya Federation of Labour in 1955, Mboya was its General Secretary, and he held that position for nearly ten years. His travels abroad in this position gave him access to scholarships for his officers, money for affiliate unions, and even netted a giant international union building in Nairobi which provided his union free office space. When the Nairobi People's Convention Party was founded—with Mboya as its President—four of the five top posts went to union leaders, and union staff and facilities were used (illegally) for party activities. Nearly all union men supported the NPCP and its successor, KANU. After KANU came to power with the eventual arrival of independence, the new Prime Minister, Jomo Kenyatta, found himself in disagreement with Mboya on many public issues. The labor movement split into two rival factions and Kenyatta himself had to bring it back into one body by governmental decree. The new union he formed, COTU, remains closely affiliated with the ruling party. While no longer the central portion of the party and closely enough tied to government that it cannot freely lobby for workers' demands, the union's leaders are at the same time in a position to receive special attention. It is important to the government to retain its links with union leadership and to prevent unions from falling into the hands of any rival political movement.

In Zambia, copper is a key element in the economy, and striking miners can effectively paralyze that industry. Government and industry have developed close working relationships with miners' union leaders. For one thing, industry looks to the pool of trade union leaders as potential high-level employees.[66] Since nationalization, the appointment of union leaders to boards of directors in industry has further reinforced this syndrome. Ministers frequently tour the country, making public appearances with top local union leaders.[67] The government also offers employment opportunities for union officials. Since the 1956 wholesale arrest of union leaders,[68] leaders have negotiated wage settlements considered conservative by many union members, and have removed from leadership men like Chief Katilungu, who led a successful strike involving

---

[65] See Richard Sandbrook, "Patrons, Clients, and Unions: The Labour Movement and Political Conflict in Kenya," *Journal of Commonwealth Political Studies* 10, no. 1 (March 1972): 3–27. Stephen H. Goodman, "Trade Unions and Political Parties: The Case of East Africa," *Economic Development and Cultural Change* 17, no. 3 (April 1969), discusses Kenya and similar phenomena in Tanzania and Uganda.

[66] Robert H. Bates, *Unions, Parties and Political Development: A Study of Mineworkers in Zambia* (New Haven, Conn.: Yale University Press, 1971). p. 93.

[67] Ibid., p. 75.

[68] Ibid., p. 101.

substantial concessions to mine workers' demands.[69] The union (with over 10,000 members) maintains only fifty-two shop stewards and fifteen branch officers[70] and holds few rank-and-file meetings. Furthermore, union leaders are expected to be members (but not officers) of the ruling United National Independence Party (UNIP).[71] Rank-and-file unionists must look not to the union, but to local UNIP leaders, for militancy. These local party leaders campaign strongly for the issues that top party and union leaders soft-pedal: Zambianization (replacement of Europeans by local workers), better wages and working conditions, even the price of fish at the market.[72] When strikes occur (usually illegally, due to agreements reached with the government by top union leaders), the UNIP leaders intervene to effect a settlement. They are actually acting as highly disciplined members of a hierarchical party that assigns them this role.[73] Hence, the party has kept considerable control over union affairs without actually controlling the unions or being controlled by the unions.

In Latin America, where competition among several parties is more common than in Africa, a primary objective of party policy is the assimilation of union leadership. Peru's strong unions have long been in a position to threaten violence against the government. Union members tend to give their support to moderate leaders who keep contact with the President and the Minister of Labor and who are sparing in their use of force in labor disputes.[74]

In Argentina, Juan Perón brought union militancy under control by his alliance with union activity. He forced rural landowners and reticent industries to accept unionization. He also forced socialist and communist unions to curtail activities and forbade unions to strike unless in support of government policy. After the fall of Perón, succeeding governments had less control over unions but kept contact with Perónists who remained powerful within the union movement.

Discussion of Brazil is continued from p. 114.

In Brazil, a corporative Estado Novo was established in 1937.[75] Under this system, *sindicatos* were created, funded by a trade union tax. (All wage earners are taxed the equivalent of one day's pay per year.) They were to represent the interests of the workers and provide them with government liaison while also serving as conduits for state welfare services—in lieu of trade unions. Their leaders thus held welfare services, government liaison functions, and access to

---

[69] Ibid., pp. 141–146.

[70] Ibid., p. 106.

[71] Ibid., p. 159.

[72] Ibid., pp. 166, 193–194.

[73] Ibid., pp. 171–181.

[74] Payne, *Labor and Politics in Peru,* pp. 120–121.

[75] Kenneth Paul Erickson, "Corporatism and Labor in Development," in *Contemporary Brazil: Issues in Economic and Political Development,* ed. H. Jon Rosenbaum and William G. Tyler (New York: Praeger, 1972), pp. 139–166. Sylvia Ann Hewlett, *The Cruel Dilemmas of Development: Twentieth Century Brazil* (New York: Basic Books, 1980), pp. 185–201.

state patronage within their grasp, and did not need to worry about competition from competing trade unions. Prior to 1964, strikes were prohibited and all labor disputes had to be settled through the labor courts (or often through the Ministry of Labor putting pressure on employers in face of threat of an illegal strike). When inflation periodically brought a precipitous lowering of the real value of earnings, strikes were threatened and wages raised. A new breed of labor leaders emerged in the early 1960s who, looking beyond the mere personal profits that had satisfied their predecessors, were anxious to establish an independent base of power for labor. When the liberal João Goulart ascended to the presidency he opened the door for them. A new law gave labor one-third of the seats in all social service agency governing councils (which controlled 100,000 patronage appointments). A series of crippling strikes which the *sindicatos* directed between 1961 and 1964 helped provoke the military coup of 1964 against Goulart. The new military regime has retained the *sindicato* system, but screens it much more carefully to see that radical individuals do not achieve leadership or patronage jobs. It has held wages tight, but expanded social services to union members. Hence, through a series of regimes, the Brazilian government has retained patron-client ties with the labor leadership.

Further discussion of Brazil may be found on p. 151.

Colombia has maintained competition between left and right political parties, and unions play a role in this struggle. Labor leaders enjoy both considerable economic mobility and political influence; many become congressmen.[76] The government has given unions in heavy industry considerable bargaining power; many leaders have access to foreign travel and scholarships. In turn, the two largest labor federations tend to be both anticommunist and antirightist.[77] Catholic clergy have supported unionization in the countryside, and several thousand acres of land have been distributed to peasants in areas where rural violence erupted. Liberal governments have depended upon active labor support to gain and keep power; moderate governments can depend upon a broader coalition and so are less in need of union support. During periods of Liberal government, real wages of unionized workers have risen markedly. This labor movement has probably benefited from the relative instability of rule in its nation. It achieves concessions, however, by its close tie to the Liberal Party. As in the other examples, the labor movement remains better organized than most other public groups. Its members are in a position to achieve larger and steadier gains than their nonunionized social peers. Its leaders lie closer to the centers of power in the major network than do most of their social peers. Yet organized labor constitutes only a small percentage of the total population.

Trade unions have some unique organizational skills which put them close to the ranks of the major network. They can organize workers to improve pro-

---

[76] Miguel Urrutia, *The Development of the Colombian Labor Movement* (New Haven, Conn.: Yale University Press, 1969), p. 142.

[77] Ibid., p. 255.

ductivity. They can also help steer disaffected peasants and workers from stances of revolt into movements that can be controlled from the center. But their rank and file perform the classic functions of minor network clients—providing resources that will produce capital.

In developing nations, then, patron-client ties provide a minor network of people with jobs, wage increases, social services, payments for commodities, parcels of land, homesites, and personal income. They provide a major network of people with investment opportunities and capital, developmental expertise, and the ability to exert political pressure. The minor network tends to comprise many more individuals than does the major network. Members of the minor network risk displacement if they do not provide the major network with what it requires; so long as they do so, their behavior is difficult to regulate. Most people are not a part of either network. The systems of reciprocity within the minor network have weakened as the complexity of its relationship with the major network has increased, so that those at the bottom who supply the steady influx of labor and material receive the most intermittent and uncertain flow of benefits in return.

THE MILITARY-MARKETING-MINING-MANUFACTURING COMPLEX

We have seen how reciprocal relationships among individuals in developing nations are used by major economic and political elites to tie together hierarchical political machines incorporating a minor network of functionaries to supply the leaders with political and economic supports. It remains for us to examine in greater detail how this major network operates. We argue in this section that politicians, bureaucrats, businesspeople, and military leaders who compose the major network tend to set themselves apart as a separate social system. That separate system has such strong symbiotic tendencies that no sector of it can be ignored in formulating national policy. A legislature composed of individuals from outside that system is likely to have little power. A president, whether civilian or military, cannot afford to ignore peers within this social system. Aside from the need to reward its clients within the minor network, this social system has few constraints to force it to share the resources which flow upward to it through the clientage system. So there is little redistribution within these nations. Most of the surplus passes to foreign investors with whom the major networks set up working relationships (and who are discussed more thoroughly in Chapters 6 through 8) or are circulated within the social system of the major network. Those few resources that get passed downward are devoured by the minor network. Even a government that wanted resources to move past the minor network into the hands of the general populace would not have the power to get them there.

Major Networks and Capital Cities

To understand this strange contradiction of a political leadership that is so powerful that it can keep most resources for itself and its allies, yet so powerless that it cannot assist its own people, one must comprehend the enormous gulf that separates developing nations and their capital cities.

Capital cities of North Atlantic nations and northern Asia tend to be either commercial centers of minor importance (e.g., Washington, D.C., Bonn, Ottawa, Bern) or major commercial centers that have long been capitals or have played a major role in shaping the cultures of their nations. Of the latter, some in smaller nations are the only major commercial center in their nation (Oslo, Athens) while most are only one of several major commercial centers (Rome, Paris, London, Peking, Tokyo, Moscow, Stockholm, Amsterdam, Vienna, Warsaw, Prague, Brussels, Belgrade). Leaders in these capitals must accommodate the interests of all the commercial centers and of the hinterlands, with which they identify culturally. In contrast, the capitals of developing nations tend to be *new* cities which are *the* major commercial center of their nation. These cities had little to do with shaping their nations' cultures.

In previous chapters we discussed villages, towns, and traditional capitals that date back many centuries and even millenia. These places have not become the capitals of today's developing nations. Today's capitals were generally founded since the fifteenth century as enclaves for foreign trade by merchants who were trying to free themselves from the political hold of traditional villages, towns, and capitals. In addition to becoming the principal centers of trade, these cities have evolved their own social systems which are quite far removed from those in other parts of their nations. *The major networks emerge from within the closed social system of the capital cities; their authoritative allocation of values takes place principally within that closed social system.* In this section we shall survey the origins of these capital cities. We shall then discuss the separation of their social systems and their major networks from the social systems of the rest of the nation. The pattern the following paragraphs show is that in country after country on continent after continent the capital cities are their nation's largest commercial center, are new, and are not traditional ruling centers. This is in contrast to the developed nations, whose capitals tend to be only one of several major commercial centers or not a major commercial center at all, and are generally old and closely identified with the nation's cultural and political traditions.

Often the capital of a developing nation is a city originally established by foreign traders. *Manila* was founded in 1571 by Spanish missionaries. *Bangkok* became the administrative center of Siam after the fall of Ayuthia in 1767; it was then a small fort surrounded by trading houses. *Djakarta* was established as a Dutch fort (then called Batavia) in 1619; the former great capital of Java, Djogjakarta, is now a tourist town. *Rangoon* became the capital of the last line of Burmese kings in 1753; it was transformed into a modern city after British ascendancy in 1852. *Singapore* was founded by British in 1819 on a nearly vacant island, and *Kuala Lumpur* began as a mining center in the 1870s. All these capitals are the major commercial and industrial cities in their respective nations. Among the principal nations of Southeast Asia, only three present capitals are traditional capitals: *Phnom Penh* (Cambodia) which superseded Angkor Wat as the Khmer capital in the fifteenth century; *Vientiane* (Laos), founded in 1707 as capital of a small Lao kingdom and chosen as capital of the French Protectorate in 1899; and *Hanoi,* which was already in the seventh century the capital from which the Chinese imposed their rule over Tonkin. These cities are now major commercial and trading centers.

New Delhi first became important when it was made the capital of the Moghul Empire in the sixteenth century.[78] It was sacked in 1739 and then receded in prominence until it was revived by the British in 1912 as an interim capital and began to grow. Today it is a major industrial city of India, conveniently located halfway between the major British-founded port cities of Bombay and Calcutta and in the heart of the chief region for commercial agriculture. *Islamabad,* a new town built since independence to house Pakistan's capital, is not a major commercial center but is located within the agriculturally dominant Punjab region and near Rawapindi, military headquarters of the army.[79] The capital of Sri Lanka, formerly Ceylon, is not the ancient Anaratapura, but the city of *Colombo* which grew principally out of a sixteenth century Portuguese trading fort. *Dacca,* capital and chief commercial city of Bangladesh, became a Moghul capital in the seventeenth century. The only continuing indigenous capital in this region is *Katmandu,* Nepal, which was founded in 723 A.D. and has served as a capital much of the time since.

The Muslim territories surrounding the Mediterranean deviate somewhat from the pattern; here the present capitals tend to be traditional capitals. *Kabul* (Afghanistan), *Amman* (Jordan), *Damascus* (Syria), *Cairo, Tripoli* (Libya), *Tunis,* and *Algiers* all have long histories—ranging from before the time of Abraham to the sixteenth century—as the capitals of sultans, beys, and various Muslim leaders, as well as earlier rulers. Concomitant with this role, however, they were also important centers for trade, dating back to Phoenician times in many instances. The Muslim religion, from Muhammad on, has been closely associated with trade. Muslim leaders tended to be semi-nomadic and involved in major trading operations. So it is not unnatural that their traditional capitals should already have been major trading centers. Muslims, in short, began the major expansion of commerce which Europeans and Chinese were to extend more thoroughly after the sixteenth century. Hence, in Muslim areas it was easier to adapt traditional capitals into centers controlled by independent commercial interests. Those Middle Eastern nations that have modernized most rapidly, however, have switched to newer capitals. *Teheran* (Iran) became a capital in 1788. The ancient capital of *Baghdad,* home of the Arabian Nights tales, began to decline shortly after these tales were written; by 1638, it had only 14,000 inhabitants. It was revived when the British created a new capital there in 1920. *Riad,* the capital of Saudi Arabia, only became important when a Muslim reformist movement began there early in the nineteenth century. Today this oasis is a nodal point of trade. *Beirut,* an important trading city since Phoenician times, only became a political capital in this century. In 1920, Kemal Ataturk set up *Ankara,* a small village that had once been an important capital, as his capital

[78] It had been headquarters for invading foreign Muslim rulers from 1196 onward.

[79] The British founded it as a major military post in 1849. It commands the road to Kashmir and the Himalaya passes and is of vital strategic importance.

for Turkey. Today it is over half the size of Istanbul. In choosing its capital, Morocco by-passed its two major traditional dynastic capitals, Fez and Marrakesh, in favor of *Rabat,* founded by pirates in the seventeenth century.

In the remainder of Africa, the trend is toward new capitals that are also the principal commercial centers. *Dar-es-Salaam* (Tanzania) was still a small fishing village (founded 1862) when occupied by the Germans in 1884. *Niamey* (Niger) was a small town on the Niger River when the French came late in the nineteenth century. *Gaborone* (Botswana) was founded in 1890 along the railroad line. *Addis Ababa* (Ethiopia) was founded in 1887 as a capital for the emperor. *Khartoum* (Sudan) was founded in 1822 as a trading center. *Mogadishu,* the capital of Somalia, was founded as a trading port by Arab colonists in the seventh century and only became involved as a political center when the Italians purchased it in 1905. *Nairobi,* capital of Kenya, was founded in 1899 by the British as a railhead camp. *Lusaka,* capital of Zambia, grew out of the wilderness as a trade center early in the twentieth century. *Lilongwe* (Malawi) was founded by European planters in 1880. *Salisbury* (Zimbabwe) was founded in 1890 as a British fort. *Cape Town,* parliamentary capital of the Republic of South Africa, was established in 1652 as a supply station for the Dutch East India Company. (Pretoria, administrative capital, was founded in 1855.) *Brazzaville* (Republic of Congo) was founded by the French in 1880 near the mouth of the Congo River. Directly across the river, *Kinshasa,* capital of Zaire, was started as Leopoldville in 1887. Men freed from a slave ship founded *Libreville* (Gabon) in 1849. The French created *Yaounde* (Cameroon) in 1888. *Fort-Lamy* (Chad) was founded in 1900 and *Bangui* (Central African Republic) in 1890. *Bamako* (Mali) began its role as a major trading center after European occupation in 1883. When selecting its capital, Nigeria by-passed all the major ancient capitals located within its boundaries in favor of two coastal islands along its western border. These islands once housed a Yoruba town that began to grow rapidly under the impetus of the slave trade in the fifteenth century and became the modern city of *Lagos.* A few miles away, *Porto Novo,* which grew out of a seventeenth century Portuguese trading post, serves as the capital of Benin. Throughout the remainder of the coast, it is port cities that serve as the capitals: *Abidjan,* Ivory Coast (built by the French in the early 1920s); *Monrovia,* Liberia (founded in 1822 by the American Colonization Society); *Bissau,* Guinea-Bissau (founded in 1687 by the Portuguese); *Maputo,* Mozambique (founded as a trading town in the late nineteenth century); *Luanda,* Angola (founded in 1575 by the Portuguese); *Freetown,* Sierra Leone (founded in 1787 by British abolitionists); *Conakry,* Guinea (occupied by the French in 1887); *Dakar,* Senegal (centered around a French fort built in 1857); and *Banjul,* Gambia (founded by the British in 1816). *Nouakchott,* Mauritania, was still a village when it became the capital in 1958.

Nearly all of these African capitals are the principal centers of foreign trade in their nations; a very few of them are rivaled by a second commercial center similar in size. Nearly all lie near the coast or along a strategic trade route. None were ever capitals of traditional political systems. In all of black Africa, only four modern capitals also served as traditional capitals: *Kampala,* Uganda, was capital of Buganda; *Ougadougu,* Upper Volta, capital of the Mosse Empire from the twelfth century, was captured by the French in 1896; *Tananarive,* on the island Malagasy Republic, became the kingly residence in 1797; and *Accra,* Ghana, was a village capital of a native kingdom when Danish, British, and Dutch forts were first built there in the seventeenth century. Each is largest city and principal commercial center in its nation.

Mexico City sits on the site of Montezuma's capital which Cortez destroyed before he began his own city. This coincidence of sites is a notable exception to the Latin American pattern. In Guatemala, a center of Maya civilization, the present capital (*Guatemala City*) was founded as a new town in 1776. *Lima,* the capital of the country (Peru) that occupies most of the former Inca territories, was founded on uninhabited land by Pizarro in 1535. *Tegucigalpa,* Honduras, was founded as a center for Spanish gold and silver mining in the sixteenth century. *Managua,* Nicaragua, was founded in 1855 as a compromise between two other feuding Spanish capitals. *San Salvador* was established early in the sixteenth century. *Panama City* was founded by 1519; *Bogotá,* Colombia, in 1538; *San José,* Costa Rica, around 1738; and *Caracas,* Venezuela, in 1567—all by the Spanish. *Montevideo,* Uruguay, stems from a Portuguese fort constructed in 1717. The Dutch founded (under another name) *Georgetown,* capital of Guyana. *Asunción,* Paraguay, was founded by Spaniards in 1536 as a trading center; similarly with *Buenos Aires,* Argentina, in 1580; and *Santiago,* Chile, in 1541. *La Paz, de facto* capital of Bolivia, was founded by the Spanish in 1548.

Each of these is the largest city in its country and the unchallenged commercial center. Brazil's experiment with a deviation from this pattern by its construction of a wilderness capital of *Brazilia* does not so far seem to be a success; principal political transactions continue to be made in the megalopolis of Rio de Janeiro (founded by Portuguese in 1567) and São Paulo (founded 1554). Only Ecuador has a traditional capital: *Quito,* a former divisional capital of the Inca Empire (though the port of Guayaquil, founded in 1535, serves as chief commercial and administrative center).

There is a consistency, then, in the pattern of siting current capital cities in developing nations, a consistency that does not jibe with the pattern of capital cities in Europe and North America. They are new commercial centers not associated with traditional political centers. The new trading classes found it comfortable to live neither in traditional villages nor in kingly capitals. So they founded towns of their own, accessible to shipping and raw material and often far from centers of culture and agriculture. The life in these new towns was much different from that in villages and older towns. While people still clustered into racially homogeneous neighborhoods, a variety of racial groups from varying parts of the world found themselves living side by side. Many foreigners with key roles in community life lived in their midst. Extended families generally disintegrated. Intermarriage among the groups created new races (mestizos, Eurasians, Baba Chinese, etc.) who had to develop new cultural moorings. A small segment of the populace began to accumulate wealth which dwarfed even that of the indigenous rulers. European languages started to rival indigenous languages in importance. The great majority of inhabitants found themselves involved in nonagricultural pursuits. Their interest in the countryside focused less on the people living there than on opportunities for mining, commercial crops, and commodities trading.

These cities are not the site of any great cultural renaissance; nor are they deculturated. Their inhabitants are better described as parochial than cosmopolitan. There are few great artists and thinkers; these are cities dominated by commercial interests. Even those who work in the large downtown office buildings often prefer to live among their own racial group, and to eat the traditional food of their ancestors for their evening meal at home. When they occasionally visit a rural cousin they feel at home; a visitor at the reunion might notice great similarities in the temperaments of all present. In fact, this continuity aids in the preservation of the patron-client networks. But salaried inhabitants of the cities have few social interactions with those outside the city, save, perhaps, for some immediate relatives. They become attached to the physical comforts of the city, and enjoy the company of those of similar educational attainment. Unlike their rural relatives, they are (thanks to proximity, language skills, and education) able to communicate easily with other residents of the capital with similar social standing, regardless of race.

In the United States, national politicians are constantly aware that the power resides "out there" with groups scattered about the nation. "It isn't the mood in Washington that's important; the mood in Dayton, Ohio, is more important."[80] China is a highly decentralized nation, with great power in regional committees. Leading Japanese commercial and political leaders reside in a number of cities. Regional and local politicians play key roles in European politics. In developing nations, the power seems to reside to a greater extent within the capital itself. In many ways, when one speaks of the political environment of a developing nation, one is speaking more of the capital city (and perhaps one or at most two additional cities) than of the nation as a whole. Some of the national leaders of developing nations come from rural areas; virtually all have become exposed to the capital city by the time they are in their formative years. Educational institutions, both civilian and military, are usually an important part of their road to power. One seldom encounters a chief executive of a developing nation who has not acquired an education past secondary school, command of a European language, and extensive contacts in the capital city before acceding to power.[81] Many leaders have attended universities in Europe or the United States. This is true even of traditional rulers.[82] They may retain privileges and wealth, but unless they pass through the formative experiences

---

[80] Richard Scammon, "Today Show," NBC, November 7, 1973.

[81] Of the 101 heads of state in developing nations as of January 1, 1974, on whom I could find data, 32 were military men, 18 were members of the aristocracy, and 50 were civilians. The great majority of the nonaristocrats—civilian and military—would appear to derive from middle-class homes. I was able to find information on the educational backgrounds of 61 of the 101. All 61 had exposure to higher education, with 30 of them attending school in Europe or the United States, and nearly all the remainder attending schools taught in European languages. As of January 1, 1980, there were 30 military men, 15 members of the aristocracy, and 69 civilians. Angola, Zimbabwe, Mozambique, Guinea-Bissau, and a number of islands had achieved nationhood in the interim.

[82] Of the 30 leaders mentioned in the previous footnote as attending school in Europe or the United States, 7 are aristocrats, 20 civilians, and 3 military men. Two of the aristocrats, 17 civilians, and 12 military men were educated in their home countries or nearby states. I could not find this kind of information for the other 40 leaders.

mentioned, they are unlikely to take on the paramount leadership positions.[83] Most modern leaders have emerged from the trading and professional classes of the city or from the families of more affluent rural landowners.

Leading civil servants also tend to be recruited from the capital cities. Colonial powers established (sometimes early, sometimes only shortly before independence) high schools, medical schools, law schools, and colleges in their colonies to develop middle-level bureaucrats, doctors, lawyers, clerks, and managerial talent. These institutions are usually located in the major city and draw much of their student body from the secondary schools of that city. A similar phenomenon occurred in countries that modernized outside a colonial setting (e.g., Latin American, Thailand). And civil servants do not like to be stationed away from the capitals and the conveniences to which they have become accustomed. Bureaucratic organizations tend to cluster their staff in the capital. Capital cities have the best schools, the most doctors, the best entertainment, and the greatest selection of consumer goods.[84]

Military academies are located outside capital cities with greater frequency than universities and may include more rural-born individuals within their student bodies. Their curricula, however, encompass modern subjects and their profession pulls them away from parochial attachments to home communities. Significantly, most military personnel derive directly from upper- and middle-class urban backgrounds (i.e., the patron-client networks), and only a fractional minority come from either rural aristocracy or peasant homes (the social classes discussed in Chapters 2 and 3).[85] Hence, the military—more than the civil service

---

[83] The nations referred to in footnote 81 as being headed by members of the aristocracy are Bahrain, Bhutan, Jordan, Kuwait, Laos, Morocco, Nepal, Oman, Qatar, Saudi Arabia, Tonga, Lesotho, Swaziland, Botswana, and Tanzania. The first thirteen are actual kingdoms; the latter two are republics whose elected leaders are offsprings of chiefs or aristocracy. The eight leaders on whom I could find information all had university educations.

[84] Of thirty developing nations surveyed in 1964, the best distribution of physicians was in Colombia, with 7.4 physicians per 10,000 population in the capital and large cities, and 3.8 in rural areas. The worst was Ethiopia with 3.3 and 0.1. Michael Lipton, *Why Poor People Stay Poor* (London: Temple Smith, 1977), p. 448. In 1964 Teheran contained 33 percent of the secondary school students, 34 percent of all literates, 69 percent of those with any college education, 73 percent of university students, 77 percent of hospital beds, 43 percent of cinemas, 62 percent of passenger cars, 71 percent of telephones, and 56 percent of all factory workers in Iran—yet it contained only 9 percent of Iran's population. Marvin Zonis, *The Political Elite of Iran* (Princeton, N.J.: Princeton University Press, 1971), pp. 139-140.

[85] José Nun, "The Middle Class Military Coup," in *The Politics of Conformity in Latin America,* ed. Claudio Veliz (London: Oxford University Press, 1967), pp. 71-77, reports that most authorities agree that most of today's officers in Latin America are recruited from the middle classes, and even those from rural areas tend to be from professional or business families or the sons of landowners. Alfred Stepans, *The Military in Politics: Changing Patterns in Brazil* (Princeton, N.J.: Princeton University Press, 1971), says that Brazilian army officers are recruited mostly from urban lower middle-class families; few have working-class, peasant, or upper-class origins. Surveying a sample of fifty-three nations throughout the developing world, Morris Janowitz, *The Military in the Political Development of New Nations* (Chicago: University of Chicago Press, 1964), pp. 49-55, found a steady tendency for military officerships to be moving from the hands of aristocratic or landed gentry groups (or, sometimes in colonial settings, minor tribal groups) into middle-class hands, with educational achievement as a criterion for selection. He found a disproportionate recruitment from among sons of small landholders, teachers, civil servants, and military officers. These results are echoed in other studies. See also John J.

and high civilian government officialdom—provides a social link between rural and urban sectors. Yet this is far from being a link between the traditional and modern orders. Save for a very small percentage, officers derive from families who have already become modernized, whether in urban or rural settings. They are as uncomfortable among the wealthy as they are among the unmodernized poor.

> In oligarchical societies the soldier is a radical; in societies dominated by the middle class the officers act as arbitrators among middle class groups; and when mass political participation is in sight the soldier protects the existing political order.[86]

The governmental elite, then—political leaders, bureaucracy, and military officers—is closely identified with the city and with families involved in modernizing activities. In addition, most major industries, banks, and export firms are in the capital city. Most white- and blue-collar workers and professional people live there along with many of the larger landowners.

Major Networks in Action

With the national leaders this cut off from the nation one would think the rest of the country would have a field day—they could settle their own affairs and tell the capital to get lost. This is not what happens. For, while the major network resides in the capital city, much of the minor network does not. And the major network can furnish that minor network with whatever resources it needs to keep the rest of the country under control.

In the United States if some individuals were unhappy because, say, they were only making 12¢ an hour, or their family was starving, and the government was giving them no assistance, they might join a group to protest. The group might get financial support from wealthy sympathetic people, organize public demonstrations that would be covered by the media, and support sympathetic candidates for political office. If the government should interfere, they could take their case to the courts. In developing nations this cannot happen. If dissatisfied individuals are associated with unions or neighborhood leaders already a part of the minor network, the government may wink at their activities; they are under control. But if they are associated with people the government does not trust, the government could order the group to cease having meetings, putting out publications, and functioning in any way. It might bring group members in for torture sessions. It might hire someone to assassinate the group's leaders, or it might choose to arrest them and put them away—temporarily or permanently—in a more formal manner. Here is a more complete list of some of

---

Johnson, ed., *The Role of the Military in Underdeveloped Countries* (Princeton, N.J.: Princeton University Press, 1962), all selections; Eric A. Nordlinger, "Soldiers in Mufti: The Impact of Military Rule Upon Economic and Social Change in the Non-Western States," *American Political Science Review* 64, no. 4 (December 1970): 1131–1148, including footnote references pages 1131–1133; and Uma O. Eleazu, "The Role of the Army in African Politics: A Reconsideration of Existing Theories and Practices," *Journal of Developing Areas* 7 (January 1973): 275–277.

[86] Nordlinger, "Soldiers in Mufti," p. 1144, interpreting Samuel P. Huntington.

the coercive techniques commonly used by governments of developing nations to keep their people in line:

1. Compulsory union membership in government-sponsored union federations; laws against strikes;
2. Security clearance as a precondition for enrolling in an institution of higher education either at home or abroad; purges of faculty; cabinet ministers becoming chancellors of universities while still in office;
3. Registration of all publications, periodical or occasional; restrictions on import of publications;
4. Government liaison with the press to suggest which stories should and should not be covered, etc.;
5. Suits against newspapers for carrying improper material;
6. Government-owned radio and television;
7. Police clearance of all gatherings of ten (or more) persons;
8. Outlawing of political parties founded by individuals who are not members of the major network;
9. Outlawing of all opposition parties;
10. Limits on which candidates opposition parties may run for office;
11. Co-option of former opposition leaders into the ruling party;
12. Preventive detention without trial for those whom the government deems to be involved in improper activities; torture; deportation;
13. Death penalties for broadly-defined treason; "death squads" hired informally to gun down political opponents;
14. Prime Ministers personally selecting all electoral candidates;
15. "Permanent" dissolutionments of parliament and/or cancellation of elections;
16. Public referenda giving the Prime Minister power to rule without limitation under a suspended constitution;
17. Military intervention to remove a Prime Minister from office and assure his swift replacement by a more friendly civilian rival;
18. Military takeover of government, involving the killing and deportation of certain key leaders in the previous regime followed by a reorganization incorporating other individuals who had been involved in the previous regime.

In western Europe and North America any of these activities would be either impossible or highly controversial. Constitutional and legal traditions and opposition from strongly entrenched middle-class groups discourage these tactics. In the Soviet Union and China such techniques are permissible, but they must ordinarily be used with caution against those in party circles who have strong popular followings in their home regions. In developing nations such traditions simply do not exist. Ironically, indigenous legal traditions that did limit the powers of rulers were overthrown by the more recent introduction of highly flexible versions of Western law and by the disintegration of indigenous political systems. Civil-libertarian intellectuals are neither numerous nor in a position to organize opposition. The courts are under control of government in the capital city, and clan groups capable of organizing resistance at the local level have long ago lost their grip. Others trying to organize opposition would find their followers easily scattered after they were arrested.

The only groups with sufficient resources to protect themselves against such activities are large business organizations and the military; this is what insures their position as members of the major network. These institutions will use their respective sources of power to protect themselves against one another and to protect any clients they might have. Beyond this, they are likely to raise little objection to the use of these techniques. Anyone in the society who is not personally needed at the moment to round up raw materials, labor, or political support is fair game—even bureaucrats, politicians, and occasional cliques of businesspeople or military officers who have offended their peers. Lesser clients who could easily be replaced with other lesser clients are also vulnerable to attack. As we shall see in the next chapter, there is little danger of mass revolt from the bottom.

When all sectors of the major networks are generally satisfied, and a minimum minor network of patron-clients is being supported, it is often possible to get by using few coercive techniques. But this is merely a sign that centralized control is operating efficiently (or, perhaps, that the regime is about to topple into the hands of someone who will be more willing and able to use the techniques). When all sectors of the patron-client network are content, that network is capable of imposing its will on the rest of the nation. When they are not, the networks will try to see that all sectors become content. In either case, they are free to ignore the wishes of other citizens. Between them, they share the means to keep everyone else in line.

In many developing nations civilian regimes have alternated with periods of military takeover (e.g., Algeria, Syria, Burma, Dahomey, Ghana, Iraq, Thailand, Togo, Uganda, Upper Volta, Yemen, Libya, Bolivia, Brazil, Burundi, Dominican Republic, Guatemala, Honduras, Indonesia, Nigeria, Pakistan, Peru, Sierra Leone, Sudan, and Argentina, to name a few). In others, there has been relatively unbroken rule by the same civil or military leader (e.g., Jordan, Tunisia, Saudi Arabia, Kuwait, Haiti, Bhutan, Cuba, Kenya, Malawi, Tanzania, Singapore) or political party (e.g., India, Vietnam, Mexico, Gabon Republic, Malaysia). Most regimes, even kingdoms and military-ruled states, govern in conjunction with a legislature. Most of these nations (even kingdoms and military-ruled states) allow political parties, sometimes only one, sometimes two or several. It is extremely rare to find instances of one political party succeeding another in executive office as the result of an election. When this has happened (in the Philippines, Brazil, Chile, Argentina, Venezuela, the Dominican Republic, Turkey, Guatemala, Nicaragua, and Sri Lanka), it has usually been a momentary aberration from one of these norms.

Regardless of what manifestations are in effect, however, developing nations tend to remain under the continuing control of a small coterie of men and women in the capital city, including military officers, civilian politicians, civil servants, and major economic elites (including labor leaders and landowners). In order to keep their ranks in order, and to facilitate their relations with the minor network, the major networks create political coalitions. Such coalitions survive military coups, "one-man rule", and attempts by political parties or legislatures to impose their will in an unwanted manner. They constitute the true government. All else is window dressing. We shall look briefly at four such coalitions, and then at four more in greater detail.

Discussion of Iran is continued from p. 89.

Today's elites in Iran have their roots in the nineteenth century. Then the most powerful figures tended to be members of the royal family with their governorships around the country, *tukuldar* tax collectors, large traditional landowners, tribal leaders, and religious leaders. In Teheran, some merchants were making new fortunes from selling opium for legal drugs, tobacco, cotton, rugs, nuts, and dried fruit to Europe, and a salaried class of government bureaucrats was also rising. They felt themselves in competition with the old elites. The Shah found he could accumulate large amounts of money for himself by granting monopolies on trading and mining rights to European businesspeople which he proceeded to do. The issue came to a head when he granted a tobacco concession to a British firm and began demanding that Teheran merchants sell all their tobacco through his firm. This naturally upset the merchants, as it did large landowners who had been left out of this and other concessions.

The religious elites were concerned that much of their land was being allowed to fall into private hands, and that the western contacts and loose morals of the royalty were leading the country away from Islamic principles. They joined forces with the merchants and called for a boycott on smoking. Smoking virtually ceased, and the Shah withdrew the concession. He was later forced to allow a parliament, which was dominated by landowners and the new urban leaders. Trying to find a balance between new forces and old, he later turned to Cossack troops to quell tribal uprisings and keep the peace. An Iranian-born officer in one of these units, with the aid of some members of parliament and the British, overthrew the Shah in 1925 and declared himself Reza Shah Pahlevi. He reenforced his alliance with the merchants, intellectuals, and bureaucrats by reducing (but not completely eliminating) the landownings of the former Shah's family, allowing newer elites to purchase government land, breaking up the foreign concessions except in oil, setting up Teheran-based government monopolies in which the elites there were given a part which would take over from the former concessions, formally registering the ownership rights of large landowners, and encouraging mechanization of the larger holdings.

After World War II it was becoming evident that Iran's economic future would be dominated by oil in the hands of the foreign concessions, that the tone of rule was secular (including repression of religious activities), and that the peasant was not benefitting from modernization. This helped forge the parliamentary alliance among urban elites, religious leaders, and left-wing groups which elected Mosaddeq to the prime-ministership. Mohammed Reza Shah Pahlevi (Reza's son, who had succeeded when his father abdicated) was deeply disturbed by this because Mosaddeq wanted to end the British oil monopoly. He engineered a coup to depose Mosaddeq, and turned the oil concessions over to seven oil companies, mostly American. He set up a strong military organization and SAVAK, a secret police force designed to seek out political dissidents. He also took land away from religious leaders and landowners who had opposed him and gave it to local leaders who would support him and to foreign agribusinesses via the White Revolution discussed later.

Local partners were established for all foreign enterprises, including many of the nation's most prominent families. But business deals began to take place within an increasingly closed circle, and SAVAK's surveillance became more oppressive with time. The alliance of urban elites, religious leaders, and the left was revitalized among discontented merchants, religious leaders, expropriated landowners, landless peasants, intellectuals, and members of prominent families who were being left out of business deals or had been harmed by SAVAK. When the Ayatollah Khomeini proved capable of attracting massive street crowds, the Shah exiled him. He provided a natural focus for the discontent. The Shah was overthrown. Leaders of the army, SAVAK, and the Shah's inner circle were executed. A prime minister was chosen from among the urban elites, and a parliament dominated by religious leaders. With dependence on oil revenues now very great, it was not easy to remove foreign concessions from the scene. People who had been shunted to the fringes of the major and minor networks were, however, able to reassert themselves to be included as local partners in those concessions, to regain access to the land market, and (in the case of the religious leaders) to reassert religious and economic roles in their communities. The concessions and landholdings taken from the Pahlevis provided considerable assets for the religious leaders to redistribute, even though the cash had been taken out of the country. For instance, the Shah had received payments from nearly all mosques in the country, and his family had partnerships in many businesses. Meanwhile, most major members of the major network would retain their position and would be needed to return the nation's flow of income.

This coalition of urban elites, religious leaders, and leading landowners has continued to function through all these regimes within the *dowreh* system. In Iran, as in many Middle Eastern countries, the busy bazaars serve as more than market places; here rumors circulate and political propaganda is disseminated. Those in the middle and upper classes feel a bit aloof from both the bustle and rumors of the bazaar. For them the *dowreh* is more important. The word *dowreh* can be translated as cycle: a cyclical meeting which gathers periodically, rotating the place of meeting. A *dowreh* usually contains twelve or more members, each of whom belong to perhaps two or three other *dowrehs*. There are professional *dowrehs*, gambling *dowrehs*, religious *dowrehs*, student, family, intellectual, and former-classmate *dowrehs*. *Dowrehs* usually meet on a weekly or monthly basis, in a social setting, to exchange ideas.[87]

Teheran also contains over 2,000 coffeehouses, each frequented by its own clientele. Only a fraction of urbanites belong to these organizations. Yet, since the turn of the century when political party organization first began, it was closely connected to these organizations. The Soviet-sponsored *Tudeh,* the British-sponsored National Will Party, and Mosaddeq's movement were all little more than chains of cooperating *dowrehs*. In 1960, the ruling Shah of Iran decided to experiment with national elections. The *dowreh*-based National Front which emerged for this exercise began to grow in popularity to the point that it had to be limited to running approved candidates.

---

[87] William Green Miller, "Political Organization in Iran: From Dowreh to Political Party," *Middle East Journal* 23, no. 2 (Spring 1969): 159–167; James Alban Bill, *The Politics of Iran: Groups, Classes, and Modernization* (Columbus: Merrill, 1972), pp. 44–51.

In 1963, the Shah created a party of his own. Some 4,500 peasants were transported to the Teheran stadium to inaugurate, via a Peasant's Congress, the New Iran Party. This party took control of most of the seats of the parliament. It commanded the support of peasants, though not, by and large, that of intellectuals, the bureaucracy, and the business community, many of whom continued to support other parties through their *dowrehs*. Yet political control remained the prerogative of a group of elite families. A *dowreh* of technocrats and government officials prepared the program of the ruling party. Every cabinet contained members who formerly belonged to other parties. Every family of consequence had at least one member who was actively opposed to the regime. He could voice some of his family's policy preferences, and the family could intercede to soften his sentence if he went to jail, at least until SAVAK agents became excessive in their operations. These same families have hierarchical economic connections throughout the country, with lower class retainers, faithful supporters, and employees. Here party competition is in a position to remain "within the families" of a few urban elites. It was possible to plan resistance as the Shah's government grew more unpopular, and to create parties after his overthrow so as to elect a new prime minister, Bani Sadr. In the style of the Shah, the religious leaders were able to organize peasant votes to dominate parliament. Also, as with the case of the Shah's parliament, they would depend on the *dowrehs* when drafting legislation. When they deposed Prime Minister Bani Sadr in 1981, they ignored the *dowrehs*. They did so at their own peril. All components of the major network are needed to successfully rule Iran. Command over crowds on Teheran's streets or in its stadium is not enough.

Further discussion of Iran may be found on p. 201.

In Morocco, the ruling monarch supports a number of patronage groups, some of which he encourages to form political parties to compete in the political arena. Should they step out of line, the king can always temporarily withdraw their patronage or help organize another political party to counter them. Or if they should break the law against criticizing the principle of monarchy, they might find themselves facing a show trial. For instance, an editor who quoted a politician as saying. "A people can live without a king, but a king cannot live without a people," found himself in jail for ten months. Another editor who criticized the Minister of Education for his policy of holding back on the Arabization of schools was hit with a heavy fine for "troubling the public order." Those imprisoned can receive amnesty from the king. If people outside the patronage circles make such independent moves, they may be shot by a firing squad. The entire political party system is a client of the king. The few members of this system all have a voice in government—within limits set by the king.[88]

Further discussion of Morocco may be found on p. 307.

---

[88] John Waterbury, "Kingdom-Building and the Control of the Opposition in Morocco: The Monarchical Uses of Justice," *Government and Opposition* 5, no. 1 (Winter 1969–70): 54–66.

When the king of Afghanistan introduced parliamentary government in 1964, he failed to bring in political parties at the same time. Candidates ran as individuals, often drumming up votes by circulating in the bazaar. Few citizens voted in the elections; for instance, only 12,000 of Kabul's 300,000 eligible voters cast a ballot in the 1969 election. One of those elected in this election was the President of the Afghanistan Students' Association, Hafizullah Amin, as the leader of what they called the People's Democratic Party.

The chambers were unorganized and leaderless. Members, who represented every facet of public opinion, had no offices or secretaries. The rule that allowed them to speak for ten minutes on any topic of their choosing made it difficult to consider bills. There was little spirit of compromise, and seldom a quorum. One of the few points of agreement came when the king presented his choice of cabinet officers for confirmation. Without this basic core agreement there could not even be a sitting parliament (with the US$86 monthly salaries to the members). This legislative anarchy made it easy for the king and his political confidantes (most of whom were probably not even in the legislature) to direct the actual formulation of policy without interference from the legislature. Legislative members themselves resisted the introduction of a functioning party system, which probably would have insured their replacement by those with more ability at functioning within an organization.[89] This lack of cohesion facilitated a military coup in 1973 which ousted both king and parliament.

The regimes that followed failed to comprehend that the roots of power lay deeper than what they had seen around the legislature. For instance, the king had worked closely with the land-owning Khans in the south to help them mechanize their agriculture, and helped those in the north make money from trade. The Daoud government failed to create any alliances with Pathan landowners of the mechanized farms to the south, or the Khans who serve as patrons, landowners, and militia organizers in the mountain passes. Daoud placed doctrinaire leftist intellectuals from Kabul into the governorships; they tactlessly antagonized these traditional leaders instead of working with them.[90] In April, 1978, Hafizullah Amin, a Columbia University educated teacher at Kabul University, helped the air force engineer a coup. They killed the former government leaders and installed their own. Within three months, all those affiliated with the Pathan landowners were purged from the Cabinet, which then proceeded to impose land reforms on the north against the wishes of the Khans there. Amin himself was purged for awhile, and then overthrew the other faction, all to the accompaniment of numerous executions. As of April, 1979, eight of the eighteen members of the Cabinet were teachers at the university. The contacts with the countryside were via Kabul leftists and Russian technicians. The Khans resisted the government, accusing it of being anti-Islam and pro-Russian. Early in 1980 the Soviet Union moved in troops, killed the Amin government leaders, and installed still another set of officials unrelated to the Khans or the countryside. Until a govern-

---

[89] Marvin G. Weinbaum, "Afghanistan: Nonparty Parliamentary Democracy," *Journal of Developing Areas* 7, no. 1 (October 1972): 57–64.

[90] Richard S. Newell, "Revolution and Revolt in Afghanistan," *The World Today* 35, no. 11 (November 1979): 432–439.

ment emerges again in Afghanistan that can establish contact with the major and minor networks (or the Russians kill much of the population), Afghanistan will remain an armed camp without government. It is as though the former legislature had tried to rule without the king.

Unlike the three preceding countries, Turkey has a long history of military rule. As early as 1876 Turkish rulers introduced a parliament. The military remained in power, however, until 1938, when a man named Inönü took office as a party leader. With the acquiescence of the military, he was succeeded in 1950 by the leader of the rival Democratic Party. The ensuing economic depression caused the military, the intelligentsia, the bureaucracy, and the press to largely shift their support to the Republican Party. The Democrats tried to suppress their opposition. In 1960 the military took over the government again, killed the Democratic Party premier and outlawed it. They passed the government along in 1961 to a Republican Party-Justice Party coalition under former ruler Inönü. He weathered succeeding years, under shifting coalitions, and presided over a national economic resurgence which increased the size of the urban middle class. In Kemal Karpat's words, the Justice Party Chairman had a large task after his party temporarily gained parliamentary ascendancy in 1965:

> He had to devise a policy within his own party which would satisfy the entrepreneureal business and professional groups' demands for political security and stability necessary for investment and economic development but without alienating the right [rural landholding] wing. . . . Moreover he had to placate the military as well as a variety of intellectuals, all too prone to read reactionary or vindictive motives in Justice Party decisions.

Under Inönü and the multiparty system, control had obviously shifted out of the hands of the military rulers; but the military had carefully cultivated and guided the situation to insure that the urban political elites could retain control of the political process.[91] It would continue to do so. Faced with continuing political agitation, it intervened to change premiers again in 1971 and 1972. When the politicians resisted its attempt to rule by decree over the head of parliament, it declared martial law. The parliament resisted its candidate for president and its attempts to place military men in the political parties. Elections were held in 1973 with eight parties competing; the vote was splintered. Bulent Ecevit, the leader of the People's Party (whose roots are primarily among more modernized middle-class elements in the city) took the premiership and became popular even though the weak ruling coalition failed. By 1978 Ecevit, following in the footsteps of Inönü, took the premiership again, this time as leader of the Republican Party. The election that brought him to office gave the Republican and Justice Parties (with their voting base among rural landowners and urban business and labor elements) 392 of the 432 seats. A high percentage of the deputies tend to be born in the provinces they represent;[92] the top party leaders tend to be from the city.

---

[91] Kemal H. Karpat, "Political Developments in Turkey 1950-70," *Middle Eastern Studies* 8, no. 3 (October 1972): 349-375.

[92] Frederick W. Frey, "Patterns of Elite Politics in Turkey," in *Political Elites in the Middle East,* ed. George Lenczowski (Washington, D.C.: American Enterprise Institute for Public Policy Research, 1975), pp. 60, 63.

Through all this, martial law continues. The military and these urban leaders rule the country.

Iran, Turkey, and Afghanistan have all had major changes in their governmental structures, yet their ruling coalitions have remained largely intact. In Afghanistan the government moved entirely out of the hands of the ruling coalition with the aid of massive direct Soviet military intervention; it was the government, not the coalition, that was isolated from the nation. In Iran, part of the ruling coalition seized power from the rest with the overthrow of Bani Sadr; the rest of that coalition can be expected to cooperate in regaining control of the government.

So developing nations operate with political systems that allocate values principally within a restricted network of patrons and clients. Authority relations between offices and positions (such as bureaucrat and bureaucrat, bureaucrat and citizen, or employer and employee), and market relations among major buyers and sellers are based less upon qualifications, legal obligations, and ability to pay than upon long-standing personal relationships among the participants. Those who are not able or willing to enter into such personal relationships are not in a position to receive the goods and services being exchanged. Those involved in traditional village life find it difficult to enter into such personal relationships because their commitments to all the members and customs of the community (e.g., to share land or food) must supercede any one-to-one relationship they establish with an outsider. A modernized man or woman is likely to find that his or her clientage status interferes with spatial mobility, free speech, and individualistic life style. Hence, the patrons and clients in these systems are neither traditional nor modern. *Two of the principal priorities of governmental leaders are use of combinations of the coercive techniques to assert political control over the populace, and expansion of industry and export agriculture to provide the means to distribute rewards to the major and minor networks.* These political systems can (and must) only reward and integrate those contributing substantially both to the market economy and centralized political control. This is bound to include major industrialists, traders, investors, landowners, and military leaders, and their functionaries (though there may be some choice as to which personalities in each of these sectors will receive the rewards). In most developing nations this is only a minority of the population—people living mostly in the capital city who have only thin roots in the various social systems of the nation. When governments fail to pursue these two priorities, they fall.

With this background, you should be ready to understand the actual dynamics of rule. The following case studies of a military regime, a tight one-party regime, a looser one-party regime, and the oldest multiparty democracy among the developing nations illustrate how rewards tend to flow within the patron-client networks. Think over the themes summarized in the previous paragraph as you read them. Note that the examples are enlightened, forward-looking regimes—not nations with a reputation for backwardness.

The details of rule in the four nations vary. What we are focusing on here is not military organizations or political parties, but the ruling coalitions that stand behind them and can even survive transitions between military and party rule.

Each of these coalitions are closely focused on urban elites (with the exception of the large landowners, who may be city dwellers as well). The social institutions used to build these coalitions are institutions to which only a propertied minority belongs. The purpose of the coalitions is to develop the nation's resources for the benefit of coalition members. One might well call them the military-marketing-mining-manufacturing complexes.

Brazil

Discussion of Brazil is continued from p. 134.

Latin American nations achieved independence decades earlier than most of the nations of Asia and Africa. For a long while the political systems of these nations tended to be dominated by the rural *hacendados* and landowners. Gradually, as the demand for raw materials spread in North America and Europe and expanded trading classes grew in the cities, the power shifted to the elites of the capital cities who controlled that trade. In Brazil, neighboring members of the rural aristocracy formed *juntas* to represent their region, often associating their *junta* with a political party. Some parties allied more with the producers in one region, or of one raw material, and some with another. Thus a change from a Liberal to a Conservative regime meant a shift in the particular regions being represented. The system was moderated by the fact that only active citizens with incomes above a defined minimum had suffrage, and by the power of the emperor (the vestige of aristocracy in the national government, who was sympathetic to rural elites) to intervene if the legislature stepped out of line.

Then in 1930, a military coup placed Getúlio Vargas in power. He swept away the emperor, removed independent state judiciaries, and took steps to end the independence of the state-governing groups. Henceforth, power would be concentrated in the city and away from the landowners. Vargas encouraged the introduction of industry and benefits for the workers and *sindicatos* (see p. 133). As his regime continued into World War II, he discovered that his urban supporters—the workers, the businesspeople, and the middle classes—had conflicts of interest among themselves just as the landowners had disagreed about former regimes. The large corporations and the army feared that he might lean too much toward labor after the war. Under intense pressure from them, he introduced in 1945 a system of free party competition with universal suffrage for all literates.

One of the new parties, the National Democratic Union (UDN), was composed basically of businesspeople, industrialists, bankers, and middle-class groups. The rival Brazilian Labor Party (PTB) and the Social Democratic Party (PSD) included some of the above, but also made a plea for support from organized labor. Since there was universal suffrage, both parties needed backing from the countryside. Paradoxically, the labor-oriented parties (Labor and Social Democratic) sought that support from among the rural aristocracy, while the party of the businesspeople (National Democratic Union) aimed their rhetoric at dissident smallholders and landless rural laborers. This orientation becomes more comprehensible when one remembers that it was initially the urban business elites who had supported Vargas' persistent whittling away of the power of the rural aristocracy. The businesspeople allied with the enemies of the rural aristocracy; the rural aristocracy allied with the enemies of those businesspeople. Also, with the army backing the businesspeople, the rural aristocracy worked closely with the civil bureaucracy. After the elections produced cabinets composed of Labor Party-Social Democratic coalitions, the rural aristocracy took advantage of the coalitions' sympathetic stance to bolster their power. They set up mutual aid groups, called *panelinhas,* with the rural bureaucracy:

> . . . this policy [the *panelinhas*] in its primary form consists in the congregation around each *grand seignor* of a following of dependents in a relationship rather like that obtaining between the Roman *paterfamilias* and his circle of protégés. The landowner receives the votes of his clientele either for himself or, more usually, for his political candidates, and in return dispenses favours, mainly in the form of government employment, pulling the strings as required through his political contacts. In a secondary form of this process, local followings are coordinated to control the political machine of the state and, in a still more advanced tertiary form, the federal administration itself. The final result is a solid organizational pyramid, for which the bartering of political support in exchange for favours dispensed through the state administrative machine serves as the bricks and mortars.[93]

It is unlikely that landowners ever achieved a "solid organizational pyramid"; the point is that with a sympathetic bureaucracy ensconced in various government agencies, the rural landowners could resist national directives that countered their interests. In 1950, backed by labor and the landowners, Vargas won back the presidency as the candidate of the Labor Party. This victory momentarily seemed to bolster the position of his backers. He promptly moved to increase the power of the labor *sindicatos* and nationalized oil drilling (perhaps favoring one sector of the business community at the expense of another). But then he moved his reforms into the bailiwicks of his own backers when he began to explore means to expropriate *latifundios* and reduce the profits being exported by foreign corporations. This apparently roused the ire of too many elites. On August 24, 1954, Vargas committed suicide, opening his suicide note with the statement:

> Once more the forces and interests against the people are newly coordinated and raised against me. They do not accuse me, they insult me; they do not fight me, they slander me and give me no right of defense . . . [94]

Two regimes, more cautious, followed. Janio da Silva Quadros, who took power in 1961, sought to weaken the power of the unions, sent troops to quash protest rallies in the hunger-ridden regions of the Northeast (where a third of all

---

[93] Jaguaribe, "Brazilian Nationalism," p. 177.

[94] John Gerassi, *The Great Fear in Latin America* (London: Collier-Macmillan, 1965), p. 425. Some consider the suicide note a forgery. Even if it was, his death abruptly ended his policy initiatives.

children die before the age of three),[95] and jailed protesting students. But he also fired government featherbedders while refusing to favor friends in replacing them, ordered government prosecutors to expose corruption, and finally in August, 1961, sent to Congress a bill calling for a 30 percent tax on all corporate earnings except those reinvested in the economically depressed Northeast (or those reinvested abroad, which would be subject to a 50 percent tax). He was branded a communist by prominent politicians, warned by the military to change his ways, and somehow ended up on a ship to England from which he wrote a letter of resignation. The army was deployed; students led strikes. After some conflicting orders, the military finally permitted Vice President João Goulart (who was visiting Singapore at the time) to return and assume the presidency. Goulart was a millionaire *latifundista* friendly to land reform (a paradox we shall seek to explain in Chapters 5 and 7). To strengthen his power, he called a national plebiscite (which he won by a vote of five to one) and placed into positions of power friendly military men and labor leaders (who promptly called the crippling strikes; see p. 134). Inflation soared.

At the same time, however, he began to lay the groundwork for the decline of the coalition between labor and the rural landowners. In the poor Rio Grande du Sol region to the south, Goulart's brother-in-law (the Governor) inaugurated a land reform including paid expropriation of a 60,000 hectare estate and an IT&T subsidiary. In 1963 the United States Congress put a proviso in a foreign aid bill forbidding the Alliance for Progress to contribute to any project involving expropriations. Goulart extended the franchise to some three million illiterates. He stated the goal of establishing 2,000 rural *sindicatos* to unionize the rural poor.[96] Finally in 1964 he expropriated all private oil companies and all land within ten kilometers of public thoroughfares. Two weeks later he was removed from power by a military coup.[97]

The military arrested a great many politicians whom they felt to be in opposition to the takeover, and purged universities of opposition voices. They left the legislature sitting and encouraged this body to pass an agrarian reform bill. When the next elections were held, new parties were formed and the candidates were screened by the military officer, Castello Branco, who retained the post of President. The patronage powers that had accrued to both the rural aristocracy and labor under the previous regimes were removed (thus ending the life blood for the Labor-Social Democratic alliance). To appease the landowners, rural peasant organizations were firmly suppressed at the same time. Although the new program emphasizing industrialization and land reform for the agrarian dissidents jibed with that of the former National Democratic Union party, many former Social Democratic Party leaders were given posts in the new ruling party. Opponents of the regime were subject to systematic arrest and torture, imprison-

---

[95] Peter L. Berger, "Policy and Calculus of Pain," in Wilber, *The Political Economy of Development and Underdevelopment,* p. 363.

[96] Robert E. Price, *Rural Unionization in Brazil,* University of Wisconsin Land Tenure Center Research Paper 14 (Madison 1969).

[97] Gerassi, *Fear in Latin America,* pp. 76–99; Paolo Roberto Motta, "Elite Control and Political Participation in the Party System," in Rosenbaum and Tyler, *Contemporary Brazil,* pp. 213–227.

ment, or assassination by informally organized death squads. Between 1964 and 1972 there were reports of 2,000 tortures, hundreds of assassinations, and accumulation of 20,000 political prisoners.[98] The regime of General Figuerido, which came to power in 1979, is attempting to decrease the repression. He has allowed exiles to return home, political parties to reorganize, students and workers to strike, and eliminated torture. This in turn has stimulated terrorist threats and bombings by right wing elements (with supporters in the military high command) who wish to stop the reforms.

In rural areas the land reform programs have not resulted in significant change. Traditional estates have been left essentially intact. "This has been politically expedient," says one author, "because it has left unaffected the regional economic foundation for the rural elite's economic power."[99] Increasing tax rates for underutilized lands have not been rigidly enforced. As a study concludes, "In sum, while land taxation theoretically could increase efficiency of land use in Brazil, in practice the measure may have little effect.[100] The expropriation program (purchase of land with bonds redeemable in twenty years) has been administered under the Ministry of Agriculture, with its many old-line ties with the *latifundistas*. There has been virtually no expropriation. Another author concludes:

> In evaluating the recent history of the agrarian reform issue and pondering the future one is left with the conviction that, faced with a number of social and economic alternatives, the political elite will choose those that serve to maintain the authoritarian system. It is doubtful that a reform of the pattern of land tenure will ever figure among such measures.[101]

The principal rural emphasis has been on mechanization, electrification, road building, and agricultural extension. A new law says that 10 percent of bank credit must go to the rural sector at 75 percent of the usual rate. Nearly all of these loans go to large planters who use them to mechanize their farms (cutting back on the need for farm labor) and to reloan to small farmers at high rates.[102] In the arid and hunger-ridden Northeast, corn, beans, rice and manioc constitute the staples of the diet. In 1976, stores serving Rio de Janiero's poor ran out of black beans, triggering street riots. To feed these urban poor, the government began to import beans from neighboring Chile (whose nutrition problems we shall examine later). In 1979, Brazil imported US$1.5 billion worth of food, and Rio housewives still stood in long lines each day to buy beans.[103]

---

[98] *Allegations of Torture in Brazil* (London: Amnesty International, 1972).

[99] H. Jon Rosenbaum, "Introduction: An Overview," in Rosenbaum and Tyler, *Contemporary Brazil*, p. 23.

[100] William R. Cline, *Economic Consequences of a Land Reform in Brazil* (Amsterdam: North Holland Publishing Company, 1970), p. 167.

[101] Marta Cehelsky, "Redistribution Policy and Agrarian Reform," in Rosenbaum and Tyler, *Contemporary Brazil*, p. 248.

[102] Kenneth D. Frederick, "Agricultural Development and the Rural Northeast," in Rosenbaum and Tyler, *Contemporary Brazil*, p. 290.

[103] Lappé, *Food First*, p. 200; Eul-Soo Pang, "Abertura in Brazil: A Road to Chaos?" *Current History* 80, no. 463 (February 1981): 59.

Yet government subsidies go only to the export crops of sugar, cotton, and hemp. Hence, there has been little increase in the output of staple food crops.[104]

> In summary, current forces and government policies should be expected to bring no major changes in the extensive cultivation of and the dominance of sugar cane in the Zona de Mata; the growth of a relatively small number of prosperous farmers who will supply a growing share of the Northeast agricultural market, using irrigation, fertilizer, and improved seeds; and a rapid growth in the numbers and deterioration in the economic condition of the great majority of farmers in the Agreste and Sertão.[105]

The most noticeable improvements seem to be in the cocoa growing sections of the coastal province of Bahia and along the new Trans-Amazon Highway. In Bahia extensive research has been conducted on new strains of cocoa that will better withstand the climate and diseases of the region. Fertilizer has been distributed extensively. Farmers with a title to their property, the right to vote, and an income tax receipt are entitled to loans for disease control replanting under a new program. During the first half of 1968, 478 farmers whose combined landholdings covered at most some 7 percent of the cocoa area (an average of 150 acres per farmer) received such loans. *Proterra,* a new program founded in 1971, is resettling some 10,000 farmers in territories along the Trans-Amazon Highway, opened by bulldozing the forest to the ground. Left with little soil and vegetation, many of these farms have failed. It is also resettling corporations like Volkswagen, Nestlé, Goodyear, Anderson Clayton, and wealthy Brazilians who have been given concessions to land along the Trans-Amazon Highway in plots ranging from 125,000 to 3.7 million acres apiece.[106] In addition to bulldozing ground for these improvements, the government has also been systematically rounding up Amazon Indians, and many have been killed in battles after they have revolted against being resettled.[107]

To place these figures in perspective, it should be noted that Brazil's Northeast contains over 23 million people. Over 4 million of these are migrants with neither land nor work (not including additional urban unemployed) and some 10 million more are landless rural workers.[108] The drought in 1970 affected over a million persons. In contrast, the government programs to which we have made reference gave new plots of land to only about 10,000 families, while wiping out as many Amazon Indians as that. The main purpose of the settlement program,

---

[104] Peter T. Knight, "Transforming Traditional Agriculture: The Ceplac Experience with Cocoa in Bahia," in Rosenbaum and Tyler, *Contemporary Brazil,* pp. 253–254. Between 1963 and 1969 beef exports rose from 18,500 tons to 79,000 tons; meanwhile the price of beef for Brazilian shoppers rose considerably. Ruy Mauro Marini, "Brazilian Subimperialism," *Monthly Review* 23, no. 9 (February 1972): 17.

[105] Frederick, "Agricultural Development," p. 294.

[106] Lappé, *Food First,* p. 43. For more on foreign investors, see Peter Evans, *Dependent Development: The Alliance of Multinationals, State, and Local Capital in Brazil* (Princeton, N.J.: Princeton University Press, 1979) and David Collier, ed., *The New Authoritarianism in Latin America* (Princeton, N.J.: Princeton University Press, 1979).

[107] Sheldon H. Davis, *Victims of the Miracle* (Cambridge: Cambridge University Press, 1977).

[108] See Josué de Castro, *Death in the Northeast* (New York: Random House, 1966).

in fact, is to colonize the area with a few non-Indian settlers so that the region's vast iron ore, aluminum, molybdenum, lumber, and rock salt resources can more safely be exploited.

The really dramatic changes have been in the industrial and trading sectors. Exports of primary products and industrial goods are rising at a rate of US$100 million per year under the impetus of export tax incentives. With the aid of new semi-public agencies and revenue-sharing with the states, public investment expenditures rose 30 percent in the first four years.[109] Multinational corporations came to control 49 percent of sales and 29 percent of assets in manufacturing.[110] There has been considerable new import-substitution industrialization, including the Northeast (under a tax incentive program); foreign participation in this sector has grown sharply.[111] The factories produce automobiles, refrigerators, television sets, and other such products affordable mainly by the rich.

Despite incentive programs, however, labor intensiveness does not seem to be on the increase, and inflation brought a decline in the real minimum wage[112] of 30 percent between 1960 and 1970. The *Wall Street Journal* reports 900,000 workers in the new factories, two-thirds earning less than the dollar a day that it costs to subsist in the city.[113] One-half of the population in 1968 earned less than 35¢ a day. One researcher reports on his visit to a factory in the Northeast:

> An initial interview at one factory in Recife at first challenged these results. The author was assured that labor absorption was a goal of the firm and that was why less capital intensive techniques were used in the Northeast than in the firm's São Paulo (Center-South) plant. In a later interview, the financial officer of the firm rejected this theory: the production manager had mistaken the author for a SUDENE official and was offering what he thought was most desired.[114]

The Brazilian military regime has expended considerable public relations effort to project an image of progress. That progress, it must be surmised, is largely limited at this point to larger landholders, industrialists, export traders, and their middle-class subordinates. Favored landholders are exempted from laws requiring expropriation of unutilized land; industrialists are exempted from laws requiring labor intensiveness. Both—throughout several past and present regimes—have succeeded in staving off political or legal challenges to their position and in using the political process to enhance their economic positions at the expense of labor and lower income consumers. There is little evidence that this

[109] Jan Peter Wogart, "Mobilizing Resources for Economic Growth: From Inflation to Tax and Debt-Asset Financing," in Rosenbaum and Tyler, *Contemporary Brazil*, p. 172.

[110] United Nations, *Transnational Corporations in World Development: A Reexamination* (New York: United Nations, 1978), p. 273.

[111] Rosenbaum, "Introduction," pp. 20, 23.

[112] Berger, "Policy and Calculus of Pain," in Wilber, *The Political Economy of Development and Underdevelopment*, p. 362.

[113] On the farm, 80 percent of all families earn less than US$50 a year. April 14 and 21, 1972.

[114] Kent Hughes, "Factory Prices, Capital Intensity, and Technological Adaptation," in Rosenbaum and Tyler, *Contemporary Brazil*, p. 132. See also Herman E. Daly, "The Political Economy of Population," in Rosenbaum and Tyler, *Contemporary Brazil*, p. 402.

regime, or previous ones, has benefited small landholders, rural laborers, or urban wage laborers who constitute the great bulk of Brazil's population.[115]

Between 1961 and 1971, the percentage of houses in São Paulo with piped water fell from 72 percent to 56 percent.[116] In 1974, Brazil had the second highest rate of illiteracy in Latin America and one of the worst infant mortality rates.[117] Between 1960 and 1970, the percentage of malnourished children in São Paulo grew from 45 percent to 52 percent. In the nondrought year of 1968, between the winter months of July and December, all of the children born in Amarizi, near Recife, died—of diarrhea, protein and vitamin deficiencies, poor hygiene, and lack of health care. But the number of automobiles in Brazil had risen to seven million by 1979, causing a US$7 billion oil import bill that year.[118] Between 1960 and 1976, the share of the richest 5 percent in national income rose from 28 percent to 38 percent; the share of the richest 1 percent rose from 12 percent to 17 percent. Nearly every other income group lost.[119]

Between 1971 and 1976, investments by multinational corporations in Brazil grew from 2.9 billion to 9 billion dollars, making it one of the most heavily industrialized of the developing nations. This nation was especially attractive to investers because it contained a large population. Few other nations have a large enough population to even be considered for such investment. It is possible to drive through Rio de Janiero and around the countryside, feeling only the vibrant modernity of the 15 percent of the population which constitutes an unusually large middle class for a developing nation. It is too easy to remain unaware of the abject poverty of the other 85 percent. Brazil has been called a Sweden superimposed on an Indonesia.[120] Most developing nations have even more of the Indonesia and even less of the Sweden.

Power in Brazil once resided with a rural land-holding aristocracy who kept the poorer rural dwellers in check through a system of clientage. Then an urban trading and commercial sector grew which, with the support of the army, took power from the landowner. Through the *sindicatos,* they developed power over their clients in organized labor. They produced industries and the export of commodities, such as coffee, to give them an independent financial base.[121] To fight

---

[115] Brazil has a population of 120 million, with around 12 million in São Paolo and Rio de Janiero and 1 million in Recife. As the next chapter indicates, 1.5 percent of farms occupy 50 percent of the land.

[116] Joan Robinson, *Aspects of Development and Underdevelopment* (Cambridge: Cambridge University Press, 1979), p. 118n.

[117] Hewlett, *Cruel Dilemmas of Development,* pp. 122, 127, 170–71, Table 14.

[118] Robert M. Levine, "Brazil: Democracy without Adjectives," *Current History* 78, no. 454 (February 1980): 52.

[119] Hewlett, *Cruel Dilemmas of Development,* Table 13. See also Ronald Müller, "The Multinational Corporation and the Underdevelopment of the Third World," in Wilber, *The Political Economy of Development and Underdevelopment,* pp. 161–162; and Adelman and Morris, *Economic Growth and Social Equity,* p. 244.

[120] Djakarta, the capital of Indonesia, is one of the most wretchedly poor cities in the world, with over a thousand people a day migrating in as squatters. Its most modern sector consists of one street about five blocks long containing a few tall buildings.

[121] *Business Week,* March 27, 1965, reported that a big share of Brazil's wealth lay in the hands of about 100 individuals or families in Rio de Janiero, 150 to 200 in São Paolo, and 50 to 150 in other parts of the country.

back, the large rural landowners made use of their system of patronage to gain control over key elements of the bureaucracy; they also allied with labor in the city to counter the power of the army and industrialists. When labor became ascendant in the city, however, it began to support movements such as land reform which would weaken the power of the large rural landowner. Hence, the large landowner allied with the businesspeople and the army to fight this threat. By turning increasingly to export crops, it became profitable for them to do so. The conflicts involved in this shifting of alliances have weakened the reciprocities owed by either industrialists or landowners toward labor. Government policies to replace these reciprocities have been inadequate. To receive what rewards are left for them, the workers must continue to operate within the clientage system. Most people are left out of it completely. In fact, as Brazil began joining other industrialized nations in experiencing increased inflation, and imports exceeded exports later in the 1970s, many within the new clientage system have found themselves dropped as clients or at least dropping in their standard of living. By 1977 the annual rate of inflation was 40 percent, by 1979, 80 percent,[122] and over 100 percent by 1981. The rate of growth had dropped below 5 percent, while 1.6 million youth enter the labor market each year. As of 1976, Brazil's external debt had reached US$30 billion, and 44 percent of her exports were devoted to paying it back.[123] The 1979 debt of US$52 billion was the largest of any developing nation, and the percentage of exports devoted to repayment had undoubtedly increased.[124]

Further discussion of Brazil may be found on p. 256.

Ghana and the Ivory Coast

Discussion of Ghana is continued from p. 112.

In 1957, having set up a constitution establishing parliamentary government and allowing the creation of a British-educated Prime Minister through electoral processes, Great Britain granted independence to the West African nation of Ghana.[125] Prime Minister Kwame Nkrumah's Convention People's Party (CPP) had largely been built from rural immigrants who had not found it easy to live in

---

[122] Hewlett, *Cruel Dilemmas of Development,* pp. 89–104, Table 7. Food and Agriculture Organization, *State of Food and Agriculture 1978* (Rome: United Nations, 1979), p. A44. Between 1960 and 1965 it stood at 60 percent. Immediately after the coup it dropped, but began to climb again after 1975.

[123] Bernard Lietaer, *Europe + Latin America + the Multinationals* (Westmead, Eng.: Saxon House, 1979), p. 75.

[124] Hewlett, *Cruel Dilemmas of Development,* Table 5. The foreign debt reached US$60 billion by the end of 1981. Eul-Soo Pang, "Abertura in Brazil: A Road to Chaos?", p. 57.

[125] The information on Ghana and the Ivory Coast comes from Jon Woronoff, *West African Wager* (Metuchen, N.J.: The Scarecrow Press, 1972); Jean M. Due, "Agricultural Development in the Ivory Coast and Ghana," *The Journal of Modern African Studies* 6, no. 4 (July 1970): 104–121.

the city—school graduates, clerks, artisans, unemployed, teachers, journalists, traders, trade unionists. This group of younger people had the rural roots, urban contacts, time, and sheer enthusiasm to drum up votes upon the introduction of wide suffrage. Traditional chiefs, urban intellectuals, and lawyer-politicians had been alarmed at the rise of this whole movement. Their party, the United Gold Coast Convention, had controlled the Legislative Council immediately after World War II and endorsed earlier British imprisonments of CPP leaders (many of whom, including Nkrumah, had constituted the left wing of the UGCC) in connection with the political unrest and labor strikes leading to independence. But the UGCC could not command the support of the electorate in a national election. Calling for a Volta River dam and electrification, roads and railroads, free education and health services, mechanization of agriculture, and good pay and jobs for all, the CPP was swept into power in the 1951 election. The Governor thereupon released Nkrumah from jail, so that he might head the new Cabinet.

During the six years that the British presided over his tutelary government, Nkrumah compromised with his political enemies. Freed by independence, however, he began to wipe out political opposition and to shift his base of power into a major patron-client network. Schools were built, but they seemed to be built principally in villages that were pro-CPP and to be run by party supporters. The new community councils were often taken over by CPP supporters, attempting to supercede the power of the chiefs (who continued to oppose Nkrumah). Since 1955, the chiefs (especially Ashanti) had been attempting unsuccessfully to establish a federal form of government to preserve their power. They retained enough command over the loyalties of their villagers to obtain seats in the legislature. They used their positions there to block many of Nkrumah's proposals.

Nkrumah reacted strongly. Some chiefs were arrested, others were threatened with investigation of alleged mismanagement of their lands and treasuries (now administered by them as salaried wards of the state, rather than as representatives of their villages). The intransigent Ashanti region was divided into two provinces. Some of the chiefs were talked into crossing over to Nkrumah's party. The community councils were brought under the supervision of the Minister of Local Government. He put a deportation act through the legislature, which he promptly used against two critical journalists. There followed a preventive detention act, a death penalty for treason, and a five-year imprisonment for sedition (with a clause providing fifteen years in prison for false statements "likely to injure the credit or reputation of Ghana or the Government of Ghana"). A government-controlled Trade Union Congress was created. An alleged conspiracy by the opposition to assassinate the Prime Minister turned up little proof but the show trial discredited the opposition.

In 1960 Nkrumah brought a referendum for a new constitution before the voters. Only about half the electorate turned out to vote, but they approved the proposal overwhelmingly, at the same time electing Nkrumah as the first President—for life. The Cabinet was responsible to the President, and the President was free to alter any law enacted by the Parliament. In 1964, Ghana formally became a one-party state, with the President personally picking the members of Parliament. He had meanwhile built up a small vanguard group within the party who were placed in charge of rounding up for detention trade unionists, small businesspeople, civil servants, and other party members who refused to go along with party decrees. Nkrumah made himself Chancellor of the University and disloyal faculty and students were removed. All publications were brought under strict control. Nkrumah's most trusted assistant became Minister of Defense, and members of the army were required to join the CPP and engage in economic development tasks. Party loyalty figured heavily in promotion. By 1966 the army had grown to 15,000 and the police to 9,000. Not fully trusting them, he gave many special favors to air force and navy leaders and organized a small Army Voluntary Force, plus his own personal Guard Regiment.

Nkrumah had pulled out all stops on coercive techniques. The result, however, was not an egalitarian state. His primary focus was on industrialization of a nation which had previously known little more than small factories like brick and tile works, fruit and fish canning, and sawmilling. He invited Kaiser Aluminum Company to help him build a giant dam and aluminum works on the Volta River. Kaiser built the smelter (investing US$32 million and borrowing US$140 million from the Export-Import Bank and the Agency for International Development) and Nkrumah built the dam (also with borrowed money). Under the agreement with Kaiser, the government must sell the electricity to the company so cheaply they barely have enough to repay the World Bank on the loan with which the dam was built,[126] and must charge their other customers high rates, while purchasing additional electricity from Ivory Coast. The dam employs only 150 people, and the aluminum smelter employs 2,550; the ore comes from Jamaica, and is exempt from import fees. At Tema, Nkrumah built a large artificial harbor to facilitate ore imports. State factories were established to produce a wide variety of consumer goods. The government also ran a ship line, an airline, and radio and TV stations. State farms, never covering more than 1 percent of cultivated land, were created for a time, largely using workers from the city. They were a financial disaster (costing US$21 million and yielding US$4 million). Good roads were built around Accra and in the region of the new dam; elsewhere roads were not well kept.

Most groups in Ghana were reaping little benefit from the new programs. Only 12 percent of Ghana's homes have electricity. The stagnant waters behind the dam breed schistosomiasis and river blindness. The Cocoa Marketing Board raised its percentage of the sale price from 40 to 50 percent at the very time that world market cocoa prices had fallen in half,[127] thus cutting its losses at the expense of the producer. Meanwhile, inflation was increasing greatly, and the

---

[126] Robinson, *Aspects of Development and Underdevelopment*, p. 86. Ghana funded US$60 million in dam construction costs and the World Bank loaned it the remaining US$117 million, yet Kaiser uses 70 percent of the dam's output. Kaiser is guaranteed the low electricity rates and exemption from import fees on ore for thirty years, renewable for twenty more.

[127] In post-war years the Cocoa Marketing Board's retained percentage had been sent to Britain and played a significant part in her economic recovery. Barbara Callaway and Emily Card, "Political Constraints on Economic Development in Ghana," in Lofchie, *The State of the Nations*, p. 75. The 1970–1971 decline in prices was due to market manipulation by the firm of Gill and Duffes, which by then controlled 40 percent of world cocoa trade. John Freivals, "Futures Market—A New Way to Price Stability," *African Development* 9 (September 1975): 27.

Board abandoned its efforts to control swollen shoot disease, bringing about a decline in cocoa production. Half a million farmers, under pressure to join, became involved in government cooperative movements for marketing cocoa, palm oil, coconut, peanuts, and bananas. All of these operated in a manner similar to the Cocoa Marketing Board. When farmers tried to abandon these cash crops in favor of food crops in demand in Accra, they discovered that the bad repair of roads and lack of sufficient marketing facilities made it impossible to get the food to the city. Many simply returned to subsistence farming.[128] A 1970 study found that 15 percent of farmers produced about two thirds of the cocoa.[129]

The government introduced a minimum wage for the urban worker amounting to US$280 a year. At the same time, it outlawed strikes and allowed inflation to increase at a rapid rate, so the minimum wage was of little benefit. New state industries and concessions to foreign concerns spread and many small artisans and businesspeople went out of business. Intellectuals were driven from the university. The regular army was receiving minimal pay and being put to work on public works projects which they felt were beneath their station.

In the face of this Nkrumah's power came to rest on the chains of clients he built up for himself. By 1965, 70 percent of all paid employees were working for the state.[130] Organizations had an exceptional number of persons at the top, serving as corporation heads, newspaper editors, heads of groups like the Trade Union Congress, heads of special indoctrination centers for public employees, and ambassadors. The government itself had thirty-two Ministers. Even the old enemies, tribal chiefs, had sometimes found posts within the CPP. These functionaries received good pay and fringe benefits. Numerous avenues for corruption gave some at the top additional opportunities to enrich themselves. Nkrumah's personal military guard was among the best paid groups in the society. Since all these individuals were chosen more for their loyalty than for their competence and were not easily removed so long as they remained loyal, many did a poor job. Excess spending, losses on the public enterprises, losses on trade deals with the Soviet Union, and other problems drove the economy into disarray.[131] While Nkrumah was on a trip to Peking in 1966, military officers staged a coup which Nkrumah's personal coterie was unable to counteract. A new regime was formed. Although it is in many ways different from the military government in Brazil, Nkrumah's government also appears to have been centralized around a network of industrialists, land developers, export traders, military men, and their middle-class subordinates. This network seems to have absorbed most resources for itself.

They were able to keep them after Nkrumah as well. The corrupt military regime that succeeded Nkrumah was soon followed by a corrupt civilian regime.

---

[128] Also see David Brokensha, *Social Change at Larteh, Ghana* (London: Oxford University Press, 1966). The real income of Ghana cocoa producers was 23 percent lower in 1969 than in 1958. Griffin, *International Inequality*, p. 147.

[129] Elliott, *Patterns of Poverty in the Third World*, pp. 53–54.

[130] Woronoff, *West African Wager*, p. 190.

[131] See Callaway and Card, "Political Constraints," pp. 82–87.

In 1972, a "reforming" military leadership took power. They closed parliament, unilaterally rescheduled their repayment of foreign debts, renewed state owner-ship of mines and banking, set up import and price controls, and campaigned to grow food at home.[132] They soon succumbed to the former corruption. Loans were going to large landowners, and the leaders were enriching themselves on proceeds from a run of good cocoa prices. The inflation rate stood at 100 percent by 1977–1978. Ghana was cut off from world trade credit, which was restored when the World Bank persuaded the government to resume international loan payments. In 1979, the military allowed elections on the condition that there would be no investigations into former corruption. Led by Hila Limann, a coali-tion composed entirely of former CPP ministers and supporters swept the elec-tions everywhere except in Ashanti territory. Enraged at what they saw as a sellout by senior officers, some junior officers asserted themselves and proceeded to put a number of senior officers to death for corruption. By the end of the year, Limann retired these junior officers, began to demand once again that dissident farmers sell their cocoa through the Cocoa Marketing Board, and began to persuade the International Monetary Fund that the new government really would institute an austerity program. The network of industrialists, land developers, export traders, military men, and middle-class subordinates was con-tinuing to assert itself.

Further discussion of Ghana may be found on p. 351.

Nkrumah's neighbor, Houphouët-Boigny, the president of the Ivory Coast, showed considerably more timidity than Nkrumah about seizing absolute power. Also left, in his case by the French, with a constitution calling for free party competition, he tried hard to operate within that system. When a series of at-tempts on his life by opposition leaders finally caused him to crack down, he did so far more gently. After jailing opposition ringleaders, outlawing rival parties, corraling trade unions into a trade union federation, creating a student union with compulsory membership, bringing all civil servants into his political party, and making it clear that henceforth he would direct national policy, he then released the offenders from jail and invited them to cooperate in his government. At the same time, he opened up new positions for these individuals to occupy. The military was deliberately kept in very small numbers; a part-time national guard type of militia composed of the most militant party members was orga-nized to handle any emergencies. To end the nation's dependence on export of cocoa and coffee, the president emphasized expansion of cotton, timber, rice, oil palm, and coconut production. Largely with the assistance of foreign capital, Houphouët-Boigny opened a number of large industries for such manufacturers as paper and cellulose production, oil refining, producing fats and soaps, etc. Some of these were state-owned, and many involved French, Lebanese, and na-tionals from other countries of Africa. A significant portion of the new employ-

---

[132] Jon Kraus, "The Return of Civilian Rule in Nigeria and Ghana," *Current History* 78, no. 455 (March 1980): 137–144; Robinson, *Aspects of Development and Underdevelopment*, p. 94.

ment was for Ivorians. He also built new Catholic churches in the countryside in a deliberate attempt to weaken the power of traditional chiefs. He built roads and encouraged the opening of virgin lands, both by plantations and small farmers. In this way he built up new jobs stemming from the policies of his regime. The growth of Abidjan from a large town into a modern city with skyscrapers, luxury villas, and the ostentatious Hotel Ivoire attested to the change.

Houphouët-Boigny's regime did not entirely neglect the small man, either. One interesting project[133] involved 700 French technical agents who gave cotton seed, instructions, equipment, and fertilizer to farmers in exchange for an agreement by the farmer to sell the cotton crop to the project at a fixed price agreed on in advance. Yields in the particular region rose dramatically. A slightly less successful project involved the training by Israeli advisers of 10,000 men and women in kibbutz techniques; not all of these returned to the countryside. Rice production doubled between 1960 and 1965 under a special program. Yet the figures tell a tale about this sector. Of the entire population of the Ivory Coast, 90 percent are still self-employed in agriculture, growing either subsistence or cash crops. Another 5 percent are farm laborers; one can surmise they are largely employed on the plantations. A small percentage of the 90 percent may own plantations and largeholdings; most must be smallholders. There seemed to be few programs for these. Early floundering attempts at cooperatives were ended in 1964, and there is little evidence of any other program directly benefiting these farmers other than some technical assistance on certain cash crops. Much of this was left to organizations like plantations which would buy fruit from surrounding farmers for their canneries—undoubtedly at low prices. The government's relation with the smallholder was more indirect. By encouraging him—sometimes a village at a time—to open up virgin lands, the government became the apparent patron of a process that had long been in operation anyway.

As to the rest of the population: "The other sectors—commerce, civil service, public works, transport, and industry, in that order—were able to provide work for the other 5 percent."[134]

> To ensure profitability of their farms, the plantation owners of all races agreed that the rates for farm labor should be kept down and the seasonal laborers, aliens for the most part, had the lowest and most stagnant end of the wage scale. The urban, unionized workers, for their part, kept trying to raise their minimum wage. This was resisted, as a concession to foreign investors and to preserve competition. Even the salaries of civil servants and government officials only moved slowly, maintaining their privileged position.

Much of the development is confined to the area around Abidjan. Richard E. Stryker[135] points out that European investors do not find it profitable to invest their money in the hinterland. Abidjan is larger than the next eighty towns com-

---

[133] Woronoff, *West African Wager*, p. 216.

[134] Ibid., pp. 220, 221.

[135] Richard E. Stryker, "A Local Perspective on Developmental Strategy in the Ivory Coast," in Lofchie, *The State of the Nations*, p. 131.

bined and has a per capita income thirty-seven times the national average and sixty times the average of the rural north;[136] it is growing rapidly. Yet the urban centers will provide jobs for only 9 percent of the economically active population.

While the Ivory Coast was having one of the highest rates of growth on the continent[137] and building skyscrapers and villas in the capital, that wealth was clearly not seeping far down among the populace. At the same time, there was a privileged set of people in a variety of newly created positions in the bureaucracy, industry, commerce, and agriculture from which they could support the needs of the regime. Once again, the government seems to be built around a centralized set of patron-client relationships that absorb much of the productivity for themselves.

Mexico

If one were to look for a political system that is relatively low on coercive restraints and high on distributive efficacy, Mexico would seem to be the prime candidate. Mexico has enjoyed uninterrupted democratic government since 1924, making it the oldest continuous democracy with free electoral competition in the developing world. The land redistribution scheme under the 1934–40 regime of General Lázaro Cárdenas is perhaps the most extensive ever undertaken in a developing nation. His successful expropriation of oil companies was also a major achievement in national independence. Today Mexico is experiencing economic growth and prosperity which rivals that of any portion of the developing world. If any nation has avoided the phenomena by which the major network monopolizes resources, it would seem on the surface to be Mexico.

Mexico's party system is built around slightly modernized *caciques.* In 1924, General Obregón (who had stepped in as president after the 1920 assassination of Venustiano Carranza) turned over the reins of government to President-Elect Plutarco Elías Calles, who pledged himself to only one term in office. Calles' attacks on church prerogatives brought an attempted counterrevolution by clerics, and in the 1928 elections rival military officers fielded candidates, including General Obregón. Obregón won, but he was assassinated by a religious fanatic before he could take office. Congress named one of his close associates to be interim president. Meanwhile, Calles formed the National Revolutionary Party (PRN). In the 1929 election this party's candidate, Pascual Ortiz Rubio, won a hotly contested election against a pro-cleric party. When Rubio later tried to assert his independence from Calles by firing some pro-Calles members from his own Cabinet, private-citizen Calles sought and obtained the resignation of Rubio. He was replaced by a wealthy landowner loyal to Calles. For the 1934 elections Calles was persuaded by the left wing of his party to support the candidacy of Cárdenas, who won easily. Cárdenas soon took party control into his

---

[136] Ibid., p. 132. Furthermore, in 1962, 79 percent of the top level and top paying civil service jobs were occupied by expatriates, usually from Europe. R. Jolly and C. Colclough, "African Manpower Plans: An Evaluation," *International Labour Review* 106 (August–September 1972): 210.

[137] Woronoff, *West African Wager,* p. 296.

own hands—changing the name to the Mexican Revolutionary Party (PRM)—
and exiled Calles to the United States. He also helped reorganize the labor movement, under the leadership of one of his supporters, and softened the attacks on
clerics. This freed him to pursue his land reforms. In 1940 he stepped aside in
favor of the candidacy of Avila Camacho, who was unsuccessfully opposed in
the election by a coalition of splinter parties, including one called the Party of
National Action (PAN), centering around clerical and business interests. During
Camacho's regime, the PRM became the Revolutionary Institutional Party
(PRI). Under a string of succeeding presidents—each serving six-year terms—the
PRI has remained in power. The PAN is their principal opposition.

Under three different names, then, the PRI has been in power since 1929;
close affiliates of its founders have held power since ratification of the Constitution in 1917. The party's highest organ is its National Executive Committee
(CEN). This unit has control over state and municipal nominating conventions
and the power to remove state and municipal party officers. The body includes a
president and general secretary, one representative each from the Senate and
Chamber of Deputies, and the top leaders of the three functioning sub-units of
the party: the Mexican Worker's Federation, the National Confederation of
Farmers and Peasants, and the National Confederation of Popular Organizations (representing middle-class groups). The biography of CEN President
Alfonso Martínez Domínguez illustrates how one rises to power in the PRI.[138]
Domínguez joined the PRI at an early age. In exchange for carrying out various
party tasks, such as distributing leaflets and arranging meetings, he was rewarded with a bureaucratic post. When one is associated with such a post under
such circumstances, it is usually possible to spend most of one's time on party
matters rather than the particular job at hand. What matters most is to be personally attached to someone who is rising within the ranks of the party and to
use one's efforts to support his or her rise (involving, in turn, development of
one's own network of clients).[139]

In this manner Domínguez became affiliated with Adolfo López Mateos,
the head of the public bureaucrat's union. When Mateos' protégé became president of Mexico in 1952, he rewarded Mateos with the job of Secretary of Labor.
Mateos in turn rewarded the members of his clique, including Domínguez, with
government posts. Mateos himself became president of Mexico in 1958. He
elevated Domínguez into the position of Secretary General of the National Confederation of Popular Organizations. Domínguez promptly used his position to
place his own followers into key governmental and party positions; one of these
in turn obtained CEN membership. At the next election Domínguez was permit-

---

[138] Kenneth F. Johnson, *Mexican Democracy: A Critical View* (Boston: Allyn and Bacon, 1971), pp.
68–70.

[139] These principles of Mexican politics are reaffirmed by a wide variety of sources. Frank Branden-
burg, *The Making of Modern Mexico* (Englewood Cliffs, N.J.: Prentice-Hall, 1964), pp. 141–165;
L. Vincent Padgett, *The Mexican Political System* (Boston: Houghton-Mifflin, 1966); Bo Ander-
son and James D. Cockcroft, "Control and Cooptation in Mexican Politics," in *Latin American
Radicalism*, ed. Irving Louis Horowitz (New York: Vintage, 1969), pp. 366–389; Robert F. Adie,
"Cooperation, Cooptation, and Conflict in Mexican Peasant Organizations," *InterAmerican
Economic Affairs* 24, no. 3 (Winter 1970): 3–25; Cornelius, "Local-Level Political Leadership."

ted by the CEN to run for national deputy. Shortly after, he became floor leader of the PRI delegation to the Chamber of Deputies. Though the President of the CEN (Lauro Ortega) had the support of the leader of a principal clique of the Mexican Workers Federation, Domínguez now decided to challenge him and seek his post. With the aid of Ortega's rivals in the labor movement and supporters within the National Confederation of Popular Organizations, his close protégé whom he had helped rise to membership in the CEN, and his position in the Chamber of Deputies, he succeeded in this challenge and became president of the CEN.

Obviously, this system is useful for retaining the party in power. Bureaucrats and political aspirants at all levels are in a position to be rewarded in exchange for their support of the PRI. The fact that the party subsumes a large number of separate cliques centering around differing personalities allows it to accommodate a number of interests and points of view. The fact that there is no official organ for representing large business interests within the party is somewhat assuaged by the existence of officially sponsored national confederations of chambers of commerce, by PRI tolerance of its rival PAN (which holds seats in the National Assembly and controls certain states and municipalities), and by government policy favoring rapid industrialization. The military has been steadily reduced in size and benefits until it now receives a smaller percentage of the national product than in any nation of Latin America save Costa Rica.[140]

The patron-client network probably includes more members (and, especially, more peasant members) than in most developing nations, and rewards appear to be distributed down to the lowest echelons. There are questions, however, as to how far they extend beyond these networks in a country with a population of nearly 50 million. Land redistribution has been extensive. As of 1941, nearly 15,000 villages accounting for a quarter of the total population—almost none of whom had owned their land twenty-five years earlier—were using nearly a half of the total crop land of the nation.[141] During a spurt of additional distribution (or confirmation of titles given only provisionally under Cardenas), Mateos distributed some 25 million acres between 1958 and 1962,[142] and other distributions have been made under other regimes.

Despite this, the amount of private cultivated land has tended to expand at a greater rate than that of the *ejidos* (the villages given land under the distribution programs). A high percentage of *ejido* land itself is leased to nonmembers (often as a result of obligations to private moneylenders).[143] Nearly all the unleased *ejido* land is individually (versus collectively) farmed. The *Ejidal* Bank gives credit for irrigated, rich land growing cash crops. The 1958 census showed only 16,670 *ejidatorios* (individual farmers) with twelve and one-half to twenty-five

---

[140] Pablo González Casanova, *Democracy in Mexico* (New York: Oxford University Press, 1970), p. 37.

[141] Charles C. Cumberland, *Mexico: The Struggle for Modernity* (New York: Oxford University Press, 1968), p. 299.

[142] François Chevalier, "The *Ejido* and Political Stability in Mexico," in *The Politics of Conformity in Latin America*, ed. Claudio Veliz (London: Oxford University Press, 1967), p. 170.

[143] Ibid., p. 173.

acres and 15,104 with over twenty-five acres. It is only some portion of these, therefore, who are eligible for the loans. Not more than 2 to 3 percent of *ejidatorios* are engaged in any significant way in cash crops or cattle raising.[144] Since PRI bureaucrats control the land distribution, credit transactions, and government dealings with the private businesspeople to whom farm produce is sold, these party members are obviously in a position to gain access to much of the better land and credit under this system. The 28,657 private (non-*ejido*) owners of twenty-five or more acres of irrigated land include many town-dwellers using farms as investments; many are undoubtedly connected with the PRI.

A huge engineering project in the northern state of Sonora created a new irrigation system there. Two of the largest landowners in the state arranged for the National Agricultural Credit Bank to delay crop credits for smallholders so they would have to plant out of season. Furthermore, the smallholders were provided with seeds that would not germinate and useless powder in place of fertilizer. Their crops failed. When the government subsequently foreclosed on them for debts owed to federal agencies, these two large landowners succeeded in buying the land for one-ninth of the market price, and they set up mechanized operations before the boom in land prices (which the irrigation would bring). By 1960, 75 percent of the people in the state were landless (versus 57 percent in the 1940s). Many were illegally crossing the United States border seeking work. The newly irrigated land was devoted to growing onions, cucumbers, squash, eggplant, strawberries, cantaloupes, tomatoes, asparagus, and other such nourishing goods—for sale in the United States. They are grown on farms ranging up to 25,000 acres. By 1975 Mexico was supplying one-half to two-thirds of many winter and spring vegetables on the United States supermarket shelves.[145]

> In fact, much of the land directly benefitted by the new hydraulic systems is owned, directly or indirectly, by prominent Mexican politicians and their friends and relatives. . . . In contrast, little has been done to bring water to the heavily populated central mesa region where most of the land is held by *ejidatorios* and the owners of private plots.[146]

Meanwhile, the 1960 census showed 899,108 smallholdings (of all kinds) of under twelve and one-half acres and a 1964 study of the National Confederation of Farmers and Peasants showed 498,399 properties of less than two and one-half acres.[147] As members of the latter organization, even these owners were expected to attend PRI rallies and other functions. Nearly half the inhabitants of *ejidos* were both landless and unemployed.[148] A 1963 Bank of Mexico study

---

[144] Ibid., p. 174. See also Johnson, *Mexican Democracy*, pp. 105–107; William P. Glade, Jr., and Charles W. Anderson, *The Political Economy of Mexico* (Madison: University of Wisconsin Press, 1963), pp. 169–178.

[145] Lappé, *Food First*, pp. 128, 129, 254, 396.

[146] Roger D. Hansen, *The Politics of Mexican Development* (Baltimore: Johns Hopkins University Press, 1971), p. 81. In 1979 the government was attempting to bring 560,000 additional acres under irrigation for these export crops. "Agriculture in Poor Shape." *Financial Times*, Survey VII, January 11, 1980.

[147] Chevalier, "The *Ejido* and Political Instability in Mexico," p. 185.

found 41 percent of rural families with monthly incomes below US$35, and 85 percent below US$105 a month.[149] Roads, schools, and medical care were increasingly available to rural Mexicans, as were programs for distributing subsidy food to the poor. The Institute of Nutrition still reports that only 35 to 40 percent of Mexicans have even a minimum calorie intake.[150]

In the city, Mexican labor unions have won far more benefits than usually encountered in developing nations. They have the right to strike, minimum wages, guarantees of collective bargaining, an outlawing of company stores, work-hour limitations, medical plans, free education, and profit sharing. Yet, as of 1964 only 10.5 percent of the total working population (and at most 6.4 percent of agricultural workers) were unionized.[151] Banco de Mexico figures from 1966 show one-third of the workers in the Federal District (Mexico City) with monthly incomes ranging from 25 to 64 dollars (U.S.), and less than 2 percent (mostly professional and managerial) earning more than 800 dollars per month. Over 80 percent earned less than 120 dollars a month.[152] At the same time, opportunities for corruption (bribes, first call on franchises, etc.) offer a chance for those in inner circles to bring in sizeable unreported incomes. In a 1960 study, the top 400 corporations (three-fourths private, one-half foreign) earned well over half of the total national income. In most years profits shipped abroad by the foreign concerns have exceeded their investments.[153] A large percentage of high-income people seem to be in a position to evade taxes, leaving much of this burden to those with lower fixed incomes.[154] In the early 1950s, the richest 20 percent of the population had ten times the income of the poorest 20 percent; by 1969, the top 20 percent had sixteen times what the bottom received.[155] In 1965, the richest 20 percent had 62.5 percent of Mexico City's income, while the poorest 20 percent received 1.3 percent.[156] One study concludes that "the material lot of the poorest 40 percent of Mexican families has changed negligibly since 1910."[157]

Some presidents have been more concerned with righting inequities than others. Even the most reformist among them has not been able to dispense with

---

[148] Ibid., p. 176.

[149] Casanova, *Democracy in Mexico,* pp. 106–107.

[150] Johnson, *Mexican Democracy,* p. 107.

[151] Casanova, *Democracy in Mexico,* pp. 121–122, 229.

[152] Johnson, *Mexican Democracy,* 169–170.

[153] Casanova, *Democracy in Mexico,* pp. 49, 141.

[154] Ibid., pp. 139–140.

[155] The richest 10 percent in 1950 had eighteen times the income of the lowest 10 percent; by 1963, thirty-two times. R. Weiskoff, "Income Distribution and Economic Growth in Puerto Rico, Argentina, and Mexico," *Review of Income and Wealth* no. 4 (December 1970): 312. Wilber and Weaver, "Patterns of Dependency," in Wilber, *Political Economy,* p. 116. The Banco Nacional de Comercio Exterior reports that in 1958 Mexico's richest 5 percent had 22 times the income of the poorest 10 percent; in 1977, forty-seven times. "Agriculture in Poor Shape," *Financial Times.*

[156] Economic Commission for Latin America, *Economic Survey for Latin America* (New York, 1969).

[157] Griffin, *Inequality,* p. 147.

the necessity to pass along considerable patronage in order to hold together the network of supporters, and prevent usurpation by someone promising to pass along greater amounts of patronage. To date, all attempts to gain a foothold of political strength outside of the PRI–PAN network have failed.

One significant attempt in this direction was made by Carlos A. Madrazo after fighting his way up within the system to become President of the PRI's National Executive Committee. He noted that if the elected executive committees of an *ejido* sent a delegate to one of the 500 local committees of the PRI, that individual could only reach power in the party (e.g., by the first step of being chosen as a member of one of the thirty-two provincial committees) by cooperating with those above him. One reason for this was the power of the central bodies to remove all leaders from office and of those leaders to choose political candidates. To counter this, Madrazo proposed late in 1965 a system whereby the local membership of the party would choose candidates via a primary election. This promptly stirred a hornet's nest among political bosses throughout the country, and President Ordaz removed him from office. His subsequent attempt to organize a movement outside the PRI was cut short by his death in an airplane crash.

In 1963, Marxists inaugurated a Popular Electoral Front (FEP) to challenge the PRI, with some help from aging ex-President Cárdenas. By the end of the decade the principal leaders had returned to the PRI; others involved in acts of violence were jailed. The Front was then largely forgotten as a tactic.[158] One important factor is PRI control of polling places; other parties are not permitted to employ pollwatchers, and ballot box stuffing and other irregularities seem to be frequent in occurrence. In Tijuana, a group of PRI leaders attempting to take control of sizeable portions of real estate encountered the defection of prominent propertied elites from the party. When the latter won the 1968 elections, the PRI again demonstrated its control over the electoral process by declaring the elections void.

In terms of representative democracy, Mexico's system definitely places it at the forefront of developing nations. Small farmers, labor leaders, teachers, students, and intellectuals from outlying provinces—members of the minor patron-client network—may actually rise to positions of substantive power in the highest echelon of the ruling party. From here they may have a decisive voice selecting the faction from which the next president will emerge. The presidents themselves, however, generally follow a higher trajectory in their rise to power. They have usually been governors or senators,[159] stemming from the large, economically prosperous, centrally located states. They generally move from the cabinet into the presidency. The recommendations of the president and cabinet are seldom rejected by the National Assembly. The President is free to replace personnel at all levels of the party and the bureaucracy, including state govern-

---

[158] Anderson and Cockcroft, "Control and Cooptation;" Adie, "Control Cooptation, and Conflict;" Johnson, *Mexican Democracy*, pp. 83, 114–122.

[159] Padgett, *Mexican Political System*, p. 138. Of the six Presidents since 1940, four have been lawyers, and one (Camacho) a wealthy landowner. The exception to the rule was Adolfo Ruíz Cortines (1952–1958) who emerged from obscure positions in the bureaucracy and the army.

ment.[160] He can force Governors to resign if they step out of line.[161] Even vis-à-vis the PRI's National Executive Committee, therefore, the president and cabinet are in a position to subordinate the interests of the minor network to those of the major network. The system has elements of Thomas Jefferson's thought: Electors of the populace choose those individuals from among the natural aristocracy whom they wish to assume supreme power until the next election. But only the natural aristocracy, moneyed, educated, and socially compatible in the higher circles, may actually govern.

Like the other systems we have surveyed, Mexico's political system is centrally governed by individuals far more advanced in social standing than average citizens. Rewards would appear to be distributed far more liberally among those directly involved in the patron-client networks than among the populace as a whole.

SUMMARY

In the course of the past three chapters we have been attempting to provide common denominators for comprehending the political systems of developing nations. We could have begun by categorizing the formal presidential/parliamentary or party systems of these states, or we could have discussed bureaucratic or military organization. As it is, you still have learned little about these aspects at this point. That is because I think that an understanding of them contributes little to your comprehension of how these political systems function. In fact, it seems to make little difference whether a nation is even under civilian or military rule, or whether it subsumes one or many political parties—unless one is a member of that small percentage of the populace which benefits most directly from patron-clientism. What counts is the informal relationships that stay hidden behind such formal institutions. And it would seem that these relationships have a number of aspects in common in the developing nations:

1. A nation where most extended families (clans) remain essentially intact will have a different political structure from one in which individual nuclear families (mother, father, and kids, as in United States suburbs) take precedence over extended families. Developing nations lie somewhere between these two extremes. It is a hindrance to understanding to attempt to define "society," "economics," and "politics" as separate spheres; the breakdown of the family by economic forces has political ramifications. In developing nations, the authoritative allocation of values (politics) is dominated by patron-client networks. Patron-clientism cannot thrive where either extended or nuclear families are strong.

2. By the 1980s, nearly every developing nation has emerged with a capital that also serves as the prime commercial and financial center of the nation. The economies of virtually all these capital cities are heavily dependent on the export

---

[160] Padgett, *Mexican Political System,* p. 150.

[161] Ibid., p. 146.

of basic agricultural commodities and minerals, the import of food and consumer goods, and manufacturing. Their social milieu is usually very different from that of the rest of the nation. Their leaders are more closely allied with the developed nations than with their own people.

3. Highest authority rests with a prime minister (or president) and a small inner circle of the cabinet, whose policy decisions are seldom challenged by courts, legislatures, state governments, or party leaders. When such challenges arise, the president can rely on his or her ties with the major patron-client network to subdue them, unless the challengers themselves have the support of that network. There are generally few constitutional/legal traditions to restrain this central power.

4. Prime ministers and presidents are fundamentally weak, however. They need money, expertise, and control over a militia to secure power. This normally depends on the export of crops and minerals, manufacturing, a bureaucratic establishment, and a loyal army. Without businesspeople, bureaucrats, and military men behind him, the president's power would be insecure. These individuals have the capability to withhold these needed assets and deliver them to a political rival. Should they be divided in their loyalties, this also weakens the president's hold on power. His or her ascendancy over courts, legislatures, and the populace as a whole depends upon their cooperation. With support from only the military, or only business, or only bureaucrats, one could not rule; nor could one rule with support from only mass sectors of the populace. Together, the members of the military, business, and the bureaucracy who cooperate with the president to rule constitute a major patron-client network. They usually live in the capital city, and identify with its social milieu and institutions.

5. To extract the raw materials on which their money and power depend, the major network relies on a minor network of middle-echelon patrons. So long as they deliver to the major network what is expected of them, they are generally immune from regulation by those above or below them. They have latitude to be inefficient or dishonest at their jobs, and to exploit their clients. If they do not deliver, they can be replaced. No patron is completely free to function as an impartial administrator of the law. Minor patrons must constantly guard to assure that those immediately below them do not take over their positions.

6. The reciprocity in patron-client relationships, placing, as it does, power at the top, causes more resources to flow upward than downward. This allows the major network to gain control of the major surpluses in the society, which they distribute principally among themselves and with their foreign cohorts. The minor network keeps enough to live somewhat comfortably. Little filters down to the populace at large.

7. The vast majority of the populace, who lie outside or at the fringes of its social milieu and patron-client network, are not in a position to challenge the political control of the major network. On rare occasions when they do succeed in organizing a trade union or peasant cooperative, it is rather easy to bring the leadership of such a group under the control of the major network. In such instances, the members of the movement are treated like the minor clients of economic patrons; they are individually rewarded with such things as employee benefits, jobs, education, land titles, social welfare programs, roads, and hous-

ing. A citizen cannot hope to benefit from the political system without fixing himself or herself to it in the status of a minor client. Those simply voting for the regime on election day may expect a ride to town and a free meal, or at least freedom from harassment aimed at nonvoters. Those who want more must do more. Most can do little for the regime, and receive little from it.

8. Those living within the traditional political structures discussed in Chapter 2 do not contribute to the patron-client networks and do not benefit from them. The patron-client networks are inherently incapable of contributing as much to their members as the traditional systems. Members of traditional villages cannot accept partial benefits as clients without opening the door to the disintegration of their village structure and exploitation as members of the lowest echelons of the patron-client system.

9. Traditional social life continues to be disrupted at a rapid rate, while the patron-client networks tend to spread benefits in this sporadic and imbalanced manner. Since these economies seldom have surpluses to filter down outside of clientist paths, and the modern sectors of employment (e.g., unionized factory jobs) expand slowly in proportion to population growth, this leaves the personal environments of much of the populace in a haphazard condition. Enough food, comfortable cultural surroundings, a satisfying job, adequate housing and income, and viable education for one's children become a perpetual uncertainty. In this sense, developing nations are not experiencing political development.

10. The greater the centralization and modernization of the patron-client networks, the more these generalizations apply. These networks have enough control over coercive techniques to use modernization for enhancing their power; they show no sign of being modernized out of existence.

It is as though governance of these nations took place from ships moored off the shore. (See Figure 4.3.) *On these ships* are government leaders, all those involved with major financial transactions, the bureaucracy, and the military. Contact is kept with those *on shore* needed to extract resources for export and intercept profits from the internal distribution of goods, and with those needed to enforce coercive measures. These shore dwellers are paid for their services, but their percentage of the populace is small. When these individuals do not perform their jobs well, or spies report they are engaged in malfeasance, they can be replaced with others. Occasionally, those beyond their ranks receive benefits; on the whole, they are ignored unless they are needed to extract goods for export or otherwise aid in creating profits for those on the ship. Minor functionaries in the bureaucracy settle civil disturbances and minor disputes over distribution. Those on the ship go back and forth to shore on an individual basis to inspect their various domains and for pleasure. Culturally, they have great affinity with those on shore, but they wish to avoid basic social interaction with them.

Basic political activities take place aboard ship. The *military* are capable of terrorizing the ship, but do not know how to keep it supplied with consumer goods, or how to build the roads, electrical power, and other services on which they depend when they occasionally go ashore to quell civil disturbances. The *client-bureaucracy* plays a key role in keeping those services (which also create the profits) flowing, and hence cannot be ignored. The *businesspeople* are the

FIGURE 4.3
Ship and Shore

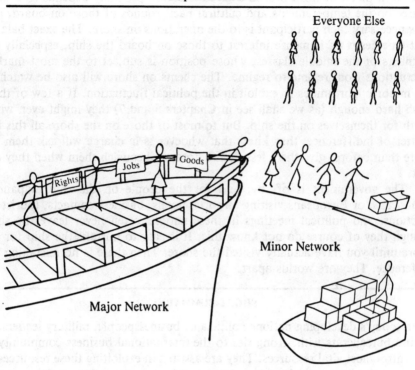

only ones capable of generating the profits that keep the ship prosperous. So the people on shipboard must keep one another happy, but do not worry about the welfare of many people on shore. They will refurbish the ship's ballroom while children on the shore starve.

The ship is not governed by any sort of international maritime code relating to mutinies. There is constant intrigue to determine who will control the helm. The military men, so long as they are supplied with arms, can grab control. But, like everyone else on board, they cannot rule alone. It makes a good deal of difference to everyone on the ship who is in charge. To them, *a good leader keeps peace and efficient operations on shore—by whatever means necessary. But on board ship, they all prefer a regime that allows freedom without constant disruptive changes in leadership.* Those few individuals with the greatest fortunes prefer to keep the distribution of assets even on shipboard as inegalitarian as possible, but they are willing to give concessions to the second- and third-class passengers in exchange for a regime that runs the shore operations efficiently.

If efforts to provide freedom lead to disruption of leadership, the next regime might cut down on the freedom. If a regime fails that did not redistribute generously on ship, the next regime may do this more effectively. There is probably no particular form of government, whether military, one-party, one-party dominant, presidential, or parliamentary, that can inherently provide these balances most effectively. We shall discuss this more extensively in Chapter 6. The form that will work best in a given situation probably depends to a large degree on the temperaments and cultural backgrounds of those on board, and how necessary each participant is to the operations on shore. The exact balance that emerges is of immense interest to those on board the ship, especially the members of the middle classes, whose position is subject to the most marked fluctuations from regime to regime. The clients on shore will also be watching for minor opportunities to exploit in the political fluctuation. If a few of them push hard enough (as we shall see in Chapters 5 and 7) they might even win a berth for themselves on the ship. But to most of those on the shore all this is a matter of indifference; they know that whoever is in charge will ask them for more than before, give them less than before, and squelch them when they object.

The government is of, by, and for the people on the ship. Japanese, Americans, or Europeans visiting airports, hotels, business contacts, tourist attractions, and political meetings in these nations often never leave the ship, though they of course do not know this. It is easy to mistake the ship for the shore until you have actually visited the shore. Then there is no mistaking the difference. They are worlds apart.

SHORT SUMMARY

In today's developing nations politicians, businesspeople, military leaders, and bureaucrats with strong ties to the international business community control most vital resources. They are assisted in exploiting these resources (for their own profit) by minor functionaries for whom they perform personal favors. All others who are not connected with these functionaries—that is to say, most people—are left out of jobs and income and find it difficult to survive.

Have you caught these definitions?

Can you answer each with one sentence?

1. Why do capital cities in developing nations tend to be located along the coast?
2. Why do government subsidies tend to go only to export crops?
3. What would happen if a village headman became a client of a king?
4. Why can't government leaders offend major patrons?

From what you have read this far, can you make and support judgments about these questions?

1. It is a basic principle of patron-clientism that more resources flow up the network than flow down, and that those at the very bottom who contribute the most labor receive the sparsest rewards. In a traditional village the opposite is usually true. Why the difference?
2. How can a king or village headman become a client?
3. Identify a major and a minor network.
4. Why do the public and governments have little control over the major and minor networks?
5. How does patron-clientism separate political from social systems?

You should now be well on your way toward fitting the various parts of this book together. With what you now know about patron-clientism, reread the entire "Book in Brief" section of Chapter 1.

CHAPTER

5

GETTING YOUR BEARINGS (see map, front of book)

1. Where could you most easily migrate by boat from Saudi Arabia? West Africa? China? India?
2. Where could you most easily go by land from Saudi Arabia? India? Nigeria? Vietnam?
3. In which developing nations might you find the most Muslims? Catholics? Buddhists? Hindus?
   (Hint: Islam comes from Saudi Arabia, Christianity from the eastern Mediterranean, and Buddhism and Hinduism from India.)

The Model

A developed nation provides most of its citizens with a stable personal environment. A developing nation does not. Today's developing nations were once developed nations. *They changed because their political systems separated from their social systems when European commerce was introduced.* If the structure of international trade changes in the near future, social and political systems may be reintegrated, promoting political development. Then the developing nations may once again become developed nations.

Why Men
Do Not Revolt

```
┌─────────────────────────────────────────────────────────────────────┐
│                    QUESTIONS TO KEEP IN MIND                          │
│                                                                       │
│   1. Why do people tend not to revolt?                                │
│   2. Who is most likely to revolt?                                    │
│   3. Why is it hard to organize a revolt around race or religion?     │
│   4. Why is it hard to organize a revolt around programs and ideologies? │
│                                                                       │
└─────────────────────────────────────────────────────────────────────┘
```

If the average citizen and family are as poorly attended to as Chapter 4 implies, why do they not revolt? One reads of guerilla movements in various countries. Usually they have few participants. In fact, although they are shaken by periodic coups and civil uprisings, developing nations seem to be characterized more by political apathy than radical discontent.

Political scientists, sociologists, anthropologists, and historians discuss this subject a good deal. They explore hypotheses about why radical revolutions occur. Some draw upon the research that has been done to predict whether revolutions will or will not occur in the immediate future. A *revolution* in a developing nation, from the perspective of our discussion, would mean the replacement of present patron-client networks by completely new membership from top to bottom, or by groups other than patron-client networks (whether modern bureaucracy and democratic party structures, modern military and authoritarian party structure, a return to kingship and kinship, or some other unforeseen arrangement). A *radical revolution* would be one which, in addition to changing networks, would begin an intelligible sustained redistribution of material assets within the society. The USSR and China have experienced radical revolution during the twentieth century; except for Cuba, Vietnam, and Cambodia, developing nations have not. In contrast, a *rebellion* (whether via coup or civil insurrection) replaces some top political leaders of the major patron-client network without disturbing the composition of top economic elites, bureaucrats, landowners, and the military officer corps (beyond those individuals most partisan to the losing side in the insurrection); it may cause some readjustment of the relative power of those elites vis-à-vis one another. A rebellion may force some read-justments—especially in racial composition—of the *minor* patron-client net-work.

The activities discussed in Chapter 3, which replaced the traditional village and kingly institutions with patron-client networks, were radical revolutions. They radically altered virtually everyone's problem-solving methods, social rela-tionships, distribution of resources, living conditions, and value systems, and brought the patron-client networks to prominence. The first elites in these net-works were merchants, export firms, and landowners. The later challenge of their new positions by urban bureaucrats and professionals, financiers, miners, manufacturers, and elected officials constituted rebellion; the end result was simply an expansion of the networks to include all of these people. The mass movements since World War II have not displaced these networks but strengthened and unified them. They, too, have brought rebellions, not revolu-tions.

The 1950s and 1960s witnessed many rebellions. Some were related to firm-ing up the control of capital cities. Others involved the expulsion of colonial powers. Still others involved infighting between civilian and military leaders, and among various economic and ethnic factions within the patron-client networks. Looking ahead into the 1980s, however, I see a diminution in the number of rebellions. With some rare exceptions (e.g., the Pacific Islands), power has generally coalesced by now around major networks. Those rebellions that do oc-cur will largely involve military intervention into civilian rule, or the toppling of one military leader by another.[1] And I side with those scholars who foresee very few revolutions in the immediate future of the developing nations. The 1960s and 1970s have produced a general improvement in the techniques for dealing with opposition discussed in Chapter 4. *Only organized groups sustained over time can counter such techniques and create revolution. The experience and motiva-tion patterns of citizens in developing nations will not sustain such organization now or in the foreseeable future.* It is the assertions in the latter two sentences that we shall explore in this chapter, so that you may formulate a judgment of your own as to their validity.

Many people in developing nations live, in the words of Franz Fanon, as "the wretched of the earth." Many others live modest but comparatively com-fortable lives, and a few live in the lap of luxury. Interestingly, it is usually from the latter two ranks that revolutionary movements emerge. I would argue that it is not so much a "scale of wretchedness" at work here as a "scale of alienation." The amount of money in one's pocket may provide a less accurate index of one's revolutionary proclivities than an analysis of the extent to which a person can cope with surroundings. Those who are least able to cope, and are hence the most alienated, are not always those who are poorest. Among the

---

[1] The average annual cost of arms imports to developing nations rose from US$1.5 billion 1964–1968 to US$4.4 billion 1974–1975. Much of this total went to the Shah of Iran, but Latin America rose from US$114 million to US$497 million, north Africa from 73 to 378, and sub-Sahara Africa 130 to 401. Joan Robinson, *Aspects of Development and Underdevelopment* (Cambridge: Cambridge University Press, 1979), p. 128.

alienated, it is generally the more affluent who join revolutionary movements. At most, such individuals support rebellion to bring themselves into the minor network. More often, their alienation prevents them from organizing effective opposition.

Alienation in simplest terms means being cut off or estranged. Karl Marx suggested that in capitalist society a person's labor ceases to be an extension of oneself—as were the gardens of the Trobriand Islanders—and becomes instead the property of his or her employer. The employer pays the worker with money. Whereas people formerly fed, clothed, and sheltered themselves with the aid of neighbors, and loved, sang, painted, and explored as an inherent part of their lives, they can now do none of these things without the aid of money. Marx called this phenomenon *alienation.*[2] When employees (or unemployed persons) lack sufficient money, they find the basic processes of their lives coming apart. Even those possessing money face the possibility of serious repercussions from alienation; they want more money, and must often give up more satisfying activities in order to earn it. Furthermore, the division of labor produced by technological society removes the satisfaction of many of a person's most basic needs from his or her own control. Marx talked of being alienated from the means of production, from one another, from nature, and from one's own body. I have written elsewhere:

> An individual needs housing that satisfies him and that he can afford. He needs neighbors and cultural facilities with which he feels comfortable. His job must offer him both security and above-subsistence income. The educational system has to promise his children the same advantages. If any of these aspects are lacking for an individual, his environment becomes unstable. At the same time, his political efficacy can be weakened, as he must devote increasing time to straightening out his personal affairs.[3]

This is what we have been referring to throughout this book as a *stable personal environment.* The more traditional political structures we discussed in Chapter 2 provided most *(but not all)* families with these ingredients. The housing may have been a thatched hut, the job little more than scratching for subsistence, and the education a series of chats and hunting trips. Yet most inhabitants appeared to be satisfied with these surroundings and roles, and identified with them. They ritualized labor and considered it a link with nature, ancestors, and progeny. They placed great value upon interactions with one another. Despite the need to devote considerable time to the basic tasks involved with staying alive, they participated in politics and an active social life. They were not dependent upon money or outside forces to look after these needs. Those same families, transferred to a modern house, a job with monetary income, and access to modern educational facilities, might find themselves far less comfortable in the new surroundings, despite the appearance of considerable

---

[2] For a convenient compilation of his thoughts on this matter, see Robert Friedman, ed., *Marxist Social Thought* (New York: Harcourt, 1968) pp. 65–107.

[3] Robert E. Gamer, *The Politics of Urban Development in Singapore* (Ithaca, N.Y.: Cornell University Press, 1972), xxiii.

economic improvement. *What you think about how you live is as important as how you live.* An individual (and here is where our definition of stable personal environment ties in with alienation) who feels uncomfortable with his or her neighbors and social contacts, and finds educational opportunities out of line with personal aspirations or available jobs, cannot achieve job security or a balanced budget, lacks housing in keeping with any of these considerations, or does not sense meaning in existence, is likely to feel alienated.

COMMENT

Marx saw alienation occurring when praxis (see p. 59) is absent. The absence of praxis certainly increases the chances for alienation to occur, but does not assure that it will. One could have a stable personal environment without praxis or alienation. A person with an unstable personal environment, however, is likely to lack praxis and to feel alienated.

Marx felt these conditions could only be righted by reuniting the worker with the means of production. Yet alienation is partly a state of mind. Whatever the basic reasons for the problem may be, if an individual is unhappy with his or her job (or neighborhood, education, etc.), one can remove the source of *personal* tension by changing one's attitude toward his job, or by changing some of her working conditions so as to induce her to change that attitude. Employee picnics, making the workplace more cheerful, or even pay increases, cannot eliminate alienation in a basic Marxian sense, but can reduce its impact on the well-being of the individual by bringing personal attitudes and environment into balance. *If, despite such efforts, an individual's values and environment do remain out of balance, he or she will continue to feel the effects of alienation.*

Alienation from surroundings is not something that can be accurately measured. Yet I venture to assert that the amount of alienation in developing nations is greater than that among inhabitants of Northern Asia, Europe, and North America. It is probably highest neither in traditional villages nor among urban industrial or white-collar workers; many of these individuals have developed personal attitudes which let them accept the poor environments in which they live. Alienation is probably highest among those who are on the *fringes* of being traditional villagers or urban workers (and who may actually be better off economically than the traditional villager or the urban worker). These people on the fringes are most susceptible to the disequilibriating influences of rapid social and economic change. The balance between their values and environment is easily disturbed. The problem is endemic because there are so many in this position and the avenues for their advancement are so few.

So let us restate the initial question. *If there are so many on these fringes, and they are frustrated, then why do they not rebel?* The answer is that they often do. But the object of their hostility is usually a particular incumbent in an office, an individual they attack in a fight, or another racial group. They often do not perceive that the patron-client networks might be responsible for their frustrations, and if they do they do not have sufficient resources to organize effective opposition. *The fact that alienated people can be counted on to vent their spleen in ineffectual directions—by fighting among themselves—relieves the government of the need to deal fundamentally with the conditions which cause their frustrations.* It even relieves authorities (except following moments of shrill violence) of the need to minimally affect environment and attitudes to reduce alienation. The government merely does the minimum necessary to prevent those few who are prone toward political action from organizing into politically effective groups.

POLITICAL ACTIVISM AND THE ALIENATED

STUDY NOTE

This section discusses the types of people who lead opposition movements.

If you have read anything about conditions in developing nations, you have probably come across shocking figures about land ownership there. According to one recent source, 7 percent of the farms in Libya occupy 50 percent of the land.[4] According to the same chart, however, 4.6 percent of the farms occupy 50 percent of the farm land in the United States. In fact, this chart shows the United States to have a more inequitable land distribution than India (with 13.1 percent of farms occupying 50 percent of the land), the Philippines (11.8 percent), South Vietnam (5.4 percent), and Panama (5 percent). To be sure, the United States is ahead of Egypt (with 1.9 percent), Honduras (2.6 percent), Nicaragua (3.6 percent), pre-revolutionary Cuba (2.2 percent), the Dominican Republic (1.5 percent), Uruguay (3.4 percent), El Salvador (1.2 percent), Brazil (1.5 percent), Colombia (1.9 percent), Guatemala (.3 percent), Argentina (1.8 percent) Ecuador (.7 percent), Peru (3.1 percent), Iraq (.7 percent), Costa Rica (.9 percent), Venezuela (.7 percent), Chile (.3 percent), and Bolivia (2.3 percent). Due to faulty reporting, the fact that large land-holding families sometimes divide titles among relatives to disguise total family holdings, and because some land reforms have taken place since some of these figures (e.g., in Cuba and Egypt) were gathered, these figures may not be exact. The country with the most equitable distribution (out of forty-seven surveyed) was Poland, where 22.3 percent of the farms occupied 50 percent of the farmland. Obviously there is great disparity in the distribution of farmland everywhere.

What these figures do not tell is how this disparity affects the social and economic life of the nation. In the United States, enormous cattle ranches spread across the Western states. In the cereal growing areas the relative size of farms is smaller. Still, mechanization has markedly increased the area that can be farmed by one person. Many smaller farmers have sold their plots to agri-businesses and

---
[4] Bruce M. Russett, "Inequality and Instability: the Relation of Land Tenure to Politics," in *When Men Revolt and Why,* ed. James Chowning Davies (New York: The Free Press, 1971), pp. 210–211.

moved on to jobs in the towns and cities. The worst rural poverty probably exists among migrant workers, plantation workers, sharecroppers, and small-town dwellers. If the larger ranches and farms were broken down (or the smaller farms amalgamated) so that all farms in the United States were identical in size, these people would not necessarily benefit unless they were included in the distribution. But if former farm workers can find jobs in town—as they often can—and if tenants and migrants can unionize, the present uneven skewing of land distribution could be made compatible with both high productivity and job stability for the great majority. *This is because many jobs are available for people who do not own farms.*

In the United States (by Russett's figures) 10 percent of the labor force is engaged in agriculture. Among developing nations this figure is much higher; in the countries just mentioned it ranges from 25 percent in Argentina to 81 percent in Iraq, with a mean of 58 percent. *The city cannot offer adequate employment to the surplus rural population,* so peasants are forced to remain behind working small plots with inadequate capital under conditions of economic peonage. Consider the figures in Table 5.1 for land distribution in Latin America in 1960 (a year when the total rural population there was 111 million):

Clearly the majority of rural residents must subsist on minimal or no land. As discussed earlier, this is often the worst land: it is the land least serviced by irrigation or credit. Sample ratios of the number of farm extension agents per farm (Mexico 1:10,000; Costa Rica 1:1,600; Nicaragua 1:1,900; El Salvador 1:3,200; Honduras 1:5,000; Guatemala 1:11,000) give an indication of how little governmental assistance can be expected by an individual peasant.[6]

Approaching the matter from an angle involving more than sheer size of plot, the Inter-American Committee for Agricultural Development identified plots of land too small to provide full employment for one family or to yield them an income sufficient to sustain a standard of living considered to be a minimum for the region concerned. These they defined as *minifundios.*

TABLE 5.1.

Latin American Land Distribution by Size of Holding[5]

SIZE OF HOLDING	PERCENTAGE OF TOTAL ARABLE LAND
22,000,000 landless heads of household	
5,445,000 holdings under 50 acres	
(averaging $12\frac{1}{2}$ acres each)	3.7
2,000,000 holdings 50–2,500 acres	31.3
105,000 holdings 2,500 + acres	65
29,550,000 heads of household	100%

[5] Jacques Chonchol, "Land Tenure and Development in Latin America," in *Obstacles to Change in Latin America,* ed. Claudio Veliz (London: Oxford University Press, 1965), pp. 81–82.

[6] Roger D. Hansen, *The Politics of Mexican Development* (Baltimore: Johns Hopkins University Press, 1971), p. 86.

Family and medium-sized farms are defined as those that offer more than the defined sub-subsistence level of the *minifundios* yet employ fewer than twelve regular workers. *Latifundios* employ more than twelve workers. Thus the figures in Table 5.2 tell us that in all the countries listed the great majority of agricultural workers are employed either on farms that are too small to support them or on family or medium-sized farms. Colombia, Ecuador, Guatemala, and Peru have a high percentage of farms in the *minifundio* category. The most economically advanced nations on the list, Argentina, Brazil, and Chile, have a higher percentage of family or medium-sized farms; this is probably related to the fact that in these nations the urban middle classes are in a better position to invest in rural real estate, hiring tenants and migrant workers. In each of these countries, a high percentage of the rural population is obviously in a position of considerable economic dependency on landlords, moneylenders, and commodities middlemen.

In general, Latin America's patterns of rural economic dependency are the most inequitable in the developing world. There are places in Africa and Southeast Asia that probably still give farm families more independence than is true in most of Latin America; statistics are difficult to find for land distribution in Africa. Still, in the most populous parts of Asia and Africa the dependency patterns are probably as bad as in Latin America.

Ecuador, Guatemala, and Peru have a large number of indigenous people with a very simple standard of living; they are mainly *minifundistas*. The family and medium-sized farms are generally more productive and more modern in appearance. It would be a mistake, however, to assume that the latter therefore offer a more adequate lifestyle to their workers. Chapter 3 indicated that both the traditional villages and workers on slightly larger farms have already encountered considerable economic disruption and breakup of traditional lands. Without knowing the details of individual cases, it is not possible to say that a *minifundista* (perhaps living in a traditional village with its traditions of self-help) is poorer than a migrant worker, or even that the owner of a family-sized farm is better off than a tenant on a nearby estate. Nor is it entirely clear that those with access to education or social security benefits or even with greater income are better off than those without such access. *What is clear is that large percentages of the rural populations of developing nations are no longer able to sustain themselves in the traditional village* and—in settings of extremely limited resources—are debtors, tenants, migrants, or hired laborers on lands to which they once had unrestricted access.

We have already examined some results of this disruption:

- The high percentage of South Vietnamese peasants paying high rents for small plots of land
- The attachment of peasants of Negros and Luzon to the sugar mills
- The marked rise in tenancy and small farmer debts in Burma
- The development of urban control over farmland and moneylending in India and Pakistan, and the economic realities behind the *panchayats* and Basic Democracies
- The acquisition of entire villages by *shaikhs* and merchants in the Middle East

TABLE 5.2.

1960s Latin American Land Distribution by Type of Holding[7]

	MINIFUNDIOS			FAMILY AND MEDIUM-SIZED FARMS		LATIFUNDIOS		
	% of farms	% of land occupied	% of labor employed	% of land occupied	% of labor employed	% of farms	% of land occupied	% of labor employed
Argentina	43.2	3.4	30	61	64	0.8	36.9	6
Brazil	22.5	0.5	11	40	68	4.7	59.5	21
Colombia	64	4.9	58	50	38	1.3	49.5	4
Chile	36.9	0.2	13	21	49	6.9	81.3	38
Ecuador	89.9	16.6	—	—	—	0.4	45.1	—
Guatemala	88.4	14.3	68	45	25	0.1	40.8	7
Peru	88	7.4	—	—	—	1.1	82.4	—

- The acquisition of prime croplands by whites and, later, wealthier Africans in African colonial areas
- The growth of plantations and small-holding estates in tropical Africa
- The superceding of tribal law by European rules of individual ownership and rent
- The introduction of slavery and, later, fiefdoms in the Caribbean and South America
- The tenancy and debt arrangements of homesteading
- The economic role of church leaders in Mudande
- The market grading system in Nigeria
- The rubber traders in Kuching and Brazil
- The nature of wage and rental agreements in Latin America
- The government marketing agencies in Africa
- The ineffectuality of rural syndicates and imbalance of rural credit in Brazil and Mexico
- The dearth of development programs for small farmers in Ghana and the Ivory Coast

Oscar Lewis lists some of the personal effects of this displacement.

. . . this constant struggle for survival, unemployment and underemployment, low wages, a miscellany of unskilled occupations, child labor, the absence of savings, a chronic shortage of cash, the absence of food reserves in the home . . . the pawning of personal goods, borrowing from local money lenders at usurious rates of interest, spontaneous informal credit devices . . . organized by neighbors, and the use of second-hand clothing and furniture.[8]

John H. Kautsky also reviews the grip of middlemen, merchants, moneylenders, and landlords over the rural dweller—how the middleman manipulates prices to keep them low, leaving the farmer insufficient income to pay off his debts to the moneylenders, merchants, and landlords, and driving him deeper and deeper into debt and peonage.[9] He notes that the middleman, merchant, and moneylender is often the same individual, and is in a position to acquire land and become a landlord as well. He concludes that "having brought to the peasant this new kind of misery, that they are not popular with him is obvious." I am not sure this is obvious. Kinship and patron-client relationships connect the peasant with those occupying these roles. The line between landlord, moneylender, and *peasant* is not always a clear one. In the words of Eric Wolf:

[7] Celso Furtado, *Economic Development in Latin America* (Cambridge: Cambridge University Press, 1970), pp. 54–55. See Solon Barraclough, ed., *Agrarian Structure in Latin America: A Resumé of the CIDA Land Tenure Studies* (Lexington, Mass.: D. C. Heath, 1973). Figures for "percentage of land occupied" do not all total exactly 100 percent across the columns; they come from different tables.

[8] Oscar Lewis, "The Culture of Poverty," in *Development and Society,* ed. David E. Novack and Robert Lekachman (New York: St. Martins, 1964), p. 253.

[9] John H. Kautsky, *The Political Consequences of Modernization* (New York: John Wiley, 1972), pp. 96–97.

... peasant's interests—especially among the poor peasants—often cross-cut any class alignments. Rich and poor peasants may be kinsfolk, or a peasant may be at one and the same time owner, renter, sharecropper, labourer for his neighbors and seasonal hand on a nearby plantation. Each different involvement aligns him differently with his fellows and with the outside world.[10]

The person oppressing you in some way may at the same time provide a valuable contact for political or economic favors, and be bound to you by reciprocal obligations. There is no assurance about where people will direct their resentments, regardless of source of aggravation.

In fact, *there is growing evidence that those demonstrating the greatest political disaffection are not those whose conditions would appear to be most miserable.* Analyzing peasant rebellions in Mexico, Russia, China, Vietnam, Algeria, and Cuba, Eric Wolf argues that the chief instigators were not the poorest strata of *minifundistas,* workers on plantations and *latifundios,* landless peasants, or wage laborers, but were instead moderately successful small cash-cropping landowners, or tenants with absentee landlords.[11] He sees such individuals as evolving from a situation in which land, labor, and wealth were integral parts of their life and social organization. The land and patterns of livelihood belonged to the ancestors and were being held as a trust. The forms of labor were carefully prescribed by custom. This has changed. Their current situation causes them to look upon land, labor, and wealth simply as commodities to be bought and sold. This seriously erodes their community ties without at the same time giving them enough land or money to be secure. They are likely to act to increase their own security—not that of those below them economically.

His is a balancing act in which his balance is continuously threatened by population growth; by the encroachment of rival landlords; by the loss of rights to grazing, forest, and water; by falling prices and unfavorable conditions of the market; by interest payments and foreclosures.[12]

Indeed, most of the members of the minor patron-client networks face a similar form of insecurity, as do most dwellers of the towns and cities. Some figures compiled by the Bank of Mexico for the average real[13] family earnings in that country in 1963 point to the economic uncertainty of people at all strata. Those in the lowest 10 percent brought home only US$18 each month. Yet even the *top* 2.4 percent of the wage earners brought home an average of only US$571 per family per month, while often spending more than the average United States citizen for items such as automobiles, housing, and appliances (which many of them own). Those in the next lowest 2.4 percent brought home only US$393 a

---

[10] Eric Wolf, "On Peasant Rebellions," *New Society* 362, no. 4 (September 1969): 351.

[11] See also James C. Scott, *The Moral Economy of the Peasant: Rebellion and Subsistence in Southeast Asia* (New Haven, Conn.: Yale University Press, 1976), pp. 193ff; and Colin Harding, "Land Reform and Social Conflict in Peru," in *The Peruvian Experiment: Continuity and Change Under Military Rule,* ed. Abraham Lowenthal (Princeton, N.J.: Princeton University Press, 1975), pp. 222–224.

[12] Eric R. Wolf, *Peasant Wars of the Twentieth Century* (New York: Harper & Row, 1969), p. 292.

[13] Adjusted to the 1950 cost of living.

month, with US$259 for the next lowest 5.2 percent, and US$156 a month for the 10 percent below that.[14] A university graduate in India can hope to earn between US$60 and US$120 a month teaching in secondary school.[15]

In Nigeria the average Lagos worker earned US$25-45 per month in 1963—half the amount a commission found necessary to provide a minimum standard of living for a family of three. The highest paid government official could hope to earn US$700 a month (plus use of a vehicle and driver, and subsidized housing), while a recent university graduate brought home US$175 a month. The 1963 inflation rate stood at 3 percent. By 1972, inflation had reached 12 percent, and average wages were US$52-81 per month. Between 1974 and 1977, inflation on food prices officially averaged 34 percent,[16] though unofficial estimates placed it far higher. Wage increases stayed much lower than this, and imported goods were being marketed for twice their European markup because of patron-client monopolies on their local marketing. Between 1963 and 1972, the average monthly wage for Nigerian managers surveyed was US$415, versus US$608 for their European counterparts sent in by multinational corporations.

Many modern writers suggest that professional people in these top income groupings may be among the most disaffected members of society. James C. Davies argues that sudden periodic recessions have the most profound effect on those who have been benefitting from previous periods of prosperity. These people have often developed rising expectations which contrast sharply with their loss in status caused by the recession.[17] Expanding on this hypothesis, Ted Robert Gurr argues that opportunities must match expectations in order to avoid personal maladjustment.[18] Mancur Olson, Jr., notes that economic growth itself can create such maladjustments, both among those who lose out to rivals, and those who gain.[19] Unstable personal environments ensue.

Interestingly, *those at lower levels of society have a number of defense mechanisms that temper their disaffection.* The sheer time and effort required to stay alive, and the general lack of leadership abilities among this strata are of course highly important factors. Workers are often competing with *one another* for scarce jobs and resources.[20] Plantation workers and rural tenants working the

---

[14] Hansen, *The Politics of Mexican Development*, p. 75.

[15] Peter C. Lloyd, *Classes, Crises and Couples* (New York: Praeger, 1972), pp. 105-108.

[16] Food and Agriculture Organization, *State of Food and Agriculture 1978* (Rome: United Nations, 1979), p. A45; Thomas J. Biersteker, *Distortion or Development? Contending Perspectives on the Multinational Corporation* (Cambridge, Mass.: MIT Press, 1978), pp. 139-142.

[17] James C. Davies, "Toward a Theory of Revolution," *American Sociological Review* 6, no. 1 (February 1962): 5-19.

[18] Ted Robert Gurr, *Why Men Rebel* (Princeton, N.J.: Princeton University Press, 1970).

[19] Mancur Olson, Jr., "Rapid Growth as a Destabilizing Force," *Journal of Economic History* 23, no. 4 (December 1963): 529-552.

[20] Wolf, "On Peasant Rebellions," p. 351: "Romantics to the contrary, it is not easy for a peasant to engage in sustained rebellion. . . . First a peasant's work is more often done alone, on his own land, than in conjunction with his fellows. Moreover, all peasants are to some extent competitors, both for available resources within the community and for services of credit from without. Secondly, the tyranny of work weighs heavily on peasants; their life is geared to an annual routine and to planning for the year to come. Momentary alteration of routine threatens their ability to face up to the routine later. Thirdly, control of land enables them, more often than not, to retreat into subsistence production if adverse conditions alter their market crops."

land of resident owners may be held back from revolutionary activity by the close presence of the landowners.[21] The sense of lord-serf relationship can be so deeply engrained in peasants that they carry it with them long after their move to the city.[22] With the arrival of new challengers for leadership (party leaders, bureaucrats, etc.) the traditional village leadership often moves to repress internal dissent among those who stay in the countryside. Those who do move to the city may not immediately experience an improvement in their standard of living, yet feel gratified at a new sense of freedom.[23] Slum dwellers and poorer peasants are often imbued with a strong sense of hope. A 1963 survey of Venezuela *barrios* found 69 percent of respondents saying they thought their situation would improve in the next five years;[24] this phenomenon has been noted by other researchers elsewhere.

Evangelina Garcia believes from her research in Venezuela barrios that advertising helps promote a sense of well-being and blurs class differences. People living in squatter shacks with dirt floors feel "I don't have a floor to wax, but I can buy the wax if I want to." When they do buy a shampoo or dishwashing liquid sloganized on the transistor radio they feel a sense of self-esteem. They feel that ownership of products is a matter of luck, and luck can change.[25]

Those slightly higher up the scale of achievement may be more prone to lash out against their condition. Gurr[26] points to research supporting this notion: In a 1940s study of Guatemalan villages Europeanized *Ladinos* responded aggressively in connection with Rorschach tests five times as often as their Indian neighbors. The authors' conclusion was that *Ladino* culture creates "wants and desires which cannot be fully satisfied by the cultural resources" of the village community. Interviews of Luo, Ganda, and Zulu peoples in Africa during the 1950s found that discontent rose along with educational level. Another study found that more Europeanized Uganda secondary students were more aggressive than less Europeanized Kenyan students. Early 1960s interviews with students in Colombia found them believing in education as a means for upward mobility, yet dissatisfied with their own prospects for achievement. Lest one hastily interpret these results to mean that education and exposure to modernization in

---

[21] Arthur L. Stinchcombe, "Agricultural Enterprise and Rural Class Relations," *The American Journal of Sociology* 67 (September 1961): 165–176, presents this argument. Landowners living on their estates may be more generous about their reciprocal obligations than those living away, too.

[22] For example, see Marcio Moreira Alves, "Urban Guerillas and the Terrorist State," in *Contemporary Brazil: Issues in Economic and Political Development,* ed. H. Jon Rosenbaum and William G. Tyler (New York: Praeger, 1972), p. 61.

[23] See Mehmet Bequiraj, *Peasantry in Revolution* (Ithaca, N.Y.: Center for International Studies, Cornell University, 1967).

[24] Talton F. Ray, *The Politics of the Barrios in Venezuela* (Berkeley: University of California Press, 1969), p. 156.

[25] Richard J. Barnet and Ronald E. Müller, *Global Reach: The Power of the Multinational Corporations* (New York: Simon & Schuster, 1974) pp. 175–176.

[26] Gurr, *Why Men Rebel,* p. 96. Leonard W. Doob, *Becoming More Civilized* (New Haven, Conn.: Yale University Press, 1960), pp. 79–84, reviewing much of this same data, reached a similar conclusion. However, he warns (p. 81) that inadequacies in the testing techniques might have hidden some aggressiveness in one or both of the test groups in each study.

themselves produce discontent, Gurr cites a number of studies to show that education accompanied by advancement in economic position produces contentment. It is the creation of new *unfulfilled* demands that leads to frustration. And neither those in traditional settings nor those who have achieved secure positions in modern society are readily susceptible to revolt because of unfulfilled demands.

> While there are demands, sometimes even very strong ones, even in remote rural areas, for material improvements, for consumer goods, and for jobs, these demands occur within a still viable context in which provision for a minimum of economic, social, and psychological security dampens whatever frustrations unfulfilled demands generate.[27]

Hence *the greatest threat to incumbent regimes comes from those in the society who seem to have achieved some degree of success, but who have encountered setbacks along the way.* In urban areas this describes many unemployed and underchallenged intellectuals. In the countryside, rebellion is most likely to emerge from among the moderately successful small cash-cropping landowner or the tenant with absentee landlord and outside income. John Duncan Powell found that 47.2 percent of the local leaders of the peasant unions he studied had lived in the city, 12.7 percent of them for over ten years. All the local leaders combined averaged eight years membership in the labor movement, and fourteen years in a political party.[28] Miners familiar with patterns of industrial organization and students played an important role in founding peasant syndicates in Bolivia.[29] Henry Landsberger observed in his study of a Chile vineyard workers' strike that "at no time was an important position of leadership, even at the local level, held by anyone who at the time was earning his livelihood as a *campesino* [peasant]."[30] The leaders in Santiago, who directed the strike, were all middle- and upper-middle-class professionals. And Cynthia N. Hewitt remarks on the peasant movement in Pernambuco, Brazil:

> The highest leadership of all factions involved in the Pernambican movement came from outside the peasant class . . . These leaders were aided on a lower level by students, who seem to have played an important role in the orientation of local peasant groups . . . It was the policy of all groups to encourage peasant leadership at the local level. . . the local leadership of the *ligas* seemed to vary. Some presidents were peasants, a few were rather large landowners [125 to 800

[27] Gurr, *Why Men Rebel*, p. 98, quoting Anthony Oberschall.

[28] John Duncan Powell, "Venezuela: The Peasant Union Movement," in *Latin American Peasant Movements*, ed. Henry A. Landsberger (Ithaca, N.Y.: Cornell University Press, 1969), pp. 81–82.

[29] Dwight B. Heath, "Bolivia: Peasant Syndicates among the Aymara of the Yungas—A View From the Grass Roots," in Landsberger, *Peasant Movements*, 193.

[30] Henry A. Landsberger, "Chile: A Vineyard Workers' Strike—A Case Study of the Relationship Between Church, Intellectuals, and Peasants," in Landsberger, *Peasant Movements*, 265.

acres of land], and one . . . was a fisherman . . . whatever the exact number of peasants in positions of leadership . . . it seems likely that they depended quite heavily on the advice and orientation of non-peasants.[31]

Shanti Tangri points to some studies of unemployment in India that showed that a higher percentage of unemployed people were literate than were literate among the population as a whole, and that literate people tended to stay unemployed longer than those illiterate.[32] He also notes that, in Indian society at least, the younger educated middle classes have fewer opportunities for sexual, artistic, and athletic outlets than the population as a whole. Writers, social reformers, artists, poets, teachers, religious preachers, dreamers, city planners, sociologists, journalists, and economists frequently live within slum neighborhoods. In this light, the following observations about the Indian Communist Party are not surprising:

> Traditionally . . . Communist Party members have tended to come from upper and middle castes and from the classes of small landlords, rich or middle peasants, and petty bourgeoisie, not from the lowest castes or from poor peasants or landless labourers. Some Communists hail from old landed families forced to the wall by modern capitalist farmers and merchants. Some, especially Brahmins, are literati who eagerly sought modern scientific education against the oppression of orthodox parents. Others—middle peasants, village merchants, or schoolteachers—saw no hope of advancement under the existing order with its backward-looking beliefs, elaborate caste ranking, and subservience to the wealthy who prospered from imperial rule.[33]

After a broad review of the literature, two authors conclude:

> Revolutionary leaders are usually men of early middle years, that is, men of considerable maturity, not yet old enough to have been co-opted into the ruling elite. Most often they are middle class in origin. . . . The rank and file of revolution are hard to categorize except to say that like their leaders they are frustrated people. It is easier to say what they are not than what they are. They are not the dregs of society, and they are usually not peasants. Under some circumstances the peasantry of a country can be revolutionized, but once their simple basic demands are met, they quickly revert to conservatism.[34]

---

[31] Cynthia N. Hewitt, "Brazil: The Peasant Movement of Pernambuco, 1961–1964," in Landsberger, *Peasant Movements,* pp. 387–388. Shepard Forman, "Disunity and Discontent: A Study of Peasant Political Movements in Brazil," in *Protest and Resistance in Angola and Brazil,* ed. Ronald H. Chilkote (Berkeley: University of California Press, 1972), p. 193, makes a similar assessment. James C. Scott and Ben Kerkvliet, "The Politics of Survival: Peasant Response to 'Progress' in Southeast Asia," *Journal of Southeast Asian Studies* 4, no. 2 (September 1973): 262–268, and Benedict J. Kerkvliet, *The Huk Rebellion* (Berkeley: University of California, 1977), pp. 262–266, indicate the same sources of leadership for Southeast Asian peasant movements.

[32] Shanti Tangri, "Urbanization, Political Stability and Economic Growth," in *Political Development and Social Change,* 2nd ed., ed. Jason L. Finkle and Richard W. Gable (New York: John Wiley, 1966), p. 216. Educated people may fail to seek jobs they deem inferior.

[33] Kathleen Gough, "The Indian Revolutionary Potential," *Monthly Review* 20, no. 9 (February 1969): 31.

[34] Carl Leiden and Karl M. Schmitt, *The Politics of Violence: Revolution in the Modern World* (Englewood Cliffs, N.J.: Prentice-Hall, 1968) p. 95.

Alienation, then, affects not only the poor. It results from imbalances that over- or under-educate individuals in terms of available jobs, placing them in cultural settings to which it is difficult to adapt, restraining them from desired lifestyles, making their economic commitments perpetually greater than income, or producing chronic insecurities with regard to the future. Unfortunately, high percentages of inhabitants of developing nations in all walks of life probably find themselves in such dilemmas. Yet, whether through habits of obeisance, fear, lack of imagination, or other reasons to be discussed shortly, most people are not prone to translate such alienation into political activism. Political activism is largely reserved for a small segment of those alienated people who are economically and educationally beyond the bottom rungs of society. This leaves the organization of dissident political movements largely in the hands of people who (unlike a poor peasant living away from passable roads, for instance) are easy to locate and isolate from popular contact. It also makes radical movements easy to co-opt into the system. Frances G. Hutchins comments:

> A revolution, though couched in terms of equality for all, usually involves the devolution of power only one step from the aristocracy to the bourgeoisie in the city, from landlord to rich peasant on the land. The rich peasants, like the bourgeoisie, are in a position to reap the most immediate material rewards from revolution.[35]

In discussing revolution, Professor Hutchins summarizes well the factor that *prevents* modern revolutions from being revolutionary. The leaders of movements, whether they are peasant syndicates or revolutionary parties, *walk a fine line between being opponents of the patron-client networks, or becoming new members of them.* This is why modern revolutionary movements often dwindle into rebellions. They are rebellions within the patron-client networks rather than against them—mutinies on shipboard rather than attempts to sink the ship.

ALIENATION AND CATHARSIS

STUDY NOTE

This section, and the next one, analyze why most alienated people do not become involved in opposition movements.

If the preceding discussion is on the right track, it would follow that considerable numbers of citizens in developing nations are alienated. We have established that some of the alienated people become political activists. What happens to the rest of them? Why aren't they activists? And if they are not, *what do they do to relieve their frustrations?* Do they constitute a vast powder keg

---

[35] Frances G. Hutchins, "On Winning and Losing by Revolution: Racism and Revolution in the United States and Comparable Developing Countries," *Public Policy* 18, no. 1 (Fall 1969): 28-29.

ready to explode some day when a spark is lit? Or are they of lesser political potential?

Obviously, the sorts of tools for repression in the hands of governments inhibit overt dissident political activity.[36] One can never be sure how many people show no signs of political disaffection simply because they are frightened to show such signs. I think it likely, however, that in addition much disaffection dissipates because it is diverted into politically ineffectual channels. Sports, sex, festivals, shows, fighting, and military maneuvers provide substitute satisfactions and distractions for discontented people. More importantly, the processes of modernization and urbanization cause mixings of racial and cultural groups that lead to prejudice and antagonisms. Paradoxically, the instability that results (including, at times, even mass rioting and killing) may help to stabilize the control of the patron-client networks rather than weaken it. We shall discuss sports and sex in this section, and the thesis that civil unrest may strengthen *status quo* rule, in the next.

Oscar Lewis, discussing the release patterns of the urban poor in developing nations, mentions gregariousness, a high incidence of alcoholism, frequent resort to violence in the settlement of quarrels, frequent use of physical violence in the training of children, wife beating, early initiation into sex, free unions or consensual marriages, a relatively high incidence of the abandonment of mothers and children, a strong predisposition to authoritarianism, relatively little ability to defer gratification and plan for the future, a belief in male superiority with a corresponding martyr complex among women, and a high tolerance for psychological pathology of all sorts.[37] It is likely that in rural villages some of the more overt forms of violence mentioned here would be restrained by public opinion. Among the urban middle class there is in general probably less gregariousness, less overt violence, later marriage, and more planning for the future. But in simplest terms Lewis has described means by which men and women relieve themselves of alienation.

Years ago, Emile Durkheim suggested that social violence may be an index of (among other things) levels of political dissatisfaction. Efforts to measure this dissatisfaction have not been very successful.[38] Anthony F. C. Wallace theorizes that periods of what he calls increased individual stress and cultural distortion (e.g., racial tension), characterized by the sorts of activities mentioned in the previous paragraph, generally precede the beginnings of revitalization via a revolutionary movement.[39] He suggests that if an individual suffering stress and distortion is not helped by a revitalization movement to reestablish a balance between his values and the realities of his environment (whether through peaceful or violent means) he or she may become politically disaffected.

I would like you to entertain an alternative possibility: Stress and cultural

---

[36] See Chapter 4, p. 143.

[37] Lewis, "The Culture of Poverty," pp. 253-254.

[38] For instance, see Chalmers Johnson, *Revolutionary Change* (Boston: Little, Brown, 1966), pp. 119-134; John Gunn, *Violence* (New York: Praeger, 1973), pp. 77-78; Emile Durkheim, *Suicide* (Glencoe, Ill.: The Free Press, 1951), pp. 348-353. It would be most difficult to relate the figures computed in these sources to political dissatisfaction.

[39] Anthony F. C. Wallace, *Culture and Personality* (New York: Random House, 1961), pp. 146-152.

distortion can simply continue as a permanent situation, with individuals relieving their frustrations on an *ad hoc* day-by-day basis. Central to Wallace's theory of revitalization is the creation of an alternative vision for society, communicated to a mass following through an organized movement. This is a common stage in successful revolutionary movements of the past century. But the sorts of coercive techniques discussed in the preceding chapter militate against the creation of such movements in developing nations, and illustrate the ease with which revolutionary leadership can be co-opted into established patron-client networks. In such situations, the individual might simply find other means to relieve stress and cultural distortions.

Violence was not a stranger to the traditional societies surveyed in Chapter 2. Nuer men killed over an insult to a cow; Trobrianders were known to wipe out entire neighboring villages during times of drought; the history of the coastal Andes is replete with continuing bloody warfare. Cannibalism has been popular in the Amazon valley, Melanesia, and elsewhere. The violence of traditional societies, however, is subject to community restraint. Warfare is carried out by the entire community and ends when the leaders declare it ended. Individual acts of violence are restrained by the community mores and adjudication, and gregariousness is far more common than is violence.

Eric Wolf and Edward Hansen describe four Latin American villages. Two are traditional, with the sorts of ties described in Chapter 2 still intact. The other two, because of their involvement with cash-cropping, are somewhat better off economically yet are less well integrated socially.[40] *Both traditional villages* provide forums to let off steam: frequent fiestas and family celebrations, chewing of coca by both sexes, frequent routine drunkenness for the men. When personal animosities arise a village council and witchcraft are used to settle disputes. Hence the homicide rate is very low in both places. *In the two villages that are more involved in cash-cropping,* it is considerably higher. Many inhabitants are newcomers and do not know one another. In one, drinking is confined to weekends in a local pub. Late evening fights resulting in stabbings and, later, blood feuds are frequent there. In the other, drunkenness is rare but explosive.

> When this occurs . . . the Totonac of Tajín exhibit a degree of violence which is in marked contrast to their everyday behavior. The Tajín drunk is dangerous; he may attack suddenly and unpredictably with machete or fire arms. To avoid such behavior, men are made to yield up their arms on public occasions, and aggressive drunks are tied up and jailed. Yet hostility breaks out in still another way, in personal vengeance and resultant homicide. Homicide is frequent; in two years more than 10 percent of the local male population has been assassinated.[41]

---

[40] Eric R. Wolf and Edward C. Hansen, *The Human Condition in Latin America* (New York: Oxford University Press, 1972), pp. 71–99, based on William W. Stein, *Life in the Highlands of Peru* (Ithaca, N.Y.: Cornell University Press, 1961): Orlando Fals-Borda, *Peasant Society in the Colombian Andes* (University of Florida Press, 1955); and Angel Palerm and Carmen Viqueira, "Alcoholismo, brujería y homicidio en dos communidades rurales de México," in *América Indígena* 14, no. 1 (January 1954): 7–36.

[41] Wolf and Hansen, *The Human Condition,* p. 98, quoting from Palerm and Vigueira, "Alcoholismo."

Modernization toned down some of the boisterousness of this village (which must be far more prone to violence than the average village experiencing the stresses of modernization) but did not provide the means to curb violence. In both the cash-cropping villages, that violence is expending itself in personal, not political, reprisals.

Discussion of Burma is continued from p. 81.

Manning Nash found a similar contrast between two villages in upper Burma.[42] In this case both villages were heavily involved in patron-clientism; but in one the kinship structure was still intact, while in the other it had disintegrated. The integrated village was composed of long-term inhabitants who still elected a headman and village council. It was, however, to the wealthiest man in town—a cotton broker and large landowner, serving on the council—that the villagers looked for leadership. When U Nu's Union Party sought to build an organization, it turned to this man. Within three months the party had thirty-nine members and closed its rolls. A survey by Nash showed that this man, his relatives, and his clients formed the core of the organization. All bargaining for favors with national and regional figures was carried on through it. The community could get quick and relatively easily-obtained services when they needed them; it voted preponderantly for the Union Party.

The land surrounding the other village was largely in the hands of a few absentee landowners. The village itself was largely composed of migrant tenants. Nash's survey found little agreement here as to who was recognized as a community leader. There were three parties active in the village, but only a total of fifteen party members; most preferred the freedom to change support for factions according to promises made. The men jockeying for power tended to represent specialized economic interests (larger landowners, smaller landowners, tenants, etc.). When land reform was announced the villagers elected a local council to implement it.

> The actual distribution of land was attended by corruption, inefficiency, favoritism, and eventually led to fighting and murder. The inept and corrupt parceling out of land pitted villager against villager, but it was not the cause of internal disruption. It was merely a symptom. A village such as this was held together only under the twin constraints of administration and military force.[43]

A study of two slum neighborhoods in Kampala, Uganda, parallels these observations.[44] An effort was made to isolate two neighborhoods of comparable size and socioeconomic level, one of which had a low rate of crime and the other a higher rate. The low crime neighborhood proved to be culturally homogeneous, with a great many inhabitants related to one another, and higher participation in religious and organizational activities. The neighborhood with the higher crime

---

[42] Manning Nash, "Party Building in Upper Burma," *Asian Survey* 3, no. 4 (April 1963): 197–202.

[43] Ibid., p. 200.

[44] Marshall B. Clinard and Daniel J. Abbott, *Crime in Developing Countries: A Comparative Perspective* (New York: John Wiley, 1973), pp. 142–165.

rate was more heterogeneous in tribal mix, and had fewer families related to one another and less participation in organizations.

Deprived of the sense of self-worth they might have experienced in traditional communities, men sometimes turn to assertiveness to enhance their own self-image. Octavio Paz, writing about Latin Americans, observes:

> It is revealing that our intimacy never flowers in a natural way, only when incited by fiestas, alcohol, or death. Slaves, servants, and submerged races always wear a mask, whether smiling or sullen. Only when they are alone, during the great moments of life, do they show themselves as they really are. All their relationships are poisoned by fear and suspicion; fear of the master and suspicion of their equals.[45]

Chingar, in Spanish, "is to do violence to another. The verb is masculine, active, cruel; it stings, wounds, gashes, stains. And it provokes a bitter, resentful satisfaction."[46] It has its roots in the *conquistador,* the *caudillo* leaders, the rural bandits: the great symbols of *machismo.* The continuing series of coups, assassinations, and kidnappings in Latin America remind one that the tradition is still alive in politics, though on a day-to-day basis it is much muted. Latin American males (who are fond of exaggerating) like to use the word *chingar* when referring to drinking, rape, and business transactions, in addition to political plots.

The expression may be translated into African and Asian settings as well. Houses of prostitution are common in most parts of the developing world. Robberies and molestations are problems in most urban slums. Most cultures have alcoholic beverages and, in smaller quantities, drugs. For areas not reached by these stimulants, governments often furnish means for releasing such aggressive instincts. Lotteries can be found in many countries. Soccer and other team sports are virtual national pastimes in many developing nations. Even urbanites frequently celebrate festivals and cultural displays. Many governments have built giant arenas in the national capital, and encourage frequent elaborate pageants, sports events, and parades. These events all provide means by which people can personally assert their own exuberance and mastery. One author, probably also exaggerating a bit, notes some middle class *macho-chingar* pastimes:

> Automobiles multiply in Rio de Janiero's streets, proudly bearing plastic emblems with the national colors which proclaim, "Brazil, you're unbeatable," or more aggressively, "Love it or leave it." In São Paulo men no longer talk of women . . . on downtown street corners. They speak of stocks, nominative, common, preferred, quotations, predictions, and dividends. The middle class, bought off by the system, has become a stockholder playing the market; it has discovered a magic formula for sharing in power. A new law prohibits newspapers from publishing "alarmist" reports on stock quotations; to do so would be "a crime against national security."[47]

---

[45] Octavio Paz, "The Sons of La Malinche," in *Conflict and Violence in Latin American Politics,* ed. Francisco José Moreno and Barbara Mitrani (New York: Crowell, 1971), p. 62.

[46] Paz, "Sons of La Malinche," p. 67.

[47] Eduardo Galeano, "Brazil and Uruguay: Euphoria and Agony," *Monthly Review* 23, no. 9 (February 1972): 32.

He also notes that in Porto Alegre the number of nightclubs grew from 12 to 200 between 1964 and 1971.

Webster's New Collegiate Dictionary variously defines the word catharsis as meaning "elimination of a complex by bringing it to consciousness and affording it expression . . . purification or purgation of the emotions by art . . . cleansing." In ancient Greece Aristotle observed that plays had an emotional effect on viewers, who, by empathizing with the actors, could purge themselves of innermost feelings that had been pent up within themselves. This was called *catharsis*. Freud referred to his sessions with patients as being cathartic when patients, recalling remote painful events, were able to conceptually link them with their current angry, anxious, or sexual responses and thus gain emotional insight into themselves. Catharsis was gaining emotional relief by putting one's feelings into words. Today, psychotherapists tend to place less emphasis on the immediate emotional relief induced by therapy than upon long-range rational insights gained by the patient. A great deal of attention is devoted, however, to the question of the role played by aggression in relieving frustration. Most psychologists accept the notion that aggression relieves frustration, but argue among themselves about the conditions under which it does so. Leonard Berkowitz is a recognized authority on the study of aggression and is especially cautious about assessing the role it plays in relieving frustration. He states in a recent article:

> Summarizing (and simplifying) a great many studies, research results suggest that angry people often do (a) feel better, and (b) perhaps even experience a reduced inclination to attack their tormenters, upon learning that these persons have been hurt.[48]

In controlled experiments a person who has an opportunity to promptly retaliate against an aggressor after being transgressed tends (sometimes, but not always) to have better feelings toward the aggressor afterwards than one who has not had an immediate opportunity to retaliate or, especially, one whose retaliation has been interrupted. Berkowitz notes, however, that this may be due to guilt, and not to a discharge of energy. Sometimes, in fact, in the long run the retaliator becomes quite hostile toward the person he or she has retaliated against. Furthermore, a person who is provoked by another cannot receive satisfaction by retaliating against a neutral party. Another potentially aggressive activity—viewing violence in films—can induce psychic relief, but only if the viewer has been experiencing frustration while seeing the film and identifies the victim in the film with his or her own tormentor.[49] Berkowitz doubts that fantasy aggression can ever be a truly satisfying means for reducing anger.

Berkowitz also notes another side of the coin. When aggression is repeatedly rewarded (whether by a parent giving in to demands or the personal achievement of catharsis as a result of retaliation), an individual can become an habitual ag-

---

[48] Leonard Berkowitz, "Simple Views of Aggression," in *Man and Aggression,* 2nd ed., Ashley Montagu (New York: Oxford University Press, 1973), p. 51.

[49] Leonard Berkowitz, *Aggression: A Social Psychological Analysis* (New York: McGraw-Hill, 1962), pp. 219–220.

gressor. This is especially true if frustration continues. Such individuals will actually seek out opportunities for aggression and will achieve tension-reduction from the new acts of aggression *if* they are angry when committing the aggression. "Aggression is all too likely to lead to still more aggression." [50]

It seems self-evident to me that all the activities mentioned—from wife beating to spectator sports—constitute potentially cathartic activities. Whether they will function as such depends upon some of the provisos mentioned by Berkowitz. Those restrictions on the occurrence of catharsis, however, seem to strengthen the argument that catharsis can weaken the proclivities of frustrated people to join revolutionary movements. If one can transform one's generalized frustrations into anger—directed against neighbor, wife, husband, another team, the stock market, another racial group, or whomever—and commit some personal aggression against these individuals, "psychic energy" could dissipate. When the energy builds up again, one is tempted to repeat the action, and to repeat it while angry. This pattern of activity does not produce socially redeeming results or solve fundamental problems. To the contrary, it uses up energy reserves that might be stored for projects inducing more long-range societal benefit. In fact, habitual aggression reduces the self-control needed to defer action until a politically propitious time. Whether the aggressor ends up liking the aggressee more, or less, is immaterial to this conclusion.

During a visit to Angkor Wat in Cambodia I met a family of peasants who were also touring Angkor on an annual holiday visit with relatives. [51] They invited me to stay with them in a village some distance from the town, and I remained there for almost a week. Their thatched house was located along a small river; we slept on a raised platform on the floor. I would judge them to be of the small land-holding class in a relatively prosperous region. The time I spent with them was far from uneventful. We (the young men and, variously, the young women) went swimming twice, got drunk once on some local whiskey, visited a modern fair (complete with a stunt motorcyclist who drove up and down the sides of a large metal drum, and a flagon of the local aphrodesiac), spent considerable time arguing about the relative merits of fruit trees in Battembang and Siem Riep, attended a traditional dance and *wayang* show (a puppet show depicting the exploits of great warriors), visited several well-attended houses of prostitution, had a vigorous family quarrel when one of the young men was given the brush-off by a young lady, and had two family quarrels over what to buy at the market for supper. There were obvious frustrations: the brush-off by the girl, a family squabble because the two young men in the group who had achieved a high school education (and, through their French, were my sources of communication) wanted to move to Phnom Penh, a field that had not yielded properly that year, a limited diet, and an uncertain future. During most of the visit my hosts were not angry or aggressive and hence were probably not achieving catharsis. The point is that they could have. Each day was potentially laced with

---

[50] Berkowitz, "Simple Views," p. 52. See also Leonard Berkowitz, "The Frustration-Aggression Hypothesis Revisited," in *The Roots of Aggression: A Reexamination of the Frustration Hypothesis,* ed. Leonard Berkowitz (New York: Atherton, 1969).

[51] I refer those who find a personal account of this type unusual in this setting to the remarks on "common experience" in Chapter 1.

opportunities for counter-aggression, whether something exceptional like the fantasy of the motorcyclist (that night the young men happened to be agitated and angry) or the *wayang* show, or something more mundane like a family quarrel, some uninhibited remarks over whiskey, a visit to a prostitute, or a discussion about the poster on the wall of one house depicting alleged American atrocities in a Cambodian border town.

Two years later I visited with one of these young men. He had moved to the capital city of Phnom Penh. I found him peddling small wares in a poorer section of the city, apparently without great success. He was living with a large number of young people in a house rented from a fairly young man who was a high-ranking officer in the Cambodian army. The officer expressed extreme dissatisfaction with his low pay and the then-low status of the army in budgetary priorities. The students in the house expressed bitterness over the relative certainty that their degrees were not going to land them a job once they graduated. There were, however, festivities and a parade that week, in which all took part with obvious relish. Three of us rode two bicycles out to visit a relative in a village some miles from town, and joined in a collective village walk to see a train pass at a nearby crossing (an *event*). And a good deal of normal spare time was obviously spent in hanging around the markets and parks of the city, usually in small groups which would purchase snacks of fruit or cane and encounter friends for talk and banter. Once again, there were frustrations; but there were also ongoing mechanisms for releasing some psychic energy.

Discussion of the Philippines is continued from p. 116.

In the early 1970s, a journalist interviewed peasants in a rural area presumably benefitting from President Marcos' new land reform program. He found that the program had not reached the area. Eight peasants who had tried to claim their land were instead arrested.

> The farmers laughed uproariously as they related the incident. They pointed out that even Jesus Christ did not win at his trial, and then they pointed out "But in the end he won."
>
> They also laughed as they told me the story they had heard of a farmer in another region. He had tried to force his landlord to give him his land in accordance with Marcos' land reform decree. Instead, he was arrested.
>
> "He could not understand this, so he went crazy. He fought against the guards in the detention camp. So they electrocuted his penis. He went even crazier, so he was taken to the warden's office and when he returned his front teeth had all been knocked out. He was certainly crazy trying to get his land."
> The laughter of those around me was wild, like repressed anger.[52]

---

[52] Bernard Wideman, "The New Society at Home," *Far Eastern Economic Review* 82, no. 52 (December 31, 1973): 18. By the end of 1971, less than 12,000 acres of land had been submitted by the big landowners to the reform, and fewer than 2,000 families had benefitted. Charles Elliott, *Patterns of Poverty in the Third World* (New York: Praeger, 1975), p. 75.

This is emotional aggression. There is hope expressed: Christ won. Yet there is an air of desperation about immediate success. In the face of this, the laughter itself might take on importance as a release mechanism.

Discussion of India is continued from p. 124.

On my first day in Calcutta, India, I made the mistake of giving a rupee to a beggar while I was walking on an open street. Instantly, several score of people descended upon the chauffered car to which I retreated. Some of them clamored over the roof and hood; hands stretched out from all directions; there was cursing and moaning for money. Chastened by the experience, the next day when I took a walk around the city by myself I resolved to give out no money. A congenitally-deformed beggar with only one full leg hobbled after me for what I later estimated to be nearly a mile before I gave him some money in a secluded spot. Later I adopted a third mistaken tactic by giving a piece of pastry to a beggar and thereby defiling him because of a caste taboo against touching food touched by foreigners. He began to curse me, a crowd gathered, and a friendly passerby suggested I make a quick retreat. I turned to see the beggar beating his head against the sidewalk.

No one could give a beggar enough money to counter-balance the sense of hopelessness he or she must feel. Crawling on the roof of a car and forcing a man to give a handout by following him are acts of desperation. Yet, like persuading themselves that a foreigner is so low in status that touching food he has touched is a defiling act, these actions might also be seen as aggressive means of asserting one's status over another. My signs of fear, handing out money, and running, were forms of submission. There is a possibility, at least, that even beggars can receive continuing psychic relief from at least part of their frustrations, a possibility that deserves some scholarly exploration. The immediate responses here to an insult are not dissimilar to the laboratory experiments in which subjects seem to have experienced some degree of catharsis.[53] A complete lack of response in these situations, leaving the frustrations unsatiated, might be better preparation for revolutionary activity than daily release in these forms.

One interesting aspect of the Calcutta confrontations was the fact that English-speaking Indians frequently came to the rescue. My visit took place during the 1967 elections in which the Communist Party carried West Bengal. One afternoon an Indian journalist took another American (a Ford Foundation employee) and myself to see a square where an anti-American play was to be given that evening as part of the Communist Party's campaign. Upon our ap-

---

[53] There have been many laboratory experiments about counter-aggression. J. E. Hokanson and M. Burgess, "The Effects of Three Types of Aggression on Vascular Processes," *Journal of Abnormal Social Psychology* 62 (1962), had a laboratory technician anger a group of college students and then gave half of them an opportunity to give him electric shocks and verbal insults while denying this opportunity to the other half (there were two other control groups as well). Tests of systolic blood pressure and heart rates showed that both groups were considerably aroused by the technician's provocation. The heart rates of the group given the opportunity to shock him subsided while the blood pressure of the other group remained high. Whether such laboratory results are cross-culturally valid is problematic.

proach, a large group of people gathered to get some accusations against the CIA off their chests, and some leaders of the evening rally came to our rescue. They insisted (over our vigorous protest—we felt we had caused enough trouble for one day) that we should return to see the play that evening. The author of the play, a prominent English-speaking Communist intellectual, personally called the other American's apartment to urge us to come. The entire square was jammed for the evening performance, and we were escorted to the front row, where we could watch the guerilla theater enactment of American atrocities in Vietnam.

The balance among ideological proclivities, tactical imperatives, and human commitments is often a delicate one. I am sure that it would be difficult for even the above intellectuals to genuinely separate the elements of the transactions from one another: to what extent they were teaching followers not to take out frustrations on individuals; to what extent they were releasing their own aggressions by becoming the protectors of someone they perhaps perceived to have higher status than themselves and exposing Americans to an anti-American play; to what extent they were cementing valuable contacts with the American community; or whether they were simply being kind to someone. And you would stretch your imagination to see how all this might fit into a grand scheme for revitalizing India. In truth, our protectors may have accomplished little of anything beyond the fact that their kindness was well received. The personal interaction may have been the most important aspect of the exchange; at least it continued the daily emotional mix that keeps people functioning in a world that seems less than fair or rational.

Further discussion of India may be found on p. 250.

Chalmers Johnson, discussing revolutionary change, talks about social equilibrium as a synchronization of one's value structure to the demands of environmental adaptation.[54] When these elements become desynchronized, the system is disequilibrated until they can be harmonized again. Johnson sees things like fights, homicide, drunkenness, and mental disease as symptoms of the disequilibrium. But beyond these lie things like exogenous (e.g., global communications, refugee migrations, works of missionaries, foreign travel, invasion) and endogenous (displacement of religions by secular authority, acceptance of creative innovation) reasons for changing values and environment.[55] The resulting disequilibria are translated into ideologies, which both verbalize the discontent and inspire movements and codes that can lead to revitalization and eventual resynchronization between the values and the environment.

Our rational Judeo-Christian Western minds like to think in terms of coping with frustrations by setting out goals and striving to attain them. Even in our own society few people actually function in this rational manner. A simpler way to remove such disequilibrium is to simply learn to live with it, even if this appears irrational and paradoxical. Those who are not in movements may find it

---

[54] Johnson, *Revolutionary Change.*
[55] Ibid., p. 65.

difficult even to articulate just which of their values are out of synchronization with their environment. Those who can articulate this may be willing to settle for rewards that are less than solutions to great problems. Acts can themselves be rewards, especially when they momentarily relieve some degree of the tension. Once the action has achieved this purpose, there is little tension left for revolutionary movements to exploit. If this is so, revolutionary leaders who demand ascetic discipline of their followers are on the right track; short-term gratifications are not the stuff of which revolutions are made.

Discussion of Iran is continued from p. 147.

In 1971, Iran spent US$100 million on gala celebrations of the 2,500th anniversary of Persian civilization. In the midst of the preparations the army was forced to occupy the main universities and arrest students who complained about such an expenditure while workers were striking for higher pay, peasants starved in a famine in the southeast, and the budget of the army rose from US$120,000 in 1953 to US$1 billion in 1973 (adjusted to constant exchange prices). The occupation of the university was followed by a series of bombings, highjackings, assassinations, kidnappings, gun battles, bank robberies, and guerilla activities. Between April 1971 and April 1973, 193 dissenters (78 college students, 29 engineers, 27 workers, 19 civil servants, 16 school teachers, 11 student draftees, 6 doctors, 2 lawyers, and 2 librarians) were executed, shot in the streets, or given life sentences.[56] The activities and the executions continued. These are some of the sorts of potentially cathartic activities mentioned earlier in this discussion, but they are tied to a revolutionary thrust. These actions may or may not be good politics. Bombing and terrorism alone do not win revolutions. At that point of time, this revolutionary movement consisted of little more than a string of aggressive acts by individuals. If action is not tied to a sustaining organizational leadership, it is unlikely to lead to a movement of national revitalization and resynchronization.

James Alban Bill notes that the patron-client network in Iran encourages both individual aggressiveness and fragmentation of the opposition as elites struggled to enter the inner circles that surrounded the Shah. Members of the inner circles (e.g., ministries, chiefs of staff, security police) tend to construct personal followings—especially from members of differing classes—to give them leverage vis-à-vis other contenders for their positions. Hence the preference for the informal *dowrehs* (discussed in Chapter 4), or groups of friends, as the basis for politics, rather than more formal committees. The influential must show that they can exert popular influence but not so much influence that they become a threat to the Shah or other members of the inner circles.

Mechanisms like the dowreh encourage plotting and omnipresent interlaced antagonisms but discourage concentrated and shattering confrontations.[57]

---

[56] Ali Jandeghi, "The Present Situation in Iran," *Monthly Review* 25, no. 6 (November 1973): 40–46.

[57] James Alban Bill, *The Politics of Iran: Groups, Classes, and Modernization* (Columbus: Charles Merrill, 1972), p. 48.

Today's member of an anti-government *dowreh* might suddenly shift his loyalties if someone to whom he is tied in another *dowreh* is successful in gaining new access to governmental circles. Bill tells, for instance, of eight middle-class friends who met in 1961 to form a *dowreh* that would discuss sociopolitical issues.[58] They mimeographed a one-page statement presenting their mutual opposition to corruption, injustice, and oppression. Each member took a copy and the rest were locked away. Five months later the Chief of the Secret Police called in one of the men and confronted him with one of the original copies of the statement. The only formal aspect of the organization had been used by one of the members to destroy it. One can well imagine how much more quickly this *dowreh* would have been destroyed had it acquired additional aspects of organization.

Toward the end of the Shah's reign, as popular support for the Ayatollah Khomeini grew, and talk of a military coup was afoot, the *dowreh* also became a useful place to seek alliances with these potential new leaders. After the Revolutionary Government came to power, *dowrehs* sought to enter the inner circles of the new government as they had the old. Certain student *dowrehs* continued guerilla activities, generally aimed at targets acceptable to a variety of other *dowrehs*. These activities had helped remove an unpopular government, and can do so again. They help individuals achieve positions within an existing government. They help governments satisfy various factions that support them. They can help people relieve frustrations. They provide those with money, resources, and talent a means of bargaining with others who have money, resources, and talent. All this is very different from spreading ideology, uprooting entrenched elites, aiding the masses, or even introducing innovative new policies. For any of that to happen, one *dowreh* would need to defeat the others. Any *dowreh* or government planning such a shattering confrontation would probably meet the fate of the group with the mimeographed manifesto—or of SAVAK after it turned to actually killing some members of *dowrehs* as it did later in the Shah's regime. When discontent within *dowrehs* became too great, even the Shah's police power was not sufficient to save him. So long as a government can command the support of *dowreh* members it will have the resources to keep down rebellion both inside and outside the *dowrehs*. If not, it will be replaced by a government that has that support. The *dowrehs* are the establishment—not the vehicles for overthrowing the establishment. Street mobs can help overthrow governments; they cannot overthrow patron-client networks. To organize a street mob, in fact, you need a *dowreh,* and the cooperation of other *dowrehs*. And your members will belong to other *dowrehs*. To organize something more, you need members whose allegiance is more firm and who can lay low until it is time to strike.

Further discussion of Iran may be found on p. 236.

The actions that help relieve personal frustrations or enhance personal aspirations are not always those which make for a sustained political movement.

---

[58] *Ibid.*, pp. 47–48.

Activities like stapling, mimeographing, traveling long hours, sitting for months in camps in the mountains, discussing strategies, lying in jail or exile, are necessary parts of winning various sorts of political battles. They are usually cathartic only to those who can be satisfied with long-delayed rewards or with subordination to charismatic personal superiors. Especially when the chances of winning are slim, simple personal means of purging frustrations may seem superior to sustained political activism. This may explain why people are apathetic to politics, or engage in politics only sporadically, even when they are highly alienated. If nonpolitical or informal actions can give continuous psychic relief from feelings of alienation, the possibility of creating sustained political movements is effectively reduced. This is especially true when leadership is easily coerced by government.

This conclusion can also be turned on its head: *If people receive psychic relief from frustrations, they may be more prone to ascribe legitimacy to their government.* This would be especially true if the government is actually helping them receive such psychic relief, and if signs that they disapprove of government might weaken what economic and social security they do have. For some, even punishment by the government for political resistance could provide a form of psychic relief and thus produce ambivalent feelings of support.[59] Government-sponsored or -condoned guerilla theater or street demonstrations, or even street riots broken up by police, can have the same effect. Hence people may develop loyalty to the political system even when the performance of that system in terms of balancing their personal environments or distributing material rewards is low.[60] Alienation may conceivably flow into political legitimacy, with neither political activism nor governmental alleviation of environmental imbalances as intervening variables. A government need not always solve basic social and economic problems to gain the support of the populace.

CULTURAL PLURALISM

Underlying the personal sources of tension in developing nations are some even more explosive ones. Nearly all developing nations are racially heterogeneous.

COMMENT

A study by Walker Connor of 132 nations found only 12 to be ethnically homogeneous.[61]

---

[59] In Singapore some of the most loyal government bureaucrats are political opponents who were jailed and later released on condition that they support the regime.

[60] Gabriel Almond and Sidney Verba, *The Civic Culture: Political Attitudes and Democracy in Five Nations* (Princeton, N.J.: Princeton University Press, 1963), p. 246, suggest that legitimacy is more important than performance in maintaining political stability. A recent study of alienation among American academics supports the hypothesis "that people whose orientations to life in American society are those tapped by standard scales of social alienation—somewhat despairing, meaningless, and even desperate—are not more alienated from the polity than are people who are more hopeful and more satisfied with their lot . . . socio-cultural and political alienation will not generally be found to be significantly associated with each other." David C. Schwartz, *Political Alienation and Political Behavior* (Chicago: Aldine, 1973), pp. 42–43.

[61] Walker Connor, "Nation-Building or Nation-Destroying," *World Politics* 24 (April 1972).

Citizens of ethnically diverse nations often view social and economic problems as stemming from racial causes. The result is sometimes civil unrest. Too much unrest can, of course, destabilize any government. But *a modicum of unrest can be useful to the patron-client networks as an outlet that prevents the populace from uniting against them.*

Each region of the developing world is, in broadest terms, divided among some major racial groupings. The principal division within the Caribbean area is among Negroes, Europeans (of French, Spanish, and British descent), and mulattoes who are a cross between whites and blacks. A small number of East Indians, Chinese, Jews, and Syrians are prominent in commerce. In Central America and the west coast of South America, the principal divisions are among those of Spanish origin, indigenous Indians, and mestizos who are a cross between the two. On the eastern coast of South America (and in Peru and Chile) where a high percentage of the populace is of European extraction there is some conscious competiton among various European groupings themselves—especially Portuguese, Spanish, Italians, and Germans—not to mention Negroes, indigenous Indians, and mestizos. In major cities there are also Europeans from other nations, Chinese, Japanese, East Indians, and some Semitic people; though their numbers are not great, they often hold key economic positions, and adhere to faiths other than the prevailing Catholicism.

Africa's principal divisions are tribal. The lighter-skinned Nilotic races living in the north (themselves highly polyglot) are also sharply divided into historic groupings characterized by differences in religion (mainly Muslim, Catholic, Protestant, Coptic, Jewish, and tribal), lifestyle (fixed farming, urban trading, nomadic), language, and historic allegiances to various rulers. The same is true throughout the Middle East. The colonial era also left behind groups of French, Spanish, Italian, and British origin, along with people of mixed racial background. Further south in black Africa the many traditional tribal groupings remain alive in memories. These divisions are more than historical-political; there are many genetically recognizable physical differences separating these groups. Nigerians alone speak 400 different languages. Belgians, Dutch, Germans, Portuguese, Britishers, Lebanese, Frenchmen, Indians, Indonesians, and others add further heterogeneity to urban Africa.[62]

The over 500 million people of India speak some 350 languages and dialects. The populace is broadly divided into earlier Dravidian inhabitants and later Aryan invaders from the Mediterranean region and contains over 20 million aboriginal people as well. While Hindu is the prevailing religion, Buddhists, Jains, Parsis, Muslims, Sikhs, Jews, and Christians also hold prominent positions in the society. Pakistan, while primarily Muslim, also contains similar divisions. In the regions along the Himalayan Mountains, mixtures of Persians, Tibetans, and various Chinese and Russian groups add further complexity to the picture.

Southeast Asia's racial pattern derives principally from the island Malayo-Polynesian people, southern Chinese groups, and immigrants from the Middle

---
[62] Robert H. Bates, "Ethnic Competition and Modernization in Contemporary Africa," *Contemporary Political Studies* 6, no. 4 (January 1974): 457–484, reviews ethnic conflicts over land, markets, trade routes and jobs, with bibliography.

East and India coming together through millenia of migrations and invasions. The result is distinct races of Burmans, Thais, Khmers (Cambodia), Vietnamese, Chams (central Vietnam), and hill tribes (along Laos), each with a feeling of racial affinity, and generally a common religion and language. In surrounding oceans, the Malayo-Polynesians, separated on many islands and scattered communities, have developed diverse languages (some twenty-seven), dialects, religious affiliations, and identities. Indonesia is composed of about 3,000 islands, and the Philippines of 7,000. Although most of the populace is concentrated on a few islands, inhabitants of neighboring islands, or neighboring regions of the same island, often consider themselves racially distinct from one another. Throughout urban areas of Southeast Asia, Chinese, Indians, Arabs, Europeans, Eurasians, and Chinese who have married indigenous people have their own neighborhoods. Hinayana and Mahayana Buddhism, Hinduism, Confucianism, Islam, Catholicism, Protestantism, Judaism, tribal religions, and others may be found in varying proportions throughout Southeast Asia.

It is difficult to think of a developing nation that does not experience serious ongoing problems with language. If business in the city is largely transacted (as is often the case) in a European language, people who do not know this language feel left out—and often are. If the reverse is true, some of the nonindigenous immigrants (who often figure prominently in commerce) feel that unfair obstacles are being strewn in their path. If schools teach in the vernacular, the lack of textbooks and outside expertise often prevents modernization of the curriculum. If they teach in the European language, children who do not speak this language at home find it hard to compete in their studies with those who do.

Differences in historic cultural development also cause problems. Some groups (e.g., those indigenous to Southeast Asia, American Indians, certain African tribes) have historically had little experience with commerce; large numbers of people in virtually every developing nation are not in a position to compete in commerce. In contrast, others are well suited for commerce. Chinese, Japanese, many castes of Indians, certain Middle Eastern Muslims and Jews, certain other African tribes, Europeans, and racial groupings that represent a cross between some of the above with indigenous peoples have a long history of commercial experience and often tend to dominate the commerce of nations they inhabit. Sometimes these commercially-dominant groups represent only a small percentage of the population of the nation and have not even been granted full citizenship.

It is not uncommon for political leadership to be in different hands from commerce and bureaucracy. In Latin America, for instance, mestizos and mulattos, standing between two cultures, have commonly sought political positions, while the highest commercial pursuits remain in the hands of those with more pure European origin. In Africa and Southeast Asia it is common for small Indian, European, Arab, or Chinese minorities to control much of commerce, while other racial groups dominate political positions. In these cases, of course, such minorities become important cogs in the patron-client networks, and hence have considerably more political power than sheer numbers or the outward setup of government would imply. They also tend to outnumber other races in institutions of higher education.

In 1972, President Idi Amin of Uganda deported the Asians who controlled that nation's economy and bureaucracy. In doing so he responded to some of these sorts of conflicts in a manner markedly different from the usual response of the leadership in a developing nation.[63] The more typical response is to assemble in the political leadership—whether through the leading political party, bureaucracy, or a military junta—representatives of the various communal groups extant in the nation. This gives all groups at least symbolic access to the political process and guards against gross racial excesses perpetrated by government.

Even when governments are committed to some process of racial accommodation, racial problems remain. When top economic positions are occupied principally by certain racial groups, any special benefits accruing to those groups (or blockage of mobility for them) easily become political issues. When the head of a nation is of a certain race, members of other races find it difficult to ignore his or her origins. Rural people often feel a cultural distance from urbanites, and articulate this in racial terms ("those Chinese in the city", etc.). Racial proximity in the city can breed distrust along with new understanding. Racial mistrust is sometimes reflected in the attitudes of rank-and-file members of political parties, the military, the bureaucracy, and elsewhere. If the central government steps in too strongly to regulate sensitive matters like curriculum in education, use of language in public institutions, or racial hiring practices of firms or the civil service, it can be accused of foisting the preferences of one racial or religious group on another. If it does not regulate these things, it opens the ground for those of parochial persuasions to control these policies in different regions of the nation, with the accompanying dangers of weakening the hold of the central government and perpetuating racial inequalities.

Each of the following scenarios may be found in at least several developing nations:

Scenario One.   Nearly all the citizens of the nation belong to race A. Race B comprises a small percentage of the populace, principally urban. During colonialism it was mainly race B that received higher education and moved into top posts in the bureaucracy and business. Today the Prime Minister and much of the Cabinet are members of race A, but the economy and bureaucracy are largely in the control of race B. Members of race A resent the fact that they comprise a majority yet race B dominates the patron-client networks.

COMMENT

In 25 of the 132 nations surveyed by Walker Connor, over 90 percent of the population belonged to one ethnic group. In another 25 nations, one group accounted for 75–89 percent of the population.

Scenario Two.   A nation is dominated by one racial group which is prominent in economic, bureaucratic, and political spheres. It is attempting to extend its

---

[63] Burma, Indonesia, and the Philippines have applied restrictions designed to squeeze out Chinese and Indians during certain periods; Thailand has attempted to promote the expatriation of Vietnamese from Northeast Thailand, and Brazil has attempted to exterminate some aboriginal groups in the Amazon Valley.

culture to all racial minorities (some of which may include principal economic influentials). In this case the minorities who are influential in the major patron-client network may accede to the submergence of their own race into the dominant culture.

COMMENT

In 31 of the 132 nations, the largest ethnic group comprised 50–74 percent of the population, and in 39 of the nations, the largest ethnic group accounted for less than half the nation's population.

Scenario Three. The population in each region is rather evenly divided among three racial groups. Two of these groups speak a European language, while the third is largely limited to an indigenous language. One of the European-speaking groups is clearly dominant in commerce, locally and nationally, while the second tends to take up white collar and bureaucratic positions, along with careers in politics. To counter-balance this influence, the third group presses for an emphasis on using the national language in conducting the nation's business and in the schools. This is regarded as retrogressive by the urban leaders of the major patron-client network, who come mainly from the first two racial groups.

Scenario Four. The population is divided among three racial groups. The capital city is almost entirely composed of two of these, while the third dominates the countryside. The major patron-client network is composed of members from all three racial groups.

COMMENT

In 53 of the 132 nations, the population was divided into more than 5 significant groups.

Scenario Five. The nation is divided among many tribal groups, of which three or four are more politically influential than others. Some of the more influential groups attempt to establish local hegemony over weaker tribes within their regions, and to obtain control of resources. Hence local government and commerce in given regions is dominated by members of the leading tribal group in that region. The major patron-client networks become dominated by the more powerful tribes, who both fight among themselves for allocation of resources and cooperate in subordinating the smaller tribes.

Scenario Six. A nation is divided among many tribal groups, yet everywhere commerce is in the hands of the same small outside minority group. This latter group tends to dominate the nation's major patron-client network, although it raises animosities throughout the nation. Sometimes this minority group will ally with one particular tribal group to give itself a regional base of support.

Scenario Seven. Most citizens of the nation are of a certain religious persuasion. Much of the economic power of the nation has fallen into the hands of secular urban businessmen. Religious leaders, who hold sway over the minds of rural villagers, still seek to exert political clout. This competition is not welcomed by the urban secular leadership which controls the major patron-client network.

Scenario Eight.   Religious institutions still own vast acreages of land. They use this control to resist investments and party organization emanating from urban leadership. Conflict ensues, and political leadership remains divided.

Under any of these scenarios, the members of the major patron-client network do not necessarily hold the top political posts. When their racial groups constitute a minority it is often safer for them not to seek these posts. When they do not hold them, they must make concessions on issues such as language and education. While this harms members of their race, it is not necessarily detrimental to their own economic hegemony. That hegemony is best preserved by seeking accommodation with the leaders of the other racial groups. Thus they do not constitute forceful spokesmen for their own race on such issues.

Obviously, all of these scenarios (and there are, of course, many other variations on these themes) can lead to conflict. The result could be periodic but scattered flare-ups of street fights, rioting, or general regional unrest. If these outbreaks are not settled by the application of persuasion, force, and concessions, such problems could become endemic. In the case of Katanga, Biafra, and Bangladesh, conflicts led to actual civil wars in which a portion of a nation attempted to secede (in the latter case, successfully). Singapore and Malaysia split apart peacefully. There are secessionist movements among Outer Islanders in Indonesia and the Philippines; hill tribes of Burma; Pathans in Pakistan; Kashmiris and Nagas in India; inhabitants of Sabah and Sarawak in Malaysia; Muslims in southern Thailand; Kurds, Armenians, and other minority tribes in Iran; the Tuareg in Mali; Sanwi in the Ivory Coast; Ashanti in Ghana; some Islamic chieftaincies in Chad; the Northern region of the Cameroons; some Sudanese regions; and Etrurians in Ethiopia, as well as a few small regions in Africa asking for border adjustments so they may shift to an adjoining nation.

Secessionist movements seldom have resources comparable to those available to the central government, which usually also commands the support of the majority of the populace for supressing them. In addition, North Atlantic nations tend to regard secessionist movements as a threat to the nation-state system and align with the central government. Usually the secessionists represent a minority within their own region and find themselves in internal conflict with other regional leaders who prefer more moderate approaches and are linked with the central patron-client networks. Bangladesh differs from all the others in that it contained the preponderance of the population and natural resources of its former nation and was separated by over 900 miles from the nearest border of West Pakistan, from which it was seceding. That 900 miles also happened to be occupied by India, with whom Pakistan was at war, and which supported the secession movement. The Katanga secession attempt became involved in the Cold War and was probably distorted in importance because of this. Etruria has historically been independent of Ethiopia for long periods of time. And Biafra was the core of a nearly autonomous federal region and was the source of much of the army high command (a rare situation of which we shall say more presently). Most seceding regions are neither as large nor populous as the ones cited here. Most developing nations do not have secessionist movements.

More worrisome to the leadership of developing nations is the concern that racial tensions short of secessionist demands will get out of hand and lead to endemic civil unrest. Paradoxically, the most effective tactic a government can take is often racial conservatism, a general perpetuation of the *status quo* economic, social, and political roles being performed by the various races. To advocate, for instance, that a racial group that has little experience in the economic realm should move to a position of economic prominence could induce more racial tension than it would displace. It is safer for the government to proceed by redoubling efforts *to assimilate disaffected leaders of the racial group into the minor patron-client networks without at the same time giving them real power*. Since such leaders seldom have the option of forming a mass movement like the American Civil Rights Movement due to the sorts of coercive techniques available to governments of developing nations, they are perhaps more prone to accept such positions than would otherwise be the case. They can use their new status especially to broaden educational opportunity, hiring practices of bureaucracy and major industries, and access to land, and thus undercut radical demands by promoting gradual progress at lower levels.

When people perceive themselves as being members of racial, social, cultural, religious, or linguistic groups that are in conflict with others, it is hard to form multiethnic opposition movements based on class. If most jobs are held by one race, for instance, and a left-wing party advocates equal employment opportunities, even jobless members of that race feel threatened and will not join. Ironically, this turns class-based parties into parties largely composed of only one race. Since members of the same race differ in dialect, religion, economic standing, and level of education, it is also difficult to create sustained movements based on racial appeals alone.[64] Should a movement based on either class or racial appeals promote unrest, or particularly violence, it is easy for the government to pin an ethnic label on it and persuade other ethnic groups (and subsets of its own ethnic group) that it should be suppressed. In the words of Samuel P. Huntington:

> In general, the more highly stratified a society is and the more complicated its social structure, the more gradual is the process of political mobilization. The divisions between class and class, occupation and occupation, rural and urban, constitute a series of breakwaters which divide the society and permit the political mobilization of one group at a time.[65]

In addition, *so long as people are conscious of racial appeals, it is possible to blame economic hardships on racism, rather than on the systematic manipula-*

---

[64] Bates, "Ethnic Competition and Modernization," pp. 467, 472, notes the class bias in African ethnic councils; they are often composed of clerks, cash croppers, and traders and retain the skills of modern elites (e.g., lawyers) to help them compete for benefits. Hence they are not representative of all members of their race.

[65] Samuel P. Huntington, "Political Development and Political Decay," *World Politics* 17, no. 3 (April 1965): 419.

tions of the patron-client networks themselves. It can be argued that racial extremists from other political parties, or traditional exclusions of some races from the economic reward system (now being "corrected" by quotas, educational policy, and other means to "equalize" mobility), or continuous unrest among minor racial groups, are responsible for the basic economic problems of the nation. To be effective, such arguments must be made by a government that has incorporated all races, religions, and major linguistic groups into its leadership structure and encourages social contacts among racial groups. Then it cannot so easily be accused of advocating dominance by a particular race, even though the patron-client network that holds power is dominated by a particular race. The presence of members of a race in the cabinet, parliament, bureaucracy, or business does not mean this race has penetrated the major patron-client network. In fact, since patron-client networks usually involve different ethnic groups at different strata levels, appeals to support such "multi-racialism" are essentially a plea to the entire nation to accept the racial hierarchy which already exists within the patron-client networks. This is especially ironic when the major patron-client network is composed principally of racial minorities. When opponents call the ruling party racist, it can simply point to all the members of minority groups with impressive sounding titles openly advocating improvements for their race. When opponents advocate the same things without holding the titles, they can be accused of overt racism rather than praised for being members of a multiethnic team, and blamed for the nation's troubles.

Donald L. Horowitz differentiates between vertical and horizontal systems.[66] A vertical system has a marked class hierarchy, with one race dominating the highest economic and political positions, another race dominating those positions a bit below, and so forth. In a horizontal system, all races may be found at all class levels. Look at the eight scenarios earlier in this section. In all of them, all races might be found at all class levels, characteristic of horizontal systems. In scenarios one, two, three, and six, one ethnic group dominates the upper class; in scenario five, three or four dominate it, characteristic of vertical systems. Scenario four suggests a system where all groups share in the major patron-client network, making this description closest to a horizontal system. Even a nation such as this, however, does not necessarily offer much class mobility. Leaders of a horizontal system can use race, dialect, religion, economic standing, and level of education to divide those below them and accuse their opponents of resorting to racial appeals. So *it makes little difference whether a system is vertical or horizontal, or what its ethnic scenario might be. Most people will get little benefit.*

Once a major patron-client network has been established it is difficult for people from other groups to break into it. Even a military coup must settle in to running the country and economy, and so must make use of people with existing

---

[66] Donald L. Horowitz, "Three Dimensions of Ethnic Politics," *World Politics* 23, no. 2 (January 1971): 232–234; idem, "Multiracial Politics in the New States: Toward a Theory of Conflict," in Robert J. Jackson and Michael B. Stein, *Issues in Comparative Politics* (New York: St. Martins, 1971), pp. 164–180.

skills.[67] Nepotism is involved; so is class background. The groups who excel in modern school curricula often succeed largely because they come from a middle-class tradition which is better attuned to this sort of activity. As mentioned, certain realms of commerce have traditionally belonged to certain races who have gained long experience in these fields, while other races are virtually unfamiliar with commerce, and hence are at a decided disadvantage at assimilating into patron-client networks. Furthermore, modern export ventures are often controlled by North Americans, Japanese, or Europeans who have developed habits for dealing with racial groups in a given country.

M. G. Smith sees Jamaica—which happens to be a vertical system—as stratified into separate cultures:

> The top ranking section consists of a hard core of employers and own-account professionals, together with superior civil servants. . . . Most members of the intermediate section are themselves either employees of "middle-income" status, or small proprietors, businessmen, farmers, contractors or such lesser professionals as teachers. The majority of this group are also themselves employers, hiring domestic labor and other types of service attendants. . . . In the lowest section, the typical employment status is a combination of wage and own-account work, and underemployment or unemployment is widespread.[68]

Those in the top echelon have employment conditions such "that dismissal or demotion are virtually inconceivable"; those in the lowest section are often hired casually and are easily dismissed. Furthermore, each of these ranks has its own distinctive patterns of mating and home life, religious observance, educational potential, language, material culture, sports, value system, and associational habits. There is some mobility between sectors; one who takes this path, however, must master all the accoutrements of the new culture. And, in a vertical system, at least, he or she must fight a racial battle as well. For in Jamaica, most of those in the top ranking section are white, most in the intermediate sector are brown (mestizo), and most in the lowest section are black. The fact that four-fifths of the populace is black gives some indication of economic conditions in Jamaica. This is what J. S. Furnivall (describing Java) called a plural society in a famous definition:

> It is in the strictest sense a medley, for they might mix but they do not combine. Each group holds by its own religion, its own culture and language, its own ideas and ways. As individuals they meet, but only in the marketplace, in buying and selling. There is a plural society, with different sections of the community living side-by-side, but separately, within the same political unit. Even in the economic sphere, there is diversity of labor along racial lines.[69]

---

[67] Ali A. Mazrui, "Soldiers as Traditionalizers: Military Rule and the Re-Africanization of Africa," *Journal of Asian and African Studies* 12, nos. 1–4 (January and October 1977): 236–258, suggests that African military regimes have more tendency than civilian ones to return a nation to tribal rule. He also feels they may be less adept than civilians at operating national institutions.

[68] M. G. Smith, *The Plural Society in the British West Indies* (Berkeley and Los Angeles: University of California Press, 1965), p. 168.

[69] J. S. Furnivall, *Colonial Policy and Practice* (London: Cambridge University Press, 1958), p. 304.

Breaking down this evident hierarchy is a laborious process. Should a "black power" movement gain ascendancy in Jamaica, it could not achieve real power until it had destroyed this economic hierarchy among the races. To do so abruptly would destroy the economy; gradualism lends itself to perpetuation of the same hierarchy. Hence such a regime would more likely limit itself to surface manifestations of ethnic revamping, while settling its leaders into the existent patron-client networks.

If the nation were more racially integrated at the top than it is in Jamaica—and most are to some degree—the problem would remain the same.

Developing nations have numerous approaches for dealing with ethnic conflict. I would suggest that nearly all of them allow some members of each ethnic group into the major patron-client network, especially the political sector of it. *Members of this and the minor patron-client network are hesitant to disturb the existing division of labor or to allow racial groups to create effective political organizations.* Those nations that began as plural societies in Furnivall's sense of the term remain so. The various groups have little autonomy and are not a part of the political system; they, and their continuing tensions, are controlled by that system, whose processes take place within the patron-client networks. There is little chance in any developing nation to mobilize the political clout needed to create mobility for all races at all levels.

| Discussion of Malaysia is continued from p. 120. |

Malaysia's approach to this problem is illustrative since it does not seem to fit this hypothesis on the surface. As of 1969, West (mainland) Malaysia was 56 percent Malay, 36 percent Chinese, and 8 percent Indian.[70] It is ruled by the Alliance Party. The Alliance Party is not one party, but three. In Malay districts there is no Alliance Party on the ballot, but rather the United Malay National Organization. The Malayan Chinese Association runs in Chinese districts, and the Malayan Indian Congress in Indian. These organizations use issues like language, education, job discrimination, and other communal issues during their campaigns. Once elected, their representatives form a coalition with one another and rule Malaysia as the Alliance Party. In the rural areas Malays constitute a majority of the populace; they tend to dominate this coalition. Meanwhile the major economic institutions of the nation—including middlemen for the Malay peasant's crops—are in Chinese hands. It would appear that each racial group participates in the political process and holds some veto power over the other groups.

Arend Lijphart suggests that some culturally diverse European nations—notably Austria, Switzerland, the Netherlands, and Belgium—should be characterized as *"consociational democracies."* The different cultural groups remain isolated and largely autonomous, each with their own organizations and leaders. There is proportional representation (giving an edge to the larger groups) yet enough autonomous organization that the individual group leaders maintain

---

[70] K. J. Ratnam and R. S. Milne, "The 1969 Parliamentary Election in West Malaysia," *Pacific Affairs* 43, no. 2 (Summer 1970): 205.

a mutual veto over one another.[71] For instance, in Belgium if a bill threatening to "harm the relations between the communities" comes before Parliament a petition signed by three-quarters of the members from one linguistic group can force the bill back to the Cabinet, which by law must have equal balance among the linguistic groups, for thirty days. Especially sensitive pieces of legislation must be passed by a "special majority": two-thirds of the total votes of both houses of Parliament, including a simple majority of each linguistic group. Each linguistic group retains a veto over serious changes in the relations between groups, and the members of each linguistic group in Parliament constitute a Cultural Council with full power over the matters Parliament defines as in their sphere (e.g., language use in public administration and industrial relations; cultural content in education, radio and television programming).[72]

Consociationalism might be considered an ideal of the Alliance Party. However, Malaysian communal groups can hardly be described as possessing a veto that protects them from incursions on their cultural and economic integrity by other racial groups. In the 1969 elections the Alliance was opposed by Malay parties demanding increased special rights for Malays (loans, quotas in university admissions and the bureaucracy, positions on boards of directors, etc.), and "noncommunal" parties asking (among other things) the formation of a special Chinese university and more cultural protection for non-Malays. These parties picked up more seats in this election than ever before, and three days later bloody race riots broke out. The government declared martial law for twenty-one months, and issued a new constitution which allows for curfews, suspension of Parliament, and press censorship and forbids further discussion of the citizenship, national language, and special position of Malay issues. This neutralized the position of both the Chinese and the Malay spokesmen. Malay was made mandatory as the language of instruction in all public schools, including those attended by Chinese. The leadership of the United Malay National Organization began weaving alliances with other more malleable Chinese political organizations, partially circumventing the Malayan Chinese Organization. Then, Malay and Chinese leaders together continued with policies that were working to the detriment of poorer Chinese and Malays.[73] For instance, a new Federal Industrial Development Authority created Pioneer Industries in which licences are granted to already-wealthy Malays who in turn hire Chinese to run the businesses. Most new employment for Malays was as garbage collectors and ditch diggers on public utilities jobs.[74] The censorship forbid public discussion of

---

[71] Lijphart discusses consociationalism in several places. Perhaps his clearest definition is in Arend Lijphart, "Cultural Diversity and Theories of Political Integration," *Canadian Journal of Political Science* 4, no. 1 (March 1971): 9–10.

[72] See James A. Dunn, Jr., "The Revision of the Constitution in Belgium: A Study in the Institutionalization of Ethnic Conflict," *Western Political Quarterly* 27, no. 1 (March 1974): 143–163.

[73] Ozay Mehmet, *Economic Planning and Social Justice in Developing Countries* (New York: St. Martins, 1978), pp. 114–116.

[74] Even with this, only 93,668 of the 588,000 new jobs created between 1970 and 1975 were for Malays, though Malays constituted over 50 percent of the population. Two out of every three Malays still lived below the official poverty line. Government of Malaysia, *Third Malaysia Plan, 1976–1980* (Kuala Lumpur: 1976), pp. 3, 58.

this phenomenon. Whereas in 1957 the richest 5 percent of Malays received 18.1 percent of Malay income and the bottom 40 percent received 19.5 percent, by 1970 those figures were 24.6 percent and 12.7 percent respectively.[75] And there is no indication that matters are moving beyond the situation described by Gullick:

> ... major merchant firms, predominantly European, at the seaports; wholesalers, predominantly Chinese, at the ports and large inland towns; and shopkeepers and local produce dealers, again mostly Chinese, in the villages ... There was a formidable concentration of economic power in the higher echelons of the system. At village level the small landholder or peasant [Malay or Chinese] found himself obliged to sell his produce to the rubber or copra dealer, the rice miller, in a word to the middleman, who was in a strong bargaining position—the stronger if, as was common enough, the Malay peasant bought goods from him on credit to tide him over until the harvest or just to meet some special expense.[76]

COMMENT

In 1957, the richest 10 percent of the populace in West Malaysia received 16 times more income than the poorest 10 percent. By 1970, that richest 10 percent received 34 times more income than the poorest 10 percent.[77]

Chinese culturally bound to Malays; Malays and Chinese economically bound to Chinese—rather than mutual veto, this sounds more like mutual interference. Control from the capital by elites from various racial groups cooperating together to protect this division of labor continues and grows firmer, even as the personalities involved change. Smith suggests that to end a situation in which top cultural sectors control the lives of lower cultural sectors it is necessary to promote intermarriage, eliminate special privileges for ethnic groups, promote equal educational and occupational opportunities for all cultural sections on a nonethnic basis, and publicly enforce freedom of worship, speech, movement, association, and work.[78] Lijphart suggests the notion of autonomous groupings with veto over infringements by others. Malaysia is clearly not in a position to explore any of these possibilities. The provocations for continuing cultural tension remain.

---

[75] D. R. Snodgrass, "Trends and Patterns in Malaysian Income Distribution, 1957–1970," in *Readings in Malaysian Economic Development,* ed. David Lim (Kuala Lumpur: Oxford University Press, 1975), p. 264. The corresponding figures for Chinese are: the richest 5 percent received 19.5 percent of the income, and the bottom 40 percent received 19.7 percent (1957). In 1970 the top 5 percent received 28.2 percent, and the bottom 40 percent received 14.3 percent.

[76] J. M. Gullick, *Malaysia* (New York: Praeger, 1969), p. 73.

[77] L. L. Lim, "Income Distribution in West Malaysia," in *Income Distribution, Employment and Economic Development in South East and East Asia* (Tokyo: The Japanese Economic Research Center, 1975), Vol. 1, p. 184.

[78] M. G. Smith, "Institutional and Political Conditions of Pluralism," *Pluralism in Africa* (Berkeley and Los Angeles: University of California Press, 1969), pp. 54, 60.

Further discussion of Malaysia may be found on p. 266. Discussion of
Nigeria is continued from p. 111.

Nigeria is another country that does not appear to be a centrally controlled
polity on the surface, nor one in which those who are in control resist racial
autonomy and equality or perpetuate communal tensions. During the colonial
period Nigeria was divided into three regions, each virtually autonomous with
regard to budgeting, laws, and governing practices. This allowed the Hausa-
Fulani empire in the north to maintain its control over most of the local tribal
groups in the area, without interfering with the autonomy of the powerful
Yorubas and Ibos in their own regions to the south.

After independence this process continued. Hausa-Fulanis took control of
the Prime Ministership; Ibos predominated in the bureaucracy, army officer
corps, and white-collar positions; many of the top commercial pursuits remained
in British hands. The Prime Minister was sensitive to dictates from the Sardauna
of Sokoto in the north. The heads of two of the main political parties worked to
control their own regional legislatures, spending most of their time in their own
region. (The parties, while ostensibly national, tended to gain principal support
from a particular region.) When Awolowo, the leader of the party based in
Yoruba territory, entrusted regional leadership to his deputy and went to Lagos
to lead the opposition in the national legislature, he soon found his deputy
challenging him for control of the party at home. The Prime Minister sided with
the deputy, an easy way to remove the leader of the opposition. Development
funds were administered locally. Government decisions could not proceed
without the support of the leaders of all three regions. Regional autonomy remained high, so up to that point there was some mutual veto. At the same time
the north was gaining ascendency over the system because of the great territory
and number of tribal groups it controlled, a politicized census which showed this
region to have the largest population, and the fact that the appropriations system
gave it the largest budget. This caused uneasiness in the south.

Then, early in 1966, there was a military coup. In one night Awolowo's
deputy and the Sardauna of Sokoto in the north were killed. In the name of wiping out corruption and modernizing the nation, the road to centralization of
power had begun. The general who headed the initial coup was an Ibo. He
promptly abolished the federal system, a move so abrupt that it led to his murder
within seven months of taking office. His successor, General Gowan, came from
a small non-Muslim northern tribe and declared that he would keep federalism
and bring back civilian rule. His road to centralization was simply slower and
more subtle. Since massacres of Ibos living in the north (touched off in the wake
of the initial military takeover) continued, the Ibo Eastern Region seceded to
form Biafra. Gowan united the north and west to fight this civil war, but he did
so only by forcing a concession from the north: Awolowo and the leaders of
northern minority tribes demanded as the price of cooperation that the north be
divided into six separate states and the east into three.

These states are being used to weaken the power of former ethnic leaders.
They are headed by federally appointed governors who are civil servants and

have patronage powers. Meanwhile the staffs of the local and regional government chiefs' councils (former kingpins in patronage) have been forbidden to take part in politics. Whereas chiefs in many regions could formerly make decisions over the objections of their councils, they are now forbidden to do so. And the councils themselves are no longer controlled by the chiefs; two-thirds of their members are elected, with candidates chosen by the national parties. The formerly powerful state of Kano has been divided into five administrative areas. While they will ostensibly be coordinated by the Kano council, the Ministries of Education, Natural Resources, Health and Social Welfare, Works, and Finance all have established offices within these areas, away from Kano. Such departments have their own professional staffs and working committees.[79] In the words of one writer (referring to a similar process in the Ivory Coast) "decentralization is only another form of centralization."[80]

These moves are designed to weaken corruption on the local level and induce efficiency. They are strongly resisted by local political influentials but seem to be moving forward at a steady pace. They do not destroy patron-clientism but instead create new networks more closely linked with the capital. They were supported by Awolowo, who saw them as a means to promote redistribution of wealth via socialism and by those on the right who welcomed the opportunity to vitalize sluggish economic growth.[81] By breaking the regional control of the Hausa-Fulanis and Ibos, the process is bringing many smaller tribes into the arena, while intensifying the efforts of the three main regions to control the federal budget.

> The Nigerian experience runs counter to the view that communalism is an historical anachronism, ultimately destined to be submerged by the "universalistic" tidal wave of modernity . . . modernization, far from destroying communalism, in time both reinforces communal conflicts and creates the conditions for the formation of entirely new communal groups.[82]

When national elections were held in 1979, Awolowo was a candidate for President. He won in most of the Yoruba districts, but was defeated by another capital-based candidate who won in most other districts. Centralization in Nigeria has promoted continuing communal rivalry, without creating safeguards for the integrity of the various communal groups. It has taken power from all racial groups, while enhancing the power of those who rule from the capital.

Further discussion of Nigeria may be found on p. 364.

"Divide and rule" is not just a matter of economic and political organization. People actually come to feel that they are supposed to be controlled by

---

[79] Edward Baum, "Recent Administrative Reform in Local Government in Northern Nigeria," *Journal of Developing Areas* 7, no. 1 (October 1972): 80–87.

[80] R. G. Lavalle, *Le Monveldu Sous-Préfet* (Abidjan, 1965), p. 5.

[81] John M. Ostheimer, *Nigerian Politics* (New York: Harper & Row, 1973), pp. 138–139, 145.

[82] Robert Melson and Howard Wolpe, "Modernization and the Politics of Communalism: A Theoretical Perspective," *American Political Science Review* 64, no. 4 (December 1970): 1113.

members of other groups, whether they trust them or not. A researcher in a village in Malaysia inhabited by immigrants from Sumatra reports on their attitudes:

> The most frequently given reason for not going to Sungei Buah is that the Javanese [who inhabit that neighboring village] are dirty, that going to the village is in itself an unpleasant experience. A somewhat grudging admiration for the capacity of the Javanese to work hard is accorded. They are likened to the Chinese in this respect and in the less complimentary (in Malay terms) respect that the Javanese, although supposedly Moslem, are given to eating pork on occasion. . . . There are two Banjarese families living in Jendram Hilir, and they are virtually isolated from all social life in the village. Banjarese, according to the stereotype held of them by Jendram Hilir villagers, are fundamentally evil and can never be trusted; they are especially prone to stealing and lying. . . . Malay villagers appear to hold to the opinion that all Chinese are dirty. . . . That many Chinese are wealthy whereas most Malays are poor is indeed a topic of concern and self-pity for Malays, but the skill of Chinese businessmen and their ability to meet all the demands placed on them is often the subject of admiration on the part of village Malays. In the same way, the evident ability of the Chinese to work harder than the Malays is admitted and admired.[83]

The villagers of Jendram Hilir do not even fully trust other Malays from differing dialect groups. Most of their commercial transactions are handled by Chinese, whom they admit to being better suited to such pursuits *and whose role they accept,* however grudgingly.

Racial stereotypes can lead people to perceive even themselves as worthy of contempt. A black woman emerging from a bus in Jamaica is almost run down by a Chinese driver, who stops just in time and then steps out to see that the woman is safe. The black women on the bus comment: ". . . the driver of the car; if it was a Black man . . . I'm woulda see the woman dead, an' leave her." "Is true; our colour noh good, y'know!"[84]

Over many decades of intermingling, the groups involved have created their own self-perceptions. Had the ancestors of the black women above not been taken as slaves to *Jamaica,* it is possible that they would have a more self-confident perception of themselves, since they would be comparing their group with other *African* groups. This would, of course, depend on which tribes they derived from. Likewise, the villagers of Jendram Hilir might have a somewhat altered status had their forebears stayed behind in Sumatra. The rank order of particular racial groups varies from country to country and, as exemplified by Nigeria, can shift over time, especially for those occupying intermediate ranks. A group's perceptions of its rank may not always coincide with economic or political realities, but are likely to be based in part, at least, on actual social standing. The modern perceptions of rank began to form in the period when

[83] Peter J. Wilson, *A Malay Village and Malaysia* (New Haven: Human Resources Area Files Press, 1967), pp. 25–26.

[84] Audvil King, "Letter to a Friend," in Audvil King et al., *One Love* (London: Bogle-L'Ouverture Publications, 1971), p. 16.

merchants challenged traditional village and kingly leadership; together with historic accidents these perceptions helped determine the ethnic composition of the new urban elites. The evolution does not seem to be entirely accidental, however; lighter skin is often a mark of higher status. Among East Indians, Chinese, Malays, Malayo-Polynesians, Latin Americans, many Negro cultures, and many other groups, a common test of beauty is the lightness of the skin. Those in these groups who hold the highest status often have fairer complexions than others of their race.[85] Nobility tend to have lighter skin than the rest of the populace. In many parts of the developing world, power has gravitated toward those of lighter skin. Colonialism definitely reinforced this tendency.[86] In places like the Union of South Africa, and even Jamaica, the pattern is very rigid and pronounced; yet it exists throughout the developing nations in a more subtle form.

Such perceptions of racial hierarchy could conceivably ease the way for revolution. Concluding a book about ethnicity, Cynthia Enloe asserts:

> The ethnically divided country most likely to transform communal unrest into political revolution is one in which ethnic boundaries are coterminous with socio-economic class lines, one ethnic group clearly dominates and exploits a numerically large but powerless have-not sector, and the oppressed ethnic group is integrated into the country's economic system and has symbolic significance for national identity. Only under these conditions will an ethnic group stand a good chance of spearheading a revolution.[87]

Enloe suggests that, among nations experiencing revolution, only Bolivia and Mexico (with Indians as the have-nots), and Cuba (where Negroes are the have-nots) meet these criteria. She concludes:

> Though the legacy and plight of the Indian crystallized revolutionary fervor in Mexico and Bolivia, in neither country were Indians the principal actors or commanders in the revolution. Perhaps for this reason the Indian's immediate circumstances were not radically altered when the revolution ended. . . . Castro and his chief lieutenants were not Negro, and their revolutionary platform was based not on an ethnic ideology but on a loose notion of socialism and anti-imperialism. But Castro made explicit appeals to Negroes and mulattoes.[88]

---

[85] Audvil King took last place among his twelve to thirteen year-old peers in a "Beauty Handsome Contest" because he was "Blacker than him," the boy awared next-to-last place. King, "Letter to a Friend."

[86] Richard Barnet and Ronald Müller suggest that even today advertising often reinforces this mentality: "In *mestizo* countries such as Mexico and Venezuela where most of the population still bear strong traces of their Indian origin, billboards depicting the good life for sale invariably feature blond, blue-eyed American-looking men and women. One effect of such 'white is beautiful' advertising is to reinforce feelings of inferiority which are the essence of a politically immobilizing colonial mentality." *Global Reach*, p. 178. Seymour Martin Lipset, "Racial and Ethnic Tensions in the Third World," in *The Third World: Premises of United States Policy*, ed. W. Scott Thompson (San Francisco: Institute of Contemporary Studies, 1978), pp. 123–148, summarizes considerable evidence that higher status has long and widely been associated with lighter skin.

[87] Cynthia Enloe, *Ethnic Conflict and Political Development* (Boston: Little, Brown, 1973), pp. 226–227.

[88] Ibid., p. 231.

It would seem that Jamaica and a number of other nations might meet Enloe's criteria for potential revolution as well. She is suggesting that an ethnic group relatively unaffected by cross-cutting cleavages (divisions in the social and economic standing of its members) can better unite to fight. However, *such groups are inherently divided by the personal obligations that tie them to their individual patrons.* They may be internally divided between those with darker and lighter skin pigmentation. And, as Enloe points out, they are easily betrayed by those from other ethnic groups whom they must often rely upon to lead them, even in revolution. Those ethnic groups divided by regions, between urban and rural dwellers, and into varying economic roles will—as Huntington observed—find it even more difficult to unite for revolt. It is far easier to think and act in terms of racial stereotypes than it is to unite a race.

Modernization, nationalism, even the processes of alienation (e.g., sale of land, moneylending, urban migration, mobility), bring groups closer together *physically.* This actually moves them farther apart *culturally,* by perpetuating old ways of life while creating a variety of new ones among those who racially and culturally intermix. Capital cities contain more cultures than other parts of the nation, yet because of the proximity of cultures in the city few are preserved in their original form. Perhaps the segment of the city with the most intermixed culture is the racially-polyglot major patron-client network. This political leadership, itself without clear cultural moorings, makes the decisions which most directly affect the well-being of the many cultural groups in the nation; they determine the housing, education, income, and social environment available to the individual citizen. Thus a cultural minority regulates the priorities of majority cultures, and—so long as those cultures remain divided from one another—does so with impunity. The biggest cultural rift of all is that between the major patron-client network and everybody else; the major network uses the other rifts to its own advantage.

STUDY AID

Notice the underscored words in the Model at the beginning of the chapter.

SYNTHESIS

Lypard P. Edwards wrote in 1927:

> As a group experiences an *improvement* in its conditions of life, it will also experience a rise in its level of desires. The latter will rise more rapidly than the former, leading to dissatisfaction and rebellion.[19]

Rebels in developing nations would indeed seem to come from among those who have experienced improvements in their conditions of life. Yet it does not seem proper to conclude that rising expectations inherently lead to rebellion. So long as the government remains better organized than the populace, it would ap-

---

[19] Lypard P. Edwards, *The Natural History of Revolution* (Chicago: University of Chicago Press, 1927).

pear that rebellion and, to a large extent, dissatisfactions can be diverted to lesser goals.

In 1965, Samuel P. Huntington published an article entitled "Political Development and Political Decay"[90] that attracted considerable attention among those interested in the politics of developing nations. He warned that the rise of urbanization, literacy, communications, voting participation, mass movements, unions, and other such phenomena was leading to *mass mobilization* that could loose desires governments would be unable to satisfy. Unless these processes were slowed by improvement in the *institutionalization* of government, bureaucracy, and especially ruling political parties, popular restlessness would lead to instability, or "political decay." To properly institutionalize, governments must develop complexity and clear hierarchies in their internal organization, autonomy from the influence of various social groups, and coherence among their component parts, leading to adaptability in meeting new problems. As part of this program to slow popular mobilization they must minimize competition among segments of the political elite, limit communications, and increase the complexity of the social structure.

Huntington's was an idea whose time had come; this institutionalization has been precisely the trend in developing nations in recent years.[91] As a means of slowing mass mobilization, however, the idea strikes me as clubbing an ant with a sledge hammer. The institutionalization of government appeared on the surface, in the aftermath of colonialism, to be a new activity of "rising nationalist elites," concurrent with new stirrings of popular disaffection. The race was on to see which group would coalesce its forces more rapidly. In reality, *the institutionalization of governmental elites began many decades before while the mobilization of societal disaffection has even now barely begun.*

The roots of patron-client networks usually go back at least to the eighteenth century. Originally composed simply of merchants and farmers or laborers, the networks gradually added landowners, bureaucrats, soldiers, politicians, white-collar workers, blue-collar workers, intellectuals, and other functionaries. The small merchant grew into the entrepreneur, industrialist, and financier. The initial hostility between these individuals and the old nobility, landowner, and religionist gradually turned into alliance after many battles. The era of colonialism further helped to freeze the emerging hierarchies, both internally and internationally. The growth of industrialization and export capital after World War II, together with the massive foreign and military aid programs of the United States, allowed for still further consolidation, while the wars for national independence produced only brief slowdowns in these processes.

In contrast, mass mobilization began much more recently. Nineteenth and early twentieth century peasant uprisings were fragile and temporary coalitions. Early in the twentieth century, Kuomingtong, Communist, and socialist organizations began largely among intellectuals and a small strata of urban

---

[90] Huntington, *Political Development*.

[91] I am not suggesting that what follows is Professor Huntington's view. I am simply leading into a counter-argument. The next chapter discusses Huntington's theory in greater detail. Huntington has been displeased with the trend he predicted; it has not produced the reforms he had hoped for.

workers. Mass literacy only started to gain impetus in the 1930s, as did trade unions. The rapid growth of cities is a post-World War II phenomenon. In most countries this is also true of the broad popular franchise. Regularized mobility of poorer youths into higher education is of recent vintage. Traditions of constitutional safeguards are far less firmly rooted than traditions of suppressing civil liberties, which predated even colonialism. Representative institutions like trade unions, interest groups, political parties, and legislatures have generally—after the brief periods of power vacuum during the wars of independence—fallen into the grip of governments and hence do not serve as autonomous instruments for mass mobilization.[92]

To be sure, representative institutions with adaptability, complexity, autonomy, and coherence existed in the traditional village. At the same time, however, as the patron-client networks were congealing, the village was disintegrating. And, in Emile Durkheim's words, subsequent history has been marked by the nondevelopment and noninstitutionalization of the precontractual elements of contracts in society:

> . . . adequate mechanisms and principles of aggregating [different levels of articulation of demands] or of regulating the conflicts attendant on their development did not develop . . . no structure of power and organization linking these individuals and the new, more articulated, demands and activities has been created—even the old structure might have broken down.[93]

In short, institutions existing in village society to effectuate mass mobilization and representation have not been recreated in today's nation states. Mechanisms to regulate conflict do exist. But they are seldom, if ever, backed by commonly shared values or by the principal feature of a contract: negotiations in which both sides bargain for concessions. One-party-dominant states with considerable control over popular movements have become virtually universal in developing nations. Once the centralization is established, even coups d'etat, while marked by extreme hatred among elite factions and disruptions in their continuity, always eventually return power to elites similar to those displaced. The fact that popular movements are not well-organized and are easy to keep in that position permits this continuity of power by the elites.

This discussion of Vietnam continues from p. 118.

Professor Huntington was an advisor in the United States Vietnam War effort and his article took a middle-line position on the debate about mass mobilization. It endorsed neither rule by military junta nor free elections there. Yet Vietnam stands virtually alone as an example of protracted civil war within a

---

[92] There can be tremendous sensitivity about this sort of assertion. In a University of Singapore class I was discussing the notion of interest groups being ancillary to political party organization and mentioned the Singapore Trade's Union Congress and the campus Democratic Socialist Club as examples. When I arrived for the next class, I found pickets from the latter organization outside my classroom door protesting this slur on their good name!

[93] S. N. Eisenstadt, "Breakdowns of Modernization," *Economic Development and Cultural Change* 12 (July 1964): 351, 357.

developing nation. The fact that it was protracted may have less to do with in-evitable mass uprising in a world of change than with being financed and par-tially fought by Great Powers, containing two separate fully formed capital cities for the same racial group, and the access of various factions to surreptitious financing from the sale of opium.[94] The biggest blunder of the United States was perhaps the extent to which it freed the major patron-client network in Saigon from its dependence on the minor patron-client network. *By feeding the major network from the outside, the United States relieved it of the necessity to support itself from exports of rice and other commodities.* This was an unnatural state of affairs. Patron-client networks, no matter how greedy their members, normally retain enough cohesion to extract the export commodities on which all the members (greedy or not) depend. After 1965, an individual in Saigon could make his fortune simply by impressing some Americans enough to obtain the right to handle outside money or supplies (there was US$150 billion in circulation), or to fly heroin from Ban Hue Sai; he did not have to cooperate with other members of his own major network, or to work at controlling the peasantry.

The patron-client network was free to totally ignore their own countryside. This paved the way for the guerilla; soldiers are less effective overseers of the countryside than landowners and financiers worried about their profits from the next crop. The patron-client ties were allowed to die. Because Hanoi did not have PX's and commissaries, highly-paid foreign troops, massive rural aid programs, contingency funds, intricate weapons and logistic support systems, and easy ac-cess to illicit drug markets, it was spared from such a threat to its internal cohe-sion. It had to keep its patron-client network alive; to survive, and win the war, it needed the support of its own people. After the fall of Saigon, its leaders turned against the traditional enemy, Cambodia (another country which suffered from massive American aid), the vast amount of military hardware it had inherited from the Americans. But still lacking massive outside aid, it must continue to tend to its patron-client network. It must extract resources, and deal with those who obstruct extraction of resources. This will both help to free it from dangers posed by internal guerilla threats and reduce its chances of harming other nations where patron-clientism remains firmly entrenched. Guerilla activities there and elsewhere, in the words of S. N. Eisenstadt, are likely to alternate "between brief periods of highly intensive eruptions and long periods of stagnation and inactiv-ity."[95]

Exports are kingpins behind the patron-client networks; this will become even clearer in Chapters 7 and 8. Should the export links be seriously weakened in the future, the firm grip of the patron-client networks on governmental in-stitutions may be pried loose. In the interim, relatively strong governmental institutions confront relatively weak institutions for mass mobilization which are constantly bickering among themselves. So long as government has the means to interrupt attempts to organize the latter sorts of institutions, mere increases in

---

[94] Alfred W. McCoy, *The Politics of Heroin in Southeast Asia* (New York: Harper & Row, 1972) documents the unique conditions which permitted several military units to finance themselves through links with international underworld syndicates.

[95] Eisenstadt, "Breakdowns of Modernization," p. 352.

communications (literacy, mass media, urbanization, voter participation) may give members of the new middle classes or religious leaders some experience in the arts of organization but will probably not cause major disruptions in present ruling structures. And *the major networks will retain this capacity to suppress challenges to their own authority so long as their earnings from exports remain secure.* Foreign policy makers would be wise to take careful heed of this before they mistake some bands of guerillas or gun-toting urban revolutionary students for genuine fomenters of radical change. The most radical of the Third World revolutionaries, Fidel Castro, would not have survived without massive support from the Soviet Union for capital and markets, and would not have needed to turn in that direction in the absence of United States embargo and blockade. The Soviet Union probably does not have the economic strength to provide this for many more Cubas. If the United States wants to help major networks defend themselves against revolution we must assure that ports are *not* blockaded and that governments are *not* given access to large amounts of money unrelated to their export economy.[96] The resulting flow of trade will assure that the patron-client networks survive and revolutions and revolutionary governments fail.

It is not easy to create adequate food, comfortable neighborhoods, secure jobs, education adjusted both to job availability and personal aspirations, balanced family budgets, and housing in keeping with all of these considerations. Even governments in developed nations with autonomous representative interest groups and high per capita incomes find it difficult to make the adjustments that provide the above conditions for wide strata of the populace. Without such institutions and resources it becomes even more difficult—especially in settings of rapid social change. Therefore it is not surprising that large percentages of the citizens of developing nations find many of the aspects in their lives to be in poor adjustment. In this sense, alienation is widespread.

Poorer segments of the populace seldom translate such alienation into political activism, whether from habit, fear, or inexperience. They find other means to dissipate their frustrations. Middle-class groups inclined in this direction must face the fact that it is easy for any government to break up their organizational efforts and either jail or co-opt their leaders. With this in mind it makes sense to many alienated people to give positive support to a government that offers them small reliefs from their tension, whether in the form of sports contests or a job, even while this government prevents them from making more frontal attacks on their problems. They can quickly turn from opponents of the regime into members of the patron-client network. When movements occasion-

---

[96] The guerilla leaders in Angola and Zimbabwe, two of the last sub-Sahara African states not under black rule, became patrons once independence was achieved, and continued firm trade ties with the North Atlantic nations, without much disturbance in the social and economic patterns inside their countries. Unless the United States blockades their harbors they are likely to be able to maintain this state of affairs. To retaliate against the detention of hostages, the United States threatened to blockade Iran's harbors. This would have harmed the businessmen who have the strongest interest in continuing trade with the United States, and made it more difficult for them to continue control over revolutionary movements. Blockades and aid infusions can influence which government will have power; so long as patron-clientism continues that is likely to make little difference in the long run. But if the blockade and aid were to weaken patron-clientism itself that would make a great deal of difference.

ally break through this inertia to gain real disruptive momentum, they will usually find it impossible to cope with the racial animosities which tend either to break them apart or temporarily unite the rest of the nation against them. In this manner small elites, composed of social and sometimes racial minorities, maintain a grip on power even as alienation may be on the increase. Patron-clientism will endure so long as export trading endures.

SHORT SUMMARY

Even frustrated people seldom choose to revolt. They turn to other things to relieve their frustrations. Those who do revolt are most inclined to respond to racial themes. Whether centered around race, religion, region, or ideology, revolutionary organizations are easy to split apart. Military coups, street demonstrations, and acts of terror will occur frequently. But they are not likely to change the status quo much; many of today's participants will become tomorrow's members of the minor network.

Have you caught these definitions?

	page
revolution	177
radical revolution	177
rebellion	177
alienation	179
minifundio	182
catharsis	196
mutual veto	213

Can you answer each with one sentence?

1. In the developing areas were there more radical revolutions in the nineteenth or in the twentieth century?
2. In the United States land ownership is more concentrated in a few hands than in Libya. Why is this less of a problem in the United States than in Libya?
3. Why is the line between landlord, moneylender, and peasant not always a clear one?
4. What types of individuals are most likely to support rebellions?
5. Might people in traditional villages be more prone to violence than those in villages affected by modernization?

From what you have read this far, can you make and support judgments about these questions?

1. Are upper-middle-class professionals in developing nations as secure as their counterparts in the United States?
2. How do unstable personal environments and alienation affect rebellion?
3. Could mimeographing be more cathartic than attending a hockey match?
4. Is Malaysia consociational?

5. How is the power of ethnic leaders being weakened in Nigeria?
6. Only organized groups sustained over time can counter the coercive techniques available to the leaders of developing nations. The experience and
   motivation patterns of citizens in developing nations will not sustain such
   organization. True?

You should now be getting an idea of how the parts of this book fit together.
Reread the entire "Book in Brief" section of Chapter 1 with particular attention
to what you have learned about rebellion and revolution.

CHAPTER
6

GETTING YOUR BEARINGS (see map, front of book)

1. Could we explain similarities in the behavior of developing nations on the basis of climatic zones they occupy?
2. Could we explain similarities in the behavior of developing nations on the basis of their access, or nonaccess, to continental land masses?

The Model

A developed nation provides most of its citizens with a stable personal environment. A developing nation does not. Today's developing nations were once developed nations. They changed because their political systems separated from their social systems when European commerce was introduced. If the structure of international trade changes in the near future, social and political systems may be reintegrated, promoting political development. Then the developing nations may once again become developed nations.

Today's Political Systems: Are They Developing?

QUESTIONS TO KEEP IN MIND

1. Do any of these theorists find some political systems preferable to others? Why? Do those systems exist anywhere?
2. Do any of these theorists disagree with this textbook about the power of government to initiate reforms?
3. Do these theorists find development occurring?
4. Which of these theorists do you like best? Why?

If you have read this far you have absorbed the basic outlines of a model of the political systems of developing nations. Science requires us to observe and experiment. Simply reading about someone's model is not the same as observing and experimenting. Unfortunately, practice in observing and experimenting is not easy to acquire.

You have been presented with the proposition that the political systems of developing nations focus on patron-client networks, and a series of theorems explaining how the systems arrived at this focus, why they stay there, how they affect personal environments, and other variables. Each theorem has been explored systematically with supportive evidence. Some alternative explanations have been broached and disputed so that you could get a feel for opposing points of view. But how do you make experiments and observations to test these explanations about processes in distant lands?

You could create your own model and theorems, figure out ways to test them, go to the field, and start your experiments and observations. This is the ultimate step. I would suggest a more practical first step: Examine the theories of authors presenting differing arguments and the facts they use to support their cases. Going straight to the other authors and reading what they have to say would not be a time-consuming process; it is a step that should not be avoided in the process of critically assessing what you read. The footnotes in this book introduce you to many such sources; they often contain specific page references to speed the process. This chapter goes even further in helping you to compare arguments. *It lays out several theories in a format that allows you to compare them with one another and with the arguments presented in the preceding chapters.*

There is more to this process, however, than simply evaluating arguments. Arguments always proceed and facts are gathered from a given perspective. A perspective is a working assumption—a desired state of affairs or an implicit hypothesis that one state of affairs will produce (or has produced) another.[1] While students know they should scrutinize arguments and facts carefully, they often fail to examine the author's perspective. Perspectives are important because they cause us to focus our attention on certain kinds of information and to pay less attention to other kinds of information. A popular current perspective is the notion that modernization is a necessary precondition for achieving political development. We are not always clear why modernization promotes political development; in this case our perspective remains unexamined. Manfred Halpern (one of the theorists to whom you are about to be introduced) feels, instead, that modernization often produces political disarray. He approaches the matter from the perspective that political development requires the will and capacity to generate and absorb continuing transformation. Halpern examines how to achieve this balance but fails to explain why political development requires this will and capacity; he does not examine his own perspective. Other authors proceed from other unexamined perspectives. John Kautsky's premise is that "modernizers" must come to power if political development is to ensue, and he explores the means by which they may be brought to power without exploring why they should be expected to contribute to political development. David Apter argues from the perspective that a balance must be struck between information and coercion. He explores how that balance might be struck without explaining why it is of central importance to political development.[2] Samuel P. Huntington's premise that mass mobilization must be balanced by political institutionalization was an unexamined perspective. He never explained why this combination should be expected to produce political development. Gabriel Almond measures political development by the degrees to which role differentiation, subsystem autonomy, and secularization come into being without explaining why this combination should mean development. This book equates political development with stable personal environments. We have tried to explain in our discussions of praxis and alienation, and at the end of the last chapter, why personal stability is

---

[1] Alan C. Isaak, *Scope and Methods of Political Science: An Introduction to the Methodology of Political Inquiry,* 3rd ed. (Homewood, Ill.: Dorsey Press, 1981), p. 78: ". . . operational definitions do not spring fully developed from the minds of scientists. Instead, they begin with an observation, or an act of intuition sparked by a touch of creative imagination. However, as he begins to examine the phenomenon more systematically, the political scientist must move beyond this intuitive grasp. And so we return to the operational definition." It is this initial intuitive grasp which focuses the attention of the definition.

[2] In David E. Apter, *Choice and the Politics of Allocation: A Developmental Theory* (New Haven, Conn.: Yale University Press, 1971), attempting to delve further behind this premise, he says that development is a set of system changes leading to an "expansion of choice" (p. 6). For this, people need control over both individual relationships and information to increase their control over nature. Perhaps his perspective, then, is an orderly expansion of choice. Why should anyone want this? He does not explain. He does not really need to. Most of his readers share this unexamined perspective. They do not think to examine it. But why should it be considered development for people to control individual relationships and information? Why not consider this to be underdevelopment? Many members of extended families consider it to be.

desirable, but then only sketchily. All of us have our own perspectives. Everyone must begin somewhere. But we must examine our perspectives. In this case we must ask ourselves *what we mean by political development, and why.*

It is fortunate that perspectives differ, because they help us to save one another from our blind spots. *When development or any other subject is approached from a variety of perspectives, more questions will be asked and more types of data will be sought.* For example, some archaeologists, trying to explain the disappearance of giant mammals from North America during the last Great Ice Age, argue that man arrived on the continent at that time from across the Bering Straits and wiped out the mammals with stone arrowheads. Others feel it more reasonable to assume that man was already here but learned at that time, from across the Bering Straits, how to make stone arrowheads. The former hypothesis spurs efforts to find more sites that are 20,000 years old (during the Ice Age) so as to explore migration patterns. The latter hypothesis has spurred efforts to find traces of man in strata older than 20,000 years. Both efforts, spawned by the existence of differing perspectives, will likely increase our knowledge about early man on the continent. Both hypotheses share a great many common assumptions (e.g., that the Clovis point originated in Asia, that hunting by man wiped out the giant mammals, that either technology or people moved freely about the continent). If arrowheads are discovered and verified in older strata, both sides would have to rethink their positions. Likewise, biologists might seek other explanations of why the animals disappeared (e.g., disease, overgrazing), or other archaeologists with other perspectives, such as that both man and arrowheads arrived by boat from elsewhere, might look in still different strata and locales to uncover evidence. Discovery of new validated artifacts in those locales would also call for a rethinking. Yet all these scientists of differing perspectives share the need to be able to communicate their findings accurately to one another,[3] to think through alternative explanations of what could have caused the artifacts they find, and to logically explain causal relationships. By examining from one another's perspectives they can broaden their understanding of man's occupation of the Americas.

In studying developing nations, differing perspectives can provide the same enrichment of knowledge. One scholar tries to explain the poverty of developing nations by pointing to deficiencies resulting from a lack of modern facilities. A second tries to explain it by suggesting that it will be reduced if two particular modern attributes are found together at the same time. Both share the assumptions that there is a relationship between modernization and poverty, and that adding to modernization can be beneficial, but they differ as to exactly how to achieve those benefits. The first will seek information on how the addition of modern facilities had helped reduce poverty. The second will seek to discover whether the coexistence of the particular attributes relates to a reduction in poverty. If one finds nations with increased modernization or the coexistence of the

---

[3] Noting that perfect objectivity is never possible in science, Arnold Brecht suggests it is sufficient that we be "intersubjective": "a type of knowledge that can be transmitted from any person who has such knowledge to any other person who does not have it but who can grasp the meaning of the symbols (words, signs) used in communication and perform the operations, if any, described in these communications." Arnold Brecht, *Political Theory: The Foundations of Twentieth-Century Political Thought* (Princeton, N.J.: Princeton University Press, 1959), p. 114.

particular attributes, yet *increasing* poverty, this might call for a rethinking of perspectives. Other scholars might seek explanations for the poverty from other perspectives, such as that certain traditions are being destroyed, that outsiders are exploiting these nations, or that there are imbalances between tradition and modernity. These scholars would seek still different kinds of evidence to deal with these hypotheses. As all these scholars communicate their findings to one another they enrich their understanding of the political systems of developing nations.

Authors proceeding from perspectives other than our own are apt to fill in gaps in our knowledge. If we compare the knowledge they amass with what we have accumulated, and their perspective with ours, it will become apparent that each of our perspectives has overlooked important ramifications. After such comparison, you or I might even change our perspective, deciding that our working assumptions were less obvious or desirable than we believed them to be at first—though it is not necessary or inevitable that we do so. That is how knowledge accumulates. When students fall into the habit of simply accepting the perspectives of their teachers, entire generations can end up approaching a subject from similar perspectives. We limit the questions being asked and hence restrict the accumulation of knowledge.

This is to say that our values need not hinder objective inquiry; they may enhance it. They provide us with motivation to explore new topics, and with a focus while doing so. But we need to recognize our values and bring them into the open, to be willing to explore questions that raise doubts about those values, and to see how they relate to the values, speculations, and explorations of others. Scholars who argue that personal values should be kept out of objective inquiry are often simply disguising the perspectives from which they approach their subjects.

I should say a word about evidence as well. The most frustrating thing about gathering evidence is that it is usually scarce and difficult to obtain. Once you have found it, the particular details that interest you most may not be there. One advantage of looking at a variety of methodological approaches to any given question is to note that everyone must work with far less evidence that would be needed to prove their point definitely. That is part of the reason for argumentation. The skill lies in using what evidence is available with as much care as possible.

The following writers agree fundamentally with the model that begins each chapter in this book, but each takes exception with some aspects of it. And, because of differing perspectives, each points to additional aspects not discussed in that paragraph. Up to this point I have introduced developing nations from only one perspective. Now they will be introduced from a variety of perspectives. You will also learn something about how the argument in this book developed, how it can be expanded upon, and why the last two chapters discuss what they do. It will quickly become apparent that *authors with similar perspectives are grouped together. There are two main groups, and the perspectives of these groups are very different.*

If you ask the following questions about each of these scholar's ideas you will find them easy to compare:

1. What sorts of political systems could exist in developing nations (i.e., those so named on the map in the front of the book)?
2. How is development achieved?
3. Which sort of political system comes closest to achieving development?
4. Do any developing nations have, or come near having, that sort of system?

To help you compare their models with the model you have been using in this book, I also discuss some contrasts between the emphases in their model and my own. All of this is designed to help you decide upon the perspectives, concepts, emphases, and models with which you are (for the moment, at least) most at ease.

THE VIRTUES OF HARMONY:
ORCHESTRATING MODERNIZATION

We shall begin by matching arguments you have already encountered with alternative viewpoints of scholars who are highly respected in the field. They represent a variety of perspectives, and a variety of schools of thought within the discipline, such as systems theory, functionalism, communications theory, dependency theory, and Marxism. As each scholar is introduced, a footnote will lead you to basic articles or books that present his approach in greater detail. After summarizing the author's approach, we shall relate it to the perspective and model of this book. At the beginning of the next section we shall review each approach in briefer, more focused form.

The mid-twentieth century was a period of optimism about the benefits to be derived from modernization. We wanted more goods, better distribution, and more freedom, and we thought modernization could provide them. In colonial areas, too, people were told that modernization would bring improvements to their lives. That optimism was reflected in the field of comparative politics of developing nations. In more recent times there has been a questioning of modernity as we discovered it inducing inflation, shortages of raw materials, pollution, warfare and civil unrest, continuing maldistribution of goods, and other problems. There is a return to interest in antiques, simpler life styles, energy saving, unprocessed foods, bicycles, genealogies, rehabilitation of homes, and the like. That questioning and search for alternatives has affected the field of comparative politics, as you will see in the next section of the chapter most clearly.

First, in this section, we shall look at two writers who see modernization of nation-states as a boon and can find little fault with it in the long run. Then we shall examine several who have begun to note some more persistent problems with modernization and see it as a blessing only if government brings some of its various chords into harmony. Both these sets of writers are in basic agreement with the first four sentences in our model printed at the beginning of this chapter, but they disagree with the last two pertaining to the future. They are all more optimistic than I am about the chance that internal reforms of economic and social institutions (in the case of Binder and Deutsch) or political institutions (in the case of the rest) can right fundamental imbalances, because they all con-

tinue to see modernization, for all its faults, as capable of producing development in the developing nations in the same way as it has done in the United
States. *Can modernization, or carefully orchestrated modernization, bring development?*

Leonard Binder and Karl W. Deutsch

Leonard Binder views[4] the Industrial Revolution in Europe as an historic threshold. Political development concerns the political consequences of crossing that
threshold. Before this threshold there was tradition. Today there is transition
into modernity. The transition involves replacing tradition with modernity.
Before the development of modernity is complete, a nation must pass through
five crises: the creation of a national identity, legitimacy for the leadership,
broad participation by citizens, fair distribution of goods and services, and
penetration of the nation-state into all its regions.

Binder has no illusions about the difficulty of this process. He thinks traditional society had some virtues; for instance, the elimination of magic will
weaken modern society in some ways (though science will strengthen it in
others). Modernization will not always have humane consequences or encourage
political development or democracy, and it can lead to empirical contradiction
and political conflict. The rise of middle-class types that modernity inherently involves is not always a good thing. Bureaucracy is not always rational. Yet "it is
evident that a society lacking a bourgeoisie, an industrial labor class, an intelligentsia, or a bureaucracy would not satisfy our general idea of a developed society." This combination will not necessarily set to work to face the five crises
and produce political development, but it is a necessary precondition for doing
so.

Binder can categorize the political systems of developing nations according
to how many crises they have passed through (i.e., from those which have passed
through none to those which have passed through all five). Development can
only be achieved after a nation has a bourgeoisie, an industrial labor class, an intelligentsia, and a bureaucracy, which can happen only after it has modernized.
The nation that has passed through all five crises comes closest to achieving
development.

While we have tended to emphasize positive features of traditional societies,
Binder tends to emphasize negative features. What he calls traditional, however,
sounds more like what we called the period of disruption in Chapter 3. He places
the changeover from traditional to modern at the point of the Industrial Revolution, not at the earlier point when world trade was introduced, as we have done.
He agrees with this book about many of the imbalances that modernity has
created. We agree on the need for legitimacy, though we disagree on the need for
broad participation, fair distribution of goods (versus land), and national identity and penetration of the nation-state, for we are less confident than he about

---

[4] Leonard Binder, "The Crises of Political Development," in *Crises and Sequences in Political
Development,* ed. Leonard Binder et al. (Princeton, N.J.: Princeton University Press, 1971), pp.
3–72. Quotes taken from and specific references to Binder in this section are from pp. 16, 20, 22, 23,
29, 34–35, 44, and 51.

the ability of modern nations to produce development. But we are far apart in defining development. Passing through the five crises, which he defines as development, may actually interfere with what we have called development, the creation of stable personal environments. The mere fact that rational national institutions with popular support penetrate to the hinterlands, even to fairly distribute goods, does not mean they will create stable environments there. They may, in fact, *disturb* stable environments.

Our disagreement about when modernization began (the Industrial Revolution versus the earlier era of European trade) may partially account for the disagreement over the direction in which reform is moving. Binder's descriptions of traditional society sound suspiciously like the early stages of patron-clientism. For instance, he states that in traditional society "it is the form of legal documents or petitions which determines whether they are to be honored and not the validity of the applicant's case. It is the form of bureaucratic communication that is more important than what bureaucrats actually write to one another. . . . It is the formal legitimacy of the government and not its performance which is important." We have suggested that in traditional villages quite the opposite was true, while this description was indeed characteristic of patron-client relations and still is. The distinction is important, for *Binder is suggesting that modernization is improving this situation, while we are suggesting that modernization created it.* From my perspective, Binder's description of modern culture has romantic[5] overtones: "By contrast [to traditional culture], the modern culture values skill, the pragmatic attainment of results, efficiency in the use of resources, the easy substitutability of similarly qualified persons, and the possibility of disregarding personality differences." Binder might argue that the nepotism, advertising deception, planned obsolescence, and favoritism in today's society must simply be a carryover from traditionalism which will end as modernization proceeds. It might, in contrast, be argued that traditional societies exhibited the qualities on Binder's list more than today's transitional societies and that the situation is getting worse rather than better.

Karl Deutsch offers another example of a scholar who sees *development as pertaining to modernizing various aspects of the political system, the economy, society, or the physical surroundings while leaving behind more traditional modes of behavior.* Deutsch sees[6] the key to development as an increase in communications. For example, in his 1980 text[7] he defines development as "the change from poverty to prosperity, illiteracy to widespread education, an obsolete technology to a modern one, inefficiency to competence, high death rates to low ones, national impotence to national power." He suggests that national power requires independence from direct or indirect "forms of foreign hegemony and military, political, and financial control." Yet most of his dis-

---

[5] Binder also has a rejoinder to Chapter 2: "Indeed, there is a school that interprets modern society by emphasizing the negative consequences of modernization, particularly in cultural terms. This school has been nourished by the writings of romantic anthropologists among other romantic rejecters of the modern world." Ibid., p. 41.

[6] Karl W. Deutsch, *The Nerves of Government,* 2nd ed. (New York: The Free Press, 1966); idem, *Nationalism and Social Communication,* rev. ed. (Cambridge: MIT Press, 1966).

[7] Karl W. Deutsch, *Politics in Government: How People Decide Their Fate,* 3rd ed. (Boston: Houghton Mifflin, 1980), pp. 536, 543, 558.

cussion about how to achieve development involves links with outside technology.

He divides *traditional societies* into three types—early transitional, advanced, and industrialized— distinguishable by the size of their per capita incomes. In all of these traditional societies, though few can be found in their pure form, communications remain largely within the conventional channels of family, locality, ritual, occupational specialty, and social class. Arts and techniques change slowly. Habits and prejudices prove "useful as well as convenient"; there is "an apparent mood of stability and security, and . . . real anxieties and fears, high rates of death, hunger, and disease." They differ among one another in their economies and technologies, their division of labor, their capacity to produce concentrations of wealth for the rulers, and the level of their intellectual and artistic culture.

Then enters the "impact of modernity" upon certain groups, localities, practices, and institutions. Markets and cities bring a growth in communications. "Money, modern commerce, banking, transport, and industry all tend to be concentrated in a few foreign or foreign-dominated economic centers." Colonialism helped perpetuate some of the old oppression and slowed some aspects of modernization. Today, demographic and economic growth, *social mobilization* (e.g., per capita income, literacy, circulation of newspapers), and *assimilation* into modern social groupings are gathering strength. If there is control to be applied to modernization, it largely pertains to imbalances between social mobilization and assimilation (e.g., children must learn modern languages to be assimilated into modern groups).

For Deutsch, political systems vary according to the extent that social mobilization has moved them away from traditionalism. Development is achieved by moving from tradition into modernity, with some care to assure a balance between social mobilization and assimilation in the process. Those systems that have moved farthest from tradition into successfully assimilating people into modern groups are the most developed.

In this book I have defined political development as the capability to provide stable environments for individual citizens and concluded that the unfolding of modernization is hindering this capability rather than helping it. Binder and Deutsch have defined political development as resulting from the processes of modernization and have concluded that these processes can be expected to produce human advancement if allowed to continue rather freely. Many take a middle position: that modernization must be regulated by government in particular ways if it is to be beneficial. They disagree on exactly what government should regulate, and how. Otherwise they, together with Binder and Deutsch, have a remarkably similar perspective on development.

According to Binder and Deutsch:

1. What sorts of political systems could exist in developing nations?
2. How is development achieved?
3. Which sort of political system comes closest to achieving development?
4. Do any developing nations have, or come near having, that sort of system?

Manfred Halpern

We have pointed to only one type of political system in developing nations: patron-clientism. Manfred Halpern sees six: the system of structured instability, pluralist interest-bartering, oligarchic interest-bartering, the ritualized system, and the extremist system, and the authoritarian modernizing system.[8] Under *structured instability* several main groups share power, but none can keep ascendancy for any long period of time. Each group harbors cleavages in opinion on how to deal with change, but agrees to let no groups into inner circles who would destroy the balance among them. The *pluralistic interest-bartering system* is similar but has achieved greater stability among its component groups. Newly emerging social groups, the poor, and the uprooted, are not likely to be found among its ranks. The bargaining usually centers "on the distribution of scarce resources and reinforcement of existing relationships rather than on the sacrifice of vested interests and of accustomed beliefs, values, and behavior." The *oligarchic interest-bartering system* is headed by an authoritarian ruler who "bases his power on a calculus of personal relations—upon the intimidation of one prominent man, the purchase of another, the expectation of future favors by a third, and the fear of losing privileges not earned on grounds of talent or skills." The *ritualized system* uses ideology and charisma to develop new solidarity networks (retribalize) among the emergent middle classes and newly literate men in the provinces. The *extremist system* "institutionalizes terror and violence to impose dogmatic certainty in the midst of rapid social change." The *authoritarian modernizing system* is similar but more temperate in its use of power.

This book has suggested that even in rapidly modernizing settings patron-client networks tend to inhibit what Halpern calls the extremist system. The other systems all seem compatible with what we have described as the nature of the political systems of developing nations. Halpern comes close to describing patron-clientism as we have defined it and all these definitions imply that the political systems do not include broad strata of the populace. This approach to describing systems, in short, emphasizes the same sorts of tendencies as the approach I have taken. However, I have simply not focused on these particular distinctions among systems; elements of all these descriptions can be found in most developing nations if they are viewed over a period of time.

Halpern himself is less interested in making these distinctions than in what he calls the central question: *the will and capacity to transform the imbalances that exist among the systems of a society in the direction of an intrinsic capacity to generate and absorb continuing transformation.* None of the five (six) systems, he feels, have this capacity. Halpern sees today's economic, social, and productive systems as in rapid flux, and often working at cross-purposes with one another. It is the role of politics to bring these systems back into balance.

---

[8] Manfred Halpern, *The Politics of Social Change in the Middle East and North Africa* (Princeton: Rand, 1963); idem, "The Revolution of Modernization in National and International Society," in *Revolution-Nomos VIII,* ed. Carl J. Friedrich (New York: Atherton, 1966); idem, "The Rate and Costs of Political Development," *The Annals* 358 (March 1965): 20–28; idem, "A Redefinition of the Revolutionary Situation," *Journal of International Affairs* 22 (1969): 54–75; idem, "Egypt and the New Middle Class: Reaffirmations and New Explorations," *Comparative Studies in Society and History* 11, no. 1. (January 1969): 97–108.

This will not happen unless leaders are motivated and capable enough to make it happen. Halpern in no way excludes the notion that as part of this process it may be necessary to shore up some traditional institutions that are disintegrating. It may also be necessary to create some new ones. Simple accumulation of infrastructures, factories, armies, rising economic and popular participation indices, or other accoutrements of modernization is not sufficient. The hard part is weaving these together into a pattern that will both look after today's populace and harness the onslaught of continuing transformation to serve even broader elements of the population.

Halpern and I are in complete agreement on this. Disagreement would probably arise, however, over the possibility of this balance emerging, and over the prime moving force to produce it. The last chapter of this book argues that the beginnings of such harnessing will have to emanate from outside the developing nations. Halpern, in contrast, looks to the new middle class within developing nations to accomplish it.[9] They are the ones who are acquiring the motivation to broaden distribution, regulate development, and recreate social institutions; they are being placed in charge of the modernized institutions with the capacity to achieve these goals.

Discussion of Iran is continued from p. 202.

A student of Halpern, James Alban Bill, went to Iran during the 1960s and came away describing what he calls the politics of system preservation in a system where the new middle class plays a prominent role.[10] Politics congregated around web (patron-client) networks. Middle-class participants in politics and bureaucracy broke down into differing personality types: the uprooter, who turned to revolutionary activity; the technocrat, who carried out his job and kept his nose clean; and the maneuverer, who engineered his way to the top by doing the right things for the right people. The occasional uprooter who slipped his way into the land reform program found himself transferred to a post abroad, or simply bypassed when graft which he had tried to eliminate was distributed. Yet the middle class was growing, and the demands for change were on the increase. Whereas previous chapters have suggested that these demands could be quashed by the power of government, Bill sees them as transforming the system:

> One of the deepest unintended consequences of the White Revolution [the land reform program] is the accelerating growth of the professional middle class. Yet this is the same class that is needed to control and guide ongoing patterns. And it is the same class that is needed to control and guide the explosive reform program. Thus, the dilemma that faces the Iranian political elite inheres in the very reform program that they dramatically chose to reinforce the traditional system. First, the elite requires the participation and commitment of the very class which threatens them, in order that the reforms be implemented and controlled. Sec-

---

[9] The new middle class is to be found among salaried professionals, "defined by its interest in ideas, actions, and careers relevant to modernization." Halpern, "Egypt and the New Middle Class," p. 99.

[10] James Alban Bill, *The Politics of Iran: Groups, Classes, and Modernization* (Columbus: Merrill, 1972). See also Chapter 4, pp. 139–140 and Chapter 5, pp. 198–199.

ond, many of those peasants who benefit from the reforms will move into the already expanding professional middle class and here they will join in a new level of criticism and demand. The forces of time reveal the inevitability of the ascendence of the professional middle class in the political system.[11]

Bill himself documents the decline of the White Revolution and the docility of the middle class which permitted that decline. And he explains why technocrats and maneuverers get ahead of uprooters in the system. It is hard to visualize what will stop them from being transferred from their posts, ignored, or co-opted when they try to effect changes. This is not simply a question of the ability of the major patron-client networks (which may not have all the expertise but do have the money and many of the tools of power) to keep the middle classes in line through force, co-optation, and interruption of organization. I also fear that once people have been uprooted from rural life styles it is difficult to return them to conditions of sustenance and social viability. It is also difficult to prevent middle-class groups from hoarding benefits for themselves. It might prove extremely difficult to wrest from them the personal sacrifices needed to accomplish a fundamental war on poverty.

Further discussion of Iran may be found on p. 304.

Halpern does not entirely disagree. He sees the new middle class caught in the "polarity of direct bargaining," a form of patron-clientism.[12] "Until this polarity has been transformed, the salaried middle class will not be able to persist in modernizing any other aspects of society."[13] But he sees more reason for hope. First, those members of the new middle class who emerge as patrons can make new kinds of demands for submission "for actions novel in substance; in return for accepting the discipline of our new political party, you will get priority in jobs." The new middle class in the Middle East has transformed a few relationships between a few men and women, between a few fathers and sons, between a few teachers and students, a few officials and other officials, a few leaders and followers. This is "incoherent change" rather than the "deliberate generation and absorption of change." Halpern would like to see it lead to the "polarity of boundary management" in which individuals have autonomous zones of jurisdiction that they can defend against one another, and later into the "polarity of transformation" with sustained efforts to "transform peasants bound to family, faction, landlord, and habit into farmers fully participating in society's modernization," under leaders "prepared to persist in transforming ideologies." But his hopes, too, are tempered. This incoherent change is more

---

[11] Ibid., p. 155. See also Chapter 7, pp. 297–299.

[12] Halpern, "Egypt and the New Middle Class," p. 104. "Each individual occupying a pole in this type of dialectical encounter in Islamic society persistently demands submission of the other but, since both cannot achieve submission and one is likely to be unequal in power to the other, a bargain is struck over the terms of the submission. This bargain is subject to change at any moment—as soon as the balance of power changes or can be made to change. It is a style of collaboration and conflict that encourages unstable assertiveness no less than unstable dependence, and the impulsive quest for high, short-term gain."

[13] Ibid., pp. 105, 108.

likely to lead to anarchy: "incoherence, i.e., the absence of polarity on any ground, and hence the absence of capacity to deal with continuity or change."[14] *He sees* some possibility that present patron-client relationships will disintegrate, though they will probably not be replaced by a system with a capacity to transform. *I see* little possibility that they will disintegrate or be replaced by a system with a capacity to transform.

According to Halpern:

1. What sorts of political systems could exist in developing nations?
2. How is development achieved?
3. Which sort of political system comes closest to achieving development?
4. Do any developing nations have, or come near having, that sort of system?

John Kautsky

Kautsky spells out in greater detail than Halpern the means by which a middle-class revolution could be accomplished.[15] The key individuals in Kautsky's model of development are the *modernizers,* "people who value material progress, equality, and widespread popular participation in politics. . . ." These modernizers want to modernize their societies, and have the qualifications to do so. In accepting alien modern values they become alienated from their own underdeveloped societies. They "have only contempt for money making." These are not merely the middle-class professionals to whom Halpern refers. They are, in fact, the leaders in many developing nations today. Nkrumah, Sukarno, Ben Bella, Kemal, Nehru, and Nasser are among Kautsky's favorite examples of modernizers. These men took power away from an older entrenched aristocracy. In contrast to the old economy based on the export of basic raw materials these leaders are committed to industrialization, land reform, and growth in the middle class. They are supported by the industrial workers, the small bourgeoisie, town-dwellers, peasants and more progressive members of the aristocracy; in fact, it is from among these classes that modernizers tend to have their origins.

Once modernizers came to power, usually after fights against colonial powers for independence, conflicts emerged. Part of these struggles grew from within their own ranks: Some preferred slower industrialization, and some a more rapid push. They disagreed over public versus private ownership, foreign alliances, the use of coercive power, continuing relations with former colonial powers, how rapidly wages should rise, and may other issues. In addition, the

---

[14] Halpern's more positive statement of this prediction has the same conclusion tacked to the end: "I would propose categories of tension-management or polarities, in which the costs and benefits of such relationships change as the problems of tradition yield to the problems of modernization *or else, modern incoherence.*" (Emphasis added.) "Egypt and the New Middle Class," p. 108. He promises to discuss five other polarities in a forthcoming book and emphasizes that the situation is extremely complex, with polarity flowing into polarity.

[15] John H. Kautsky, *The Political Consequences of Modernization* (New York: John Wiley, 1972). Quotes taken from and references to Kautsky in this section are from pp. 83, 106, 168, 171, 188, 194–195, 197, 199–200, 222, and 235, unless otherwise indicated.

modernizers have to compromise with aristocrats, industrialists, the military, and a new breed of managerial modernizers whose commitment to their own professions is stronger than their revolutionary zeal.

These conflicts can only be resolved if industrialization proceeds. Some nations that are *slow to industrialize* may experience civil unrest and discontent into the indefinite future. But in nations where *modernizers make rapid strides in industrialization* the story may be different. The regime can rely on mass terror, regimentation, and persuasion, with little worry about mass opposition. The workers can be induced to work hard for slowly rising wages, and the peasants to produce what is needed for the state. In return for the sacrifices the regime repeatedly promises a society of abundance and equality. With growing production, consumer goods spread, the feverish pace of initial industrialization slackens, and public satisfaction increases. Peasants become agricultural managers, technicians, and skilled workers. Service employees, white-collar workers, and scientific, professional, and technical specialists emerge from the ranks of the industrial workers. People are working less hard and receiving a larger share of their product. An increasingly smaller proportion of the population is subject to terror tactics and regimentation.

Kautsky depicts still a third scenario that involves neither unsuccessful industrialization nor rapid industrialization. While Kautsky's first scenario sounds vaguely like Halpern's structured instability, and the second like his extremist system, this third does not seem to appear on Halpern's list of types. In this case, various groups of modernizers compete for support among workers and peasants. The workers are offered higher wages, shorter hours, and better working conditions. The peasants are promised land reform. As industrialization proceeds, modernizers might even become leaders and ideologists of groups like capitalists, aristocrats, and townspeople. A technical elite also emerges. Modernizers increasingly serve as the representatives of the various organized interests in the society. Kautsky calls this a *regime of balance.* Less firmly in control than the regime with rapid industrialization, this regime must constantly work to balance all the major groups in society. It must offer material incentives to everyone at an earlier stage in development because it must use less terror and regimentation. In a regime of balance, industrialization is likely to be slower. Mexico, Turkey, India, Argentina, Brazil, and Chile are cited as examples. Unfortunately, such a regime is unlikely to wipe out all aristocratic or parochial interests. This leads to the possibility of a new revolution by second-wave modernizers, who will replace the period of balance by a regime similar to the second scenario. The longer the balance is able to persist, however, the less the chance for such a second wave revolution; the entire nation simply turns into modernizers.[16]

---

[16] Kautsky sees yet a fourth possibility: that the aristocrats (especially the military, the bureaucracy, the church, bankers, and big capitalists) reassert their influence and set up a fascist regime. But they would have to base their support on propertied peasants, the petty bourgeoisie, and some intellectuals, who are frustrated but in many ways do not share big-business proclivities. What heavy industry and banking there is may well be under foreign control. Furthermore, the townspeople and petty bourgeoisie are less numerous than they were in Europe, and less able to form a fascist movement. The propertied peasants received their land fairly recently and are not well established. Hence a fascist movement is "almost impossible to imagine in the future of underdeveloped countries." So fascism is not really an option. *Political Consequences of Modernization,* pp. 213–214, 224.

Where does it all lead? At some distant future, Kautsky says, Mexico might have a political regime not unlike that of the United States. For the present, however, the best that can probably be hoped for are regimes of balance in which the modernizers gradually blend with the other elements of the populace. Modernizers in less industrialized nations will have more independence than in nations with more industry, where they can govern "only by balancing various already-organized interests against each other, including not only the more modern native industrial, commercial, and professional ones, but also the aristocracy and the church—and the military, which contain[s] adherents of both the modern and traditional elements." [17] In fact:

> The bases of support of any regime of successfully industrializing modernizers, communist, or noncommunist, are likely to shift much as did those of the Soviet regime. It loses what support of workers and peasants it had in its beginnings and replaces it by that of the rapidly growing bureaucracies of the single party, the government, the police, the military, and industry. [18]

If there is any point of agreement between Kautsky and this book, it lies in these last statements. The governments of developing nations came to power under many circumstances, and usually after overthrowing the hegemony of land-owners and traditional aristocrats. Once they achieved power they had to create a coalition between government, bureaucracy, the military, industry—and the land-owners and aristocrats. It is what lies between, and after, that constitutes the areas of disagreement.

Our look at Nkrumah's Ghana in Chapter 4 raised serious questions about the possibilities for Kautsky's second scenario. His third scenario seems a bit more familiar, but we have noted little evidence of a regime of this type moving toward land reform, redistribution of job potential or balanced development of all segments of the society. The term "modernizer" is a deceptive one. If these people who only care for reform and not for money or power exist, they would probably find themselves soon divided into Bill's uprooters, technocrats, and maneuverers. In fact, Kautsky himself differentiates between revolutionary mod-ernizers and technocratic modernizers. But revolutionary modernizers who want to get ahead in politics would surely need to learn something of the arts of man-euvering; how else, in fact, can they create their alliances with the commercial and other elites? Otherwise they are liable to be on the outside of the regime looking in. And maneuverers do not achieve reform.

COMMENT

In discussing his first scenario, slow industrialization, Kautsky says the independence of the modernizers is reduced by the need to compromise with aristocrats and educated people more committed to their professions than to change. Later he says modernizers have more independence when industrialization is slow than when it is fast. He is, in effect, suggesting that modernizers never have much independence to promote progress and equality.

---

[17] Ibid., p. 223.
[18] Ibid., p. 248.

The basic problem here, as with Halpern, is why we should rely on these middle-class individuals, admittedly alienated from their own societies, to promote balance in those societies. Their only claim to producing salvation is industrialization, which Kautsky admits they can only deliver in measured and often erratic doses. Since they have little feel for their own societies, how are they to apply this industrialization in a form that would be useful to their people? He does not elaborate on how they are to be absorbed into other groups. Meanwhile he fails to analyze the nature of the one coalition in which he finds hope: that between modernizers, military, and industry, which excludes peasants and workers, in a setting of successful industrialization. It is simply a comment in a postscript. And regimes with unsuccessful industrialization are seen as merely formless and chaotic (ignoring many such regimes that have endured for some time). The almost exclusive preoccupation with the middle class and industrialization leads to pessimism by default: one cannot promise any very clear results from middle-class industrialization, so there is little left to promise. If industrialization is the only road to political development and industrialization is halting, then political development is halting. The question remains: Is industrialization the only road to political development?

Halpern, of course, does not concur with Kautsky's preoccupation with industrialization. He sees the problem of the will and capacity to absorb continuing transformation as more complex than this. However, he offers as little as Kautsky by way of analysis of why it is the middle classes who should be the most reliable purveyors of this will and capacity, or how the middle classes will gain the power to carry out this objective. And he and Kautsky both fail to explore whether the objective might be achieved by other means. Both simply assume that whatever is done, it must surely involve building the infrastructure and the modernized sector. And they agree that this sector is not being built.

According to Kautsky:
1. What sorts of political systems could exist in developing nations?
2. How is development achieved?
3. Which sort of political system comes closest to achieving development?
4. Do any developing nations have, or come near having, that sort of system?

David E. Apter

No scholar studying developing nations today can ignore the forces of modernization. There are scholars, however, who have departed from a preoccupation with relating political development to indices of modernization, or positing stages through which modernization progresses. They have turned instead to describing how regimes achieve and hold power. David Apter is an example of one of these individuals.[19]

Apter's central premise is that a regime must achieve a *balance between*

---

[19] David E. Apter, *The Politics of Modernization* (Chicago: University of Chicago Press, 1965); idem, "A Comparative Method for the Study of Politics," *American Journal of Sociology* 64 (November 1958): 221–237.

coercion and information. It must have the power to enforce its edicts, and at the same time to find out what problems need attention. Unfortunately, the more the government coerces the populace, the less vital information it receives from them, and vice versa. To be sure, Apter seems confident that if a proper balance is achieved between these two variables, modernization can progress smoothly. He has not abandoned a concern over modernization, but has rather made it a secondary issue to be dealt with only after the primary objective of achieving the balance between coercion and information has been analyzed—and to be dealt with by other authors. Like Huntington and Almond (to be examined shortly), and unlike Halpern and Kautsky, he has little interest in the relationship between government and different interest groups and social classes or in any particular policy objectives. He has a great deal of interest in how the component parts of government interact with one another.

Apter suggests that many developing nations operate within what he calls a *mobilization system*. In such a system, power is centralized within an executive, who leaves the courts and legislature in a subordinate position. For information, the executive generally relies on a single political party. That political party (the party of solidarity) is tightly disciplined and helps to control special interests, and distribute patronage and resources.[20] The military and civil service help to coerce and carry out functions of government. But the military officer "is clearly a functional subordinate of the party and the state." Because of their monopoly on technical expertise, civil servants must be permitted some corruption as the price paid for their political subordination. The nation does not necessarily move smoothly toward its goals. There is a tendency to personal government; "ideologized justifications cover up capriciousness."

The balance between coercion and information in the mobilization system is unstable. The party is apt to slant the information it passes along, and citizens may be afraid to tell it what they really feel. The personal favoritism weakens the power to use coercion equitably on everyone and helps promote factionalism. In time the mobilization system can break down. One of the directions this breakdown could take is the *reconciliation system*. The executive and party still play the central roles under this system, with the military and civil servants playing important roles. But there is more reliance on private enterprise than state enterprise (not that either system is composed exclusively of either type). The leadership circle is widened. The use of punishment as a political device declines. Resource allocation takes place more at the local levels. Corruption increases. The government is more willing to accommodate goals to public demands. Political parties and voluntary associations proliferate and place demands on government. The party of solidarity engages in purges against dissident factions, and loses some of its reformist zeal.

> But the party of solidarity does not suddenly disappear. Its apparatus remains, becoming the basis for a network of client-patron relationships. Nepotism, kinship, and favoritism result. Government acts as a superpatron.

The reconciliation system also has a bad balance between coercion and information. The information available is greater than under the mobilization

---

[20] Apter, *Politics of Modernization,* p. 363. Other quotes from or references to Apter in this section are taken from pp. 371-372, 375-376, 381-384, 397-398, 400, 404, 410-414, and 421.

system, but so is the factionalism, which prevents the translation of the information into goals and policies. Hence the system is not an efficient modernizer, and not always stable. Many reconciliation systems (and mobilization systems) are in turn moving in the direction of a *neo-mercantilist system*. Coercion is increased, so that the government can once again speed along the process of modernization. Authority is ritualized, retribalized. Private enterprise will be controlled in some measure, and a large part of public enterprise will be directly controlled by government. Some of the voluntary associations remain, but coercion is used against them when they question authority.

> Politics is organized around the civil service and the party, each with its own bureaucracy and each in competition for the favor of the presidential monarch. . . . A small group around a "presidential monarch" may become the equivalent of a royal lineage. They may choose incumbents to office by very particularistic means. Only if they fragment their authority by conflict between themselves and their supporters will instability result and induce a different form of government.

Many developing nations are accumulating attributes of modernization without yet being heavily industrialized. Until such time as they are ready to industrialize, the neo-mercantilist system provides a framework for the optimal balance between coercion and information in a modernizing nation, and hence is the optimal and most stable system.

Note that Apter's description of political systems differs from Halpern's and Kautsky's in that no mention is made of particular social classes. He does not conjecture how a government might go about producing balanced modernization, or balance among social groups. There is more attention given to the individual units of government, including the political party, and how they interact with one another. He has avoided conjectures about how particular types of individuals are prone to act, and replaced this with conjectures about how particular institutions are prone to act, perhaps a safer area for prediction.

In the effort to avoid entangling an analysis of society and economics with the analysis of political power, however, some valuable elements for explaining the political system may be lost. What are the possibilities of conflicts between government leaders and supporters under a neo-mercantilist system? This is a key question if one is to assert that a neo-mercantilist system is more stable than others, and it may be a question largely unrelated to a balance between information and coercion. The "capriciousness" which tempers the ideology can certainly not be understood without knowing something about the pattern of payoffs to supporters. Apter talks about the party limiting civil servants by defining their roles "within a fairly narrow range of competence." How does one do this when, as in the example of Mexico in Chapter 4, the civil servant also has an outside patron to whom he owes higher loyalty than to his immediate superior? Apter talks of using centralized power to transform a nation in accordance with ideology. One needs to know something about the society to visualize how to extend this control to major economic elites. In Guinea, he says, the mobilization system "tries to eliminate traders, private enterpreneurs, and the like as anti-social elements" and has "raised the status of dock workers, porters, and the like, through the trade union movement. It has tried to eliminate ethnic discrimination through a drastically expanded educational system. Although it has not succeeded in many of it objectives, Guinea gives the general impression of wanting to achieve a revolution, populist in nature, from above." Kautsky talks of modernizers continuing to use pro-labor symbols while actually submitting workers to regimentation and compulsion. "What are now the regimes's labor organizations continue to be referred to as trade unions."[21] Our earlier descriptions of unions in Kenya, Zambia, Brazil, and elsewhere suggest that Kautsky's interpretation may be closer to the mark in this situation than Apter's.

It is interesting that Apter and Almond both think of themselves as functionalists. Functionalists claim to be less interested in how institutions are organized or what they should do than in how it is that they function and how people behave in politics. Functionalism is a reaction against earlier approaches to understanding which described government in a purely formal way, or prescribed how government should function and tried to project how it might achieve this. Yet both Apter and Almond tend to examine only those interactions that take place within formal channels. Apter talks more about the structure and ideals of parties than about how they function. Especially since Apter suggests that there are special relationships between government officials and private individuals, it seems unfortunate that he does not analyze those relationships. And while he suggests that goals and costs are a part of understanding the functioning of the political system, he fails to examine any particular goals and costs to see how they relate to the functioning of the system. He may be *neither* a functionalist *nor* an institutionalist.

In this book we have attempted to be specific about the kinds of special relationships that surround government, and the sorts of limits these might place upon policy, both in general and in terms of specific policies. Rather than suggesting that a place "gives the general impression of wanting to achieve a revolution," we have sought to determine whether it is indeed achieving one, and why or why not.

We have found some grounds for disagreement as to how Apter's models might apply to specific facts. For instance, we have suggested that while executives in developing nations formally appear to be at the top of a tight pyramid of power, an examination of the patron-client networks surrounding them will often reveal that they are beholden to other members of the major patron-client network. This could only be verified if one is to broaden one's investigation beyond the boundaries Apter sets for himself. Apter suggests that in the neomercantilist system the government enterprises are "the largest employer of trained individuals;[22] there is probably no developing nation with these characteristics. And we have suggested that developing nations do not contain the sorts of free voluntary associations implied in the reconciliation system. It would be difficult to show that any one country belonged entirely to one of these systems, and did not share in the characteristics of another.

Yet Apter's systems are similar in outline to what has been described in this book: centralization of power, patron-client networks, weak legislatures and courts, generally weak voluntary associations, a proclivity to modernize,

---

[21] Kautsky, *Political Consequences of Modernization*, p. 189.

[22] Apter, *Politics of Modernization*, p. 413. Nkrumah's Ghana, which Apter studied firsthand, was a rare exception in this regard.

breakdown of traditional authority structures, a prominent role for the military and civil service, dominant hierarchical political parties, low information and high coercion. The two models—Apter's and mine—differ in some particulars. But they share basic grounds of agreement. Not the least of these is the fact that Apter nowhere contemplates the possibility that popular dissent will in the near future transform any of these systems into democracies, or that modernization will somehow solve their social, political, or economic problems.

> According to Apter:
> 1. What sorts of political systems could exist in developing nations?
> 2. How is development achieved?
> 3. Which sort of political system comes closest to achieving development?
> 4. Do any developing nations have, or come near having, that sort of system?

Samuel P. Huntington

We have already introduced you to Huntington at the end of Chapter 5. But it is important to point to some similarities between Huntington, Apter, and Almond, and to say a bit more about Huntington. All three of these scholars place great emphasis upon the stability of governmental institutions. Apter would achieve it through balancing coercion and information; Huntington by *balancing mass mobilization and governmental institutionalization;* and Almond by balancing the feedbacks of government in relation to public demands. All three see this stability as a prerequisite for the solution of more fundamental social and economic problems, including stable economic growth and (at least they imply) stable personal environments. All three are more concerned that government be stable than that industrialization and other attributes of modernization proceed—with one exception: Huntington and Almond are both very concerned that government institutions be modern.

Huntington's 1965 article came as a shock to many people.[23] He stated the unthinkable: that such attributes of modernization as urbanization, literacy, communications, voting participation, mass movements, and unions (the social mobilization which Deutsch sees as a sign of development) might be instruments of decay rather than of progress. The decay to which he referred was not economic or social, but political. In calling for complexity, clear hierarchies, autonomy, coherence among component parts, and adaptability on the part of government, he was calling for modernization of government. Hence he does not oppose modernization, provided that it begins within the government. In reality if often does not. "Modernization in practice always involves change in and usually the disintegration of a traditional political system, but it does not necessarily involve significant movement toward a modern political system. . . . Yet the tendency is to think that because social modernization is taking

---

[23] Samuel P. Huntington, "Political Development and Political Decay," *World Politics* 17 (April 1965): 386–430. See also idem, *Political Order in Changing Societies* (New Haven, Conn.: Yale University Press, 1968).

place, political modernization also must be taking place."[24] Clearly countries which have high levels of both social mobilization and economic development are more stable and peaceful politically;" yet the very attempt to modernize may be the principal cause of instability in developing nations. Economic development raises living standards; it also disrupts traditional social groupings, creates personal tensions, and places new demands on government. And very often social mobilization moves more rapidly than economic development. Corruption, too, seems to flourish most intensely during the initial phases of modernization. Political institutionalization is needed to control all this.

Political institutions must have the capacity both to resist entrenched traditional interests and to absorb new social forces which result from modernization. At the same time they must have the power to promote reform.[25] In achieving these ends, Huntington is wary of both *military* and *one-party* rule. "More *competitive two-party* and *multiparty* systems may have considerable capacity for expansion and the assimilation of groups but less capability for the concentration of power and the promotion of reform." Yet "two-party systems assimilate rural masses into the political system, and thus produce the bridge between rural and urban areas which is the key to political stability in modernizing countries." He reviews a number of instances in developing nations where, with rural support, one party swept another from power in elections (e.g., the Turkish elections discussed earlier), and is impressed with their ability to assimilate large numbers of social groups and to redirect policy after the election. He argues that one-party states tend to become lax both in working with a mass following and in nurturing reform. He states that "societies which have created large-scale modern political institutions with the capability of handling much more extensive political participation than exists at present are presumably stable." He would hover somewhere between the one-party state and the full two-party state, perhaps supporting a situation where *one party is dominant* over others. This is optimal for centralizing power and creating stability, and a second choice for assimilating groups and promoting reform. The centralization is probably a more important key to stabilization for him than the assimilation or the reform.

So, while it may be a secondary concern, Huntington does, in this book, want to break up patron-client networks and replace them with a political system that has deeper popular roots. My viewpoint—which shares this concern— has suggested that this cannot be accomplished merely by broadening the party system by a few notches. I have expressed fears that limited liberalization of party systems will only serve to stabilize existing elites who will control the new parties. An open party system, whether desirable or not, would be impossible to achieve because the patron-client networks have the coercive capabilities to stop unwelcome parties. I have suggested that electoral switches within limited two-party systems do not result in important changes in leadership or policy. Rather

---

[24] Huntington, *Political Order in Changing Societies*, p. 35. All other quotes from or references to Huntington in this section are taken from pp. 40, 57–70, 147, 398, and 460.

[25] In a later article he says he meant to imply here that in some states the traditional political systems had been highly institutionalized and hence would be able to "survive modernization and accommodate broadened patterns of participation." Samuel P. Huntington, "The Change to Change: Modernization, Development, and Politics," *Comparative Politics* 3, No. 3 (April 1971): 315. We discuss this article at the end of this chapter.

than the party reforms bringing patron-clientism under control, they are liable to fall under the direction of powerful patrons. Besides, I feel no special need for stabilizing political participation; I see little potential for serious disruptions from mass uprising, while Huntington is more ambivalent about this potential.[26] As you will see at the end of the chapter, he later ended this ambivalence. He has given up his fears about mass uprisings, and his hopes that institutions can produce reform.

Huntington parallels my observations when he notes the existence of factions controlling government, the emergence of centralized power, and the breakdown of traditional authority structures. In his discussion of revolution he agrees that the possibilities of peasant revolution are remote, and that revolution without peasant participation is not likely. Nor does he feel that modernization in itself will solve social, economic, or political problems.

According to Huntington:
1. What sorts of political systems could exist in developing nations?
2. How is development achieved?
3. Which sort of political system comes closest to achieving development?
4. Do any developing nations have, or come near having, that sort of system?

Gabriel A. Almond

Gabriel Almond's approach has gained a good deal of popularity in the field of comparative politics.[27] It combines extreme simplicity with a sense of inclusiveness and makes it possible to discuss political systems everywhere in the same terminology. In basic terms, his definition of a political system is contained in the next paragraph.

Political systems are divided into input and output functions. On the input side is the general populace; on the output side, the government. The general populace articulates and aggregates (i.e., gathers together and expresses a variety of demands in the same format) demands and communicates them to the government. It also becomes socialized by the political culture in which it operates to behave and formulate demands in certain ways, is the recruiting ground for future public servants, and supports government with material, obedience, participation, and deference. The government, in turn, makes, applies, and adjudicates rules. It extracts (both resources, and services from the public), regulates, and distributes. In doing so, it attempts to be in some degree responsive to the demands.

---

[26] Huntington, *Political Order in Changing Societies,* pp. 264–343.

[27] Gabriel A. Almond, Taylor Cole, and Roy C. Macridis, "A Suggested Research Strategy in Western European Government and Politics," *American Political Science Review* 49 (December 1955): 1042–1049; Gabriel A. Almond and G. Bingham Powell, Jr., *Comparative Politics: A Developmental Approach* (Boston: Little, Brown, 1966); Gabriel A. Almond, Scott C. Flanagan, and Robert J. Mundt, eds., *Crisis, Choice, and Change: Historical Studies of Poltical Development* (Boston: Little, Brown, 1973); Gabriel A. Almond, ed., *Comparative Politics Today: A World View* (Boston: Little, Brown, 1974.)

Without drawing labels, the present study has described all of these functions. Yet it has contended that there are some rather uniform limits to their expression in developing nations. Articulation and aggregation are usually tightly supervised. Central executives and bureaucracy tend to monopolize the "rule" functions at the expense of courts and legislatures. The principal inputs come from major networks composed of investors, entrepreneurs, landowners, the military, and their clients. Government tends to extract from and regulate those beyond these networks, without responding and distributing to them in any significant degree.

In a general sense Almond would seem to agree about the existence of most of these limits in developing nations, though he does not discuss patron-client networks. He suggests that democratization has been frustrated, and that one-party rule has become the norm.[28] He also sees a tendency to suppress welfare in order to protect business profits, the accumulation of investment funds, and upper-class groups.[29] He notes the presence of endemic violence, yet fails to comment on whether it might lead to revolution.[30]

Almond also presents a theory of political progression. It centers around four concepts: differentiation between political and societal structures, specialization of functions, secularization, and subsystem autonomy. These have all been discussed in this book:

- *Political vs. societal structures.* We noted in Chapters 2 and 3 that it was difficult to differentiate between societal and governmental institutions in village political systems, while the rise of kingship removed the institutions of government farther and farther from those of society.
- *Specialization of functions.* We argued that in village society functions and roles were clearly designated to various ritual leaders, who would each handle a variety of them; as kingship and trade advanced, the number of such functions increased, and individuals began to specialize in only one or two rather than handling several.
- *Secularization.* In the village, people had only one set of norms, laws, and mores, with religious and political norms heavily interrelated; over time, conflicting sets of norms began to appear, with a single town accommodating several religions and conflicting sets of values.
- *Subsystem autonomy.* In the village, various kinship groups, and associations, by custom had clearly specified powers, which gave them sub-system autonomy. With the introduction of kingship, these powers began to slip, and with the breakdown of the village virtually ceased to be. Recent attempts to introduce free voting, and the independence associated with middle class status, have begun to reintroduce subsystem autonomy.

Almond discusses some different kinds of data than what we have seen; his definitions of political progression differ somewhat from mine.[31] He sees the

---

[28] Almond, *Comparative Politics Today*, p. 35.

[29] "The strategy followed by these countries is to suppress dissent and demands for welfare, and accumulate resources for investment . . ." Ibid.

[30] Ibid., pp. 64–65.

[31] Almond, *Comparative Politics*, pp. 213–298.

earliest *primitive systems* as characterized by limited differentiation, specialization, secularization, and subsystem autonomy. I would tend to argue about the limited subsystem autonomy, and perhaps see more differentiation and specialization than he does.[32] *Traditional systems* (he divides them into patrimonial systems, bureaucratic empires, and feudal systems) continued the fusing of norms, but increased in specialization and differentiation. This agrees with my assessment. *Modern systems,* in varying degrees, have increased all four attributes. There is still a great deal of variation in the degree of secularization and subsystem autonomy, however, ranging from the premobilized democratic to high autonomy democratic and radical totalitarian. Developing nations tend to be premobilized authoritarian or democratic (with limited differentiation in roles and limited secularization), modernizing authoritarian, or democratic with higher differentiation and secularization but low subsystem autonomy. Hence, while he sees some developing nations as having low secularization and others more, and all as having low subsystem autonomy, we see virtually all developing nations as having high secularization *in their capital cities,* and low subsystem autonomy for everyone *except the patron-client networks.*

In short, Almond's approach does not differ greatly from the approach of this book. He would, however, have given far less attention to patron-client relationships, and far more to inputs and outputs. It is Almond's major premise that political development implies a *balance between input and output functions*—that those powerful enough to make demands receive part of what they want. He explores how governmental activities relate to demands made on government, and the communication processes between private citizens and government. But he is indifferent as to who receives what in the process. He is interested in seeing that negotiations begin on sensitive issues, and that they are concluded to the satisfaction of the parties involved. He is interested in distribution, for instance, only up to the point that a decision is made about it. He is not interested in how actual distribution is made (e.g., whether it involves wholesale benefit to the populace, or simply a division of the pie among those sitting at the negotiating table) until such time as a lack of it results in another set of demands. His is the politician's bias: He is interested in an issue only up to the point where it quiets down. At that point there is a balance between inputs and outputs, because the elites who made the demands are satisfied and the rest of the populace (who have little subsystem autonomy or free articulation) can do little about what has been agreed upon. In contrast, I am very interested in what gets distributed to whom after the agreement has been reached because I suspect that what has been agreed may entail a great deal going to those directly involved in the negotiations and very little to anybody else. I also am concerned that many of the most important problems never even become demands because the elite is not interested in dealing with them.

Almond is sensitive to this, but suggests that the solution lies in modernizing

---

[32] With reference to subsystem autonomy, both Apter and Almond distinguish between "pyramidal" and "hierarchical" systems. See Apter, *Politics of Modernization,* pp. 92–93. In the former the village chief has many of the same inherent powers as the paramount chief (i.e., subsystem autonomy), while in the latter "subordinates have power at the leader's pleasure" (i.e., no subsystem autonomy). I question that before the advent of extensive commerce there were any hierarchical societies and suggest that subsystem autonomy was then the norm.

interest groups and parties: ". . . the development of something like a modern interest-group or party system seems to be the prerequisite to a high development of responsive capability."[33] He sees parties and interest groups in developing nations as less than fully modern. Once they become so, he implies, all types of demands could be handled in formal channels; by watching the expansion of demands being handled in the formal channels one can watch the gradual expansion of responsiveness. I reply that the mere growth of modern interest-group or party systems does not assure responsiveness. One must find out who the government is responding to, and also investigate why some problems never become translated into demands. The transformations needed to control modernization are not necessarily among the demands being made on government, even those made by modern interest groups.[34] These groups, like their predecessors, may be under the control of a small powerful elite. If one is merely interested in short-term stability (making sure that those few powerful enough to make demands get rewarded), following inputs and outputs is sufficient; if one is interested in satisfaction of need, one must know more. Among the things that must be known are who is in a position to control the inputs and outputs, who benefits from the outputs, and how these people might be pressured to implement the policies in which one has an interest (such as those needed to control the transformations of modernization).

Discussion of India is continued from p. 200.

To illustrate: Thomas E. Headrick, using Almond's approach, discusses two crises in India during the 1960s over language and food.[35] Some 45 percent of Indians (mostly from the North) speak Hindi-related languages. Around the time of Nehru's death in 1964 a movement was afoot in the legislature to make Hindi the national language, replacing English for all official functions. In regions where Hindi was not spoken, riots broke out in the streets. The protesters did not wish to be forced to learn the language, and did not like the increased power the move might bring to Northern leaders. Working through leaders of his own and opposition parties, and a variety of ad hoc committees, Prime Minister Shastri tactfully brought leaders of the extreme positions together and worked out a compromise. Headrick concentrates on describing Shastri's tactics. A compromise was reached; Hindi would not become the national language but would increase in importance. All sections of the country benefited. If there were any special deals among the leadership, they are not discussed. Nor does Headrick discuss the social or economic consequences of the settlement, such as our suggestion in Chapter 5 that a deal of this kind might be a means of tightening elite control over the economy or of enhancing the power of some ethnic group.

The food crisis developed because some wheat-growing states in the North

---

[33] Almond, *Comparative Politics*, p. 324.

[34] In Manfred Halpern's words, ". . . The question does not merely become 'interest aggregation' but aggregation or else transformation of interests for the sake of tension-management in society relevant to fundamental problems of historical change." Halpern, "Egypt and the New Middle Class," p. 108.

[35] Thomas E. Headrick, "Crisis and Continuity: India in the Mid-1960's," in *Crisis, Choice, and Change*, ed. Almond et al. pp. 560–618.

were rather self-sufficient in food production, but were under pressure to distribute their food at relatively low prices to urban areas, and to other rural areas suffering from drought. Recurring drought and the Pakistani conflict intensified the situation into a crisis. Gradually the center negotiated a consensus among the state leaders and they worked out a compromise. ". . . At no time during the crisis period were the center's resources great enough to impose its policies." But "it was the incremental increase in the center's resources [due to the desire of the leaders to resolve the deepening crisis] and the decline of polarization—which was never great, even in the beginning [one reason being, perhaps, that the richer Northern farmers were benefitting from hoarding and economies of scale and hence differed from some Northern urban leaders]—that led to the consensus shifts in policy."[36] Almond concludes that if the leadership had less legitimacy to begin with (Shastri's accession was itself the result of compromises among the state leaders), or if the sides had been more polarized (e.g., the North taking one side on all the issues and the South the other) the issues would not have been as readily resolved.[37] Headrick notes that the major political roles were held by land-owning members of dominant castes (which had greater membership in the North), the small town middle classes, and upper-class industrial and commercial leaders;[38] that some of the greatest gains from the compromising were made by the landlords with five to fifteen acres of land raising commercial crops with borrowed capital;[39] and that the compromises were probably not particularly effective in redistributing food, but did at least create an institutional framework for doing so in the future.[40]

COMMENT

Notice that our discussion of Indian cooperatives and *panchayats* in Chapter 5 helps explain why particular groups of people are negotiating, and what they hope to get from the negotiations. Headrick is not so interested in why these groups are negotiating, or why other groups are left out of the negotiating. Nor is he interested in what happens after the negotiations are over. He is interested in the negotiations themselves—how the elites sitting around the table bargain with one another.

He sees Indira Gandhi putting together a new coalition in which the legislature is not so heavily dominated by rural landlords and includes members of a new generation interested in "politics and social work";[41] the old elite will have to include them in the consensus, which will hopefully bring "new policy departures."

Further discussion of India may be found on p. 312.

---

[36] Ibid., p. 596.

[37] Gabriel A. Almond and Robert J. Mundt, "Crisis, Choice, and Change: Some Tentative Conclusions," in *Crisis, Choice, and Change,* ed. Almond et al. p. 622.

[38] Headrick, "Crisis and Continuity," p. 565.

[39] Ibid., pp. 562, 586, 601.

[40] Ibid., p. 595.

[41] Ibid., p. 611.

Headrick's study goes into far more subtle dissection of arguments among various elites and the formal procedures by which they are resolved than anything you will find in this book. While I have not suggested that elites agree on all issues, the lack of discussion about the matter might cause you to forget the many issues that divide members of patron-client networks. Their arguments are the stuff of which day-to-day politics in developing nations is made. This is why I constantly find myself returning to Almond; he helps me organize in my mind the mass of material that CBS News and *The Evening Gazette* throw my way about political conflicts. I think he does this better than my own or other approaches discussed in this chapter. What bothers me is that he does not look far enough. I suspect these issues were settled not simply because they were "salient" (i.e., hot), or "multiple" (with a variety of overlapping factions, instead of just two), and the leaders good at "aggregative strategies." There were also personal payoffs, which perhaps meant more to the participants than finding a solution to the problems. And there was a personal advantage to the participants in holding together a lucrative coalition. And so long as people with strong financial interests control the *panchayati raj* and the system of banking has firm ties with the bueaucracy, I suspect that bringing social workers to the legislature will not greatly change policy. What we have here is a discussion of some of the surface compromises that hold the patron-client networks together, minus an analysis of what constitutes these patron-client networks or how these compromises translate in terms of the allocation processes (who gets what, when, and how; e.g., how much grain did the grain-rich states end up giving to the grain-poor states?). I feel a need to dig deeper.

Almond's functional approach allows him to do some things we could not do with the conceptual tools provided in this book. It lets him study formal political coalitions and the management of conflicts surrounding the issues they raise. At the same time, it ignores both the context within which these exchanges are institutionalized, and the actual functions (e.g., distribution of food, building of roads, healing of tensions, investment of funds) they affect. Ironically, this functionalist may be so absorbed in the exchange processes that he ignores the functions themselves. And because he focuses only on formal institutions (parties, pressure groups, legislative committees) and exchanges (laws, agreements), while ignoring such informal institutions as patron-client relationships and their informal exchanges, he is in a tenuous position for explaining what the formal exchanges mean. If you are interested in functions, you may need to start with functions (distribution of food, allocations of housing, transformations needed to control modernization) and ascertain how both formal and informal institutions and exchanges affect them, all the while insisting on knowing who gets what, when, and how. Otherwise it is easy to get sidetracked into simply discussing how a government holds itself together. If combined with attention to informal relationships and policy results, however, Almond's approach might well break new ground. It is worth some thought.

Almond has moved farther than any of the authors discussed so far from the problems of how to deal with the social disruptions caused by modernization. His approach recommends itself comfortably to those who might prefer to ignore questions about how regimes, political systems, and social systems transform themselves (or even what functions they perform) and to focus instead simply on how regimes institutionalize various relationships with elites and how they keep the peace. As Headrick intones, "The political leadership needs to be alert to keeping the political system from hardening into dualistic cleavages or fragmenting into a multiplicity of politicized social differences and interests."[42] You must decide. Is this simply a call for the major patron-client networks to be careful to keep themselves intact? Or does it inherently involve benefits for the populace at large?[43]

According to Almond:
1. What sorts of political systems could exist in developing nations?
2. How is development achieved?
3. Which sort of political system comes closest to achieving development?
4. Do any developing nations have, or come near having, that sort of system?

Helio Jaguaribe

Halpern, Kautsky, Apter, Huntington, and Almond, we have suggested, have many common focuses in their analyses. They disagree slightly on the role that middle-class groups should play, on how to describe some of the differences among political systems, and on the attention that should be given to mass mobilization. Some of them, especially Kautsky, make predictions and assertions with greater specificity than others. Yet, paradoxically, each, in an effort to be comprehensive, omits important areas from purview. It is difficult to use any of their theories to obtain a rounded picture of political systems. Helio Jaguaribe has attempted to pull all these ideas together into one theory. As a Brazilian, his work is not well-known in the United States. He is a prodigious scholar. His charts and texts contain virtually every theoretical construct we have discussed up to this point, and many more.[44] He provides a sort of Bacchanalia for those who want to get an overview on ideas about politics in the developing nations.

Hovering over all of Jaguaribe's terminology are three "systems mac-rovariables"—operational, participational, and directional—that refer to how systems operate, who participates, and the direction in which they are moving. If you identify these variables, the rest of the theory falls readily into place. The *operational variables* are rational orientation (e.g., degree of secularization), structural differentiation, and level of capability (of the government to adapt).

---

[42] Ibid., p. 616.

[43] He continues: ". . . full franchise also emphasizes performance and accountability . . . political performance will increasingly depend on objective evidence of expanding opportunity and a subjective sense of a just political order." Ibid., pp. 616–617. The key question is whether there is any reason to believe that the elites doing the bargaining must pass any benefits beyond themselves. Why might they have more reason for doing so in the future than in the past? Mull it over.

[44] Excerpts and condensation in this section are taken from *Political Development: A General Theory and a Latin American Case Study* by Helio Jaguaribe. Reprinted by permission of Harper & Row, Publishers, Inc., New York, pp. 148–151, 159, 208, 217, 381, 475, 476, 499, 520, 523, 525, 530, 542, 545, 546, 549, 553.

The *participational variables* are political mobilization, political integration, and political representation. The *directional variables* are political superordination (the extent to which the political system controls other societal systems such as economic and cultural) and development orientation (toward modernization and institutionalization). You will note that these are familiar terms in the discussion by this point.

The directional variables are not only one of three sets of macrovariables; they are also the indicators of political development, which Jaguaribe defines as "the cumulative process of political modernization and political institutionalization." In general, he sees each of the characteristics of all macrovariables as increasing with political development. For instance, rational orientation is low in primitive societies, higher in traditional societies, and highest in modern societies; and so forth with structural differentiation and the rest of the variables (and subvariables; see Table 6.1). He parallels Huntington in his pairing of modernization and institutionalization. "In modern polities increasing institutionalization requires increasing modernization, although modernization, by itself, is not a sufficient condition for institutionalization."

While a developed political system must exhibit all the characteristics in Table 6.1, it is by no means inevitable that all of these aspects will develop at the same rate. The development of one may set back the development of another. Hence no nations are fully modern, and none are steadily advancing in the direction of modernity. For most nations, political development is a long way off:

> Maximum general political development is achieved when the concerned polity, besides maximizing its capability, at the available scientific-technological level (first aspect of political development), and besides contributing to the overall development of the society (second aspect), also achieves maximum political consensus and opens the way to maximum social consensus (third aspect). This stage, which no modern political system has ever achieved and which can only be viewed as an ideal type, is the expression of the highest ideal level of general political development.

Jaguaribe's definition of political development seems more comprehensive than those we have encountered so far. Unfortunately, of the three aspects discussed in this quote, Jaguaribe gives full attention to only one: the capability of the government to adapt (I.C in Table 6.1). This is also the aspect to which Huntington, Halpern, and Almond devote greatest attention. Jaguaribe gives some attention to the third aspect, development of the responsiveness of the political system (approximately D to F in Table 6.1). He gives little attention to the second aspect, which he defines more fully elsewhere as: "Development of the contribution of the political system to the overall development of the concerned society, which corresponds to the development of whole society by political means." If he had done so, his theory might have opened new parameters of the discussion. As it is, Jaguaribe reveals only one major new parameter concerning the international environment within which developing nations operate: *If the cultural, participational, political, and economic leaders cannot work together, they will not be able to make proper use of the resources that are*

TABLE 6.1
Jaguaribe's Macrovariables[45]

I. OPERATIONAL VARIABLES
   A. Rational orientation
      Secularization
      Controllability
   B. Structural differentiation
      Independence
      Autonomy
      Complexity
      Subsystem autonomy
   C. Capability
      Viability
      Dependability
      Effectiveness
      Adaptability
      Flexibility
II. PARTICIPATIONAL VARIABLES
   D. Political mobilization
      Socialization
      Politicalization
      Participation
      Political equality
      Political commitment
   E. Political integration
      Societal integration
      Value integration
      Mass-elite integration
   F. Political representation
      Legitimacy of authorities
      Legitimacy of regime
      Legitimacy of system
III. DIRECTIONAL VARIABLES
   G. Political superordination
      Economic statization
      Social statization
      Cultural statization
   H. Development orientation
      Modernization
      Institutionalization
      Speed for change or antichange

---

available and the nation will not be "viable."[46] *Latin American nations are not viable because they are satellite dependents,* "characterized by informal but actual political subordination to a superpower," the United States. The superpower is only interested in the formal and mechanical aspects of public order, not in the quality of that order. The elites exploit land and labor, and do not

---

[45] Table 6.1 is compiled from information in Helio Jaguaribe, *Political Development: A General Theory and a Latin American Case Study,* Harper & Row, New York, 1973, pp. 148–151. The author gratefully acknowledges permission of the publisher to reprint a modified form of the table.

[46] "National viability": "Existence . . . of sufficient human and natural resources to allow the autonomous and predominantly endogenous national development of that society."

broadly distribute gains. National markets prove too small to sustain full internal industrial development. There is stagnation in overall economic growth. The military is supported from outside, and citizens are culturally denationalized. Many middle-class people themselves become marginalized. Therefore the state "is compelled to maintain its cartorial [see Chapter 4, note 1] characteristics, forging parasitic public jobs to accommodate the middle class." This system of patron-clientism is inflationary and rapidly exhausts the fiscal possibilities of the state. The contrast between the concentration of wealth and privilege in a tiny elite and the marginality of the relevant sectors of the subelite—who are an essential part of any revolutionary activity—inhibits revolution. If a revolution were to occur, the lack of national viability would prevent domestic actors from making radical internal changes. Even in Cuba (a small, isolated island) current elites are alert to prevent a recurrence of the Cuban revolution. As it is, the leaders continually decrease the possibilities of revolution by increasing the degree of coercion and the extent of dependence.

Discussion of Brazil is continued from p. 158, and of Peru from p. 129.

So the problem is to envisage what more modest road to *reform* might be available. Jaguaribe examines some of the populist efforts at reform in Brazil, Mexico, Bolivia, and elsewhere (which we have examined in Chapter 4) and finds them to be failures. Their principal limitations are a lack of clear goals and an inability to command enough support from *those sectors of the elite and subelite which would benefit most directly from populism.* However he is impressed with reform efforts in Chile, Venezuela, and Peru (which we also discuss in Chapter 7, but with less enthusiasm). He feels that the Chilean and Venezuelan efforts are products of an exceptionally high degree of social integration and development. Their model may be applicable to Uruguay and Argentina. The Peruvian model could not apply in the nonviable nations of the Caribbean and Cental America, but it may apply in Brazil, Argentina, Ecuador, Colombia, and Bolivia, where elites and resources are better integrated. These nations must move in this direction in the next thirty years or they will grow too dependent to do so.

Jaguaribe sees Chile, Peru (the book was written before the overthrow of the reformist regimes in those countries), and Venezuela as making a start toward increasing political participation by the masses (especially rural), accelerating economic development (including agrarian reform) and bringing a nationalist orientation to the economy. In Peru he is especially impressed by the manner in which the military officers developed a unity of action, capable of rising above the subsystem of political domination ("the president . . . the party leaders, the top military administration and the civil government, including certain high-ranking administrators and technocrats"). He sees the military in the five countries above as capable of the same independence. The Peruvian army is intensely nationalistic, as are the others mentioned in this paragraph. But there are ideological constraints: anticommunism, the fear that all nationalistic formulations are leftist, intense loyalty to free enterprise, and a desire for efficiency. These viewpoints make the military fear asserting too much independence from the United States and her corporations, and involving themselves too heavily in the economy. But they have succeeded in building a powerful and efficient state machinery, with a level of political and administrative capability never reached before.

> . . . with just a few adjustments, that same machinery if reoriented toward social and national developmental goals, mobilized by a new reformist spirit, and supported by popular participation, could become a decisive instrument for the promotion of the autonomous national development of these countries.

Jaguaribe is optimistic about these developments in Peru. "As long as a free discussion of the crucial issues and policies at stake is allowed to continue in the armed forces, particularly in the army, it is rather probable that the nationalist and social-reformist views will come to prevail in the military establishments of these countries in a couple of years."

Further discussion of Peru may be found on p. 300, of Brazil on p. 369, and of Chile on p. 294.

Likewise, Jaguaribe sees winds of change stirring in the United States. He thinks that the nation—and especially the ruling circles—will come to see that the maintenance of its interests abroad and the very existence and survival of American society call for a tighter management of the empire abroad.

> Along with many other important functions, the empire is, economically, an outlet for capital surpluses, an instrument for preventing scarcities or price rises in raw materials, a favored market for finished goods, and, for these reasons, a decisive factor in socioeconomic stability at home.

In a positive vein, says Jaguaribe, is the opportunity to extend American democracy in the field of private rights, personal advancement, welfare services, and redistributing wealth and power. Johnson and Nixon could not see this; Kennedy "without mentioning its ascriptive and imperial features but taking into account its real needs" did.

While this new imperialism (Jaguaribe likens it to the Roman Empire, which both looked after the needs of its provinces and left them a degree of local autonomy) would benefit the Americans and the middle classes in the developing nations, he sees it offering little to the unskilled masses save the opportunity for some of them to attain mobility in the armed forces. They "will tend to have much more to lose than to gain with populist imperialism." But it is the best hope for reform that Jaguaribe finds feasible.

Jaguaribe is the only native of a developing nation whom we have surveyed up to this point, and his tone is more blunt than that of the others. If modernization is to be the savior, then one must ask whom it will benefit and how one might ultimately make it benefit more people.[47] Jaguaribe's answer may be inconclusive. Yet he is the first among these thinkers to even attempt a response.

---

[47] To put it another way, if a fundamental problem in describing what political development is concerns the relation of modernization to the process, then one must actually analyze that relationship rather than simply introduce it.

He is also the first to explore the influence of the informal networks of power and the international environment upon policy, and to examine the relative strengths and weaknesses of various types of military machines, bureaucracies, and interest groups with reference to the policies they might support.

You will recall, however, that I stated earlier that Jaguaribe does not really discuss a problem he purports to be most fundamental in defining political development: "Development of the contribution of the political system to the overall development of the concerned society, which corresponds to the development of the whole society by political means." In Venezuela, Peru, and Chile he sees land reform, economic development, and increased political participation as the answers, but never really explains why. After a prodigious examination of variables which went into explaining why the societies became unbalanced, this seems to be a serious omission. He is far more interested in examining how the government can develop the will and capacity to develop than in examining what sort of development might be needed. Indeed, by this definition, he admits that the populist imperial system which he sees as the best hope would mean anything but development; the unskilled masses would "have much more to lose than to gain."

According to Jaguaribe:
1. What sorts of political systems could exist in developing nations?
2. How is development achieved?
3. Which sort of political system comes closest to achieving development?
4. Do any developing nations have, or come near having, that sort of system?

Irving Louis Horowitz

Some United States' scholars share Jaguaribe's interest in the international environment, and focus a bit more than he does on what is necessary to develop the whole society by political means. Irving Louis Horowitz is one example.[48]

Horowitz sees Four Worlds. "What is meant by the *First World* is basically that cluster of nations which were 'naturally' transformed from feudalism into some form where private ownership of production predominated." This includes the United States. The *Second World* is the Russian orbit. They have moved quickly but incompletely from feudalism to state ownership of modern means of production, and stand on a pivot between the First and Third Worlds. The *Third World* is a self-defined group of nations seeking to choose between capitalism and socialism economically, and libertarianism and totalitarianism politically. The "formal systems are nearly always and everywhere republican in character, while their real systems are nearly always authoritarian." The Fourth World is the world of undevelopment: "tribal societies which for one or another reason are unconscious of alternatives to their own ways of life."

---

[48] Irving Louis Horowitz, *Three Worlds of Development: The Theory and Practice of International Stratification* (New York: Oxford University Press, 1966). Quotations taken from Horowitz in this section are from pp. 5, 19, 25, 26, 28, 35, 66, 68, 352, and 357.

> *Social development* . . . implies transformation in human relations, in the economic and political status in which men relate to each other, irrespective of the level of industrialization. Industrialization does produce stress and strain in human relationships which in turn has a large-scale effect on the over-all process of social development. But to identify industrialization with development is to run the grave risk of offering prescriptions for economic growth independent of social inequalities.

Horowitz is careful to separate the concept of development from the concept of modernization. Development involves improvements in the lives of people; modernization can occur without creating such improvements. But when those improvements do occur, they are the result of modernization. "Development implies a genuine break with tradition—perceptible disruptions of the 'static' equilibrium. . . . Development . . . implies a new technology which makes available consumer goods."

The Third World nations generally have a single metropolitan center that represents a highly developed city-state with a backward countryside surrounding it. These urban centers "are parasitic rather than promoters of development. They tend to exploit, through the domestic bourgeoisie, the labor and produce of the countryside." As export-import centers they are in turn exploited on the international sphere. Underdeveloped societies, characteristic of the Third World, combine sectors of low productivity with sectors of high productivity, behavior governed by both law and custom, and status based both on achievement and inherited patterns. Exact mixtures vary. "Development . . . is often preceded by social disorganization." Some nations, such as India, have underdevelopment accompanied by starvation. In other underdeveloped nations, such as Argentina, "everyone is essentially well-fed and well-clothed." To become developed, people must attain the sorts of educations, achievement motivation, and life styles that will help them adapt to industrialization. (He is describing something like Deutsch's balance between social mobilization and assimilation.) Governments can help push them in this direction, so long as they learn to distinguish between necessary coercion and terrorism. The United States and European nations could help by opening up markets to imports of manufactured goods from Third World nations, providing technical assistance to modernize plants, and "a self-imposed screening by the leading powers of their own private-enterprise foreign holdings." But "they simply do not operate this way." At bottom, Third World governments must "impose order and independence on the economy" by expropriating and redistributing those industries which are not promoting development.

According to Horowitz:
1. What sorts of political systems could exist in developing nations?
2. How is development achieved?
3. What sort of political system comes closest to achieving development?
4. Do any developing nations have, or come near having, that sort of system?

All of these theories operate within what is to me an uncomfortable vacuum. Whether examining institution-building, participation, or distribution of goods, they assume the functions will benefit people without even exploring whether that is the case. Participation (from the perspective of these authors) may be harmful to political development because it interferes with, say, institution-building, but not in and of itself; likewise with industrialization, secularization, or any of the other variables. Nowhere is there a discussion of how functions that are listed at the more modern end of a scale of values might be harmful to some human beings. Distribution is perhaps the most interesting variable in this regard. It is difficult to be against improved distribution of material goods: Deutsch virtually equates political development with the number of hospital beds and newspapers; Halpern implies that an important part of controlling modernization is broader distribution; Kautsky stresses the importance of land reform and a broader distribution of consumer goods; Apter values resource allocation at the local level; Almond sees the challenge of distribution; Horowitz stresses consumer goods. None have any clear analysis of what will most enhance distribution. Yet, simply stated, an early distribution of hair driers and beautician supplies in a primitive economy can have detrimental effects on personal environments (by diverting family incomes, destroying some traditional values, weakening family solidarity, etc.). If the kinds of distribution these men propose enhance the sale of hair driers before other types of distribution more essential to stable personal environments ensue, this distribution might lead less to social development than to social decay. Because there is no analysis here of what human needs are, there is no basis for determining how political systems relate to human need. The authors agree that modernization must be orchestrated, harmonized, and fine-tuned. No one has analyzed how this coordination is to contribute to human well-being or political development.

THE VIRTUES OF DISCORD: TRADITION AND MODERNITY

In contrast to analyses of political development that leave the solution of human problems as their last highly-abstracted theoretical spinoff, I have sought in this book to begin with human problems and then proceed to relate political systems to these problems. Rather than assuming that some reasonable solution is in the works and seeking to find out what the key to that solution will be, I am trying to establish what solutions the problems require before proceeding to seek a cure.

I began by suggesting that the citizens of developing nations are faced every day with a set of related needs: feeding, housing, educating, recreating, and finding meaningful social relationships on a level with which they feel comfortable. Finding a balance among these variables is a fundamental problem among all modern men and women. But with scarce resources and excessive dependency it is an especially great problem among citizens of developing nations. Then I noted that, whatever else might be said about precommercial societies, an establishment of a comfortable balance among these variables was not so serious a problem as it is today in those countries. And I suggested that this is more than an academic problem, since many individuals in developing nations are only in the initial phases of being hit by commerce. So I asked: *Would it be better for these nations to retain some of the features of their traditional society, or would it be better to introduce modernization all the way?*

Though they are sophisticated analysts of comparative politics in developing nations, all of the authors reviewed above have given only the most cursory treatment to the nature of traditional societies. The only solid data we have concerning precommercial societies comes from anthropologists. So I reviewed the material available from the anthropologists. That data seems to suggest that those societies might be more "advanced" than they have normally been given credit for outside of anthropological circles. Then I asked how functions performed in traditional settings were performed after these people became more modernized. The results were not encouraging; benefits were accruing to a relatively limited number of indigenous people, and in a manner which created imbalances in their environment. This took me to the doorstep of inquiry into political development with the opening question: *Why do the benefits accrue to the few privileged people who do receive them? Is it inevitable that they will continue to so accrue? And is this skewed accrual more likely to occur under conditions of increased modernity, or in settings where tradition is left more to itself? If the former, are other advantages of modernization sufficient to make up for this?*

None of the authors we have just reviewed will argue with the conclusion that the benefits are skewed. Aside from Jaguaribe, none of them particularly asks why they are skewed. All simply take it for granted that they will cease to be quite so skewed after modernization, or after modernization is brought into some kind of harmony, and then proceed to extrapolate as to what conditions will best promote harmonious modernization.

It has been brought clearly to our attention in preceding pages that there is a good deal of difference between modernization and political development, and that modernization is not a boon unless it is brought into harmony. It has not been clearly brought to our attention that there is a difference between bringing *modernization into harmony*—transforming the imbalances among the systems of society in the direction of an intrinsic capacity to generate and absorb continuing transformation, or whatever you want to call it—and bringing *personal environments into harmony*. This might amount to the same thing, and it might not. It calls for further examination.

For me, there is a hollow sound when Huntington suggests (describes, predicts, prescribes—take your pick) that nations should slow down mobilization so as to build up government institutions, political consensus, and potentials for reform. He does not give any clues as to how those actions will affect the skewing of benefits or the personal environments of members of the society. Nor does he give any idea how these activities will affect or transfer functions performed in traditional society. For the same reason, I am unmoved when Deutsch talks of balancing assimilation and social mobilization, when Kautsky says that a regime of balance may promote industrialization, when Apter compares the potentials for augmenting the flow of information under various regimes, when Jaguaribe extols the advances of the Peruvian regime, or when Horowitz talks about expropriating industries. These men are discussing aspects of the political system, but they do not seem important if I cannot apply the activities they are talking about to something that seems important to me: who gets what, when, and how.

Some Policy Questions

To deal with this issue, it is necessary to ask some policy questions. When dealing with policy questions we are testing the waters of the possible—who *could* get what, when, and how, if the policy were adopted.

The Presidential Commission on World Hunger in its March 1980 Report[49] states that it wishes to "make the elimination of hunger the primary focus of [United States] relations with the developing world." They have made a value judgment to use in analyzing who could get what; they want to know whether the hungry could be fed. The Commission recommends the following policy:

1. ". . . that the United States press for an early resolution of the issues impeding the establishment of a global system of [food] reserves, and support the efforts of developing countries which might wish to create their own reserves."

Suppose the Commission hired you as a scholarly consultant, and asked you to explore whether this policy suggestion—to set up silos of spare food in developing nations to use for emergencies, with money and/or grain provided by the United States—could help feed the hungry. To deal with this suggestion, one needs to choose some country or countries, and some particular information about those countries, to analyze; where might the policy work, and how? Asking yourself some questions about the models we examined in the previous section can be a useful starting point in making those choices.

Which of Manfred Halpern's or David Apter's systems would be most likely to set up such silos and distribute the food to the needy during emergencies? Which type of leader discussed by John Kautsky might be most likely to push for such a plan? Which of Apter's or Huntington's party systems might best promote this? Might either of the two types of coalitions in the India case study discussed under Gabriel Almond be looked to for carrying out such a plan? What combination of Jaguaribe's variables would be needed to make such a reform "viable"? Now, looking at this list of potential people and groups to be counted on, can you think of any countries where such individuals or groups might have enough power to carry out such a plan? How might United States policy-makers assist them toward such goals?

Asking these questions, and answering them tentatively, is only a start on policy analysis. If it helps you identify some people who might be counted on to implement such policy, and think of how they might become involved with such a plan and how the political system might affect their participation, it is a useful start. It helps you formulate hypotheses, focus on particular people and places to study, and begin to devise a strategy for validating your hypotheses.

Here is another policy suggestion by the Commission on World Hunger:

---

[49] Presidential Commission on World Hunger, *Overcoming World Hunger: The Challenge Ahead* (Washington, D.C.: Government Printing Office, 1980), pp. 3, 63, 100, 129.

2. "The United States should support agrarian reforms both directly and indirectly through bilateral and multilateral food and development assistance programs. It should also support a multilateral institution or arrangement that would provide capital and technical assistance to facilitate changes in inequitable land tenure patterns."

Bilateral programs involve only the United States and the recipient country; multilateral programs involve many countries, such as United Nations programs. To find out whether the policy suggestion could support the Commission's stated objective, you would want to know whether it would reduce hunger if the United States supported land reform programs, to break up some of the inequalities in land distribution we have been looking at.

Which political participants discussed by Halpern, Kautsky, Apter, and Jaguaribe would be least likely to support land redistribution? Most likely? Least and most likely to support other agrarian reforms like cooperatives, low interest loans, and irrigation? How would their opposition or support affect the goal of eliminating hunger? Which of the systems discussed by Halpern, Kautsky, Apter, or Almond would put these participants in the best positions to allow for the promotion of such reforms? Where do such systems exist? Where are nations "viable" for such reforms in Jaguaribe's sense of that term?

3. "The Commission recommends that the United States support continuing international efforts to create price-stabilizing agreements for those commodities of particular interest to the developing nations . . . and should adopt an affirmative attitude towards the producers' price concerns."

Here you would need to decide whether making the wholesale market price of commodities like coffee, cocoa, sugar, rubber, tea, tin, copper, bananas, and peanuts higher and less subject to fluctuation will help relieve hunger. Which political participants discussed by Halpern, Kautsky, Apter, and Jaguaribe would benefit most from high and stable prices for such products? How could such high stable prices affect hunger? Which of Huntington's or Apter's or Almond's party systems are most likely to spread the benefits from such a reform? Would Huntington's or Almond's notions of modernizing government increase the possibilities of achieving this policy objective?

You will get still more information on these three policies, and many more policy suggestions to think about, in the remainder of the book. To prepare yourself to begin to think about them critically it will help if you think about these questions (or another we will give you in a moment) just enough to see how to arrive at critical judgments, no matter how tentative.

The exploration need not end here. Because they have focused on fine-tuning and harmonizing modernization, these particular authors (both the theorists and the Commissioners proposing these policies) have ignored some other important questions that might be asked in approaching policy alternatives. In fact, these authors have made a strong case for looking beyond harmonizing modernization. Each of them may be lending support to the argument that *governments of developing nations are unlikely to seek to harmonize modernization.* If that is true, one needs to look elsewhere for a solution:

Binder.   It is the formal legitimacy of the government and not its performance that is important to traditional (i.e., patron-client) societies. Modernization produces a bourgeoisie that can (though will not necessarily) seek to improve that performance. Without vigorous performance, government will not be able to tackle the traditional forces holding back the creation of national identity, broad participation by citizens, fair distribution of goods and services, and penetration of the nation-state into all regions. If it does act vigorously in these directions, its legitimacy will be challenged by traditional forces. The odds for success are not high.

Deutsch.   Finding a balance between assimilation and social mobilization, and spreading these two phenomena uniformly throughout a nation, requires some policy initiatives from government. Developing nations have moved with surprising speed toward social mobilization, and toward assimilation. There is little evidence, however, that their governments are prepared to take the policy initiatives needed to strike a balance between the two.

Halpern.   Those with the greatest tendency to desire to transform imbalances so as to absorb continuing change are those suffering personal maladjustments. Those who attain highest power are able to relieve many personal frustrations; this diminishes their desire to transform imbalances. These elites do not have the capacity to concentrate on absorbing continuing transformation because of reciprocal obligations with middle-echelon individuals who demand elites' time and resources if they are to stay in power. Those middle-echelon individuals at intermediary levels of power are in turn forced to reward themselves and their institutions (business, the bureaucracy, the military) rather than to distribute rewards to broad constituencies. Developing the capacity to absorb transformation requires the power to regulate many of those who, because of reciprocal obligations, one is least able to regulate. The political system includes many who not only have no desire to promote the sorts of policies involved in absorbing continuing transformation, but who are themselves involved in modernizing activities which they do not wish regulated.

Kautsky.   There are definitely middle-class types in power in developing nations who have a strong proclivity to modernize. That proclivity, if it is to be fulfilled, requires them to make concessions to investers, technicians in the bureaucracy, and producers of basic commodities. It does not require them to make concessions to workers, peasants, or poor urbanites. And if some leaders are not particularly interested in modernization they still do not need to make concessions to powerless masses as long as they have a steady alliance with the military, bureaucracy, and large landowners. So they do not make these concessions. The same personal maladjustments which make some peasants and poor urbanites favor reform also help keep them politically weak.

Apter.   Citizens in developing nations are not in a position to furnish the government with accurate information about the imbalances that affect their lives *regardless* of the form of government under which they operate. This is partly because the maladjustments are often so severe as to inhibit their participation in politics, partly from fear of retaliation, and partly because those who represent them in politics distort the information because of their own reciprocal obligations. Simple reductions in coercion without changes in the pattern of reciprocal obligations will not significantly increase the amount of information. Government policy may be more affected by the ties of top government leaders with bureaucracy, the military, and economic elites than by the type of party system. And the stability of a political system may depend more on the degree of accommodation reached among key elites than on ability to coerce or receive information from the general populace. Hence stability could be achieved without significant concessions to the general populace.

Huntington.   Modernization disrupts traditional social groupings, creates personal tensions, and places new demands on government. But government institutionalization cannot control this process in developing nations precisely because government is committed to the very modernization that carries out the disruption. Institutionalization cannot resist entrenched interests because it is controlled by entrenched interests. For the same reasons, two-party systems cannot promote reform. Political systems in developing nations cannot deepen their popular roots to resist special interests because they represent strong government dealing with a weak populace. Personal maladjustments among the populace generally inhibit mass mobilization in developing nations from achieving staying power or firmness; it is difficult for rural movements to link up with urban.

Almond.   The conversion processes between inputs and outputs in developing nations have less to do with unstructured pressures and counterpressures than with predetermined patterns of reciprocal obligation. A rather select body of people communicates demands; the types of responses also benefit a limited body of people. Subsystem autonomy is low everywhere and among all classes. Rural areas remain far less secularized than urban regions. Past attempts to alter this pattern in the direction of broader participation and distribution by extending the suffrage have not been successful. The political systems of developing nations remain tightly fused with disparately wealthy portions of societal structures.

Jaguaribe.   It is precisely in nations with the greatest viability—sufficient human and natural resources to allow for endogenous development and complementarity of social subsystems—that systems of reciprocal obligations will be strongest and most centralized. Colonial powers are especially in need of local allies to carry out their work. If elites are complementary and much of the populace marginal, it is easy for them to keep resource distribution to themselves. If elites are not complementary but the populace is marginal, they too do not have the capability to redistribute beyond themselves. Even populist or provincial empires must work through reciprocal obligations with local elites. These obligations tend to limit policy. And even liberal military establishments cannot rule without the aid of key economic elites. The patterns of dependency and marginality in developing nations will not be broken simply by changing the attitudes of those who control the political systems.

Horowitz.   Dominent minorities in the metropolitan centers build roads, communications systems, and the like to ship raw materials to First World countries. This process disrupts traditional society, but it requires few people and produces little industrialization, which is the prerequisite for social development. Even though these authoritarian regimes emulate the industrial progress of the First and Second Worlds, they have no firm motivation for aiding either those who do not help them exploit those natural resources, or those who do. So the prognosis for spreading social development is not good.

In short, the fundamental problem with modernization in developing nations is that it is spread with the aid of a small number of special interests who are more interested in creating stable environments for themselves than for others. The primary advantage of traditional systems is that they left a greater percentage of the populace with greater potential to affect the stability of their own personal environments. Increased modernity means increased reciprocal obligations at the top, and decreased personal stability for those not at the top.

The natural next step, then, is to examine whether any benefit might be derived from leaving some aspects of traditional society intact, so as to reintegrate political and social structures and thus help stabilize personal environments. Perhaps we should be more cautious about modernization and more careful to assess what we are destroying when we modernize. There might be advantages in preserving part of the tradition.

This discussion of Malaysia is continued from p. 215.

When I first went to Singapore in 1964, I drove my Humber Super Snipe up the East Coast of Malaysia. Much of it was dirt and sand. The sand I remember well; at one point virtually the entire male polulation of a village helped me and my companions push the car—an enormous relic of colonialism that once belonged to the British High Commission and was pawned off on me by a British army officer for the sum of $250—out of this sand. We visited the markets and brought home pictures of a medicine doctor putting on his show with the heads and skins of exotic animals. Wherever we went people were curious. I saw the cues of integrated community life that were to become familiar to me over the years as I visited places relatively untouched by modernization: families congregated around doorsteps, the children playing in groups, the conferences among elders, the flowers in the yard, the vigorous activity interspersed with abject leisure.

The following year the Canadian Government helped build a road up the same East Coast. As a result, timber and mining operations boomed. On my two subsequent trips I witnessed a rapid influx of modernizing influences, but little that made me feel there had been a tangible improvement in life styles or standard of living. There were new signs of generational disaffection, economic displacement, spending beyond means, dissension, neglect of property. The Canadian Government did not have to build that road. Some officials made the decision. Perhaps I was simply being nostalgic. I asked: Was the road a good idea?

That was my account. Phil Shinn, a student at Brown University, traveled on the same road a few years later. This is his:

I also traveled up the east coast of Malaya, and I think the people were happy with the new road, hospitals, schools, and mosques. They were curious about the land from which I'd come, and were glad to make money off of the few tourists who were beginning to come through. In a kampong (village) a few miles off the road, there was malaria. The hospital was two days' journey away, and there was no doctor. The well was collapsing and the animals roamed around, dropping their waste for flies and feet. A woman, bent from labor and lined from the sun looked forty as she drew muddy water by hand from the well. She was twenty-four and had had five children. Two had not lived to see their first birthday.[50]

The two of us saw the same road, but, having differing perspectives, we noticed different things about it. We are back to asking policy questions again—who gets what, when, and how. Should a road be built? First, we must be clear what goals we are testing. Both Shinn and I are looking at the road in terms of the villagers (the "who") and their welfare (the "what"). Our notions of "what and how" is good for them differ.

Shinn and I both like health and stable personal environments in a modern setting. Shinn, however, does not like one aspect of stable personal environments offered by traditional societies—what he sees as a culturally induced lack of choice. "The societies in *Brave New World* and *1984*," he writes, "had stable personal environments (I'm glad I'm an Epsilon),[51] yet so do animals in zoos have stable personal environments. . . . I think people should be given the freedom of choice and equality of opportunity . . . call it the myth of self-determination." He feels "it does not seem possible to stem the tide of change. If one sets himself up in the position of determining the fates of others, becomes the arbiter, we risk tyranny." He compares those wishing to preserve the kampong to wealthy people joining the Sierra Club—trying to preserve some wilderness "while advocating admittedly higher energy costs for the working classes." I, in turn, see little chance that further disruption of traditional society will lead to greater freedom of choice for the villagers. Nor do I see how urban working classes can benefit from the new road. In contrast to Shinn, I see an intrusion on freedom of choice when North Americans, citing "the tide of change" and "self-determination", foist a road on people against the will of many of them; "keep out" signs are also a form of self-determination. When, on top of this, we claim we are doing them a favor by disrupting their lives with little apparent benefit to them, we risk becoming tyrants. The former colonial rulers cloaked their lucrative transactions in such humanitarian rhetoric, too. And I do not think the road is inevitable.

QUESTION

Why not have the road, health care, and *minimum* personal disruption, by planning carefully?

---

[50] Phil Shinn, Take-Home Final Exam, Political Science 142, January 15, 1978. Most of the quotes that follow are from a letter he wrote me on October 1, 1980.

[51] The Epsilons in *Brave New World* were to be found in the futuristic society there. The kampong is more like the Pueblo Indian Reservation, which Huxley suggests may have had a measure more freedom than the futuristic society. That Reservation had been disrupted by modernization, but not yet transformed by it.

As in most such debates, there is more heat here than fire. We share the goal of wishing the villagers to have health and stable personal environments, and would prefer those stable environments exist in a modern setting if possible. Anyone who makes successful input into any policy debate is foisting their views on others should their proposals be carried out, so neither of us can claim immunity from that. If we can translate our perspectives into operational questions about these goals we share, and subsequently gather facts to answer the questions, such a debate can be the starting point of science rather than an emotional ritual to display our disdain for all who see the world in any different vein from us, and our intention to stay clear of all stimuli which might challenge our pet notions about how the world operates. It is tolerance, curiosity, and a dedicated, systematic search for verification that separates the scientist from the bigot. Shinn and I, in fact, have a great deal in common in our curiosity about how the lives of individuals are affected by modernization. The fact that he and I have differing perspectives means that we will ask more questions and think of more sources of information than would either of us alone. Then it is incumbent upon us both to seek the most reliable information available to deal with one another's hypotheses.

Shinn surmises that with the road, villagers can move to town and find new opportunities; an Indonesian student told him that roads allow kampong dwellers to go to Djakarta and then return with "money, skills, and knowledge." The question becomes: How many of them do so, who are they, and what do they then do with their lives?[52] Shinn suggests that the road, by promoting economic development, will improve the livelihoods of workers elsewhere in Malaysia. Is there evidence of this happening? He emphasizes the lack of opportunities for free expression and individual personal development in the kampong. I emphasize the lack of opportunities for free expression and personal development in the atmosphere of cultural disintegration that exists after the kampong is displaced. How does personal development compare in these two situations? He and I both see creativity resulting from modern anxieties and educational opportunities; I also see it in the praxis to be found in traditional societies. How does creativity compare in the two settings? He might emphasize the health advantages to be derived from new wells and latrines; I wonder whether the new well would soon look like the old (which was itself built since the original disruption of the original kampong). Both matters need investigation. He would emphasize the advantages to be derived from immunization; I would wonder about the dangers of malaria from the standing water that always seems to result from the bulldozing activities surrounding roadbuilding.[53] He would be interested in the new access to markets; I would wonder whether the new road will further deteriorate the kampong's access to land and hence food

---

[52] United States Agency for International Development, *Liberia: Rural Roads,* Project Impact Evaluation No. 6 (June 1980) found that the new roads enabled some peasants to become involved in cash-cropping and to send occasional children to town. Outsiders bought land and thus pushed many original settlers inland away from the roads and new facilities.

[53] *Idem.,* pp. 8–9, found that clinics which accompanied the new roads reduced the number of mothers dying during childbirth. However, there was an increase in traffic accidents, malaria and schistosomiasis bred in standing water, lung diseases from dust, and tuberculosis when people closed thier shutters to avoid the dust.

and money.[54] We would want to know where the doctors and clinics are located and how the villagers could reach them; I would want to know how many villagers could take advantage of these facilities, for what, and how often. He emphasizes the capabilities of modern medicine; I would emphasize the capabilities of traditional medicine. We would want to find out what each can do for the kampong dwellers, under what circumstances. What kinds of educational and job opportunities would open to the kampong youth after the road, and what kinds would cease? We would both want to know more about the social, nutritional, and health conditions just before this road was improved (versus after) to help us judge future roads.

Once again, the authors in this chapter can help us ask questions to place the situation in its political and social context. Which of Halpern's or Apter's political systems would be most likely to take advantage of the road to distribute health care and education to the villagers? Is that the type of system in Malaysia? Which type of leader discussed by Kautsky, or Apter's or Huntington's party systems, might be most likely to do this? Is Malaysia's leadership like this? Are either of the two types of coalitions in the India case study available in Malaysia? Are there "viable" factors in Jaguaribe's sense of the term? Which of Apter's or Huntington's party systems would be most aided by the road, and how might that affect health and education? In Jaguaribe's terms, how would the road strengthen or weaken the villagers' autonomy, and how would this affect the government's effectiveness in meeting their problems? From Deutsch's angle, would the road add to both the kampong dwellers' social mobilization and their assimilation? In Almond's terminology, how would the road contribute to the villagers' secularization, and how might that affect their health and education?

Discussion of Malaysia is continued on p. 281.

Despite all these questions, a great deal has still escaped our attention up to this point. That is because we have been paying little attention to history, or the nature of traditional society. Are there, in fact, possibilities for these people that go beyond those we have explored here? We have usually begun with the assumption that those with more commerce are potentially better off than those with less. Perhaps the reverse is true. Suppose Malaysia *both* abandoned its road improvement program *and* cut back on its exports of rubber, tin, timber, and manufactured goods. Suppose it retreated from international trade somewhat in order to emphasize its more traditional elements and the domestic portions of its modern economy. What then? And maybe those nations which *right now* have fewer exports are better off than those with more.

Reducing dependence on, or maintaining independence from, an export economy does not mean a "return" to traditional society. *Modernization in one form or another is here to stay.* But when the export sector is weak the tradi-

---

[54] *Idem.*, pp. 10–16, found that the roads greatly improved access to markets for cash crops, but much of the land near the road fell into the hands of village chiefs and outsiders, while many of the original villagers were forced to move away from the road (and the new schools and clinics) to obtain land. Those peasants who started cash-cropping often received barely enough cash to purchase the rice they had formerly raised on the cash-cropped land.

tional society is stronger. To find out whether there might be benefits to be derived from a stronger traditional society requires asking some new questions, beyond "What happens as modernization progresses?" or "How do you orchestrate modernization?" We must ask about the traditional forces that remain in society, what roles they played before modernization, what roles they continue to play, and what roles they could play in the future, especially if they did not have to compete much with an export economy. We have a tendency to ask only what role traditional forces play now and see them only as fighting modernization, instead of comprehending the roles they played before that fight. We look on tradition as bringing discordant tones to our symphony of modernization. Yet modernization, in turn, brings discordant tones to the symphony of tradition. Why not give some attention to that?

In Illinois in the 1950s we looked upon windmills as relics cluttering up farmyards; in Illinois in the 1980s people are using them again because someone took another look at the advantages they offered when they were first built. In Malaysia, what hope would there be for health or education or personal environments or other human aspirations if the traditional sector were given some opportunity to perform functions it used to perform? To broaden such vision of the future we must broaden our vision of history. None, perhaps, is more lively and challenging on this subject than Fred Riggs. He focuses on what happens when traditional societies come into contact with modern societies. We will look at Riggs and three other theorists and then return to the question about whether to build the road. Riggs has a different line of questioning. He is not asking how to harmonize modernization, but, rather, what happens when modernization and tradition clash. *Might there be human benefits in the dissonance and discord which results when the former symphony tries to drown out the latter?*

Fred W. Riggs

You will note immediately that Riggs speaks in his own idiosyncratic dialect.[55] The reason is simple. When he is talking about things that other comparative politics scholars talk about, he tends to use their language. He is especially fond of the terminology of Gabriel Almond, Max Weber, Harold Lasswell, and David Easton. When he talks about his original subject matter he defines his own terms and (in keeping with his personality) he defines them colorfully. His analyses sometimes become quite involved, but once you have mastered the terms, they become relatively easy to comprehend. The terms themselves are based on everyday experience.

Riggs builds his thinking around three ideal types, states of being that have never existed but which combine the characteristics of places that have existed. Significantly, all three of his ideal types are built around places that have already experienced extensive commerce and patron-clientism. He calls his three political systems, fused, prismatic, and diffracted. The *fused* society approximates the

[55] Fred W. Riggs. *Administration in Developing Countries.* Copyright © 1964 by Fred W. Riggs. Reprinted by permission of Houghton Mifflin Company. Quotations taken from Riggs in this section are from pp. 95, 148, 171, 173, 183, 204, 209, 210, 216, 219, 234–236, 263, 271, 281, 283, 300, and 304.

Etsu Nupe's state. The *prismatic* is the present state of affairs in developing nations. The *diffracted* society is the ideal stage at which advanced industrial societies may someday arrive. His choice of words comes from optics: If you aim a fused beam of light at a prism, it emerges from the prism as numerous diffracted rays. Inside the prism, the light shares the characteristics of both the fused ray and the diffracted beams. The developing nations are the prism, where tradition and modernity blend.

In fused societies the exchange and price of goods are heavily influenced by the power, prestige, and solidarity of ruling groups; Riggs calls these *arena factors*. Diffracted societies have business concerns where prices are determined by *market factors* such as supply and demand, or monopolies when they exist. In prismatic societies, prices are controlled neither by kings and courts, nor by the interactions of business concerns. Instead, they are characterized by bazaars, where one bargains for price, and canteens (as on plantations and in the army) which serve limited clientele under special fixed pricing conditions. Here both arena factors and market factors control price. In the bazaar, price fluctuates according to the relationship between buyers and sellers, their relative power, prestige, solidarity ties, skill in bargaining, value system, and the need for time—all arena factors—as well as in response to market factors of supply and demand. A canteen sets its price lower when its intent is to subsidize a particular group to which it owes favors (the subsidized canteen), and higher when it has a captive clientele dependent on it for all supplies and credit, as in a company store (the tributary canteen). The same factors work outside of formal marketplace settings. The price of land, or cost and availability of a loan, may fluctuate according to race, place of residence (stranger vs. local), and political connections—all arena factors. Or someone may find it necessary to pay a bribe to achieve the right to import goods or to safeguard their property.

These arena factors in the bazaar-canteen contribute to what Riggs calls *negative development*. To get ahead economically or politically the citizen must cultivate special relationships. Those who already have wealth must buy protection from those who have power. Those with power find ample opportunity to use it to attain wealth from those buying protection. "By circular causation, insecurity weakens the social position of the entrepreneur, making him vulnerable to official persecution, hence highly dependent upon particularistic favors and protection."

Riggs calls the developing nations exo-prismatic because they were initially modernized by outsiders. The scope of power refers to the range of the values it affects. "If we call formal power *authority* and informal power *control,* we can say that in our exo-prismatic model, authority has a narrow scope whereas control has a wide scope. . . . A 'law' . . . may formally prescribe a specific policy, but officials charged with its implementation may regularly permit its violation." The law may attempt to narrow the range of values over which the government may exercise authority, but the law may simply be conveniently ignored, especially for those with whom the officials have special reciprocal relations. All this leads to the *dependency syndrome*. The chief characteristic of this syndrome is "the proportionately large share of the total national product which is consumed by a small segment of the population, the elite, which does not itself make a proportionate contribution to economic production." The dependents in this case are both those at the top of the ladder and those at the bottom. Those at the bottom are paying out more than they are receiving back because they owe more obligations to their superiors than their superiors owe to them. Those at the top of the ladder are in a deficit situation because they must increase their spending above their income to keep their position. They cannot depend on rising productivity to insure their position, and must instead rely on transferring income away from those who actually produce it (peasants, plantation workers, craftsmen, etc.). They do this through control of price via arena factors.

The bureaucracy, pariah (one who is despised by society) entrepreneurs, and politicians are at the top of the dependency syndrome. It is they who constantly have a dependency ratio with one another, as well as with the general populace. The dependency ratio of the general populace toward these elites is very great. The dependency ratio of these elites toward one another is relatively narrow. The peasant, plantation worker, craftsman—the actual producers—give everything they have and more to pay off their obligations. The elite take this surfeit and pass it around to one another in a continuous circle in the form of bribes, taxes, parties, public works, sinecures, etc. In this way they can live well on relatively limited resources without making significant strides in real economic productivity. Likewise, this approach leaves little money aside for capital investment. And it makes it difficult for elites to control one another's activities: everyone is too dependent upon someone else for bribe money, imports, paychecks, tax rebates, or political positions. Hence the paradox exists of a powerful central executive who has little control over the activities in the provinces, of the mass ideological party that has no real control over affairs, of the legislature controlled through the back door, and of the seemingly powerless bureaucracy that exercises massive powers. It also accounts for the inability of the bureaucracy to carry out laws like land reform and welfare distribution; any individual bureaucrats who tried to carry out the law can be fired, transferred, or chastised by an immediate superior who is responsible for them having their job and who expects them to carry out their arena obligations.[56] Hence there is an inadequacy in any investigation that looks only at *formal* responsibilities and powers; hence we find the anomaly of abject poverty at the foot of the door of lavish wealth.

COMMENT

This explains why Almond does not go far enough when he looks only at formal decision-making processes.

Those involved in a dependency syndrome find it difficult to escape. They would need to acquire some new means of support, and their very activities inhibit the accumulation of capital and a rational approach to business-governmental relations. It would be difficult to know where to begin. If you try to enforce the laws, the system will deliberately recruit individuals into the bureaucracy who will invoke double-talk and say one thing while doing another.

---

[56] "Given a choice between loyalty and competence in a subordinate, the sala official chooses loyalty. Thus the pressure to appoint relatives and friends . . . should not be attributed so much to a 'culture lag' of traditional institutions or the compulsions of kinship, as to the need of sala officials to reinforce their power position by recruiting men on whom they can rely." Ibid., p. 273.

"Were [a superior] to delegate authority to zealous subordinates, intent upon enforcing laws assigned to their care, he might lose a major source of personal income." If you try to change recruitment patterns, business will keep two sets of books and continue the same patterns through informal networks. If you tried to eliminate government intrusion into business, the arena aspects of the bazaar would help insure a continuation of the old practices. And behind all this stands the power of the *clects*. A clect is a cross between a clique and a sect.

> Each clect draws its membership from a particular community [a clique characteristic]; it applies its norms selectivistically to members of that community [a sect characteristic]; and its poly-functional goals always include a communal-orientation [a clique characteristic] as well as whatever economic, religious, political, educational, or social objectives constitute its manifest functions [sect characteristics].

There are official clects, and "combative, feckless, and pariah clects" in adversary position. They want the recruitment and advancement of their own communal members. They oppose reforms that might threaten this. They stand at the center of the dependency syndrome. They are composed of people who have already gained some access to the system of reciprocal obligations; hence their ideals and policy objectives are constantly watered down by their own ambition to succeed. When these individuals enter political parties, they never forget their attachment to their clect. This makes it especially difficult for opposition parties to stay united around any political platform. "The official bureaucracy itself has many clect-like characteristics, and cooperates closely with official clects." Whatever goals they advocate to improve the nation are always tempered by the necessity to serve their own clects first.

This pattern could conceivably be broken if outsiders were to come into the country and impose proper business procedures. Since Riggs did most of his field work in the Philippines in the late 1950s, he had not yet seen the massive influx of United States, western European, and Japanese investment in industrialization. However, he implies that this might not help the situation; these latter countries are also victims of the dependency syndrome. If they are to keep alive a political atmosphere in which economic investment is comfortable, they must keep the dependent elite in power. The easiest and cheapest way, in fact, to extract cheap labor and raw materials from the general populace is to continue the pattern of dependency and buy into the pattern of reciprocity among the elite. The developed nations must give favors to that elite in the form of aid, military forces, and the like. "The elite's ability to buy price-gifts in bazaar and canteen, and the pariah's ability to charge price-tributes to primary producers sets the 'terms of trade' in favor of powerholders, against the weak."

> The assumption here is that the dominant imperial power or national power center is also characterized by negative development, hence needs to extract unrequited tributes to maintain its own higher standards of consumption.

The foreign investing power raises productivity somewhat, and keeps this increased productivity for itself. Meanwhile, it does not disturb the dependency syndrome. "The shift to *positive development,* correspondingly, requires that the powerful be restrained by the rule of law so they cannot convert their power into wealth, and that the wealthy be protected by the rule of law so they need not buy protection." *This is not in the cards.* Even if it were, "when laws are drafted on the basis of inadequate data or a misunderstanding of local problems—perhaps through mimesis [imitation] of foreign models—their intent remains obscure and their goals unfeasible." The clects stay in control.

In an earlier day when kinship groups performed the roles now performed by clects, it was possible to combine reciprocity with a redistribution policy, for everyone belonged to a kinship group. Today the clects contain only a small percentage of the population. The official clects respond only to one another. Pariah (opposition) clects are discounted. "If a pariah clect reveals its interests by petition, legislators drawn from a dominant community are as likely as not to enact the opposite, either in the artless hope of suppressing the pariah group, or the artful expectation of squeezing them more." Nonclect interest groups have even less effectiveness. "The processes of articulation and aggregation work inefficiently." And besides, their inputs will be blocked by some clect. "It would distort the prismatic model to suggest that there is no connection between inputs and outputs"; there is only such a connection when it is a clect making the input. Meanwhile rising political elites feel that "since the formal channels of political control through the rule-making process are so ineffective, intervention in administration is the only method by which they can actually make their influence felt." "A powerful bureaucracy is administratively weak"; it is powerful only in helping its friends—not in carrying out broad policy objectives.[57] It is composed of clects.

> Perhaps enough has been said . . . to illustrate the basic proposition that . . . no single function or aspect of the system can be adequately understood without taking into account other aspects which form, not discrete and relatively autonomous systems, so much as merely different ways of viewing a single complex totality.

The dependency syndrome, then, is deeply rooted:

> The prismatic need for strategic spending [negative development], not some cultural or personality idiosyncrasy, compels the elite and semi-elites to exact tribute in order to be able to spend. Any who fail to exact tributes lack the means of acquiring elite status. . . . Price indeterminacy is not just an accidental characteristic of the prismatic model, it is indispensable to maintenance of a dependent elite since it makes possible the transfer of wealth from primary producers through pariah middlemen to the power-holder, all in the form of market transactions.

COMMENT

James Alban Bill's example earlier in this chapter of the uprooter reformer who is simply bypassed in the distribution of graft, and Thomas Headrick's suggestion about improving Indian politics by putting people interested in

---

[57] "Statements are evaluated in terms of their authorship rather than their intrinsic meaning." Ibid., p. 279.

"politics and social work" into the legislature are worth thinking about here. Do you reform by including uprooters or social reformers in the clects? See pages 236 and 251.

Riggs is suggesting not merely that modernization must be controlled to benefit the populace, but that it *cannot* be controlled without fundamental changes in the social, economic, political, and cultural systems *taking place in unison; there must be reintegration of these spheres.* Economic development and political institutionalization alone cannot help the situation; *by giving an elite that had once survived on petty cash larger profits and armies, one simply entrenches more firmly their power and their ability to avoid reform and popular participation:*

"The degree of administrative efficiency of a bureaucracy varies inversely with the weight of its power." Riggs distinguishes the *chamber* bureaucracy of the fused society, the *sala* bureaucracy of the prismatic, and the *office* bureaucracy of the diffused society. The fused bureaucracy can be thought of as the men of the chamber who surround the king and carry out his bidding. In the office, one is assigned to functionally specific roles and is relatively insulated from outside forces that weaken the resolve to perform according to the rules. Sala is a Spanish word for the French *salle,* or public rooms in a home, in which the interlocked members of a family nonetheless carry out their own personal functions. The clects make demands; the bureaucrats work them out within the sala, and intermingle them with their own goals before they emerge as policy. Those goals include keeping open their special relationships with economic elites. And they involve paying off their network of subordinate bureaucrats.

> Statements about "overcentralization" of power reflect one surface of this pattern. The other surface might just as well be called "undercentralization," for in respect to effective control the prismatic bureaucracy is almost anarchic, offering few substantial curbs to the expediency interests of subordinate officials. Thus, on balance, power in the sala is neither centralized nor localized, neither concentrated nor dispersed, but highly *equivocal.*

So you cannot tackle the problem of overcentralization simply by reorganizing in a decentralized fashion. (See our case study on Nigeria.) "No program of reform which does not first seek a closer reengagement or reintegration of authority and control can hope to achieve significant results merely by manipulating authority structures." And no government can reintegrate authority and control without changing its entire base of power. If an economy does increase in productivity, the size of its bureaucracy increases at an even faster rate, as does the budget of the bureaucracy. Budgets "reflect substantively not the relative priority of program needs so much as the relative power position of bureaucratic elites." Specialized revenues and sales of certain goods and services become automatically earmarked for particular bureaucratic programs, helping to perpetuate and enlarge their domain. Clects are in control.

Riggs offers little by way of solution to the problems he elucidates, yet he seems to indicate that one cannot achieve reform of political structures without a reform of social and economic structures as well. He sees a developed future; he implies that it will arrive only after major economic changes transform all the links on this chain—not merely party systems, political leadership, or balances between mobilization and institutionalization. He is by no means clear as to how, or whether, such a transformation can take place in developing nations. He opens the door to another possibility, however. Present forms of modernization have made power flow out of the hands of kinship structures and simple patrons into the hands of clects and bureaucracy. This process can only be stopped by reaching a diffracted society with so many resources that they can be widely distributed, or by some kind of outside intervention or inside competition to countervail this aggrandizement of clect-bureaucratic power.

In short, it is possible that the dependency syndrome might change to allow for broadening of clects and greater reintegration of authority and control. Riggs does not know what would happen, but he notes that today's political systems are very loose fusions of traditional and modern, and that the traditional portion has enough resiliency that it might be able to bring greater unison to the social, economic, political, and cultural systems. So reintegration of authority and control is possible. Patron-clientism may be superceded by new forms of political leadership.

According to Riggs:
1. What sorts of political systems could exist in developing nations?
2. How is development achieved?
3. What sort of political system comes closest to achieving development?
4. Do any developing nations have, or come near having, that sort of system?

André Gunder Frank

André Gunder Frank[58] also sees a role for tradition in development. He speaks of the *undeveloped,* the *now-developed,* and the *underdeveloped* nations: those with no modern economic development, those with modern economic development, and those which may or may not have been developed economically but are now satellites of now-developed nations. The now-developed nations were once undeveloped in terms of modern economic institutions, but have never been satellites of other now-developed nations. The underdeveloped nations are not likely to achieve economic development even if they should cease to be satellites.

In underdeveloped nations, capitalism has penetrated into every region and segment of the society, culture, and economy. The underdevelopment is not due to the survival of old institutions. The greatest industrial development in Argentina, Brazil, Mexico, and Chile, he argues, took place during the two world wars and the great depression of the twentieth century, and the depression in Europe during the sixteenth century, when ties to the metropolitan centers in Europe were weakest. When the metropolitan centers revived after the crises, the industrial development in the satellites declined and emphasis returned to export crops and minerals. If the metropolitan centers later pull out after, say, depleting

---

[58] James D. Cockcroft, André Gunder Frank, and Dale L. Johnson, *Dependence and Underdevelopment: Latin America's Political Economy* (Garden City, New York: Doubleday, 1972).

the minerals of a region, they leave behind debilitated political and economic institutions that are incapable of keeping alive a vital economy. These institutions would need to revive some of their original self-sufficiency in order to do so.

Development means a self-sustained process of industrialization. Undeveloped states such as those in medieval Europe had strong political and economic institutions which could support their development. Today's underdeveloped states lack this, and could only develop it by seeking to recreate such institutions for themselves.

QUESTIONS

1. Which of Frank's categories of nations exist in developing nations?
2. How does he suggest development is achieved?
3. Can any of the developing nations achieve development in this manner?

Immanuel Wallerstein

Immanuel Wallerstein, in a book that has received considerable scholarly attention,[59] sees the capitalist world-economy to be divided into four zones: the *core,* the *semi-periphery,* the *periphery,* and the *external arena.* Those at the core extract cheap labor and natural resources from those at the periphery, and hence are more prosperous. Those in the semi-periphery have somewhat less extracted from them than those at the periphery. Those in the external arena are ouside the area of extraction, but this arena has just about disappeared by the 1980's.

A *world-economy* is different from a *world-empire;* the former is divided into separate nation-states, while the latter is completely under the control of one political center. The existence of nation-states induces a creative tension. What is good for the world-economy and thus for the nation-states at the core is only partially good for the nation-states at the periphery. The governments in periphery states are almost entirely dependent on income produced by the capitalist world economy, and they design their institutions and policies to help promote the development of that economy. The division of labor in their nations, and their attitudes, are adapted to that economy. But their behavior, attitudes, customs, bureaucracy, and army, still retain many pre-capitalist elements. So their relations both with their own domestic bourgeoisie and with the international bourgeoisie constitute a balancing act reflecting their dependency on the outside powers and their desire to preserve old ways.[60] The more the government leans in the direction of the bourgeoisie, the more they weaken their army and bureaucracy and contacts between city and countryside. The more they lean in the direction of the old landed aristocracy, the weaker the international

---

[59] Immanuel Wallerstein, *The Modern World-System: Capitalist Agriculture and the Origins of the European World-Economy in the Sixteenth Century* (New York: Academic Press, 1974). Quotations taken from Wallerstein in this section are from pp. 309, 348, and 357, unless otherwise indicated.

[60] Wallerstein does not like to use the word *tradition,* which he calls "an aspect of and creation of the present, never of the past. . . . In a one-class system, the 'traditional' is that in the name of which the 'others' fight the class-conscious group" (i.e., the nonbourgeoisie fight the bourgeoisie who control the world-economy). *The Modern World System,* pp. 98, 356.

trade and income to support themselves. They lose either way, so the nations on the periphery are inherently weak. In contrast, the governments of the core nations can depend on a strong internal tax base and income from the peripheral nations. Their armies, bureaucracies, and everyone else have benefited for many decades and centuries from the capitalist world-economy. It makes the core nations both strong and wealthy, so they need not feel ambivalent about it.

So, viewed from the perspective of the core states and their citizens, the development of the world-economy and of their own nation-states go hand in hand. Viewed from the perspective of the peripheral nation-states and their citizens, the world-economy is a mixed blessing. It leaves some of these individuals prosperous but all of them weak. The only counterforce to the world-economy is the states. The states in peripheral areas are weak. Those with the highest skills live in the core states, which also absorb the prime resources and the investment capital which accrue from exploiting low-paid labor and low market prices for resources of the peripheral states. Strengthening the latter requires strengthening those elements of the army, bureaucracy, religious leadership, and landowners least dependent on the world-economy. It also requires strengthening the individual culture[61] of the nation so people can rally to it against outsiders, and against internal forces causing tension by attempting to organize class interests. These strengthened elements can form alliances which force the core nations to give them concessions. The welfare of the people in peripheral nations requires maintaining this balancing act because the capitalist world-economy will continue.

For capitalism itself to continue, this balancing act is also necessary. Should the peripheral nations become too weak, the world-economy could be converted into a world-empire which might try to squelch the very technological inventiveness on which capitalism is founded; the continued refusal of these less-dependent elements to take orders from a center is part of what prevents a world empire from coming into being. "Capitalism has been able to flourish precisely because the world-economy has had within its bounds not one but a multiplicity of political systems." So those forces that resist capitalism are actually beneficial to it. The health of these states also prevents socialism from developing its own world-economy. Individual states on the periphery cannot develop national socialist economies and retain any strength while surrounded by a capitalist world-economy. For core states to institute socialism they would need to reintegrate political and economic decision-making (versus capitalism where the political entities absorb losses and private hands receive gains) and thus to transform the governments of the peripheral states away from putting gains into private hands. This means overcoming resistance from within those states from pre-capitalist elements which would not like this. *So a developed capitalism requires states on the periphery which are weak, but not too weak. And that in turn requires individual cultures and pre-capitalist groups there to reassert themselves.*

---

[61] By emphasizing language, tradition, and distinctive life styles, for example, peripheral nations can emphasize their distinctiveness from the core nations, and also keep down left-wing class-based challenges ("We Muslims of_____must not fight among ourselves.") This perpetuates social stratifications, behavior patterns, and attitudes out of step with the capitalist world economy but in step with pre-capitalist institutions.

The peripheral nations and their people will remain poorer and weaker than the core nations, and the state machinery of the peripheral nations will remain weaker than informal elites there. But these nations and their nonbourgeoise elements must resist somewhat to retain some privileges. "The mark of the modern world is the imagination of its profiteers and the counter-assertiveness of the oppressed." He is talking about a balance between elements which will strengthen the forces of "modernity" and elements which will weaken them.

According to Wallerstein:
1. What sorts of political systems exist in developing nations?
2. When is the world-economy strongest?
3. What kinds of peripheral nation-states contribute most to keeping the world-economy strong?
4. Do any such peripheral nation-states exist or come close to existing?

S. N. Eisenstadt

Shmuel N. Eisenstadt, of the Hebrew University of Jerusalem, is, like Riggs, interested in bureaucracy.[62] He is famous for his monumental study of the political systems of ancient empires—a study that points to such focal roles played by bureaucracies in these empires that he labeled them bureaucratic empires.[63]

Eisenstadt sees the principal problem in contemporary developing nations as an adjustment between tradition and modernity. New elites are taking on new modern roles in the economic, organizational, and political spheres; these new elites must establish a *modus vivendi* with older elites without disrupting their cohesion.[64] Instead, there is a rapid growth of interaction among different groups and strata—including a breakdown of some older groups—without new mechanisms to deal with the problems that arise from the interaction.[65] This results in oscillation between repression and giving in to the exaggerated demands of various groups.

The destruction of traditional groups "tends to lead to disorganization, delinquency, and chaos, rather than to the setting up of a viable modern order."[66] These groups learn, instead, to adapt to the problems of modernization, and to one another. In India, for instance, occupational and caste groups on the periphery did learn to adapt to modern occupations and demands, but these adapted groups were never adequately organized with reference to one another. Those who achieved such organization were elite groups (e.g., merchants allied with religiously orthodox sects). Their accommodation was largely political. The

[62] S. N. Eisenstadt, *Essays on Comparative Institutions* (New York: John Wiley, 1965); idem, *Modernization: Protest and Change* (Englewood Cliffs, N.J.: Prentice-Hall, 1966); idem, *Tradition, Change and Modernity* (New York: John Wiley, 1973); idem, "Cultural Molels and Political Systems," *European Journal of Political Research* 2, no. 1 (March 1974): 1–21.

[63] S. N. Eisenstadt, *The Political Systems of Empires* (New York: The Free Press, 1963).

[64] Eisenstadt, *Tradition*, p. 38.

[65] Ibid., p. 58.

[66] "So-called traditional societies are no more lacking in entrepreneurship, specialization, and differentiation than are advanced societies. Many once-prosperous societies are now underdeveloped as a result of the intervention of imperialistic interests in their economies." Ibid., pp. 104–105.

links between the center and the periphery become "increasingly direct, decreasingly mediated by traditional ideological and structural links."[67] The mechanisms to deal with the problems of all groups—elite and nonelite—have not been forged. Groups are increasingly scrambling for access to the political center, rather than working together to solve the problems presented by change. "The major means of political struggle tended to become more and more that of cooptation, change or extension of the clientele networks."[68]

> Notice the parallel between this and Riggs' pariah clects.

Eisenstadt feels it important to develop a strong center to the political system, to keep social groups intact and autonomous (with their own strong centers), and to develop adaptability to change among their members. The lower the solidarity and cohesion of any social system, the lower the adaptability to change of its members.[69] Eisenstadt has seen the development of some strong new political centers since World War II which are highly adaptable to change (e.g., those just mentioned in India). They are good at developing symbols and charisma, but poor at establishing working relationships with intact and autonomous social groups. Many other regimes have weak centers with traditionalistic, nontransformative elites; the social groups in these nations suffer the same disability. They tend to "conceive of their own legitimation in terms of maintaining this restricted range of status symbols." They "tend to emphasize one component of center-building—especially the regulation of center-group relations and the development of new goals and symbols of common identity."[70]

Developing nations, in short, are not concentrating on inducing the adaptation of traditional cultural and social groups to modernization or creating modern groupings that can so adapt. They are instead intent on forging limited alliances among elite groups with a virtual monopoly on the distribution of resources and status positions.

Eisenstadt agrees with Halpern on the importance of middle-class innovators and of developing the capacity to transform the imbalances caused by modernization.[71] Yet he contends that the problem is not simply to take over the reins of government and apply checks on modernizing activities; it involves developing viable groups within society that can be used to countervail the power of vested interests in government. It involves preserving some former functions of traditional groups that cannot easily be reproduced in modern form, such as becoming the nucleus for a sense of identity (incorporating national symbols into the context of one's own group) and a place to turn when one faces personal crisis. And it requires more than attention to the problems of modernization as they arise. It necessitates *the construction of strong social, cultural, and economic centers, led by elites who can maintain autonomy for their own sphere*

---

[67] Ibid., p. 299.

[68] Ibid., p. 319.

[69] Ibid., p. 341.

[70] Eisenstadt, "Cultural Models," p. 19.

[71] He calls it the capacity to forge out or crystallize new institutional frameworks for adapting to changing conditions. Eisenstadt, *Tradition,* p. 329.

while at the same time adapt to the needs of the others.[72] This is a far different notion from Huntington's concept of the political institutions, or Apter's of party institutions, becoming dominant over all others. Huntington thinks it is important for parties to develop popular roots. He is wary of those roots being controlled by autonomous leaders who deal with but are not an intrinsic part of political institutions. Apter sees his parties—whether of solidarity or reconciliation—controlled by the elites of the *political* center. Kautsky finds positive virtue in the fact that his modernizers are cut off from their societal roots. Almond expresses interest in subsystem autonomy. Yet this autonomy is seen in political rather than social or cultural terms. He is indifferent to the question of whether those who lead articulation and aggregation have viable social roots. And Jaguaribe is at least sensitive enough to raise this problem but leaves it on the sidelines when he formulates his conclusions.

According to Eisenstadt:
1. What sorts of political systems could exist in developing nations?
2. How is development achieved?
3. Which sort of political system comes closest to achieving development?
4. Do any developing nations have, or come near having, that sort of system?

As we move into the final chapters of this book that deal with reform, we shall be returning frequently to Jaguaribe's concern about complementarity and marginality of indigenous elites in the international arena, the informal networks and dependency syndrome analyzed by Riggs, Frank's underdeveloped and Wallerstein's peripheral nations, and the links between societal and political structures discussed by Eisenstadt. This is because these five authors notice something fundamental about the leading elites of developing nations: In the greater scheme of things, they are weak and dependent on individuals and institutions outside their countries over which they have no control. At best they are clients of these outsiders; at worst they are suppliers or debtors who can be discarded or foreclosed on at a moment's notice. At the same time the people they are leading are also weak, even though they once were strong. *No matter what party systems or governmental institutions these countries devise, it is the weak leading the weak without the resources to help their people. Part of the weakness derives from the decline of traditional institutions with the power to keep resources inside the nation.*

Discussion of Malaysia is continued from p. 269.

Is a road improvement valuable for Malaysia's East Coast? We now have some new questions to ask. Will it strengthen, or weaken, the dependency syndrome? How might that affect the power of Malaysia's elites to aid villages? What might it do to clects within the villages? The bazaar-canteen? How might it affect the adaptability to change of villagers? How do the clects and bazaar-

---

[72] Eisenstadt, *Tradition,* p. 346.

canteen relate to health care? Could elites and villagers be put into a position to be more autonomous after (or without) the introduction of a road? Could they construct strong social, cultural, and economic centers? How would the presence or absence of such centers affect the health, education, and personal environments of the villagers? What can or could elites do for the villagers in the presence or absence of such centers? What can or could villagers do for themselves? Would the road strengthen or weaken the power of Malaysia vis-à-vis the core nations? How could that affect the personal environments of the villagers?

These questions we have asked about the Malaysian road, both here and earlier in this section, are the sorts of questions we shall be asking in the closing two chapters. See what tentative answers you might have to some of them right now. We will continue to be interested in the internal issues of synchronizing and coordinating modernity within a patron-client framework discussed by Halpern and the others. However, to deal fully with the policy issues that surround developing nations it is also necessary to view them as part of a broader international arena and to recognize that the minor changes taking place since World War II are part of more sweeping changes viewed over a slightly longer time frame—to recognize that patron-clientism has a limited history, is inherently tied to the world economy, and is not the only potential form of rule for developing nations in the near future.

SYNTHESIS: THE STAGNATION OF CHANGE

Some political scientists are beginning to back away from the implications that modernization and political development are somehow inevitably intertwined ongoing processes and from their nearly exclusive preoccupation with the activities of political institutions. For instance, in an article entitled "The Change to Change,"[73] Samuel P. Huntington recants the notion that "tradition" and "modernization" are mutually exclusive dichotomies. Instead of the chief balancing act in politics being the modernization-induced conflict between political institutionalization and popular mobilization, he sees a number of components in flux and maintains that it is difficult to predict how they will relate to one another. In fact, he suggests dropping the terms "modernity" and "political development" from the vocabulary since they are such complex constructs and their parts may be going in different directions. "A political system can be thought of as an aggregate of components, all changing, some at rapid rates, some at slower ones."[74]

While he refuses to predict how any components will react in a given setting, he does suggest relationships among them centering especially upon *culture* ("the values, attitudes, orientations, myths, and beliefs relevant to politics and dominant in the society") and *institutions* ("the formal organizations through which the society makes authoritative decisions, such as political parties, legislatures, executives, and bureaucracies"). In a *stable political system* culture and institutions may change slightly more slowly than groups, *leadership* ("the individuals in political institutions and groups who exercise more influence than others on

---

[73] Huntington, "The Change to Change."
[74] Ibid., p. 316.

the allocation of values"), and *policies* ("the patterns of governmental activity which are consciously designed to affect the distribution of benefits and penalties within the society"). *Revolution* would mean rapid changes in all components. A rapid change in culture and institutions accompanied by slower change in leadership and policies would result in *instability*. Should there be little or no change in culture and institutions, but rapid change in leadership and policies, *political stagnation* would be the result.[75] He sees little likelihood of stagnation, since "the absence of change [in a component] is simply one extreme rate of change, a rate rarely approximated in practice." Each component may be going in a different "direction" (though he does not elaborate on this term); but we may be sure of continuing change.

Huntington's definition of *groups* ("the social and economic formations, formal and informal, which participate in politics and make demands on the political structures") leaves open the question of what elements participate in politics. If large numbers of people participate, then institutions could become vital forums for absorbing group pressures and coordinating changes in policy and leadership. *If only small numbers participate, then groups would not be much larger than leadership and it would be hard for political institutions to have much autonomy from them.*

Our analysis would seem to suggest that few people participate in politics in developing nations. Ties between the center and autonomous social groups, needed for effective participation, do not exist outside of leadership circles. So groups, as defined by Huntington, are small. The export economy and dependency syndrome keep dominant values ("culture") similar and constant. *Hence groups, leadership, bureaucratic institutions, culture, and actual policies are closely intertwined and change very slowly.* Political institutions and their formal leaders, and their policy declarations, may or may not change frequently. In either case, they have little influence over the allocation of values. This hardly sounds like revolution, stability, instability, or a "change to change." Huntington's term "stagnation" fits it best. Rather than being caught up in an irreversible movement toward urban progress, or lost in a period of open-ended flux, perhaps we are caught instead in the doldrums of a particular social and economic order. *Groups are stagnant, so politics is stagnant.*

According to "The Change to Change":
1. What sorts of political systems could exist in developing nations?
2. How is change achieved in a political system?
3. Which sort of political system has the most rapid, and which the slowest, change?
4. Do any developing nations that you can think of have, or come near having, either of these sorts of systems?

It is healthy for the social sciences to move away from the notions of inevitable progress through modernization, needing only periodic adjustments from leadership. One need not jump from this to the equally shaky position that we know nothing about how the components of political activity will interrelate

---

[75] Ibid., p. 318.

and that the future could take us almost anywhere. Much knowledge about how political activity interrelates has been accumulated. It is incumbent upon us to use it.

We are short of food and energy, long on population and armaments, and surrounded by poverty and imbalanced environments. There is a crying need to enlarge the agenda of politics, to give authoritative responses to a wider variety of issues, to coordinate our responses so as to meet grave new challenges. Many have hoped that modernized political institutions would somehow help to enlarge that agenda. The plain cruel truth may be that they cannot. *The constant changes in leadership and institutions which fill the newspapers will accomplish nothing as long as groups remain stagnant.* The so-called policy departures that leaders periodically announce may be just public relations campaigns. For all the heat and talk, we may be moving neither forward nor backwards. We may simply be moving nowhere. *Yet, rather than explore new alternatives, we have a tendency to want to continue to turn to leadership and institutions to solve our problems.* In 1975 and 1976 Huntington brought out two books in which he shows this habit.[76] In *No Easy Choice* he cites studies that conclude that economic development does not promote greater equality. If the poor can organize in conjunction with middle-class groups, he believes they could potentially gain more than they do, but in reality the middle class steals most of those potential gains. He suggests a class-based party of the poor

> . . . is the most effective channel for altering the attitudes of the poor and improving their condition in the long run. But the most striking fact about such participation is its rarity. In most of the developing nations, for some time to come, the poor are less likely to become involved in politics through this than through other patterns.[77]

The other patterns to which he refers are primarily patron-clientism, which he surveys at great length through many of the sources we have been discussing here. He feels that patron-clientism ignores most needs of the poor, but at least deals with some urgent needs on a personal level. He suggests that political elites can control groups and organizations and thus weaken participation by individuals in politics. But:

> From the standpoint of the broader political system, followings based on traditional leadership, patron-client networks, or machines may provide a basis for the engineering of coalitions and consensus in nations where most of the population cannot yet be expected to respond to "modern" appeals to class or occupational interests.[78]

In the other book, *The Crisis of Democracy,* writing about a nation where people can be expected to respond to class and occupational appeals—the United

---

[76] Samuel P. Huntington and Joan M. Nelson, *No Easy Choice: Political Participation in Developing Countries* (Cambridge: Harvard University Press, 1976); Samuel P. Huntington, "The United States," in *The Crisis of Democracy: Report on the Governability of Democracies of the Trilateral Commission,* ed. Michael Crozier, Samuel P. Huntington, and Joji Watanuki (New York: New York University, 1975). Introduction by Zbgniew Brzezinski.

[77] Huntington, *No Easy Choice,* p. 158.

[78] *Idem.,* pp. 130–131.

States—he indicates his reaction to that sort of response. He suggests that it is possible (and, he implies, advisable) to elect a president on the basis of slogans like human rights, and then virtually ignore the voters starting "the day after the election." This would make it possible to institute a large defense budget and give support to large corporate interests while cutting back on welfare programs. He is suggesting that appeals to class or occupational interests should be subdued even in modern settings where they are successful—something akin to balancing mass mobilization with institutionalization. In developing nations, patron-clientism, unrestrained by even middle-class influences, is the best system possible.

QUESTION

Does Huntington think any particular type of change is more useful than other types of change?

Clearly his 1965 fears that popular participation would overwhelm the system have subsided, as have his 1971 notions that the international system is going into a period of unpredictable flux. We may be going nowhere, but at least the system which benefits the rich benefits the poor more than the system which has greater participation by the middle class.[79]

Huntington cites data comparing 13 "democratic" and 31 "nondemocratic" developing nations. A higher percentage of the democractic nations have the poorest 20 percent of the population getting below 5 percent of income than of the nondemocratic nations ($14 \div 31 = 45$ percent). The percentage going to the poor is lower in the democractic nations, though this tells us little about the actual condition of the poor. He concludes: "In less developed countries, in short, democratic institutions enhance the power of the middle class and make the poor as well as the rich worse off than they are likely to be in nondemocratic societies.[80]

Huntington has moved far afield from thinkers like Kautsky, Halpern, and others who extolled the virtues of middle-class participation in politics. He has moved a good distance from his own earlier preoccupation with the need to control mass participation, though not from his conviction that mass participation must be balanced by institutionalization. He has come to recognize the patron-client nature of the status quo. Yet that recognition virtually constitutes an endorsement. He, like the other theorists in this chapter, gives no notion of how to move beyond this status quo.

So we shall try.

---

[79] *Idem.*, pp. 75–78.

[80] *Idem.*, pp. 76–77, 71. Figures are from I. Adelman and C. T. Morris, *Economic Growth and Social Equity in Developing Countries* (Stanford, Calif.: Stanford University Press, 1973); Adelman and Morris, "An Anatomy of Patterns of Income Distribution in Developing Nations," Part III, Final Report, Grant AID/csd-2236, February 12, 1971.

SHORT SUMMARY

The theorists in this chapter, from those analyzing only internal systems to dependency theorists, from functionalists to Marxists, all basically agree in their analysis of the main features of the political systems of developing nations. They differ, however, in their definitions of development. Some see development as taking place only when nations leave behind traditional modes of behavior, while others feel that development occurs when a balance is struck between tradition and modernity. Before we start to look at reform attempts it is useful for us to examine the works of writers from both these camps, because each raises questions and points to information about people and their problems which the other might ignore. And tolerance for, and curiosity about, conflicting viewpoints is a prerequisite for fruitful scientific inquiry.

Can you match these words and phrases with these theorists?

political decay	Leonard Binder
secularization	Karl W. Deutsch
satellite dependent	Manfred Halpern
extraction	John Kautsky
clect	David E. Apter
political superordination	Samuel P. Huntington
level of capability	Gabriel A. Almond
input-output functions	Helio Jaguaribe
social mobilization	Irving Louis Horowitz
social consensus	Fred W. Riggs
social development	André Gunder Frank
aggregation	Immanuel Wallerstein
endogenous development	S. N. Eisenstadt
exo-prismatic	
cultural denationalization	
dependency syndrome	
modernizer	
cartorial	
incoherent change	
negative development	
peripheral nations	
subsystem autonomy	
assimilation	
autonomous social group	
complementary elites	
functionalism	
viability	
the crisis of legitimacy	
arena factors	
marginal populace	

Can you answer each with one sentence?

1. Which of Halpern's five types of political systems in developing nations are not patron-clientism?
2. According to Kautsky are all members of the new middle classes modernizers?
3. In developing nations does Apter see the balance weighted in the direction of information or of coercion?
4. Can you find a canteen in Chapter 4?
5. How does negative development lead to the dependecy syndrome?
6. What is a peripheral nation?
7. Why does Jaguaribe differentiate between participational and cultural leaders?
8. Is social development the same as a balance between social mobilization and assimilation? Social mobilization and institutionalization?

From what you have read this far, can you make and support judgments about these questions?

1. Have you answered the questions under at least one of the Presidential Commission on World Hunger policy recommendations?
2. Have you answered some questions about the road in Malaysia?
3. How does Almond explain the fact that not all government output produces responsiveness to aggregated demands?
4. How might one of Riggs' clects interfere with one of Kautsky's modernizers?
5. Riggs talks about pariah (outcast) entrepreneurs as having power. Are there any pariahs discussed in Chapter 5? How can you be both outcast and powerful?
6. Do Huntington, Wallerstein, and Eisenstadt think it matters whether the national center is highly institutionalized or weakly institutionalized?
7. Do you think Huntington disagrees with the other authors about the role that should be played by the middle class? With which author do you most agree on this?

Reread the entire "Book in Brief" section of Chapter 1, thinking about how its emphases differ from those of some of the theorists you encountered in this chapter.

CHAPTER

7

GETTING YOUR BEARINGS (see map, front of book)

1. Where are the world's biggest deserts? Mountain ranges? Jungles?
2. Where is Morocco? Indonesia? Ethiopia? Egypt? Cuba?

The Model

A developed nation provides most of its citizens with a stable personal environment. *A developing nation does not.* Today's developing nations were once developed nations. They changed because *their political systems separated from their social systems when European commerce was introduced.* If the structure of international trade changes in the near future, social and political systems may be reintegrated, promoting political development. Then the developing nations may once again become developed nations.

Reform: Policies Tried

QUESTIONS TO KEEP IN MIND

1. Is there enough food to feed everyone in the world?
2. Why do land reform programs do little to help malnourishment?
3. Why does expansion in agricultural production not help poor people?
4. Why doesn't industrialization expand in developing nations like it did in Europe and the United States?

Feeding a growing population is the most serious challenge faced by the modern world. Our response to this challenge will affect all our other relationships.

I have suggested that the present worldwide web of political interactions makes this and other problems relating to the stability of personal environments virtually insoluble. Now we shall explore that contention in greater detail. A number of countries have instituted reforms to improve the standard of living of their citizens. Some of these reforms are aimed at augmenting rural inhabitants' access to land and control over the products of their own labor. Some are designed to increase agricultural productivity. Still others attempt to improve the productivity of other sectors of the economy. And additional reforms try to make political processes more responsive to the needs of the populace. We shall look first at the reforms of agriculture. Next, we shall explore the impact of industrialization, mining, and other forms of economic growth. Then we shall make some observations about political reform in the light of what we have learned from these first two investigations.

LAND AND FOOD

There is virtually no developing nation that has not attempted some sort of land reform or government program to stimulate agricultural productivity. Each of these programs has its unique aspects. Each has produced some kind of accomplishments. None appear to me as solutions to the problem. I shall briefly discuss the food crisis, and then look individually at some of the more successful land reform programs before attempting to generalize about the reasons for their failures. Once again, I shall try to present some of the facts and opinions needed if you are to challenge this interpretation.

Food production is rising; so is population. As this chapter indicates, it is probably possible to achieve some balance in production between the two, but obtaining a balance in distribution will be more difficult. While one part of the world's population practices weight control, another part starves.

The problems of famine, malnutrition, and subsistence nutrition are so staggering that they are difficult to reduce to comprehensible terms. In late October of 1974, for instance, at least 150,000 people were already estimated to have died of starvation in a Bangladesh famine, with the likelihood that 800,000 more would follow them to their graves within another few months.[1]

> Just how many are dying is a matter of some dispute in Dacca's bars and on the cocktail party circuit. But people who actually visit some of the gruel kitchens, where everyone who receives food is on the verge of death through hunger, have no doubt that the figure is enormous. Photographers, who accompany Red Cross helicopters to stricken areas in the north, such as Rangpur, and who bring back roll after roll of evidence sometimes too sickening to be published, agree with the critics: The situation is completely out of control.[2]

The gruel kitchens were offering as little as one chapatti (like a small pancake) per day to 3 million people. The boat of supplies which is normally sent up the river to relieve the Rangpur district did not even leave the dock; critics charged government-connected hoarders, smugglers, and black-marketeers with this oversight. A single Red Cross helicopter arriving with powdered milk in late October was the first relief to reach the area. In Dacca itself, around the bars and cocktail parties, an estimated seventy to one hundred persons die of starvation each day. Meanwhile (with 7 percent of the nation's farms already controlling 31 percent of the land) rich landlords stood in line all night at land registry offices to buy land forfeited by small farmers who could not pay their mortgages.[3] The United States government had been temporarily withholding food loans to Bangladesh on condition that it stop selling gunny sacks to Cuba.[4] By year's end the government responded by declaring one-party government and locking up dissidents.

In the bordering state of West Bengal in India, a minister

> has estimated that about Rs 1,000 million (US $111 million) in black money has surged into the foodgrains trade in his state alone. The amount must be much

---

[1] "Starving Huddle in Bangladesh," *Kansas City Star,* November 7, 1974, p. 3B.

[2] "Starvation: Pointing the Finger," *Far Eastern Economic Review* 86, no. 44 (November 8, 1974): 26.

[3] Swadesh R. Bose, "The Strategy of Agricultural Development in Bangladesh," in *The Economic Development of Bangladesh,* ed. E. A. G. Robinson and Keith Griffin (New York: Macmillan, 1974), p. 14.

[4] Frances Moore Lappé and Joseph Collins, *Food First: Beyond the Myth of Scarcity* (Boston: Houghton Mifflin, 1977), p. 337.

greater in states that are agriculturally more prosperous. . . . To make matters worse, many *jotedars* (big farmers) have stopped selling rice on a retail basis to local villagers. One villager, Girish Mahato, from Lagda in the chronically-distressed Purulia district of West Bengal, tells how he could previously buy rice from the *jotedars,* or at least borrow it and repay it after harvest. But for this season the *jotedars* would rather take the stock to Purulia town and sell it to the wholesale trade.

[The wholesale traders] control not only the wholesale food trade but also the trade in items such as mustard oil, fertiliser, seeds, pesticides and kerosene. Such traders often enjoy overt as well as covert political support, and sometimes enlist the services of local *mastans* (thugs) to protect themselves.[5]

Prime Minister Indira Gandhi said that "what food we have in the country is not far short of what we need, provided hoarded stocks are unearthed." She started a de-hoarding operation, "but some politicians and a section of the administration have ensured that it does not go too far." The black market has enough money to avoid the need for bank financing; much of its funds are undeclared, untaxed earnings from big farms and businesses.

In the Sahel, which spreads across the central third of Africa, at least 250,000 people died in a drought during the early 1970s (see page 42); the actual figure is probably much higher. Great additional numbers had their lives shortened and their health severely impaired. In 1979, practically no farmers in war-torn Cambodia could plant rice, and a million people could well have died. Most of the relief supplies that entered the country seem to have gone to troops and affluent residents of the capital city. In 1978, Kenya, Tanzania, and other nations along the east coast of Africa had bumper crops of grain. Government marketing boards exported substantial quantities of it to raise foreign exchange (while Kenya cut back the price it paid farmers for grain). In 1979 and 1980, the coastal rains failed, and several million people faced starvation. In nearby Uganda the problem was compounded by the presence of marauding bands of soldiers—both supporters of former leader Idi Amin and the new government—seizing food and killing villagers.

These are just examples from a brief span of time. They are neither unusual nor seasonal; incidents of this sort are constantly being reported somewhere on the globe. Far from receding with time, their magnitude seems constantly on the increase.

Furthermore, food is a constant problem in areas not affected by droughts or crop failures. In West Malaysia (an area relatively fortunate in food production and distribution) friends of mine in the Peace Corps found it difficult even to keep rural children awake in school until they began feeding them in class (a problem shared in many innercity schools of the United States). In half of seventy-two households studied by Iain Buchanan in lower-income Singapore neighborhoods (one a modern housing estate), the food budget was below

---

[5] Jayanta Sarker, " 'Black Money' Corners India's Grain Stocks," *Far Eastern Economic Review* 86, no. 44 (November 8, 1974): 47–48.

US $.25 per day per adult ($.12½ per child), the minimum standard set by the Singapore medical profession.[6]

Using a similar standard set by the Food and Nutrition Center in Manila, another study shows that the number of people in Manila with incomes insufficient to purchase minimal food needs grew from 17 percent in 1965 to 25 percent in 1971, and from 39 to 48 percent in the rural areas.[7] The Food and Agriculture Organization estimates that 455 million people in developing nations, about a fourth of the total population, have inadequate intakes of calories or protein.[8] It calls its own figures conservative. Studies show that if there is not enough food for the whole family, the working adults tend to take the largest share for themselves. Hence about half of all children, and a high percentage of pregnant and nursing mothers, have insufficient calorie and protein intake. Many children suffer from roundworms, hookworms, and amoebic intestinal parasites that consume much of the protein that they do ingest; so many of the children who do live never mature properly (e.g., they have weak bones or internal organs). In addition, several hundred million people suffer from goiters, anemia, pellegra, beri-beri, scurvy, blindness, and other diseases and disabilities caused by vitamin and mineral deficiencies. Josué de Castro's estimate that 85 percent of the population of developing nations suffers from malnutrition may not be far from the truth.[9]

Some 70 percent of the population in the developing nations consists of small farmers (a rough approximation). Their personal environments are frequently shaky. The peasant just referred to in West Bengal illustrates this vulnerability:

> Mahato cannot remember rice prices as high as the current Rs 3.30 a kilo. A landless labourer, his wage rate has now dropped to Rs 2.50 a day or less—without the food which used to supplement the cash payment. During the sowing season from June to August he somehow managed, but August to November are the lean months; he has no job, no earnings and no savings. Like many others in the village, he and his family are managing on one meal a day. And it will be like this until at least the end of this month, when harvesting will begin and he might again find employment.[10]

Ernest Feder estimates that in 1970 out of a total Latin American rural population of 114 million, 86 million were living at subsistence levels (over half of these landless); and these figures are growing.[11] He sees the paradox that while the number of peasants owning land is on the increase, nearly all of these new

---

[6] Iain Buchanan, *Singapore in Southeast Asia: An Economic and Political Appraisal* (London: G. Bell and Sons Ltd., 1972), pp. 230–231. See Ernest Feder, *The Rape of the Peasantry: Latin America's Landholding System* (Garden City, N.Y.: Anchor, 1971), pp. 26–27, for more gloomy statistics on urban diets in Brazil.

[7] Keith Griffin, *International Inequality and National Poverty* (London: Macmillan, 1978), p. 171.

[8] Food and Agriculture Organization, *Fourth World Food Survey* (Rome: United Nations, 1977), p. 53.

[9] Josué de Castro, *The Geography of Hunger* (Boston: Little, Brown, 1952), p. x.

[10] Sarker, "India's Grain Stocks," p. 48.

[11] Feder, *Rape of the Peasantry*, pp. 3–7.

landowners are poor; hence, despite the rise in the number of landowners (often simply due to division of land through inheritance), the percentage of the rural population living below subsistence level is on the increase.[12] Even the most optimistic researcher will agree that the problem is severe; the argument centers around how fast it is growing, not whether it is growing.

My own pessimism, however, does not stem from statistics such as these. I am more concerned about overall personal environments than about family income. If I could be convinced that stable personal environments can continue even in the face of inadequate monetary income, I would be less concerned. If I could find an experiment, no matter how small in scale at the present time, which I thought might open the door to solving these problems, I would feel relieved. I find none. A review of some of the best of these land-reform experiments will help explain my position.

The experiments share two goals: raising the standard of living of farmers, and producing more food. The goals sometimes conflict. When small farms and the notoriously inefficient *latifundios* are replaced with large-scale mechanized farms in order to increase productivity, the surplus farmers are often relegated to unemployment. The literature on whether this trade-off is necessary remains inconclusive. When *latifundios* are divided among peasants in land reform movements, they are apt to cultivate much more intensively than before, and thus increase output.[13] For instance a study of Central America shows that farmers who own ten or fewer acres cultivate 72 percent of the their land, while farmers with over eighty-six acres cultivate only 14 percent.[14] The new "miracle" grains require a good deal of artificial fertilizer and a regular supply of water. Small farmers usually have trouble obtaining these; hence, their productivity per acre is much lower than that of a mechanized irrigated farm with adequate working capital. But when small farmers can obtain adequate water, seed, and fertilizer, their labor intensiveness and ability to use greater percentages of the total land available give them an advantage over the larger mechanized operations; under these conditions, and given equally fertile land, adequate credit, marketing and extension services, and price incentives, "traditional" peasants often produce more per acre than larger modern farms.[15] Europe and Japan, with small

[12] Ibid., pp. 11–18. Implicit in his calculations is the assumption that all families inhabiting *minifundios* are poor. This is not necessarily true. He quotes from a number of intensive detailed case studies of families in Colombia, Brazil, Guatemala, Peru, and Ecuador which show that family incomes of *minifundistas* were inadequate to purchase necessities in a great majority of cases studied. One could argue that the researchers, because of liberal leanings or research biases, chose cases to study which were worse than normal. Feder himself admits that *minifundistas* (whose numbers are growing) are at least better off than those without any land.

[13] E.g., see Melvin Burke, "Land Reform and its Effect Upon Production and Productivity in the Lake Titicaca Region," *Economic Development and Cultural Change* 18, no. 3 (April 1970): 410–450.

[14] Food and Agriculture Organization, *Agricultural Development and Employment Performance: A Comparative Analysis* (Rome: FAO Agricultural Planning Series no. 18, 1974), p. 124.

[15] Kenneth L. Bachman and Raymond P. Christiansen, "The Economics of Farm Size," in *Agricultural Development and Economic Growth*, ed. Herman M. Southworth and Bruce F. Johnston (Ithaca, N.Y.: Cornell University Press, 1967), pp. 244–248, provide a good bibliography and discussion on this and conclude that the small farm is more productive, although less prof-

farms as the norm, tend to have higher yields per acre than the United States, which has principally large farms. So until more conclusive evidence is in, one way or the other, it is probably wise to keep an open mind on whether large or small farms could raise the most food. What is startling about the following experiments is that, whether emphasizing modern mechanized farming or division of land among smaller farmers, they tend *neither* toward a rapid increase in food supply *nor* toward an increased standard of living for the peasant. The reasons are economic and political more than they are technological or social. The reforms are carefully designed to enhance the prosperity and power of small groups of people.

Chile

Discussion of Chile is continued from p. 257.

Chile in 1978 contained some 11 million people (mostly of European extraction), $3\frac{1}{2}$ million of whom were in agriculture.[16] In 1967 farms covered around $61\frac{1}{4}$ million acres of land.[17] On one extreme: In 1955, 4.4 percent of Chilean landholders owned approximately 80.9 percent of the total farm land, 77.7 percent of the agricultural land, 51.5 percent of the arable land and 43.8 percent of the irrigated land. On the other end of the scale, 36.9 percent of the holdings contained roughly 0.3 percent of the total farm land, 0.3 percent of the agricultural land, and 2.3 percent of the irrigated land.[18] The 1955 agricultural census showed over

itable. Montague Yudetman, Govan Butler, Ranadey Bonerji, "Technological Change in Agriculture and Employment," in Development Centre of the Organization for Economic Cooperation and Development, *Developing Countries,* Employment Series #4, pp. 27–31, see the small farm as less productive; Robert R. Kaufman, *The Politics of Land Reform in Chile, 1950–1970* (Cambridge: Harvard University Press, 1972), pp. 116–117, reminds one that such statistics are often gathered in a charged political atmosphere. Stanislaw Wellisz, Bernard Munk, T. Peter Mayhew, and Carl Hemmer, "Resource Allocation in Traditional Agriculture: A Study of Andhra Pradesh," *Journal of Political Economy* 78, No. 4:1 (July/August 1970): 671–672, find the large farmer less productive than the small in Andhra Pradesh. John MacRae, "The Relationship Between Agriculture and Industrial Growth, With Special Reference to the Development of the Punjab Economy from 1950 to 1965," *Journal of Development Studies* 74 (July 1971): 402, shows a similar conclusion. See also Folke Dovring, *Land Reform and Productivity* (Urbana: University of Illinois, 1966). J. N. Sinha, "Agrarian Reforms and Employment in Densely Populated Agrarian Economies: A Dissenting View," *International Labour Review* 108 (March 1973): 395–421, argues that small farms absorb more labor and use land more intensively than commercial farms. Feder, *Rape of the Peasantry,* pp. 61–106, shows that in Latin America the larger the landholding, the smaller the percentage used for crops. Comparing crop-land only, average yield per acre is about the same on smallholdings as on middle or largeholdings. The reasons are social and economic in nature. Keith Griffin, *The Political Economy of Agrarian Change* (London: Macmillan, 1974) devotes a whole book to this contention, and World Bank, *The Assault on World Poverty: Problems of Rural Development, Education, and Health* (Baltimore: Johns Hopkins, 1975), pp. 215–217, cites a number of studies showing that productivity is greater on smallholdings than largeholdings.

16 Jeannine Swift, *Agrarian Reform in Chile* (Lexington, Mass.: D. C. Heath, 1971), p. xi.

17 Ibid., p. 64.

18 Marvin J. Sternberg, "Chilean Land Tenure and Land Reform," unpublished Ph.D. Dissertation, University of California, Berkeley, September 1962, p. 34.

300,000 landless agricultural workers in Chile.[19] The Ministry of Agriculture estimated that from 1955 to 1960, while population was growing by 2.7 percent, agricultural production grew by 2.29 percent. In 1963, agricultural produce accounted for 25.2 percent of imports and only 6.2 percent of exports. These figures show that Chile is plagued with the typical problems of developing nations: inequitable land distribution, rural unemployment, and the need to import food.

There are also more problems. The working class in Chilean agriculture makes up 87 percent of the active agricultural population but receives only 34 percent of income from agriculture.[20] The large landholder consumes over 60 percent of his own disposable income—a quarter of this for imported products.[21] Hence much of the agricultural income is not reinvested, and in fact adds to the balance-of-payments deficit. There are at least 175,000 *minifundistas,* families owning parcels of land too small to support them.[22] Division of land upon the death of a family head causes continuing land fragmentation. A great deal of farm land remains unused, or inefficiently utilized, both on large holdings and small.

The first formal governmental approach to these problems began in 1925 with a program of planned colonization. Individuals, primarily graduates of universities or agricultural colleges, were offered government land to colonize and purchase with a reasonable mortgage. By mid-1962, this program had settled 4,206 colonists (an average of 124 a year), only 15 percent of whom had been sold land in the central nucleus, which was the best farming area.[23] In 1962, the legislature passed a new Agrarian Reform Law, changing the Caja de Colonización Agrìcola into the Corporación de la Reforma Agraria (CORA), charged with acquiring land for division among small farmers and former workers on *latifundios,* and creation of agricultural cooperatives. Between November 1962 and November 1964, CORA distributed land to 1,066 families in the form of 781 parcels and 285 garden plots.[24] Meanwhile the Catholic Church set up four experimental colonies on former church lands, with a total of 182 families.[25]

When Eduardo Frei of the Christian Democratic Party came to power in 1965, he was determined to speed up the process of land reform. The backbone of this program was the formation of *asentamientos,* or cooperatives. The idea was to buy aggregates of land and keep them under cooperative management assisted by technicians and bureaucrats, until the members were ready to profitably assume ownership of their own plots of land. The program would have the power to expropriate inefficiently-used land, paying the former owners. Frei

---

[19] William C. Thiesenhusen, *Chile's Experiments in Agrarian Reform,* Land Economics Monograph Number 1 (Madison: University of Wisconsin Press, 1966), p. 41.

[20] Sternberg, "Chilean Land Tenure," p. 56.

[21] Ibid., p. 151.

[22] Thiesenhusen, *Experiments in Agrarian Reform,* p. 41.

[23] Ibid., p. 36.

[24] Swift, *Agrarian Reform,* p. 35.

[25] Thiesenhusen, *Experiments in Agrarian Reform,* p. 202.

hoped to provide adequate-sized farms for some 100,000 families under this program.

One particular *asentamiento,* described by Jeannine Swift as the best of the twenty she studied, consisted of 2,125 acres, 1,400 of which were cultivated.[26] Forty-five families had previously resided on this estate; they had served as clients *(inquilinos)* of the *patrón* who owned it. In mid-1965, when CORA officials visited the farm to determine whether to expropriate it, they reported that "there are no crops or even animals except about sixteen horses." There were twenty-six houses for the forty-five peasant families, all but four in a state of disrepair. A barn with a capacity for 150 to 200 cows was being used to house four families. Though CORA estimated the par value for tax purposes at US $15,200, the owner was awarded US $235,400 for the land, payable over twenty-five years at 4 percent interest, adjusted each year according to the cost of living. By June of 1966, the *inquilinos* voted into office a committee of five of their number who, together with two representatives of CORA, would manage the farm for the coming year. Each year this committee is reelected; within five years the land is to be individually distributed to member families or groups of families. The role of the CORA officials varies according to their personalities. On this particular farm the main CORA official was a young man in his late twenties, with agricultural training, who gave the committee leeway in managing their affairs but set aside demonstration plots to persuade them to try innovations.

Except for $2\frac{1}{2}$ acre garden plots surrounding each house, the *asentamiento* is farmed as a unit, with work assigned to each *asentado* on a daily basis. This was similar to the system under the former owner, except that the committee now carried out his functions. CORA provided 90 young heifers, 23 work animals, 155 male calves, fertilizer, machinery, and other goods which, after a grace period of three years, would be repaid over a period of thirty years with some interest adjusted according to inflation. CORA also provided about US $23,000 as interest-free advances for individual peasants, on the basis of the number of days worked by each, plus a total of about US $5,075 to use for family allowances for the forty-four peasant families on the *asentamiento.* At the end of 1967 each family received its share of the profits, minus advances; CORA took 15 percent for itself. In the future these profits would go to the social security administration, which would pay the families. Income was figured as the sum total of sales, inventory, changes, crops not yet harvested, and valuation of increased weight of animals. The November 1967 figures for this *asentamiento* were approximately (i.e., translated to U.S. dollars at an exchange of five escudos to one dollar) that shown in Table 7.1.

CORA's share in this case came to nearly what it estimated administrative expenses to be. It should be noted that the *asentamiento* was not yet repaying their indebtedness for the livestock and other goods borrowed from CORA (a total indebtedness of US $300,300) and CORA also was making the heavy land payments for the first three years after the title was conferred. The *asentamiento* used US $800 of its US $18,700 to repay CORA on its indebtedness and US

---

[26] Swift, *Agrarian Reform,* pp. 41–48.

TABLE 7.1
1967 Asentamiento Income

Income	US$152,500
Expenses	103,400
Profits	49,100
CORA's share (15 per cent)	7,400
Asentamiento share	41,700
Minus advances	23,000
To be distributed	18,700

$1,800 to purchase animals for individual members; the rest was distributed in cash to the forty-four members. When combined with income from garden plots and private animals, this gave each family an average annual income of about US $1,626. This compares with a rough estimate of US $1,108 for the 1965 income of *inquilinos* on traditional estates in two nearby provinces (the figure includes housing, grazing rights, land, and other payments in kind also received by the *asentados* but *not* included in their income estimate). Hence the *asentados* received a higher income than their neighbors. It must be noted, however, that they were not yet faced with the considerable burden of repaying CORA and the high purchase price of the land. And this was one of the most successful *asentamientos* studied by Professor Swift. Some others were making less profit than the advances paid to the peasants. In most cases, peasants simply consumed the advances and remained unclear when interviewed as to how the debt was to be repaid. For the time being, CORA let bad debts ride.

Because of poor data-gathering, little accurate data exist to allow for a comparison of production before and after *asentamientos*. From the meager information available, Professor Swift was unable to detect any noticeable production trends either up or down.[27] She noted that the fear of expropriation may have had some beneficial effect on productivity of the *latifundios* and that some more recently acquired farms were getting better production than those expropriated earlier. In Chile as a whole, production of barley, rice, corn, and green peas improved between 1964–1965 and 1966–1967, while corn production decreased. The rice increase was due to the output of one *asentamiento,* which had such high operating costs that its profits were highly negative. It is impossible to trace the source of the other increases.

The total cost of CORA's *asentamiento* program in 1966 amounted to some 0.4 percent of the total GNP of Chile.[28] By December 1967, 1,945,000 acres of land containing 8,252 families were included in *asentamientos;* 209,528 of these

---

[27] Ibid., pp. 61, 70. The CORA report referred to earlier, describing the poor conditions of the former estate, may well have been exaggerated to assist in the expropriation. Since the recommendation was also made to pay the former owner US$235,400 for land valued at US$15,200, there would have been little point in his contesting the report.

[28] Ibid., p. 103.

acres were irrigated.[29] By November 1970, those figures had grown to 8,184,917 acres, 275,940 irrigated, with 20,970 families.[30] Farms occupied an estimated 61,250,000 acres in all of Chile in 1967.[31] Hence the *asentamientos* occupied about an eighth of the farm land but contained little of the rural population and had an uncertain effect on agricultural productivity or rural well-being, while costing a considerable amount of money. A good deal of this money was going toward repaying the former owners of the land.

Late in 1970, Salvador Allende was elected President, and began to move Chile in a Marxist direction. During the first four months in office, his regime claimed to have expropriated 3,508,860 acres, 163,725 irrigated, for 6,382 families:[32] 1,810,000 of these consisted of a single sheep ranch expropriated in the south.[33] The land taken, as under the previous program, went to those already occupying the land, and hence would have little effect on the estimated 30 percent of the labor force who were still unemployed, or on two-thirds of the *campesinos* who are landless laborers or *minifundistas*.[34] Furthermore, the reform was not destined to proceed. Large landowners, fearful of Allende, seem to have driven several hundred thousand head of cattle across the border to Argentina. With political unrest and uncertainty in the countryside, an economic embargo by the United States, exhaustion of exchange reserves, and other difficulties, Chile soon experienced a meat shortage and a decline in agricultural activity. Government pressure upon *asentamientos* to absorb more labor was resisted.[35] Soon the large rural landowners combined with urban forces to oust Allende and institute a nonreformist military regime.

Until the 1960s, despite the fact that an urban majority had developed in Chile, a rural oligarchy tended to dominate Chilean politics. As the Christian Democratic Party rose to challenge this dominance, it was convenient for the party to support land reform as a means both of obtaining peasant adherents and weakening the political base of the landowners. But their support for land reform was fragile. The Christian Democrats derived their electoral strength largely from the urban working and middle classes. The working-class segments of the Communist and Socialist parties were principally interested in urban wages and workers' rights and had little contact with peasant segments of the parties. The radical wing of the Christian Democratic Party consisted largely of the lower middle class: primary school teachers, government bureaucrats, and white-collar employees.[36] Their primary interest was in issues like prices and wages; the nationalization of copper, transportation, and education; and

---

[29] Ibid., p. 64.

[30] James Petras, "The Transition to Socialism in Chile: Perspectives and Problems," *Monthly Review* (October 1971): 54.

[31] Swift, *Agrarian Reform*, p. 64.

[32] Petras, "Transition to Socialism," p. 54.

[33] Stanley Plastrik, "Chile: A Way to Socialism?" *Dissent* (December 1971): 546.

[34] Solon Barraclough, "Agrarian Reform and Structural Change in Latin America: The Chilean Case," *Journal of Development Studies* 8, no. 2 (January 1972): 170, 176.

[35] Dudley Seers, "Chile: Is the Road to Socialism Blocked?" *The World Today* (May 1972): 205.

[36] Robert R. Kaufman, *The Politics and Land Reform in Chile, 1950–1970: Public Policy, Political Institutions, and Social Change* (Cambridge: Harvard University Press, 1970), pp. 232–233.

changes in the social security system. The right wing of the Christian Democrats and the other parties to the right were generally unfriendly to land reform; they, too, had their clients among the middle classes and the workers.

The situation in the countryside was even more tenuous. Marxist politicians there generally derived from the urban middle classes. They established alliances with middle landholding peasants and derived support from a small coterie of landless peasants by performing patron-client functions for them like protesting a dismissal, obtaining payment of social security benefits, or securing a property title;[37] they contained many factions. As part of their land reform effort, the Christian Democrats created rural peasant unions that were meant to compete with leftist and Catholic organizations. Cleavages soon grew between the *inquilinos, asentados, minifundistas,* and landless workers in these organizations. *Inquilinos* fought among one another regarding whose petitions for expropriation would receive highest priority. *Asentados* resisted pressures by landless workers to incorporate them into their settlements. Some 31 percent of labor on the *asentamientos* was performed by landless workers;[38] yet they were given low wages, unsteady employment, and no share in profits, and few of them were employed. *Minifundistas* had nothing to gain from the reforms and could therefore not be expected to support them.

In the late 1960s, Chile was plagued with high inflation. Frei's strategy was to increase Chile's share of income from the country's principal export, copper, and to permit wage readjustments equal to price increases of the preceding year, combined with a matching tax increase. The higher taxes would be used for the land reform program and various industrial development and welfare programs; at the same time they would cut down the popular proclivity to spend money on nonessentials and thus help stabilize prices and eliminate trade deficits. The strategy worked from 1964 to 1967, partly because of an increase in world copper prices. Then copper prices leveled off, while domestic inflation rose sharply. The government responded with a proposed forced savings plan that would plow wage increases into a "fund for national development." The left wing offered to endorse this only if employers were to add contributions. Legislators to the right demanded a cut in government spending as the price for their support. As a result, the government proposed to cut the budget for land reform. Those on the left were angered by the unions sponsored around the *asentamientos* (which were competing with their own rural organizations), concerned about high taxes, and clamoring for more attention to urban welfare problems; most of them offered little resistance to this budget cut. The defense of the land reform budget largely came from the bureaucrats charged with administering it. They managed to get the cut reduced from 25 to 15 percent and to negotiate a US $20 million loan from the United States, which at that time was supporting land reform.

It is probable that the more radical Allende regime which replaced the Frei government in 1970 suffered from similar disabilities with regard to land reform. Between 1965 and 1967, the Frei government spent almost 100 million dollars on

---

[37] Ibid., p. 210–211.

[38] David Lehmann, "Political Incorporation vs. Political Stability: The Case of the Chilean Agrarian Reform 1965-70," *Journal of Development Studies* 7, no. 4 (July 1971): 380.

land reform, or US $12,500 for each family affected.[39] But despite the large expenditures the results in increased productivity and income for the participants were far from certain. The Allende government proposed to do far more. It could drastically reduce the main expense, land acquisition, by paying the landowners less. But runaway inflation would partly neutralize that gain. Allende's attempts to totally nationalize copper cut off American assistance and diminished income from copper. Meanwhile, urban workers wanted benefits. The Frei regime had been careful to pick on only a few landowners at a time, and to pay them well. Allende was challenging all landowners, and at the same time all big business, while doing nothing to ease the economic losses among the middle classes. This made it easy for their leadership to unite against him. Meanwhile he could unite neither peasants nor workers.

Chile's *asentamiento* program depended upon a heavy infusion of funding and a tight administrative organization, extended over time. The country's political climate made that unlikely. It also required a great deal of land per settler. Even if all $61\frac{1}{4}$ million acres were included in the program, there would not have been room for all 3 million of the rural population. This is because the reform program had changed ownership of the former *latifundios* without actually opening them to new settlers; the *asentados* themselves resisted such a policy initiative. CORA's administrators had never learned to transform landless peasants into successful farmers. Nor had it yet taught the *asentados* to farm without outside subsidies. Some 36.9 percent of the holdings continued to occupy 0.3 percent, or less, of the total farm land.

The military regime that overthrew Allende totally abandoned the land reform program. And, as of 1977, the annual inflation rate in food prices stood at 175 percent,[40] while increasing amounts of land were being used to grow food for export to the United States and other parts of Latin America.

> Further discussion of Chile may be found on p. 369.
> Discussion of Peru is continued from p. 257.

Peru

Chile's neighbor to the north, Peru, is plagued with the same problems. It has around 17 million people, about half of whom are in agriculture.[41] Its coastal plain contains only 1.6 million cultivated acres (along the mouths of small rivers as in pre-Inca days); yet over half the population—mostly of European extraction—lives there. Most of this land is irrigated; 80 percent of it lies within 920 *latifundios*.[42] The rest of the country is mountainous and inhabited by American

---

[39] Kaufman, *Politics and Land Reform*, p. 99.

[40] Food and Agriculture Organization, *State of Food and Agriculture 1978* (Rome: United Nations, 1979), p. A–45.

[41] Solon Barraclough, ed., *Agrarian Structure in Latin America: A Resumé of the CIDA Land Tenure Studies of Argentina, Brazil, Chile, Colombia, Ecuador, Guatemala, and Peru* (Lexington, Mass.: D. C. Heath, 1973), p. 252.

[42] *Idem.*, p. 254.

Indians. Here is where most of the nation's 46.5 million cultivated acres lie. Some 60 percent of this land has belonged to 181 proprietors.[43]

At least 700,000 families, 500,000 of them in the mountains, are landless.[44] Over 300,000 families are *minifundistas,* mostly on unirrigated plots under $2\frac{1}{2}$ acres; using current techniques, it takes about $16\frac{1}{2}$ *irrigated* acres to support a family in this dry terrain.[45] In addition, about 10 percent of rural families—not over 100,000—worked full-time on the *latifundios.* Our story concerns this latter group.

The mountain regions have the smallest yields, and the smallest yields per capita; yet they ship over half their yields to the coast.[46] Between 1959 and 1962, 77 percent of short-term loans, and 60 percent of all loans granted by the Agricultural Development Bank went into cotton and rice for export.[47] The government sold *guano* at subsidized rates, but half was used to fertilize cotton, rice, and sugar, mostly on coastal *latifundios.*[48] Meanwhile, between 1948 and 1963, the yield of potatoes, corn, barley, and cattle declined while sugar cane, cotton, and rice crops showed increases. Of the net agricultural income in 1959, 46 percent was destroyed by blight, disease, and poor storage; losses on smaller farms were proportionately greater.[49] The foreign exchange obtained from exporting the sugar, cotton, and rice crops was used to pay (premium prices) for imports of other agricultural products, including wheat, meat, fruit, and milk. In 1962, 72.3 percent of the wheat and 40 percent of the beef consumed in Peru were imported.[50]

Land reform attempts in Peru went back to the 1920s, and were largely the work of urban middle-class and business groups promoting commercialization of agriculture. They recognized that land reform could provide access to land for the more ambitious tenants and workers on the old *latifundios,* and for commercial interests who wished to modernize and expand production on those *latifundios.* It could also help quiet dissent from within the villages on whose land these estates infringed.

During the 1920s, the land reform program did little more than expropriate

---

[43] John Stephen Gitlitz, "Impressions of the Peruvian Agrarian Reform," *Journal of Inter-American Studies and World Affairs* 13, no. 3–4 (July-October 1971): 466.

[44] Colin Harding, "Land Reform and Social Conflict in Peru," in *The Peruvian Experiment: Continuity and Change Under Military Rule,* ed. Abraham F. Lowenthal (Princeton, N.J.: Princeton University Press, 1975), p. 237.

[45] Barraclough, *Agrarian Structure in Latin America,* p. 287.

[46] *Idem.,* p. 277.

[47] Solon L. Barraclough, "Agricultural Policy and Land Reform," *Journal of Political Economy* 78, no. 4:2 (July/August): 914: "One Peruvian *agronomo* reported that his technical courses focused on the large plantation crops—cotton, rice, and sugar—and that he graduated from the university without having been taught anything about corn and potatoes or having been told they were Peru's two leading crops."

[48] Barraclough, *Agrarian Structure in Latin America,* p. 278.

[49] Ibid.

[50] Barraclough, "Agricultural Policy," p. 906: "Agricultural production per head in Latin America has been some 10 percent below its pre-World War II level for the past two decades. . . While Latin America's agricultural exports are estimated to have increased by 16 percent since the 1930s, agricultural imports, mostly foodstuffs, have gone up by more than 80 percent in volume, with serious balance-of-payments consequences in many cases."

a few small abandoned *latifundios*. During the 1930s, APRA, a political party, pushed for more secure tenancy agreements. Its *Aprista* agitations caused unrest on estates where landlords (both traditional *latifundistas*, and more modern estates who wished to convert to mechanization and part-time wage labor) resisted these initiatives. In 1959, a government institute led by commercial estate landlords was set up to start land reform. They recommended creating small and middle-sized farms from the more traditional (they called them "feudal") *latifundios*. Commercialized estates were not to be touched. In 1964, an Agrarian Reform Law was promulgated to carry out this objective: those who were working the land on the feudal estates would be given those estates to modernize. Some 100,000 such tenants and full-time wage earners promptly seized their estates from absentee owners. They were initially backed in their agitation by part-time wage laborers. The national leader of those part-time laborers, Hugo Blanco, was arrested, and his followers were left landless.

In 1968, a group of reform-minded generals seized power, determined to end the agitation and to further shift power out of the hands of the traditional rural aristocracy. By the time it had been overthrown, the civilian regime had awarded 14,631 of the tenants and full-time laborers legal occupancy to 950,000 acres.[51] Special courts set up by the new military regime raised this to 28,000 families and 1,375,000 acres; many of these had, in fact, occupied this land for many years. The courts' actions finally removed the land claims of *latifundistas* who had moved to the city many years before, and were reaping little economic benefit from their land anyway. The new regime also removed the former regime's taboo on expropriating commercial estates by promptly expropriating eight of the fourteen largest sugar and cattle estates on the coast, where APRA was still heavily agitating.[52] Then they proceeded to expropriate other estates. The former landowners were paid cash plus bonds amortized over twenty years plus shares of stock in state industries; the bonds could be converted to cash if invested in new industrial plants. In this way, it was hoped, the landowners would be integrated within the urban-based leadership. The government also purchased or expropriated all banks (where many of the traditional *latifundistas* had investments), and outlawed APRA.

About half of the reformed estates were set up as production cooperatives.[53] They must pay the former owners for the land over a twenty-year period. They are governed by administrative councils, resonsible to the government, consisting of larger property owners from nearby villages, in addition to former full-time wage earners and tenants on the estates. Part-time wage earners are not represented. Land is held in common on most of the cooperatives; in the moun-

[51] James F. Petras and Robert La Porte, Jr., *Cultivating Revolution: the United States and Agrarian Reform in Latin America* (New York: Vintage, Random House, 1971), pp. 257, 293.

[52] The first expropriation was the Cerro de Pasco Corporation cattle ranches. In 1922, this copper mining firm opened a huge smelter. It emitted fumes of arsenic, lead, zinc, and hydrogen sulfide, which killed most of the plant life within a fifty-mile radius. Having rendered the land worthless, the company bought much of it at drastically reduced prices and turned it into a 70,000 acre cattle ranch (after then installing pollution control on the stacks). This was to be one of the only large inland acquisitions. Jeffrey M. Paige, *Agrarian Revolution: Social Movements and Export Agriculture in the Underdeveloped World* (New York: Free Press, 1975), p. 189.

[53] Alfred Stepan, *The State and Society: Peru in Comparative Perspective* (Princeton, N.J.: Princeton University Press, 1978), p. 223.

tains members are also allotted some private plots of land. If there is a profit it goes to those represented on the administrative council. Villagers would receive their share collectively for road repair and the like; in addition, they might sometimes be permitted to graze their cattle on estate land. The cooperatives had access to more irrigation water than the surrounding villages.

At the time of the expropriations many former landlords stripped their lands of livestock and equipment.[54] Full-time laborers were frequently declared part-time or dismissed so they would not share in the distribution. Sometimes owners parceled out the land among relatives, instead of letting it be turned into a cooperative. Such actions spurred intense agitation among peasants, who demanded faster expropriations and inclusion of more people in the new cooperatives. By the time the reform was completed in 1977, all farms of over 70 acres in the mountains and 120 acres on the plain had been distributed.[55] Some 80,000 workers had received about one-fourth of the $46\frac{1}{2}$ million acres in Peru devoted to agriculture (an average of about 135 acres per worker), plus an additional 3 million acres of pasture land. An additional 275,000 village families benefitted by no longer having to pay rent, and by having access to pasture land. So about 20 percent of the rural population benefitted.

There were problems, however. First of all, the reform had done nothing for the over 300,000 *minifundistas;* nor had it helped most of the landless. Employment was becoming even harder to find since the management committees wished to employ as little outside labor as possible in order to keep up profits. Furthermore, the new owners of the estates were increasingly dissatisfied.[56] There was no expansion of agricultural extension services.[57] Fertilizer was in short supply.[58] There were no improvements in irrigation. Both foreign investors and former landowners withdrew their money from the agricultural banks, so loans were difficult to obtain and tended to go to larger estates. The government, wishing to control urban food prices, paid the cooperatives low prices for food. This encouraged still further increases in export crop production, and food imports increased.[59] Between 1974 and 1977, the inflation rate on the price of food rose from 33 percent to 40 percent per annum.[60] And, whereas some of the

---

[54] E.g., Harding, "Land Reform and Social Conflict in Peru," p. 238n; Susan C. Bourque and David Scott Palmer, "Transforming the Rural Sector: Government Policy and Peasant Response," in Lowenthal, *The Peruvian Experiment,* p. 214.

[55] J. M. Caballero, *Agrarian Reform and the Transformation of the Peruvian Countryside,* Working Papers Series no. 29 (Cambridge: Centre of Latin American Studies, 1977).

[56] A public opinion poll administered in the same two cooperatives in 1969 and 1974: "Do you think that in general what the government does helps to improve the country?" In 1969, 33 to 50 percent said yes, while the rest gave qualified or negative responses; in 1974, the yes answers were 7 to 13 percent. Stepan, *The State and Society,* p. 308.

[57] Rosemary Thorp and Geoffrey Bertram, *Peru 1890-1977: Growth and Policy in an Open Economy* (London: Macmillan, 1978), p. 307.

[58] Between 1961 and 1976, fertilizer use grew from 94,000 tons to 129,000 tons a year in Peru; in the same time it grew from 224,000 to 2,371,000 tons in Brazil. In Chile it grew from 95,000 to 158,000 tons under Allende, and then dropped to 116,000 by 1976. Food and Agriculture Organization, *The State of Food and Agriculture 1978* (Rome: United Nations, 1979), pp. 2-38.

[59] Until 1971, the government encouraged transfer of coastal lands from export crops to food. It reversed this policy for reasons you will see in the next chapter. Thorp and Bertram, *Peru 1890-1977,* p. 315.

[60] FAO, *State of Food and Agriculture,* pp. A-45, A-11.

workers in the plains had been able to own their own cattle, or cultivate their own plot of land under the old system, they were now expected to simply cultivate and tend the collective fields and herds, the economic benefit of which was uncertain. This also put them into tension with the wealthier villagers whose cattle were allowed to graze on the estates.[61]

Before the reform, .00025 percent of Peru's population owned the *latifundios;* now some 3 percent of the populace owned them. One-third to one-half of these new owners, who got in on the program early, had received individual plots of land. Unable to obtain fertilizer, agricultural extension, access to irrigation, bank loans, or high market prices, their temptation to sell their land might be great. The remaining 50,000 families are receiving salaries at least two or three times what they were before, and perhaps some new services like schools and medical care. They finally have secure tenancy. Many of them cannot tend private plots or their own cattle. Surrounding villages may be sharing in some fringe benefits like schools and roads, and some in some places still have grazing access for their cattle on estates. Meanwhile, at least 300,000 families are trying to farm plots of less than $2\frac{1}{2}$ acres, and at least 600,000 other families are still landless and largely unemployed. No new programs serve these latter groups. Yet the inland regions of Peru still contain 54 million unused arable acres,[62] enough to supply *every* Peruvian family, rural and urban, with fifteen acres.

Despite a major effort by dedicated reformers, the fall from power of whom we shall examine in the next chapter, Peru has achieved little redistribution of land or personal income,[63] and still remains heavily dependent on food imports.

Further discussion of Peru may be found on p. 370.
Discussion of Iran is continued from p. 237.

Iran

By the rules of the numbers game, the most successful land reform would appear to be the program instituted by the Shah of Iran. At the beginning of the program around 1951, about 70 percent of the fertile land in Iran was owned by a few landowners.[64] By 1966 land had been redistributed to about 520,000 families in 14,000 villages. A second phase was initiated in which land was no longer to be expropriated; instead, landowners were called upon to sell their land to peasants; to give them a percentage of the land they tilled, based on the percentage of the crop they had formerly received in kind; or else to write clear tenancy agreements that spelled out the tenant's tenure and responsibilities and the owner's obligations in clear and fair terms. According to official sources, 3,238 landlords sold

[61] Stepan, *The State and Society,* pp. 306–307.

[62] Barraclough, *Agrarian Structure in Latin America,* p. 277.

[63] I. Adelman and C. T. Morris, *Economic Growth and Social Equity in Developing Countries* (Stanford, Calif.: Stanford University Press, 1973), p. 247, found the richest 5 percent receiving 48.3 percent of income, while the poorest 40 percent received 8.8 percent.

[64] Julian Bharier, *Economic Development in Iran 1900–1970* (New York: Oxford University Press, 1971), p. 136.

land to 46,000 families;[65] 153,000 tenants were given a percentage distribution of land; and 203,049 landlords wrote tenancy agreements with over a million peasant families. This program ended in January 1967. In 1960, the FAO estimated Iran's rural population at 15.4 million; hence, a high percentage of the total population was affected by the land reform program. About 15 percent of them had actually become landowners.[66]

The Shah initiated the program in an attempt to neutralize the power of the rural land-owning aristocracy and to diminish communist political organizations, especially in the north where much of the program was activated. This has been discussed in previous chapters. As the Shah gradually succeeded in this objective and began to form a political movement composed of the new landowners, urban middle-class elements, and the armed forces, the impetus behind the program slowed. The most committed personalities were dismissed from the program; efforts were made to stabilize the position of the new clients who had emerged from the program. The recipients from the last phase received very little. The percentage distribution for the 153,000 former tenants was in most cases such a small parcel of land as to provide only a garden plot to back up other forms of employment the new owner would need to seek. There was little left of an aggressive bureaucratic apparatus to insure that the tenancy agreements would be respected. Nonetheless, that over 600,000 families in about one-fourth of Iran's 60,000 villages received parcels of land at least approaching sustenance size is no small achievement.

It is important to note who received land and who did not. Before land reform, villages were either owned by one man or divided among a handful of men who were usually absentee landlords. Each absentee owner had an agent in the community who would rent the land to several nonlaboring renters. Laborers who owned a pair of oxen would vie for favor with the village headman and these renters to become the heads of work teams. Each work team was assigned a parcel of land, often by lot; four or so years later a new lot would be drawn and new parcels assigned. The work teams were composed of workers with varying degrees of status, ranging from those with some cattle to those who would simply sign on as day laborers.

The land reforms largely eliminated the absentee landlords from the politics of the village. The land was distributed principally to village agents, renters, heads of the work teams, and higher status members of those teams. This left a great many people, probably around ten million, with no land or less than ten acres of poor land.[67] Fifteen acres is the normal minimum needed for family subsistence in Iran. Later laws permitted the biggest land recipients to buy land from those who received less land and thus further increased the program's disparities. The method of implementation permitted the former landowners to keep 75 to 375 acres of the best land around each village for themselves and often to control water resources that were potentially a more lucrative source of income and power than land.

---

[65] Nikki R. Keddie, "The Iranian Village Before and After Land Reform," *Journal of Contemporary History* 3, no. 3 (July 1968): 87.

[66] Ibid., p. 87.

[67] Ibid., p. 79.

Furthermore, under the old system of assigning by lot a family which had received a poorer plot of land could hope for a better one on the next drawing. Families with and without land could use the communal land around the village for grazing. But this land was not redistributed in the reform program and the chances for villagers to use it might be jeopardized by the fact that the former landowners were no longer chief patrons in the community. There is definitely an advantage in the fact that the peasants no longer have to give large gifts to the landlords; they still need to devote a percentage of their yield to paying the former landlords for the land. There is disadvantage to the peasant in that landlords who were formerly obligated to provide their peasants with seed, fertilizer, and water no longer are. The former landlords are receiving payments for water, in addition to purchase payments for the land, and have been given opportunities to participate in Teheran's commerce. All recipients of land are required to join cooperatives, which often fall into the control of wealthier members of the community. The cooperative regulations permit much larger loans by the cooperative to those who contribute larger shares to it;[68] hence, the fairly large loans extended to cooperatives by the Agricultural Bank may have gone principally to the larger landowners. Those larger and middle-range peasants who received loans could in turn become moneylenders to smaller peasants at high interest rates and thus induce dependency. They could even use the money to buy out smaller peasants. Whereas the former owners of entire villages, in the interest of harmony, were probably interested in distributing favors to all segments of the populace, the high percentage of each village who are still landless or poorly landed may have little protection against subjection by the middle peasantry and bureaucrats whose powers increased with the reforms.

It is questionable how much the Iranian land reform succeeded in breaking the power of the older landowners. It strengthened a minor network of bureaucrats, entrepreneurs, and middle landowners. It did not provide a basis for raising the living standards or productivity of the peasantry. Many of the new land recipients seem to have sold out to large landowners or the Shah Pahlevi Foundation; it may have owned about one-fifth of the cultivated land when the Shah left Iran in 1979.[69] The Shah's family, the multinationals with whom his family and associates did business, and those whose landholdings were increased by the reforms were able to enhance their power vis-a-vis other members of the major and minor network. For example, their supermarkets diverted business away from merchants in the Teheran bazaar, their imports competed with local manufactures, and they were in a position to control many exports. This left many merchants, businessmen, religious leaders, and former landowners angry. Many displaced rural dwellers moved to Teheran to create raw materials for the mobs who would later oppose the Shah.

Further discussion of Iran may be found on p. 341.
Discussion of Morocco is continued from p. 147.

[68] Ibid., p. 85.

[69] John Shaw, "The Vanishing US$20 Billion," *Far Eastern Economic Review* 108, no. 14 (April 4, 1980): 34.

Morocco

One of the principal failures of the Iranian reform was the lack of a follow-up program to provide the peasantry with seed, water, fertilizer, and technical and marketing assistance. Morocco's reform efforts have focused more on this realm than on land redistribution. Between 1945 and 1957, the *Paysanat Scheme* selected 137,000 acres for an intensive concentration. Here social overhead capital was spent on schools, clinics, and the like. For a nominal charge, farmers could receive assistance in plowing and harrowing. Credit assistance and agricultural extension services were available.

In 1957, *Operation Plow* commenced. A thousand tractors were purchased and spread around among work centers, which were administered by local committees. Farmers participated on a voluntary basis. They had to agree to plant wheat, maize, beans, and peas on their best soils, while leaving the poorer soils for wheat, barley, and fallow. They were to use improved seed and chemical fertilizers. Tractors from the center plowed and disked. Fertilizing, sowing, plowing under seed, harrowing, and harvesting were up to the peasant. First-year costs for plowing and disking were payable over a two-year period; fetilizer was provided at cost price. Yields were reviewed each year; farmers with better yields were then charged a bit more for the services so that those with poorer yields could be charged less. The program was tried mostly in regions with fairly steady rainfall.[70]

Yield increases were significant on those farms where everything went smoothly. Yet these farmers did not see any immediate net profits because their costs were up. Bad weather, the wrong choice of plowing depths, fraud in seed distribution, a tendency for some farmers to sell the fertilizer on the open market for the higher prices and to skip harrowing, and the use of the wrong fertilizer (readily-available phosphate was used, yet nitrogen was needed) caused crops to fail on many other farms. When the payment schemes were made progressive to cover these failures, many of the more successful farmers withdrew from the program. Supporters in the government had hoped the scheme would pay its own way; it did not. By 1961, interest had been lost both in government and among farmers. The program faded away.

Indonesia

Discussion of Java is continued from p. 77.

When the Suharto government came to power in 1966, 60 percent of Java's irrigation canals (discussed in Chapter 3) were so badly silted as to be operating at half their capacity.[71] Deforestation was removing watersheds. Money formerly used to improve irrigation had been spent on schools and mosques. The district

---

[70] Herman J. Van Wersch, "Rural Development in Morocco; Operation Labor," *Economic Development and Cultural Change* 17, no. 1 (October 1968): 36–45.

[71] Gary E. Hansen, "Rural Administration and Agricultural Development in Indonesia," *Pacific Affairs* 44, no. 3 (Fall 1971): 392, 393.

irrigation committees had for the most part ceased functioning and tertiary canals had frequently been plowed under into the fields. Villages near a canal would take all the water during the dry season, leaving little for the other villages.

The World Bank supplied money to repair this canal network. A January 1969 decree revived the district irrigation committees and empowered provincial governments to levy a tax on peasants for canal maintenance.[72]

In 1968, the Indonesian Government also hired the Swiss pharmaceutical firm CIBA to saturate 750,000 acres with improved seed, fertilizer, and pesticides. CIBA subcontracted part of the work to Hoechst, AHT, Mitsubishi, and a mysterious company named Coopa, which later proved to be a front for transferring funds to members of President Suharto's personal staff.[73]

The peasants would repay with one-sixth of their yield.[74] The firms acted in concert with the indigenous bureaucracy, giving each farmer the same amount of fertilizer and pesticide per acre. To be certain that these elements were applied, the fertilizer was to be transported directly to the field and the pesticide sprayed from airplanes.

The irrigation program soon hit a snag. The approach of the July 1971 elections made the government hesitant to levy the new tax. There was also a fear that enforcement of the new tax would mean a decline in payment of debts peasants already owed on a former unsuccessful rice program, and that would translate into a decline in other categories of revenue. Some of the money given by the World Bank had already been used for other purposes by the military and civilian bureaucracy.[75]

The Department of Agriculture extends to the subdistrict level, where the one or two officers are so poorly paid they are lucky to have a bicycle. There are three or four villages and several hundred peasants in each subdistrict for these one or two officers to supervise on foot or by bicycle. In contrast, at higher levels the bureaucracy tends to be overstaffed; these officers often seem not to like to serve in rural areas and use their influence to avoid such assignments. Under this program the companies had only five to ten representatives in each *province*. Meanwhile there was great peasant resistance to being forced into a new program for which they would have to pay.[76]

The aerial spraying was applied when planes were available, over large areas of land within which peasants exhibited great variability in their periods of planting. No regard was shown for crop and planting variables. As a result, the spray was frequently applied at the wrong time and had a negligible impact upon pest control. Fish were poisoned and there were other ecological problems.[77] The

[72] Ibid., p. 393.

[73] Richard W. Franke, "Miracle Seeds and Shattered Dreams in Java," *Natural History* 83, no. 1 (January 1974): 86.

[74] Gary E. Hansen, "Indonesia's Green Revolution: The Abandonment of a Non-Market Strategy Toward Change," *Asian Survey* 12, no. 11 (November 1972): 937.

[75] Hansen, "Rural Administration," p. 393.

[76] Hansen, "Indonesia's Green Revolution," p. 939.

[77] Ibid., p. 941.

miracle rice proved especially vulnerable to certain Indonesian pests. It was not considered tasty by Indonesians, and hence brought less at the marketplace than conventional rice (e.g., 1,100 rupiahs per quintal versus 1,800 for conventional). Market fertilizer was priced lower than government fertilizer so people therefore preferred to get it on the open market. The understaffed subdistrict offices were having difficulty collecting the repayments. Peasants lied about their yield, or failed to pay altogether. By August 1969, rice repayments were falling 35 to 90 percent below projections. To remedy the problems of judging yields, the government turned in September to charging fixed payments for the services. Worst of all, even in the best agricultural areas, harvests had fallen from $2\frac{1}{2}$ tons per acre in 1965 to 2 tons in 1968–69, and a major famine hit Java's north coast.[78] A groundswell of resistance grew. Local parliaments, political parties, and the press joined in opposition.

Hence this program, involving the foreign firms, was scrapped and a new program devised. Aerial spraying was discontinued. The peasant would select the amount of seed and fertilizer he needed, within a certain range. He could choose some new Indonesian-developed strains of seed. Village banks would be established to dispense low-cost credit.[79] The government-owned Indonesian People's Bank established village units in villages involving 82,000 acres and enlarged its fleet of mobile units which could move from village to village. Wealthy landowners who did not wish the peasants to find alternate sources of credit and wanted the money themselves kept the notices about the bank loans within family circles and saw to it that local meetings to publicize the loans were never called. This would also permit them to increase their holdings by foreclosing on those in debt, and buying up land.[80]

Before 1970, a government firm had a virtual monopoly on fertilizer, but no sales organization. In May of 1970, the market was opened to private competitors but with no safeguards to prevent them from carving out territories for themselves. The government floor price on rice was raised, with the Bureau of Logistics placed in charge of making purchases from traders and millers to maintain this price level. There was no agency established to record prices at the village level and hence insure that the peasant benefits from the program.[81] Several instances soon occurred where the provincial governors tried to avoid complying with instructions from the central government concerning the regulation of rice prices. All this provides extra incentives for bureaucrats to remain at middle echelons, where most of the manipulation takes place; the one to two subdistrict officers, with or without bicycle, remain the link at the village level. Java, with a population of over 70 million, has only about 1,600 agricultural extension officers.[82]

[78] Franke, "Miracle Seeds," p. 86.

[79] Hansen, "Indonesia's Green Revolution," pp. 943–946.

[80] Franke, "Miracle Seeds."

[81] Economic Research Service, United States Department of Agriculture, *The World Food Situation and Prospects to 1985,* Foreign Agricultural Economic Report No. 98, Washington, D.C. (December 1974): 30, reports that Indonesian, Thai, and Burmese farmers receive less for their rice than farmers in other countries.

[82] Hansen, "Rural Administration," p. 395.

SPECIFIC EXAMPLE

Richard W. Franke[83] gives an indication of what agricultural extension could do. In 1963, a group of twelve student radicals moved to three villages near the College of Agriculture where they were studying, worked in the fields, offered suggestions, and interceded with local government and private institutions on the peasants' behalf. Without miracle seeds, yields rose from 1,984 to 2,866 pounds per acre.

At the outset of the 1968 program, the most frequent peasant complaints were a lack of instruction from extension services, problems in procuring fertilizers and pesticides in time for planting, annoyance with fixed payments for services whether the crop was good or not, successful demands for increased payments by corrupt officials, and low market prices.[84] I wonder whether the new program has diminished any of these problems.

As of 1960, average consumption of protein per person was at 1.34 ounces per day per person; by 1967 this had fallen to 1.17. By 1972, after the expenditure of US$100 million on rural development, the figure was even lower.[85]

Beginning in 1972, landowners throughout Java devised a new way to avoid their obligations both to the government and to landless laborers in their villages—*tebasan*.[86] Prior to this it had been the custom at harvest time to allow any villagers who wished to assist in the harvest to do so, using a small finger knife which cut one stalk at a time. In a half hour, 200 people could harvest an acre of land; each would retain a percentage. When sickles were introduced in the 1930s, they were bitterly resisted because they cut many stalks in one swipe and thus reduced the number of people who could share in the harvest. Now, with *tebasan*, the crop is sold to a merchant the week before harvest. The merchant brings in a few workers with sickles, who turn in all the rice to the merchant and get paid in money. The landless villagers are left out. And the government is left out unless it can work a deal with the merchants.

Ethiopia

Ethiopia contains 5 million Amhara people. The Amhara social hierarchy relegates low caste artisans to positions of tenancy. The elites have large estates called *gult*. They divide these estates, giving each person in the middle of the social hierarchy a share of land, called *rist*. *Rist* holders pay taxes to the elite and accept their judicial and administrative authority.[87] Both *gult* and *rist* holders support the local churches. Nearly all the land in Amhara areas is under this system.

---

[83] Franke, "Miracle Seeds," p. 18.

[84] Hansen, "Indonesia's Green Revolution," p. 936.

[85] Franke, "Miracle Seeds," pp. 11-12. The minimum daily requirement is 1.94 ounces.

[86] William L. Collier, Soentoro, Gunawan Wirodi, and Mikali, "Agricultural Technology and Institutional Change in Java," *Food Research Institute Studies* 13, no. 2 (1974): 169-194.

[87] Allan Hoben, "Social Anthropology and Development Planning—A Case Study in Ethiopian Land Reform Policy," *Journal of Modern African Studies* 10, no. 4 (December 1972): 561-582.

In 1966, Ethiopia established a Ministry of Land Reform and Administration. Its plan of action was to produce cadastral survey maps and individually register land titles that could then be used by the owner as collateral for credit or to sell the land. This would, the government felt, provide capital to improve production. It would also end the inequities of the caste system; lower caste people would be entitled to own land, and middle caste people would no longer be subject to the higher castes.

When Allan Hoben went into this region, he soon discovered a number of anomalies. While men spoke with fervor about their hereditary *rist* and their willingness to fight and die for it, they could not tell you where their ancestors lived or how they came to own the land. Many of the largest landowners were born of humble parents. There was frequent litigation over rights to particular plots. Almost half the fields in the community had been obtained from people who were not even relatives. None of this matched the government's impressions of the meaning of *rist*. Hence Hoben spent some months producing the first written explanation of this landholding system. It does not differ greatly from Trobriand *pokala* or a great many village distribution systems discussed in Chapter 2.

A corporation's land covers $\frac{1}{2}$ to $1\frac{1}{2}$ square miles and bears the name of its first holder (a titled noble, famed warrior, or priest); this is the *rist*. Most members of the corporation do not even recognize one another as kin, although they all claim to be related to the first holder; their only common obligation is the payment of taxes. Each member of the corporation occupies a strip of the corporation's land. They may have obtained it from a parent, by litigation, by clearing it, or even through tenancy. Their ultimate claim to the land is that the officers of the corporation have recognized them rather than someone else as the rightful occupants. In practice, each *rist* is usually divided into several segments, with a segment officer making the final decision about who gets what land. The average person owns a strip of land in each of two or three different corporations; an influential leader, in four or five; and a leading regional politician in twenty or thirty. Several contiguous corporate *rists* form a *gult*.

Most farming households cultivate two or three fields, each averaging three acres. One household in four has eighteen acres; one in seven, thirty acres, and one in fifty, over forty-five. Only artisans, who produce various wares, are landless. A young man usually gets land through inheritance or pre-inheritance gifts. Later, if he has initiative, he may accumulate more, using his wife's pedigree or his leadership talents. Elders and officeholders usually claim more land on the basis of their position. No matter how many children a man has, all have a claim on land. If all land in a corporation or region is full, one can move on to another. One's relations with one's neighbors govern access to land. Giving the peasant different fields, spatially separate and of differing qualities, helps him diversify crops and avoid total crop failure; it also provides work for the entire family. Most of the peasants Hoben interviewed were not using their land to full capacity; they blamed low market prices. All were raising basic foodstuffs.

In 1968, when the government tried to introduce the cadastral-based freeholding system, there was armed rebellion in the village Hoben studied. This system would have frozen ownership to individual plots of land. A peasant could not switch plots without selling the old one and buying a new one; those with larger plots and more cash would be in a better position to buy. Children could inherit only the property their parents owned. Each farmer would have no control over land use of adjoining plots. Regional politicians would not be dependent on the good will of their neighbors to keep their positions. There would no top limit on the amount of land any one person could own. There would no longer be any incentive for community cooperation. I wonder whether the new system would equalize rural incomes and increase the food supply.

India and Pakistan

Discussion of India is continued from p. 251.

India, with its 650 million people, is frequently viewed as the kingpin in the "Green Revolution." Between 1966 and 1973, the number of acres planted there in Mexican "miracle" wheat rose from 7,400 to 25,295,200. Acreage in Taiwan and Philippine rice rose from 150 to 21,347,200.[88] Since 1951, India has increased its area under cultivation by 20 percent, doubled its irrigated area (to 70 million acres), and increased fertilizer use thirty-fold. According to some Indian government sources, rice, corn, and wheat harvests rose 105, 265, and 340 percent respectively, up from 72 to 118 million tons.[89]

In addition, between 1951 and 1974, the population of India grew from 380 million to 580 million. Food imports declined in that period by 60 percent,[90] and had declined even further by 1978; many of these had been furnished free by the United States. The increase in grain production was accompanied by a critical reduction in acreage devoted to high-protein legumes. In the interim, India became the world's largest exporter of nutritionally-rich peanut cake (supplying 42 percent of the total world trade, primarily to western Europe) and a heavy exporter of copra and milk products. So the supply of protein may be more tenuous than before.

While average per capita income rose 1.8 percent,[91] the poor rural sectors did not share equally in this gain. From 1961 to 1971, the number of day laborers rose by 20 million while the number of tenants declined by 15 million.[92] Meanwhile the cost of food rose at a much greater rate (300 to 400 percent from 1971 to 1974 for cereal grains), and the average Indian spends 60 to 90 percent of his income on food.[93] One researcher reports that an average Indian family needs

---

[88] Harry W. Blair, "The Green Revolution and 'Economic Man': Some Lessons for Community Development in South Asia," *Pacific Affairs* 44, no. 3 (Fall 1971): 355. Dana G. Dalrymple, "The Green Revolution: Past and Prospects," USDA Source Paper, Washington, D.C., July 22, 1974 (mimeo), p. 4.

[89] Roger Revelle, "Food and Population," *Scientific American* 231, no. 3 (September 1974): 163. Other figures, given later in this chapter, place the total yields from *all* grains at 110 million tons. I use those more conservative figures there.

[90] Ibid., p. 170.

[91] Ibid., p. 164.

[92] Lappé and Collins, *Food First,* p. 129.

[93] Revelle, "Food and Population," p. 163.

US$4 to US$5 a month for an adequate diet, and 60 percent fall below this line.[94] Obviously the problem of poor food distribution remains pressing, and land distribution may be more inequitable than ever. Land reform measures passed during the 1950s and varying from state to state call for greater security of tenancy (with fixed fair rents and first option on purchasing land), the abolition of intermediaries in the collection of rent, a ceiling on holdings, and distribution of surplus land. Studies during the mid-1960s in about a dozen Indian states show widespread ploys to circumvent the reforms.[95] Tenants can be asked to voluntarily surrender land after a year or so to prevent them from claiming rights to it.[96] A landholder can farm the land using day laborers, who are not generally covered by the tenancy laws, and pay them one-sixth to one-eighth of the gross produce (versus one-half paid to tenants) without any danger that they will claim land rights.[97] To further bolster his position under such circumstances, the landholder can report that he is tilling his own land.[98] The laws generally cover only rent paid in crops; hence, cash rent is becoming more popular. The law says only one-third of the crop may be charged as rent, while the going rate is one-half; to obtain enforcement, the peasant would have to complain, often to authorities on good terms with his landlord, and endanger his continuance as tenant.[99] As a result, tenants are often more insecure than they were before, continue to pay more than the maximum legal rent, and feel their relations with the landowners are no longer cordial.

The new miracle wheat program is concentrated in the Punjab and Uttar Pradesh. To avoid spreading scarce resources too thinly, 48 percent of the "miracle" wheat was concentrated in two states and 40 percent of the "miracle" rice in two others where conditions were most suitable. These grains require a constant water supply (meaning irrigation) and fertilizers rich in nitrogen; otherwise they do not produce superior yields. They are also highly susceptible to disease and require insecticides. The average farm needs an initial investment of US$1,000-$2,500 to adapt for optimal growth of these grains.[100] It is customary for tenants to pay the costs of production; fertilizer, water, and pesticides are production costs. It is generally only the larger farmers who can obtain loans of this magnitude. This increases the tendency for farms using the miracle grains to turn to the day laborer alternative.[101] The government subsidized mechanization on even middle-sized farms, and mechanized farmers tended to evict tenants and

[94] Alan Berg, *The Nutrition Factor: Its Role in National Development* (Washington, D.C.: The Brookings Institution, 1973), p. 43.

[95] J. S. Uppal, "Implementation of Land Reform Legislation in India—A Study of Two Villages in Punjab," *Asian Survey* 9, no. 5 (May 1969): 360-361.

[96] Ibid., p. 368.

[97] Ibid., p. 367.

[98] A similar law passed in 1872 brought similar ploys. Elizabeth Whitcombe, *Agrarian Conditions in Northern India: Vol. 1, The United Provinces Under British Rule, 1860-1900* (Berkeley: University of California Press, 1972), pp. 144, 159.

[99] Uppal, "Implementation of Land Reform Legislation," pp. 369-370.

[100] Francine R. Frankel, "India's New Strategy of Agricultural Development: Political Costs of Agrarian Modernization," *Journal of Asian Studies* 28, no. 4 (August 1969): 698.

[101] Ibid., p. 706.

to buy out smaller landowners so as to expand the size of fields.[102] Even so, the raise in average wheat yields from below 700 pounds per acre on land growing ordinary wheat in 1961 to around 1,400 pounds per acre on land growing "miracle" wheat in 1974[103] was below the United Kingdom's average of 3,500 pounds.[104] Once the wheat is sold on the private market, it can be hoarded—often in poor facilities where much rotting takes place—or is sold locally while neighboring states are suffering from starvation conditions. Meanwhile cooperatives are often short of agents to collect on loans and less than 10 percent of all loans advanced by credit cooperatives in 1965 and 1966 were recovered.[105] These programs have not led to major advances in the distribution of food, land, or income.

COMMENT

Notice how this ties in with Thomas Headrick's case study on p. 250 and the discussion about elite control of *panchayats* and cooperatives on p. 118.

A look at an earlier period of Indian history gives another dimension on what is happening. Prior to the arrival of the British, irrigation was carried out using bullocks and well lifts. The bullocks could only raise enough water for $1\frac{1}{2}$ acres per well and could hardly affect the overall water table. Along with the private land ownership discussed in Chapter 3, the British introduced a series of grand public works. The first irrigation canal was built in 1820. By the 1880s, the canals had irrigated 8 million acres of land.[106] The millets and pulses on which much of the populace depended for food were not well adapted to irrigation. Instead, much of the irrigated land was used to grow wheat, sugar cane, cotton, indigo, tobacco, and opium.[107] Due to the financial pressures discussed in Chapter 3, a tendency to overcrop these lands brought a rapid diminishing in fertility, often within two to three years. Much land was once covered with lush forests; these were chopped down to build railroads and plant crops. The increase in evaporation caused capillary action to raise salts from substrata of the soil and further lowered soil fertility; water soaking through the bottoms of the irrigation canals saturated subsurface areas and helped push up the salt, as did the rapid evaporation caused by flooding fields with insufficient water to fully soak the surface soil.[108] Because the government's second greatest source of revenue was

---

[102] Francine R. Frankel, "The Politics of the Green Revolution: Shifting Patterns of Peasant Participation in India and Pakistan," in *Food, Population, and Employment—The Impact of the Green Revolution,* ed. Thomas T. Poleman and Donald K. Freebairn (New York: Praeger, 1973), pp. 132–133.

[103] Dalrymple, "The Green Revolution," pp. 23, 27.

[104] David Grigg, *The Harsh Lands: A Study in Agricultural Development* (New York: Macmillan, 1970), p. 257.

[105] Frankel, "India's New Strategy," p. 700.

[106] Whitcombe, *Agrarian Conditions in Northern India,* p. 2.

[107] Ibid., pp. 8–12.

[108] According to an 1876 government commission report: ". . . the whole surface-soil is brought into the condition of sun-dried bricks; the more water that is applied to the land, the harder the soil

from the sale of table salt, it would not even let this be converted into nitrate of potash and nitrate of soda for fertilizer for fear that table salt would be produced surreptitiously on the side. (Today the hesitancy to convert the salts to fertilizers relates more to keeping the nation dependent on petrochemicals for fertilizer.) The deforestation removed firewood; hence, dung, which had been used for fertilizer, was increasingly needed for fuel. The water table dropped due to the decrease in ground cover and the increase in evaporation. It became increasingly necessary to have irrigation in order to grow crops. Roads and railroads often cut off drainage of unirrigated fields and caused them to swamp during rainy seasons, destroying their crops and spreading malaria. No government inquiry was begun until 1877 (a Department of Agriculture to look into such matters was not established until 1874, with a staff of two European officers for all of India). The first agricultural chemist to explore the problem, in 1891, found 4,000 to 5,000 square miles significantly affected. This report gained little official recognition.

The increased acreage of these export crops (even wheat started to be exported after 1870) was at the expense of acreage in peas, millets, sorghum, and other native grains.[109] An 1878 government report indicated that wheat is

> . . . not the food of the masses. They live either on the millets of the autumn crops or the coarse mixed grains (barley, gram, and peas) of the spring harvest. The urban population undoubtedly did consume a large proportion of wheat for their numbers and the richer proprietors or tradesmen in the villages also use wheaten flour. But to the millions wheaten flour is a luxury, untasted perhaps from birth to death or only at high festivals and holidays.[110]

During droughts, only the irrigated fields yielded. An 1877 writer reports the "melancholy sight to see acre upon acre of magnificent indigo and sugarcane, while hardly a blade of any food crop was to be seen."[111] Meanwhile those growing millets and sorghums would lose their crops and the wheat on the irrigated fields could be hoarded and sold at high prices. Even sorghum and millet could be sold at high prices to the landless.[112] To compound the problem, the peasant was often sold inferior seed by the traders, insuring that the next crop would also be bad.[113] Furthermore, the British imported manufactures which brought a sharp decline in the Indian clothmaking and other industries. So there were few jobs to which to turn if one was forced from the land. And between 1900 and 1950, *per capita* food production would decline 42 percent.[114] All of these prob-

---

becomes, and while its powers of absorption and radiation are reduced, those of reflection and retention of heat are increased . . . capillary attraction . . . is increased." Whitcombe, *Agrarian Conditions in Northern India*, p. 89.

[109] Ibid., p. 190.

[110] Ibid., p. 73.

[111] Ibid., p. 74.

[112] Ibid., p. 190.

[113] Surgit S. Sidhu, "Economies of Technical Change in Wheat Production in the India Punjab," *American Journal of Agricultural Economics* (May 1974): 22, reports noting "mixing of lower quality seed with better seed at more than one level of distribution" since 1968.

[114] K. Mukerji, *Levels of Economic Activity and Public Expenditure in India* (Bombay: Asia Publishing House, 1965).

lems continue today. They contradict Sir John and Richard Strachey's conclusion about the remarkable expansion of public works:

> . . . it is not the least remarkable part of the story that the accomplishment of
> all this work, and the expenditure of all this money, which have increased to an
> extent absolutely incalculable the wealth and comfort of the people of India,
> have added nothing to the burden of taxation.[115]

Further discussion of India may be found on p. 324.
Discussion of Pakistan is continued from p. 126.

When Ali Bhutto became President of Pakistan on December 20, 1971, in
the wake of the loss of Bangladesh, he decided to make a frontal attack on the
rural landlords who had supported the former military regime. Within three
years he had expropriated 2,352,716 acres from some 600 landowners and
distributed 1,600,000 of these to 200,000 persons, including 150,000 former
tenants.[116] Pakistan has about 67 million inhabitants, 80 percent of whom are involved in agriculture.

Of the expropriated acres 1,067,690 were in the desert regions to the north-
west,[117] which contain 16 percent of the population.[118] In the most intensively irrigated section of the country, the Punjab (which together with the Frontier
Provinces contains 51.8 percent of the population), only 211,000 acres had been
expropriated as of February 1973 and only 40 percent of this distributed. Hence,
the small amount of land distributed was probably not even of the best quality
nor were the parcels likely to have been very equal in size.

In Dadu District of the Sind, where statistics are available, over 100,000
peasant families are landless.[119] The government planned to expropriate 7,800
acres here, much of it wasteland, and distribute it to 488 peasants.

COMMENT

Bhutto nationalized shipping lines, oil distribution companies, and the
country's fifteen domestic banks, too. He developed a popular following.
In July 1977, he was overthrown by the Pakistani army, and in 1978 was
condemned to death for treason in connection with some executions he had
ordered during his regime. Despite pleas on his behalf from world leaders
he was put to death.

---

[115] Sir John and Richard Strachey, *The Finances and Public Works of India, 1882*, p. 8. Quoted in
Whitcombe, *Agrarian Conditions in Northern India*, p. 2.

[116] Bruce J. Esposito, "The Politics of Agrarian Reform in Pakistan," *Asian Survey* 14, no. 5 (May
1974): 433–434.

[117] Ibid., p. 435. Pakistan contains 155 million acres.

[118] Shahid Javed Burki, "Development of Towns: The Pakistan Experience," *Asian Survey* 14, no. 8
(August 1974): 753.

[119] Esposito, "Politics of Agrarian Reform," p. 434.

Already by 1968 and 1969, 57 percent of the area in intensive agriculture was growing Mexican wheat primarily on the farms of the middle farmers.[120] Their incomes were often doubled, and they could buy or rent additional parcels of land from both the very large and very small farmers. The need for labor was not reduced, but there was a tendency to dispense with the use of the landless laborer in favor of family members. In addition, large loans from the World Bank and the United States AID program were helping the big farmers mechanize. So it is not surprising that demographers are finding an increasing movement of people from the village into the towns and cities.

In 1962, CPC, International (Skippy Peanut Butter, Mazola Corn Oil) purchased the largest corn grinding and processing company in Pakistan.[121] This company then expanded with the aid of loans from the Pakistan government and US AID. It worked out contracts with small- and middle-sized farmers under which it could supply on credit miracle seed, pesticides, and fertilizer, in exchange for the right to purchase all their corn crop at the time of harvest (when the price is lowest) and store it in modern silos. This left no corn for eating by local citizens, which had been the traditional use of the crop. The corn would now be used as a sweetener in soft drinks and snack foods. All this is classified as rural development.

Egypt and Cuba

All of the programs we have looked at up to this point have been generally unsuccessful in redistributing land or rural income, in shifting production and distribution to accommodate national food needs, or in providing the peasant with secure tenure. The last two programs we shall survey, in Egypt and Cuba, seem to be more successful in these regards.

When Gamal Abdul Nasser took power in Egypt in 1953, he moved quickly to remove the influence of the rural landowners who had supported the former King Farouk and to build popular support for his regime. A land reform program was part of this effort. In 1950, 6 percent of the landowners owned 65 percent of the arable land; their tenants often rented from middlemen on short-term leases, paying rents that sometimes exceeded the net income of the land.[122] By 1966, 735,307 of Egypt's 7,847,500 arable acres had been distributed to 303,624 families (containing over 1,500,000 persons).[123] Egypt's estimated 1973 popula-

[120] Burki, "Development of Towns," p. 756.

[121] Lappé and Collins, Food First, pp. 285–287.

[122] Elias H. Tuma, Twenty-Six Centuries of Agrarian Reforms: A Comparative Analysis (Berkeley: University of California Press, 1965), pp. 148–149. See also Bent Hansen and Girgis A. Marzouk, Development and Economic Policy in the UAR (Egypt) (Amsterdam: North-Holland Publishing Company, 1965), pp. 13–112; Patrick O'Brien, The Revolution in Egypt's Economic System: From Private Enterprise to Socialism, 1952–1965 (London: Oxford University Press, (1966), pp. 115–123; 136–147; 249–253; 294–296; Tai Hung-Chao, Land Reform and Politics: A Comparative Analysis (Berkeley: University of California, 1974).

[123] Gabriel S. Saab, The Egyptian Agrarian Reform 1952–1962 (London: Oxford University Press, 1967), pp. 3, 188; Doreen Warriner, "Employment and Income Aspects of Recent Agrarian Reforms in the Middle East," International Labour Review 101, no. 6 (June 1970): 615.

tion was 35,625,000, 70 percent of whom were rural and about 17 million of whom were in agricultural work. This reform could not begin to accommodate the 8 million estimated landless during the 1950s.[124] It does represent nearly a tenth of total arable land and agricultural population. To prevent future estate-acquisition, the sale of over five acres of land to any single individual was forbidden.

In Egypt the arable land directly adjoins the Nile; it is all irrigated and highly fertile. To both sides of this fertile narrow valley—only inches away—is completely arid desert. There is nothing in between. In Egypt, an acre potentially produces two to four crops in two years; in Iran, one. In addition, the yield per acre for each crop is three times higher than in Iran. So it takes considerably less land to produce the same yield. The standard holding under the redistribution is 2.3 acres,[125] though the majority may own fewer than one[126]; four to five acres is considered the minimum viable holding. Ten thousand families continued to own one-eighth of the arable land, and the top 5.2 percent own one-third.[127]

All peasants receiving land were required to join a cooperative. Each local cooperative is managed by an individual appointed by the agrarian reform authorities in Cairo. He is usually a graduate of an agricultural institute and often a former employee of the expropriated landlords.[128] These individuals watch to see that peasants do not surreptitiously harvest crops to avoid repaying loans; peasants are not permitted to enter their fields on their own during the growing period. Part of income has been invested in new pumps to improve irrigation and in fertilizers.[129] According to Saab, efforts to dredge canals on a voluntary basis usually proved unsuccessful.[130] The managers bring concert to the crops that are planted; by law, only one-third of the fields in a cooperative may be devoted to cotton, one-third must remain fallow, and the rest must grow foodstuffs. (Elsewhere in Africa, marketing boards also push farmers into planting certain crops; in this case, the pushing helps insure that *more* food will be grown, rather than less.) Fields must be rotated triennially. The government distributes low-cost credit, seed, fertilizer, pesticides, farm equipment, and agricultural extension services. Farmers work collectively to plow, apply fertilizer and pesticides, water, and harvest; each farmer sows, weeds, hoes, and harrows his own piece of land. Each farmer markets part of his crop himself and part through the cooperative. Each farmer is paid according to his output.

Since 1952, the rate of output per agricultural worker has been rising at 2 to $2\frac{1}{2}$ percent a year. By 1960, the use of fertilizer was double the pre-war level.[131] A 1966 study by the Ministry of Agrarian Reform found that in reform areas a

[124] Saab, *Egyptian Agrarian Reform*, p. 13.

[125] Warriner, "Recent Agrarian Reforms," p. 616.

[126] Elias H. Tuma, "Agrarian Reform and Urbanization in the Middle East," *Middle East Journal* 24, no. 2 (Spring 1970): 170.

[127] Charles Elliott, *Patterns of Poverty in the Third World: A Study of Social and Economic Stratification* (New York: Praeger, 1975), p. 76.

[128] Saab, *Egyptian Agrarian Reform*, p. 54.

[129] Warriner, "Recent Agrarian Reforms," p. 615.

[130] Saab, *Egyptian Agrarian Reform*, p. 75.

[131] Warriner, "Recent Agrarian Reforms," p. 616.

number of major crops registered greater output increases since 1952 than in nonreform areas, despite the fact that before reform the reform areas had lower yields of all crops except rice than did the nonreform areas.[132] Supervised cooperatives have been extended to all farms of Egypt, including those with tenants. Attempts to enforce maximum rent laws do not seem successful.[133] The cooperative managers appear to have kept some control of irrigation and the distribution of crops. These efforts, however, have not helped unemployment. Income for owners and tenants has risen to some degree, due to the more efficient use of land and increasing productivity. There is no desire on their part to share the wealth, and owners and tenants have generally dispensed with the use of casual laborers.

Despite the successes, Doreen Warriner concludes that unless Egypt's land area is increased, there will be "unemployment, inadequate incomes and widespread misery among the agricultural population of Egypt."

> As a summing up of the result of a policy which by comparison with other contemporary reforms is remarkably successful in that it increased production and efficiency of land use, this may seem a pessimistic conclusion; but so far as the direct effects are concerned, it is exact. Unemployment still exists, and farm incomes are still low.[134]

With the aid of over US$1 billion in loans from abroad, Egypt constructed the Aswan Dam. This added 750,000 new acres of arable land and brought perennial irrigation to another million acres (thus permitting two crops a year instead of one) or a total of four-fifths of the arable land.[135] Still more land will be needed. The technology has its drawbacks. According to Georg Borgstrom, one-third of the water supply is needed just to drain away salty water and slow down the inevitable salination of the land. The elimination of dry periods on irrigated land has created a permanent epidemic of the parasitic disease schistosomiasis, which inflames the liver, bladder, and intestines and weakens the body's ability to retain nourishment.[136]

Egypt probably has a more capable bureaucracy than most countries. Its land is far more fertile than average. As an irrigation source the river gives the state more control over water supply than in a place like Iran which depends on wells. Egypt is one of the oldest farming areas and her farmers are hard-working and skilled. The country is strategically located politically and has benefited from more foreign aid than the average developing nation is able to receive. All this has helped to give Egypt something of a head start.

Between 1969 and 1974, the number of undernourished in Egypt rose from 1.3 million to 2.5 million in official estimates.[137] Between 1938 and 1974, real

---

[132] Tai Hung-Chao, *Land Reform and Politics,* pp. 317–318.

[133] Warriner, "Recent Agrarian Reforms," p. 615.

[134] Ibid., p. 616; see also Doreen Warriner, *Land Reform and Development in the Middle East* (London: Oxford University Press, 1962).

[135] Warriner, "Recent Agrarian Reforms," p. 616.

[136] Georg Borgstrom, *The Food and People Dilemma* (Belmont, Calif.: Duxbury, 1973), p. 41.

[137] FAO, *Fourth World Food Survey,* pp. 127–128.

wages in agriculture have not increased. They rose to their highest point in 1966, when the land reform was completed, and then declined by 26 percent by 1974. Landless families accounted for 60.6 percent of rural families in 1950, fell to 45.3 percent in 1961, and were up again to 50 percent in 1972.[138]

The economy of pre-Castro Cuba was dominated by sugar cane, cattle, and tobacco. The 1955 harvest of sugar cane was some 4.4 million tons.[139] From 80 to 90 percent of Cuba's exports were sugar, while 30 percent of its imports were food (often processed), and many of the rest were luxury goods.[140] Many of the profits were invested abroad. Many of the rest went into railroads and electricity to serve the sugar estates and Havana, and into real estate and industry in Havana. The laborers on the sugar estates were unemployed most of the year. Many other peasants were poor, landless, and unemployed. There were no government programs to serve them. Much of the land lay fallow.[141]

When Fidel Castro came to power in Cuba in 1959, he declared that the countryside, not Havana, would be the center of his regime. Unlike every other country among the developing nations, the population movement in Cuba is toward the countryside, rather than away from it.[142] That is where the new building and the new jobs are to be found. Havana's percentage of the total population is steadily declining; more people move out each year than move in. While production of the export crop, sugar, has not markedly increased, production of beef, milk, eggs, and fish has risen sharply.[143] By 1968, three million acres had been added to land available for production of sugar cane, rice, citrus fruits, and coffee by clearing out scrub areas.[144] The capacity of dams grew from 28.8 million to 862 million cubic meters.[145] With the important exception of wheat (of which it imports about a pound per person per day), fats, and oils, Cuba could supply all of its own basic food needs.[146]

Castro's regime nationalized all holdings over 167 acres;[147] these were turned into state-run estates, managed by graduates trained at the university for such tasks. By 1962, there were 330,000 workers on state farms.[148] Some 11,000

---

[138] Griffin, *International Inequality and National Poverty,* p. 147.

[139] Hugh Thomas, *Cuba: The Pursuit of Freedom* (New York: Harper & Row, 1971), p. 181.

[140] Ibid., p. 188.

[141] Some 50,000 of United Fruit's 147,770 acres lay fallow, and thousands of acres were used for grazing. Andres Branchi, "Agriculture—PreRevolution," in *Cuba: The Economic and Social Revolution,* ed. Dudley Seers (Chapel Hill: University of North Carolina, 1964), p. 90.

[142] Petras and LaPorte, *Cultivating Revolution,* p. 337.

[143] Edward González, *Cuba Under Castro: The Limits of Charisma* (Boston: Houghton Mifflin, 1974), p. 194. In 1970, Cuba produced 8.5 million tons of sugar, and production has stayed close to that level until 1980, when cane rust reduced output to below 7 million tons. The fish catch has risen steadily except for sharp declines in 1975 and 1979. Sergio Roca, "Revolutionary Cuba," *Current History* 80, no. 463 (February 1981): 53.

[144] Thomas, *Cuba,* p. 144; 8,750,000 vs. 5,750,000 in 1958.

[145] Petras and LaPorte, *Cultivating Revolution,* p. 347.

[146] Thomas, *Cuba,* p. 1441. There are no statistics available to indicate whether malnutrition exists among any segments of the populace.

[147] Ibid., p. 1439.

[148] Roberto M. Bernardo, "Managing and Financing the Firm," in *Revolutionary Change in Cuba,* ed. Carmelo Mesa-Lago (Pittsburgh: University of Pittsburgh Press, 1971), p. 192.

additional farms have been nationalized since that time.[149] The state farms finance a great many welfare programs for their members. This still left 150,000 to 200,000 small private farmers.[150] About one-quarter of them are subsistence farmers, while others produce most of the country's fruit, coffee, tobacco, and almost half of Cuba's livestock. They keep their land and a measure of their profits, but must grow the crops they are told to grow. Cuba's 1973 population was around 8,870,000. Hence, about one-third of the population is directly occupied in agriculture. The government has created a number of new jobs to support its many rural welfare and construction programs, but it is unclear just how many.

Until the end of the 1970s, Cubans paid little or no rent, no doctors' bills, no school fees, no taxes, no bus fares, and low prices for food;[151] (e.g., $.06 each for eggs, $.20 a liter for milk). Codfish is plentiful and unrationed. Adults are rationed to fifteen eggs and six liters of milk a month and $\frac{3}{4}$ pound of stewing beef every nine days; but everyone in the country receives the same allotment and has this food available to them.[152] Luxury goods are almost nonexistent. The middle class is reduced to relative poverty; some million people have left the island since the revolution.[153] Castro is generally oblivious to economics. Projects are often pursued without much cost accounting. As of the end of 1979, Cuba was some US $10 billion dollars in debt to the Soviet Union, which continues to support his regime with considerable aid funds.[154] Cuba's debt to the USSR will probably reach US$15 billion by 1986. She also owed US$1.5 billion to private international banks as of 1979. Her annual revenues from sugar exports (which once again account for 80 percent of exports, though only 20 percent of gross material product) are around US$2 billion, almost half of which are used to import petroleum,[155] so the debt keeps growing. Rising petroleum prices, and potential declines in output of sugar could leave Cuba's favorable balance of trade in peril, even though the Soviet Union subsidizes her sugar prices.

Castro is constantly spending his time working on schemes to improve milk production or plant more vegetables, interjecting himself into technical matters relating to such projects and changing course on the way programs are set up. When his technical experts insisted that cows must be fed corn and molasses in barns, he continued to insist that they could be adequately fed in pasture (saving much infrastructure cost, as well as much humanly edible corn and molasses). With the aid of some private farmers, he produced his own detailed data to

---

[149] Thomas, *Cuba,* p. 1439.

[150] Ibid., p. 1440.

[151] Barry Reckord, *Does Fidel Eat More Than Your Father* (New York: Praegar, 1971), p. 144.

[152] Ted Morgan, "Cuba," *The New York Times Magazine,* December 1, 1974, p. 100. It is not clear that all can take advantage of their full allotment. In India, the average 1969 *annual* per capita consumption of eggs was eight. Berg, *The Nutrition Factor.*

[153] George Volsky, "Cuba Twenty Years Later," *Current History* 76, no. 444 (February 1979): 83.

[154] Ibid., pp. 55-56.

[155] Ibid., p. 55. Cuba has built four new sugar mills since 1976, and is expanding mechanization of sugar cutting and raising wages of sugar cutters. It is also improving its methods of extracting sugar from the cane. All this raises production, though also the costs of production and the need for petroleum. And, if not checked, the cane rust which reduced the 1980 crop could threaten future output.

counter that of the experts.[156] Sugar cane waste products and food wastes are being used to feed pigs. He is the only leader of any developing nation to devote such great attention and energy to matters such as this. It is obvious that a great many more children drink milk and eat fish, meat, and eggs than before the revolution.

In 1974, Western diplomats estimated that 80 percent of the populace was satisfied with the regime.[157] Since then the foreign debt and low labor productivity have forced price increases, and charges for many formerly free services. Between 1970 and 1980 Cuba's growth rate in social product slowed from 12 percent to 3 percent.[158] Unemployment, too, seems to be on the rise. Relatives allowed in for visits from the United States have increased exposure to Western influence and the demand for Western consumer goods and culture. At the same time, whereas in 1971, 90 percent of average household income was spent on rationed goods, and there were only 230 consumer goods on the market, by 1980 only 30 percent went for rationed goods and 800 consumer goods were on the market. In mid-1980, a million workers received pay increases, while prices of many consumer goods were drastically reduced (further reducing government revenues as well). For a time, emmigration was also permitted, and 125,000 people left.

Cuban culture is probably better attuned to Fidel's *machismo tour de force* than some others would be. Without the massive influx of Soviet aid, which represents a high percentage of their total foreign aid and would probably not be forthcoming if Cuba did not lie on the very doorstep of the United States, he would probably not have survived, if only because of the need for the heavy grain imports. The climate is tropical, so the periodic neglect of housing programs can take place with less discomfort than in colder climes. The country had been exceptionally poor and oppressively ruled, so whatever improvements have been made seem all the bolder by comparison. The nation is an island, and therefore is less susceptible to illegal entry by immigrants from bordering states than if it were on a continent. A million refugees could not normally be so handily transferred to another country. And while the sentiments and goals come through strongly, the results are still hard to calibrate.

The Peasant and Land Reform

Land Reform did not begin in the 1950s. It has its roots in the sixteenth century when commercial interests started to disrupt the community life of Africa, Asia, and Latin America. The programs of the 1950s and 1960s have merely served to augment and deepen the commercialization of agriculture and the decline of the

---

[156] Reckord, *Does Fidel Eat More,* pp. 143–161.

[157] Morgan, "Cuba," p. 112.

[158] Between 1970 and 1977, Cuba experienced a 1 to 2 percent a year decline in agricultural productivity. FAO, *State of Food and Agriculture,* pp. 1–8. Sergio Roca, "Revolutionary Cuba," p. 53. Absenteeism, drunkenness, stealing from job sites, and laziness are widely acknowledged problems. In 1978, more houses were destroyed due to lack of repair than were built. Leaky roofs in new industrial plants and public buildings are common. In Havana, people spend four to five hours commuting to work because busses do not run properly.

community. They are placing the finishing touches on the centralization of the patron-client networks. They have generally not proven effective in returning the land to food production or raising the peasant's standard of living or absorbing a growing population. Rather than restoring the land to the peasant, these programs have moved the power to make decisions further away from the local level and destroyed incentives to produce. They are using the peasant's land to grow materials which he cannot eat and from which he will derive little benefit.

And beneath all this lies a supreme irony: Those in the capitals who control power show an interest in the peasant only when they are consolidating power or looking for new means to turn a profit. Yet on the rare occasions that they show that interest, they demand that *he* pay the costs of the innovations they deem appropriate. If the innovations fail, the peasant has already paid the bill; if they succeed, the patrons pocket the profits. As we shall soon see, that principle also applies in relations between the developed and the developing nations.

ECONOMIC GROWTH

Today there is increasing willingness to admit that land reform is a failure. But another argument waits in the wings: If industrialization of the city is successful, the surplus population can be absorbed. The early phases of the Industrial Revolution involve pain; later the cities will prosper, and the populaiton will eventually shift to them. As Arthur W. Lewis puts it, "In industrialization, one has to cross a desert to get to the promised land."[159] In the case of the developing nations, this may require a few new policy initiatives to speed the process. It may be necessary to expropriate foreign drilling, mining, and agribusiness operations so that prices may be raised and profits retained at home. Profits of remaining foreign businesses may have to be taxed more heavily. The middle classes will grow and wealth and consumer goods spread. The rural masses will be absorbed as workers in the new industries and support-services for this middle class. Gradually, economic growth will provide income and welfare for most of the populace, even if they do not have land.

This is, to put it politely, a pipe dream.

The technological capabilities to feed, clothe, and shelter everyone on the globe already exist. First, let us look at food. Human beings need a minimum of about 2,200 calories a day and about 2 ounces of body-soluble proteins, not over 80 percent of them from cereal grains. A pound of cereal grain will generally supply, after milling and baking, at least 1,500 calories and about 1 ounce of body-soluble proteins (rice provides only $\frac{3}{4}$ ounce of body-soluble protein while hard dry-land winter wheat, oats, and barley supply $1\frac{1}{4}$ ounces). If provided with this daily pound of cereal, an individual can round off a bland but above- subsistence diet of 2,500 calories and $2\frac{1}{2}$ ounces of body-soluble proteins by consuming, say, six tablespoons of bean or oilseed sauce, 4 ounces of fish or chicken, a cup of milk and a banana, plus some trace amounts of vitamins and minerals and some vegetable roughage. The exact additional condiments would depend on

---

[159] *Reflections on Nigeria's Economic Growth* (Paris: Development Centre of the Organization for Economic Cooperation and Development, 1967), p. 27.

what was easiest to obtain in a given area; even many plants currently classified as weeds contain protein and can provide roughage.[160] So does poultry, which can forage around farm yards. The quantities beyond the pound of cereal need not be great.

> A United States Department of Agriculture survey found that Americans eat about 6.4 ounces of red meat, 2 ounces of poultry, 0.7 ounces of fish, half a pound of cereals, 0.5 ounces of nuts and beans, 1.9 ounces of fats and oils, 2 eggs, and 6 cups of dairy products *per capita* each day.[161]

The 1978 world production of cereal grains was 3.5 trillion pounds, enough to feed a pound a day to over $9\frac{1}{2}$ billion people, or over two pounds a day (twice the calculation in the previous paragraph) to the entire 1980 world population.[162] *In terms of dietary needs, there is a vast surplus of cereal grains on the planet.* Furthermore, food production is on the increase. Between 1948 and 1978, world grain production increased by more than 385 percent while world population grew by only 76 percent.[163] Looking at staple foods in general, in 1975–1977 the per capita food production in developed countries was 15 percent above the 1961–1965 average.[164] Even in developing nations, the average supply of calories and proteins per capita was higher in 1975–1977 than in 1961.[165] Food production in developing nations is growing faster than population.

> Discussion of India is continued from p. 316.

Furthermore, there are strong possibilities for expanding production in the future. Some 2.75 billion acres can potentially be added to the 3.5 billion acres currently under cultivation on the planet—an 80 percent increase.[166] India in

---

[160] For instance, Indian peasants eat dried blossoms of the Mahwa tree, stones of mangoes and other fruits, the leaves and tops of gram, and millet stalks. These are the sorts of items they lose from their diets when they move to urban areas.

[161] Food and Agriculture Organization, *Review of Food Consumption Surveys 1977,* Vol. 1 (Rome: United Nations, 1977), pp. 72, 145–146. The United States survey was conducted in 1965. It showed an increase in meat and bakery product consumption (to 2.5 ounces of sugar and sweets per day) since the 1955 survey. These are the averages. The survey shows that those in higher income brackets eat more meat, fish, and dairy products, and less cereal, than this.

[162] FAO, *State of Food and Agriculture,* pp. 1–9.

[163] Borgstrom, *People and Food Dilemma,* p. 29; Economic Research Service, *The World Food Situation,* p. 2; Food and Agriculture Organization, *Production Yearbook 1978* (Rome: United Nations, 1979). The gains in cereal production outstripped population growth everywhere in the world, with Africa the closest.

[164] Economic Research Service, *The World Food Situation,* p. 1; FAO, *Production Yearbook 1978.*

[165] *Assessment of the World Food Situation: Present and Future,* United Nations World Food Conference, Rome, November 5–16, 1974, p. 58; FAO, *Production Yearbook,* p. 247. Between 1970 and 1977, the gain was 0.2 percent, with gains of 0.6 percent in Latin America, 0.5 percent in Asia, and a decline of 1.3 percent in Africa. FAO, *State of Food and Agriculture,* pp. 1–13.

[166] Economic Research Service, *The World Food Situation,* pp. 58–59; Revelle, "Food and Population," pp. 168–169. There are a number of major studies on this. I am using the most conservative projections, those of Revelle.

1978 was growing about $1\frac{1}{4}$ pounds a day of grain per capita. Africa is eleven times larger than India, has about half its population, can more than treble its present cultivated area, and has over five times the arable land per capita. South America is six times larger than India, has about a third its population, can more than quadruple its cultivated area, and has five times the arable land per capita. Their *combined* populations approximately equal that of India. With improved seed, irrigation, fertilizer, and farming techniques, there is considerable room for additional improvement of yields without even expanding cultivated areas. The first improved wheat varieties were released in 1948, in Mexico. Within five years 50 percent of Mexican wheatland had been planted in the new varieties, and by the early 1960s Mexican wheat yields had quadrupled.[167] Whereas the Indian land planted in traditional varieties of wheat in 1973–74 averaged 530 pounds to the acre, those planted in high yielding varieties averaged 1,400 pounds; comparable figures for rice are 850 pounds and 1,400 pounds.[168] As of 1972–73, India had 46,642,400 acres planted in high yielding varieties of these two crops.[169] With better fertilization there is considerable room for improvement in these yields.[170] India has around 70,000,000 acres under irrigation[171] and 58 percent of all the acreage planted in high yielding wheat and rice in all of Asia and Africa.[172] The twelve major irrigating developing nations[173] have about 175 million irrigated acres, so there is room to expand the acreage planted in high-yielding varieties.

| Further discussion of India may be found on p. 356. |

There are serious limits on the methods currently being employed to expand food output. The developed nations have used vastly increased amounts of fertilizer, much of it derived from petroleum and coal. The developing nations have introduced improved seeds heavily dependent on fertilizer and irrigation, the supplies of which cannot expand far beyond present amounts. They have also opened new land to intensive cultivation in a manner which is destroying it. Some 250 million acres of forest in Africa, 20 million in Asia, and 15 to 25 million acres in Latin America have been destroyed. The organic topsoils of tropical forests are very fragile and not easy to rejuvenate. Erosion of topsoil has reached serious dimensions on around 15 percent of the world's agricultural land, and another 15 percent combines serious erosion with serious mineral

---

[167] Economic Research Service, *The World Food Situation*, p. 66.

[168] Dalrymple, "The Green Revolution," pp. 27–28.

[169] Ibid., p. 4.

[170] In 1967–1968, when a few fields with a general higher level of fertilization were planted in high-yielding wheat, they averaged 2,300 pounds per acre. Experimental farms in India have yielded 3,600 pounds per acre for rice and 5,800 pounds per acre in the Philippines. Asian Development Bank, *Southeast Asia's Economy in the 1970's* (New York: Praeger, 1971), p. 121.

[171] Grigg, *Harsh Lands*, pp. 276–277.

[172] Dalrymple, "The Green Revolution," p. 4. Africa and Asia have 81,304,500 acres in high yielding rice and wheat.

[173] India, Pakistan, Indonesia, Iran, Mexico, Iraq, Egypt, Thailand, Argentina, Turkey, Chile, Peru. Economic Research Service, *The World Food Situation*, p. 70.

depletion. More than half of India's topsoil is affected by such erosion, and within twenty-five years the topsoil may have vanished from a quarter of her tilled land if preventive measures are not undertaken. Overgrazing and excessive plowing are the chief culprits. In the Philippines, more than 75 percent of the farmland is regularly damaged by erosion from torrential rains, and in Somalia nine-tenths of all farmlands are reported eroded or threatened.[174] Since the end of the 1880s, the world's desert area has more than doubled, largely because of human farming practices.[175] Extensive irrigation and concreting of natural runoff areas have seriously lowered water tables and endangered water supplies; they have also rendered large tracts of ground unusable due to salinization. By creating contiguous belts of farming, instead of isolated patches, man has facilitated the spread of pests and diseases. The chemical sprays he has created to destroy these have in turn created other ecological imbalances and dangers.

If humankind continues to plow tropical soils indiscriminately, destroy forests, poison the water with nitrates, overirrigate and overgraze, the results could be disastrous. Without soil and adequate water, the human race cannot support itself on the planet. Soil has developed slowly over many thousands of years by complex processes; once destroyed, it cannot be recreated, even by modern technology.

Production can expand without destroying the land. Soil contains many, many elements; most basic to good soil is a balance among phosphorus, potassium, and nitrogen. These are the three principal elements that artificial fertilizers reinforce. Phosphorus is to be found in urine, straw, blood from rendering works, and bones; certain plants can help microorganisms produce it. Potassium can be obtained from sea water, sea weed, manure, wood ashes, straw, and urine. Legumes fix nitrogen in the soil; manure, peat moss, urine, and activated human sludge can also serve as sources of nitrogen. As we shall see presently, slash-and-burn agriculture, if combined with proper fallowing periods, does not disturb the balance of nature in tropical forest areas. Grasslands are sometimes more safely farmed using hoes than plows. As we shall also see presently, irrigation is not the only way to obtain yields from marginal lands. Mulch can be beneficial in preserving water and fertilization. Pests and diseases can be reduced by rotating crops and thus depriving them of hosts during alternate seasons; birds and ladybugs can also help. Man has the technological capability to use approaches such as these to protect the soil and water. Technological prospects for producing an adequate food supply are good.

There is some danger that these potentials may be nipped in the bud by the weather. The years from 1930 to 1960 involved massive improvements in technology. They were also perhaps the warmest years in centuries. In the fifteenth century the climate of the northern hemisphere (where most the planet's grain is grown) turned colder than it had been. During the seventeenth century the Thames froze over eight times; during the American Revolution the British shuttled artillery from Manhattan to Staten Island not on the Staten Island ferry, but on ice.[176] Today, a period in the earth's orbit which puts it farthest from the

---

[174] Borgstrom, *Food and People Dilemma,* p. 39.

[175] Ibid., p. 106.

[176] Geoffrey Lean, *Rich World, Poor World* (London: G. Allen & Unwin, 1978), p. 26.

sun during the northern hemisphere's summer (which tends to cool the temperature), and a radical increase in the amount of carbon dioxide in the atmosphere from the burning of fossil fuels (which tends to warm the temperature) brings questions about whether the planet's growing potentials will remain the same. This could cause a change in these projections.

Meanwhile, plant life in the sea offers a vast potential as a food source which remains largely unexplored. There are many other unexplored sources of food as well, as the !Kung have proven in the Kalihari Desert.

Discussion of the !Kung is continued from p. 92.

Most !Kung today, while working for ranchers in exchange for milk, meat, tobacco, and pay, or simply squatting on land, spend the rainy season gathering and hunting in their traditional manner.[177] Of the forty species of larger mammal in the region, they hunt wart hogs, antbears, porcupine, small antelope, and springhares. Of the eighty species of birds they hunt guinea fowl, francolin, korhaan, kori bustard, sandgrouse, cape turtle, dove, and red-billed teal. Among the twenty-four species of reptiles and amphibians they hunt rock python and the leopard tortoise. Of the seventy species of high-protein insects with which they are familiar they use bees for honey, flying ants and click beetles for delicacies, and poison beetles to provide poison for the arrows with which they hunt the larger game. There are over one hundred species of edible plants, including thirty species of roots and bulbs, thirty species of berries and fruits (including the abundant, delictable, and vitamin-and-mineral-rich baobabs and sour plums), and an assortment of melons, nuts, leafy greens, and edible gums. They know where the food is each season, and how to get it. They eat thousands of pounds of the mangodango nuts, which are 27 percent protein after shelling. Tons of these nuts rot on the ground each year. The wild tsin bean is equally high in protein, and may be stored for months. The vegetable ivory fruit and the !giva berry yield hundreds of pounds annually. All this is unbeknownst to the "modern" ranchers, who are chronically undernourished, come close to starvation when the water is insufficient for their herds, and think of the !Kung as primitive. So even if the worst weather forecasts come true, there may still be plenty of food if we can think where to look for it.

The problem, then, is not that we cannot produce enough food. The problem is that we waste much of the food that is produced. Some food is wasted by the poor, especially due to poor storage. Most is wasted by the relatively affluent. The waste does not come from leaving food on our plates. Most of it comes from eating meat fed in feedlots, from snacks, from undereating and overeating, and from institutional waste. Let me explain:

Waste through Feedlots. Before World War II only about a third of the beef that reached American tables had been fed anywhere other than the range or pasture. Today per capita beef consumption has more than doubled,[178] and

---

[177] Richard B. Lee, "The !Kung Bushmen of Botswana," in *Hunters and Gatherers Today,* ed. M. G. Bichieri (New York: Holt, Rinehart and Winston, 1972), pp. 326–368.

[178] Geoffrey Barraclough, "The Great World Crisis I," *The New York Review of Books* 21 and 22 (January 23, 1975): 26.

about three quarters of the beef we eat has been fed in a feedlot. Feeding these valuable proteins to livestock has been instituted largely for economic reasons: America has had a huge surplus of grain. Livestock feedlots will pay the farmer more for grain than would the world's poor. In the next chapter we will explore alternatives to such economics. Such feeding does not necessarily improve the nutritional value of the meat. Most of a cow's protein comes from grass, leaves, stalks, and other plants not digestible by humans. Much of the feed the cow eats on the feedlot creates saturated fats, which add a delicious taste to the meat, but at the same time reduce the proportion of polyunsaturated fats.

Before World War II most American chickens were fed in barnyards; now the great majority come from enclosed buildings where they are fed entirely on fodder. The same change in feeding habits has taken place with pork. And these new feeding policies have spread around the globe to affluent people everywhere.

The problem with all this is that *sixteen pounds* of grain and soybeans fed to a steer turns into only *one* pound of meat![179] A pig must be fed six pounds for each pound of meat, and a chicken three. If I feed a cow twenty-one pounds of protein in grain, soybeans, oilseeds, fishmeal, or milk, it will be reduced to one pound of protein. The results are devastating, as Table 7.2 makes clear.

The fish, grain, milk, soybeans, oilseeds, and pulses currently fed to livestock in fodder worldwide converts into enough protein to give 157 million

TABLE 7.2
How Fodder Wastes World Protein Production[180]

1976–1978 Average Annual World PROTEIN PRODUCTION (million metric tons)		Percent Used as Fodder	No. of People (in millions) Getting MDR* of Protein:	
			through the fodder	if the PROTEIN PRODUCTION used as fodder were eaten directly
Fish	14	40%	8	173
Grains	166.5	33%	79	1274
Milk	15.7	25%	6	124
Soybeans	26	90%	34	552
Oilseeds	18	60%	16	209
Pulses	15.8	60%	14	183
			157	2515

*MDR = minimum daily requirement

[179] Frances Moore Lappé, *Diet for a Small Planet,* rev. ed. (New York: Ballantine, 1975), p. 382n.
[180] We have divided total tonnage of the commodities as reported in the FAO *Production Yearbook 1978* by a conservative estimate of the percentage of protein they contain (fish, 15 percent; grains, 8 percent; wet milk, 3 percent; soybeans, 35 percent; oilseeds, 25 percent; pulses, 30 percent; to get the figures in the first column. The percentage fed to livestock (worldwide) is the lowest estimates

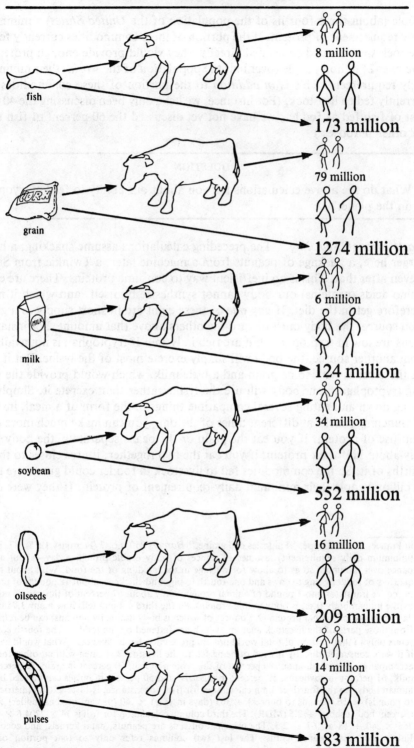

CHART 7.1
How Fodder Wastes World Protein Production

fish

8 million

173 million

grain

79 million

1274 million

milk

6 million

124 million

soybean

34 million

552 million

oilseeds

16 million

209 million

pulses

14 million

183 million

people (about three-fourths of the population of the *United States*) a minimum daily requirement of protein. If the portion of these commodities currently fed to livestock were instead consumed directly, they would provide enough protein to give over $2\frac{1}{2}$ billion people (over half the population of the *world*) their minimum daily requirement. This is *in addition* to the portion of these commodities not currently fed to livestock. (For instance, we have only been discussing the 40 percent of fish fed as fodder; we have not yet discussed the 60 percent of fish used for other purposes.)

QUESTION

What do the above calculations tell you about our ability to feed everyone on the planet?

Waste through Snacking.   The preceding calculations assume snacking: a hamburger here, a package of peanuts from a machine later, a Twinkie from Seven Eleven after that. This is an inefficient way to consume proteins. There are eight amino acids (proteins) our body cannot synthesize by itself, and which it must therefore get in the diet. If *any one* of these eight are in short supply in a given food source, the body must discard the others above that amount. For instance, beans are low in tryptophan, but are rich in lysine. If tryptophan is not available from another source, the body will simply excrete most of the lysine. But if you eat these beans with some grain and a little milk, which would provide the missing tryptophan, your body will use the lysine rather than excrete it. Simply by sitting down and eating several compatible things in the form of a meal, instead of munching snacks at different times of the day, you can make much more efficient use of protein. If you eat the grain or the beans separately, the body uses only about half their protein; if you eat the two together, it uses closer to three-fourths of it. So the commodities fed to livestock in fodder could give more than $2\frac{1}{2}$ billion people their minimum daily requirement of protein. If they were con-

---

in Frances Moore Lappé, "Fantasies of Famine," *Harpers* 250, no. 7 (February 1975): 87. MDR (minimum daily requirement) assumes $2\frac{1}{4}$ ounces of body usable protein a day—about a half ounce over minimum so as to allow for wastage in the handling of the food. With about three-quarters of fodder going to cows and one-fourth to pigs and chickens, about 18 pounds of protein in fodder translates into 1 pound of animal protein. Only about 67 percent of this can be utilized by the human body (i.e., is body usable protein). So the third column tells how many 3.75 ounce daily portions of animal protein (2.5 ounces of which is body usable by humans) can be retrieved from those parts of the livestock anatomy which are fattened by the fodder. The fourth column refers only to that portion of total world protein production fed to livestock: What would happen if it were consumed directly instead of being fed to the livestock? If eaten without other food to accompany it in a meal, about 80 percent of the protein in fish, 60 percent in grain, 82 percent in milk, 61 percent in soybeans, 50 percent in oilseeds, and 50 percent in pulses can be used by the human body. So the fourth column calculation for fish, for instance, is 14 × 2204.6 (metric tons to pounds) × 16 (pounds to ounces) ÷ 365 (days in year) × .40 (percent used as fodder) × .80 (percent body usable) ÷ 2.5 (MDR). The third column calculation for fish is 14 × 2204.6 × 16 ÷ 365 × .40 ÷ 18 × .67 ÷ 2.5. The principal oilseeds are peanuts, palm kernels, and coconuts. Pulses are peas, beans, lentils. The last two columns refer only to that portion of the catch/yield/crops fed to livestock.

sumed together in meals, they could conceivably feed up to 3 billion people their minimum daily requirement of protein.

In fact, if we were to eliminate entirely these two post-World-War II habits of snacking and feeding high-protein commodities to livestock, we would have sufficient protein *just from the commodities discussed thus far* to feed close to 7 billion people, as Table 7.3 indicates. Elimination of snacking alone would free up enough protein to feed close to 900 million people—the population of China.

Americans snack by choice; Indians often "snack" from necessity. By replacing bean fields with wheat fields, the Green Revolution robs protein from people who would otherwise eat their grain together with beans. Mixing beans and wheat can increase the body's utilization of their proteins by up to one-third.[182] The consumption of legumes in India declined 31 percent between 1956 and 1971.[183]

These figures do not even include the large additional quantities of potatoes, vegetables, fruits, and other plants that contain protein and are both tasty and edible for humans. Cows are well designed to transform grass, corn and sorghum stalks, potato starch, cellulose, sucrose, and much else into protein in their rumen (cud); they do not need protein from the sources that compete with humans. Enough corn and sorghum stalks are unused each year in the United States alone to feed 12–30 million head of cattle.[184] Cattle survived for many cen-

TABLE 7.3
How Snacking Wastes World Protein Production[181]

1976–1978 Average Annual World PROTEIN PRODUCTION (million metric tons)		No. of People (in millions) Who Could Get MDR* of Protein:	
		with snacking	without snacking
Fish	14	432	432
Grains	166.5	3862	4505
Milk	15.7	498	498
Soybeans	26	613	704
Oilseeds	18	348	417
Pulses	15.8	305	366
		6058	6922

*MDR = minimum daily requirement

[181] The first column and the minimum daily requirement are the same as in Table 7.2. The second column uses the same percentages as the fourth column in Table 7.2, except the percentage used as fodder; here we are talking about the entire annual protein production. In column three we are assuming the body could use 80 percent of the protein in fish, 70 percent in grain, 82 percent in milk, 70 percent in soybeans, 60 percent in oilseeds, and 60 percent in pulses if they are mixed together in the same meal. This is a conservative estimate based on reading Lappé, *Diet for a Small Planet,* 78–82, 95–117.

[182] Lappé, *Diet for a Small Planet,* p. 81.

[183] Lappé, *Food First,* p. 142.

[184] Research by Dr. Harlow Hodgson, W. F. Wedin, and N. L. Jacobsen. Seth King, *New York Times,* February 8, 1975.

turies without feedlot feeding. We can quit this practice and still have our cows, minus some of the marbling that tastes good but increases the risk of cancer and heart attack. The same holds for chickens and hogs. The reasons for not doing so are economic and social—not nutritional.

Waste through Undereating.   This whole discussion so far has simply pertained to protein. Proteins build and restore tissue. People, of course, also need calories to burn for energy. Calories are available from all the sources we mentioned, and many others we have not such as sugar cane, cassava (which in itself could provide nearly enough calories for everyone on the planet if raised everywhere it likes to grow), and many additional roots, fruits, and vegetables. The body normally creates energy from carbohydrates and fats. *If they are insufficient the body will make use of whatever protein is available to produce energy.* So the malnourished are often doubly robbed. Even the small portion of body-usable protein they do receive can be burned up as energy instead of being used to construct body tissue. Their bodies are using a scarce and expensive fuel when a cheap and plentiful fuel would do—were more of it made available to them. Protein malnutrition is often accompanied by calorie malnutrition, so the malnourished are receiving even fewer proteins than the consumption figures suggest.

Waste through Overeating.   Meanwhile, at the other extreme, Americans eat 6.4 ounces of red meat a day (40 percent of which derives from a full 41 ounces of grains and soybeans in fodder which if eaten directly would in themselves provide a minimum daily requirement of protein) contributing 0.8 ounces of usable protein; 2 ounces of poultry (containing 6 ounces of grains and other human food) with 0.4 ounces usable protein; 0.7 ounces of fish with 0.1 ounces usable protein; 8 ounces of cereals with 0.5 ounces usable protein; 0.5 ounces nuts and beans with 0.1 ounces usable protein; 2 eggs with 0.5 ounces usable protein, and 6 cups of dairy products with 1.4 ounces usable protein. Total daily protein consumption: 3.8 ounces. A large male needs about $2\frac{1}{2}$ ounces of usable protein a day, even if he is active. For the extra activity he needs more glycogen from carbohydrates, not protein. Most people, especially if they are smaller and do not jog every day, need less protein than this. So Americans eat twice as much protein as they need; if you count in the fodder used for feeding the livestock they consume three times the protein they need. Since they also eat far more fats and carbohydrates than necessary, all this surplus protein is simply flushed down the stool. Georg Borgstrom estimates that the *livestock* in the United States excrete enough protein to supply 2 billion additional people with $2\frac{1}{2}$ ounces of protein a day; little of this is even used for fertilizer.[185]

Most of this overconsumption takes place in the developed nations. Some 25 million tons of cereals could add 500 calories a day to the diets of the 455 million malnourished people in the world, bringing them above subsistence levels on

[185] Borgstrom, *Food and People Dilemma*, p. 104. The United States Department of Agriculture's much more conservative estimate is that they excrete as much protein as is contained in the United States soybean crop. Since animals excrete much more protein than they absorb into their meat, Borgstrom's estimate sounds closer to the mark. Some excrement is fed to pigs.

caloric intake and allowing them to make full use of the proteins already in their diets.[186] Meanwhile, the United States alone feeds 140 million tons of cereals to livestock.[187] We are the world's largest importer of livestock, most of which come from developing nations;[188] in 1978, the United States imported 1,252,388 head of cattle and exported 122,573 head, while all of Africa imported 1,033,153 head and exported 1,076,170 head.[189] Over one-third of all cereal grown on the planet goes into meat for consumption in the developed nations; the developing nations with China included eat about as much grain as the cows of the North Atlantic nations. In 1974, for instance, the people of developing nations, including China, directly consumed 520 million tons of grain; that same year livestock consumed 480 million tons of grain.[190] Total world grain production that year was 1,325 million metric tons. In 1972 to 1974, the United States fed 88 percent of its grain to livestock, and Europe and the Soviet Union 67 percent. About half the increase in cereal production since 1961 has occurred in the developed nations (excluding China) with about 1.2 billion people, and the other half in the developing nations (including China) with about 2.8 billion people.[191] Yet, with one-third of the population, the developed nations consume about two-thirds of the world's grain and agricultural production.[192] In 1978, Japan and Western Europe, with one-sixth the world's population, imported 40 percent (versus 20 percent a decade earlier) more grain than all the developing nations combined;[193] their meat consumption is rapidly increasing. Even though the United Kingdom grows more grain per capita than India, it imports 25 times more grain than India.[194] The Netherlands imports over 400 times more grain per capita than India, though its per capita production of grain is about half that of India; it uses this to grow meat. The North Atlantic nations, Australia, and New Zealand import well over 1 million metric tons more protein other than meat from developing nations each year than they export to them[195] and the proteins imported (oilseeds, fishmeal) are superior to those exported (grain).[196] It is not

[186] Economic Research Service, *The World Food Situation*, pp. 50–51.

[187] G. Barraclough, "Great World Crisis I," p. 26.

[188] Borgstrom, *Food and People Dilemma*, p. 128. An example of the result is that while Costa Rica's meat production rose 92 percent from the early 1960s to 1970, per capita consumption went down 26 percent. Much of the beef went to franchised restaurants in the United States. Berg, *The Nutrition Factor*, pp. 65–66.

[189] Food and Agriculture Organization, *Trade Yearbook 1978* (Rome: United Nations, 1979)

[190] FAO, *Fourth World Food Survey*, pp. 8–10.

[191] Revelle, "Food and Population," p. 165.

[192] Borgstrom, *Food and People Dilemma*, p. 65.

[193] FAO, *Trade Yearbook*.

[194] 1976–1978. FAO, *Trade Yearbook* and *Production Yearbook*.

[195] Ibid., p. 64. This simply refers to the exchange of oilseeds and fishmeal for grain. If one adds on trade in meat and dairy products, the deficit becomes a good deal worse.

[196] In 1978, India, Senegal, Brazil, Argentina, and the Sudan supplied nearly all peanut cake and meal for world trade; nearly all of this went to west Europe. Nearly all palm oil comes from west Malaysia and west Africa and goes to western Europe. Nearly all coconut in world trade comes from the Philippines and India and goes to the United States and western Europe. Nearly all oilseed cake comes from South Africa, India, and other developing nations and goes to western Europe.

surprising that seventy-eight out of ninety-five developing nations have average protein intakes below $2\frac{1}{2}$ ounces a day and thirty-six have caloric intakes below 2,200.[197]

Institutional Waste. The waste does not even stop here. Not all of these excess proteins and calories imported into Europe and north America are even consumed. As of 1978, European community nations had a surplus of 869,000 metric tons of powdered milk, 129,000 of butter, and 382,000 of beef.[198] These were being withheld from the market to keep prices high. In 1974, Europe spent US$53 million to destroy vegetables as part of a program to keep up prices.[199] Over two-thirds of fruits and vegetables produced in Central America fail to meet size, color, and smoothness tests for the North American market and are destroyed or fed to cattle (also for export to the North American market.)[200] Large amounts of produce in supermarkets and leftovers in restaurants are disposed of. In some countries, this could at least be used to feed pets. The 30 million cats and 35 million dogs in the United States are however involved in still an additional food-waste program. They consume large quantities of fish, soybeans, grain, dry milk, and other nutritious food in specially processed pet foods.

SPECIFIC EXAMPLE

Over half of the 14 million tons of protein in the 1976–1978 average annual fish catch was shipped to the United States. Americans eat about 0.1 ounce of fish protein a day. Even the imported fish not fed to livestock would feed about 250 million people a full ounce of protein a day. So a great deal of this must go into pet food. Most of the world's fish catch originates off the coasts of South America and Africa. Most of this catch, which would provide 1.35 billion people an ounce of protein a day, ends up in the stomachs of American cats, cows, and other beasts, or in our shrimp cocktails.

Besides the feedlot, our biggest institution for destroying protein is the flour mill. The germ of the grain contains the most protein, but will spoil. By remov-

---

[197] United Nations, *Assessment of the World Food Situation*, pp. 52–53. United States Secretary of Agriculture before the American Pork Congress: "Will we accede to the plaintive—and misleading—cries of some to adopt 'meatless Tuesdays' or similar schemes in an effort to release grain for direct human feeding around the world? . . . In the first place people don't eat very much hog feed. More significantly, the inadequate transportation systems, the archaic distribution systems and the incentive-killing economic systems that prevail in much of the world would still prevent any substantial improvement in diet or affluence among the masses of people. Meat eating is not something to be ashamed of. Instead, it is fortunate that more and more of the world's people can now have meat to eat and very unlikely that consumer tastes will be drastically altered here in the United States." "Butz Criticizes 'Meatless' Idea," *Kansas City Star,* March 20, 1975.

[198] Bernard Lietaer, *Europe + Latin America + the Multinationals* (Westmead, Eng.: Saxon House, 1979), p. 164n.

[199] Lappé, *Food First,* p. 260.

[200] Ray Goldberg, *Agribusiness Management for the Developing Countries—Latin America* (Cambridge: Ballinger, 1974), pp. 160–161.

ing it the mill can produce flour which keeps on store shelves but is lower in nutritional value. Some of the removed germ is used in other food designed for humans; some is fed to livestock; much is wasted.

In the 1980s, a new way to use up food is emerging: gasohol. The United States is devoting wheat, and Brazil sugar cane, to the production of gasohol. This saves on fuel imports. Like fodder, it is profitable. It is still another way of diverting food away from the hungry. It allows those who do not care to grow fat to use up food while driving around in their cars.

Yet, even with all this, we have still not hit upon the most depressing point. The problem would be less deplorable if someone were doing something to remedy it. Far from it. *Our so-called programs of reform are deliberately designed to take from the poor to feed the rich and waste even more extravagantly than before.*

As income rises in the developed nations, and among the wealthier citizens of developing nations, their ability to corral available food supplies increases. And demand for animal products, sugar and fruits and vegetables increases faster than that for cereals, roots, tubers, and beans.[201] If grain prices go up, fewer citizens of developing nations can afford to buy it. If grain prices go down, the profitability of feeding grains to cattle for middle and upper-class consumption increases. So people in developing nations lose out when grain prices are high, and when they are low; either price is too high, or the crop is being fed to livestock. As people in developed nations grow wealthier, their demand for items like cotton, jute, strawberries, and asparagus also increases, along with the temptation to produce those commodities even at the expense of soil, water tables, ecological balance, and food to feed the hungry, in developing nations.

Much of the improved fertilizer, irrigation facilities, farm machinery, and farming techniques in developing nations grows products for consumption in the developed nations. Sugar and cotton acreage is increasing in Peru; hemp acreage in Algeria and Brazil; peanut and cotton acreage in Nigeria, Senegal, Mali, and Gambia; tea acreage in Uganda; tobacco and asparagus acreage in Uganda and Zambia; cotton and tea acreage in Kenya and Tanzania;[202] jute acreage in Bangladesh and India; palm oil in Malaysia; carnations in Colombia;[203] roses and pompoms in Guatemala; soybeans for fodder in Brazil; cotton acreage in Nicaragua—the full list would be very long. Many of these are heavily-populated nations with especially severe hunger and drought problems. An irony in all this is that while the volume of agricultural exports by developing nations rose by over one-third between 1952 and 1970, the net gain in cash income from these exports was only 4 percent.[204] Most of this benefits only the upper strata of the society and is more than counterbalanced by the cost of imports. In the Ivory Coast, for instance, imported protein in canned meat, milk, and fish costs eleven

---

[201] Economic Research Service, *The World Food Situation,* p. 77.

[202] I. A. Svandize, "The African Struggle for Agricultural Productivity," in *Africa: Problems in Economic Development,* ed. J. S. Uppal and Louis R. Salkever (New York: The Free Press, 1972), pp. 131, 134, 138, 139.

[203] Richard J. Barnet and Ronald E. Müller, *Global Reach: The Power of the Multinational Corporations* (New York: Simon & Schuster, 1974), p. 182.

[204] Borgstrom, *Food and People Dilemma,* p. 66.

times more than revenue derived from the equivalent amount of exported proteins in peanuts and oilseed cakes. The cost of the imported food increases faster
than the revenues derived from the exported food. Between 1951 and 1978,
cereal imports of developing nations rose from 12.4 million tons to 66 million
tons,[205] and may rise to 90 million tons by 1985. The cost of United States wheat
and Thai rice has doubled to quadrupled since 1972.[206] The cost of cereal imports
to developing nations rose from US$3 billion in 1971–1972 to an estimated
US$27 billion in 1978. The increase in cost for sixteen of these nations studied by
UNCTAD—with 40 percent of the developing world's total food consumption—amounted to over 30 percent of their gross export earnings. Much of these
imports goes to feed members of the middle classes, not the undernourished. In
addition, the increased price of oil is placing a radical strain on the import bills
of most developing nations (those not producing oil), who were spending US$100
billion more on energy each year by 1975 than they were in 1970.[207]

Before 1972, one-third to one-half of the import tonnage—and a high proportion of those imports that did *not* go to middle-class groups—came from
United States farmers. After the lowering of United States food reserves due to
the 1972 drought and the opening of trade with the USSR and China, most of
this source dried up. By 1974, the United States was shipping one-sixth as much
food to developing nations as ten years before; it proved more profitable to sell
the food in these new markets.[208] Only 20 percent of the 4 million ton fiscal 1974
Food for Peace program went to famine-stricken countries; more than 50 percent
was sent to Cambodia, Israel, Jordan, Laos, Malta, and South Vietnam,[209] while
much of the rest went to India, Bangladesh, Pakistan, the Philippines, Morocco,
Republic of Korea, and Indonesia.[210] Strategic considerations are obviously important in determining aid recipients; using food as a weapon is not a new idea.

Furthermore, little of the Food for Peace is donated any longer; under the
new concessional sales program, the recipient nation is lent the money at low in-

---

[205] Revelle, "Food and Population," p. 165; FAO, *State of Food and Agriculture,* pp. 1–2, 1–37.

[206] United Nations, *Assessment of the World Food Situation,* pp. 12, 22.

[207] Benjamin Higgins and Jean Downing Higgins, *Economic Development of a Small Planet* (New York: Norton, 1979), p. 5.

[208] United States Secretary of Agriculture Earl Butz, *The Today Show,* February 10, 1975: "Food exports are now our biggest source of foreign exchange. . . . Some people want us to give away more
than we can afford. . . . We are going to meet the real human needs of the world. On the other
hand [our food program] is aimed to expand our own commercial markets, too, because we get
foreign exchange that way." Of the $13\frac{1}{2}$ million tons of wheat sold to the top ten United States
wheat customers in fiscal 1974, $10\frac{1}{2}$ million went to Japan, China, USSR, the Netherlands, and
Britain. Foreign Agricultural Service, United States Department of Agriculture.

[209] Transnational Institute Report, "World Hunger: Causes and Remedies," Amsterdam, October
1974, p. 57.

[210] Economic Research Service, *The World Food Situation,* p. 55. The top ten recipients of wheat
were South Vietnam, Israel, India, Bolivia, Bangladesh, Colombia, Pakistan, Morocco, Jordan,
and South Korea; a total of 785,000 tons, ranging from 135,000 to 39,000. All but India were concessional sales. Foreign Agricultural Service, USDA. Meanwhile, United Nations, *Assessment of
the World Food Situation,* p. 67, described Angola, Somalia, Tanzania, some of the sub-Sahara
countries, Bangladesh, India, Indonesia, the Philippines, Afghanistan, Saudi Arabia, the two
Yemens, Bolivia, El Salvador, and Haiti as the worst sufferers from malnutrition. In 1978–1979,
total food aid by all developed nations amounted to only 9.6 million tons. FAO, *State of Food
and Agriculture,* pp. 1–19.

terest to buy the food on the open market from U.S. suppliers at commercial prices. Development assistance agencies are increasingly turning to concessional loans in dealing with the poorest developing nations. These poorest nations are meanwhile faring much poorer than other nations in the terms of trade when they sell their agricultural raw materials in exchange for imports.[211] So these loans will be harder to repay. And they will have little money to devote to welfare projects.

SPECIFIC EXAMPLE

The 1974 Food for Peace program lent enough money to buy 22 million people a pound of grain a day—$2\frac{1}{2}$ million of them in drought-stricken countries. Put another way: The food purchased could add 400 calories (but only about one-eighth of protein needs) to the diets of 80 million people—15 million of them in drought-stricken countries. The countries had to buy most of this food from United States suppliers at regular market prices (which were then very high) and later repay the loans. Many of the individuals arranging these purchases were themselves involved in grain hoarding and speculation.

Even in nations like India, Pakistan, Kenya, the Republic of Niger, and Malaysia, which are making notable increases in their cereal grain production, much of the best land remains in the hands of wealthier landowners. Such individuals also control marketing and hence gain control of much of the surplus harvested. These individuals hold out for the best price on their cereal. This is often to be obtained in the cities rather than in the countryside with its masses of landless and unemployed people. Feeding an adequate diet to the majority of people who have little ability to pay entails cutting down on money that could be earned from foreign exchange or from selling to the smaller percentage of the populace who have money in their pockets. It would diminish the potential for developing growth capital. Since, in addition to the high cost of imports, many nations are already paying back heavy payments on debts incurred in the past to international lending agencies or to governments of developed nations, they feel pressured to maintain a tight fiscal policy.

The situation tends to be aggravated further when multinational corporations enter the picture. They, too, are interes   in producing for the developed nations market, where the profits are. Their latest aproach is to set up marketing agreements whereby they give farmers loans to buy seed and fertilizer, in exchange for which the farmer agrees to grow what the corporation wants and to sell the crop to the corporation. This prevents the corporation from being nationalized, allows it to leave the market at any time, and shifts the risks of a bad crop to the farmer. And it tends to shift land out of food crops. For instance, under the influence of such agreements, two-thirds of Colombia's Green Revolution rice in 1973 was being fed to livestock for the United States market, or being made into beer. Ralston Purina added 200,000 acres to growing soybeans and sorghum, 42,000 of which had formerly grown beans for local consumption. The soybeans

[211] Idem., pp. 140–42, I-51.

and sorghum were turned into chicken feed to produce mayonnaise and snack food.[212] Meanwhile, it would take the entire weekly earnings of over one-fourth of the families in Colombia to buy a two-pound chicken and a dozen eggs. In Senegal, even during the Sahel drought, the House of Bud was airfreighting food to Europe grown under such agreements. Gulf and Western grows sugar in the Dominican Republic this way. And there are many more.[213]

And multinationals advertise heavily; by the early 1970s, one-third of United States advertising agency revenues were derived from abroad.[214] Much of this was from developing nations. Most of the products advertised are expensive processed foods with less nutrition than basic diets. The poor are encouraged to buy Ritz crackers with the money they would normally spend on rice and beans. "It is not uncommon in Mexico, doctors who work in rural villages report, for a family to sell the few eggs and chickens it raises to buy Coke for the father while the children waste away for lack of protein."[215]

So *a disproportionate share of the improved world agricultural production is going to developed nations or to urban jobholders.* For landless people to eat, they must earn. Even land reform has allowed few of them to do this. Hence, many of them look to the city. One study showed quite accurately that Latin America's population would grow from 130 million to 374 million between 1940 and 1980; while the rural population doubled in that period, large cities increased nine times. Africa's population grew from 192 million to 449 million, with rural population doubling and large cities multiplying fifteen times. South Asia's growth is from 610 million to 1,366 million, with rural population doubling and urban population up eleven times.[216] Some of these people find jobs in the city which, though better than those available in the countryside, are often menial. Most do not. For instance, between 1950 and 1960 factory employment absorbed only nine percent of the growth of the labor force in Latin America and an even lower percentage thereafter.[217] International Labour Organization studies conducted between 1970 and 1973 surmised that in Colombia, if present trends continue, 31 to 37 percent of the labor force would be unemployed by 1985, as opposed to 21 percent in 1970.[218]

A CEPAL study found that the proportion of workers in Latin America employed in manufacturing in 1975 was no greater than in 1925.[219] In Sri Lanka,

[212] Robert J. Ledogar, *Hungry for Profits: U.S. Food and Drug Multinationals in Latin America* (New York: IDOC/North America Inc., 1975), pp. 94–98.

[213] See Susan George, *Feeding the Few: Corporate Control of Food* (Washington, D.C.: Institute for Policy Studies, 1978), pp. 44–56.

[214] Sylvia Ann Hewlett, *The Cruel Dilemmas of Development: Twentieth Century Brazil* (New York: Basic Books, 1980), p. 148.

[215] Derrick B. Jelliffe, "Commerciogenic Malnutrition?" *Nutrition Reviews* 30, no. 9 (September 1972).

[216] Richard M. Morse, "Trends and Issues in Latin American Urban Research, 1965–1970, Part II," *Latin American Research Review* 6, no. 2 (Summer 1971): p. 31.

[217] Rural Development—Report of a Working Group," *Journal of Administration Overseas* 9, no. 1 (January 1970): 15, Between 1925 and 1970, the percentage of the Latin American work force employed in the manufacturing sector decreased. Barnet and Müller, *Global Reach*, p. 169.

[218] Erik Thorbecke, "The Employment Problem: A Critical Evaluation of Four ILO Comprehensive Reports," *International Labour Review* 107, no. 5 (May 1973): 398.

[219] Lietaer, *Europe + Latin America + the Multinationals*, p. 95.

between 1969 and 1970, 90 percent of secondary school graduates under twenty, and two-thirds between twenty and twenty-four were unemployed.[220] In Nairobi, Kenya, 8 to 14 percent of the urban labor force was unemployed.[221] In fourteen countries studied by H. A. Turner, industrial output was increasing by 7 to 8 percent, employment by 3 percent, and unemployment by 8.5 percent.[222] Nigeria has only about one million of its over eighty million population working for salaries and wages; even if this sector expanded at the rate of 10 percent, this would create only 100,000 jobs for the 700,000 leaving school each year. Firms claim that it costs US$5,000 to $7,000 just to create one job in a low-technology industry. This would require US$4 billion—one-fourth Nigeria's annual oil revenues—simply to provide jobs for one year's school leavers. Nigeria's largest industrial holding company has only about US$7 million invested in the country.[223] Between 1960 and 1970, the United Nations estimates that the percentage of unemployed and underemployed in developing nations rose from 27 percent to beyond 30 percent, and that figure is still rising.[224]

When the Industrial Revolution began in England, Germany, the United States, Russia, northern Italy, and Scandinavia, raw materials were readily available and inexpensive, and markets could be found around the world among the new traders and landowners there. Manufactures were not kept out by tariffs. The addition of labor movements and welfare programs helped workers gain more than a marginal return on their labor and turned them into accessible consumers. In the United States the land grant programs created many small farmers whose yields from their rich land gave them buying power. Control of the principal profits from mines, plantations, and commercial crops around the globe largely fell into the hands of nationals from the North Atlantic nations; these profits did not need to be shipped abroad and could be reinvested at home. With control of investment capital, resources, principal industries, and technical skill concentrating in the North Atlantic region, it is not surprising that buying power there spread to wider strata of the populace.

Currently, it is difficult for industries in developing nations to compete on the international market. Most of the products they produce are already being manufactured in the technologically-advanced nations. Tariffs, economies of scale, well-established marketing arrangements, and big-power diplomacy protect industries in the latter nations. When the occasional nation like Singapore, Brazil, or Mexico finds itself producing heavily for the European or North American market, it must operate within strict quotas which place an unpredictable ceiling on its production.[225] Because most developing nations are attempting to industrialize, they erect tariffs and quotas against one another. The

[220] Thorbecke, "The Employment Problem," p. 399.

[221] Ibid., p. 401.

[222] H. W. Singer, "Dualism Revisited: A New Approach to the Problem of the Dual Society in Developing Countries," *Journal of Development Studies* 7, no. 1 (October 1970): 67.

[223] Louis Turner, *Multinational Companies and the Third World* (New York: Hill & Wang, 1973), pp. 51, 161–162; see chapter 8, pp. 348–349.

[224] United Nations Economic and Social Council, *Development Digest* #4 (New York: United Nations, 1969).

[225] Between the mid-1950s and the mid-1970s, the developing nations' share in world trade dropped from one-third to one-fifth, according to Lappé, "Fantasies of Famine," p. 87.

internal market for a given product within any particular developing nation is usually not great and does not allow for economies of scale sufficient to compete with foreign-made products. This means that the principal industries in developing nations tend to be those that can convert an indigenous raw material into commodities for export: things like aluminum plants, rubber and cotton mills, shipyard facilities, sugar and oil refineries, canning plants, commercial agriculture and fertilizer plants and dam complexes to serve them, railroads and road networks, and engineering and construction firms to build these. Household consumer goods are cheaper to import from abroad, and usually imported goods are preferred by consumers. Some foreign firms will set up installations such as auto assembly plants and packaging plants in connection with selling their products on the domestic market, and then seek protective tariffs so they can wipe out local competition and have the local market to themselves. The trend among multinationals in the 1970s was toward building such plants; they raise the country's cost of living without increasing its revenues.[226]

The trend in industrial research and development in recent years in the United States has been to emphasize reduction in the amount of labor needed to produce a product. To do this, it is often necessary to use an increased amount of petroleum and other resources. European and Japanese research and development has been more preoccupied with reducing the amount of resources used in production, and therefore their energy efficiency has been greater. Both regions tend to use more resources and less labor, and to revolve around a larger plant, than is necessary in developing nations. They do not adapt this technology to local marketing conditions when they open a plant in the developing nations because the market is too small to warrant big start-up costs; nor do they try to devise products especially for developing nations.[227] So all plants use less labor and more energy resources than is possible and those not designed for export produce products not especially designed for the local market. As the technology becomes more sophisticated, the amount of capital required to employ one worker keeps on rising.

An indigenous investor in a developing nation can usually reap the greatest profits from investing in a capital-intensive enterprise that is involved with shipping raw materials, raw or semi-refined, abroad. Other investments are far more risky unless guaranteed a monopoly on the local market, which inhibits growth. Should an investment prove lucrative, as in the case of oil, greater returns can be realized by investing the profits abroad in the North Atlantic region than from devoting them to a riskier enterprise at home. And one of the riskiest forms of investment conceivable would be an expensive program to produce jobs or food for people who are presently virtually penniless.

One could argue that an increase in sophistication in the aggregation process through greater democracy and adeptness in organizing political parties and interest groups, more freedom of the press, and improved education might force these investors to leave their money at home and use it to improve food output and distribution. At present, however, the patron-client networks coalesce

---

[226] Lietaer, *Europe and Latin America and the Multinationals,* pp. 232, 216.
[227] Idem., pp. 16–17.

around those very investors. They control the communications media, the army, governmental institutions, and other instruments capable of channeling aggregation. Unless there were new forces at work to remove these instruments from their control, there seems little reason to believe that these patterns will change. No such new forces seem imminent.

Economic growth in itself is of neutral value. If used to increase agricultural productivity and distribution and generally raise the standard of living, it could be a blessing. However, if, as has been true for some centuries now, it is used to increase the concentration of land in a few hands, divert land away from the growing of foodstuffs, divert food out of the mouths of growing percentages of the populace, upset the stability of social life without creating new mechanisms to return it, and continually decrease the power of citizens to reverse these trends, it cannot be looked upon as a blessing. Technology has markedly increased man's ability to organize and extract benefits from nature. If it were to be seriously applied to the problem of relieving the food shortage or disparities in distribution, it could probably overcome the considerable obstacles in its way. The problem is that while economic growth has increased for several centuries, it has not been so applied. And nothing on the horizon indicates that it will be. The widespread dissemination in recent years of health care, transistor radios, movies, literacy, and factory-made clothing has been a benefit to the common citizen. This dissemination, however, hardly seems to provide a means to roll back the continuing accumulation of wealth, land, and political power into a few hands. Often it has used up funds which the peasant could have spent better for other purposes. Nor does there seem reason to believe that the addition of a few hundred thousand landowners, office workers, and wage laborers to involvement in these investments will turn this tide.

Discussion of Iran is continued from p. 306.

If money and technology could buy general prosperity, one would expect to find some in the oil-rich OPEC nations. Iran's annual profits from oil had risen to US$17 billion by 1976. In 1977, *Fortune* classed National Iranian Oil as the seventh largest company in the world. Iran is no longer going through the early growing pains of capital accumulation; yet two-thirds of the families in Teheran, the most prosperous city, earn less than US$200 a year.[228] The number of physicians rose from 3,722 in 1964 to 9,500 in 1974, half of them in Teheran, mostly with rich clientele (leaving about 4,750 to serve the nation's remaining 30 million people). The expensive new medical school turned out 600 graduates a year, half of whom left the country. The infant death rate in 1975 was substantially worse than the rates in Pakistan, India, Egypt, and Ethiopia.[229] No more than 40 percent of land has adequate water resources. Only about half the potential water resources are exploited, and only half that delivered to the fields. The giant

---

[228] Frances FitzGerald, "Giving the Shah Everything He Wants," *Harpers* 249 (November 1974): 55–57, 72, 77–78. Saudi Arabia and the two Yemens—who should also be making oil money—are described by the United Nations as especially malnourished. See footnote 210.

[229] Karl W. Deutsch, *Politics and Government: How People Decide Their Fate,* 3rd ed. (Boston: Houghton Mifflin, 1980), p. 602.

Pahlevi dam, opened in 1972, was designed to serve fourteen foreign-owned agribusinesses[230] with 12,000 to 60,000 acres apiece. Two of these projects were in bankrupcy by 1976, and the others were unable to begin production because of incredible management blunders and corrupt deals. Meanwhile, restrictions on loans from government cooperatives were so tight that many farmers were being forced to take loans from small moneylenders and banks at exorbitant rates of interest. There were only a thousand agricultural extension agents in the entire country. Between 1974 and 1976, agricultural exports dropped by a third, while food imports grew from US$400 million in 1970 to US$1,400 million in 1976. Meanwhile, 15 percent of the population was reported to be undernourished in 1974 (at least, down from 23 percent in 1969).[231] Between 1973 and 1978, the Shah purchased some US$18 billion in arms. At the time of his overthrow he had outstanding orders in the United States alone for US$12 billion more arms, and US$6 billion in other goods.[232] He was building a steel mill, a gas liquefication plant, nuclear reactors, a petro-chemical complex, a diesel engine plant, and airports that cost billions and were mostly built by foreign construction workers. But there were no industries to put this infrastructure to productive use. An estimated US$4 billion a year was leaving Iran for personal bank accounts abroad, not counting the Shah's own personal transactions.[233] The money was being spent, but not to raise the living standards of the people. And the explanation lies much deeper than just the personal quirks of the Shah.

Further discussion of Iran may be found on p. 345.

One urban phenomenon in recent times is the decline of the small factory. Small factories are characterized by family ownership, reliance on basic nearby resources, labor intensiveness, simple production techniques, skills acquired outside the formal school system, unregulated and competitive markets, and sloppy buildings and waste disposal techniques. Far from encouraging the small business sector, there is a tendency for business leaders to ignore or hamper it (unless the owners have important political connections). Small labor-intensive cigarette, furniture, chemical, clothing, repair, boatbuilding, and food processing facilities are put out of business by the introduction of larger competing firms from abroad (most of them less labor intensive), regulations, bribes, and demolition of informal-sector buildings. The Punjab, the section of India with the fastest-growing industrial and agricultural sector, had 15,000 small-scale industries with 52,000 workers in 1956; by 1959, there were 20,000 with 100,000

---

[230] Among them: Hawaiian Agronomics (C & H), the Diamond A Cattle Company, Mitsui, Chase Manhattan, Bank of America, Dow Chemical, John Deere, and Shell. M. G. Weinbaum, "Agricultural Policy and Development Politics in Iran," *Middle East Journal* 31, no. 4 (Autumn 1977), pp. 434–450.

[231] FAO, *Fourth World Food Survey*, pp. 127–128.

[232] John K. Cooley, "Iran, the Palestinians, and the Gulf," *Foreign Affairs* 57, no. 3 (Summer 1979): 1023–1024.

[233] James A. Bill, "Iran and the Crisis of 78," *Foreign Affairs* 57, no. 2 (Fall 1978): 334n.

workers; by 1966, that number had barely grown to 21,424 small factories.[234] Even if this sector has grown markedly since that time, it does not represent a substantial number of jobs. Similar trends may be noted elsewhere. In Tanzania, the real income of those depending on this sector fell by about a half between 1969 and 1975; that of smallholders declined by 17 percent.[235] While big industry is unable to absorb the labor force, small industries are likewise unable to do so and often succumb to competition from larger firms on which the major patron-client networks can make more money.

The trade union movement does little to help to markedly spread the wealth. By inducing higher wages and welfare legislation for its members, it increases the tendency of industry to avoid labor-intensiveness. If foreign firms must pay high wages, they often prefer to bring in their own white-collar staff from abroad. Even those unions receiving more moderate and gradual pay increases are liable to prefer not to expand the numbers, and hence the competition, within their ranks.

Today fuels and metals are becoming difficult to obtain but increasingly in demand. Nations without these resources will have to expend higher percentages of their income to obtain them. Nations with these resources will try to derive as much profit as possible from them. Neither are likely to use the profits to feed or employ the poor. This is tragic. Nigeria, for instance, moved into the oil age in 1978 with US$9.5 billion and 1979 with US$15 billion in oil revenues. By the year 1999, the oil will be gone.[236] If it wastes the revenues, they will be gone forever.

Economic growth has produced modern buildings, roads, dams, electrification, mines, factories, and enterprises in developing nations. It has provided people with education, watches, radios, television sets, clothing, medical care, and many modern accoutrements. But it has also left many unemployed, homeless, decultured, and short of food. The latter problems are not easily solved in a manner which promotes profits. In fact, the labor intensiveness, diversions of land and imports, and redistribution of wealth needed to solve them are liable to reduce both profits and investment capital. Hence, rather than economic growth being a solution to these problems, these problems endanger economic growth. The easiest way to avoid that danger is to ignore them; so long as these people do not encroach on land needed for economic development, they may be ignored

---

[234] John Macrae, "The Relationship Between Agricultural and Industrial Growth, With Special Reference to the Development of the Punjab Economy from 1950 to 1965, *Journal of Development Studies* 7, no. 4 (July 1971): 410. A survey of a stratified sample of 173 of the 533 tubewell manufacturers in Pakistan's Punjab province found that only six 4–6 worker operations had received loans, while thirty-two larger firms had. "Large-scale industries have been nurtured by a variety of subsidies, licensing procedures, tax concessions, special credit arrangements, and protection from import competition . . . [This] threatens the growth and even the survival of small-scale engineering firms." The entire industry only employs 6500 workers. Frank C. Child and Hiromitsu Kaneda, "Links to the Green Revolution: A Study of Small-Scale Agriculturally Related Industry in the Pakistan Punjab," *Economic Development and Cultural Change* 23, no. 2, (January 1975): 252, 266, 273. In addition, to get a loan to purchase a tubewell a farmer must have 12.5 acres, which excludes 80 percent of landowners. Griffin, *The Political Economy of Agrarian Change*, p. 27.

[235] Griffin, *International Inequality and National Poverty*, p. 147.

[236] Jean Herskovits, "Democracy in Nigeria," *Foreign Affairs* 58, no. 2 (Winter 1979–1980): 327.

with impunity. Economic growth produced these problems; it does not have a cure for them.

POLITICAL LEADERSHIP

Some people argue that a change in the internal politics of developing nations will help insure that efforts will be expended to solve problems like unemployment, food shortages, homelessness, and deculturation. In the previous chapter a number of arguments were presented to this effect. Political scientists like to refer to these as "primacy of politics" arguments, the notion that one can create social and economic changes by changing political leadership. Some prefer to see a political structure directed by more liberal members of the middle class. Some advocate military control. Others wish to intensify party competition. There are those who feel that political stability and institutionalization of government institutions are a prerequisite for transforming the imbalances created by modernization. There are suggestions to improve the bureaucracy, strengthen legislatures, enhance the flow of information, expand mass participation in politics, and give poorer folk greater access to political careers.

Any political regime, however, must maintain economic stability. In developing nations, such stability generally depends on a healthy export economy. Any program that weakens the nation's ability to reap profits from its exports leaves the government in a vulnerable position.[237] Those who control the export economy control the patron-client networks. Replacing one set of members of the patron-client networks with others is one thing. Making a frontal attack on the patron-client networks by removing their sources of profit is another. A government that reduced the profitability of exports, mining, and agriculture and consumer industries by devoting national income to raising food productivity and general popular welfare would incur the wrath of the patron-client networks. It would probably also lose access to foreign aid. For instance, the Goulart regime in Brazil was denied international economic aid. Within hours after his overthrow, the United States Agency for International Development extended the new regime emergency funds, and the International Monetary Fund and World Bank quickly came up with loans.[238] From 1961 to 1970, Chile received 9.9 percent of the loans of the Inter-American Development Bank; in 1970, after the political ascendency of Salvadore Allende, and his attempts to expropriate foreign industries, that figure dropped to 0.63 percent.[239] Short-term credit from foreign banks shrank from US$220 million to US$35 million during Allende's first year in office.[240] Chile also dropped from being one of the highest

---

[237] As Henry L. Bretton, *Power and Politics in Africa* (Chicago: Aldine, 1973), p. 35, puts it: "In so many ways Senegal's profile in its general outline is typical of that of most other underdeveloped countries: for years to come, whoever rules Senegal is compelled to come to terms with the main commodity, the peanut. To attempt to ignore the economic and social demands flowing from its production, collection and distribution and sale is to invite economic, hence political, disaster."

[238] Jan Knippers Black, *United States Penetration in Brazil* (Philadelphia: University of Pennsylvania, 1977), pp. 49, 50n.

[239] Turner, *Multinational Companies*, p. 41.

[240] Barnet and Müller, *Global Reach*, pp. 83, 140.

recipients of direct United States foreign aid to one of the lowest. Meanwhile, the aid to the Chilean military jumped from US$800,000 in the last pre-Allende year to US$12 million two years later. The military overthrew Allende; within hours ships left New Orleans harbor with food for Chile. By 1976, the new military regime there was receiving US$90 million in direct aid alone, and six times the food aid of all the rest of Latin America. Chile also stepped up its luxury food exports.[241] Intelligence agencies of developed nations, hostile on ideological grounds to such "leftist" regimes, are also prepared to lend assistance to attempts to overthrow them. It is dangerous for a reformist regime to broaden human rights, since its opponents within the patron-client networks can use these rights to promote economic and political chaos. It is, in fact, difficult for such reformist regimes not to allow such rights; they are unlikely to have support from the military in suppressing them, and they often depend on labor unions who contain within their ranks many devoted enemies of such reforms. Calls for human rights are, in essence, calls for the right of patron-client networks to operate without interference from governments. So, to guarantee human rights successfully a regime must avoid reforms that interfere with the patron-client networks.

This discussion of Iran is continued from p. 342.

In Iran, the Shah suppressed civil liberties of many within the patron-client networks. This helped lead to his overthrow. The regime that followed tried to disband the military and showed some reformist tendencies, such as a broadening of the social base of parliament and increases in wages, though most commerce was severely disrupted. It contained within its ranks various elements of the patron-client networks, but others within these networks found it offensive. The cutoff of oil exports deprived the regime of new revenues. Without money and a military establishment the government could not easily resist attempts from within the patron-client networks to overthrow it. Those who tried the tactic of holding American hostages did so partly out of the mistaken belief that this would make it more risky for those conducting covert operations to launch an overthrow attempt. In response, overthrow attempts proliferated, and Iraq attacked, making the growth of military forces even more necessary. With increased military activities it was all the easier to steer toward non-reformist government which would reduce social benefits and rely more heavily on original elements of the patron-client networks to effect economic recovery. The religious radicals attempted to counter these initiatives.

---

[241] Lappé, *Food First,* pp. 359–360. William F. Buckley, Jr., "Chile's Economy is Unmistakably Healthy," *Kansas City Star,* November 25, 1980: "The minister of finance for Chile, Sergio de Castro, is a youngish man who learned his economics at the University of Chicago. . . . The critics of Mr. de Castro said in 1974 that Chile would not be able to pay off its debts. Chile did. . . . The critics said that de Castro's drastically lowered tariffs . . . would ruin Chilean manufacturing. Since 1976, Chilean manufacturing has increased at a rate of 10 percent per year. . . . In Allende's best year, Chileans bought 192,000 television sets. Last year they bought 457,000 television sets. In Allende's best year, 23,000 cars were bought. Last year, 48,000. Radios? Allende—177,000; last year, 933,000. . . . What is going on in Chile is the most exciting economic recovery since that of West Germany after the war."

The discussion of Iran is continued on p. 361.

Mobs may take over the streets, terrorists take over embassies, and fanatics take over governments, but the patron-client networks continue to control arms and resources. In so doing, they ultimately control government.

Covert operations by international intelligence agencies, and public acts of violence sponsored by members of patron-client networks, designed to topple governments but also posing the threat of confrontations between the super-powers, can (by stirring popular passion) slow down the reassertion of patron-client control rather than speed it up. Leftist unions or radical students are likely to be a part of the support that brings some new governments to power, for reasons we have seen. But a government that took their programs seriously would simply find itself unable to carry out those programs, and throw power back to the patron-client networks. Whatever the scenario, the patron-client networks regain the power.

Since World War II many radical reformist regimes have come to power in developing nations: Nasser in Egypt, Mrs. Bandaranaike's Freedom Party in Sri Lanka, Boumedienne in Algeria, the 1968–1976 regime in Peru, the 1972–1980 Manley regime in Jamaica, and the People's Democratic Republic of Yemen are clearly in this category. Sooner or later all of these have toned down their rhetoric or lost power without North Atlantic military involvement. All have remained patron-client states supplying raw materials to the North Atlantic nations. In Zimbabwe, the most left wing of the guerilla leaders came to power in 1980 and promptly began to turn to the right; it was soon fighting remnants of its own guerillas. The Soviet and Cuban backed Popular Movement in Angola and Mariam regime in Ethiopia, and the Maoist regime of Machel in Mozambique, continue heavy trading with the North Atlantic nations. The leftist Nicaraguan Mercado regime, which purged itself of even its moderate leftist elements, finds it necessary to court United States trade and aid. Though the Soviet Union gives assistance to these nations, as it did to Nasser, Zimbabwe's guerillas, Boumed-ienne, South Yemen, and others, it clearly does not have the resources to offer them the massive aid it lends to Cuba, which remains the only nation outside its borders receiving massive ongoing Soviet economic assistance. There is nothing to indicate that these nations will take routes different from those followed by their leftist predecessors.

By the mid-1970s, many developing nations were paying back more in foreign loans than they were receiving. From 1965 to 1967, 87 percent of all aid to Latin America was used to cover debt repayments. Comparable figures for East Asia and Africa are 52 percent and 73 percent.[242] As we shall see in the next chapter, those figures are much higher now. A reformist government could endanger these repayments. At the point that support from both the local patron-client networks and foreign aid sources declines, it would not matter whether the government was middle class, or military, or had problem-solving potentials, or a skilled bureaucracy, or a particular political party system, or had access to much information, or did or did not possess democratic institutions. Unless it

---

[242] Turner, *Multinational Companies,* p. 56.

could command enough popular support to contravene the entrenched position of the patron-client network and defy the international bill collectors, it could not carry through its reforms beyond the moderate and generally ineffective reforms we have surveyed up to this point.

A regime, such as that in Peru, that has been forced to backtrack from reform might actually more safely allow human rights to members of the patron-client networks than one that has forcibly overthrown a reformist regime, and thus provide a better investment climate. North Atlantic governments that use covert agents to aid coups may ironically be slowing down an improvement in investment climates, which would take place more rapidly without the interference. It is like using the old method of applying leeches to suck the patient's blood, and then claiming you are responsible when the patient recovers anyway. Given stability within the ranks of their major and minor networks, regimes can be counted on to support continuing modernization and to suppress popular calls for reform. Foreign intervention by spies, saboteurs, and rapid deployment forces is unlikely to speed this process. Governments with a sense of assurance that there is no plot by foreign governments to overthrow them can proceed more quickly to establish stability within the ranks of their patron-client networks. If they do not succeed in doing so they will not last anyway. If they do, one can be sure that there will be no reforms.

V. I. Lenin was the first major twentieth century popularizer of the notion of the primacy of politics—that political leaders could produce reform. His mentor, Karl Marx, believed that revolution must wait until economic forces had paved the way for revolution. A bourgeoisie could not seize political power until it had begun to attain economic power. Lenin disagreed. He felt that a properly organized coterie of political activists could take power even in a peasant-based society and then build an industrial economy and an equitable distribution of goods later. This is what we are sometimes warned could happen in Angola, Yemen, Nicaragua, El Salvador, or Guatemala, leading them away from the fold of the West. But Russia was rapidly becoming an industrial society when Lenin's forces seized power in 1917, and he took power away from a modern leadership with the aid of industrial workers. Hitler, Mussolini, and Tojo strengthened scholarly emphasis on the role that could be played by revolutionary political parties. It was clear, however, that these latter parties were also heavily dependent on the support of industrialists, the aristocracy and the military. In Russia, even Stalin's reign of terror and purges within his own political party depended on a class of technicians who could run industry and on a professional military and secret police. These political leaders were all dependent on clients and an industrialized economic base *that already existed*. The reforms had to be paid for and implemented by this supporting network. Without it, the reforming regimes had neither the money nor the personnel to proceed.

After World War II, "charismatic" leaders like Nkrumah, Sekou Touré, Sukarno, Nasser, and Nehru came to power in developing nations, and revived talk about the primacy of politics. They would lead their nations into reform. They organized their parties among the young and enthusiastic; their rhetoric spoke of sweeping away the old order. The old order which they swept away, however, was that which had been crumbling for several centuries: the village chief, the ethnic asociation, the rural aristocracy. And the new order they ushered in had been on the rise for centuries. The small trader was replaced with the big businessmen. The bureaucracy and military increased in size and strength. Power was increasingly centralized in the capital city. In the countryside, schoolteachers, middle farmers, and export-oriented landowners were strengthened in their positions. These trends would have continued with or without anyone's charisma.

Who was wagging whose tail? Nkrumah, Touré, Sukarno, Nasser, and Nehru—even Mahatma Gandhi—were born into the new middle classes; they did not create them. The impetus toward expanding trade and industry was begun under their colonial predecessors. The subsequent modernization of their countries has largely been carried out by members of the private sectors of their economies. The beneficiaries of this modernization have largely been members of those same private sectors. The young and enthusiastic supporters who swept these individuals to power are aging and moving into obscurity; the rhetoric has turned low key. Governments rely on bureaucracies and military leaders; organized political parties are strictly controlled from the top. Presidents and prime ministers come and go with little change in politics. Dependency on trade continues to increase. Many of those who have seemed strongest in building up their own personal base of power appear weak when it comes to their ability to produce an egalitarian distribution of resources in society. Perhaps they are really creating a primacy of politics, but must wait until their nations produce a certain level of industrial capacity before they can use their reservoir of power to force broader distribution (in which case it is Marx, and not Lenin, who is correct). There is little sign of such an industrial base emerging. Perhaps they do not have a primacy of power but are instead sharing it with other civilian and military patrons who are not free individually or collectively to effect such reforms. "Primacy of politics" may just mean "politics as usual." Behind the flashy leaders and movements we like, and those we hate, lay thoroughly entrenched political systems which show no sign of moving out of the orbit of the North Atlantic nations, or "endangering" our position by promoting reforms.

SUMMARY

The attempts to broaden the standard of living in developing nations have largely involved land distribution, efforts to raise agricultural yields, industrial expansion, and political reform. Little land has been redistributed, and to only a small proportion of peasants. When yields are raised, the crops have often been for export or consumed by a small percentage of the populace. Industrial employment has grown far less rapidly than the labor force. The profits from agriculture and industry are seldom invested in activities which improve the distribution of food, housing, or self-sufficiency to the general populace; such activities are not as profitable as other investments. If a government attempts to force investment in these unprofitable arenas, it runs the risk that its capital will dry up, along with its political support, regardless of the political arrangements through which it is operating.

SHORT SUMMARY

The Green Revolution has left the peasant with less food than he had before. The White Revolution has left the peasant with less land than he had before. The Industrial Revolution has left the peasant with fewer jobs than he had before. Charismatic leaders help the rich more than the poor; so do noncharismatic leaders.

Have you caught these definitions?

	page
malnutrition	292
expropriation	295
salination	314
concessional sales program	336
domestic market	340
capital accumulation	341
capital-intensive industry	340

Can you answer each with one sentence?

1. How many people could get 2 daily ounces of usable protein from the 1976–1978 protein production? (Many nutritionists call 55 grams, or 1.94 ounces the minimum daily requirement.)
2. Why would large farmers stop selling food to local villagers and giving food rations to their laborers during a famine?
3. Why are infants, and infants who grow up, often the worst sufferers from malnutrition?
4. Are "miracle" grains useful to small farmers?
5. Why are urban workers' groups not stable advocates of land reform?

From what you have read this far, can you make and support judgments about these questions?

1. For all the statistics, does the book present any evidence that rural dwellers in Chile or Peru (or any other country) have imbalanced personal environments?
2. Over 600,000 families received land in Iran's land reform. Does this mean a better life for these families or a worse life for any others?
3. Do the land reforms in developing nations during the 1960s differ from the land reforms there during the eighteenth and nineteenth centuries?
4. Where are jobs being destroyed in developing nations? Being created?
5. If the developed nations were to end their aid and loan programs to developing nations and shut them off from international commerce how would that affect the citizens of those nations?

Reread the entire "Book in Brief" section of Chapter 1 with particular attention to whether reforms might be accomplished short of changing the structure of international trade.

CHAPTER

8

GETTING YOUR BEARINGS (see map, front of book)

1. Suppose the United States were cut off from everywhere south of the Tropic of Cancer. What commodities would we be deprived of?
2. From where may the Soviet Union reach the developing nations by sea?
3. Where are the regions of modern agriculture in developing nations?

The Model

A developed nation provides most of its citizens with a stable personal environment. A developing nation does not. Today's developing nations were once developed nations. They changed because their political systems separated from their social systems when European commerce was introduced. *If the structure of international trade changes in the near future, social and political systems may be reintegrated, promoting political development. Then the developing nations may once again become developed nations.*

Reform: Policies Not Yet Tried

QUESTIONS TO KEEP IN MIND

1. Can international trade continue?
2. If multinational corporations were to decline would world standards of living decline?
3. If left to themselves could developing nations produce enough goods and distribute them equitably?
4. Could we survive without the developing nations?

A first step in changing unsatisfactory trends is to seek alternatives. In this chapter I will seek an alternative. It, too, may be unsatisfactory; it is an initial exercise in an attempt to think the matter through. After presenting this alternative, I will discuss its feasibility. I hope you can take it from there, deciding whether the situation calls to mind any other kinds of alternatives and, if so, what their strengths and weaknesses might be.

This alternative may sound radical—even bizarre—especially to someone who has not ingested the earlier chapters of this book. As one observer comments in another context, "for observers surrounded by . . . steel, glass and concrete, it requires a leap of the imagination and considerable openness of mind to perceive the informal sector as a sector of thriving economic activity."[1] It takes imagination to picture this sector—the shantytown, the cottage industry, the isolated village—even taking care of itself or surviving among the accoutrements of modernity. Perhaps we "moderns" should find out more about this informal sector; then we might not need so much imagination. But, there is still another complication. We are thinking about the future; that, too, requires imagination. Hence the occasion calls for some openness of mind. We are speculating more than we are projecting—trying to broaden thinking about the future rather than to pinpoint it. The speculation is this:

The developed nations of western Europe, North America, and Japan are

---

[1] Eric Thorbecke, "The Employment Problem: A Critical Evaluation of Four ILO Comprehensive Reports," *International Labour Review* 107, 5 (May 1973): 411.

becoming increasingly dependent on developing nations for vital metals, fuels, raw materials, and manufactured goods. Whereas in the past foreign aid programs were largely profitable to the developed nations, the combination of defense spending, aid, commitments to loan programs, failures of recipient nations to repay loans, higher costs for raw materials, and competition for markets may make them less so in the future. Multinational corporations are increasingly earning and retaining their profits outside the developed nations, and inflation makes it difficult to cater even to domestic priorities without deficit spending imbalances. Fuel imports are shifting capital into the hands of oil exporting nations and making both western Europe and North America more dependent on outside capital; they do not have regular balance-of-payments surpluses. Their energy consumption rises quickly, while their GNP's grow more slowly. As a result of all these forces, their currencies become less stable. In the face of this, heavy imports and expenditures to maintain markets and supply bases abroad may seem less attractive to them than in the past. If supplies can be obtained at home, it would help the balance of payments, decrease the necessity of aid and defense spending abroad, weaken the independence of multinational corporations, and slow the diversion of capital to the oil-producing states by lowering their exports. The economies of western Europe, North America, and Japan are so intertwined that moves by one major nation—say the United States—in this direction might necessitate similar moves on the part of the others. This might happen slowly by indirection, or forcefully by plan.

The effect of such moves would be a rapid diminishing in the power of the patron-client networks in developing nations. They are heavily dependent on their markets in and capital from the developed areas. The multinational corporations are also heavily dependent upon the developed nations for markets and military, capital, and logistic support. To weather the storm, the leaders of developing nations would need to look in one of two directions: to the Soviet Union and China, or inward. China is reaching near self-sufficiency, but it is in a poor position to be supportive of outside regions. The Soviet Union has a vast reservoir of natural resources; its technology and capital reserves, however, are not on a firm footing and it is dependent upon food imports to grow meat it feels it needs. If the Soviet Union could not improve its position in those regards, this would leave the leaders of developing nations the option of turning inward. There is a potentially viable manner in which they could do this.

The *crux* of this inward approach would involve a return to, or reemphasis upon, communal (i.e., as in Chapter 2) land tenure in major portions of their territories. This would allow nations to give back to large numbers of their people local control over land, the power to cooperate in solving agricultural problems, and incentives to produce. *Second,* some of the best land could remain under individual or state ownership for intensive production of cereals and other foodstuffs. And *third,* there would be urban areas. These would continue to supervise exploitation of minerals and other natural resources for domestic use and perhaps some export, but would resist exports based on agriculture unless their own people were provided for. Urban sectors would produce—generally through small industries—consumer goods for sale to both the urban and the rural populace. And they would devote considerable attention, research, manufacturing, education activity, and organizing to improving the productivity and living standards of the rural sectors.

QUESTION

What is the plan being proposed here? What are the three sectors?

Such an approach in developing nations would weaken the political powers of the export-import sectors of the economy, centralized armies, multinational corporations, and urban white- and blue-collar workers. It would halt the centralizing of the patron-client networks and return greater power to regional leaders. The return to communal tenure, however, would make the model for leadership closer to that of the kingly states than of early patron-clientism. The existence of modern technology would allow greater flexibility than before in assuring healthy villages on which that regional power would need to be based. Initially, the introduction of that technological assistance might involve some pressure from the central urban sectors and reliance on North America to provide a buffer food bank. Later, as villages reachieved some self-sufficiency and integration, they, themselves, would be in a position to resist incursions on their own self-sufficiency and perhaps even demand government assistance to augment it. In addition, a return to social stability forms a viable basis for reestablishing birth control.

Under such circumstances, the developed nations might need to eliminate waste and inefficiencies from their life styles. This could mean eating food grown closer to home, less elaborate packaging, living closer to work, eliminating planned obsolescence, less conspicuous consumption, and greater population dispersion. New energy sources would need to be tapped. Four of the most underutilized energy sources, the sun, photosynthesis, human and animal labor, would probably be better utilized than in the past. Otherwise (or in addition), developed nations might turn to Siberia, Canada, Antarctica, and the ocean for resources to use and waste. The United States and the Soviet Union could continue their rivalries and arms race if they felt so disposed. If they are able to limit the arms race, their combined resources could easily provide the entire northern hemisphere with a standard of living comparable or superior to that in the past.

REDEVELOPMENT: A POTENTIAL DIRECTION

The United States contains cities, farms, small towns, and Indian reservations. The speculation I am about to make has something in common with this structure, if you can imagine the Indian reservations as much larger in size, more populous, and culturally diverse than they are at present. Developing nations generally contain cities, zones of surplus food and raw material production, and hinterland with subsistence farming. Current plans call for gradually absorbing the latter into the former two areas. My approach differs in that it would try to preserve and expand the latter.

North America contains 1,125 million cultivatable acres.[2] If 400 million of them were devoted to cereal grains at a yield of 1,800 pounds per acre (a very moderate yield by North American standards) they would produce enough grain to feed nearly half the 1980 world population of 4.3 billion people a pound a day. If Asia used 800 million out of its 1,150 million arable acres to produce cereal grains at an average of 600 pounds per acre (also a very moderate goal[3]) this would provide the same quantity of food for another 1.2 billion people. If Africa did this on 250 million of 1,500 million cultivatable acres at an average of 450 pounds to the acre, another 300 million people could be added to this total.[4] South America has 925 million arable acres; 400 million of these yielding a 500-pound average would extend this ration to a half billion more. By using high-yielding seed, better fertilizers (whether organic or artificial), and scientific farming techniques, farmers could hope to increase yields on part of the acreage and thus raise these averages. Europe, with 425 million cultivatable acres and yields traditionally higher than any of these, and the USSR, with 875 million cultivatable acres and Australia/New Zealand with 300 million cultivatable acres could add even more to these figures. In fact, as we have noted, the picture is already brighter than this: the actual 1978 world production of 3.485 trillion pounds of cereal grains could already feed a pound a day to $9\frac{1}{2}$ billion people. There are also 5 ounces of potatoes, $1\frac{1}{2}$ ounces of oilseeds or beans, $\frac{3}{4}$ ounces of fish, and uncounted (and substantial) additional quantities of edible vegetables and range-fed animals currently produced per capita per day for $9\frac{1}{2}$ billion people.[5] This is true even though much of the best land is used to raise cotton, hemp, sugar cane, cacao, coffee, tea, pineapples, bananas, tobacco, carnations, chrysanthemums, tropical house plants, and urbanization. North America had 600, South America 200, Asia 1,175, Africa 775, Europe 375, the USSR 575, and Australia/New Zealand 50 million acres under cultivation in 1965.[6]

---

[2] Roger Revelle, "Food and Population," *Scientific American* 231, no. 3 (September 1974): 168. That is, already cultivated or capable of being cultivated.

[3] Some 42 percent of India's cereal-growing land (1972–1973) is planted in sorghum, pearl millet, maize, gram, small millets, and barley. Most of this is on unirrigated land. The average 1967–1973 yields on these grains in pounds per acre are 433, 373, 931, 724, 334, and 881 respectively. The percentage of total cereal growing land occupied by each is 15 percent, 12 percent, 6 percent, 2 percent, 4 percent, and 3 percent respectively. Averaged with wheat and rice (one-third the acreage of which is in high-yielding varieties at 1,400 pounds per acre and the rest averaging 530 and 850 pounds to the acre), this means that at present ratios India's cereal-growing lands produce 750 pounds per acre. Directorate of Economics and Statistics, "Estimates of Area and Production of Principal Crops in India, 1972-73," Ministry of Agriculture, Government of India, 1974, pp. 4–8 (mimeo). Cereal grains grew on 257 million of India's 662 million arable acres in 1978. Portions of Asia to the west of India have nearly the same amount of irrigated land as India and probably fairly comparable overall yields. The monsoon portions of Asia to the east of India grow primarily rice on their cereal lands and have higher average cereal yields.

[4] The United Nations estimates that Africa has 1,544 million acres which could produce crops without irrigation. A billion of these are primarily suited for cassava and sweet potato, though corn could grow on some of this land. Currently, only 485 million acres are under cultivation. Food and Agriculture Organization, *The State of Food and Agriculture 1978* (Rome: United Nations, 1979), pp. 1–60.

[5] Food and Agriculture Organization of the United Nations, *FAO Production Yearbook 1978* (Rome, 1979). 1976–1978 average production figures. There are large additional unused acreages. E.g., see footnote 4 and p. 324.

[6] Revelle, "Food and Population," p. 168.

Thomas Malthus warned in 1798 that the population was increasing faster than the supply of food. So, he said, the world is doomed to famine. In fact, the opposite is happening. The 1974 world agricultural production would feed about $7\frac{1}{2}$ billion people the pound of cereal, 5 ounces of potatoes, and $\frac{3}{4}$ ounces of fish. The 1978 production would feed this to $9\frac{1}{2}$ billion people. Yet between 1974 and 1978, population rose by 700 million. The number who could be fed rose faster than the number of mouths.

I would hope, of course, that it would not become necessary to feed such large numbers of people, that the surface of the planet would not have to be devoted to food production, that diets might have variety, and that there would be no need to transport large quantities of food to distant points on the globe. With these *current food surpluses* there is a great deal of flexibility. It is possible that these worries may take care of themselves if we start to solve the problem by turning our priorities away from food production, population control, and economic growth, and concentrate instead on the social environments within which individuals live.

Here is the number of acres per family of five, 1974 population figures, in some selected countries:

Iran	$62\frac{1}{2}$
Peru	105
India	$7\frac{1}{2}$
Bangladesh	$2\frac{1}{2}$
Indonesia	19
Nigeria	$12\frac{1}{2}$
Mexico	45
Pakistan	$17\frac{1}{2}$
Afghanistan	40

There is still a good deal of land per family in the developing nations. Except for the peaks of mountains and the highly arid regions, most of it is habitable. Among developing nations, only in North Africa and the Middle East do arid regions compose a high percentage of the national territory; these particular nations are generally not populous (Egypt, with 35 million people on about one *highly arable* acre per family of five, is the most populous of them). The following nations contain these indicated acreages of *arable* land per family of five:[7]

Mali	104		Venezuela	30
Ivory Coast	48		Brazil	25
Ethiopia	47		Ecuador	13
Senegal	37		Colombia	13
Morocco	14		Haiti	2
Kenya	8		Indonesia	3
Argentina	95		India	4
Bolivia	69		Bangladesh	$1\frac{1}{2}$
Mexico	36			

---

[7] A Transnational Institute Report, "World Hunger: Causes and Remedies," October 1974, p. 38. Figures on Bangladesh are from Harvey Stockwin, "Why Charity Goes Astray in Bangladesh," *Far Eastern Economic Review* 88, no. 14 (April 4, 1975): 39.

If you begin with the question of how best to distribute these people, a good many options are open. Some of them could move across national boundaries to equalize numbers. Even leaving this notion aside, there is still room for change in locating people. One innovation might be a return to (or, in some cases, a reemphasis upon) the communal-tenure village.

Discussion of India is continued from p. 325.

Consider India. Even if one removes from consideration its 125 million uncultivatable acres[8] (which are usable for other purposes), is still has 662,400,000 acres. Setting aside 25 percent of this for cities, mines, factories, and individually owned farms (e.g., for the 70 million acres currently irrigated), this *still* leaves about 500 million acres that might be returned to communal tenure. If villages were provided on the average with enough land to give six acres to each family of five, this area could accommodate 400 million people, or over two-thirds of India's current population. Sorghum and pearl millet, which averaged 433 and 373 pounds per acre in 1967–1973 in India (see note 3) are 11 to 20 percent protein and will grow on the poorest and driest land. They can be interplanted with pigeon peas, which average 530 pounds to the acre in India, and are 18 to 32 percent protein (or chickpeas: 310 pounds per acre, 20 to 22 percent protein) and also grow in the poorest and driest soil. The intercropping adds nitrogen to the soil.[9] Maize will produce much higher yields than sorghum and millet (an average of 931 pounds per acre) on comparable land almost as poorly watered, but is poor in lysine. New research to cross "opaque-2," a high-lysine corn, with some new strains that are resistant to pests, diseases, and drought, may make this an even more suitable crop.[10] Barley (an average of 881 pounds per acre) grows on some of the driest, poorest land; new strains have been developed that are 20 percent protein.[11] Some new strains of these grains are also being developed which have shorter growing periods and hence raise yields via double-cropping. So these communal farmers, without purchased fertilizer or irrigation, and using one-third of their land allotment to grow grain, could conceivably produce enough grain for their families; with improved seed and fertilizer they could even create surpluses for sale. There would still be room for legumes, vegetables, bearing trees, and animals to round out their diets and produce fertilizer, fuel, and fallow. India grows many leafy vegetables, cucumbers, melons, gourds, garlic, mangoes, bananas, guavas, tamarinds, jackfruit, pomegranates, figs, and citrus fruits on trees, bushes, and vines that occupy peripheral areas of fields. It was once common to use sweepings, refuse, and dung to fertilize such vegetable plots.[12] The mixed usage of the land would allow for a return of some natural ecological balance.

---

[8] David Grigg, *The Harsh Lands: A Study in Agricultural Development* (New York: Macmillan, 1970), p. 270.

[9] Consultative Group on International Agricultural Research, *International Research in Agriculture* (New York, 1974), pp. 51–55.

[10] See Anthony Wolff, "A New Earful," *Saturday Review World* (December 14, 1974): 14.

[11] *International Research in Agriculture*, p. 32.

[12] Elizabeth Whitcombe, *Agrarian Conditions in Northern India: Vol. 1, The United Provinces Under British Rule, 1860-1900* (Berkeley: University of California Press, 1972), p. 30.

Further discussion of India may be found on p. 360.

If Iran did the same with half its total land, giving twenty-acre plots to each family, it could provide land for 50 million people, or half again its current population. Nigeria, using half its land area and seven-acre plots, could accommodate 80 million, or about its present population. Virtually all Latin American and African countries could give even larger plots and accommodate their entire populations.

Would people want to live this way? In many areas of many nations they still do, except often under economic arrangements which make them less than masters of their own lands. A high percentage of additional people in developing nations live with neither land nor job; to them such an arrangement might well seem a vast improvement.

Why communal tenure? Communal land tenure gives villages control over their land and their community. Village leaders, rather than outsiders, can decide what is to be done with the land and who is to work it. If a family errs in its use of the land, it is responsible to the community and can be assessed by the community. If a village leader errs in his distribution of the land, he, too, is responsible to the community. There is an additional ecological reason. Opening vast new stretches of land to modern agriculture could drastically alter the ecology of the planet. We have seen how the timbered land of India was turned into virtual desert, how irrigation wastes water and salinates land, and how easy it is to destroy the frail topsoil when uprooting jungle. A modernized traditional agriculture would change ecology less drastically. For instance, savannah land keeps its cover best when the grass can grow back each year. A combination of grazing and small-plot gardening there can effect this process better than intensive cultivation. Slash-and-burn can be ecologically beneficial in tropical forest areas providing there is ample fallow in between. It also involves leaving trees standing in the midst of fields and mixed crops and produces a far milder environmental impact than bulldozing and single-crop farming.[13] Birds in trees and bushes, and elimination of large stands of the same crops repeated without rotation, can contribute to reducing pests and plant diseases.

Henry Bretton raises an important objection to communal tenure:

Communal ownership, increasingly favored, still cannot escape the pervasive presence of the traditional rulers or ruling class. Too often, in order to secure stability even enlightened modern rulers allow communal ownership to be undermined and reduced to where it is "nothing but a screen for the semi-feudal exploitation of the peasants" . . . In prevailing conditions, recognition of the rights of such traditional landlords as the Nigerian obas, the tendana priests, the

---

[13] Grigg, *Harsh Lands,* pp. 212–217; 216: "Intercropping, whilst appearing untidy and inefficient, has three virtues. The crops grown include roots, cereals, shrubs, and trees. These grow rapidly and provide a layered cover to the soil, protecting it from sun and rain. The crops have different requirements of the soil and thus serve a similar function to the crop rotation of temperate lands. . . . The larger trees provide some cover during cropping, and their existence hastens regeneration. . . . The failure to cultivate the soil . . . reduces the chances of erosion. Burning the debris . . . makes the topsoil friable and spreads the plant nutrients of the vegetation cover evenly over the surface. Only nitrogen and sulphur are lost. Burning also reduces acidity."

Ashanti hierarchy and others in Ghana, and the marabouts in Senegal merely
sets the stage for the emergence of a new class of real estate operators in traditional garb.[14]

I agree. This is why I cannot picture communal tenure as a solution to anything
under present world conditions. As Bretton himself points out, it was the power
of local leaders to collect rubber, peanuts, and the like that "tied local functionaries to the territorial and eventually national centers" and produced their
ability to exploit the peasants.[15] Once these regional leaders—whether they were
traditional rulers converted into patrons, or newer forms of patrons—found
their profits from the sale of goods to the capital gone their ability to exploit
peasants would be greatly reduced. Perhaps they would dream up some effective
new way to exploit the peasants; they would certainly try. But they would find it
much harder to interfere with communal land tenure.

Still, one might object, the old communal communities were notorious for
their adherence to subsistence agriculture. Not all of them were. It was they,
after all, who provided the surpluses that supported the kingly states, and with a
minimum of help from the kings. If a village's land happened to be more fertile
than average, and outside assistance with credit, agricultural extension, and fertilizer were available, it might well be that the community would want to avail
itself of the extra income that could thereby accrue to it. Studies of peasants have
not shown them to be without motivation to produce when they can see visible
rewards for themselves.[16] As we have seen earlier, viable communities can
develop their own internal motivations to produce. Given the benign neglect that
surrounds them, the fact that rural folk survive at all is testimony to their
resourcefulness; with some outside assistance, perhaps they can do even better.

If communities did not produce much beyond subsistence under this approach, they would at least be feeding themselves and thus removing themselves
from bread lines. Those communities that did produce extra would create a built-
in internal market for more modern sectors of the economy. The improvement
of their productivity might also provide a focus for the health and educational
institutions, factories, and bureaucratic organizations of the nation. The more
their productivity is improved, the less the nation's reliance on importing food
from North America or other places.

If any village were to become overly reliant on outside help, this could be its
undoing. Communities in semi-arid regions, for instance, would need more land,
perhaps for grazing, than those in regions with more constant rainfall. Here,
tubewells that work only during periods of average rainfall, or complete reliance
on trade (e.g., of cotton) with outsiders, could prove fatal, should either the
water supply or the markets dry out. Such a community would better be left

---

[14] Henry L. Bretton, *Power and Politics in Africa* (Chicago: Aldine, 1973), pp. 156, 157.

[15] Ibid., p. 146. See also pp. 191-192.

[16] In addition to the discussion at the beginning of Chapter 7, see Raanan Weitz, *From Peasant to
Farmer: A Revolutionary Strategy for Development* (New York: Columbia University Press, 1971),
pp. 68-78; John H. Cleave, *African Farmers: Labor Use in the Development of Smallholder
Agriculture* (New York: Praeger, 1974).

without the tubewell[17] or outside trade until it could achieve subsistence (many seemingly prosperous communities are actually *below* the subsistence level—they cannot even feed themselves in an emergency because their energy is diverted into other forms of production). In this situation, some other types of technical assistance might be more appropriate; it might mean setting up local grain reserves such as those under the Incas, or turning to hunting and gathering. Short of this, it might even be better to let members die of diseases which modern medicine could cure. This is preferable to artificial increases in numbers and prosperity which could turn into complete oblivion for all members, should a drought occur (such as that in sub-Sahara Africa in the mid-1970s or in Bihar in 1967) for which the government could not provide aid.

This brings up the question of population control in general. In settings of extreme poverty, population control has little impact. Parents often wish to have a lot of children so that someone will support them in old age, and there is little that can be done to stop this. Traditional villages, we have seen, had population control in the form of infanticide, extended periods of nursing, contraception using native lore and medicine, war, and drought. They did not have population control in the form of starvation due to sheer lack of money to buy food. For the indigent, the former might be preferable to the latter. But for those villages able to convert some surplus crops into income a new form of population control could also develop, that which derives from personal stability. In developed nations and among the middle classes in developing nations, modern families who experience a degree of prosperity tend to start holding down the number of their children. Once the stability and desire are created, it would be considerably easier to establish modern birth control facilities than it is at present.[18] And, with the aid of modern satellites and research methods, it might be possible to help

---

[17] In pre-British India farmers used to build their own wells by digging a round hole, lining it with straw, and setting up a wooden structure by which cattle could lift water in buckets. As communities were destroyed, and canal irrigation progressed, many communities ceased building these wells and became reliant on outside water supplies. If those who build the well live in the community, the villagers are more likely to know what to expect and what not to expect from it and plan accordingly.

[18] "The latest fad is the faith in population control as the sole answer to Bangladesh's many problems. Advertisements . . . appear in the English-language papers . . . preaching to the converted, the members of the urban elite . . . native Bangalee medicine . . . has evidently long since come up with a crude version of the contraceptive interuterine device (IUD). Belatedly, some research is being done to discover if the crude device is effective. This is not enough. Native medicine is the only medicine for the vast majority of Bangalees. Precious little is known about it in any scientific sense, but there is no doubt that it is effective in some ways. It is also certain that the vested interests of modern Western medical practitioners in Bangladesh resists such increased understanding . . . some feel that Western medicine is what the 'natives' should have—rather than thinking in terms of what the masses know, can afford, and are likely to get for the foreseeable future . . . is it necessarily logical or wise in the Bangladesh context to go straight for population control *per se?* What about the demographic view that fertility rises in times of hunger, to offset deaths by starvation, but falls when food becomes more plentiful? Does this merely mean that food, clothing, and shelter must also be part of population planning? Is even this too simplistic? . . . it is a waste of time giving contraceptive devices to people who instinctively know that more children wither away or die from endemic complaints." Extract from Harvey Stockwin, "Why Charity Goes Astray in Bangladesh," *Far Eastern Economic Review* 88, no. 14, (April 4, 1975): 40–41. Tanzania and Sri Lanka are the only countries to officially recognize traditional healers. Charles Elliott, *Patterns of Poverty in the Third World: A Study of Social and Economic Stratification* (New York: Praeger, 1975), p. 338.

communities in over-grazed and over-cultivated regions to move into areas which are less intensively used.

We have by no means suggested placing all land under communal control. In Africa and parts of Latin America, for instance, communal lands have long existed side-by-side with individually controlled lands. Some of the best (e.g., irrigated) lands might well remain in individual hands, producing high yields of cereal grains, supplementary food crops, or crops for export. And if villages in the countryside did grow too large, some of their members might move to the cities as in the past.

H. W. Singer argues that 98 percent of the research and development expenditures in the richer countries go toward solving the problems that concern richer countries.[19] Hence technology in developing nations tends to be most up-to-date in those sectors that are most similar to the richer countries while virtually no technology is devoted to problems that are important to the developing countries, such as tropical agriculture; small-scale production; adapting miracle seeds, pest control, and fertilizers to local conditions; small-farm irrigation; adapting contraceptives and drugs to various cultural settings; inexpensive food additives to round out diets; utilization of natural raw materials for fertilizer and small consumer products; special pumps and storage devices; and subsistence farming.[20]

Discussion of India is continued from p. 357.

The Indian farmer once used the shallow furrow plow (which does not disturb subsurface moisture), a harrow to scratch up the surface, a club for clods, a pick axe for drainage and irrigation ditches, a trowel for planting and a hoe for weeding, a bucket for irrigation, a pair of bullocks to pull the plow and work the well lift (fed on chaff, some fodder crops, and by grazing the fallow fields), and a pull cart. He grew millets, barley, peas, sorghum, gram, fruits, and vegetables.[21] When the Department of Agriculture was established in 1874 it opened experimental farms. These tried to develop new strains of wheat, cotton, sugar, and cattle for export. They tried steam-driven farm implements and lightweight ironshare plows, and used irrigation and heavy fertilizer which the peasant could not possibly afford.[22] The farmer might have been better served with experiments on how to use the tools he already had to improve the output of staple foods.

---

[19] "Dualism Revisited: A New Approach to the Problems of the Dual Society in Developing Countries," *Journal of Development Studies* 1 (October 1970): 62–64. See also Bernard Lietaer, *Europe + Latin America + the Multinationals* (Westmead, Eng.: Saxon House, 1979), pp. 35–38.

[20] A study based on seventy-eight American investments in developing countries showed that no technological adaptations had been made in any of these regards. Rolf Sutter, "Technology Transfer into the LDC's," *Intereconomics* no. 12 (December 1974): 380–383.

[21] Whitcombe, *Agrarian Conditions*, p. 35.

[22] Ibid., pp. 106–110. In comparison, Whitcombe mentions a certain Maharajah who contemplated sending an elephant to an old pensioner in England who complained of no longer being able to get around on foot and being too poor to keep a conveyance.

Discussion of Iran is continued from p. 346.

Iranian peasants use nailplows, handmade from local materials. These plows can maneuver irregular plots bounded by irrigation ditches without leaving a furrow to cut off the flow of water. The peasants' small animals can easily pull them. Moldplows introduced to replace them do not work so well on small irregular fields and cannot be pulled by the smaller animals. To use them the peasant must hire a neighbor with larger animals, and lose a percentage of his crop in the process. Tractors and threshers only work well on the fields of larger landlords. There they compete with cattle owners who rent their beasts for field work. The increased yields these technological improvements bring are accompanied by decreased wages, so the sharecroppers do not benefit. Less grain is left on the ground for the landless peasants to retrieve as part of their traditional share in harvesting. So there is little reason for the peasant to be supportive of such innovation. Were peasants supplied with their own land *and* new technology *adapted to their needs,* they would have much more reason to support it. This would make it possible for them to maintain themselves and for their richer neighbors to help feed the others. An agricultural college was begun near Teheran in 1929. Almost no sons of peasants attended, and nearly none of those who did returned to the land. The college introduced European and Australian livestock, and worked to improve sugar beets, tobacco, silk, and tea, most of which (except the sugar beets) was grown on land owned by the Reza Shah. It also introduced modern agricultural machinery.[23] None of this was useful to the peasant or improved Iran's ability to feed itself.

As energy costs rise, so will the cost of producing food via large-scale agriculture; while the North American grain that could feed $1\frac{1}{2}$ billion persons each year will still be available, its costs will be higher. This will make it increasingly an economic proposition for developing nations to find ways to feed themselves. Those countries with more land and fewer people will have an economic advantage over those with the opposite situation, even if the latter are blessed with more minerals and fuels. Those countries with an urban infrastructure devoted to increasing yields from available resources will have an advantage over those absorbed in producing products their own people do not need and the developed nations find redundant. Cities devoting great attention to the internal problems of their nations are likely to be scattered about their hinterlands rather than located as monoliths on their peripheries. Developing nations will try to apply local resources to local problems and to become dependent on other nations only for those resources and activities needed to develop independent national economies.

The Rockefeller Foundation helped found the International Maize and Wheat Improvement Center in Mexico, where the first breakthroughs were made on high-yielding grains. By 1972, US$15 million was being spent world- wide on this research, and US$34 million in 1974 went to eight such centers in Mexico,

---

[23] Amin Bononi, *The Modernization of Iran 1921–1941* (Stanford, Calif.: Stanford University Press, 1961), pp. 124–125.

the Philippines, Nigeria, Colombia, India, Peru, Kenya, and Ethiopia. While much of the research to date has been applied to strains usable principally by middle farmers with irrigation, fertilizer, and advanced equipment, some research is finally underway on strains designed for poorer lands as well. This probably constitutes the most notable exception to Singer's generalization that attention goes only to the problems of rich countries. Total expenditures have not been great, but the results have already been significant. For instance, upland and rain-fed rice accounts for 65 to 70 percent of the world's rice lands. This land has the advantage of not needing elaborate irrigation, but yields only an average of 900 to 1,300 pounds per acre. New research in the Philippines and Africa is producing drought-resistant strains with $3\frac{1}{2}$-month growing cycles, well-suited to upland conditions, and yielding 3,500 pounds per acre. Sweet potatoes are being developed which can yield 26,000 pounds per acre in dry season. As mentioned earlier, pigeon peas, which can be interplanted with sorghum in semi-arid regions, are being improved in India so that they will have the same growing time as sorghum and will lend themselves to double-cropping; they contain 18 to 32 percent protein. Chickpeas, which thrive in dry weather, are being given increased fungus resistance. The International Potato Center in Peru, which is finally ending the inattention alluded to by a young man in Chapter 7, is increasing the protein content (as high as 25 percent in some varieties) and growing range of potatoes.[24] Genetic engineers are trying to transfer nitrogen-fixing genes from legumes into grains so as to produce partially self-fertilizing cereals (something the prairie grasses did on their own through the mixture of species they created). Algae, yeast, and plant leaves might also be transformed into human food containing usable protein using new enzymes. Experiments are underway in India to make alfalfa and water hyacynth edible for humans.[25]

Even these first attempts to use international facilities for adaptation to local needs point, ironically, to the need for greater local self-sufficiency. Patents for the miracle seeds have been granted to seed companies who, in turn, have been purchased by large multinational corporations. The same multinationals often hold drug, seed, pesticide, and fertilizer companies. Local strains of seed, adapted for centuries to local diseases and weather, are being taken out of production and may at times be simply eaten and vanish, while seeds are imported from other countries to replace them. Vast acreages of the same seeds are susceptible to blights that could sweep through the countryside. So the farmer becomes dependent on foreign multinationals both for seed and expensive pesticides. In Europe, there is even discussion of outlawing plants without patents. Dr. Erna Bennett of the FAO estimates that by 1990 three-quarters of all the vegetable varieties grown in Europe will be extinct because of enforcement of patenting laws.[26] In 1980, the United States Supreme Court ruled that bacterial strains may be patented here. Already the companies are discussing patents on the nitrogen-fixing grains and some of the seeds mentioned in the previous paragraph. So the peasant in the most remote hinterland, too, might need to begin buying his seeds

---

[24] *International Research in Agriculture,* pp. 18, 37, 39–40, 60–61.

[25] N. W. Pirie, "Leaf Proteins: A Beneficiary of Tribulation," *Nature* 253 (1975): 239–241.

[26] Presidential Commission on World Hunger, *Overcoming World Hunger: The Challenge Ahead* (Washington, D.C.: Government Printing Office, 1980), p. 221.

from abroad. And there is more. Satellites are capable of sensing whether a field of corn is diseased before this is evident on the ground. They can also survey the growth of crops around the globe. The United States government and the Latin American Agribusiness Development Corporation, with about fifteen multinational stockholders, have permanent staffs to compile such data for sale to corporations.[27] Those subscribing to such services can know ahead of others the size of annual yields so they can adjust their commodities buying and selling accordingly. They can plan to pull their contracted harvest out of one country to send to another. They can make deals with government marketing boards before it becomes evident the price is going to be high that year. And they can tell when their patent rights are being infringed.

The Chinese began working right in peasant villages in 1961 to develop high-yielding strains of wheat and barley that are resistant to cold and high altitudes. They have developed over 1,200 strains of rice as well. India, Sri Lanka, and Brazil have developed new strains of rice, and Brazil, Tunisia, Egypt, Iran, and Iraq, have developed new wheat.[28] These indigenous improvements require cooperation between town and countryside, and entail no foreign indebtedness for seed, fertilizer, machinery, and irrigation. They would benefit from having agronomists and engineers who spent part of their time in the countryside and knew its problems. The hero of tomorrow may be patterned on a functionary almost nonexistent in today's developing world: the agricultural extension worker. It is he and she who will best be able to help communities adapt new technologies to local growing conditions, using the resources closest at hand.

OUTSIDE INFLUENCES

The forces that govern developing nations are not entirely internal. Governments of richer nations, commodities exchanges in Europe and North America, and directors of international corporations all have an important effect upon the policies of developing nations. They, like the current leaders of developing nations, can hardly be expected to be enthusiastic about an approach such as that just proposed. Reports from international agencies like the World Bank, the International Monetary Fund, and other groups concerned with the problems of developing nations place primary emphasis on quite different issues: improving communication, population control, installing technological innovations, increasing exports, capital formation, improving health (especially tap water) and education (especially basic literacy), and raising urban employment. They speak of raising agricultural productivity but often devote most of their attention to the export sector.[29] They do not talk of redistributing land to peasants with no im-

---

[27] Susan George, *Feeding the Few: Corporate Control of Food* (Washington, D.C.: Institute for Policy Studies, 1979), pp. 46, 56-59.

[28] Frances Moore Lappé and Joseph Collins, *Food First: Beyond the Myth of Scarcity* (Boston: Houghton Mifflin, 1977), pp. 123, 138-139.

[29] Of all World Bank loans in 1974, only 18 percent went to agriculture. Frances Moore Lappé, "Fantasies of Famine," *Harpers* 250, 1497 (February 1975): 89. Even much of this went to export agriculture.

mediate prospect of economic return, or returning land to food production which is involved in production for export, or exporting North American food supplies in a manner less profitable than other potential uses, or of cities concentrating on human needs in their hinterlands.

It is common knowledge that certain companies have had a strong influence on certain countries: Firestone in Liberia; United Fruit in Guatemala; Unilever in Nigeria; ITT, Anaconda Copper, and Grace & Company in Chile and Peru; Anderson & Clayton in Brazil, Peru, Bangladesh, and elsewhere; oil companies in their various drilling areas; Rockefeller interests in Latin America; and Alcoa Aluminum in Jamaica or Kaiser in Ghana. The list is long. Many of these companies have had such a tight hold on the economies of individual nations that they could virtually dictate policy to their local clients, the national leaders.

Discussion of Nigeria is continued from p. 216.

In recent years the policies of some of these firms have become more subtle, but their basic dominance actually increases. For instance, Unilever, one of the world's largest conglomerates, first went to Nigeria through its subsidiary, the United Africa Company, to obtain palm oil for their margarine business in Europe, using their own ships.[30] The ships returned from each run laden with Unilever products and the company soon became Nigeria's largest importer; by the 1960s it was four times larger than its nearest rival. As competition grew from other foreign imports, the company began a new tactic, import substitution. It would set up a plant in Nigeria and see to it that the Nigerian government gave this plant tariff protection from foreign competition. Its first local plants made beer, trucks, and bicycles. It diversified into department stores, earth-moving and civil-engineering machinery, air conditioning, and other electrical goods and office equipment—twenty-eight industries in all. Gradually the parent company sold its transport and plantations—the original investment—to Nigerians. Meanwhile, its gross investment remained much the same—fluctuating between US $5.6 and $7.8 million.[31] In each of its ventures Unilever sought a Nigerian partner. By the late 1960s, it was in printed textiles, cotton yarn, sugar, cement, vehicle batteries, cigarettes, fiberboard packaging, foam rubber, radio assembly, reconstituted milk, beds and mattresses, ice cream, pigs and meat products, sewing thread, building contractors, plastic products, timber, plywood, and furniture, in addition to the businesses mentioned above. All of these firms are Nigerian "owned." All have little or no competition.

[30] Louis Turner, *Multinational Companies and the Third World* (New York: Hill & Wang, 1973), pp. 50–53. Unilever now controls 80 percent of the international oilseed market. Carl Widstrand, ed., *Multinational Firms in Africa* (Dakar: African Institute for Economic Development and Planning, 1975), p. 308.

[31] Henry L. Bretton, *Power and Politics in Africa* (Chicago: Aldine, 1973), p. 113, says of an earlier era in Africa: "Astonishingly modest expenditures in money, men, and material were required to maintain control over so vast an area." Thomas J. Biersteker, *Distortion or Development?: Contending Perspectives on the Multinational Corporation* (Cambridge: MIT Press, 1978), p. 86, examining fifteen Nigerian firms which had over 50 percent of capital owned abroad, found that 95 percent of their total debt capital was raised locally.

Unilever's total capital investment in Nigeria has not increased, but it virtually dominates Nigeria's modern sector.

Further discussion of Nigeria may be found on p. 369.

In recent years there has been a marked increase in overseas investments by multinational corporations.[32] Today, their overseas operations may account for over one-quarter of total world production.[33] *This does not mean a great influx of capital into developing nations, however.* One study found that during the 1960s, 46 percent of the investments by multinational corporations in Latin America went to buy out local businesses.[34] Multinational subsidiaries tend to be less labor-intensive than local firms.[35] A study of 257 Latin American firms found that the multinational subsidiaries used about half the number of employees per $10,000 in sales as local firms.[36] A retired executive of one of the three largest multinational banks indicates that his bank always tried to use 95 percent local savings sources for its local loans, and no more than 5 percent from its home base.[37] Multinational subsidiaries find it easier to get bank loans than do locally owned firms.[38] Furthermore, a high percentage of transactions by multinational subsidiaries are with their parent corporations.[39] Since pricing decisions are made in the home offices of the companies, it is easy for them to avoid local taxation at both ends of export transactions. They can underprice exports, so that the subsidiary makes less money on them, and then mark up the

---

[32] For instance, a study of 125 United States multinationals showed that their fixed investments in overseas subsidiaries was 21 percent of fixed domestic investment in 1960; this rose to 25 percent in 1966, and 41 percent in 1970. Richard J. Barnet and Ronald E. Müller, *Global Reach: The Power of the Multinational Corporations* (New York: Simon & Schuster, 1974), p. 259.

[33] Lietaer, *Europe + Latin America + the Multinationals,* p. 11.

[34] Barnet and Müller, *Global Reach,* p. 408. This does not improve productive capacity, and any profits accruing to the local businessmen from these transactions can easily be transferred to foreign banks, further depleting local investment capital.

[35] Ibid., pp. 169, 444.

[36] Ronald Müller, "The Multinational Corporation and the Underdevelopment of the Third World," in *The Political Economy of Development and Underdevelopment,* 2d ed., ed. Charles K. Wilber (New York: Random House, 1979), p. 160.

[37] Barnet and Müller, *Global Reach,* p. 154. Raymond Vernon, "The Economic Consequences of U. S. Foreign Investment," in *The Economic Consequences of Multinational Enterprises: An Anthology,* ed. Raymond Vernon (Boston: Division of Research, Harvard Business School, 1972), p. 69 agrees that "three out of four dollars" are raised in the countries themselves, but suggests (p. 79) that the money would not otherwise have been well invested.

[38] For instance, during Argentina's 1971 credit squeeze, local firms cut their borrowing by 42 percent, while subsidiaries of multinational corporations increased their borrowing by over 20 percent. Ibid., p. 141. From 1965 to 1969, Guatemalan multinational subsidiaries absorbed 28 percent to 38 percent of total annual local bank loans to the manufacturing sector; multinational utilities, 75 percent to 100 percent. Barnet and Müller, *Global Reach,* p. 408.

[39] In almost half the foreign trade transactions involving United States-based multinational firms, the buyer and the seller are part of the same multinational firm. Ibid., p. 229. Barnet and Müller estimate that 75 percent of United States-based multinationals conduct all of their exports through subsidiaries. Ibid., p. 158. According to U.S. trade statistics, during 1970, 70 percent of United States exports and 42 percent of imports were handled through multinationals, with at least 27 percent of these involving subsidiaries. Ibid., p. 266.

price via another subsidiary at a tax-free port (e.g., the Bahamas, the Cayman Islands, or Panama) or at sea so that the home company appears to be paying more for them.[40] The home company can also substantially overcharge the local subsidiary for imported goods and charge them fees and royalties on patents. (See Figure 8.1). Only 6 percent of the estimated $3\frac{1}{2}$ million patents active in 1972 were granted by developing nations, and less than one-sixth of those were owned by nationals of developing nations.[41] A Federal Reserve Bank study indicates that fee payments for patent rights accounted for some 25 percent of the total returns from investments of United States multinational corporations in 1970.[42] The local firms pass these costs along to their consumers. In this way investment funds are derived from local sales while profits are repatriated without being reported.[43] Afterwards, even the reported profits can be repatriated. One study shows that United States-based multinational corporations in Latin America derived 83 percent of investment capital locally between 1957 and 1965,

FIGURE 8.1
A Way to Hide Profits

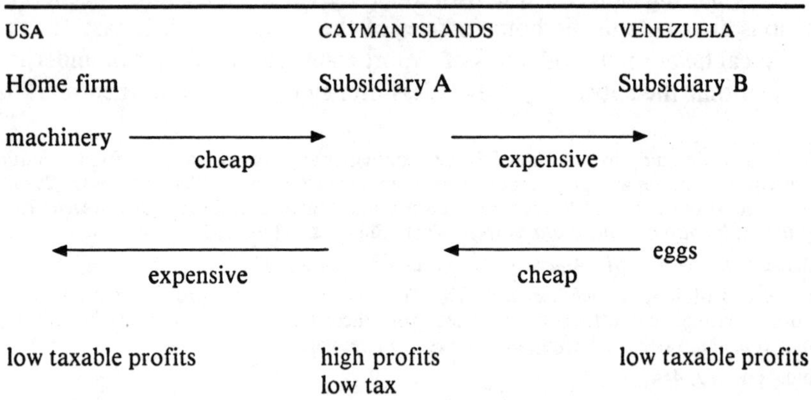

USA	CAYMAN ISLANDS	VENEZUELA
Home firm	Subsidiary A	Subsidiary B

machinery ———————→ cheap   ———————→ expensive

←——————— expensive   ←——————— cheap   eggs

| low taxable profits | high profits low tax | low taxable profits |

---

[40] The study of 257 firms mentioned earlier in the paragraph, with 25 percent of Latin America's exports in 1969, found that three-quarters of them exported to subsidiaries of the same group, and underpriced the goods by an average of 40 percent. About US$47 million in funds were removed from these countries in this disguised manner each year. R. Müller and R. D. Morgenstern, "Multinational Corporations and the Balance of Payment Impact of LDC's: An Econometric Analysis of Export Pricing Behavior," *Kyklos* 27 (April 1971): pp. 304–321.

[41] Frances Stewart, *Technology and Underdevelopment* (London: Macmillan, 1977), p. 119.

[42] Susan B. Foster, "Impact of Direct Investment Abroad by United States Multinational Companies on the Balance of Payments," *Monthly Review of the Federal Reserve Bank of New York* (July 1972), p. 172. Often the rights are to use equipment that is larger and more capital-intensive than appropriate, when simpler technology would be more appropriate and would not involve patent fees.

[43] Constantine V. Vaitsos, "Interaffiliate Charges by Transnational Corporations and Intercountry Income Distribution," Ph.D. Dissertation, Harvard University, 1972, found that subsidiaries of United States drug firms in Colombia had an effective annual rate of return averaging 79.1 percent. They were reporting average profits of 6.7 percent to Colombian authorities. See Barnet and Müller, *Global Reach*, p. 160.

yet between 1960 and 1968 took 79 percent of their net profits out of Latin America.[44] Calculations based on *reported* repatriations show an estimated US$235 million in new direct investment in Latin America each year (most of it probably derived locally), vs. US$1 billion being repatriated out of Latin America.[45] Unreported patriations make this disparity even greater.

EXAMPLE

A firm can use machinery until its cost is completely depreciated on the books in the developed nation, and then sell this to its foreign subsidiary for a tidy profit—classing it as a gift on the books at home, and as an expensive cost on the books of the foreign subsidiary. They can also charge an annual fee for the use of the patents on this machinery. A study of thirteen countries with 65 percent of the population and 56 percent of the GNP of developing nations found their total cost for patents, licenses, trademarks, knowhow, and management service fees to exceed US$1.5 billion, and increasing 20 percent annually. So these countries were *annually* paying out *just for these services* more than twice the *total* amount of money that foreign banks and firms had invested in them.[46]

Even when firms are owned by local entrepreneurs, they often need supplies that only firms in advanced technological nations can provide. In many instances they must sign a sole supplier agreement, stating that the firm will buy from only one supplier (some versions of which we encountered in the last chapter in agriculture). Studies in India and Colombia have shown that these agreements are common and often cause these companies to pay considerably more than

---

[44] Ibid., p. 153.

[45] Ibid., p. 161. Another study found $2.70 leaving for every dollar invested. Theontonio Dos Santos, "The Structure of Dependence," *American Economic Review* 60 (May 1970): 234. Another study of forty-three developing nations between 1965 and 1970 found that inflow was 30 percent of outflow. United Nations Department of Economic and Social Affairs, *The Impact of Multinational Corporations on Development and International Affairs* (New York: United Nations, 1974), p. 88. Another study by the Bank of Brazil of eleven firms found that while they remitted US$502.4 million abroad in the form of dividends between 1965 and 1975, they also remitted US$272.1 million as technology payments. Lietaer, *Europe + Latin America + the Multinationals,* p. 247. Another study for all of Latin America, including all inputs of investments, grants, and loans from both governmental and private sources, and outputs of loan repayments and repatriation of profits, found that in an average year from 1961 to 1968, US$130 million dollars more flowed out of Latin America than flowed in. US$360.5 million was invested by private capital each year versus US$1063.1 million repatriated, but US$1069.4 million came in through foreign aid while loan repayments took out US$497.7 million (including only US$186.8 million interest). Today, with loan interest repayments vastly higher, that imbalance is undoubtedly worse. Keith Griffin, *International Inequality and National Poverty* (London: Macmillan, 1978), pp. 57–58. Griffin suggests that if Latin America were to forego all foreign aid, renounce the debt, and confiscate all foreign investments, it would gain US$1000 billion a decade. None of this even takes into account the higher costs of imports and lower revenues from exports that often result from aid programs.

[46] Lewis D. Solomon, *Multinational Corporations and the Emerging World Order* (Port Washington, N.Y.: Kennikat Press, 1978), p. 91.

open market prices for the supplies.[47] When Mexico passed a law requiring auto plants to buy local components whenever possible, the former foreign suppliers of such components were still needed, since all components could not be produced locally; they simply raised their prices to compensate.[48] Another tactic is to buy local plants on a joint-partnership basis.[49] Furthermore, foreign-owned firms usually have contacts abroad and can therefore find greater success in their export business than local firms, giving them greater volume and making them more competitive on the local market, as well. According to José de Cubas, between 1957 and 1966 United States subsidiary firms with local plants in Latin America increased their exports of manufactured goods by 704 percent, while all other, locally-owned, firms increased theirs by 51 percent.[50] Yet, on those products which it does not want to leave the country, the parent company can set up export restrictions when it sells technology contracts to its subsidiaries. A study of 400 such contracts in Latin America found 81 percent to contain such restrictions, as did 40 percent of those in an India study and 63 percent in a Philippines study.[51]

---

[47] Constantine V. Vaitsos, "Transfer of Resources and Preservation of Monopoly Rents," in *Development Advisory Service: Economic Development Report 168* (Cambridge: Harvard University Press, 1970); Michael Kidron, *Foreign Investments in India* (London: Oxford University Press, 1965).

[48] Turner, *Multinational Companies,* p. 60. A study of thirteen components imported by Mexican firms found most of them marked up from 100 to 1,000 percent above world prices. Lietaer, *Europe + Latin America + the Multinationals,* p. 47.

[49] One company founded a "dummy" firm in Mexico, smuggled the manufactured goods across the border, and then blamed their high retail prices on the "start-up" costs for the "dummy" factory. Barnet and Müller, *Global Reach,* pp. 186–187.

[50] José de Cubas, "It Pays to Speak Out," *Columbia Journal of World Business* 5, no. 5 (September/October 1970): 61–68. Other studies show that most of this extra sales performance by the multinationals took place from Argentina, Brazil, and Mexico to other countries in Latin America. On sales to developed nations (which did not involve much total volume) the domestic industries outperformed the multinationals. Müller, "The Multinational Corporation and Underdevelopment in the Third World," p. 168.

[51] Solomon, *Multinational Corporations and the Emerging World Order,* pp. 83–84. Because they bring in technology and have marketing facilities abroad, multinationals can increase total exports of a nation above what they would otherwise be. They usually export several times more than they import. This helps a nation's balance of payments, and thus its ability to get trade credit from financial institutions. So long as most of that credit, however, goes into the pockets of the multinationals abroad, it does not help the country's overall financial standing. Part of this credit does stay in the country. For instance, the Bank of Brazil study mentioned in footnote 45 found that the eleven companies brought a total of US$298.8 million into Brazil and remitted US$774.5 million abroad. But they had also reinvested US$693 million of profits in Brazil. So they invested more than they brought in. These are mostly high-technology manufacturing concerns (Volkswagen, Pirelli, General Electric, etc.) selling primarily to the local market and thus not generating foreign exchange. Firms that export raw material or pajamas tend to be lower-technology industries who do less investing within the country once their initial exploration and mines are in place. In fact, much of the reinvestment by these companies was in mines (see p. 135), so such a high rate of reinvestment could not be anticipated in the future. So, basically, more capital was leaving the country than was coming in or staying. Local capital was being shipped abroad. Another study of Brazil multinational corporations from 1960 to 1968 found 79 percent of their net profits repatriated, plus royalties and fees; in manufacturing for domestic use, the repatriations were lower, but rose from 42 to 52 percent during the period. Müller, "The Multinational Corporation and Underdevelopment of the Third World," p. 164. The problem is compounded by the fact that local members of the patron-client network who share in the profits find it unprofitable to invest at home, given the presence of the multinationals as competition. They, too, invest their money abroad.

SOMETHING TO THINK ABOUT

Keith Griffin hypothesizes that as the profits of multinational corporations increase, the supply of capital in developing nations declines.[52]

It is easy for foreign-owned firms to multiply their advantages. In Nigeria, Bookies (using local tobacco and pages from the Holy Book) were the favorite cigarettes during the nineteenth century. Beer was produced from local corn and millet, and wine from kola nuts. Cotton was grown, spun, and dyed for centuries. Potters supplied most households with cooking utensils. Laterite mud compounds and baked mud bricks were used in building construction. And mothers nursed their babies. All these artisan goods lost their markets when tastier foreign cigarettes, beer, liqueurs, cloth, pots, cement, and baby formulas were imported. Later, plants were created locally to produce these goods, but with profits being repatriated abroad and foreign exchange lost on imports of raw materials. These industries employ far fewer people than had the artisan industries. Nigerians, even poor ones, were spending considerably higher percentages of their income to buy these products than they had before.[53] In the nineteenth century thousands of Ghanians were employed in mining salt, building canoes to transport it, marketing it, and the like. The salt was grey. When mechanized factories using few workers introduced white salt, they wiped out the local salt industry.[54] The members of the patron-client networks can make more money from the larger industries than from the smaller.

Discussion of Nigeria is continued from p. 365 and concludes on p. 389. The discussion of Ghana is continued from p. 162, of Brazil from p. 257, and of Chile from p. 300.

In the nineteenth century Chile and Brazil both had fairly extensive manufacturing sectors. Then, between 1868 and 1888, foreign investors came in to exploit nitrates, copper, and agriculture. They used their own ships, and the Chilean merchant fleet was reduced from 276 to 21 ships in eight years, copper smelters from 250 to 69, and flour mills from 507 to 360.[55] The manufacturers preferred to use their own ships, smelt the copper abroad, and divert grain land to other purposes. It is hard to reverse such processes. To create its own plants, Chile would need to import its copper smelters and flour mills from abroad. It could buy them on the open market, as did Ghana and Nigeria in several instances, only to discover they did not possess the technical skills to keep them open and could not get replacement parts.[56] A developing nation cannot easily

[52] *International Inequality and National Poverty,* pp. 3–6.

[53] Biersteker, *Distortion or Development?,* pp. 104–116.

[54] Joan Robinson, *Aspects of Development and Underdevelopment* (London: Cambridge University Press, 1979), pp. 114–115.

[55] André Gunder Frank, *Latin America: Underdevelopment or Revolution* (New York: Monthly Review Press, 1969), p. 102.

[56] Turner, *Multinational Companies,* pp. 62–63.

compete with international shipping interests. And diverting land back to grain would momentarily lower foreign exchange. Furthermore, although Chile has considerable coal, petroleum, and hydraulic resources, it cannot exploit them without outside technical help, and it cannot receive this aid without coming to terms with multinational corporations and the skills they control. Between 1937 and 1967, the percentage of Chilean patents owned by foreign concerns rose from 65 percent ot 95 percent.[57] In addition, it is easy for the firms with international backing to weather periods of economic depression and then buy out struggling local competitors who have faltered.[58] Salvador Allende was determined to end this dominance, but was overthrown before he had done much. In neighboring Peru, the military regime that took power in 1968 put on what is probably the most carefully conceived and determined drive to date to control multinationals. Its failure demonstrates many of the difficulties facing developing nations.

Discussion of Peru is continued from p. 304.

Peru, too, had the capabilities to develop its resources. Before the arrival of foreign capital, Peru had its own sugar, cotton, wool, coffee, and rubber estates for export, together with cotton and wool textile, and sugar milling industries. It also manufactured hats, cottonseed oil, soap, cigarettes, matches, shoes, lumber, spaghetti, leather, furniture, soft drinks, wine, liquor, beer, and petroleum. Truck farmers served Lima, which did import rice and wheat. Most of these ventures belonged to European immigrants. There were well-developed silver, gold, and copper mines and smelters.[59]

During the 1890s, the owners of mines began selling them to United States firms. The largest of these investors, which bought Cerro de Pasco mine, brought about US$9.5 million into the country, of which at least US$3 million seems to have been immediately taken abroad by the former mine owners.[60] Standard Oil of New Jersey bought most major oil rights just before World War I; it covered its entire operating costs from local sales,[61] and had Peruvian competitors on some land the rights to which it had failed to purchase.

By 1968, much of Peru's industry and mining was under the control of foreign capital. The new military regime was determined to take back that control. By 1975, it had expropriated the sugar estates, the mines, the petroleum

---

[57] Barnet and Müller, *Global Reach,* p. 140. By 1967, 51 percent of the largest 160 Chilean firms were effectively controlled by multinational corporations. In each of the seven key industries of the economy, one to three foreign firms controlled at least 51 percent of the production. Of the top twenty-two multinationals operating in the country, nineteen either operated free of all competition or shared the market with other multinational corporations. Idem, p. 147.

[58] Of the 717 new manufacturing subsidiaries established in Latin America by the top 187 United States-based multinational corporations, 331 were established by buying out existing local firms. Ibid., p. 139. Cf. J. W. Vaupel and J. P. Curhan, *The Making of Multinational Enterprise* (Boston: Harvard Business School, 1969).

[59] Rosemary Thorp and Geoffrey Bertram, *Peru 1890-1977: Growth and Policy in an Open Economy* (London: Macmillan, 1978).

[60] Idem., pp. 91–94.

[61] Idem., p. 103.

rights, and all banks—often without compensation. As we saw in the previous chapter, the sugar estates were taken over by cooperatives. Occidental Petroleum and other firms were given contracts to explore for oil. Volvo got a contract to build cars and Massey Ferguson for tractors. Local firms were put in charge of a big new copper mining venture. These firms were not invited on ordinary terms. First off, the state would own 50 percent of the shares. They would run the businesses in conjunction with workers' councils, on a Yugoslav model. Each year they would give the workers shares of stock, until after fifteen years they would bow out, leaving the business to the state and the workers. Meanwhile, they would only be allowed to repatriate 14 percent of profits; 15 percent of profits would go to a special workers' fund. Romania, Japan, and others would help supply loans and markets. For every dollar of goods they imported, they would be expected to export a dollar of goods, so as not to harm balance of payments; 60 percent of all inputs would need to come from local enterprises. The plants would be built away from Lima, to help other regions. Despite these restrictions, the government received seven tenders for each contract.[62]

But the Peruvian government ran out of money: The oil wells were mostly dry. In 1972, ocean currents shifted and fishing export profits dropped to a third. Except for 1975, world sugar prices stayed low. The new copper mines were not yet ready to open. Locally-expropriated capitalists had been paid largely with government bonds. Foreign banks had been closed. Between 1968 and 1976, the government had succeeded in borrowing over US$3.5 billion from Japan, Romania, private banks, and the like at high interest. But it was now looking at payments of about a billion dollars a year to repay the loans. The international agencies would lend no money until the expropriated companies from abroad had been reembursed. In 1974, there was a temporary reprieve when the World Bank granted a short-term loan to pay for loan repayments; one condition was that certain expropriated companies be reembursed.

At home, the poorest strata of the nation was unhappy because it had received nothing from the reforms. The rural cooperatives were not receiving enough capital assistance to prosper. The urban middle class and investors were unhappy with the new rules, the 33 percent to 40 percent rate of inflation in food prices each year,[63] and their exclusion from politics. (All political parties had been shut down to quiet opposition in connection with the reforms.) And the traditional bureaucratic links with villages had been severed. The government's rapport with some in labor unions, and with urban squatters in Lima, gave it a small working base. Besides, the workers themselves were engaging in an increasing number of industrial strikes each year, contributing to inflation and industrial instability.

Meanwhile, Chile, Brazil, Argentina, Ecuador, and Bolivia all acquired antagonistic governments. These are traditional military border enemies. They were also friends of the United States. Foreign reserves were nearly exhausted. In August 1975, a new general, less committed to reform, became premier. During

---

[62] Alfred Stepan, *The State and Society: Peru in Comparative Perspective* (Princeton, N.J.: Princeton University Press, 1978), p. 280.

[63] FAO, *State of Food and Agriculture*, p. A-45. Prices rose progressively from 33 percent in 1974 to 40 percent in 1977.

April 1976, the government imposed a wage freeze, devalued the currency, cut the budget, cancelled the right to strike, removed all radicals from the Cabinet, ended its ban on new oil contracts with foreign firms, announced the first sale of a state company to the private sector, and agreed to pay compensation for an expropriated mine. Within thirty days, an international loan was approved. The reforms were over.[64]

The multinational corporations frequently have the backing of North American and European governments. Not only do they maintain strong lobbies and personnel ties with these governments, but their access to markets and inexpensive raw materials strengthens the material prosperity of the developed nations. Some 80 percent of Alliance for Progress funds were actually given to United States businessmen; the agreements required that the money be spent to buy United States products.[65] The same was true of the Food for Peace program. This is a common practice in giving both aid and loans on a bilateral basis. Funds from international agencies are often given for specific projects that require importing major components from the lending nations. So the recipient not only must pay for imports at above-competitive prices; it must also pay interest to the lending nations.

SPECIFIC EXAMPLE

In 1974, the Overseas Private Investment Corporation, a United States government agency that insures overseas investors, lent the Star Kist division of Heinz money to buy a fleet of modern fishing vessels. Heinz purchased a canning factory in Ghana that had been canning mackerel. Heinz converted the plant to canning tuna for export to the United States. About one-fourth of the output is for cat food.[66]

Furthermore, marketing boards and exchanges in North America and Europe have controlled the price of most basic commodities, keeping their values low while the price of manufactured goods and foodstuffs for developing nations is on the increase. The effects of these measures is to reduce the amount of earnings retained in developing nations. According to one source, between the 1950s and early 1970s, the *volume* of exports by developing nations increased by about a third, while their *value* rose by only 4 percent.[67] During the 1970s, the volume rose much more slowly than value—reversing that situation. But increased revenues for developing nations were eaten up by increased dependence on imports at even more inflated prices; the quadrupled price of wheat or 600 percent increase in oil prices, and the 500 percent rise in pharmaceuticals, would,

---

[64] E. V. K. Fitzgerald, *The Political Economy of Peru 1956-78: Economic Development and the Restructuring of Capital* (London: Cambridge University Press, 1979); Richard Charles Webb, *Government Policy and Distribution of Income in Peru 1963-1973* (Cambridge: Harvard University Press, 1977).

[65] John Gerassi, "The United States and Revolution in Latin America," in *Struggle Against History: U. S. Foreign Policy in an Age of Revolution,* ed. Neal D. Houghton (New York: Clarion, 1968), p. 172.

[66] George, *Feeding the Few,* p. 47.

[67] Lappé, "Fantasies of Famine," p. 87.

for example, wipe out the advantage of the 250 percent increase in revenues from selling coffee or cocoa or the other local commodity.[68] In 1973, the developed nations made US$29 billion on exports of primary products other than oil, while developing nations made US$11 billion.[69] In the 1960s, the global Gross International Product increased by more than US$1 trillion; 80 percent of this went to countries with per capita incomes above US $1,000, while 6 percent went to those with per capita incomes below US $300.[70]

In recent years developing nations have begun to fight back against this dominance. OPEC, the Organization of Petroleum Exporting Countries, has had the most conspicuous success. During the 1960s, Libya and Iran made deals with oil companies in which their countries received a higher percentage of the price than had been normal. With western Europe heavily dependent on oil imports, and the United States increasingly so, the other members of the organization began to assert their power in a unified manner and were able to obtain a considerably higher payment for their oil. They have surprisingly little to show for it. Between 1974 and 1980, OPEC nations earned close to a trillion dollars from exports.[71] Yet in 1980, their reserves assets were around US$250 billion.[72] We will see in the next section where those reserves are. What happened to the rest of the money? They spent it—on elaborate buildings, airports, cars, yachts, personal fortunes, meat, armaments, jewelry, and a variety of other things. Some OPEC countries have actually been spending more on imports than they earn from exports. Most of the money spent ends in the hands of the multinational corporations. The buying binge benefits only a few people within the OPEC nations themselves. The (accidental, but true) fact that the principals in OPEC—Saudi Arabia, Kuwait, Libya, Oman, and Qatar—have two-thirds of its oil and half its output, but only 4 percent of its population, serves to underscore that fact. So does our more detailed analysis of Iran earlier. By the end of the century most of the oil will probably be gone, leaving behind some fancy buildings and many impoverished people. And, as we shall see shortly, OPEC solidarity has had a dramatic effect on *increasing* the dependency of the non-oil developing nations. So, as a means of fighting back OPEC has worked, but only for a few people.

Further discussion of OPEC may be found on p. 382.

---

[68] Between 1970 and 1977, the volume of agricultural products as exports rose nearly one-third, while their value tripled. FAO, *State of Food and Agriculture,* pp. 1–39.

[69] Lappé, "Fantasies of Famine," p. 87.

[70] Ibid.

[71] Dennis Healey, "Oil, Money, and Recession," *Foreign Affairs* 58, no. 2 (Winter 1979-80): 221–222; Howard W. Wachtel, *The New Gnomes: Multinational Banks in the Third World* (Washington, D.C.: Transnational Institute, 1977), pp. 16, 23; Walter J. Levy, "The Years That the Locust Hath Eaten: Oil Policy and OPEC Development Prospects," *Foreign Affairs* 57, no. 2 (Winter 1978-79): 292.

[72] "The Uncontrollable 'Stateless Money,'" *Far Eastern Economic Review* 105, no. 38 (September 21, 1979): 47. Former British Chancellor of the Exchequer Dennis Healey's estimate (previous footnote) is closer to US$150 billion. In 1970, the Arab states had US$5 billion in reserves. Barnet and Müller, *Global Reach,* p. 225. As of 1974, the combined reserves of all free-world governments came to US$200 billion. Priscilla S. Meyer, "Arab Investors," *The Wall Street Journal* (March 5, 1974).

The oil producers have largely been successful because their product is in short supply and is a vital necessity in technologically-advanced nations, and because the oil companies share their interest. All they have asked of the oil companies is a higher percentage of a higher wholesale price. Once the price is marked up several times at the retail level, the oil companies make even more than the OPEC nations. Other such efforts have had less impact. The four leading copper-producing countries, Chile, Peru, the Congo, and Zambia, formed CIPEC in 1967; copper can be recycled and replaced with synthetics, but they did affect prices somewhat, especially before the end of the Vietnam War. In 1977, however, Gen. Pinochet withdrew Chile from the association and lowered prices. Because Chile has open pit mines, its production costs are lower than elsewhere. In 1974, banana-producing countries tried to cooperate in imposing an export tax; the banana producers destroyed bananas on the estates and docks, and the governments finally backed down. Ecuador, which produces 30 percent of the world's banana exports, never joined.[73] Mexico and Peru have been unable to interest other silver-producing countries in an association to limit production; elsewhere, silver is often a by-product of lead, zinc, or copper veins, so the quantity is not easy to regulate. The most successful producer's cartel has been the International Bauxite Association, whose members have succeeded in imposing 8 to 10 percent export taxes on bauxite, at a time when aluminum is both running short in Europe and the United States and needed for commercial and military applications of lightweight metals technology.[74] With petroleum-based synthetic rubber becoming more expensive, and natural rubber needed to produce radial tires, long-time rivals Indonesia and Malaysia are trying to control rubber prices, which they may succeed in doing until coal-based synthetic rubber or latex made from a New Mexico desert plant called guayule becomes available. Since Malaysia produces most of the world's tin, and new industrial needs for it are constantly arising, Malaysia may be able to keep its price high, if it can resist OPEC offers to buy cartel rights.[75] Various regional organizations—ASEAN in Southeast Asia, LAFTA and the Andean Pact in Latin America (Chile also withdrew from this in 1976, objecting to Peru's attempts to limit profit repatriations of multinationals to 14 percent of investment), CACM and CARIFTA in Central America and the Caribbean—have tried to set up common markets and to organize against multinationals, but with limited success. Their own internal rivalries weaken them.

The biggest threat that developed nations have posed to the markets of developing nations up to now is synthetics. Freezer wraps, corn sugar, cocoa

---

[73] Robinson, *Aspects of Development and Underdevelopment,* p. 70. United Brands used a US$1.25 million bribe on Honduran officials to lower the export tax. The tax was cut in half. Lappé and Collins, *Food First,* p. 195.

[74] In 1973, the United States imported 86 percent of its bauxite, Japan 100 percent, and Europe 60 percent. Club of Rome, *Reshaping the International Order* (New York: E. P. Dutton, 1976), p. 106.

[75] "Cartels 1984: The Cloning of OPEC," *Far Eastern Economic Review* 107, no. 2 (January 11, 1980): 40. Saudi-led Arab oil producers offered Thailand, Malaysia, and Indonesia US$1 billion of development aid if they would cut back their rubber replanting 40 percent per year for five years and reduce tin production by 15 percent. Malaysia is by far the wealthiest of the three, and with much of the rubber and most of the tin, is unlikely to bite. So the other two nations will not get their $1 billion.

made of soybeans, roast grain additives, spun glass and lasers, fabricated plastic parts, vinyls and nylons, and synthetic fertilizers have weakened the demand for tin, cane sugar, cocoa, coffee and tea, copper, iron, cotton, hemp, wool, phosphates, and nitrates. The countries that lose from this are those that export these products. Those that gain are those that export the oil needed in the manufacture of most of these synthetics. Far from being an example for other raw materials exporters to follow, OPEC may be compounding the export problems of those nations. The oil exporting nations have, in essence, become competitors with nations that export rubber, cotton, phosphates, and other products being replaced with oil-based synthetics. Until the oil-importing nations develop synthetics from materials found at home, they will still be at the mercy of the suppliers of the materials from which the synthetics are made.

Studies sponsored by UNCTAD on copper, cobalt, manganese, and nickel have raised another doubt about the potential effectiveness of cooperation to raise world prices on basic commodities; these four metals might potentially be mined from the sea in sufficient quantities to keep world prices down.[76] Within the United Nations developing nations have set up UNCTAD as a potential nucleus for a development bank independent of North America and western Europe. It has had little money to work with. If it were to receive some, say from OPEC members (who have as yet tended to distribute through the more established International Monetary Fund), those few members would play the same sort of dominating role now enjoyed by North American and European nations in the current international funding organizations. As we shall see shortly, the possibilities of that are increasingly remote.

Governments have sometimes taken advantage of rivalries by inviting several firms from different nations to set up competing plants; this can easily flood what is already a small market. Demands for a substantial initial investment, or limits on exports of profits abroad, can cause companies to simply invest their money elsewhere. Laws that require a majority of stock in enterprises to be locally owned are also easy to circumvent. One way is to overvalue the contribution made from abroad (e.g., ship in forty-year-old machinery worth $170,000 and value it at $1.7 million).[77] A multinational can put a large share of the capital of its local subsidiary into interest-bearing loans payable to itself. Or it can keep perhaps 25 to 45 percent of the stock and then spread the local holdings among large numbers of investors so that the multinational retains the largest single block. If some individuals with political connections can be added to the list of local investors, they help the business to compete as well.[78] The Rockefeller International Basic Economy Corporation is a refinement of this idea. It is set up with separate branches in different countries, about half of them developing nations. The local IBEC in turn owns supermarkets, companies that build middle-class housing, produce hybrid seeds, milk, etc. And they share the profits with their local partners. Nationalizations like copper in Zambia and

---

[76] "Seabed Riches Pose a Threat to Asia," *Far Eastern Economic Review* 87, 3 (January 17, 1975): 59–60.

[77] Turner, *Multinational Companies*, p. 58.

[78] It is sometimes possible to pool resources to bribe Cabinet ministers. See Barnet and Müller, *Global Reach*, p. 187.

Peru and aluminum in Guyana, and oil and nickel in Indonesia have proven successful. However, the country is still dependent upon foreign concerns to run the operation; they are still in a position to extract a price for their services, and to extract even more by assisting in the marketing of the raw materials, often to their own subsidiaries.

SPECIFIC EXAMPLE

The Latin American Agribusiness Development Corporation, according to a consultant's report, supports "businessmen whose success is predictable" and produces goods "for upper middle, upper class consumption, or for export," like cattle ranches, supermarkets, cut flowers, and frozen vegetables. Stockholders include John Deere, CPC International, Gerber, Goodyear, Bank of America, Chase Manhattan, Borden, and Ralston Purina. US AID lent them US$17 million. About one-quarter of their operations were in Nicaragua. There they lent US$300,000 to a firm whose Nicaraguan partners were relatives of President Somoza; it raised frozen vegetables for Safeway and Seven-Eleven.[79]

Movements toward greater autonomy from multinational corporations are more likely to strengthen patron-client networks than to weaken them. The national leaders remain as dependent as ever on income from exports, corporate taxes, and exploiting natural resources. They need the multinational corporations for marketing and technical assistance, spare parts and supplies, direct or indirect assistance in obtaining capital, and business expertise. In fact, local partners or managers of firms are themselves often tied in with politics. They must obtain licenses and favorable interpretations of regulations and procedures from local officialdom and mediate with local financial institutions. There are nations in which three or four key local individuals or firms, originating from high-placed families, are the local "partners" of all the major multinational corporations operating in the country.[80] Nothing more clearly illustrates the manner in

---

[79] Lappé and Collins, *Food First,* pp. 355–356.

[80] Turner, *Multinational Companies,* p. 106. See also 131–139. M. L. Chaterpadhya, "Letter From London," *Far Eastern Economic Review* 87, 6 (February 7, 1975): 62, reports that Jahurual Islam, believed to be the richest man in Bangladesh, is a close friend of former British Privy Councillor John Stonehouse, who left Britain under strange circumstances. Islam earned his fortune through construction, jute, shipping, import-export, insurance, and oil. According to Chaterpadhya, a Bangladesh newspaper, which was later brought under the strict guidance of the Information Ministry's executive cell when one-man rule was declared in Bangladesh early in 1975, reported that Stonehouse "had a hand in, and a percentage of, nearly every single major contract signed between British and other foreign firms and the new Government of Bangladesh;" he had been active in dramatizing the plight of Bangladesh in 1971. For instance, shortly after independence, the World Bank offered Bangladesh a multimillion dollar irrigation scheme for the impoverished northwest region. The two main contenders for the pumps contract were KSB and Dacca Fibers. The Bangladesh Agricultural Development Corporation awarded the contract to KSB, who had submitted the lowest bid of $8 million. Shortly afterward, the entire top management of the Agricultural Development Corporation was fired, and the contract was subsequently awarded to Dacca Fibers: for $12 million. Dacca Fibers belongs to Jahurual Islam. "People in Dacca allege that Stonehouse, who was a close friend of Prime Minister Sheikh Mujib, was a 'persuasive influence in getting the contract shifted to Islam and Dacca Fibers.'" The Dacca branch of the World Bank urged cancelation, but it was feared this would endanger the whole scheme and create embarrassing political problems, according to Chaterpadhya's sources.

which movements to bring multinational corporations under national control can be part of a program to strengthen the power of centralized patron-client networks.

Multinational corporations have developed some products specifically for developing nations. Dow Chemical is creating pesticides; Monsanto and BASF, herbicides; British Leyland, a 25 h.p. mini-tractor; Ford, a tractor run by a lawn-mower engine; Phillips, simple radios. H. J. Heinz has introduced a bean and pea plant in Turkey and pineapple and chile plants in Mexico for export to the developed nations; a Danish firm is shipping asparagus from Kenya to Denmark; and Duncan, Gilbey, and Matheson is developing a coconut and chocolate liquer for export for a consortium of African distilleries.[81] Monsanto has created a bottled drink based on soybean to add protein to diets. American International Flavors and Fragrances has worked on rice-flavored protein to add to children's food in Algeria and Nigeria. British Petroleum has developed animal food from oil; Tate and Lyle has done the same with carob beans. The Bank of America has financed a number of large fertilizer projects. The Agribusiness Development Corporation is seeking to improve marketing and warehouse facilities.

These activities are valuable for promoting exports and providing products to the small middle-class sectors; they have little significance for the less affluent members of these societies. In fact, while these corporations do little to add nutrition to the diets of lower income people, they also deplete their diets by luring part of their incomes into low-nutrition foods like colas and white bread, which are made attractive through advertising media. And they divert into packaged products food which might otherwise be eaten by low-income people. The experiment of H. J. Heinz with fishmeal cakes in Peru (other commercial experiments with fishmeal have already been abandoned), and General Foods' high-protein macaroni being tested in Latin America, may prove to be exceptions to this rule, but probably not; Nabisco's Ricetein (rice reenforced with soybean) is "priced higher than rice, but is less expensive than meat."[82] All of these schemes involve working through local partners closely allied to patron-client networks; none so far show a tendency to aid in the spread of needed resources to wide strata of the populace.

SPECIFIC EXAMPLE

Brazil is the world's largest exporter of orange juice—mainly to the United States and Coca Cola's Minute Maid and Snow Crop divisions. Meanwhile, Coke's biggest seller after Coca Cola is their Fanta orange, which contains no orange juice. A study of working class families in São Paulo found about half deficient in vitamin C. The companies have fought government attempts to demand a minimum amount of real juice in soft drinks.[83]

Brazil, Mexico, Puerto Rico, and Singapore, are the sites of another phenomenon, which began earlier in Japan, Hong Kong, South Korea, and

[81] Turner, *Multinational Companies,* pp. 149–171, 268.

[82] George, *Feeding the Few,* p. 64.

[83] Lappé and Collins, *Food First,* p. 306.

Taiwan. American, European, and Japanese firms, faced with rising labor costs at home, are establishing plants for export to their home markets. This provides these particular nations with a greater expansion of employment and exports than is available to other developing nations. It also makes them peculiarly sensitive to economic indices in the United States and Europe; for instance, the economic downturns of 1975 and 1980 lowered the exports of these nations and created unemployment among their wage earners. The companies are attracted to these particular nations because of the availability of a skilled working force, a suitable economic infrastructure, and the potentials for government cooperation. Their existence also helps strengthen the economic and political control both of existing governments and of foreign corporations.

Both these outside influences *and* the efforts to contain them *strengthen* the control of the patron-client networks. And they increase the dependence of the developing nations on outside sources of control, rather than weakening it.

STABILITY—PERSONAL, NATIONAL, AND GLOBAL

Developing nations would like to be more independent. So would the developed nations. There are good reasons for this concern on both their parts.

One has to do with *fuel.* Interdependence requires much transport and sophisticated machinery; it uses fuel. Many of the manufactured products sold on international markets use fuel. Fuel is becoming more expensive and in shorter supply. Obtaining it may require a tradeoff of valuable land space, investment capital, or economic subservience to those foreign powers who are the chief fuel exporters.

Another reason has to do with *the role of multinational corporations.* They are becoming more mobile. They have power to affect prices, demand for labor, availability of goods, and political options in all nations. Increasingly they are not based in any one nation.

A third reason relates to *national defense.* If a nation is dependent on outside sources for materials needed to feed, clothe, or shelter itself, its security is diminished. If its military machine needs outside supplies, weapons, or fuel, it is diminished even more. With the possible exception of the Soviet Union and Canada, which have vast land and raw material resources, the more technologically advanced a nation becomes, the greater the likelihood that this dependency will increase.

A fourth reason concerns *international debts.* Already the developing nations are so heavily in debt they must take out new loans, often at full banker's rates instead of the lower concessional ones of international agencies, just to repay old loans. If these institutions stop lending, they assure default on the old loans and a closing of legal trade between developed and developing nations. Yet they cannot continue to lend indefinitely if the debts mount. The economic results could be catastrophic.

There is a basic incompatibility between national independence and the present international system of interdependence. Multinational corporations are interested in resources (including both material goods and human labor) they can combine in the easiest manner possible and for the highest profit possible. They are interested in resources they can bring under organizational control and distribute themselves. A great many human, plant, animal, solar, soil, water, and mineral energy resources are physically scattered, deposited in small quantities, and isolated from the basic communications infrastructure on which corporations depend. A great many people are equally cut off from that communications network and from a money economy. As the cost of bringing both these marginal resources and marginal markets into the corporate economy increases, it is more profitable to focus on drawing profits from accessible, easily controlled resources and markets. Urban dwellers are entirely dependent on corporate intermediaries for food, clothing, and shelter;[84] they are also compactly located for distribution purposes. Because they are a captive market and are susceptible to advertising, packaging, and other promotions, they will pay considerably more money for commodities than it costs to produce them (i.e., "effective demand" = ability plus willingness to pay = higher profits from presently-developed markets than from potentially-developed markets). Hence the corporation is free to exploit those mines, fields, modes of production, and labor most convenient to it, even if the cost is fairly high and many people and resources are excluded from the process. The higher the prices, the less the chance that those outside the corporate economy will be able to afford them. Compactly deposited resources are sought for development while other resources that cover most of the earth's surface remain unused, and most of the earth's population is unable to buy the finished products. A Ford Foundation report[85] states that between 1870 and 1950, GNP per capita in the United States rose sixfold from a mere doubling of energy use while between 1950 and 1973 growth in energy use per capita actually exceeded the per capita growth in production. This phenomenon is largely beyond the control of national leadership, but it weakens that leadership's ability to influence either its national budget or the distribution of goods to its people. *A nation that is neither in a position to exploit most of its energy resources nor to distribute goods to most of its people is not really independent.*

The sun is the longest-range source of energy, available to all nations. It does not need to be transported across international boundaries, and hence it is difficult for floating multinational corporations to corner the market on it. In fact, when trapped by plants, solar batteries, human skin, and dark surfaces, it can be directly mined by individuals without the need for corporate intermediaries. This would help to increase the self-sufficiency of nations; it would not enhance international interdependence. Oil and natural gas are easy for multinational corporations to control; by 1973, these sources accounted for 77 percent of the energy consumption in the United States (which was then consum-

---

[84] Professor Howard Perlmutter of the Wharton School estimates that by 1985, 200 to 300 multinational corporations will control 80 percent of all productive assets in the non-Communist world. Barnet and Müller, *Global Reach*, p. 26.

[85] Energy Policy Project of the Ford Foundation. *A Time to Choose: America's Energy Future* (Ballinger, 1974.)

ing 30 percent of the world's total energy output).[86] Some 35 percent of the oil used was imported. In 1973, the United States paid US$8 billion for foreign oil; in 1980, over US$60 billion.[87] About one-third of the energy consumption was through electricity—something else easy to corner. In 1973, 37 percent of United States electricity was produced by oil and gas.[88] About 65 percent of the energy units of the original fuel are lost in the generation and transmission of electricity.[89] Europe's dependence on oil, gas, and electricity is even greater. This sort of energy use requires international interdependence; it makes nations dependent on multinational corporations.

One of the great ironies about food production in the United States is that more energy units are used to produce the food than are contained within it. For instance, United States tractors burn 32 gallons of gasoline for every man, woman, and child in the nation. Between 1940 and 1965, electrification increased fivefold on American farms (to the equivalent of 14 gallons of gasoline per capita for the national populace). Artificial fertilizers consume 40 gallons per capita. The cost of creating, storing, and repairing the farm machinery must also be added in, raising the total figure to 150 gallons per capita. According to Georg Borgstrom, this constitutes several times more (nonrenewable!) energy than the calories in the food produced.[90] European farms, which are smaller and more labor intensive, use somewhat less energy and have considerably larger yields. In recent years, Japan, France, and Bulgaria have greatly increased their agricultural output, partly by investing in tractors, artificial fertilizer, pesticides, and irrigation (though retaining labor intensiveness).[91] Their increased independence in food production was purchased at the cost of increased dependence on Arab oil. David Pimentel says that if we were to use modern mechanized agriculture to feed 4 billion people we would use 1 to 2 billion gallons of fuel per day and soon deplete all the planet's reserves.[92] From the perspective of a multinational corporation there is no tension here—it is all progress. From the perspective of national independence, any of these gains which could have been attained using wind, organic fertilizer, or animal or human labor would have improved the progress.

---

[86] *A Time to Choose,* p. 5. Per capita energy consumption in the United States is six times the world average, three times that of Switzerland, twice that of West Germany. Richard N. Gardner, *The World Food and Energy Crisis* (Renssilaerville, New York: Institute on Man and Science), p. 41, says that oil accounted for 60 percent of all United States energy consumption in 1970.

[87] "The Uncontrollable 'Stateless' Money," p. 46.

[88] *A Time to Choose,* p. 28.

[89] Tad Szulc, *The Energy Crisis* (New York: Franklin Watts, 1974), pp. 28–29.

[90] Georg Borgstrom, *The Food and People Dilemma* (Belmont, Calif.: Duxbury, 1973), pp. 89–91. E.g., Iowa farms use 2.35 to 3.5 times more fuel per acre than the calories in the harvested soybeans. Gerald Leach, *Energy and Food Production* (Guilford, Eng.: IPC Science and Technology Press, 1976) says primitive societies use one calorie to produce five to fifty calories of food, while industrialized nations use five to ten calories, mostly of fossil fuel, to produce one calorie of food.

[91] Transnational Institute, "World Hunger," pp. 42–46.

[92] Wilson Clark, "U.S. Agriculture is Growing Trouble as Well as Crops," *Smithsonian Magazine* (January 1975): 63, 64.

A field that lies deep in a hinterland can only be made interdependent if it is connected with the outside world by a road. That road is economically feasible only if the field can provide the outside world with more than enough income to pay back the cost of constructing it. If it can merely provide its own inhabitants with sustenance, it is useful to them and to their nation. But it is not compatible with the international system of interdependence.

As the multinationals develop relationships with an increasing number of nations, their reliability as suppliers to any particular nation during wartime might be decreased. The United States, for instance, could have its oil supplies obstructed. So major powers may find their sovereignty diminished in an unfamiliar area: their right to wage war. They would be interdependent under circumstances that call for independence and suffer the same constraints as small nations in earlier conflicts.

The United States and European nations have fought in the past to keep governments in power friendly to them and undoubtedly will in the future. It has often been profitable to do so. Lester Brown states that by 1985 the United States will be primarily dependent on imports for nine of the thirteen basic raw materials required by a modern industrial economy: iron ore, aluminum, tin, copper, nickel, cobalt, lead, petroleum, and natural gas.[93] This will make the OPEC approach to supplier dictatorship feasible in more realms than previously. As these friendly governments find it increasingly necessary to apply pressure to raise the prices of their raw materials and expand their markets, and as they use up energy resources, and unite against the North Atlantic powers over regional issues, the profitability of shoring up these friendly governments may decrease. Balance-of-payments problems, costs of foreign wars, inflation and recession cycles, and decreasing ability to control multinational corporations may also make it seem less attractive for developed nations to expend dollars, munitions, or lives to defend international interdependence. *The costs of the support activities needed to keep raw materials coming may actually grow higher than the value of raw materials received.* So long as nineteenth century colonialism required little outlay of resources by the colonial powers, it was an economic proposition; as the cost rose, so did the propensities of the colonial powers to pull out.

In 1961, the United States had a net capital inflow (repatriated profits, interest, royalties, and technical fees, minus new investments abroad) of US$1.2 billion; in 1967, US$1.4 billion; in 1973, US$6.2 billion.[94] We export US$20

---

[93] Lester R. Brown, "The End of American Independence," *Saturday Review World* (December 18, 1973): 16. Barnet and Müller, *Global Reach,* pp. 126, 209, in tables deriving from a number of official sources, largely agree. Their figures show an additional 1985 dependency on outside sources for most zinc, tungsten (in very short supply worldwide), potassium, manganese, and chromium. They do suggest that the United States can be self-sufficient in copper and obtain all its aluminum from Australia. Developing nations would appear to supply most of the world's antimony, aluminum, tin, manganese, and nickel. Club of Rome, *Reshaping the International Order,* p. 106, says that Europe and Japan are already basically dependent on them, and the United States already derives most of its bauxite, chromium, cobalt, manganese, natural rubber, nickel, tin, tungsten, and zinc from them.

[94] Barnet and Müller, *Global Reach,* p. 297.

billion in agricultural products each year. This must be measured against a number of liabilities. Our agricultural imports amount to US$10 billion each year, about $6 billion of which are commodities we could grow ourselves.[95] Large numbers of jobs formerly held by North Americans are being shifted to low-wage laborers abroad.[96] The Vietnam War cost well in excess of US$150 billion. The continuing commitment to supply arms to local troops around the world costs considerable amounts of money. Oil imports cost the United States close to US$60 billion a year as of 1980.[97]

According to the Federal Reserve Board, nine New York banks (six of them in the Rockefeller-Morgan group) accounted for 26 percent of all commercial and industrial lending in 1973; about half their loans go to multinational corporations.[98] Many profits from multinationals have been invested in European bonds and currencies (Eurodollars); their Eurodollar pool is probably several billion. The sales of United States and European multinationals in 1976 totaled US$1372 billion.[99] Whereas in the early 1950s corporations had $8 for every $10 borrowed, by 1969–1973 they had $2,[100] and can use Eurodollar investments to back loans from New York banks. Corporations in 1974 had US$160 billion to US$268 billion in liquid assets—more than twice that in the hands of all non-OPEC governments combined;[101] that figure, and ratio over governments, is higher now.[102] So governments can no longer control corporate borrowing and spending habits by adjusting interest rates. If a government releases money into the hands of the public, the corporations (which have eliminated much of their competition) can absorb this simply by raising prices. If the government tries price controls, the companies can concentrate on foreign sales and force an end to the price controls. Hence inflation becomes an endemic worldwide phenomenon. The result is fewer jobs, higher prices, and a slowdown in the dissemination of consumer goods in the advanced industrialized nations. Despite this, the Overseas Private Investment Corporation guarantees with United States government money two-thirds of American nonpetroleum corporations against war damage and expropriation—their biggest risks.[103] This gives incentive to our government to use its military and foreign policy to prevent these risks from occurring.

---

[95] Economic Research Service, *Foreign Agricultural Trade of the United States* (April 1976), pp. 26–27; United States Department of Agriculture, *United States Agricultural Trade Statistical Report.*

[96] Ibid., pp. 303–333.

[97] See footnote 87.

[98] Barnet and Müller, *Global Reach,* p. 271, 259.

[99] Lietaer, *Europe + Latin America + the Multinationals,* p. 12.

[100] Barnet and Müller, *Global Reach,* p. 271.

[101] Ibid., p. 286. The lower figure comes from First National City Bank, and the higher from the Senate Finance Committee.

[102] In 1974, the United States government had US$14 billion and the German government US$34 billion in international reserves, foreign exchange, and gold. In 1978, the industrialized nations had balance of trade surpluses of US$31 billion, which then turned into a US$49 billion deficit by 1980. Ho Kwon Ping, "North and South: Poles Apart," *Far Eastern Economic Review* 108, no. 19 (May 2, 1980): 40.

[103] Lappé and Collins, *Food First,* p. 293.

Where are these billions? Where are the US$250 billion in OPEC reserves? As we have seen, little of them are tied up in investment projects like mines or factories. You can't go to your corner bank and borrow them. Some have been converted into gold, the sale of which itself converts into liquid assets for some banks and corporations. Some get tied up in short-term speculation on commodities markets. But for the most part banks and corporations, oil-rich governments and sheikhs, if they are to make money on their liquid assets, must find someone to whom they can loan their money in large quantities at high interest. That "someone" is governments seeking funds with which to pay off deficits.

As of 1970, the share of commercial banks in loans to developing nations was about 20 percent;[104] the rest came from international lending agencies like the World Bank. These nations owed a total of about US$60 billion.[105] By 1980, developing nations owed commercial banks 60 percent of their US$315 billion debt.[106] What had happened? The price of imports was overburdening the developing nations. In 1980, for instance, the non-oil developing nations paid around US$65 billion for imported oil—more than the US$50 billion trade surplus that year of OPEC nations.[107] The amount of money taken out of their nations by multinationals continued to exceed that brought in. The market prices of their raw materials were uncertain, and rose in value more slowly than the cost of manufactured goods, grains, and processed food imports. Often their imports exceeded their exports, which left them with balance of trade deficits. Their current balance of trade deficits went from US$11 billion in 1970, to US$37 billion in 1978, to US$67 billion in 1980, and kept rising.[108] And they found themselves unable to repay their loans to the international agencies. To avoid forfeiture, both on loans and trade, the international agencies would extend payments and loan additional amounts. When it still remained difficult to repay, countries like this turned to commercial banks for assistance. For instance, even though its entire gross national product totaled US$48 billion in 1977, Turkey owed US$13.5 billion to international agencies, and could not pay its current principal and interest. It turned to commercial banks who, in 1979, refinanced US$3 billion of the debt.[109] (Peru's debt exceeds US$8 billion; 53 percent of her export earnings go into repayment. In addition, Soviet bloc debt to the West reached US$100 billion by 1980.[110]) The commercial banks have been able to attract investment money to make such loans by offering good-interest-bearing bonds in which corporations and OPEC nations could safely invest. The banks would earn back their money by charging the developing nations even higher rates of interest than the bonds paid. The international agencies also accumulated money to lend by

[104] Lietaer, *Europe + Latin America + the Multinationals,* pp. 73n, 77.

[105] *Overcoming World Hunger,* p. 97.

[106] Ibid. Healey, "Oil, Money, and Recession," p. 220.

[107] Idem., pp. 222–223.

[108] Ho Kwon Ping, "Caught in the Oil-debt Trap," *Far Eastern Economic Review* 106, no. 42 (October 19, 1979): 58.

[109] Dwight James Simpson, "Turkey Moves into the 1980's," *Current History* 78, no. 454 (February 1980): 7.

[110] David P. Werlich, "Peru: The Lame Duck Revolution," *Current History* 76, no. 444 (February 1979): 63. James Whitmore, "A Threat to the West: the Polish Debt Syndrome," *The New Leader* (November 3, 1980): 8.

selling government securities to corporations, banks, and OPEC investors; the citizens of their nations back these securities.

The ultimate safety of all this, of course, depends on the ability of the recipient nations to repay. They are caught in a strange trap. The same entities that are removing investment capital from their countries and charging them high prices for imports are loaning them money at high rates of interest so they can repay loans (also from these same entities) from which they received little benefit. It is a problem with which peasants in developing nations have long been familiar, now transferred to their patrons. Peasants must often solve such a Catch-22 problem by bowing out of the economic system. A few of these nations will benefit from oil strikes, or growth in exports to developed nations. Most will not.

SPECIFIC EXAMPLE

Bangladesh, whose food availability dropped from 17 ounces per capita per day in 1961 to 15.4 ounces in 1978, and who imported 2.9 million tons in fiscal 1979–1980, is beginning to develop natural gas resources. World Bank aid averages US$1 billion to US$2 billion a year. An American firm has asked permission to make urea fertilizer from this natural gas—100 percent for export.[111]

The total indebtedness continues to grow, as does the proportion of indebtedness going into interest, and the percentages of gross national products and balance-of-trade earnings that must go into debt repayment. And most of these nations see little sign of opportunity for increases in their trade balances or their retained earnings. Nor is there any way to restrain spending excesses within the patron-client networks, who have the same independence toward the international agencies as the minor networks have toward the major networks. The International Monetary Fund foresees that their balance of trade situation will continue to worsen and that new loans will have to be granted each year. By 1990, it seems these nations will be US$1278 billion in debt, 40 percent of it to international agencies and another percentage to commercial banks being underwritten by the international agencies.[112] This means the international agencies are now lending money primarily to help repay loans to private banks—not for "development."

This mind-boggling work of modern-day nonfiction gets little attention in the media. It is on the agendas of the nearly 6,000 international meetings (with their million pages *per annum* of documentaion) which meet each year.[113] The Brandt Commission, set up by the World Bank to study the problem, titled its report *North-South: A Programme for Survival*. It suggests a tax on trade, sea-bed minerals, and arms sales; a tax on industrialized nations; and the use of In-

---

[111] S. Kamaluddin, "Second Thoughts on Aid," *Far Eastern Economic Review* 108, no. 19 (May 2, 1980).

[112] Ho, "Caught in the Oil-dept Trap," p. 58.

[113] "A Thousand Tons of Paper & a Whole Lot of Words," *Far Eastern Economic Review* 108, no. 19 (May 2, 1980): 43.

ternational Monetary Fund gold as collateral to help finance new loans to the developing nations.[114] The Report of the President's Commission on World Hunger[115] calls for lowered tariffs, price stabilization agreements on world commodities, increased foreign aid grants, and placing some amounts owed the United States government into local currency accounts to be used for development purposes. Other strategy papers have suggested that the banks and international lending agencies better coordinate their lending activities, that the lending agencies should underwrite some loans by the private banks (i.e., guarantee to repay them if the recipient fails to repay), that interest rates be made adjustable, and that there should be more supervision of how loans are spent. I have seen no suggestions that the banks use any of their interest earnings to help refinance the loans, or that the corporations and OPEC use part of their considerable liquid assets to simply pay off the loans and then give no more of them, before the situation gets completely out of hand. These discussions are buried in statistics and humanitarian platitudes which leave the layperson who should stray upon them deeply confused.

If a company mismanages its affairs, or gambles and loses on the silver or commodities markets, the public would feel no obligation to bail them out. Nor would we if a bank lost money to a poor credit risk. In this case, corporations and banks and OPEC nations accumulated billions of dollars which they could have put in bank vaults if they could not find worthwhile investment opportunities. Instead, they chose to lend them to obviously poor credit risks, hoping to prevent themselves from losing on past investments and to earn interest on their new investment at the same time. Meanwhile they themselves are using the money that has been lent to these poor credit risks, in order to finance new ventures; they are taking the money away from the debtors before the loans can be repaid. They call this "recycling petrodollars." It is gambling. The amount owed at the crap table keeps rising. In the end, outsiders are called in, the citizens of developed nations, to help bail them out. We, and our governments, with considerably fewer assets than theirs, are asked to underwrite their adventures. And we do so because we think it is humanitarian and necessary for international peace and security, or for our own welfare. Then, of course, we too find ourselves in a Catch-22 situation. Where do we get the money for this rescue mission? By raising our own national debt past the trillion-dollar mark. Like the peasant in debt to the landlord, we only delay the inevitable a bit longer.

> Put another way: If the multinationals or OPEC loaned the money directly to developing nations they would be taking the risks. If their creditors defaulted, American citizens would not feel obligated to pay off the debt. Why should we pay off the debt simply because banks become involved in the transactions?

There is another way out. We may take it with planning and forethought, or we may have to take it out of desperation after the geese who lay the golden eggs

---

[114] Ho, "North and South: Poles Apart," pp. 40–43.
[115] *Overcoming World Hunger.*

(the geese with the stable personal environments) join everyone else in the starvation cycle. The key to our salvation lies in the fact that the *publics of Japan, Western Europe, and the United States are the chief consumers on whom these corporations depend.* The multinationals could survive if we stopped paying for roads, power plants, and armies in developing nations to back their investments. They may not ultimately survive if we do not bail them out of their bad investments in the international loans, but they can probably maneuver us into doing so until we, too, are overburdened with them. They cannot survive, however, without markets. They must have customers for their products. Those customers lie in the developed nations. Without us as customers, the multinationals go under. We may cease to be customers because low tariffs, high taxes, and inflation render us incapable of purchasing anymore—or we might cease to be customers with a policy strategy clearly in mind.

The North Atlantic nations and Japan have political systems closely embedded in their social systems. This means that their political systems are in a position to rely on popular support to exert some control over the multinationals. Multinationals call for "consumer democracy." At the same time, their executives join liberals in advocating that the power to regulate be moved into the hands of world government, which would be easier to manipulate by multinationals than by consumers. Multinationals want taxes from those in developed regions to build roads and armies in less developed regions so as to extract resources; if they had to build these roads and armies themselves they would reduce their profits. They want the power to manipulate tariffs and import quotas so they can bring their products in to sell. So they prefer to keep control of taxes and trade as far from the hands of the public as possible; they fear intervention in these matters by democratic governments.[116] They want help on guaranteeing their loans to the developing nations. In a crunch, they could get by without all this, but they cannot get by without markets. They must have someone to whom they can sell their wares. People in developing nations simply cannot afford to buy enough of them. We in the developed nations are their market. *By controlling their own consumption, publics in developed nations can control multinational corporations.* This is the Damoclean sword we can dangle over the multinationals. *Do as we ask or we will no longer buy from you.* Without us as a market your operations will come to a grinding halt. We may dangle the sword, or it may dangle us. If the publics in the developed nations are confronted with lowered tariffs that rob them of jobs, combined with inflation and tax hikes which keep prices high anyway, they may not be able to make the choice of removing the market from the multinationals; they may be forced into it because they cannot afford to buy. Either way, the end results need not be gloomy if we have a *policy strategy* clearly in mind:

The United States government gives tax incentives to multinational corporations to encourage them to invest abroad. Backed by a change in public sentiment it could instead offer incentives to companies *not* to invest abroad, but to seek resources in Antarctica and under the ocean which would not involve in-

---

[116] For a frank discussion of these fears see Michael Crozier, Samuel P. Huntington, and Joji Watanuki, *Report on the Governability of Democracies of the Trilateral Commission* (New York: New York University, 1975). Introduction by Zbigniew Brzezinski.

vestment in developing nations. Rather than spending money on sending arms to developing nations, or on standing armies, it could spend more on *naval power* to protect such explorations. It could *eliminate its contributions to international lending agencies.* It could examine the Japanese model of encouraging *nationally based corporations,* closely identified with the nation, and encourage such companies to buy needed resources on the free world market rather than creating subsidiaries abroad. It could *restrict imports* of nonessential commodities, especially agricultural products. It could *discourage conglomerates,* and encourage the reemergence of moderately sized competitive industries, not to mention small business. It could encourage buying domestically manufactured goods, and *focus on agricultural rather than manufactured exports.* (As it stands, despite numerous tie-ins with government programs that force foreign nations to buy American products, America's 500 largest companies only exported 6.5 percent of their 1976 sales.) [117] It can subsidize exploitation of *the sun, the wind, and human and animal labor.* In short, it could devise a program of national independence.

The multinationals would undoubtedly retaliate by moving their headquarters to Europe. But Europe would find it difficult to support the international agencies and military commitments on its own. It, too, suffers from the export of jobs, the inability to fully tax corporate profits, the unfavorable balances of trade, inflation, and the other side effects of corporate hegemony. And if we do not bail these speculators out of their bad loans to the developing nations, they are not likely to either. They are likely to follow suit in asserting national independence.

The idea behind this policy strategy is not to weaken capitalism, but rather to strengthen it by bringing it back home to serve us by making us, and it, more autonomous. The idea is not to harm the developing nations, but rather to weaken those who exploit the developing nations, and help them put their institutions back into proportion with their needs. *The idea is to help nations produce for their own consumption.*

Such moves would bring special focus upon five regions of the globe. With only 21 million people and 5.1 million square miles, Siberia is a great largely-untapped storehouse of accessible oil, gas, iron ore, gold, diamonds, copper, hydroelectric power, coal, timber, tin, lead, zinc, nickel, asbestos, aluminum, salt, cobalt, platinoids, mercury, antimony, and other resources, especially for the Soviet bloc.[118] Canada, with 3.8 million square miles and 22 million people, and Australia with 3 million square miles and 13 million people, have great quantities of copper, lead, nickel, zinc, uranium, iron ore, asbestos, potash, gold, silver, aluminum, tin, timber, gas, oil, and coal.[119] Antarctica, with around 5.5 million square miles, is permanently under ice, yet apparently rich in minerals.

---

[117] Lietaer, *Europe + Latin America + the Multinationals,* p. 19n.

[118] See Alan Sanders, "Tapping Siberia's Riches," *Far Eastern Economic Review* 87, no. 5 (January 31, 1975): 58–61.

[119] See George W. Wilson, Scott Gordon, and Stanislaw Judek, *Canada: An Appraisal of Its Needs and Resources* (New York: Twentieth Century Fund, 1965), pp. 241–249. Japan already imports high percentages of the aluminum, copper, iron, lead, manganese, and tin she uses from Canada, Australia, New Zealand, South Africa, and Zimbabwe. William Schneider, *Food Foreign Policy and Raw Materials Cartels* (New York: Crane Russak, 1976), p. 50.

And then there is the sea. Copper, cobalt, manganese, nickel, and molybdenum can be mined from the sea bottom; as of 1974, the United States already was extracting 45 million tons from the seabed. Sea water contains in solution huge amounts of magnesium, potassium, bromine, copper, uranium, nickel, silver, and gold. Silver, copper, zinc, and cadmium may be found in silt in the trenches deep in the ocean.[120] If the developed nations wish to continue their former life style and arms race, or to continue to expand their standards of living, there are resources for them to do so. For it is they who will have prime access to these resource-rich regions. The Soviet Union would have to develop her railroads and perhaps closer ties with Japan; the United States and western Europe would need to expand their navies. Canada and Australia would play a greater role in world affairs.

These major shifts in national policies would not only weaken the multinational corporations; they would also seriously jeopardize the position of the present patron-client networks in developing nations. Their access to technology would be endangered, as would their access to munitions. Markets for their minerals and agricultural products would become uncertain, as would the payrolls for their white collar and bureaucratic clients. They, too, would be forced to seek greater national independence. If they could not afford to import food, they would need to grow it. Without markets abroad, they would need to create markets within. Dividing land among people and helping them improve production would be the most efficient means to these ends.

Rule in developing nations depends on urban-rural coalitions. The rural components of today's coalitions involve large individual landowners and middle peasants. *With the export-oriented urban allies of these social groups weakened political parties might spring up which in contrast were composed of the more traditional aristocracy and peasantry; urban middle-class elements interested in national independence might join them in forming these parties.* Once such coalitions come to power—perhaps quickly, perhaps after some years of sparring with their political rivals—they could start policy initiatives toward communal tenure. It is conceivable that their rivals would have started such initiatives in the process of sparring with them. When such reforms were completed, the regimes might more resemble the Moghul and Inca Empires in their agrarian policy than the regimes surveyed in Chapters 4 and 7. The local aristocracy would need the peasantry for support, both political and material. The central government would have a lively interest in preventing that aristocracy from conquering neighboring territories or producing a landless or impoverished peasantry trying to move to the city. With communal tenure, local peasant councils would be revived. Such political events—given the growth of education and communications—open the possibility that the peasants themselves would come to participate in national party politics. This would further their chances for governing local affairs, fair taxation, and outside assistance in improving productivity. The continuing existence of private landowners and urban manufacturers, laborers, and middle-class groups—needed by both aristocracy and urban sectors for food, clothing, and shelter, but without financial control from abroad— would

---

[120] Lietaer, *Europe + Latin America + the Multinationals,* pp. 110–111.

enliven the interest in improving the national market and make it harder to impose one-party rule.

Such moves might require a simplification of life style everywhere in the world. All nations would need to devote more to growing food and developing their own energy sources; those with food and energy surpluses would be the only ones assured of foreign markets. Consumption habits that wasted food or energy (whether fossil fuels, human labor, wind, or plow oxen) would be counterproductive for national independence rather than a desirable aspect of international economic growth, because they would make the nation more dependent on foreign markets. Nations could no longer count on markets abroad for other products. Notions of unlimited growth based on inexpensive raw materials and expanding markets abroad would give way to ideas of making the most of whatever materials were available. People would need to trade the luxury of quickly discarded consumer products for the security of steady supplies of food, clothing, and shelter emanating from materials attainable close to home. They would need to learn to do more things for themselves. To do this, they might have to choose settlement patterns that abandoned megalopolis for more scattered urban and rural settlements. The Chinese learned to do all this long ago; it can be done.

Discussion of Nigeria is continued from p. 369.

Let me use Nigeria as an example. Much of northern Nigeria has a system of communal tenure.[121] The state owns the land, the Hausas form farming villages, and the Fulanis graze cattle. With shifting cultivation, many of the fields lie fallow, while other large stretches of potentially arable land are not farmed at all. There are few fences, and the cattle graze freely. But population levels have reached the point where the World Bank Mission suggests the combination of shifting cultivation and herding cannot support the people. Some 40 percent of the farmers hold less than 2.5 acres. The land that is used is overused. It is difficult to open new areas to cultivation. Urban employment cannot support these folk.

"If a *rural transformation* is to take place, it necessarily will involve not only the absolute expansion of agricultural activities but the whole range of changes necessary to raise the level of agricultural productivity and incomes."[122] To cope with these momentous problems, the mission suggests a switch to individual land ownership (though without land reform), commercial grazing areas, and a 1.75 percent increase in peanut and 2.5 percent increase in cotton acreage each year.[123] These are common suggestions in such reports. (In fact, one-third of World Bank agricultural credit projects, and 70 percent of those in

---

[121] World Bank Mission, *Nigeria: Options for Long-Term Development* (Baltimore: Johns Hopkins University Press, 1974), pp. 79, 129, 130.

[122] Ibid., p. 31.

[123] Ibid., pp. 79, 127–128, 130. In nearby Mali, which is ravaged by the drought, marketed food dropped from 60,000 tons in 1967 to 15,000 tons in 1973, while peanut exports increased, according to the World Bank. Geoffrey Barraclough, "The Great World Crisis I," *The New York Review of Books* 21, nos. 21 & 22 (January 23, 1975): 24–25.

Latin America, have been for the livestock industry.[124] Ranching accounts for half the arable land in Latin America, where it shores up the *latifundio* system,[125] and increasing amounts of it in Africa.) Note was taken of an average Nigerian diet containing 2,200 calories;[126] no mention was made of the disastrous drought that was decimating the northernmost regions in 1973.

I question that the land cannot support the people. Northern Nigeria is a semi-arid region. Fallow and fertilizer (likely techniques of a modernized agriculture) may not always be of value in arid regions; periodic hoeing can sometimes better prevent moisture loss (through the leaves of weeds) and turn manure and weeds into humus.[127] Planting of legumes in between cereal crops can provide a substitute for fertilizer by adding nitrogen to the soil (which also improves its water-holding capacity), and provide grazing for cattle.[128] Legumes are high in protein. Cattle herding on the edges of the semi-arid regions, making use of nonarable land, the stubble from harvested fields and the legumes grown on fallow land can be beneficial, provided the herds do not grow too large.[129] As to land left entirely for grazing, six times as much meat can be produced per acre, with less ecological damage, if the wild animals are left intact. (See footnote 129). This, and grazing, also turns otherwise inedible plant life into human food.[130] As explained in Chapter 2, the Hausa and the Fulani once developed a symbiosis along these lines. With some help from the former kingly capitals—especially in the form of thinning the cow herds, redistributing people, and keeping down civil warfare—and a gradual sharing of some of the more beneficial manifestations of modernization, they might be able to do so again. The kingly capitals might have more incentive to do so if they themselves were once more dependent on the well-being of the villagers and herders rather than on their relationship with Lagos or the sale of cotton and peanuts.

The World Bank report found some 900,000 households in cottage industry in Nigeria (versus 77,000 employed in large-scale manufacturing).[131] This cannot

---

[124] World Bank, *The Assault on World Poverty: Problems of Rural Development, Education, and Health* (Baltimore: Johns Hopkins University Press, 1975), pp. 125-126.

[125] George, *Feeding the Few*, p. 50.

[126] World Bank Mission, *Nigeria*, p. 127.

[127] Grigg, *Harsh Lands*, pp. 170-171.

[128] Ibid., p. 173. The International Institute of Tropical Agriculture in Ibadan, Nigeria, has already found cowpea strains that will yield 1,800 pounds per acre. Cowpeas presently average 325 pounds to the acre. Cowpeas are a legume that grows on relatively dry, poor lands. Humans can eat the green pods, dried peas, and sprouted seedlings, and livestock the rest. Or the stalks can be used for fertilizer.

[129] The United Nations estimates that a tse-tse control program, costing US$2–2.5 billion dollars over twenty years (US$30 million a year over the first five years) could add 1,750,000 acres to agricultural productivity in Africa by making permanent human habitation possible. This land could then carry a supplemental 120 million head of cattle, producing 1.5 million tons of meat, valued at least US$750 million, as well as crops. U.N., *The World Food Problem*, pp. 8, 115. At a cost of US$60–US$70 per acre per year, this might be a feasible sort of program to undertake, with cooperation at the international, national, regional, and local levels. It would, however, use pesticides that pose health and ecological risks. And the cows eat all forms of grass, thus endangering the savannah more than the existing wild animals, which specialize in particular grasses (so they will not completely strip an acre of all vegetation), and which can produce six times as much meat per acre. Geoffrey Lean, *Rich World, Poor World* (London: G. Unwin, 1978), p. 35.

[130] Grigg, *Harsh Lands*, pp. 175-176.

even begin to accommodate the unemployed in a country with eighty, perhaps a hundred million[132] people—at least one-fourth of the entire population of Africa.

A 1978 report of the Food and Agriculture Organization[133] advocates increasing Africa's cultivated area by one-third between 1975 and 1990, and using most of this land to grow corn, millet, sorghum, pulses, and some rice. The plan calls for expanding irrigation from 18.8 million acres to 22.5 million acres, at a cost of over US$10.5 billion. Only 40 percent of this land would grow cereals, rootcrops, and pulses, and many of the pulses would be exported. Much of this irrigated land is to be in the Sudan and used to benefit Arab nations.[134] In the Sahel, irrigation would come from huge dam projects and lakes, despite the uncertainty of rainfall and 30 percent levels of evaporation.[135] Cattle stocks would grow (with investments of US$6.5 billion). Meat would be exported from the Sahel even though west Africa is short of meat. Central Africa would export cassava. In Nigeria, modest increases in cropped area would combine with increased use of fertilizer, irrigation, and pesticides. Eight billion dollars would be invested on mechanizing agriculture, while less than one billion would be spent on nonirrigated land. Much of the capital would come from loans. Much of the new food produced under the program would go to the middle-class groups. Still, Africa would be importing US$11 billion in food in 1985, and US$15 billion in 1990. There is no indication how any of this will increase food supplies for the undernourished.

Talk of kingly capitals undoubtedly has a Rousseauian ring for many "modern" men and women. Our myopia, compounded by the shocks of burgeoning technological advance, often creates an inability to imagine the simple fact that many people cooked today's dinner on a dung heap instead of a kitchen range. I would suggest instead that there is a true romantic spirit involved in the notion that a *"rural transformation"* (the emphasis is the Mission's, not supplied by me) can arise from a stodgy continuation of a policy of driving more people off the land by individual ownership, expanding peanut[136] and cotton fields, commercializing livestock farming for export, and leaving 40 percent of

---

[131] World Bank Mission, *Nigeria*, p. 82.

[132] Nigeria has not had an accurate census because of corruption and a desire to overcount some tribes while undercounting others, to affect distribution of federal benefits. The official estimates have been 80 million, but the nearly 50 million who registered for the 1979 election forced upward revision in those estimates.

[133] *Regional Food Plan for Africa* (Rome: United Nations, 1978); FAO, *State of Food and Agriculture*, 2, 3-17.

[134] Idem., pp. 2-51.

[135] In the desert, it is preferable to keep scarce water underground until it is used. Evaporation from irrigation already amounts to 350 gallons per day for every living person. Mihajlo Mesanovic and Edward Pestel, *Mankind at the Turning Point: Second Report to the Club of Rome* (New York: E. P. Dutton, 1974), p. 150.

[136] These peanuts would be highly nutritious if they were consumed at home (about 840 calories and $1\frac{1}{4}$ ounces protein per cupful); but they are for export. Furthermore, while oilseeds (peanut/palm oil) contain 26 to 40 percent protein, 60 to 70 percent of world production is fed to livestock; a third of the African peanut crop is eaten by European livestock. Lappé, "Fantasies of Famine," pp. 52, 54, 87. Despite 1 to 1.9 percent annual increases in Nigeria's agricultural production between 1970 and 1977, Lagos housewives in 1978 were faced with high inflation on the price of nuts and oils. FAO, *State of Food and Agriculture*, pp. 1-8, 1-15.

the farmers on plots smaller than 2.5 acres, while admitting that the employment problem must be solved through the rural sector rather than the urban.[137] It may also be romantic to think that Hausas and Fulanis, left more to their own devices, could benefit both from their centuries of experience in living off the land and from their exposure to modernization in overcoming some of the new problems with which they have been confronted—or that they would have the motivation to do so. To me, there is a thread of more hardheaded realism in the latter suggestion. And there is more hope of using resources to their fullest capacity. We must seriously ask ourselves who is the romantic when charges of romantic idealism are aired.

AN EXAMPLE OF ROMANTIC THINKING BY HARDHEADED REALISTS

Around Kirman, Iran, overgrazing and the addition of trucks to help in gathering firewood caused the supply of wood for fuel to dwindle. Kerosene was meanwhile (in this oil-producing country) far too expensive for the average peasant. A government commission assigned to study the problem nevertheless recommended that the villagers take their goats and sheep off the land (thus depriving them of their last means of livelihood) and then proceed to purchase kerosene for heating. Villagers were telling jokes about this commission for years after. It is like Marie Antoinette telling the peasants and workers to eat cake.[138]

Not all groups have retained as much of their traditional culture as those in northern Nigeria. It would be far more difficult for those in shantytowns or for unemployed villagers to return to a rural way of life. Yet on those rare occasions when agrarian reforms—in Chile, Cuba, Israel, and Egypt, for instance—have permitted such people to do so, it would appear that they did adapt and learn to carry on effective agriculture. If they could adapt to the shantytown, why can they not readapt to the village? If they did not adapt to the shantytown they will be all the more ready to return to the village. Besides, no groups that would ever assemble in new villages could be the same as former ones. The days of fixed norms and cultural isolation are over. No longer is there immunity from technological innovation. The life style and social consciousness of tomorrow can in no event be the same as it was yesterday or is today. The identities of traditional life—the traditions, rituals, and stories, the gatherings, friendships, and kinship ties—were not born at the dawn of history either. Many of the traditions had their origins in very recent times; many of the kinship ties were fictions to solemnize an accidental coalescence of individuals. After war, famine, and migrations there were regroupings, and life would begin anew; the entire Hausa people are such a regrouping. What is important is that village and nomadic set-

---

[137] A World Bank Mission reports on "the chief crops of the Caribbean: sugar and bananas." They are the only crops discussed in the report. World Bank Mission, *The Commonwealth Caribbean: The Integration Experience* (Baltimore: Johns Hopkins University Press, 1978), p. 134.

[138] Paul Ward English, *City and Village in Iran: Settlement and Economy in the Kirman Basin* (Madison: University of Wisconsin Press, 1966), p. 108.

tings invite such regroupings; urban environments, with their anonymity and constant mobility, often inhibit them.

Sometimes we have the image that preindustrial villages, like Medieval Europe, somehow gained their ability to function from noble lies—fixed norms and never-questioned beliefs. Without the lies, the peasants would cease their toil.[139] Once the Renaissance has arrived (the former organic communities are scattered by modernization) one cannot put the pieces together again. The city dwellers would not know how to return to the countryside. And, once returned, they could never reestablish a community order. Perhaps we fool ourselves in two ways. What makes us think that these people (save for brief experiments like the Inca Empire) ever experienced the intellectual monolithism of the Holy Roman Empire (which may itself be somewhat fictitious), or that just because they have been physically uprooted they have turned into Renaissance men and women? Perhaps they toiled more because the toil and the land were theirs, rather than because of a series of ideas; the ideas may have been as much the outgrowth of the toil as the food they ate, not its cause. And what makes us think that modern ideas cannot live side-by-side with fixed norms? Why, in fact, should these people not feed themselves even more effectively now than before their exposure to other normative systems? A weekend in the Missouri countryside—or even time spent in a Missouri city—should be enough to reinforce such questioning.[140] People who have lived in the city can return to the country. And modern rural communities, even plural ones, can both enforce norms and innovate.

Furthermore, there is growing prestigious support for the notions expressed in this book that traditional societies contained modern elements, modern societies contain traditional elements, and history is not moving inexorably in one direction or the other[141]—if, indeed, one can separate the notions of "modern" and "traditional." They may mean little more than "papal" versus "anti-papal," an appendage from earlier European intellectual history. The Talcott Parsons model is falling into question. The fact that traditional villages have been physically disrupted does not mean that traditional cultures, economic

---

[139] Today we have a new breed of intellectuals who argue that it is vitally important to create new noble lies: "efficiency," "economy of scale," "a better life for your kids."

[140] Fred Riggs talks of formalism—where people say one thing and do another. There is some of this in Missouri towns. But there are also things that people say which they also do—quite consistently. And few who grow to adulthood there ever think seriously about alternatives to their way of life.

[141] Reinhard Bendix, "Tradition and Modernity Reconsidered," *Comparative Studies in Society and History* 9 (April 1967): 293–346; Lloyd and Suzanne Rudolph, *The Modernity of Tradition* (Chicago: University of Chicago Press, 1967); Joseph R. Gusfield, "Tradition and Modernity: Misplaced Polarities in the Study of Social Change," *American Journal of Sociology* 72 (January 1966): 351–362; S. N. Eisenstadt, "Breakdowns of Modernization," *Economic Development and Cultural Change* 12 (July 1964): 345–367; J. C. Heesterman, "Tradition in Modern India," *Bijdragen Tot de Taal-, Land-, en Volkenkunde,* Deel 119 (1963); Rajni Kothari, "Tradition and Modernity Revisited," *Government and Opposition* 3 (Summer, 1968): 273–293; C. S. Whitaker, Jr., *The Politics of Tradition: Continuity and Change in Northern Nigeria, 1946-1966* (Princeton, N.J.: Princeton University Press, 1970); Samuel P. Huntington, "The Change to Change: Modernization, Development, and Politics," *Comparative Politics* 3, 3 (April 1971): 283–322; Wilber, *The Political Economy of Development and Underdevelopment;* James C. Scott, *The Moral Economy of the Peasant: Rebellion and Subsistence in Southeast Asia* (New Haven, Conn.: Yale University Press, 1976).

practices, and social customs are not still flourishing or that traditional values are on the decline. The most modern sectors of modern nations still incorporate many traditional elements; why should they and the less modern sectors not accommodate the additional traditional element of communal land tenure?

The history of transition from aristocratic to patron-client political systems itself could have been different. Muslims, Catholics, and Confucian rulers had science budding within their realms but forbade it to expand. A few of these leaders came close to allowing it to do so. Had this expansion taken place in their realms, they, rather than Spain and northern Europe, might have begun the world trade which broke up the integrated community. In this case, their regions, rather than the North Atlantic areas, might have gained control over the magnified surpluses and history would have been much different. Had the British and French taken a different approach on colonial land policy, or concentrated less on the field of engineering and more on biology in administering their technical services, this could also have brought much different results. The discovery of patterns in past history does not predestine a continuance of such patterns in the future. These patterns may have resulted partly from historic accident.

IS SCIENCE TRADITIONAL OR MODERN?

During the Nigerian Civil War, Biafra was blockaded and the managers of multinationals went home. Biafran entrepreneurs began to produce gin and brandy, soap, pharmaceuticals, and salt. They devised a technology to process cassava which was to be used in large-scale production after the war; for twenty years prior to that, attempts to create this technology had failed. They created armored vehicles, guns, land mines, aerial bombs, rockets, grenades, and even a tree-mounted schrapnel device capable of destroying a company of men. They distilled crude oil into usable fuels in large water tanks set on trestles. And they machine tooled replacement parts for equipment.[142]

A world containing industrialized and less-industrialized nations need not be a divided world. Aside from automobile, office building, and factory counts it might become increasingly difficult to tell one group from the other as each both began to offer more frugal but stable personal environments. That stability can become the ground for commonality. Ideas and some trade, even mutual assistance, would continue to flow. Independent entities do not inherently cease to interact and get along with one another. In fact, if the interaction becomes less desperately necessary, it might flow from more natural motivations like sympathy, curiosity, even mutual advantage.

And emphasis on the countryside need not bode a decline of the city. Rural communities in control of their own land and jobs would still find many reasons for interacting with the city. Urban centers can offer the countryside consumer goods, health and educational services, and numerous aids in improving produc-

---

[142] Biersteker, *Distortion or Development?*, pp. 98–100.

tivity. Rural communities that control their own skills and resources can, in fact, derive the greatest benefit from such contact. They have something important to offer the city, without being forced to offer virtually everything they have.

SPECIFIC EXAMPLES

Using 2,200 pounds of petroleum per acre in heavily mechanized farming, Japanese farmers produce 5,177 pounds of rice per acre. Philippine farmers were getting 1,115 pounds of rice per acre without any mechanization. Using some limited technology, and only 353 pounds of petroleum per acre, these same Philippine farmers have increased yields to 2,454 pounds per acre.[143]

In Kenya both the traditional methods of grinding flour (which take practically no investment) and the modern roller mills for sifting flour (which take great investment) remove the germ from the grain and cut down its nutritional value. A hammer mill, which can be set up in town, takes moderate investment and modernization, and leaves the germ and nearly all nutrients in the grain. Most rural dwellers in Kenya use grain ground on the hammer mill. More sophisticated city dwellers prefer the nutritionally inferior and more expensive sifted flour.[144] The town dweller thus makes a contribution to improving rural diet.

What we are talking about is taking maximum advantage of this planet's resources, including human talent and energy. This means using labor, land, sunlight, wind, and other resources that have long lain idle. It means elimination of duplications like using more nonrenewable energy to produce food than the food contains, only to have fifteen-sixteenths of food value destroyed by feeding it in turn to cattle, and then using more energy to transport this food long distances. Just as tradition is not the opposite of modernity, and industrialization is not the antithesis of countryside, conservation is not the enemy of cows. Feeding livestock cornstalks, orange juice squeeze remainders, cocoa residue, bark, wood pulp, overripe bananas, potato starch, ammonium salts, sucrose, urea, pea vines, vegetable tops, treated manure, and on open range can eliminate the cow's competition for human food—can, in fact, make the cow a partner in collecting food—without eliminating cattle. With some concerned attention to problem-solving, solutions could be found for many of the enigmas that presently stump us.

As indicated earlier, these thoughts are speculative, not predictive. They involve broadening our imagination about what is possible, not pinpointing what is probable. It is very possible that the world will go on much as it has, piling mission report upon mission report, building new engineering marvels to accommodate the minority, fighting wars to maintain alleged power zones, compounding the number of poor—and perhaps making *all* nations marginal to the power of the multinationals. The point is that this is not inevitable. None of us has thought enough about what other options the future might hold.

---

[143] FAO, *State of Food and Agriculture*, pp. 2–24.
[144] Stewart, *Technology and Underdevelopment*, pp. 208–238.

All this is not strictly an "outsider's" opinion. For instance, arguing that "we are living in a world with no truly credible 'development models,'" a study by the European Centre for Study and Information on Multinational Corporations to serve as a discussion guide at conferences for leaders of multinationals argues that the time is at hand to explore bold new alternatives for developing the hinterlands.[145] It talks of adapting stoves to burn a variety of fuels, of helping villagers dig irrigation canals by hand and paying them with food, of communal villages issuing "work coupons" to replace money (which it says allowed a Chinese village to build itself a project that would have cost US$1 million if financed by an international aid agency), and other ways to avoid international borrowing and help industry serve the poor.

> Statements in official documents often represent only the tip of the iceberg of true sentiments. This report gives some insight into the art of interpreting bureaucratic language: "The situation has now become so precarious that central banks are quite obviously worried. The ultimate nightmare is of a massive debt default by some countries, plunging the vulnerable banks into insolvency. . . . Money will simply have to be pumped into near-defaulting countries. . . . But that merely delays the potential catastrophe. . . . Several weeks ago central bank governors from the major industrialized nations took the unusual step of issuing a public warning about a financial crash. At the conclusion of one of their secret monthly meetings at the Bank for International Settlements in Basle, Switzerland, the governors said: 'Individual banks, or the international banking system as a whole, could in the future be [exposed] to greater risks than in the past.'"[146]

Robert McNamara, former President of the World Bank, ended his 1973 "Nairobi Speech," widely publicized as heralding the beginning of a new emphasis on the small farmer, by saying: "It would be a great disservice if the aid agencies were to try to convince either these countries or themselves that policies for alleviating rural poverty can be fashioned and delivered from abroad. The problem must be perceived and dealt with by the countries themselves."[147]

The Preface of the Report of the Presidential Commission on World Hunger states: "Until poverty and inequality are replaced by sustained and self-reliant development undertaken by men and women who are in charge of their own future, there will never be a real hope of eliminating hunger." The Report later argues: "Not only must more food be produced in these nations, but it must be produced in a fashion that develops self-reliance for individual citizens as well as the nation itself. Fortunately these are not far-fetched or unattainable goals."[148] Four of the Commissioners preferred a fuller explanation of "self-

---

[145] Lietaer, *Europe + Latin America + the Multinationals,* pp. 151–200. For a large bibliography on the huge emerging body of literature on multinationals, and a defense of multinationals, see Biersteker, *Distortion or Development?*

[146] Ho Kwon Ping, "Alarm Bells are Ringing Over the Massive Debt Crisis," *Far Eastern Economic Review* 108, no. 19 (May 2, 1980): 41.

[147] World Bank, *The Assault on World Poverty,* p. 98.

[148] *Overcoming World Hunger,* pp. x, 36.

reliance," and quoted in their comments from still another such report, the Cocoyoc Declaration of 1974:

> We believe that one basic strategy of development will have to be increased national self-reliance. It does not mean autarchy. It implies mutual benefits from trade and cooperation and a fairer redistribution of resources satisfying the basic needs. It does mean self-confidence, reliance primarily on one's own resources, human and natural, and the capacity for autonomous goalsetting and decision-making. It excludes dependence on outside influences and powers that can be converted into political pressure. It excludes exploitative trade patterns depriving countries of their natural resources for their own development. There is obviously a scope for transfer of technology, but the thrust should be an adaptation and the generation of local technology. It implies decentralization of the world economy, and sometimes also of the national economy to enhance the sense of personal participation. But it also implies increased international cooperation for collective self-reliance. Above all, it means trust in people and nations, reliance on the capacity of people themselves to invent and generate new resources and techniques, to increase their capacity to absorb them, to put them to socially beneficial use; to take a measure of command over the economy, and to generate their own way of life.[149]

Denis Goulet explains the need for rethinking:

> As long as privileged classes or nations continue to regard the emancipation of the world's poor as the fruit of productivity gains alone or mere increases in GNP, without altering the present arrangements governing access to resources . . . rapid worldwide development remains impossible. Only massive restructuring of productive priorities, allied to major changes in the distributive norms governing wealth, skills, and access to resources, can produce universal development.[150]

One can achieve global stability of sorts by creating powerful links among governments, military organizations, multinational corporations, and technocrats, even if these groups are surrounded by legions of semistarved peasants. That has been amply demonstrated. There is always the possibility, if we think about it, that it might be purchased in another manner. More amazing still, that other manner might some day (perhaps soon) come to seem the more realistic course even to those with "modern" minds. A world packed with people, tobacco fields, and loans due, and rapidly dwindling in fuel and food, may remold the image of what is considered modern just as Americans have already remolded their image of what is considered a sensibly-sized automobile. Some 36 percent of the earth's land surface is arid or semi-arid; much of this is not irrigatable. When arid lands—and oceans, and tropics, and savannahs and other underoccupied spaces—become the last frontiers on the planet, it may be those frontiersmen who abandon urban definitions of life style and progress who will

---

[149] Idem., p. 212, quoting from the Cocoyoc Declaration. This is contained in remarks appended to the report by Commissioners Harry F. Chapin, Senator Patrick Leahy, and Congressman Richard Nolan.

[150] Denis Goulet, *The Cruel Choice: A New Concept in the Theory of Development* (New York: Atheneum, 1971), pp. 282–283.

become the "modern" men and women, with the urban regions falling in line behind them. If they realize that they are not the first to make this journey and the aboriginese whom they encounter along the way may be men and women of wisdom and even foresight, their pathfinding will be the more rewarding.

At the heart of all this is our perspective on what constitutes the good life. I would contend that greed is unduly interlaced into that perspective. Primitive and early-commercial societies exhibited their share of greed. The Nuer acquired cattle; the Navajo, sheep; Trobrianders, land parcels and yams; the *Etsu Nupe,* swords and gold; the Inca collected gold objects and discarded sacred robes that took months to make after only one wearing. Some, like the Inca, the Bantu and Nupe noblemen, Kachin headmen, and the Chief of Omarkana also displayed a lust for power. Except in the latest years of their rule, this greed did not involve coveting the land or means of sustenance of their subjects and was balanced by obligations owed to each of those subjects; it was nonetheless greed.

That greed had some important utility: it increased productivity, saved resources, and helped provide meaning to life. We have evidence that the Nuer genuinely liked their cattle, the Navajo their sheep and hunting prey, the Trobrianders their yams and gardens, the Bantu their banana gardens, and the Incas their metal plows and carefully-tended fields. These were their means of production, and precious resources. Their names, their songs, their social connections, their ritual acts, their leisure play concerned these entities. The Nuer made use of every portion of the cow, even washing their face and curdling their cheese with its urine. The cows that gave more milk were considered better cows, but all the cows received affection. The Navajo performed elaborate ritual when they killed their prey, and killed only the prey they needed. The Bantu banana garden doubled as a social garden, and the Trobrianders took time after many hours of hoeing and weeding to decorate their fields with banners. These people enjoyed being with their means of production and gave great attention to the details of productive processes. They devoted considerable time to training their young to do the same. They took pride that they were carrying on in these traditions from their ancestors. They wove their social life into their productivity.

"Modern" men and women do not do the same. Corporate executives see little of the machines they use or the products they produce; machines and products are viewed as discardable and quickly consumed expediencies. Most individuals feel uncomfortable around means of production. People look forward to the end of the day, when work will be finished. They waste resources to save labor. They laugh at the notion that people should have affection for tools, and often are careless in their handling and storage of tools. Jobs are performed away from family and friends. People do not associate "job," "meaning," and "pleasure." Nor is much attention given to products. People eat beef, but do not necessarily take time to savor it; in fact, as corporate affluence spreads, diets often deteriorate as people overeat processed starches and fats. People want to acquire products, but often pay little attention to their quality. With the possible exception of the automobile and stereo receivers people feel little personal involvement with products. This acquisitiveness is greed. It affects productivity; people work to buy products. But it can hardly be associated with frugality in the use of resources. Its role in providing meaning to life is qualitatively different.

There is an anomaly about a person who finds neither job nor the products he or she buys especially fulfilling, yet continues to work hard to buy these products. Greed may be becoming *an end in itself,* a continuing search for lost meaning that keeps on producing more of itself. It is a peculiar search that spreads beyond the individual. In a sense, it has become the foundation of our entire social order and sense of stability. A stable person wants to keep increasing his or her income. A stable interest group constantly makes new demands. A stable nation constantly increases its production output. A stable corporation or bank invests money in shaky financing of developing nations to turn a profit. A spread of this greed to everyone will bring "productivity" and rewards to everyone. Mendacity builds world order out of mendacity. Stability derives from everyone being dissatisfied with what they have.

But should too many people stop to savor the quality of what they produce—the food they eat, the homes in which they live, the educations they pass along to their children, and their relationships with one another—the stability of the entire system is endangered. The same is true if we stop to investigate the quicksand economics on which the structure is built. Obviously, such activities are counterproductive because they are the opposite of greed—not a continuing search for more acquistion but a thorough utilization of and satisfaction with what we already have. Our system not only lacks praxis; it is at war with it.

Activity that is not greedy produces paranoia and fear. It is something to be stamped out, to be branded as retrogressive and counterproductive, not something to be examined as a replacement for the present nonmeaning. What are perhaps the most unstable of personalities and wasteful of systems, the excessively greedy ones, become the norm on which the so-called stable society, economy, and global balance is based.

The primitive community seems stable, not only because of the food, clothing, shelter, and continuity of relationships that it provided. It was stable because it was content with what it had. There was more identity with self and one's own kind than with self-aggrandizement, even at the expense of one's own kind. Perhaps because of this contentment, it was able to *provide* itself with food, clothing, shelter, and continuing relationships and to use resources more efficiently than they have been used since. Far from being retrograde, romantic, and shortsighted, that contented, culture-bound personality might offer a model for a stability more relevant to today's needs than that propounded by "modern" men and women.

The mother enters the hospital and sees a large poster of a healthy baby nursing with a bottle—the same she has heard about on radio commercials. After her baby is born she is visited by a nurse urging her to bottle-nurse her child with Nestlé Lactogen. She does not know that this is one of 4,000 or 5,000 nurses earning extra money by working for Nestlé after hours, and that though the nurse is in uniform it is not a professional call. She is told that the formula, with cow's milk, has almost three times the protein of human mother's milk; she is not told that calves grow faster than human babies and may need more protein, or that only 1 to 5 percent of even poor women have breast feeding problems (which is what wet nurses are for), and these are usually women so poor they could not possibly afford Lactogen.[151] Nor does she understand that Lactogen contains no immunizing factors like mother's milk, to protect the child from disease, or that an adequate supply would take more than her family's income and cost four times what it would cost to feed herself for lactation. She wants the best for her baby, and trusts that the modern way is better than the old way. So she switches to the bottle and stops lactating. She abandons milk she has for milk she must buy.

Then she discovers that she cannot afford enough Lactogen. She waters it down, or simply feeds water or tea or cola in the bottle. Cooking on a mud floor with a small fire, she can make little sense or use of the instructions to boil ten minutes immersed in a pan of water. The baby develops diarrhea and dies.

Some Swiss consumer advocates put out a pamphlet exposing this problem. Nestlé is unhappy. They have eighty-one formula plants in twenty-seven developing nations. They have spent a lot of money promoting their product. High percentages of urban women have been converted to bottle feeding. Nestlé sues. Investigators around the world find that the story of this mother is a common one.

> . . . The dramatic decline in breast feeding in urban areas has a dramatic impact on child malnutrition in low-income groups. . . . The consequence of bottle feeding is a high prevalence of diarrhea and gastrointestinal tract infections which, coupled with frequent overdilution of the milk, leads to increased incidence of protein-energy malnutrition [and] an earlier age of onset of malnutrition. . . . Mortality is much higher in never breast fed and prematurely weaned infants. . . . Breast milk is a commodity of very high nutritious value and low production cost which is potentially almost perfect.[152]

In 1976, the court holds that the pamphlet title, "Nestlé Kills Babies," is defamatory since the misuse, and not the product itself, are to blame. The consumer advocates are fined US$120 and two-thirds of court costs. Nestlé must pay one-third of court costs and change its marketing practices so as to prevent further misuse of its products.

King Solomon, in a child custody case, threatened to split the child in half and divide it between the litigants, so that the true mother would show herself by giving up her claim so as to save the baby. Play Solomon. Will this problem be solved in Deutsch's fashion by the forces of modernization gradually improving the overall situation of the mothers? Halpern's removal of imbalances in modernization by, say, regulating advertising? Does it require Eisenstadt's viable groups within society to countervail the power of vested interests? Or Waller-

---

[151] Food and Agriculture Organization, *Fourth World Food Survey* (Rome: United Nations, 1977), p. 44: "As for lactation, the output of milk may be reduced in malnourished women, although the composition in terms of major nutrients does not seem to be grossly affected, except for fat. It is only under conditions of particularly severe dietary deprivation that lactation does cease. Although prolonged lactation constitutes a heavy burden on the mother's nutritional stores, it has the advantage of retarding resumption of ovulation, and thus acting as a child spacing factor."

[152] Idem., pp. 44–45. For more information on this subject see Lappé and Collins, *Food First*, pp. 310–319; Calvin Tudge, *The Famine Business* (London: Faber and Faber, 1977), pp. 109–110; Herman Nickel, "The Corporation Haters," *Fortune* (June 16, 1980). These contain many additional bibliographical references.

stein's notion of strengthening individual national cultures, and those elements of the army, bureaucracy, religious leadership, and landowners least dependent on the world economy? Would the policy strategy outlined in this chapter solve it? Is there some other solution? How do we achieve any of these objectives? If not, where is the money coming from which is buying all that Lactogen year after year? Can you grow old peacefully and prosperously if this problem is not solved?

SHORT SUMMARY

Before developing nations can develop they must become less dependent on the rest of the world. If developed nations are to stay developed they, too, must become less dependent on the outside world. Nations can do this without giving up many of the blessings which modernization has made possible.

Have you caught these definitions?

	page
communal land tenure	352
repatriation of profits	366
subsidiary	365
marginal resources	379
marginal markets	379
captive markets	379

Can you answer each with one sentence?

1. Why is it more difficult to exploit communal-land villagers when export agriculture and mining for export do not exist?
2. How can a multinational invisibly remove profits from a subsidiary?
3. How does a multinational corporation operating within a developing nation derive investment capital locally?
4. How can indigenous-owned firms become dependent on multinationals without being purchased by them?
5. Which nations are in the best position to exploit energy resources without the aid of multinationals?
6. To feed the planet must we stop eating cows?

Can you make and support judgments about these questions?

1. Was Thomas Malthus correct about population outstripping food supply?
2. Do multinationals and foreign aid add to the investment capital of developing nations and their business firms?
3. Given a choice, will a corporation exploit an expensive mode of production and consumption that it can control, or a less expensive one that it cannot? Is there such a choice, and how might it affect personal environments?
4. Who loses when copper, cobalt, iron, manganese, nickel, and molybdenum are obtained by dredging nodules from the 2,600 × 800 square miles of ocean floor between Hawaii and Mexico? Who gains?

5. The *conquistadores* may have brought guns and exploitation. They also brought priests, schools, and hospitals. If you knock out the trade patterns that promote patron-clientism do you not also knock out the schools and hospitals?

6. Do developed and developing nations need greater independence or greater interdependence?

7. Is political development possible if we continue to promote improved communications, exports, capital formation, and urban employment in developing nations?

8. What policy strategy does this book propose for the United States, and what results does it hope to achieve? How could this affect stable personal environments?

Now reread the entire "Book in Brief" section of Chapter 1, and see where you agree, and where you disagree, with it. Look again at the policy questions in Chapter 6 and see how you respond to them.

Index